THE WISDOM IN FEELING

EMOTIONS AND SOCIAL BEHAVIOR

Series Editor: Peter Salovey, Yale University

The Wisdom in Feeling

Psychological Processes in Emotional Intelligence

Edited by

LISA FELDMAN BARRETT
PETER SALOVEY

Foreword by John D. Mayer

THE GUILFORD PRESS
New York   London

© 2002 The Guilford Press
A Division of Guilford Publications, Inc.
72 Spring Street, New York, NY 10012
www.guilford.com

Printed in the United States of America

This book is printed on acid-free paper.

Last digit is print number: 9 8 7 6 5 4 3 2 1

Library of Congress Cataloging-in-Publication Data

The wisdom in feeling : psychological processes in emotional intelligence / edited by Lisa Feldman Barrett, Peter Salovey.
    p. cm. – (Emotions and social behavior)
Includes bibliographical references and index.
  ISBN 1-57230-785-4
 1. Emotional intelligence. I. Barrett, Lisa Feldman. II. Salovey, Peter. III. Series.
BF576 .W57 2002
152.4–dc21

                                                        2002006983

Out of the marriage of reason with affect there issues clarity with passion. Reason without affect would be impotent, affect without reason would be blind
—SILVAN S. TOMKINS, *Affect, Imagery, and Consciousness*
(1962, Vol. 1, p. 112)

The emotions are of quite extraordinary importance in the total economy of living organisms and do not deserve being put into opposition with "intelligence." The emotions are, it seems, themselves a high order of intelligence.
—O. HOBART MOWRER, *Learning Theory and Behavior*
(1960, p. 308)

About the Editors

Lisa Feldman Barrett, PhD, is Associate Professor in the Department of Psychology at Boston College. She received her undergraduate degree from the University of Toronto and her PhD in clinical psychology from the University of Waterloo. Dr. Barrett's research focuses on the generation and representation of emotional experience, but she has also published papers in related areas, including the structure of affect, interpersonal relationships, experience sampling procedures, and, more generally, the role of retrospection in the self-report process.

Peter Salovey, PhD, is the Chris Argyris Professor of Psychology, Professor of Epidemiology and Public Health, and Chair of the Department of Psychology at Yale University. He is also Director of the Department of Psychology's Health, Emotion, and Behavior Laboratory and Deputy Director of the Yale Center for Interdisciplinary Research on AIDS. Dr. Salovey has published over 175 articles in the scientific literature and is past Associate Editor of *Psychological Bulletin,* as well as Editor of the *Review of General Psychology,* and Associate Editor of *Emotion.* A recipient of the National Science Foundation's (NSF) Presidential Young Investigator Award, he has served on the NSF Social Psychology Advisory Panel. His recent work on emotion has focused on the ways in which feelings facilitate adaptive cognitive and behavioral functioning.

Contributors

Nalini Ambady, PhD, Department of Psychology, Harvard University, Cambridge, Massachusetts

Jo-Anne Bachorowski, PhD, Department of Psychology, Vanderbilt University, Nashville, Tennessee

Kimberly A. Barchard, PhD, Department of Psychology, University of Nevada, Las Vegas, Nevada

John A. Bargh, PhD, Department of Psychology, New York University, New York, New York

Lisa Feldman Barrett, PhD, Department of Psychology, Boston College, Chestnut Hill, Massachusetts

Robert James Richard Blair, PhD, Mood and Anxiety Program, National Institute of Mental Health, Bethesda, Maryland

Mark E. Bouton, PhD, Department of Psychology, University of Vermont, Burlington, Vermont

Julia Braverman, MA, Department of Psychology, Northeastern University, Boston, Massachusetts

Gerald L. Clore, PhD, Department of Psychology, University of Virginia, Charlottesville, Virginia

Nathalie Dalle, MA, LAPSCO/UFR Psychologie, Université Blaise Pascal, Clermont-Ferrand Cedex, France

Susanne A. Denham, PhD, Department of Psychology, George Mason University, Fairfax, Virginia

David DeSteno, PhD, Department of Psychology, Northeastern University, Boston, Massachusetts

Erin Driver-Linn, PhD, Department of Psychology, Harvard University, Cambridge, Massachusetts

Hillary Anger Elfenbein, PhD, Program in Organizational Behavior, Harvard University, Boston, Massachusetts

Melissa J. Ferguson, PhD, Department of Psychology, Cornell University, Ithaca, New York

Barbara L. Fredrickson, PhD, Department of Psychology, University of Michigan, Ann Arbor, Michigan

Daniel T. Gilbert, PhD, Department of Psychology, Harvard University, Cambridge, Massachusetts

Carol L. Gohm, PhD, Department of Psychology, University of Mississippi, University, Mississippi

James J. Gross, PhD, Department of Psychology, Stanford University, Stanford, California

Oliver P. John, PhD, Department of Psychology, University of California–Berkeley, Berkeley, California

Anita Kochanoff, PhD, Department of Psychology, Temple University, Philadelphia, Pennsylvania

Richard D. Lane, MD, PhD, Department of Psychiatry, University of Arizona, Tucson, Arizona

Abigail A. Marsh, MA, Department of Psychology, Harvard University, Cambridge, Massachusetts

James B. Nelson, PhD, Department of Psychology and Counseling, University of Central Arkansas, Conway, Arkansas

Paula M. Niedenthal, PhD, LAPSCO/UFR Psychologie, Université Blaise Pascal, Clermont-Ferrand Cedex, France

Michael J. Owren, PhD, Department of Psychology, Cornell University, Ithaca, New York

W. Gerrod Parrott, PhD, Department of Psychology, Georgetown University, Washington, DC

Branka Zei Pollermann, PhD, Department of Liaison Psychiatry, University Hospitals, Geneva, Switzerland

Anette Rohmann, Dipl-Psych, Department of Psychology, University of Munster, Munster, Germany

James A. Russell, PhD, Department of Psychology, Boston College, Chestnut Hill, Massachusetts

Peter Salovey, PhD, Department of Psychology, Yale University, New Haven, Connecticut

Cary R. Savage, PhD, Cognitive Neuroscience Group, Department of Psychiatry, Massachusetts General Hospital, Charlestown, Massachusetts

Norbert Schwarz, PhD, Institute for Social Research, University of Michigan, Ann Arbor, Michigan

Michele M. Tugade, PhD, Department of Psychology, Boston College, Chestnut Hill, Massachusetts

Timothy D. Wilson, PhD, Department of Psychology, University of Virginia, Charlottesville, Virginia

Foreword

A fractal is a design that possesses "self-similarity"—that is, the design's exact geometric properties are repeated at the smallest level, at midlevel, and at high levels. The Sierpinski triangle (see Figure 1), for example, is a triangle made from smaller triangles repeated at several levels of scale. At first glance, most people see a triangle with an upside-down triangle in its middle. The large triangle, however, is made of four smaller, inner triangles, with each of the three triangles around the perimeter having its own upside-down triangle in its middle. Drop down still another level, and the pattern is the same. The Sierpinski triangle's self-similarity arises because it is itself built up from smaller Sierpinski triangles.

FIGURE 1. A Sierpinski triangle. Computer art by Joseph Kamm. Used with permission of the artist.

The field of emotional intelligence, it seems to me, possesses a self-similarity analogous to that of the Sierpinski triangle and other fractal shapes. That is, there is a thematic "shape" of a discussion that is carried on at several levels of analysis simultaneously. The central debate concerns whether intelligence is more important to one's life, whether emotion is, or whether the two can be synthesized in some way. This exchange of ideas takes place at a societal level, at the level of psychology as a discipline, and at the level of individual programs of research.

LEVEL 1: SOCIETAL CONTEXT

Most people first heard of emotional intelligence through Daniel Goleman's (1995) lively popularization of the field. Goleman's book went on to become one of the best-selling books on psychology to date. There were several reasons for this interest in emotional intelligence. First, Goleman's work was well written and exciting. Second, Goleman himself was a distinguished science writer, with strong ties to the *New York Times,* and he and his publisher were able to generate considerable excitement for the book. None of that would have mattered, however, if emotional intelligence did not play into a critical issue in many cultures. That issue concerned the perceived conflict between a person's thoughts and feelings. We may never know when the debate first arose, but we do know that it is represented in early Greek thought. The ancients identified with their intellect in part because it seemed central to distinguishing humanity from animals; Aristotle argued that intellect is "the highest thing in us" (Aristotle, 1976, p. 505). Stoic philosophers regarded emotional information, in contrast, as unreliable (Payne, 1986, pp. 17–19). Any educated person, they believed (somewhat naively) could reason to the same conclusion as any other. Reason, they believed (somewhat hopefully), was universal, dependable, and reliable. Emotion, on the other hand, was idiosyncratic, self-oriented, and undependable. "The sage will rule his feelings, the fool will be their slave," wrote Publilius Syrus in the first century BCE (Syrus, ca. 100 BCE/1961, p. 19). These thinkers set out to banish emotions from everyday life, or at least restrict their influence, so as to create a rational way to live. There are few people who would acknowledge being adherents to stoicism today, of course. The movement died out, but certain among its central tenets influenced the religions that would, ultimately, supplant the Greek pantheism of the time. Judaism, and especially Christianity, employed stoic philosophy. Those ideas then became a part of Western religious tradition. As a consequence, stoic philosophy is often embedded in Western thinking (Guttman, 1964; Payne, 1986, p. 15).

At the same time, there have been rebellions (antitheses) against the logical, stoic thesis. In Western Europe, these included the Chassidic rebellion against the cerebral emphasis of Judaism in the early 1800s. Several decades later, it included the Romantic rebellion against the logical emphasis of European classicism. Closer to the present, in the 1960s (when some of the contributors to this volume were coming of age), the student revolutions, and the surrounding conflicts between "youth" and "the establishment" often had an explicit quality of valuing emotions over intellect (Herman, 1992). Thus, Western culture has a thesis—that intellect is superior to emotion; an antithesis—that emotions are what make life worth living; and perhaps several attempts at synthesis—simply keeping heart and head "in balance," or more complex humanistic transcendence of the conflict, and the like. Emotional intelligence, however, would prove to be a different, perhaps more complete sort of synthesis, a synthesis that would arise from a more complete understanding of underlying cognitive and emotional processes.

LEVEL 2: THOUGHT AND EMOTION IN PSYCHOLOGY

The same debate about emotion and intellect as occurred at the societal level was recapitulated in the discipline of psychology. Academic psychology dates roughly from 1887. Shortly thereafter, the area of intelligence and intelligence testing predominated. Emotion was treated sometimes as a curiosity and sometimes as too subjective to measure. Even William James's influential theory of emotion concerned how it arose rather than what it meant (James, 1892/1920). In fact, the first mood scales were not introduced until the 1960s. When intelligence and emotion were compared, intelligence was viewed as the absence of emotion. Thus, Young (1936, p. 263), described emotion as an "acute disturbance of the individual as a whole." Young's textbook described emotions as causing a "complete loss of cerebral control" and containing no "trace of conscious purpose" (Young, 1943, pp. 457–458). Another text described it as "a disorganized response, largely visceral, resulting from a lack of an effective adjustment" (Schaffer, Gilmer, & Schoen, 1940, p. 505). In this vein, Woodworth (1940) suggested that scales measuring IQ should contain tests demonstrating the *absence* of fear, anger, grief, and other emotions characteristic of "younger children."

As in the culture at large, psychology had no shortage of proponents of the value of emotion as well. Leeper (1948, p. 17) suggested that emotions "arouse, sustain, and direct activity." During the 1970s and 1980s a number of precursors important to emotional intelligence emerged. There was a growing recognition of the role of emotion as a universal signal system rooted in evolution (Ekman & Friesen, 1975). There was a recognition that emotional knowledge was necessary to understanding human interactions and, hence, would need to be formalized for computers to be able to read and comprehend stories (Dyer, 1983). There was a growing understanding of the interaction of emotion and cognition (Bower, 1981; Clark & Fiske, 1982; Isen, Shalker, Clark, & Karp, 1978; Zajonc, 1980). Finally, there was a loosening of the concept of intelligence to broader categories of symbol systems. For example, Howard Gardner (1983; see also Sternberg, 1985) published a volume that suggested scientists should place a greater emphasis on the search for multiple intelligences rather than focusing on a monolithic general intelligence. Gardner did not deal with an emotional intelligence per se, and he explicitly denied the possibility of its existence after it was introduced (Gardner, 1999, p. 75). Yet he had written that a central aspect of his suggested intrapersonal intelligence was "access to one's feeling life" (Gardner, 1983, p. 239).

In 1990 my colleague Peter Salovey and I drew together those psychological (and cultural) literatures and proposed the first published, formal definition of emotional intelligence, along with a demonstration of how aspects of it might be measured as an ability (Mayer, DiPaolo, & Salovey, 1990; Salovey & Mayer, 1990.). We wrote an editorial in the journal *Intelligence* (Mayer & Salovey, 1993) as well, calling for its further study.

LEVEL 3: FOUNDATIONS UNDERLYING EMOTION AND THOUGHT

The opposition of intellect and emotion occurred at a third level of self-similarity. That level involved studying the underlying (e.g., more molecular) mental processes within three smaller areas: the cognitive system, the emotion system, and their interaction. The research area that examined these was known as "cognition and affect." As noted, the 1970s and 1980s saw the emergence of research into this interaction. At the societal level and the general psychological level, as this area emerged, intellect was viewed as primary and moods were viewed as biasing thought (e.g., Bower, 1981). Again, there was a loyal opposition. In an unusual reversal of primacy, Beck argued that irrational cognition could be viewed as a cause of depression. No longer was emotion disrupting intellect, but rather the reverse (Beck, Rush, Shaw, & Emery, 1979). And, of course, there were arguments that emotion might make people—or computers, or robots—think better (Alloy & Abramson, 1979; Mayer, 1986; Sloman & Croucher, 1981).

The term "emotional intelligence" had been used sporadically at least from the early 1960s forward, but without any clear explanation as to what it might mean, how to define it, or how to measure it (for an early use, see Van Ghent, 1961, p. 103). It existed in a sort of science fiction purgatory until the research could catch up. It was the area of cognition and affect, and its neighboring fields, that began to delineate and focus on the specific relations between passion and reason that would finally permit a logical analysis of the term. As noted earlier, the areas, concepts, and terminology were integrated into the emotional intelligence concept during the period from 1990 to 1993. However, the original research lines that led to it continued, and in those years and the years since, have continued to reveal the synthesis between the heart and the head (e.g., Niedenthal & Kitayama, 1994). The present volume brings together many of the researchers who first laid the foundations of the field and others who, more recently, have attempted to explain the processes of emotional intelligence.

The editors of this volume are my esteemed colleagues Lisa Feldman Barrett and Peter Salovey. Dr. Salovey and I had the great joy and privilege of working together writing the first articles on emotional intelligence—and we continue to delight in our collaborations today, on measuring emotional intelligence as a set of individual differences in ability with the Mayer–Salovey–Caruso Emotional Intelligence Test (MSCEIT) and the Multifactor Emotional Intelligence Scale (MEIS), and in our further work in the area. I have known Dr. Barrett more briefly, and I admire her sophisticated, energetic, and highly regarded research in the area of cognition and affect. It is she and her colleague James Gross who have called for the examination of the basic processes underlying emotional intelligence addressed in this book (Barrett & Gross, 2001).

The editors bring a wealth of experience to this volume, and they have assembled a top-notch group of contributors. As a consequence, you will have a rewarding experience herein watching over the shoulders of these great researchers as they unlock some of the mysteries of emotional intelligence.

JOHN D. MAYER, PhD
Department of Psychology
University of New Hampshire

REFERENCES

Alloy, L. B., & Abramson, L. Y. (1979). Judgment of contingency in depressed and nondepressed students: Sadder but wiser? *Journal of Experimental Psychology, 108,* 441–485.

Aristotle. (1976). *Ethics* (J. A. K. Thompson, Trans.). London: Penguin Books.

Barrett, L. F., & Gross, J. J. (2001). Emotional intelligence. In T. J. Mayne & G. A. Bonanno (Eds.), *Emotions: Current issues and future directions* (pp. 286–310). New York: Guilford Press.

Beck, A. T., Rush, A. J., Shaw, B. F., & Emery, G. (1979). *Cognitive therapy of depression.* New York: Guilford Press.

Bower, G. H. (1981). Mood and memory. *American Psychologist, 36,* 129–148.

Clark, M. S., & Fiske, S. T. (Eds.). (1982). *Affect and cognition: The 17th annual Carnegie Symposium on Cognition.* Hillsdale, NJ: Erlbaum.

Dyer, M. G. (1983). The role of affect in narratives. *Cognitive Science, 7,* 211–242.

Ekman, P., & Friesen, W. V. (1975). *Unmasking the face: A guide to recognizing the emotions from facial cues.* Englewood Cliffs, NJ: Prentice-Hall.

Gardner, H. (1983). *Frames of mind: The theory of multiple intelligences.* New York: Basic Books.

Gardner, H. (1999). Who owns intelligence? *Atlantic Monthly, 283,* 67–76.

Goleman, D. (1995). *Emotional intelligence.* New York: Bantam Books.

Guttman, J. (1964). *Philosophies of Judaism.* New York: Holt, Rinehart & Winston.

Herman, E. (1992). Being and doing: Humanistic psychology and the spirit of the 1960s. In B. L. Tischler (Ed.), *Sights on the sixties* (pp. 87–101). New Brunswick, NJ: Rutgers University Press.

Isen, A. M., Shalker, T. E., Clark, M., & Karp, L. (1978). Affect, accessibility of material in memory, and behavior: A cognitive loop? *Journal of Personality and Social Psychology, 36*(1), 1–12.

James, W. (1920). *Psychology: Briefer course.* New York: Holt. (Original work published 1892)

Leeper, R. W. (1948). A motivational theory of emotions to replace "Emotions as a Disorganized Response." *Psychological Review, 55,* 5–21.

Mayer, J. D. (1986). How mood influences cognition. In N. E. Sharkey (Ed.), *Advances in cognitive science* (pp. 290–314). Chichester, West Sussex: Horwood.

Mayer, J. D., DiPaolo, M. T., & Salovey, P. (1990). Perceiving affective content in ambiguous visual stimuli: A component of emotional intelligence. *Journal of Personality Assessment, 54,* 772–781.

Mayer, J. D., & Salovey, P. (1993). The intelligence of emotional intelligence. *Intelligence, 17*(4), 433–442.

Niedenthal, P. M., & Kitayama, S. (Eds.). (1994). *The heart's eye: Emotional influences in perception and attention.* San Diego, CA: Academic Press.

Payne, W. L. (1986). A study of emotion: Developing emotional intelligence: Self-integration; relating to fear, pain and desire. *Dissertation Abstracts International, 47*(01), 203A. (University Microfilms No. AAC 8605928)

Salovey, P., & Mayer, J. D. (1990). Emotional intelligence. *Imagination, Cognition, and Personality, 9,* 185–211.

Schaffer, L. F., Gilmer, B., & Schoen, M. (1940). *Psychology*. New York: Harper.

Sloman, A., & Croucher, M. (1981). Why robots will have emotions. In *Proceedings of the seventh international joint conference on artificial intelligence* (pp. 197–202), Vancouver.

Sternberg, R. J. (1985). Human intelligence: The model is the message. *Science, 230*(4730), 1111–1118.

Syrus, P. (1961). Sententiae. In J. W. Duff & A. M. Duff (Eds.), *Minor Latin poets* (pp. 14–111). Cambridge, MA: Harvard University Press. (Original work of Syrus published ca. 100 BCE; Original Duff & Duff volume published 1934)

Van Ghent, D. (1961). *The English novel: Form and function*. New York: Harper & Row Publishers.

Woodworth, R. S. (1940). *Psychology* (4th ed.). New York: Holt.

Young, P. T. (1936). *Motivation of behavior*. New York: Wiley.

Young, P. T. (1943). *Emotion in man and animal: Its nature and relation to attitude and motive*. New York: Wiley.

Zajonc, R. B. (1980). Feeling and thinking: Preferences need no inferences. *American Psychologist, 35*(2), 151–175.

Acknowledgments

Preparation of this volume was supported by NSF Grant Nos. SBR-9727896 and SES-0074688 to Lisa Feldman Barrett, and by NIMH Grant Nos. P01-MH/DA56826, R01-CA68427, and P50-DA84733, as well as support from the Andrew W. Mellon Foundation and Ethel F. Donaghue Women's Health Investigator Program to Peter Salovey.

Contents

Introduction

LISA FELDMAN BARRETT
PETER SALOVEY

The concept of emotional intelligence has emerged as an area of intense interest, both in scientific (Mayer, Salovey, & Caruso, 2000; Salovey & Mayer, 1990) and lay (e.g., Goleman, 1995, 1998) circles. Because emotionally intelligent individuals are socially effective, definitions of the concept in trade books and the popular press have included personality attributes more generally associated with adaptive personal and social functioning that may or may not be related to skills and abilities in the emotional arena (Mayer et al., 2000). Scientific treatments have defined emotional intelligence in terms of mental abilities rather than broad social competencies. For instance, Mayer and Salovey (1997) defined emotional intelligence as the ability to perceive, appraise, and express emotions accurately; the ability to access and generate feelings to facilitate cognitive activities; the ability to understand emotion-relevant concepts and use emotion-relevant language; and the ability to manage one's own emotions and the emotions of others to promote growth, well-being, and functional social relations.

The concept of emotional intelligence has been useful as an organizing framework in diverse contexts. It has been helpful to educators designing curricula for the purposes of improving children's social and emotional functioning (Mayer & Cobb, 2000; Salovey & Sluyter, 1997). It has been used by the human resources and organizational development fields to characterize skills important in the workplace other than specific job-related competencies (Caruso, Mayer, & Salovey, 2002; Cherniss & Goleman, 2001). Yet we wonder whether the excitement about the heuristic value of emotional intelligence has overshadowed a careful study of what it is, and in particular, the underlying psychological components that when brought together emerge as emotional intelligence. We expect that with a detailed explication of the multiple processes that characterize emotional intelligence, it will emerge as an organizing framework for investigators who study phenomena in which emotions play some role. The purpose of this volume is to examine these component processes using the model outlined by Mayer and Salovey (1997) as a starting point: (1) perceiving and appraising emotion, (2) using emotion to facilitate thought, (3) understanding and communicating emotion concepts, and (4) managing emotions in oneself and others. By establishing the underlying processes that characterize each of these domains of emotional intelligence, the construct validity of emotional intelligence as a whole can emerge.

As research on emotion progresses at many levels of analysis, from neuroscience to culture, the concept of emotional intelligence continues to evolve. The chapters in this book reflect some of these developments. One issue is whether it makes sense to talk of "accuracy" when referring to the representation of emotional events. Emotions are contextualized, emergent phenomena, such that there are no right or wrong responses—no accuracy in an absolute sense. However, some responses are better than others. Usually, judgments about the desirability of a response are culturally and temporally situated. Thus, it is sensible to measure emotional intelligence in terms of an individual's understanding and use of this consensual knowledge.

A second issue concerns the harnessing of emotions to encourage rational thought, stimulate creative problem solving, and motivate behavior. It is not a new idea that emotions play a pivotal role in assisting good decision making (e.g., Damasio, 1994; DeSousa, 1987), but the multiple ways in which this can occur are still being delineated. To begin with, emotional intelligence is more than just relying on feeling in reasoning. It is also harnessing the motivating properties of affect in everyday life. Traditional discussions of passion and reason assume a strong boundary between the two. Although thinking and feeling are certainly experientially distinct, recent neuroscience investigations suggest that they may be less neuroanatomically separable than originally assumed (Lane & Nadel, 2000). As a consequence, the relationship between emotion and cognition may need to be reconsidered. Moreover, less attention has been paid to the role of emotion in instigating behavior when the behaviors in question are not related to immediate survival. Unless one lives in a war-torn part of the world or in a distressed urban center, the probability of confronting stimuli that threaten survival and provoke prototypical emotional events (of the kind described by Darwin, 1872/1998) is relatively low. A useful theory must account for those events, but should also be able to capture the more frequent, but perhaps less dramatic, emotional responses that characterize modern daily living.

As for the structure of emotion knowledge, we do not know whether emotion concepts have the functional properties of concepts in other domains such as animals, automobiles, and food, or whether they have unique properties. If emotion concepts are like other concepts, then are they best described as traditional feature-based categories (Clore & Ortony, 1991), fuzzy sets with prototypes (Russell, 1991), or theory-based groupings (Medin, 1989)? Are they permanent or fluid, changing in response to situational contingencies in the immediate external environment (Barsalou, 1983) or phenomenological experiences in one's internal environment (e.g., Niedenthal, Halberstadt, & Innes-Ker, 1999)? Of course, the most important questions concern the relations between how emotional information is represented and the manner in which such representations influence diverse elements in an emotional response.

Finally, theories about coping, mechanisms of defense, finding meaning in adversity, resilience, and flexible responding all converge on the notion that components in an emotional response often require active management. This idea is reflected in the fourth branch of emotional intelligence concerning the regulation—often strategic—of feelings and emotions in oneself and other people. Typically, theorizing on these issues focuses on the prevention, abbreviation, or transformation of negative emotion, but is this really the dominant motivation for emotion management? It is plausible, even likely, that negative emotional responses allow us to function effectively in certain situations. Even more likely is the notion that cultivating positive emotions can have adaptive value in its own right, over and above the amelioration of negative responses.

The chapters included in this volume link ongoing basic research on affect and emotion to the ideas embodied in the emotional intelligence concept. In doing so, they provide evidence for the value of emotional intelligence as a framework for organizing and advancing theory and research on emotion. These chapters also stretch the boundaries of the emotional intelligence idea in new and important ways.

Part I of this volume deals with the processes involved in perceiving and identifying emotions in oneself and others. Bachorowski and Owren describe the functional acoustics in an emotional signaling system. They argue that there are direct and indirect ways in which perceivers attribute emotion to targets on the basis of their nonlinguistic vocal properties. Especially interesting are the ways in which declarative knowledge about the vocalizer interact with prosodic features of the vocal cues to produce an emotional impression in the listener. Perhaps even more apparent are the emotional cues provided on the canvas of the face. Elfenbein, Marsh, and Ambady describe the crucial role of reading facial expressions in emotional intelligence. Their chapter addresses how the meanings of facial expressions are interpreted against a contextual backdrop. Although facial expressions may provide some signal in an emotional transaction, they are not impervious to the influence of the relationship between sender and receiver, culture, social class, gender, and other features of the social environment. In the final chapter of Part I, Nelson and Bouton argue that the types of judgments described in the first two chapters may have their basis in associative learning. They detail the associative processes that modify or change the affective value of a stimulus. On the basis of the evidence they present, Nelson and Bouton argue that our learning histories are always with us. Although the affective significance of a stimulus may change, that change is often contextual (and therefore conditional in nature). As a result, learning histories are accumulative and to some extent indelible. These properties of acquisition and change in the affective significance of stimuli have profound implications for other aspects of an emotional response. Together, these three chapters begin to characterize how we come to view certain kinds of cues as emotionally meaningful, and certain types of information as emotionally relevant.

Part II describes how affective experiences come to influence thought and action. Gohm and Clore provide an explicit framework for understanding how individuals rely on affective feelings as a source of information in social judgment. They suggest that there is significant variability in this process, however. Those individuals who report attending to their feelings, and experiencing those feelings in a clear, intense way, use them in the judgment process differently than do others. Gilbert, Driver-Linn, and Wilson also describe the informational value of affective experience, specifically the value of anticipated affective states. They describe the processes involved in "impact bias," the tendency to misjudge both the duration and the intensity of predicted affective reactions. They suggest that similar biases may play out in retrospective accounts of emotional reactions as well, leading to the idea that prospective and retrospective judgments have more in common with each other than they do with actually experienced affective states.

Schwarz's analysis suggests that the states of mind accompanying everyday moods are best suited for different kinds of cognitive tasks. The expansive orientation facilitated by pleasant affective feelings encourages top-down information processing that is creative and heuristic driven. In contrast, the detail-oriented focus facilitated by unpleasant affective feelings encourages bottom-up information processing that is stimulus driven, deductive, and engenders the careful scrutiny of incoming information. Schwarz's ideas about how moods tune the cognitive system have implications for a range of outcomes, including stereotyping, attitude change, and analytical reasoning. Niedenthal, Dalle, and Rohmann also discuss how feeling tunes cognitive processing. The emotional aspects of stimuli form a core organizing principle around which they can be grouped into concepts. Discrete emotional experiences function as the "glue" in perceiving these concepts. The implication is clear: People literally perceive the world differently depending on how they are feeling. Discrete emotions influence not only categorization processes, but other cognitive processes as well. DeSteno and Braverman discuss the various ways in which discrete emotional experiences affect attitude change. They argue that individual differences in emotional intelligence influence the mechanisms by which emotions have their impact. In doing so, they synthesize the affect-as-information perspective with the cognitive-tuning approach to provide an emotional spin on the popular elaboration-likelihood model of attitude change.

The final chapter in Part II provides a neuroanatomical basis for the idea that feelings influence strategic information processing and planned behavior. Using examples from psychopathology, especially obsessive–compulsive disorder, Savage details how one area of the prefrontal cortex, called the orbital frontal cortex, allows individuals to harness affective information during the early stages of responding to stimuli, especially those that are novel or ambiguous in some way. In a preliminary sense, Savage lays the anatomical foundation for how emotional information influences thought and behavior.

Part III deals with emotion concepts—individuals' knowledge base about emotion and their ability to represent symbolically elements of the emotional response. This issue has been a focus of systematic research in developmental psychology. Denham and Kochanoff describe much of this research in their review of the developmental milestones in children's understanding of emotion—how this understanding develops from the ability to label emotional expressions, identify emotion-eliciting situations, comprehend probable causes of emotion, appreciate the consequences of emotion, and infer the emotional experiences of others. These authors provide a useful summary of the development of an emotional knowledge base that may be involved in other aspects of emotional intelligence. Lane and Pollermann describe the different levels of sophistication that characterize individuals' understanding of emotional experience. Using a Piagetian framework, they suggest that there are different levels of development, from understanding emotional experience in simplistic ways (e.g., in global or physical terms) to a more complex conceptual system that is precise and multifaceted. The complexity of a person's conceptual framework will determine, in turn, both the degree to which emotional experience can be represented mentally in a complex fashion and the complexity of the experience itself.

When laypersons think about emotional intelligence, they likely focus on regulation. In fact, managing the potential array of elements in an emotional response, and attempting to influence the feelings of others, are central aspects of competence in the emotional domain. Part IV of this volume concerns managing emotion. Gross and John are especially concerned with providing a framework for understanding the range of strategies involved in emotion regulation. Specifically, they contrast those strategies focused on managing the potential antecedents of an emotion response with those that change the response once it has occurred. They are also concerned with the effects of such strategies, in particular the consequences of suppression. Next, Tugade and Fredrickson point out the value of positive emotions. They suggest that positive emotions provide a powerful antidote to negative reactions. In addition, they highlight the intrinsic adaptive value of positive emotions themselves. Their broaden-and-build model suggests that positive emotions provide us with the psychological resources to engage in the more adaptive antecedent-focused strategies described by Gross and John. The final chapter in Part IV explores the consequences of challenging the deeply held belief that hedonism alone is the primary motive for emotion regulation. Knowing that certain types of cognitive and behavioral tasks are accomplished better when our cognitive system is tuned by negative emotion, Parrott argues that there may be circumstances in which it is useful to cultivate negative emotions and unleash their functional power. Contrary to being "hijacked" by negative emotion (e.g., Goleman, 1995), Parrott's analysis suggests that we may benefit from our negative feelings, which can sometimes be the guide to thinking clearly and behaving appropriately.

A good theory is generative. And although it is too early to know whether emotional intelligence is a foundation for creative research in emotion, Part V of this volume provides three illustrations of interesting directions for future research. Russell and Blanchard suggest that a person cannot be intelligent unless he or she knows what to be intelligent about. They argue that *emotion* is a category too broad for scientific discourse and suggest a lexicon for parsing the emotion domain that is consistent with many theories of emotion. Just as a well-developed emotion lexicon is important for functionally effective emotional behavior, these authors suggest that the definitional clarity resulting from a precise scientific lexicon can be important for effective future research on emotional intelligence.

The final two chapters provide examples of how emotional intelligence can make contact with research that is traditionally considered outside the realm of affect science. Ferguson and Bargh describe their work on automatic attitudes. They discuss the mechanisms through which individuals effortlessly integrate evaluative information from individual features of a novel object to provide an evaluative summary response to it. Aspects of this process appear to occur outside of consciousness and likely contribute to the initial affective appraisal of a stimulus. Blair reviews some of the literature on Theory of Mind, the ability to represent the mental states of self and others, and examines potential links to the various facets of emotional intelligence. Using examples from autism, where Theory of Mind is impaired, and examples from sociopathy, where emotional intelligence is impaired, Blair examines whether Theory of Mind is necessary for emotionally intelligent behavior.

Much of the popular media attention to the idea of emotional intelligence has focused on the measurement of an "EQ" (e.g., Gibbs, 1995). Although assessing individual differences in the abilities that constitute emotional intelligence is a useful endeavor, it is our view that the field will benefit from a deeper understanding of the processes that subserve these different skills. Such an analysis allows research on emotional intelligence to be better situated in the field of affect science, rather than merely a provocative contribution to the intelligence testing literature. Once situated there, emotional intelligence has the potential to organize what we know and stimulate new questions about how emotional phenomena serve adaptive personal and social functioning at many levels of analysis. Regardless of one's core theoretical preferences, there is a convergence of thought that emotions are functional. One cannot study the processes by which people emote or assign emotional value without considering their effectiveness. And, as learning theorist O. H. Mowrer (1960, p. 308) noted, the emotions "do not at all deserve being put into opposition with 'intelligence.'" The spirit of Mowrer's comment is clear: We cannot understand the workings of the mind and their influence on behavior without understanding the role of emotional processes. Emotional intelligence may be an important conceptual framework for guiding research on emotional phenomena and their influence on the range of things that concern us as psychologists.

REFERENCES

Barsalou, L. W. (1983). Ad hoc categories. *Memory and Cognition, 11,* 211–227.

Caruso, D. R., Mayer, J. D., & Salovey, P. (2002). Emotional intelligence and emotional leadership. In R. E. Riggio, S. E. Murphy, & F. J., Pirozzolo (Eds.), *Multiple intelligences and leadership* (pp. 55–74). Mahwah, NJ: Erlbaum.

Cherniss, C., & Goleman, D. (Eds.). (2001). *The emotionally intelligence workplace.* San Francisco: Jossey-Bass

Clore, G. L., & Ortony, A. (1991). What more is there to emotion concepts than prototypes? *Journal of Personality and Social Psychology, 60,* 48–50.

Damasio, A.R. (1994). *Descartes' error: Emotion, reason, and the human brain.* New York: Putnam's.

Darwin, C. (1998). *The expression of emotions in man and animals* (3rd ed.). New York: Oxford University Press. (Original work published 1872)

DeSousa, R. B. (1987). *The rationality of emotion.* Cambridge, MA: MIT Press.

Gibbs, N. (1995, October 2). The E.Q. factor. *Time,* pp. 60–68.

Goleman, D. (1995). *Emotional intelligence.* New York: Bantam Books.

Goleman, D. (1998). *Working with emotional intelligence.* New York: Bantam Books.

Lane, R. D., & Nadel, L. (Eds.). (2000). *Cognitive neuroscience of emotion.* New York: Oxford University Press.

Mayer, J. D., & Cobb, C. D. (2000). Educational policy on emotional intelligence: Does it make sense? *Educational Psychology Review, 12,* 163–183.

Mayer, J. D., & Salovey, P. (1997). What is emotional intelligence? In P. Salovey & D. Sluyter (Eds.), *Emotional development and emotional intelligence: Implications for educators* (pp. 3–31). New York: Basic Books.

Mayer, J. D., Salovey, P. & Caruso, D. R. (2000). Emotional intelligence as zeitgeist, as personality, and as mental ability. In R. Bar-On & J. D. A. Parker (Eds.), *Handbook of emotional intelligence* (pp. 92–117). San Francisco: Jossey-Bass.

Medin, D. L. (1989). Concepts and conceptual structure. *American Psychologist, 44,* 1469–1481.

Mowrer, O. H. (1960). *Learning theory and behavior.* New York: Wiley.

Niedenthal, P. M., Halberstadt, J. B., & Innes-Ker, A. H. (1999). Emotional response categorization. *Psychological Review, 106,* 337–361.

Russell, J.A. (1991). In defense of a prototype approach to emotion concepts. *Journal of Personality and Social Psychology, 60,* 37–47.

Salovey, P., & Mayer, J. D. (1990). Emotional intelligence. *Imagination, Cognition, and Personality, 9,* 185–211.

Salovey, P., & Sluyter, D. (Eds.). (1997). *Emotional development and emotional intelligence: Implications for educators.* New York: Basic Books.

PART I

Perceiving Emotion

 CHAPTER 1

Vocal Acoustics in Emotional Intelligence

JO-ANNE BACHOROWSKI
MICHAEL J. OWREN

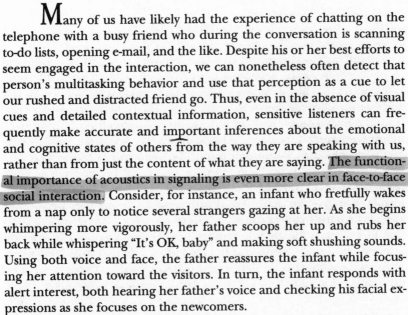

Many of us have likely had the experience of chatting on the telephone with a busy friend who during the conversation is scanning to-do lists, opening e-mail, and the like. Despite his or her best efforts to seem engaged in the interaction, we can nonetheless often detect that person's multitasking behavior and use that perception as a cue to let our rushed and distracted friend go. Thus, even in the absence of visual cues and detailed contextual information, sensitive listeners can frequently make accurate and important inferences about the emotional and cognitive states of others from the way they are speaking with us, rather than from just the content of what they are saying. The functional importance of acoustics in signaling is even more clear in face-to-face social interaction. Consider, for instance, an infant who fretfully wakes from a nap only to notice several strangers gazing at her. As she begins whimpering more vigorously, her father scoops her up and rubs her back while whispering "It's OK, baby" and making soft shushing sounds. Using both voice and face, the father reassures the infant while focusing her attention toward the visitors. In turn, the infant responds with alert interest, both hearing her father's voice and checking his facial expressions as she focuses on the newcomers.

In each of these examples, one or both parties has responded to nonlinguistic aspects of vocal behavior. Not only in these, but in many other types of situations, infants, children, and adults all demonstrate that they are affected by sounds that others produce and can themselves effect similar influences. How sounds are used, and the exact ways in which listeners perceive, appraise, and respond to sounds, thus constitute an important part of emotional intelligence (EI). We will refer to this aspect as "vocal EI," a term that is meant to include both the use of sounds by vocalizers and responses to sounds in listeners. Vocal EI may be considered part of what Mayer and Salovey (1997) refer to as the perception or identification of emotion in their four-branch model of EI. However, in this chapter, our overall focus is a bit more on listeners, particularly as they perceive and respond to the affective states of others in negotiating social interactions (Lane, 2000; Salovey, Bedell, Detweiler, & Mayer, 2000; Walker-Andrews, 1997). The underlying processes are, of course, very complex and as yet poorly understood, whether the sounds in question are explicitly nonlinguistic, as in the cases of crying and laughter, or acoustic cues that occur against the backdrop of linguistic speech. Even less is known about possible individual differences in vocal EI, on either the production or perception side. However, in reviewing several pertinent areas of expression and perception of vocal emotion, it becomes clear that such differences must exist.

SOUND AND AFFECT

The abilities to perceive and express emotion are together considered to be the most basic component of EI (Ciarrochi, Chan, & Caputi, 2000; Mayer, Caruso, & Salovey, 1999). As articulated by Salovey, Mayer, and Caruso (2002; Mayer & Salovey, 1993, 1997), this aspect is nonetheless extremely complex, including registering, attending to, and deciphering emotional messages. Although the focus of such discussions is often speech-based communication, the topic can be addressed as a much more general problem, namely, that vocal EI can include both using acoustics to influence others and producing functional responses to such sounds. Our goal here is to flesh out this broader perspective and particularly involves using an "affect-induction" framework to show that EI reflects both the inherent influences that a sound can have on listener emotional systems and the mediating role that the ability to appraise the significance of that sound plays in the effectiveness of an individual's response.

The Affect-Induction Framework

The affect-induction perspective argues that nonlinguistic vocal behavior is fundamentally a means by which a signaler can modulate the behavior of a listener by using sound to influence the latter's attentional, arousal, and emotional states (Owren & Rendall, 1997, 2001). In other words, it is explicitly not assumed that vocal signals are meaningful as a result of having the linguistic-like property of carrying symbolic information. Instead, the "meaning" or "message" that can be ascribed to a vocal event is taken to reflect a combination of its impact on a listener's affect and the appraisal processes that this individual can bring to bear. This approach thus explicitly avoids ascribing to nonlinguistic signals the linguistic-like property of having encoded, representational value. Although originally developed as a model of nonhuman primate vocal signaling, it can be equally well applied to human vocal behavior (e.g., Bachorowski & Owren, 2001; Owren & Bachorowski, 2001a). In each case, vocalizers are thought to be able to influence listeners both through the "direct" effects that acoustic events can have on listener affect, and because of more "indirect," learned emotional responses resulting from previous pairings of an individual's sounds with subsequent affect-inducing events.

Direct Effects

Direct effects of sound come easily to mind—for instance, as illustrated by acoustic-startle responses to loud or abrupt-onset sounds. Humans experience this reflex as an involuntary attentional shift toward the source of the triggering sound, which is often a somewhat unpleasant experience. It is also an arousing one, in the sense that sounds can trigger general organismal activation due to stimulation of low-level neural circuitry such as the pontine nuclei of the brainstem. However, this reflex is not limited to humans. Rather, it is believed to occur in every species that can hear (Eaton, 1984) and demonstrates that particular kinds of acoustic features can engage the listener response systems directly. In their most general form, these effects can thus include drawing the listener's attention, modulating overall activation level either up or down, and inducing emotional responses as in the form of positive or negative feeling states (for further discussion of these terms, see Russell & Feldman Barrett, 1999).

Although few vocal sounds are likely used specifically to elicit acoustic startle, vocalizations can readily exhibit features like abrupt onset, high pitch and amplitude, and dramatic frequency and amplitude modulation—each of which is effective in capturing attention and inducing arousal (Owren & Rendall, 2001). These powers are quite evident for environmental sounds like thunderclaps, as well as artificially constructed warning sounds like car honks and wailing sirens. Just as these sounds can directly "tweak" listeners, human vocalizations such as infant cries, laughter, shrieks of pain, and even emblematic exclamations of disgust or fear can also readily grab attention and induce arousal.

Indirect Effects

Sounds can also exert an impact on listeners through more indirect means, based on associative learning. Here the premise is that both humans and nonhumans alike routinely learn emotional responses to acoustic stimuli that are distinctive sounding and predict some other affectively significant event. Vocalizers, for instance, regularly produce individually distinctive sounds that are paired with behavior that affects others in important ways, thereby creating the foundation for conditioned affective responses in those individuals. For example, the soothing tone that a parent adopts when comforting a distressed child is effective in part because that tone has in the past been paired with warmth, physical contact, and gradual calming. The distinctive features of this individual's voice also clearly plays a role, as that learned affect has not been attached to just any vocalizer who might adopt a similar tone in speaking to the child. Similarly, a child's emotional response to an abrupt "no" varies, depending on whether the sound is uttered by a parent who has previously followed it by physical deterrence or punishment or by a sibling who has not followed with such behavior. Even the individually distinctive sigh produced by a romantic partner has quite a different emotional impact on the listener than the same sound heard from a professional colleague.

Sound-Induced Affect

Recent empirical work on the psychophysiology of sound-induced affect nicely demonstrates that sound can routinely affect listener arousal and emotion (Bradley & Lang, 2000; see also Bradley & Lang, 1999). Although these studies did not draw a comparable distinction between direct and indirect effects of sounds, the authors found clear evidence of separable effects on arousal on the one hand, and positive or negative emotional valence on the other. The study also showed correlations between listener ratings of sounds on these two dimensions and several standard measures of psychophysiological responding. In other words, using stimuli as disparate as machine noises, nonhuman vocalizations, nonlinguistic human vocalizations, and sounds associated with appetitive human behaviors, the work indicated that both nonspecific nervous system activation effects and specifically positive or negative responses occurred in listeners. That listener evaluations of many of the stimuli used reflected learned affective responses is illustrated by the strong positive ratings given to the distinctive sound of beer being poured. Although the sound itself is quiet and unobtrusive, it is nonetheless distinctive and routinely paired with subsequent pleasurable ingestion of beer.

THE FOUNDATIONS OF VOCAL EI

Although previous applications of the affect-induction approach have focused on vocalizers using sounds to elicit attention, arousal, and emotion in listeners, the preceding observations set the stage for considering at least four separable, but complementary, contributors to vocal EI. We first briefly describe these threads, and then go on to consider a series of examples from nonlinguistic and linguistic vocal behavior in humans. Specifically of interest here is how individual differences in vocal EI can arise from variation in each of these four components, and likely in others as well.

Four Components of Vocal EI

In our view, the most basic contributor to vocal EI is that humans are susceptible to direct effects of sound. In other words, both in exerting an influence on listener affect and in intelligent evaluation of vocalizer behavior, the process is grounded in responsiveness to salient acoustic features. It is also likely that there are significant individual differences at this level. It is, for example, clear from acoustic-startle studies in nonhumans and humans alike that significant variation occurs in the probability of eliciting this reflex with a given sound (e.g., Blumenthal, 2001). This variability undoubtedly reflects both genetic and environmental influences, as shown in rodent strains that are specifically inbred for susceptibility to startle responses that then trigger audiogenic seizures (e.g., Bjork & Tacke, 1985). In other words, human listeners likely vary significantly in the degree to which they are inherently responsive to acoustic features like abrupt onset, high frequency and amplitude, or dramatic frequency and amplitude modulation. Thus, although sirens are designed to have a direct, affectively significant impact on all individuals within earshot, some listeners find them excruciatingly noxious whereas others are much less affected. Although the direct impact of human vocalizations is typically, but not always, more subtle, listener response can be expected to vary in the attentional, arousal, and emotional domains.

The second component is the acquisition of learned responses to

affectively significant sounds—both using and responding to vocalizations is likely fundamentally grounded in previous experience with
these sounds. Here again, significant individual variation can be expected. In other words, some human listeners can be expected to form immediate, strong, and durable affective responses to distinctive and predictive sounds produced by those with whom they interact. However,
there are likely others who would form such associations more slowly
and attain a more modest and shorter-lived affective response from exactly the same pairing experience.

Moving to a higher level, a third important component of vocal EI
is the extent to which an individual is able to empathize with or draw accurate inferences concerning the vocalizer's state. Both direct and indirect effects are likely contributors, as illustrated by "emotional contagion." This phenomenon is said to occur when synchronization of
expressions, vocalizations, postures, and movements contributes to attentional and affective convergence of two or more individuals (e.g.,
Hatfield, Cacioppo, & Rapson, 1994). Both direct and indirect effects
of vocalizations that modulate the attention, arousal, and valenced
emotion of a listener can thus also induce an affective state that more
closely resembles that of the vocalizer—in effect, producing empathy.
However, listeners inevitably also bring more active processing to bear.
In addition to drawing inferences based on their own affective responses to a vocalizer's sounds, listeners can draw on cues available from
other aspects of the vocalizer's behavior, contextual cues, and any
knowledge they may have from past experience with that individual.
Again, one can expect significant individual variation in critical traits,
not only in the degree of "contagion" that occurs, but also in the extent
and sophistication of the more evaluative, inferential processes.

Finally, vocal EI must include the extent to which listeners can respond flexibly and functionally in the face of their own directly and indirectly induced affective responses to the vocalization they hear. As discussed later, for example, a parent will likely respond more effectively
by being able to harness the activation and unpleasant feelings induced
by a grating, high-amplitude infant cry in the service of caregiving behaviors rather than acting on the negative emotion per se. In this case,
the caregiver must override the most immediate effects of the vocalizations in evaluating how to respond. The converse must also be the case,
as vocalizations like laughter can also induce positive affect in listeners
and thereby influence their behavior. However, although vocalizers
may thereby promote a more positive stance toward themselves on the
part of listeners, it is not a given that the latter also benefit. Instead, a
listener's most functional response is to modulate that response, thereby being able to weigh concomitantly the costs and benefits involved in

the interaction. In this case too, we suspect important individual differences in the degree and effectiveness of the critical processes.

Vocal EI Includes Multiple Processing Levels

As implied by the enumeration of the four components, a significant amount of the response processing involved in vocal EI is likely to be comparatively low-level and to occur outside the realm of conscious awareness (see also Bargh & Chartrand, 1999). The affect-induction view, for example, emphasizes the benefit that vocalizers can derive by using the direct and indirect effects of sound to induce affect in listeners, thereby helping to shape the behavior of those individuals. These are effects over which the listener has little or no direct conscious control. In addition, nonconscious processes in the listener are also likely important in more active responding: deploying auditory and visual attention, engaging appraisal processes involved in stimulus assessment, regulating physiological responses elicited by sound, and selecting among behavioral response options. Each of these elements should also be sensitive to the context in which vocalizations are occurring. Thus, even low-level responses to sounds are known to be subject to strong "top-down" modulation effects—for instance, dramatically affecting whether or not a sound elicits attention, arousal, or a particular valenced emotional state (reviewed by Kryter, 1994).

Whereas the direct and indirect effects we have outlined are "bottom-up" sorts of events, a listener's more sophisticated evaluation and inference reflects higher-level processing. Here the listener's pre-existing knowledge of the particular vocalizer involved and the context of vocalization must be extremely important, with ample opportunity for modulating emotional and behavioral responses. For example, the listener may respond quite differently to an emotionally evocative sound depending on who has produced it and the context in which it has been heard. The significance of a given sound produced in a particular context may thus be open to quite different interpretations, depending on the relationship between vocalizer and listener, whereas virtually identical sounds heard in distinct contexts may evoke quite different appraisals.

One upshot of this overall approach is that nonlinguistic vocal behavior need not be seen as having linguistic-like symbolic or referential value in order to function as communication (see Owren & Rendall, 2001). Instead, the "meaning" that can be said to attach to a particular vocal event emerges from a combination of effects occurring at each of these levels, including affective responses elicited by the vocalizer and appraisal processes occurring in the listener. In this view, nonlinguistic vocalizations do not convey fixed, encoded messages, but rather rely on particular sorts of acoustic properties to trigger low-level responses in listeners that are then subject to both automatic and more flexible, higher-level processing. In this sense, vocal EI is a central construct for understanding nonlinguistic communication in general. In the next sections, these ideas are illustrated in the context of both nonlinguistic and linguistic vocal behavior in humans, including infant crying, laughter, infant-directed speech, and modal speech. In each case, we attempt to illustrate how the various levels we have sketched out contribute to an overall construct of vocal EI.

Vocal Acoustics

In considering these examples, a few points should be noted about the vocal-production process itself. Most work in this area is guided by the source-filter model of speech production (for a detailed overview, see Kent, 1997), which views vocalization as a linear combination of a source energy and subsequent filtering effects—both of which can contribute to the phenomenon of vocal EI.

In many cases, the source energy of vocalization is produced through regular vibration of the vocal folds, which produces energy at the basic rate of vibration (the fundamental frequency, or F_0) and at integer multiples of that frequency (the higher harmonics). F_0 is a primary contributor to the listener's perception of pitch, and sounds with measurable F_0 are said to be voiced. However, source energy can also be produced through irregular vocal fold vibration or through turbulent airflow in the vocal tract, in which case the resulting sounds are noisier, lack a measurable F_0, and are referred to as being unvoiced. As will be seen, both mean F_0 and F_0 modulation are prominently involved in emotion-related vocal signals. Although these cues can reflect a vocalizer's internal state (see Johnstone & Scherer, 2000), it is also the case that humans have considerable control over both.

Filtering effects exerted by resonances of the cavities above the larynx are the other component of the source-filter model of vocal production. These resonances are referred to as formants, which are regions of the frequency spectrum that selectively pass energy while damping it out elsewhere. Articulatory gestures such as tongue and lip movements alter the shape of this supralaryngeal filter, thereby giving rise to linguistic contrasts in speech. Filtering effects are also of interest because of their prominent role in providing individual distinctiveness to vocal signals (Bachorowski & Owren, 1999; Bachorowski, Smoski, & Owren, 2001b).

Although less well studied, nonlinear phenomena are also highly likely to be important in vocal EI. For example, vocal fold vibration need not be regular and stable, but can instead become chaotic or undergo discrete F_0 jumps (e.g., Wilden, Herzel, Peters, & Tembrock, 1998). Although these effects are considered antithetical to effective linguistic signaling in speech (e.g., Baken, 1995), they may be central to nonlinguistic aspects of vocal behavior. Nonlinear phenomena are frequently observed in sounds like infant crying (e.g., Mende, Herzel, & Wermke, 1990) and human laughter (Bachorowski et al., 2001b), for instance, making them grating, shriek-like, tinny, or wheezy. We suspect that sounds with nonlinearities are especially effective in engaging listener attention and arousal processes and are important to listener attributions concerning vocalizer affect.

NONLINGUISTIC VOCALIZATIONS

Humans produce a variety of nonlinguistic, emotion-related vocal signals, with crying and laughter being two obvious examples. Although both have clear links to vocalizer emotion, each is also a compelling example of how vocal acoustics can induce affect in listeners and thereby shape their behavior. Traditionally, sounds like cries and laughs have been thought to convey representational information, with listeners extracting differentiated meanings from different acoustic versions within each signal class. The affect-induction approach, in contrast, posits that the foundation of the communication event is the impact that each sound type can have on listeners, who "understand" these signals based on a combination of their own arousal and emotional responses, the context in which the signal has been produced, and any relevant knowledge they have about the vocalizer.

Infant Crying

Crying is one of the primary means by which human infants can prompt parenting behaviors from their caregivers. There is general agreement that cries are specifically associated with negative states, including irritability, distress, hunger, and both minor and acute physical illness (Bisping, Steingrueber, Oltmann, & Wenk, 1990; Zeskind & Lester, 1978). Caregivers are thus ostensibly able to distinguish between pain, hunger, and "wet-diaper" cries (Berry, 1975; Wasz-Höckert, Lind, Vuorenkoski, Partanen, & Valanné, 1968), with some researchers going so far as to propose that cries are akin to a universal language learned early in life (Berry, 1975; see also Zeskind & Marshall, 1988). However, there is little empirical work to support this representational perspective (Gustafson, Wood, & Green, 2000). Although it would clearly be advantageous for both infants and their caregivers if cries had linguistic-like referential value, inferences about the significance of cry acoustics are more likely made on the basis of contextual cues (Barr, Hopkins, & Green, 2000a; Brennan & Kirkland, 1982; Zeskind & Collins, 1987).

Infant cries are nonetheless potent signals, whose salient acoustics are very effective in drawing the attention of caregivers. As discussed by Gustafson and colleagues (2000; see also Barr, Hopkins, & Green, 2000b; Leger, Thompson, Merritt, & Benz, 1996), acoustic variability in crying is correlated with listener perceptions of distress and urgency, which in turn are likely important for the probability and latency of caregiver response. However, listeners in perceptual experiments make these sorts of evaluations no matter the original underlying cause of the crying (Protopapas & Eimas, 1997; Zeskind & Collins, 1987), meaning that cry acoustics themselves are important in shaping listener inferences concerning infant states and needs. For example, F_0-related measures and the presence or absence of nonlinear phenomena appear to be important in both inducing affect in listeners and in their perceptions of infant distress. Both naïve adults and experienced caregivers routinely rate high-F_0 cries as being more urgent, grating, aversive, and piercing than low-F_0 versions (e.g., Dessureau, Kurowski, & Thompson, 1998; Huffman et al., 1994; Zeskind & Collins, 1987; Zeskind & Lester, 1978). Cries showing nonlinearities in vocal fold vibration are similarly rated as being more aversive than comparatively tonal cries with fewer such irregularities (Gustafson & Green, 1989; see also Hirschberg, 1999; Mende et al., 1990).

In combination, the acoustic manifestations of infant urgency, resulting physiological responses in listeners (Zeskind, Sale, Maio, Huntington, & Weiseman, 1985; see also Gustafson et al., 2000), contextual information, and the highly developed cognitive abilities of caregivers can thus make crying a very effective communication system. Some data also indicate that cries can be individually distinctive. For example, Gustafson, Green, and Cleland (1994) reported that adults can recognize the cries of familiar infants, even when cry quality is degraded by both distance and signal manipulation. If so, specific conditioned emotional responses can be added to the list of elements that contribute to caregiver evaluation processes.

Both child-abuse offenders and those people at risk for perpetrating child abuse have been found to respond quite differently to these sounds than do nonabusive adults. Frodi and Lamb (1980), for example, found that parents with a history of child abuse do not make distinctions among cries, instead regarding all cries as noxious. These investigators also reported that in comparison to nonabusers, those with a history of abuse or neglect had stronger cardiac and electrodermal responses to cries—consistent with the notion that they were either more aroused by infant cries, unable to regulate the arousal induced by cry acoustics, or both. In a similar vein, Crowe and Zeskind (1992) found both cardiac and electrodermal distinctions between adults deemed to either exhibit or not exhibit child-abuse potential, which were particularly apparent in responses to cries with very high F_0s. Taken together, these findings indicate that caregivers who maltreat or who are at risk for maltreating their offspring may be impaired in any of several kinds of processes that we are arguing to be important contributors to vocal EI, including affective responses to crying, the ability to modulate those reactions, and appraising the significance of the sounds. It therefore appears that abusive individuals may actually be particularly vulnerable to infant cry acoustics, rather than being unresponsive caregivers, but lack the resources to effectively manage the arousal and emotion that these sounds can provoke.

Optimal responding to infant crying thus brings each component of vocal EI into play. We suspect that first-time caregivers, in the absence of much experience with crying infants, are likely haphazard in responding to newborns. Affective responses to cry acoustics are probably not as well managed as they later become, and caregivers may not be particularly sensitive to telltale variation in the sounds. However, over time, caregiver vocal EI can increase through improved modulation of their own affect in response to crying, better discrimination among the acoustic features involved, and more experience with the relationships between vocalizations, infant states, and the effectiveness of various attempted remedies. Each of these dimensions creates the opportunity for more effective inferences about a given situation, and individual variation in the requisite perceptual and appraisal abilities likely leads to different eventual levels of adeptness on the part of different caregivers (see also Gustafson & Harris, 1990).

Laughter

Despite the virtually ubiquitous occurrence of laughter in human social interactions, surprisingly little is known about the functional significance of this vocalization. There has nonetheless been no shortage of speculation about why we laugh, typically emphasizing the purported meaning or representational information being conveyed (e.g., Darwin, 1872/1998; Deacon, 1997; Grammer, 1990; Grammer & Eibl-Eibesfeldt, 1990). However, a fundamental problem with this approach is that the purported messages involved appear to vary widely, without mapping onto corresponding acoustic variation (reviewed by Owren & Bachorowski, 2001a). For example, although laughter has been proposed to convey that the laugher is experiencing a positive state like being happy, feeling playful, or getting a joke, it is also associated with more negative feelings like anxiety, self-deprecation, and derision.

From a representational standpoint, listeners should be able to discern each possible message from the laugh acoustics involved. In our own work, we have instead found that laugh sounds are highly variable (Bachorowski et al., 2001b), even when laughers are consistently experiencing positive affective states (Bachorowski, Smoski, & Owren, 2001a). In these studies variation in laugh rate and acoustic form was, however, associated with the relationship between the laugher and the social partner present at the time. Here, two important factors were laugher and listener sex, and whether the two individuals were friends or strangers. As in the case of infant crying, subsequent experiments showed that listeners produced consistent ratings of the laughs based on acoustic characteristics of these sounds—in this case, the presence or absence of voicing (Bachorowski & Owren, 2001). In other words, although the laughter had all been produced by vocalizers in similar emotional states, listener affective responses to these same sounds were quite different, depending on the acoustic features involved. Regardless of whether listeners were asked to rate the laughs according to their own emotional response, the likely emotional response of others, or inferred attributes of the individual producing the laugh, voiced laughs invariably elicited more positive evaluations than did unvoiced laughs.

The affect-induction approach therefore proposes that laugh production is grounded in a vocalizer strategy of eliciting listener arousal and emotion through both direct and indirect effects (Owren & Bachorowski, 2001a). The occurrence of laughter naturally engages active listener appraisal processes as well, which are then important in modulating affective responses and subsequent behavior. In this view, the function of laughter is to induce or accentuate positive emotion in another individual (Bachorowski & Owren, 2001), thereby encouraging the listener to have a favorable dispositional stance toward the vocalizer (Owren & Bachorowski, 2001b). Once again, however, the listener's response should reflect a combination of the lower-level effects the laugher can induce and the higher-level evaluative processes that the listener brings to bear.

To illustrate, consider a flirtatious, high-pitched laugh produced by a female in conversation with a mixed group of males and females whom she has just met at a cocktail party. In line with common sense and experience, we suggest that these various listeners respond quite differently—not because the laughter carries multiple representational messages that are independently sent to the various listeners, but because both induced affective responses and concomitant appraisals and inferences can be quite different among these individuals. Males, for example, are notorious for their tendency to interpret friendly behavior by unfamiliar females as being indicative of sexual interest (e.g., Koeppel, Montagne-Miller, O'Hair, & Cody, 1993), arguably reflecting an inherently positive affective stance when interacting with stranger females. The latter can then accentuate that bias by producing laughs with acoustic features that tend to activate the male listener's nervous system. While encouraging interest and approach behavior in males, the same arousing effects may produce a quite different effect in a female listener. The latter does not have the male's affective bias and may even have the opposite predisposition—an inherently negative stance resulting from intra-sex competitiveness (e.g., Burbank, 1987). If so, the same arousing acoustic features can accentuate that negative predisposition, promoting withdrawal or competitive behavior rather than a more positive response.

Inferences concerning the "meaning" of the laughter may be similarly divergent, based not only on this lower-level interaction of acoustics and an affective response system, but also on the listener's implicit and explicit knowledge or biases about human behavior. Those processes can in turn dramatically change a listener's ultimate appraisal. A male, for example, may explicitly recognize that the female's laugh is not inherently indicative of interest, in spite of feeling the pleasant tweak produced by its acoustics. Based on past experience, that individual may in fact experience both responses simultaneously, with resulting behavior then reflecting the extent to which the male can use this explicit realization to modulate the impact of his lower-level responses. Similarly, a female experiencing a spurt of competitiveness prompted by the activating effects of these laugh acoustics may draw any of a variety of implicit or explicit conclusions concerning the vocalizer and her behavior, with past experience and higher-level modulation effects also playing a significant role. As outlined earlier, vocal EI can thus be said to reflect a combination of these effects, beginning with the listener's susceptibility to these acoustics, learned affect resulting from past experience, the ability to modulate those responses, and the accuracy of inference concerning the significance of the sounds vis-à-vis the vocalizer's motivations and states.

LINGUISTIC VOCALIZATIONS

Although its pervasive referential content and grammatical structure may distinguish human speech from other known signaling systems,

spoken language nevertheless always includes nonlinguistic components as well. In certain cases, in fact, the linguistic content of speech
may actually be less important in influencing listener behavior than are
other aspects. That may particularly be the case when caregivers speak
to preverbal infants. Although these offspring cannot comprehend this
speech, they are nevertheless affected by its acoustic properties. It is
also clear that when speech occurs among fully competent language
users, nonlinguistic aspects of the signal can play an important role in
the overall communication process. In both such instances, using and
responding to these nonlinguistic aspects of the speech signal exempli-
fies the phenomenon of vocal EI.

Infant-Directed Speech

In many cultures, the speech caregivers use with infants is notably different from that used with adults and older children. Perhaps the most
noticeable of the many features that characterize this infant-directed
(ID) speech are its high mean F_0 values and dramatic F_0 modulation—
properties associated with high overall pitch, exaggerated pitch contours, and stronger prosodic cueing (Fernald & Kuhl, 1987; Katz,
Cohen, & Moore, 1996). Both these and other characteristics are
known to play an important role in regulating affect in infant listeners
who are too young to recover linguistic content, but are nonetheless
susceptible to the impact that ID speech can have on attention, arousal,
and emotion (Fernald, 1991, 1992; Walker-Andrews, 1997). The
melody is the message in such speech, according to Fernald (1989), a
characterization that also captures the essence of our argument that the
acoustics of vocalizations can themselves be important because of having direct effects on listeners.

In fact, early in infant development, vocal cues are more powerful
than facial expressions in eliciting responses or modulating infant states
(Fernald, 1991; Papoušek, Bornstein, Nuzzo, Papoušek, & Symmes,
1990). For example, when caregivers attempt to draw infants' attention
or engage them in a joint activity, their speech becomes dominated by
rising pitch contours. Conversely, when the speech is meant to be
soothing, predominantly falling pitch contours are used. Controlled
laboratory experiments with synthetic stimuli have requisitely confirmed that upward-sweeping stimuli increase or maintain infant
arousal, whereas downward sweeps have the opposite effect (e.g., Kaplan & Owren, 1994). These effects can be considered a latent form of
EI, because although an infant has very limited ability to regulate its
own affect, its susceptibility to caregiver sounds and expressions facilitates the development of these and other emotion-related abilities (Fer-

nald, 1992; Walker-Andrews, 1997). By about 8 months of age, for instance, infants are able to actively use the emotional expressions of others to guide their own affective and behavioral responses, a phenomenon referred to as "social referencing" (Walker-Andrews & Dickson, 1997).

Although there is as yet little direct evidence of individual variation in this infantile form of EI, work by Camras and her colleagues is at least suggestive in this regard. For instance, infants have been found to be more likely to reference relatively expressive than inexpressive day care providers, especially in fear-related circumstances (Camras & Sachs, 1991). Work with older children has further shown that maltreated children tend to be less competent in recognizing and deliberately posing emotion-related facial expressions (Camras, Grow, & Ribordy, 1983; Camras et al., 1990; see also Camras, Sachs-Alter, & Ribordy, 1996). Izard and his colleagues have confirmed the implications of such results, finding that competence in these abilities during the preschool years subsequently mediates both social behavior and academic performance in school-age children (Izard et al., 2001). Although it is not yet known whether the relatively poor emotion recognition shown by abused children results from differences in perceptual or inferential processes, both can certainly be involved. It is therefore of interest for future work to examine the relative importance of vocal, facial, and other expressive gestures at each stage of development, particularly as it is not yet known whether infants and toddlers make equal use of all the available cues or instead weight them differentially (see Mumme, Fernald, & Herrera, 1996).

The use of ID speech is, of course, another important domain of vocal EI in this intertwined system of communication between caregivers and infants. Not only must caregivers be motivated to use prosodic cues to regulate infant attention and arousal, they also need to be requisitely sensitive to infant state and able to modulate their own affective state so as to produce the appropriate sounds at the most auspicious moments. Some caregivers may, for example, be better able than others to produce short, shushing sounds and other calming vocalizations in the face of aversive crying, noxious odors, and a possible range of annoying behaviors shown by the infant. In this view, ID speech does not itself constitute emotional speech, as has recently been suggested (Trainor, Austin, & Desjardins, 2000). Rather than being a direct reflection of vocalizer state, our claim is that ID speech is produced because its acoustic features affect infant states. It is thus a form of vocal EI to be able to use ID speech effectively in regulating the infant's affect no matter what the caregiver's own internal state is at that moment.

In that vein, it is of interest to note that because ID speech can be used to attract an infant's attention to important features in his or her environment, it may play an important role in learning and cognitive development. Here again, a caregiver's ability to produce effective vocal signals at appropriate moments can have a significant impact on those processes. For example, depressed mothers on average produce ID speech with lower mean F_0s and less F_0 modulation than do nondepressed mothers (Bettes, 1988; Kaplan, Bachorowski, & Zarlengo-Strouse, 1999). These differences may have important functional consequences, as laboratory learning studies have further shown that ID speech recorded from depressed mothers is relatively less effective in facilitating simple voice–face associations in infant participants (Kaplan et al., 1999). However, even infants of depressed mothers show evidence of this learning when trained with the ID speech of an unfamiliar, nondepressed mother (Kaplan, Bachorowski, Smoski, & Hudenko, 2002). In other words, it is the acoustics of the ID speech involved rather than some difference in the infants' processing that is critical.

This particular example represents a relatively extreme case, but it illustrates that important components of vocal EI may be compromised by depression and probably other psychopathologies as well. Although exploring such effects in detail is beyond the scope of this chapter, the larger point is that some caregivers, for any number of reasons, may be less able to take advantage of the beneficial impact that judicious use of vocal acoustics can have on their infants. As a result, these offspring may endure longer periods of emotional distress than other infants, be less likely to use others' facial and vocal signals to regulate their own emotional states, and miss out on learning that would otherwise be facilitated by a caregiver's use of acoustically salient vocalizations in the normal course of interaction.

Modal Speech

Although linguistic content has played only a small part in the examples of infant crying, laughter, and ID speech that have been considered so far, it is obviously paramount in normal, or modal, speech. Nonetheless, it is also clear that acoustic aspects of speech that are not inherently phonetic also play an important role in the communication event. For example, paralinguistic speech features such as prosody are routinely considered to carry affect-related information from which listeners draw inferences about talker arousal and emotion. A considerable number of studies involving "emotional" speech produced by actors have demonstrated that listeners can infer the emotion that is intended with at least some degree of accuracy (e.g., Banse & Scherer, 1996; Scherer, Banse, Wallbott, & Goldbeck, 1991; for review, see Johnstone & Scherer, 2000). However, it is also the case that listener error rates are often quite high—much higher, in fact, than is usually observed when participants are asked to perform the same task based on photographs of posed facial expressions.

The most robust results have again primarily revolved around F_0 properties. For example, when Scherer and colleagues (1991; see also Banse & Scherer, 1996; Leinonen, Hiltunen, Linnankoski, & Laakso, 1997) examined the acoustic features of neutral and emotional nonsense sentences spoken by four actors, portrayals of fear, joy, and anger were all associated with higher mean F_0. In contrast, the actors' portrayals of sadness resulted in lower mean F_0. Parallel effects were also noted for vocal amplitude in each case. Across studies, the most robust findings have thus been that portrayals of high-arousal emotions are associated with increases in mean F_0, F_0 variability, and overall amplitude, whereas low-arousal emotions produce the opposite effects. Some additional differentiation among individual emotions has been found by examining pitch contours, but these outcomes are less reliable.

Given the remarkable acoustic complexity of linguistic utterances, it should probably not be surprising that neither perceptual nor acoustic studies have shown altogether convincing evidence of invariant cues to emotion in speech. In fact, as Scherer (1986) points out, perceptual performance is actually somewhat better than expected as compared with the objectively identifiable acoustic cues that are present. Although there is admittedly much yet to be learned, taking these data at face value suggests that arousal per se may be playing the most important role. Clearly, talker arousal state plays an important role on the production side, affecting aspects like overall pitch, speech rate, and vocal amplitude. These characteristics are all in turn very salient to listeners, but by themselves do not clearly differentiate between valenced emotions involving similar arousal levels. The implication is that although speech signals do provide some cues to talker state, more accurate emotion-related inferences from naturally occurring speech probably rely heavily on a combination of contextual information and the listener's own expertise in making such judgments.

If so, there is a considerable role to be played by vocal EI both in production and perception—arguably more so, in fact, than is the case for any of the other vocal signals we have considered. For example, it is clear that higher-level cortical circuitry is much more important in speech communication than in nonlinguistic vocalizations like crying and laughter. If speech has fewer links to affect-related brain regions like the limbic system, talkers are likely better able to deliberately produce speech with acoustic features that sway listener affect and inference (see also Neumann & Strack, 2000). Conversely, listeners face the requisitely more challenging task of trying to infer accurately specific emotional states from cues that are mostly arousal- rather than valence-related. They must furthermore be able to tease apart emotion-related effects from the use of the same F_0 and amplitude cues for purely linguistic emphasis (Cauldwell, 2000). The ongoing speech stream must thus be evaluated not only based on the talker's particular linguistic characteristics, but also talking into account the particular context in which the speech is being heard.

Although there is little direct evidence available concerning individual differences in vocal EI as applied to modal speech, some individuals may exhibit much greater control over the extent to which they can either inject or inhibit affect-related cueing in their voices, including professional actors and accomplished liars. Examining lie detection from vocal cues is thus one way to better understand vocal EI (see Mayer & Salovey, 1997). Experiments conducted by Ekman and his colleagues (reviewed by Ekman, 1996) show that on average it is a remarkably difficult task for naïve participants to discern reliably when a person is lying or stating a belief to which he or she does not actually subscribe. In fact, the same is true even for professionals whose careers involve direct interactions with deceptive individuals. However, a few people can be identified who are especially astute in this regard, including some law enforcement agents and clinical psychologists (Ekman, O'Sullivan, & Frank, 1999; Frank & Ekman, 1997). Although these highly skilled lie detectors probably attend to a variety of cues, vocal characteristics are likely to be important in identifying deceit. The fact that most listeners are more routinely duped is thus at least suggestive evidence of important individual variation in sensitivity to vocal correlates of talker state in modal speech (see Louth, Williamson, Alpert, Pouget, & Hare, 1998).

CONCLUSIONS

To summarize briefly, we have outlined a concept of vocal emotional intelligence that encompasses a range of components. This construct of vocal EI must include production of sounds whose acoustic features influence the behavior of others. Yet perceiving and responding to such characteristics must be at least as important. Furthermore, we consider vocal EI to include processes of differing complexity, including responsiveness to direct and indirect effects of sounds, modulation of the affective consequences of those effects, and the ability to draw inferences about the significance of the vocal event by incorporating both previous knowledge and the context in which the sound is heard. In taking this approach, we have treated vocal EI as an inherent part of any communication process that involves nonlinguistic elements. Among nonhumans, in fact, it may be difficult to distinguish between the construct we have outlined and the normal course of acoustic communication.

Vocal EI in an Evolutionary Context

Having adopted this broad perspective, it is also appropriate at least to consider briefly vocal EI in an wider evolutionary context. On the one hand, there is a natural temptation to infer that vocalizers and listeners should benefit uniformly from both producing signals that include veridical acoustic correlates of their internal states and accurately perceiving and responding to such cues. Consistent with this approach, we have at least implicitly suggested that vocal EI confers a number of advantages on both parties. Infants typically cry, for example, precisely because they are distressed and need attention from caregivers. The latter can then benefit from the attention-getting, arousing, and even noxious aspects of these sounds precisely because natural selection has favored those who respond effectively to their offspring's needs.

On the other hand, no trait can possibly confer only benefits and no costs—if only because a trait in one form precludes some alternative version that would provide a different set of advantages to the organism. The observation holds for vocal EI as well, at least as outlined here. For example, we have argued that infant crying is a strategy of eliciting parental care by using highly salient sounds that have a direct impact on listener nervous systems. Although obviously effective, it is also energetically costly and puts the infant at some risk of physical abuse from these same caregivers. An alternative strategy would be to produce sounds that are less salient, reducing both metabolic costs and risk of maltreatment. However, such sounds would presumably be less reliable in eliciting the attention needed, particularly when the caregiver is sleeping, distracted with other tasks, or simply lacks the motivation to respond. For the listener, being vulnerable to the salient acoustic features of the sounds is, of course, also beneficial—except in those circumstances when caregiver and infant interests are in conflict or susceptibility to ongoing crying leads to abuse.

Generalizing, one can thus never simply assume that either producing veridical cues to one's internal state or responding to those cues from others is uniformly beneficial (e.g., Krebs & Dawkins, 1984; Owren & Bachorowski, 2001b; Owren & Rendall, 2001; cf. Fridlund, 1994). Instead, one should consider both vocalizers and listeners to be behaving strategically, noting that the two parties never have exactly the same fitness interests in every circumstance. For the vocalizers, produc-

ing signals that are direct, veridical readouts of internal state is sometimes beneficial but also makes them extremely predictable to others
and creates the risk of exploitation. Conversely, perceivers who are sensitive to vocal cues to signaler state benefit by being able to "read" those
individuals, but also leave themselves vulnerable to being swayed in
ways that are more advantageous to the vocalizer. In this sense, vocal EI
represents a double-edged sword of benefits and costs, which further
underscores the likelihood that individual humans will show significant
variation in its component traits.

What We Need to Learn

It is also worth considering how further progress may best be made in understanding vocal EI. As the concept itself is new, vocal EI is not currently part of most available tests of EI, including the Mayer–Salovey–Caruso
Emotional Intelligence Test (MSCEIT) (Mayer, Salovey, Caruso, &
Sitarenios, 2001; Salovey, Mayer, Caruso, & Lopes, in press; although see
Davies, Stankov, & Roberts, 1998). However, in accordance with the
component-based perspective proposed here, one strategy is to devise a
corresponding set of measures. Given the recent availability of normed
acoustic stimuli (Bradley & Lang, 2000), for example, it is now possible
to compare arousal- and emotion-induction among individual listeners.
Another trait of interest to measure is how quickly and efficiently a listener can regulate acoustically induced psychophysiological responses,
for instance, by measuring the power of sound to interfere with task performance in some other domain. It is, of course, particularly important
to measure how well listeners can take contextual information into account in drawing inferences about other individuals' affective state from
their vocal acoustics, with the hypothesis being that individual differences on this variable should have predictive value for the nature and
quality of social interactions.

However, one approach that we strongly feel should be avoided is
the hitherto heavy reliance on artificial stimulus material such as emotional speech produced by actors. Although it is of central importance
to better understand how and to what degree listeners can make inferences about emotional state from vocal acoustics, it is also essential that
the speech samples represent naturally occurring emotional states. It is
the nature of acting to portray affective states using cues that are as
salient as possible while remaining convincing. Through experience
with such portrayals, audiences naturally become requisitely familiar
with the way in which such states are represented in a given acting style.
The inevitable result is then that the relationship between apparent
vocal EI in and from acted vocalizations and naturally occurring sound

production and perception remains unknown. Given the intimate relationship we have proposed between EI and communication in general, we must advocate experimental approaches that avoid introducing the confounding effects of deliberate portrayal on one side and volitional suspension of disbelief on the other. Instead, we suggest that testing occur with stimuli whose authenticity can reveal both the sensitivities that are present and their limitations. Exploring the two facets together must be the means through which vocal EI and its likely variation across individuals ultimately can be understood.

REFERENCES

Bachorowski, J.-A., & Owren, M.J. (1999). Acoustic cues to gender and talker identity are present in a short vowel segment produced in running speech. *Journal of the Acoustical Society of America, 106,* 1054–1063.

Bachorowski, J.-A., & Owren, M.J. (2001). Not all laughs are alike: Voiced but not unvoiced laughter elicits positive affect in listeners. *Psychological Science, 12,* 252–257.

Bachorowski, J.-A., Smoski, M.J., & Owren, M.J. (2001a). *Laugh rate and acoustics are associated with social context: I. Empirical outcomes.* Manuscript under review.

Bachorowski, J.-A., Smoski, M.J., & Owren, M.J. (2001b). The acoustic features of human laughter. *Journal of the Acoustical Society of America, 110,* 1581–1597.

Baken, R. J. (1995). Between organization and chaos: A different view of the voice. In F. Bell-Berti & L. J. Raphael (Eds.), *Producing speech: Contemporary issues* (pp. 233–245). New York: American Institute of Physics.

Banse, R., & Scherer, K. R. (1996). Acoustic profiles in vocal emotion expression. *Journal of Personality and Social Psychology, 70,* 614–636.

Bargh, J. A., & Chartrand, T. L. (1999). The unbearable automaticity of being. *American Psychologist, 54,* 462–479.

Barr, R. G., Hopkins, J. A., & Green, J. A. (2000a). Crying as a sign, a symptom and a signal: Evolving concepts of crying behavior. In R. G. Barr, B. Hopkins, & J. A. Green (Eds.), *Crying as a sign, a symptom, and a signal* (pp. 1–7). New York: Cambridge University Press.

Barr, R. G., Hopkins, J. A., & Green, J. A. (2000b). The crying infant and toddler: Challenges, emergent themes and promissory notes. In R. G. Barr, B. Hopkins, & J. A. Green (Eds.), *Crying as a sign, a symptom, and a signal* (pp. 210–217). New York: Cambridge University Press.

Berry, K. K. (1975). Developmental study of recognition of antecedents of infant vocalizations. *Perceptual and Motor Skills, 41,* 400–402.

Bettes, B. (1988). Maternal depression and motherese: Temporal and intonational features. *Child Development, 59,* 1089–1096.

Bisping, R., Steingrueber, H. J., Oltmann, M., & Wenk, C. (1990). Adults' tolerance of cries: An experimental investigation of acoustic features. *Child Development, 61,* 1218–1229.

Bjork, E. A., & Tacke, U. (1985). Sounds with harmonic spectra are more effective than pure tones in inducing audiogenic seizure in rats. *Hearing Research, 17,* 95–98.

Blumenthal, T. D. (2001). Extraversion, attention, and startle response reactivity. *Personality and Individual Differences, 31,* 495–503.

Bradley, M. M., & Lang, P. J. (1999). *International affective digitized sounds (IADS): Stimuli, instruction manual, and affective ratings.* (Tech. Rep. B-2). Gainseville: University of Florida, Center for Research in Psychophysiology.

Bradley, M. M., & Lang, P. J. (2000). Affective reactions to acoustic stimuli. *Psychophysiology, 37,* 204–215.

Brennan, M., & Kirkland, J. (1982). Classification of infant cries using descriptive scales. *Infant Behavior and Development, 5,* 341–346.

Burbank, V. (1987). Female aggression in cross-cultural perspective. *Behavior Science Research, 21,* 70–100.

Camras, L. A., Grow, G., & Ribordy, S., (1983). Recognition of emotional expressions by abused children. *Journal of Clinical Child Psychology, 12,* 325–328.

Camras, L. A., Ribordy, S., Hill, J., Martino, S., Sachs, V., Spaccarelli, S., & Stefani, S. (1990). Maternal facial behavior and the recognition and production of emotional expression by maltreated and nonmaltreated children. *Developmental Psychology, 26,* 304–312.

Camras, L. A., & Sachs, V. (1991). Social referencing and caretaker expressive behavior in a day care setting. *Infant Behavior and Development, 14*(1), 27–36.

Camras, L. A., Sachs-Alter, E., & Ribordy, S. C. (1996). Emotion understanding in maltreated children: Recognition of facial expressions and integration with other emotion cues. In M. Lewis, M. W. Sullivan (Eds.), *Emotional development in atypical children* (pp. 203–225). Hillsdale, NJ: Erlbaum.

Cauldwell, R. T. (2000).Where did the anger go? The role of context in interpreting emotion in speech. *Proceedings of the ISCA Workshop on Speech and Emotion: A Conceptual Framework for Research,* 127–131.

Ciarrochi, J. V., Chan, A. Y. C., & Caputi, P. (2000). A critical evaluation of the emotional intelligence construct. *Personality and Individual Differences, 28,* 539–561.

Crowe, H. P., & Zeskind, P. S. (1992). Psychophysiological and perceptual responses to infant cries varying in pitch: Comparison of adults with low and high scores on the Child Abuse Potential Inventory. *Child Abuse and Neglect, 16,* 19–29.

Darwin, C. (1872/1998). *The expression of the emotions in man and animals.* New York: Oxford University Press.

Davies, M., Stankov, L., & Roberts, R. D. (1998). Emotional intelligence: In search of an elusive construct. *Journal of Personality and Social Psychology, 75,* 989–1015.

Deacon, T. W. (1997). *The symbolic species.* New York: Norton.

Dessureau, B. K., Kurowski, C. O., & Thompson, N. S. (1998). A reassessment of the role of pitch and duration in adults' responses to infant crying. *Infant Behavior and Development, 21,* 367–371.

Eaton, R. C. (Ed.). (1984). *Neural mechanisms of startle behavior.* New York: Plenum Press.

Ekman, P. (1996). Why don't we catch liars? *Social Research, 63,* 801–817.

Ekman, P., O'Sullivan, M., & Frank, M. G. (1999). A few can catch a liar. *Psychological Science, 10,* 263–266.

Fernald, A. (1989). Intonation and communicative intent in mothers' speech to infants: Is the melody the message? *Child Development, 60,* 1497–1510.

Fernald, A. (1991). Prosody in speech to children: Prelinguistic and linguistic functions. In R. Vasta (Ed.), *Annals of child development* (Vol. 8, pp. 43–80). Philadelphia: Jessica Kingsley.

Fernald, A. (1992). Human maternal vocalizations to infants as biologically relevant signals: An evolutionary perspective. In J. H. Barkow, L. Cosmides, & J. Tooby (Eds.), *The adapted mind* (pp. 391–428). New York: Oxford University Press.

Fernald, A., & Kuhl, P. K. (1987). Acoustic determinants of infant preference for motherese speech. *Infant Behavior and Development, 10,* 279–293.

Frank, M. G., & Ekman, P. (1997). The ability to detect deceit generalizes across different types of high-stake lies. *Journal of Personality and Social Psychology, 72,* 1429–1439.

Fridlund, A. J. (1994). *Human facial expression: An evolutionary view.* New York: Academic Press.

Frodi, A. M., & Lamb, M. E. (1980). Child abusers' responses to infant smiles and cries. *Child Development, 51,* 238–241.

Grammer, K. (1990). Strangers meet: Laughter and nonverbal signs of interest in opposite-sex encounters. *Journal of Nonverbal Behavior, 14,* 209–236.

Grammer, K., & Eibl-Eibesfeldt, I. (1990). The ritualization of laughter. In W. Koch (Ed.), *Naturlichkeit der Sprache und der Kultur: Acta colloquii* (pp. 192–214). Bochum: Brockmeyer.

Gustafson, G. E., & Green, J. A. (1989). On the importance of fundamental frequency and other acoustic features in cry perception and infant development. *Child Development, 60,* 772–780.

Gustafson, G. E., Green, J. A., & Cleland, J. W. (1994). Robustness of individual identity in the cries of human infants. *Developmental Psychobiology, 27,* 1–9.

Gustafson, G. E., & Harris, K. L. (1990). Women's responses to young infants' cries. *Developmental Psychology, 26,* 144–152.

Gustafson, G. E., Wood, R. M., & Green, J. A. (2000). Can we hear the causes of infant crying? In R. G. Barr, B. Hopkins, & J. A. Green (Eds.), *Crying as a sign, a symptom, and a signal* (pp. 8–22). New York: Cambridge University Press.

Hatfield, E., Cacioppo, J., & Rapson, R. (1994). *Emotional contagion.* New York: Cambridge University Press.

Hirschberg, J. (1999). Dysphonia in infants. *International Journal of Pediatric Otorhinolaryngology, 49*(Suppl.1), S293–S296.

Huffman, L. C., Bryan, Y. E., Pedersen, F. A., Lester, B. M., Newman, J. D., & del Carmen, R. (1994). Infant cry acoustics and maternal ratings of temperament. *Infant Behavior and Development, 17,* 45–53.

Izard, C., Fine, S., Schultz, D., Mostow, A., Ackerman, B., & Youngstrom, E. (2001). Emotion knowledge as a predictor of social behavior and academic competence in children at risk. *Psychological Science, 12,* 18–23.

Johnstone, T., & Scherer, K. R. (2000). Vocal communication of emotion. In M.

Lewis & J. M. Haviland-Jones (Eds.), *Handbook of emotions* (2nd ed., pp. 220–235). New York: Guilford Press.

Kaplan, P.S., Bachorowski, J.-A., Smoski, M. J., & Hudenko, W.J. (2002). Infants of depressed mothers, although competent learners, fail to learn in response to their own mothers' infant-directed speech. *Psychological Science, 13,* 268–271.

Kaplan, P.S., Bachorowski, J.-A., & Zarlengo-Strouse, P. (1999). Infant-directed speech produced by mothers with symptoms of depression fails to promote associative learning in four-month-old infants. *Child Development, 70,* 560–570.

Kaplan, P.S. & Owren, M. J. (1994). Dishabituation of visual attention in 4-month-olds by infant-directed frequency sweeps. *Infant Behavior and Development, 17,* 347–358.

Katz, G. S., Cohen, J. F., & Moore, C. A. (1996). A combination of vocal f0 dynamic and summary features discriminates between three pragmatic categories of infant-directed speech. *Child Development, 67,* 205–217.

Kent, R. D. (1997). *The speech sciences.* San Diego: Singular.

Koeppel, L. B., Montagne-Miller, Y., O'Hair, D., & Cody, M. J. (1993). Friendly? Flirting? Wrong? In P. J. Kalbfleisch (Ed.), *Interpersonal communication: Evolving interpersonal relationships* (pp. 13–32). Hillsdale, NJ: Erlbaum.

Krebs, J. R., & Dawkins, R. (1984). Animal signals: Mind-reading and manipulation. In J. R. Krebs & N. B. Davies (Eds.), *Behavioural ecology: An evolutionary approach* (2nd ed., pp. 380–402). Oxford: Blackwell Scientific.

Kryter, K. (1994). *The handbook of hearing and the effects of noise.* San Diego: Academic Press.

Lane, R. D. (2000). Levels of emotional awareness: Neurological, psychological, and social perspectives. In R. Bar-On & J. D. A. Parker (Eds.), *The handbook of emotional intelligence: Theory, development, assessment, and application at home, school, and in the workplace* (pp. 171–191). San Francisco: Wiley.

Leger, D. W., Thompson, R. A., Merritt, J. A., & Benz, J. J. (1996). Adult perception of emotion intensity in human infant cries: Effects of infant age and cry acoustics. *Child Development, 67,* 3238–3249.

Leinonen, L., Hiltunen, T., Linnankoski, I., & Laakso, M.-L. (1997). Expression of emotional–motivational connotations with a one-word utterance. *Journal of the Acoustical Society of America, 102,* 1853–1863.

Louth, S. M., Williamson, S., Alpert, M., Pouget, E. R., & Hare, R. D. (1998). Acoustic distinctions in the speech of male psychopaths. *Journal of Psycholinguistic Research, 27,* 375–384.

Mayer, J. D., Caruso, D. R., & Salovey, P. (1999). Emotional intelligence meets traditional standards for an intelligence. *Intelligence, 27,* 267–298.

Mayer, J. D., & Salovey, P. (1993). The intelligence of emotional intelligence. *Intelligence, 17,* 433–442.

Mayer, J. D., & Salovey, P. (1997). What is emotional intelligence? In P. Salovey & D. J. Sluyter (Eds.), *Emotional development and emotional intelligence* (pp. 3–31). New York: Basic Books/HarperCollins.

Mayer, J. D., Salovey, P., Caruso, D. R., & Sitarenios, G. (2001). Emotional intelligence as a standard intelligence. *Emotion, 1,* 232–242.

Mende, W., Herzel, H., & Wermke, K. (1990). Bifurcations and chaos in new-born infant cries. *Physics Letters A, 145,* 418–424.

Mumme, D. L., Fernald, A., & Herrera, C. (1996). Infants' responses to facial and vocal emotional signals in a social referencing paradigm. *Child Development, 67,* 3219–3237.

Neumann, R., & Strack, F. (2000). "Mood contagion": The automatic transfer of mood between persons. *Journal of Personality and Social Psychology, 79,* 211–223.

Owren, M. J., & Bachorowski, J.-A. (2001a). *Laugh rate and acoustics are associated with social context: II. An affect-induction account.* Manuscript under review.

Owren, M. J., & Bachorowski, J.-A. (2001b). The evolution of emotional expression: A "selfish-gene" account of smiling and laughter in early hominids and humans. In T. J. Mayne & G. A. Bonanno (Eds.), *Emotions: Current issues and future directions* (pp. 152–191). New York: Guilford Press.

Owren, M. J., & Rendall, D. (1997). An affect-conditioning model of nonhuman primate signaling. In D. H. Owings, M. D. Beecher, & N. S. Thompson (Eds.), *Perspectives in ethology: Vol. 12. Communication* (pp. 299–346). New York: Plenum Press.

Owren, M. J., & Rendall, D. (2001). Sound on the rebound: Bringing form and function back to the forefront in understanding nonhuman primate vocal signaling. *Evolutionary Anthropology, 10,* 58–71.

Papoušek, M., Bornstein, M. H., Nuzzo, C., Papoušek, H., & Symmes, D. (1990). Infant responses to prototypical melodic contours in parental speech. *Infant Behavior and Development, 13,* 539–545.

Protopapas, A., & Eimas, P. D. (1997). Perceptual differences in infant cries revealed by modifications of acoustic features. *Journal of the Acoustical Society of America, 102,* 3723–3734.

Russell, J. A., & Feldman Barrett, L. (1999). Core affect, prototypical emotional episodes, and other things called emotion: Dissecting the elephant. *Journal of Personality and Social Psychology, 76,* 805–819.

Salovey, P., Bedell, B. T., Detweiler, J. B., & Mayer, J. D. (2000). Current directions in emotional intelligence research. In M. Lewis & J. M. Haviland-Jones (Eds.), *Handbook of emotions* (2nd ed., pp. 504–520). New York: Guilford Press.

Salovey, P., Mayer, J. D., & Caruso, D. (2002). The positive psychology of emotional intelligence. In C. R. Snyder & S. J. Lopez (Eds.), *Handbook of positive psychology* (pp. 159–171). New York: Oxford University Press.

Salovey, P., Mayer, J. D., Caruso, D. R., & Lopes, P. N. (in press). Measuring emotional intelligence as a set of abilities with the MSCEIT. In S. J. Lopez & C. R. Snyder (Eds.), *Handbook of positive psychology assessment.* Washington, DC: American Psychological Association.

Scherer, K. R. (1986). Vocal affect expression: A review and model for future research. *Psychological Bulletin, 99,* 143–165.

Scherer, K. R., Banse, R., Wallbott, H. G., & Goldbeck, T. (1991). Vocal cues in emotion encoding and decoding. *Motivation and Emotion, 15,* 123–148.

Trainor, L. J., Austin, C. M., & Desjardins, R. N. (2000). Is infant-directed speech prosody a result of the vocal expression of emotion? *Psychological Science, 11,* 188–195.

Walker-Andrews, A. S. (1997). Infants' perception of expressive behaviors: Differentiation of multimodal information. *Psychological Bulletin, 121,* 437–456.

Walker-Andrews, A. S., & Dickson, L. R. (1997). Infants' understanding of affect. In S. Hala (Ed.), *The development of social cognition* (pp. 161–186). East Sussex, UK: Psychology Press.

Wasz-Höckert, O., Lind, J., Vuorenkoski, V., Partanen, T., & Valanné, E. (1968). *The infant cry: A spectrographic and auditory analysis* (Clinics in Developmental Medicine, No. 29). Lavenham, UK: Lavenham Press.

Wilden, I., Herzel, H., Peters, G., and Tembrock, G. (1998). Subharmonics, biphonation, and deterministic chaos in mammal vocalization. *Bioacoustics, 9,* 171–196.

Zeskind, P. S., & Collins, V. (1987). Pitch of infant crying and caregiver responses in a natural setting. *Infant Behavior and Development, 10,* 501–504.

Zeskind, P. S., & Lester, B. M. (1978). Acoustic features and auditory perceptions of the cries of newborns with prenatal and perinatal complications. *Child Development, 49,* 580–589.

Zeskind, P. S., & Marshall, T. R. (1988). The relationship between variations in pitch and maternal perceptions of infant crying. *Child Development, 59,* 193–196.

Zeskind, P. S., Sale, J., Maio, M. L., Huntington, L., & Weiseman, J. R. (1985). Adult perceptions of pain and hunger cries: A synchrony of arousal. *Child Development, 56,* 549–554.

CHAPTER 2

Emotional Intelligence and the Recognition of Emotion from Facial Expressions

HILLARY ANGER ELFENBEIN
ABIGAIL A. MARSH
NALINI AMBADY

Emotional intelligence—the "accurate appraisal and expression of emotions in oneself and others and the regulation of emotion in a way that enhances living" (Mayer, DiPaolo, & Salovey, 1990, p. 772)—encompasses a set of interrelated skills and processes. Because the face is the primary canvas used to express distinct emotions nonverbally (Ekman, 1965), the ability to read facial expressions is particularly vital, and thus a crucial component of emotional intelligence.

Facial expressions are privileged relative to other nonverbal "channels" of communication, such as vocal inflections and body movements. Facial expressions appear to be the most subject to conscious control (Zuckerman, DePaulo, & Rosenthal, 1986). Individuals focus more attention on projecting their own facial expressions and perceiving others' facial expressions than they do on other nonverbal channels (Noller, 1985) and often more than they focus on verbal communication (Friedman, 1978). We are so primed to read facial expressions that we often read expressions into neutral faces, perceiving static facial features as indicative of emotional or personality traits (Laser & Mathie, 1982; Zebrowitz, 1997). People are more accurate in recognizing facial expressions relative to other kinds of expressive information (Boyatzis

& Satyaprasad, 1994; Fridlund, Ekman, & Oster, 1984). Moreover, information from the face is privileged relative to other communication channels. For example, when inconsistent or mixed messages are communicated via different channels of communication—such as a positive facial expression with a negative spoken message—the facial information tends to carry relatively more weight (Carrera-Levillain & Fernández-Dols, 1994; Fernández-Dols, Wallbott, & Sanchez, 1991; Mehrabian & Ferris, 1967).

PERCEIVING IS FOR DOING

Overall, the ability to perceive faces accurately serves important adaptive functions. Information acquired from facial expressions promotes efficient interpersonal behavior that can help to maximize social outcomes (McArthur & Baron, 1983). Although the ability to perceive emotion from all channels—and particularly the face—shows reliable individual differences (Buck, 1976; Rosenthal, Hall, DiMatteo, Rogers, & Archer, 1979), often these differences are adaptations structured by the situational context.

We attempt to review these phenomena in this chapter. We begin by discussing briefly the evolution and development of the ability to recognize facial expressions, and then review findings on the relationship between the expresser and perceiver of facial expressions as well as cross-group differences. We then summarize methodological issues that provide the backdrop for understanding how the recognition of facial expressions in real life settings can differ from that in experimental studies. Later, we review evidence that the ability to recognize facial expressions has important consequences for interpersonal functioning. Given the enthusiastic reception that emotional intelligence has received in organizational contexts (e.g., Goleman, 1995, 1998), we emphasize the link between organizational outcomes and recognizing facial expressions of emotion. Finally, we discuss the recognition of facial expressions in the context of other components of emotional intelligence.

UNIVERSALITY AND EARLY DEVELOPMENT OF
RECOGNIZING FACIAL EXPRESSIONS

The ability to recognize emotion from facial expressions appears at least partially inborn. Newborns prefer to look at faces rather than other complex stimuli and thus may be programmed to focus on information in faces (Fantz, 1961; Kagan & Lewis, 1965). Infants also appear able to discriminate between facial expressions, to imitate them, and to comprehend their emotional tenor (Field, Woodson, Greenberg, & Cohen, 1983; Fridlund, Ekman, & Oster, 1984; Meltzoff & Moore, 1983; Zebrowitz, 1997). It seems, then, that we are born with the tendency and capacity to focus on facial expressions. However, infants' recognition skills are rudimentary, and the ability to read faces improves greatly with age (Feldman, Coats, & Spielman, 1996; Lenti, Lenti-Boero, & Giacobbe, 1999; Philippot & Feldman, 1990). This improvement has been attributed to development of relevant cognitive and perceptual capacities, as well as increasing practice and exposure over time (Nelson & De Haan, 1997; Walker-Andrews, 1997). On the basis of this and other evidence, evolutionary theorists have argued that natural selection may have favored a predisposition toward attending to information expressed in the face (Fridlund, 1997).

Facial expressions also likely serve a social function. Some basic expressions may have developed and maintained their particular appearance because they elicit reactions and attributions beneficial to the person who expresses them. For example, fear may make a person look more submissive, and anger may make a person look more dominant (Keating, Mazur, & Segall, 1977; Marsh & Kleck, 2002; Zebrowitz, 1997). In this way, expressing fear may serve to limit the aggression of another person, whereas expressing anger may induce submission. Thus, the tendency to perceive basic facial expressions in consistent ways may be an adaptation permitting social interactions to run more efficiently and smoothly. There may also be a social function to more complex facial expressions. Ambiguous messages can sometimes be useful, and the flexibility of many facial expressions allows for the communication of indirect, tactful, or duplicitous messages.

THE RELATIONSHIP BETWEEN THE EXPRESSER AND THE PERCEIVER OF FACIAL EXPRESSIONS

In the recognition of facial expressions, it matters *whose* face is being judged. The relationship between the expresser and the perceiver of a facial expression has important consequences for accuracy. Two particular aspects of this relationship are shared cultural background and acquaintanceship.

Familiarity with a Group

Emotional communication is generally more accurate among people who share similar cultural backgrounds. Although classic studies conducted by Ekman (1972), Izard (1971), and their colleagues have demonstrated that facial photographs of Americans expressing "basic" emotions can be recognized with above-chance accuracy by both liter- ate and nonliterate groups, these studies also provide evidence for cul- tural differences. Non-American samples generally did not recognize the photographs of American facial expressions as accurately as did Americans (Elfenbein & Ambady, 2002; Russell, 1994). For example, in Izard's (1971) large-scale study, American and European groups identi- fied 75–83% of the facial photographs, whereas Japanese scored 65% and Africans correctly identified only 50%.

Recent research on recognizing emotional expressions across cul- tures has attempted to integrate evidence for both cross-cultural univer- sals and differences (e.g., Fiske, Kitayama, Markus & Nisbett, 1998; Markus & Kitayama, 1991; Mesquita & Frijda, 1992; Scherer & Wallbott, 1994). Along these lines, a recent meta-analysis found evidence for both universality and cultural differences in emotion recognition (Elfenbein & Ambady, 2002).

Although emotions are recognized at above-chance levels across cultural boundaries, there is also evidence for an "in-group advantage," such that emotion recognition is more accurate when individuals judge emotions expressed by members of their same national, ethnic, or re- gional group. To explain this in-group advantage, we suggest a meta- phor of "emotional dialects." Although emotional communication may be a universal language, there may also be subtle differences in this lan- guage across cultural groups such that we can better understand people expressing themselves using a similar "dialect" to our own. Further, there is evidence that cross-cultural exposure can reduce the size of the in-group advantage in emotion recognition (Elfenbein & Ambady, 2001, 2002), just as familiarity with a dialect improves understanding of a spoken language.

Familiarity with an Individual

Acquaintance with an individual's cultural group appears to improve the accuracy of perceiving facial expressions, as subtle differences in emotional expression across cultural groups may aid in communica- tion, implicitly or explicitly. There is less evidence, however, that famil- iarity with any single person improves the recognition of his or her fa- cial expressions. People exhibit roughly equal accuracy in judging the facial expressions of strangers versus acquaintances (Ansfield, DePaulo, and Bell, 1995; Zuckerman, Lipets, Koivumaki, & Rosenthal, 1975), dat- ing partners (Sabatelli, Buck, & Dreyer, 1980), and even themselves (Ansfield, DePaulo, & Bell, 1995; Lanzetta & Kleck, 1970).

The ability to perceive expressive behavior may actually be hindered by familiarity with a person's past behavior. Kenny and Acitelli (2001) have argued that familiarity may improve accuracy but increase bias. In the particular example of lie detection, personal familiarity decreases the ability to detect deception (Brandt, Miller, & Hocking, 1980; Millar & Millar, 1995). Individuals may become overloaded when they possess too much information about an interaction partner's behavioral patterns (Millar & Millar, 1995). This may cause perceivers to attend selectively to expected behavioral cues only, potentially overlooking other cues, which may result in biased interpretation. Sabatelli, Buck, and Dreyer (1982) provide an alternate explanation for the absence of large acquaintanceship effects in emotion recognition. They hypothesize that accurate understanding of nonverbal expressions may increase intimacy early on, but later declines in importance. Thus, acquaintanceship effects may exist only up to a certain threshold, after which people with differing levels of familiarity should be on roughly equal footing.

GROUP DIFFERENCES IN RECOGNIZING FACIAL EXPRESSIONS

As with any form of "intelligence," there are individual differences in the ability to recognize facial expressions of emotion (e.g., Rosenthal et al., 1979). Further, there are systematic differences in the ability across demographic groups and personality types.

Gender

As early as 3 years of age, and across many cultures, females have greater ability than males to perceive facial expressions of emotion (Babchuk, Hames, & Thompson, 1985; Boyatzis, Chazan, & Ting, 1993; Hall, 1978, 1984; Kirouac & Doré, 1985; Rotter & Rotter, 1988). Explanations of this gender difference have proved controversial. Psychologists have linked the finding to a wide range of other gender differences, including women's greater empathy, greater expressiveness, greater practice, greater tendency to accommodate others, greater breadth in using emotional information, and subordinate role in the larger culture (Noller, 1986; Hall, 1979).

The *subordination hypothesis,* asserting that women's traditional social subordination causes their superior skills in detecting emotions, has been particularly controversial (Henley, 1977; LaFrance & Henley, 1994; Snodgrass, 1985, 1992). The logic is that it is more valuable for subordinates to understand their superiors' emotions than the reverse

(Keltner, Gruenfeld, & Andersen, 2001). In favor of the subordination hypothesis is experimental evidence that assigning subordinate versus superior status to experimental participants does alter sensitivity to certain types of nonverbal cues (Snodgrass, 1985; Snodgrass, Hecht, & Ploutz-Snyder, 1998). Recent evidence also suggests that the in-group advantage in emotion recognition is not symmetric for ethnic groups, as members of majority groups were relatively worse at reading emotions expressed by minority group members than the reverse (Elfenbein & Ambady, 2002). However, empirical evidence also argues against the subordination hypothesis. First, males are more accurate than females with certain types of expressions, such as anger (Mandal & Palchoudhury, 1985; Rotter & Rotter, 1988; Wagner, MacDonald, & Manstead, 1986). Further, the experimental manipulation of subordination status does not always reliably improve emotion recognition skills (Kombos & Fournet, 1985). Evidence considering subordinated groups other than women has generally demonstrated that they often achieve lower—rather than higher—accuracy in emotion recognition (Hall & Halberstadt, 1994; Hall, Halberstadt, & O'Brien, 1997; Kirouac & Doré, 1985).

Rosenthal and colleagues have proposed an alternative to the subordination hypothesis, termed the *accommodation hypothesis* (Rosenthal & DePaulo, 1979). This stemmed, in part, from the finding that women's superior emotion recognition skills do not apply equally to all forms of emotional expression. In particular, men are superior at recognizing nonverbal "leakage"—information that is expressed inadvertently, usually through poorly controlled channels of communication such body movements. This gender disparity increases with age. Although young boys and girls detect leaked information at roughly equal levels, over time girls grow less sensitive to leakage relative to boys (Blanck, Rosenthal, Snodgrass, DePaulo, & Zuckerman, 1981). Such a difference in skills allows women to be more accommodating socially by, among other things, not "eavesdropping" on information unintentionally transmitted (Rosenthal & DePaulo, 1979). Correspondingly, women adept at detecting leaked information appear to be less socially successful than women poor at understanding such leakage. The accommodation hypothesis may also account for men's superiority in judging anger, especially in other men. Because stringent display rules exist for the expression of anger, particularly in women (Feinman & Feldman, 1982; Maccoby & Jacklin, 1974; Underwood, Coie, & Herbsman, 1992), anger is more likely than some other expressions to leak from behind a more controlled facade.

Taken together, the preceding evidence suggests that using or judging emotions "intelligently" involves the regulation of the ability to recognize facial expressions. Although it is important to know the nonverbal dialect being "spoken," it is perhaps equally important to know when to recognize and when to ignore what is being communicated.

Socioeconomic Status

Individuals of a higher socioeconomic status (SES) appear to perform better on tests of nonverbal skill in general (Hall, Halberstadt, & O'Brien, 1997; Michael & Willis, 1968) and on tests of facial expression more specifically (Izard, 1971) than do lower SES individuals. It may be that SES is itself a type of cultural difference leading to segregation in American society. Because most standardized tests of emotion recognition use expressers from relatively affluent private universities, the in-group advantage could lead to better performance on standardized instruments for higher-SES participants. Although differences across ethnic groups are often accompanied by socioeconomic differences as well, both of these factors exert independent effects on emotion recognition (Elfenbein & Ambady, 2002).

Personality

Attempts to link general emotion recognition ability with individual differences in personality traits have met with mixed success (Cunningham, 1977; Hall, Gaul, & Kent, 1999; Rosenthal et al. 1979). With reference to faces specifically, Snyder (1974) did find a slight tendency for participants high in self-monitoring—the tendency to focus on situational appropriateness—to recognize facial expressions more accurately. Similarly, Nowicki and colleagues (Nowicki & Hartigan 1988; Nowicki & Richmond, 1986) found that internal locus of control predicted greater accuracy in recognizing expressions. Also focusing on the face, Matsumoto and colleagues recently found evidence that of the Big Five personality traits, Openness, and to a lesser extent Conscientiousness and Extraversion, predicted accuracy with facial expressions. The trait Neuroticism, on the other hand, predicted lower accuracy (Matsumoto et al., 2000). Taken together, this evidence suggests that individuals more predisposed to attend to social and situational cues may be better able to recognize others' facial expressions.

MEASURING THE ABILITY TO RECOGNIZE FACIAL EXPRESSIONS

Considering how researchers measure the ability to understand facial expressions of emotion is crucial to understanding the limitations of such methods to gauge emotional intelligence. In most of the studies discussed earlier, researchers selected particular expressions as stimulus materials, presented them to participants, and elicited tightly defined types of responses. The ecological validity of each of these steps affects the degree to which a measure is a valid representation of the perception of facial expressions in everyday life.

First, the selection of stimuli requires many choices by researchers. Expressions in the social world are generally subtle, embedded in a particular context, spontaneous, dynamic, fleeting, and exist in combination with other expressions, words, and behaviors. It is difficult for researchers to choose photographs or videos that accurately reflect this true phenomenon. Stimulus materials used are often posed, static, stripped of context, seen only from a full-frontal vantage point, shown while the target is alone, and may consist of "prototypical" combinations of gestures that actually occur at a low frequency in natural interactions. Any of these variables can qualitatively change the interpretation of an expression (Carroll & Russell, 1996; Ekman, Hager, & Friesen, 1981; Fujita, Harper, & Wiens, 1980; Gosselin, Kirouac, & Doré, 1995; Hess & Kleck, 1990; Kappas, Hess, Barr, & Kleck, 1994; Motley, 1993; Motley & Camden, 1988; Russell, 1994). Even seemingly small details, such as the frequent presentation of stimulus faces in gray scale rather than color, may alter the perceived intensity of the emotion (Barr & Kleck, 1995), which can in turn influence the emotion that is perceived (Hess, Blairy, & Kleck 1997).

The sample of participants is the next detail for researchers to choose. Many participants are college students, who come from a relatively narrow range of age, ethnicity, SES, and even gender, as females volunteer more often for psychological experiments. Researchers also choose how to record responses from participants. Most tests for facial emotion recognition require an explicit emotional label from participants, often based on a forced-choice response format. This presupposes that recognition of nonverbal behavior is accompanied by the ability to verbalize the judgment, which may not necessarily be the case (Walden & Field, 1982). Further, as Russell (1993, 1994) has argued, forced-choice responses often overstate consensus among participants, and the use of forced choice has been the subject of ongoing debate (e.g., Ekman, 1994; Elfenbein, Mandal, Ambady, Harizuka, & Kumar, 2002; Frank & Stennett, 2001; Haidt & Keltner, 1999). Finally, in scoring participants' responses, researchers must decide which answer is "correct." Psychologists have a tradition of multiple perspectives on the nature of accuracy in social judgments (Funder, 1987, 1995; Kruglanski, 1989). Whereas the realistic approach assumes that there is a "right answer" that the experimenter can use for comparison, the constructivist approach views judgments as social constructions and assesses accuracy in terms of consensus among observers (Funder, 1995). Neither of these two perspectives considers explicitly what expressers believe they are expressing, which often, but not always, corresponds to the answers suggested by the realistic or constructivist approaches (Wagner et al., 1986).

Each of these methodological issues requires researchers to make choices, and each provides an opportunity for experimental settings to differ from the everyday context of recognizing facial expressions. In spite of these issues, the measurement of emotion recognition ability has developed over several decades and is generally believed to be valid and reliable (Nowicki & Duke, 1994; Rosenthal et al., 1979). Unlike areas of psychology that use pencil-and-paper questionnaires, the study of emotion recognition uses a nonverbal measure that recreates the phenomenon itself rather than a self-report or verbalization of the phenomenon. Most likely for this reason, recent empirical work attempting to validate the basic components of emotional intelligence has demonstrated that emotional perception measures show high reliability and validity, particularly relative to pencil-and-paper instruments (Ciarrochi, Chan, & Caputi, 2000; Davies, Stankov & Roberts, 1998[1]). More recent emotional intelligence tests, such as the Mayer–Salovey–Caruso Emotional Intelligence Test (MSCEIT; Salovey, Mayer, Caruso, & Lopes, in press), incorporate measures using facial expressions of emotion.

DIFFERENCES BETWEEN EMOTION RECOGNITION IN EXPERIMENTS VERSUS REAL-LIFE SETTINGS

It is worthwhile to consider how several of the choices discussed here may affect how participants judge facial expressions. The judgment of facial expressions can differ considerably between real-life settings and traditional experimental studies.

Motivation and Attention

One difference between the experimental context and real life is the researcher's request for the participant to make a judgment and record a response. The request focuses participants' conscious attention on decoding emotional stimuli. This additional attention and motivation can serve to create certain individual and group differences in recognition

---

[1]Editor's note: Note that there are serious flaws in the analysis of Davies et al. (1998)—LFB.

ability where there are none in more ecological settings. Such requests can also serve to hide certain differences that do exist. For example, several studies suggest that women's greater nonverbal sensitivity in general—and with the face in particular—may stem largely from greater motivation. Hall (1984) argued that women gaze at others more frequently than men do, which is what permits them to pick up larger amounts of nonverbal information and results in their apparent decoding advantages. Similarly, Ickes, Gesn, and Graham's (2000) review found that in empathic accuracy exercises testing nonverbal sensitivity, women outperformed men only in experiments that made them aware and more motivated to perform well. Equalizing status roles or the amount of time attending to relevant cues may also equalize the decoding abilities of men and women (Snodgrass, 1992). Mufson and Nowicki (1991) found that men recognized facial expressions less accurately than women, but that this difference was smaller for men informed that the task measured their social competence. In other studies testing facial expression recognition, individual differences have a smaller impact once situational variables are measured and taken into account (Kenny & La Voie, 1984). For instance, Sabatelli, Buck, and Kenny (1986) found that much of the variability due to differences in recognition ability decreased when they asked participants to pay explicit attention to targets' facial behavior.

Some theorists have gone as far as to argue that all humans possess the necessary tools for adept nonverbal decoding (Gibson, 1979) and that individual differences in emotion recognition are simply differences in the motivation to attend and use nonverbal cues (Buck, 1988). Even without going this far, it is still important to consider how experimental measurements of ability may also inadvertently measure attention and motivation to understand others' facial expressions.

Context and Situations

Facial expressions are normally interpreted within a larger context that includes the situation precipitating the expression, concurrent verbal messages, and other information likely to affect expectations and thus the interpreted meaning of an expression. But most experimental measurements of emotional expressions do not include this bigger picture. Although participants generally report that they do not make extensive use of contextual information when making a judgment (Nakamura, Buck, & Kenny, 1990; Watson, 1972), such contextual information has a major impact on judgments when it is available (Carroll & Russell, 1996). For instance, the perceived verbal or emotional context paired with an expression of emotion can alter its interpretation (Carrera-

Levillain & Fernández-Dols, 1994; Friedman, 1978; Knudsen & Muzekari, 1983; Motley, 1993; Motley & Camden, 1988; Nakamura et al., 1990). Moreover, differences in perceived status or other factors can influence perceivers' attributions of a particular expression (Algoe, Buswell, & DeLamater, 2000; Hess, Blairy, & Kleck, 2000).

Besides immediate contextual variables, more long-term situational factors also influence facial expression recognition. In general, it seems that we develop skills adapted to our own particular environments. For example, siblings tend to show similarities in terms of nonverbal decoding skills (Blanck, Zuckerman, DePaulo, & Rosenthal, 1980). One reason for such similarity could be a common family environment. Children with relatively inexpressive families become better at understanding facial expressions than do children from expressive families, because it pays to learn to recognize subtleties in less expressive families (Halberstadt, 1983, 1986). Children who are heavy consumers of televised programs decode facial expressions better than lighter viewers, but they also tend to interpret emotional information more simplistically (Coats, Feldman, & Philippot, 1999; Feldman et al., 1996). Because televised emotions are somewhat exaggerated and simplistic, these children may be unaccustomed to considering factors such as display rules or impression management when interpreting expressions. Family contexts can affect the recognition of facial expressions in other ways as well. Children who grow up in violent households show a reduced ability to recognize positive expressions (Camras, Grow, & Ribordy, 1983; Hodgins & Belch, 2000). Hodgins and Belch (2000) suggest that these children do not learn to recognize facial expressions that are infrequent and consequently less useful to understand. Utility, then, seems fundamental in learning to recognize facial expressions. People adapt to their surroundings by developing the communication skills that serve them best. However, tests of emotion recognition are often based on a "normative" sample of perceivers, and individuals who have learned to recognize expressions in unusual contexts may appear deficient by comparison to this normative standard. What appears deficient in one setting may in fact be adaptive and appropriate in another, but unappreciated by the criteria that define emotionally intelligent responses.

PERSONAL EFFECTIVENESS AND RECOGNIZING FACIAL EXPRESSIONS

The final part of Mayer et al.'s (1990, p. 772) definition of emotional intelligence—the "accurate appraisal and expression of emotions in oneself and others and the regulation of emotion in a way that enhances living"—is that the skill should serve to improve personal and social effectiveness. A wide range of research demonstrates a generally positive association between social adjustment and mental health and the ability to recognize facial expressions (e.g., Carton, Kessler, & Pape, 1999; Cooley & Nowicki, 1989; Denham, McKinley, Couchoud, & Holt, 1990; Field & Walden, 1982; Nowicki & Duke, 1994; Rosenthal et al. 1979). It is beyond the limited scope of this paper to review these findings in detail. In light of the particularly enthusiastic reception for emotional intelligence in organizational contexts, we focus next on evidence regarding to what extent this enthusiasm is warranted. In general, the ability to recognize facial expressions of emotion predicts greater success both at work and in school.

School Outcomes

School performance is perhaps the earliest type of workplace outcome that we experience. Many studies have documented a positive association between academic performance and nonverbal sensitivity (e.g., Halberstadt & Hall, 1980), and for facial expressions in particular (e.g., Izard, 1971; Izard et al., 2001; Nowicki & Duke, 1994). For example, the greater skill in interpreting facial emotions in 5-year-old children positively predicted social and academic outcomes 4 years later (Izard et al., 2001). Interestingly, in some studies nonverbal sensitivity was strongly related to academic achievement—especially teachers' ratings of students—but only weakly related to traditional measures of cognitive skill (Halberstadt & Hall, 1980; Nowicki & Duke, 1994). Halberstadt and Hall (1980) found that nonverbal sensitivity predicted teacher-rated academic ability much more strongly than did social maturity ratings. Over time, students with greater nonverbal skills improve in cognitive abilities as well, possibly because they are better able to respond to favorable expectations from teachers (Conn, Edwards, Rosenthal & Crowne, 1968).

Adult Workplace Outcomes

Skill in emotion recognition has long been associated with positive workplace outcomes. A number of empirical studies have documented that individuals' ability to understand general nonverbal behavior predicts a range of important workplace outcomes (e.g., Campbell, Kagan, & Krathwohl, 1971; Costanzo & Philipott, 1986; Rosenthal et al., 1979; Schag, Loo, & Levin, 1978). Although some studies have reported null results, it is interesting to note that these studies made use of laboratory-based outcomes rather than real workplace performance (e.g., Hill,

Siegelman, Gronsky, Sturniolo, & Fretz, 1981; Lee, Hallberg, & Kocsis, 1980). However, studies using laboratory outcomes that were previously validated assessment tools have replicated the positive relationship (Costanzo & Philipott, 1986; Schag et al., 1978). Therefore, it is possible that ecologically valid outcome measures are necessary to observe this phenomenon.

The findings are somewhat more complicated for studies examining the relationship between workplace effectiveness and the recognition of facial expressions in particular. Because the face contains the information that is the most controllable, and consequently the most subject to deliberate falsification, accuracy at recognizing facial expressions is valued in some organizational settings but penalized in others. DiMatteo, Friedman, and Taranta (1979) found that patient ratings of bedside manner were much more strongly related to their doctor's ability to read cues expressed by the body than by the face. Because facial expressions are more deliberate than body movements, they concluded that patients value the ability of doctors to "eavesdrop" on their feelings—especially those feelings that the patient may be unwilling or unable to volunteer. More recently, Tickle-Degnen (1998) examined how the importance of skill in different nonverbal channels can vary according to the demands of particular workplaces. She found that interns doing pediatric fieldwork received *lower* ratings for accuracy with facial cues and higher ratings for accuracy with body cues. By contrast, interns doing psychosocial fieldwork received marginally *higher* ratings for accuracy with facial cues and lower ratings for accuracy with body cues. Tickle-Degnen argues that different patient populations place different demands on interns. Because children are limited in their ability to express difficulties, pediatric field-workers are held back if they are too experienced with—and consequently dependent on—controllable information expressed through the face. By contrast, psychosocial patients can better articulate what they actually want their field-workers to know. Being able to "eavesdrop" on unintended signals from distressed patients may actually impair the effectiveness of the relationship. Elfenbein and Ambady (in press) recently found that members of a public service organization received lower performance ratings if they could eavesdrop on negative emotions, but better ratings if they could eavesdrop on positive emotions. Given that the face provides the most highly controllable form of nonverbal communication, it may be valuable to understand negative emotions when they are expressed intentionally, but not when they are expressed inadvertently. Likewise, it may be counterproductive to be highly skilled at reading the controllable positive messages most likely to be falsified or exaggerated for public consumption.

EMOTIONAL INTELLIGENCE AND FACIAL
EXPRESSIONS: THE BIGGER PICTURE

A wealth of time and talent has been spent determining how well emotion in the face can be recognized in the research laboratory. Emotion recognition is just one component of Mayer et al.'s (1990) definition of emotional intelligence—the "accurate appraisal and expression of emotions in oneself and others and the regulation of emotion in a way that enhances living." We hope that future research emphasizes how the ability to recognize basic expressions relates to the other components, such as the expression and regulation of emotions.

The relationship between emotion recognition and expression is worth mentioning briefly, although a complete discussion is beyond the scope of this chapter. Although there was once considered to be a theoretically logical link between skill in emotional expression and perception, empirical work has demonstrated that the connection is likely more complex. Viewing facial expressions of emotion can evoke imitative muscle movements (Lundqvist & Dimberg, 1995) that, in turn, can induce corresponding moods (Cappella, 1993; Wallbott, 1991; Zajonc, 1985). One may thus speculate expressive ability to evoke greater empathy, which may then lead to better recognition of other people's emotions. Some evidence does indirectly support a small positive correlation between the two skills. For example, women are better at both encoding and decoding facial emotions (Fujita et al., 1980; Rotter & Rotter, 1988). However, a number of other studies suggest that the skills are unrelated (Daly, Abramovitch, & Pliner, 1980; DePaulo & Rosenthal, 1979; Rosenthal et al., 1979; Zuckerman, Hall, DeFrank, & Rosenthal, 1976; Zuckerman et al., 1975; Zuckerman & Przewuzman, 1979) or even inversely related (Cunningham, 1977; Lanzetta & Kleck, 1970; Lee et al., 1980). The ability to express emotions and to perceive facial emotions may simply result from separate processes (Blairy, Herrera, & Hess, 1999; Boyatzis & Satyaprasad, 1994). The complexity of the relationship between these two core components of emotional intelligence highlights the multifaceted nature of the construct.

Likewise, emotional *regulation* skills are also crucial. Poor use of the information gained from recognizing facial expressions can be worse than the inability to perceive the emotional information at all (e.g., Hall, 1979). For example, as discussed earlier, skill in "eavesdropping" on unintended emotional expressions can be associated with poor social functioning as well as workplace performance. Further, some social relationships may function better with "rose-colored glasses" than with accurately reflective ones (Sabatelli et al., 1982). Although the ability to recognize facial expressions is a useful component of emotional intelligence, it is valuable only within its context and adaptive environment. The most important issue is how people use emotional information, not merely that they can perceive it.

Overall, the research reviewed in this chapter suggests that emotional intelligence, as reflected in the process of judging information from the face, is not a global construct. It is a multidimensional skill—not an isolated or simple ability—encompassing a range of skills with complex relationships to each other. Such complexity suggests that the popular trend of emphasizing emotional intelligence in applied settings may have the potential to cause unintended negative consequences. An emphasis on emotional intelligence has encouraged organizations to consider hiring, training, and rewarding individuals for high levels of skill based on standardized settings. Such an emphasis may, unfortunately, be counterproductive in a range of situations in which the skills required are more nuanced, and contextually defined, changing along with shifting contexts. It is important for the various constructs within emotional intelligence to be considered together. Although this may complicate the research process, psychologists cannot afford to overlook the other components of emotional intelligence. Indeed, it will make what we know about the recognition of emotion in the face more interesting and relevant to the way in which we live our lives.

ACKNOWLEDGMENTS

The names of the first and second authors, who contributed equally to this chapter, appear in alphabetical order. Preparation of this chapter was supported by two National Science Foundation (NSF) graduate fellowships and a Presidential Early Career Award for Science and Engineering (PECASE) award (Grant No. BCS-9733706).

REFERENCES

Algoe, S. B., Buswell, B. N., & DeLamater, J. D. (2000). Gender and job status as contextual cues for the interpretation of facial expression of emotion. *Sex Roles, 42,* 183–208.

Ansfield, M. E., DePaulo, B. M., & Bell, K. L. (1995). Familiarity effects in nonverbal understanding: Recognizing our own facial expressions and our friends'. *Journal of Nonverbal Behavior, 19,* 135–149.

Babchuk, W. A., Hames, R. B., & Thompson, R. A. (1985). Sex differences in the recognition of infant facial expressions of emotion: The primary caretaker hypothesis. *Ethology and Sociobiology, 6,* 89–101.

Barr, C. L., & Kleck, R. E. (1995). Self–other perception of the intensity of facial expressions of emotion: Do we know what we show? *Journal of Personality and Social Psychology, 68,* 608–618.

Blairy, S., Herrera, P., & Hess, U. (1999). Mimicry and the judgment of emotional facial expressions. *Journal of Nonverbal Behavior, 23,* 5–41.

Blanck, P. D., Rosenthal, R., Snodgrass, S. E., DePaulo, B. M., & Zuckerman, M. (1981). Sex differences in eavesdropping on nonverbal cues: Developmental changes. *Journal of Personality and Social Psychology, 41,* 391–396.

Blanck, P. D., Zuckerman, M., DePaulo, B. M., & Rosenthal, R. (1980). Sibling resemblances in nonverbal skill and style. *Journal of Nonverbal Behavior, 4,* 219–226.

Boyatzis, C. J., Chazan, E., & Ting, C. Z. (1993). Preschool children's decoding of facial emotions. *Journal of Genetic Psychology, 154,* 375–382.

Boyatzis, C. J., & Satyaprasad, C. (1994). Children's facial and gestural decoding and encoding—Relations between skills and with popularity. *Journal of Nonverbal Behavior, 18,* 37–55.

Brandt, D. R., Miller, G., & Hocking, J. (1980). The truth–deception attribution: Effects of familiarity on the ability of observers to detect deception. *Human Communication Research, 6,* 99–110.

Buck, R. (1976). A test of nonverbal receiving ability: Preliminary studies. *Human Communication Research, 2,* 162–171.

Buck, R. (1988). Nonverbal communication: Spontaneous and symbolic aspects. *American Behavioral Scientist, 31,* 341–354.

Campbell, R. J., Kagan, N., & Krathwohl, D. R. (1971). The development and validation of a scale to measure affective sensitivity (empathy). *Journal of Counseling Psychology, 18,* 407–412.

Camras, L. A., Grow, J. G., & Ribordy, S. C. (1983). Recognition of emotional expression by abused children. *Journal of Clinical Child Psychology, 12,* 325–328.

Cappella, J. N. (1993). The facial feedback hypothesis in human interaction: Review and speculation. *Journal of Language and Social Psychology, 12,* 13–29.

Carrera-Levillain, P., & Fernández-Dols, J. (1994). Neutral faces in context: Their emotional meaning and their function. *Journal of Nonverbal Behavior, 18,* 281–299.

Carroll, J. M., & Russell, J. A. (1996). Do facial expressions signal specific emotions?: Judging emotion from the face in context. *Journal of Personality and Social Psychology, 70,* 205–218.

Carton, J. S., Kessler, E. A., & Pape, C. L. (1999). Nonverbal decoding skills and relationship well-being in adults. *Journal of Nonverbal Behavior, 23,* 91–100.

Ciarrochi, J. V., Chan, A. Y. C., & Caputi, P. (2000). A critical evaluation of the emotional intelligence construct. *Personality and Individual Differences, 28,* 539–561.

Coats, E. J., Feldman, R. S., & Philippot, P. (1999). The influence of television on children's nonverbal behavior. In P. Philippot, R. S. Feldman, & E. J. Coats (Eds.), *The social context of nonverbal behavior* (pp. 156–181). Paris: Cambridge University Press.

Conn, L. K., Edwards, C. N., Rosenthal, R., & Crowne, D. (1968). Perception of emotion and responses to teachers' expectancy by elementary school children. *Psychological Reports, 22*, 27–34.

Cooley, E. L. & Nowicki, S. (1989). Discrimination of facial expressions of emotion by depressed subjects. *Genetic, Social, and General Psychology Monographs, 115*, 449–465.

Costanzo, M., & Philippot, J. (1986). Predictors of therapeutic talent in aspiring clinicians: A multivariate analysis. *Psychotherapy, 23*, 363–369.

Cunningham, M. R. (1977). Personality and the structure of the nonverbal communication of emotion. *Journal of Personality, 45*, 564–584.

Daly, E. M., Abramovitch, R., & Pliner, P. (1980). The relationship between mothers' encoding and their children's decoding of facial expressions of emotion. *Merrill-Palmer Quarterly, 26*, 25–33.

Davies, M., Stankov, L., & Roberts, R. D. (1998). Emotional intelligence: In search of an elusive construct. *Journal of Personality and Social Psychology, 75*, 989–1015.

Denham, S. A., McKinley, M., Couchoud, E. A., & Holt, R. (1990). Emotional and behavioral predictors of preschool peer ratings. *Child Development, 61*, 1145–1152.

DePaulo, B. M., & Rosenthal, R. (1979). Telling lies. *Journal of Personality and Social Psychology, 37*, 1713–1722.

DiMatteo, M. R., Friedman, H. S., & Taranta, A. (1979). Sensitivity to bodily nonverbal communication as a factor in practitioner–patient rapport. *Journal of Nonverbal Behavior, 4*, 18–26.

Ekman, P. (1965). Differential communication of affect by head and body cues. *Journal of Personality and Social Psychology, 2*, 726–735.

Ekman, P. (1972). Universals and cultural differences in facial expressions of emotion. In J. Cole (Ed.), *Nebraska symposium on motivation, 1971* (Vol. 19, pp. 207–282). Lincoln: University of Nebraska Press.

Ekman, P. (1994). Strong evidence for universals in facial expressions: A reply to Russell's mistaken critique. *Psychological Bulletin, 115*, 268–287.

Ekman, P., Hager, J. C., & Friesen, W. V. (1981). The symmetry of emotional and deliberate facial actions. *Psychophysiology, 18*, 101–106.

Elfenbein, H. A., & Ambady, N. A. (2001). *Practice makes perfect: Evidence for cultural learning in emotion recognition.* Manuscript under review.

Elfenbein, H. A., & Ambady, N. (2002). On the universality and cultural specificity of emotion recognition: A meta-analysis. *Psychological Bulletin, 128*, 203–235.

Elfenbein, H. A., & Ambady, N. (in press). Predicting workplace outcomes from the ability to "eavesdrop" on feelings. *Journal of Applied Psychology.*

Elfenbein, H. A., Mandal, M. K., Ambady, N., Harizuka, S., & Kumar, S. (2002). Cross-cultural patterns in emotion recognition: Highlighting design and analytical techniques. *Emotion, 2*, 75–84.

Fantz, R. L. (1961). The origins of form perception. *Scientific American, 204*, 66–72.

Feinman, J. A., & Feldman, R. S. (1982). Decoding children's expressions of affect. *Child Development, 53*, 710–716.

Feldman, R. S., Coats, E. J., & Spielman, D. A. (1996). Television exposure and children's decoding of nonverbal behavior. *Journal of Applied Social Psychology, 26,* 1718–1733.

Fernández-Dols, J., Wallbott, H., & Sanchez, F. (1991). Emotion category accessibility and the decoding of emotion from facial expression and context. *Journal of Nonverbal Behavior, 15,* 107–124.

Field, T. M., & Walden, T. A. (1982). Production and discrimination of facial expressions by preschool children. *Child Development, 53,* 1299–1311.

Field, T. M., Woodson, R., Greenberg, R., & Cohen, D. (1983). Discrimination and imitation of facial expressions by neonates. *Annual Progress in Child Psychiatry and Child Development, 16,* 119–125.

Fiske, A. P., Kitayama, S., Markus, H. R., & Nisbett, R. E. (1998). The cultural matrix of social psychology. In D. T. Gilbert, S. T. Fiske, & G. Lindzey (Eds.), *The handbook of social psychology* (Vol. 2, 4th ed., pp. 915–981). Boston: McGraw-Hill.

Frank, M. G., & Stennett, J. (2001). The forced-choice paradigm and the perception of facial expressions of emotion. *Journal of Personality and Social Psychology, 80,* 75–85.

Fridlund, A. J. (1997). The new ethology of human facial expressions. In J. A. Russell & J. M. Fernández-Dols (Eds.), *The psychology of facial expression* (pp. 103–129). Paris: Cambridge University Press.

Fridlund, A. J., Ekman, P., & Oster, H. (1984). Facial expressions of emotion. In A. W. Siegman & S. Feldstein (Eds.), *Nonverbal behavior and communication* (2nd ed., pp. 143–223). Hillsdale, NJ: Erlbaum.

Friedman, H. S. (1978). The relative strength of verbal versus nonverbal cues. *Personality and Social Psychology Bulletin, 4,* 147–150.

Fujita, B. N., Harper, R. G., & Wiens, A. N. (1980). Encoding–decoding of nonverbal emotional messages: Sex differences in spontaneous and enacted expressions. *Journal of Nonverbal Behavior, 4,* 131–145.

Funder, D. C. (1987). Errors and mistakes: Evaluating the accuracy of social judgment. *Psychological Bulletin, 101,* 75–90.

Funder, D. C. (1995). On the accuracy of personality judgment: A realistic approach. *Psychological Bulletin, 102,* 652–670.

Gibson, J. J. (1979). *The ecological approach to visual perception.* Boston: Houghton Mifflin.

Goleman, D. (1995). *Emotional intelligence.* New York: Bantam Books.

Goleman, D. (1998). *Working with emotional intelligence.* New York: Bantam Books.

Gosselin, P., Kirouac, G., & Doré, F. Y. (1995). Components and recognition of facial expression in the communication of emotion by actors. *Journal of Personality and Social Psychology, 68,* 83–96.

Haidt, J., & Keltner, D. (1999). Culture and facial expression: Open-ended methods find more expressions and a gradient of recognition. *Cognition and Emotion, 13,* 225–266.

Halberstadt, A. G. (1983). Family expressiveness styles and nonverbal communication skills. *Journal of Nonverbal Behavior, 8,* 14–27.

Halberstadt, A. G. (1986). Family socialization of emotional expression and nonverbal communication styles and skills. *Journal of Personality and Social Psychology, 51,* 827–836.

Halberstadt, A. G., & Hall, J. A. (1980). Who's getting the message?: Children's nonverbal skill and their evaluation by teachers. *Developmental Psychology, 16,* 564–573.

Hall, C. W., Gaul, L., & Kent, M. (1999). College students' perception of facial expressions. *Perceptual and Motor Skills, 89,* 763–770.

Hall, J. A. (1978). Gender effects in decoding nonverbal cues. *Psychological Bulletin, 85,* 845–857.

Hall, J. A. (1979). Gender, gender roles, and nonverbal communication skills. In R. Rosenthal (Ed.), *Skill in nonverbal communication* (pp. 31–67). Cambridge, MA: Oelgeschlager, Gunn, & Hain.

Hall, J. A. (1984). *Nonverbal sex differences: Communication accuracy and expressive style.* Baltimore: Johns Hopkins University Press.

Hall, J. A., & Halberstadt, A. G. (1994). "Subordination" and sensitivity to nonverbal cues: A study of married working women. *Sex Roles, 31,* 149–165.

Hall, J. A. Halberstadt, A. G., & O'Brien, C. E. (1997). "Subordination" and nonverbal sensitivity: A study and synthesis of findings based on trait measures. *Sex Roles, 37,* 295–317.

Henley, N. M. (1977). *Body politics: Power, sex, and nonverbal communication.* Englewood Cliffs, NJ: Prentice-Hall.

Hess, U., Blairy, S., & Kleck, R. E. (1997). The intensity of emotional facial expressions and decoding accuracy. *Journal of Nonverbal Behavior, 21,* 241–257.

Hess, U., Blairy, S., & Kleck, R. E. (2000). The influence of facial emotion displays, gender, and ethnicity on judgments of dominance and affiliation. *Journal of Nonverbal Behavior, 24,* 265–283.

Hess, U., & Kleck, R. E. (1990). Differentiating emotion elicited and deliberate emotional facial expressions. *European Journal of Social Psychology, 24,* 367–381.

Hill, C. E., Siegelman, L., Gronsky, B. R., Sturniolo, F., & Fretz, B. R. (1981). Nonverbal communication and counseling outcome. *Journal of Counseling Psychology, 28,* 203–212.

Hodgins, H. S., & Belch, C. (2000). Interparental violence and nonverbal abilities. *Journal of Nonverbal Behavior, 24,* 3–24.

Ickes, W., Gesn, P. R., & Graham, T. (2000). Gender differences in empathic accuracy: Differential ability or differential motivation? *Personal Relationships, 7,* 95–109.

Izard, C. E. (1971). *The face of emotion.* New York: Appleton-Century-Crofts.

Izard, C. E., Fine, S., Schultz, D., Mostow, A., Ackerman, B., & Youngstrom, E. (2001). Emotion knowledge as a predictor of social behavior and academic competence in children at risk. *Psychological Science, 12,* 18–24.

Kagan, J., & Lewis, M. (1965). Studies of attention in the human infant. *Merrill-Palmer Quarterly, 11,* 95–127.

Kappas, A., Hess, U., Barr, C. L., & Kleck, R. E. (1994). Angle of regard: The effect of vertical viewing angle on the perception of facial expressions. *Journal of Nonverbal Behavior, 18,* 263–280.

Keating, C. F., Mazur, A., & Segall, M. H. (1977). Facial gestures which influence the perception of status. *Social Psychology Quarterly, 40,* 374–378.

Keltner, D., Gruenfeld, D. H., & Anderson, C. (2001). *The experience of social power: Consequences for affect, cognition, and behavior.* Manuscript under review.

Kenny, D. A., & Acitelli, L. K. (2001). Accuracy and bias in the perception of the partner in a close relationship. *Journal of Personality and Social Psychology, 80,* 439–448.

Kenny, D., & La Voie, (1984). The social relations model. In L. Berkowitz (Ed.), *Advances in experimental social psychology* (Vol. 18, pp. 141–182). Orlando, FL: Acadmic Press.

Kirouac, G., & Doré, F. Y. (1985). Accuracy of the judgment of facial expression of emotions as a function of sex and level of education. *Journal of Nonverbal Behavior, 9,* 3–7.

Knudsen, H. R., & Muzekari, L. H. (1983). The effects of verbal statements of context on facial expressions of emotion. *Journal of Nonverbal Behavior, 7,* 202–212.

Kombos, N. A., & Fournet, G. P. (1985). Effects of dominance–submissiveness and gender on recognition of nonverbal emotional cues. *Educational and Psychological Research, 5,* 19–28.

Kruglanski., A. W. (1989). The psychology of being "right": The problem of accuracy in social perception and cognition. *Psychological Bulletin, 106,* 395–409.

LaFrance, M., & Henley, N. M. (1994). On oppressing hypotheses: Or differences in nonverbal sensitivity revisited. In H. L. Radtke & H. J. Stam (Eds.), *Power/gender: Social relations in theory and practice* (pp. 287–311). Thousand Oaks, CA: Sage.

Lanzetta, J. T., & Kleck, R. E. (1970). Encoding and decoding of nonverbal affect in humans. *Journal of Personality and Social Psychology, 16,* 12–19.

Laser, P. S., & Mathie, V. A. (1982). Face facts: An unbidden role for features in communication. *Journal of Nonverbal Behavior, 7,* 3–19.

Lee, D. Y., Hallberg, E. T., & Kocsis, M. (1980). Decoding skills in nonverbal communication and perceived interviewer effectiveness. *Journal of Counseling Psychology, 27,* 89–92.

Lenti, C., Lenti-Boero, D., & Giacobbe, A. (1999). Decoding of emotional expressions in children and adolescents. *Perceptual and Motor Skills, 89,* 808–814.

Lundqvist, L., & Dimberg, U. (1995). Facial expressions are contagious. *Journal of Psychophysiology, 9,* 203–211.

Maccoby, E. E., & Jacklin, C. N. (1974). *The psychology of sex differences.* Stanford, CA: Stanford University Press

Mandal, M. K., & Palchoudhury, S. (1985). Perceptual skill in decoding facial affect. *Perceptual and Motor Skills, 60,* 96–98.

Markus, H. R., & Kitayama, S. (1991). Culture and the self: Implications for cognition, emotion, and motivation. *Psychological Review, 98,* 224–253

Marsh, A. A., & Kleck, R. E. (2002). *Why do fear and anger look the way they do? Form and social function in facial expressions.* Manuscript under review.

Matsumoto, D., LeRoux, J., Wilson-Cohn, C., Raroque, J., Kooken, K., Ekman, P., Yrizarry, N., Loewinger, S., Uchida, H., Yee, A., Amo, L., & Goh, A. (2000). A new test to measure emotion recognition ability: Matsumoto and Ekman's Japanese and Caucasian Brief Affect Recognition Test (JACBART). *Journal of Nonverbal Behavior, 24,* 179–209.

Mayer, J. D., DiPaolo, M., & Salovey, P. (1990). Perceiving affective content in ambiguous visual stimuli: A component of emotional intelligence. *Journal of Personality Assessment, 54,* 772–781.

McArthur, L. Z., & Baron, R. M. (1983). Toward an ecological theory of social perception. *Psychological Review, 90,* 215–238.

Mehrabian, A., & Ferris, S. R. (1967). Inference of attitudes from nonverbal communication in two channels. *Journal of Consulting Psychology, 31,* 248–252.

Meltzoff, A. N., & Moore, M. K. (1983). Newborn infants imitate adult facial gestures. *Child Development, 54,* 702–709.

Mesquita, B., & Frijda, N. H. (1992). Cultural variations in emotions: A review. *Psychological Bulletin, 112,* 197–204.

Michael, G., & Willis, F. N., Jr. (1968). The development of gestures as a function of social class, education, and sex. *Psychological Record, 18,* 515–519.

Millar, M. G., & Millar, K. (1995). Detection of deception in familiar and unfamiliar persons: The effects of information restriction. *Journal of Nonverbal Behavior, 19,* 69–84.

Motley, M. T. (1993). Facial affect and verbal context in conversation: Facial expression as interjection. *Human Communication Research, 20,* 3–40.

Motley, M. T., & Camden, C. T. (1988). Facial expression of emotion: A comparison of posed expressions versus spontaneous expressions in an interpersonal communication setting. *Western Journal of Speech Communication, 52,* 1–22.

Mufson, L., & Nowicki, S., Jr. (1991). Factors affecting the accuracy of facial affect recognition. *Journal of Social Psychology, 131,* 815–822.

Nakamura, M., Buck, R., & Kenny, D. A. (1990). Relative contributions of expressive behavior and contextual information to the judgment of the emotional state of another. *Journal of Personality and Social Psychology, 59,* 1032–1039.

Nelson, C. A., & De Haan, M. (1997). A neurobehavioral approach to the recognition of facial expressions in infancy. In In J. A. Russell & J. M. Fernández-Dols (Eds.), *The psychology of facial expression* (pp. 176–204). Paris: Cambridge University Press.

Noller, P. (1985). Video primacy: A further look. *Journal of Nonverbal Behavior, 9,* 28–47.

Noller, P. (1986). Sex differences in nonverbal communication: Advantage lost or supremacy regained? *Australian Journal of Psychology, 38,* 23–32.

Nowicki, S., Jr., & Duke, M. P. (1994). Individual differences in the nonverbal communication of affect: The diagnostic analysis of nonverbal accuracy scale. *Journal of Nonverbal Behavior, 19,* 9–35.

Nowicki, S., Jr., & Hartigan, M. (1988). Accuracy of facial affect recognition as a function of locus of control orientation and anticipated interpersonal interaction. *Journal of Social Psychology, 128,* 363–373.

Nowicki, S., Jr., & Richmond, D. (1986). The effect of standard motivation and strategy instructions in the facial processing accuracy of internal and external subjects. *Journal of Research in Personality, 19,* 354–364.

Philippot, P., & Feldman, R. S. (1990). Age and social competence in preschoolers' decoding of facial expression. *British Journal of Social Psychology, 29,* 43–54.

Rosenthal, R., & DePaulo, B. M. (1979). Sex differences in eavesdropping on nonverbal cues. *Journal of Personality and Social Psychology, 37,* 273–285.

Rosenthal, R., Hall, J. A., DiMatteo, M. R., Rogers, P. L., & Archer, D. (1979). *Sensitivity to Nonverbal Communications: The PONS Test.* Baltimore, MD: Johns Hopkins University Press.

Rotter, N. G., & Rotter, G. S. (1988). Sex differences in the encoding and decoding of negative facial emotion. *Journal of Nonverbal Behavior, 12,* 139–148.

Russell, J. A. (1993). Forced-Choice Response Format in the Study of Facial Expression. *Motivation and Emotion, 17, 1,* 41–51.

Russell, J. A. (1994). Is there universal recognition of emotion from facial expression?: A review of the cross-cultural studies. *Psychological Bulletin, 115,* 102–141.

Sabatelli, R. M., Buck, R., & Dreyer, A. (1980). Communication via facial cues in intimate dyads. *Personality and Social Psychology Bulletin, 6,* 242–247.

Sabatelli, R. M., Buck, R., & Dreyer, A. (1982). Nonverbal communication accuracy in married couples: Relationship with marital complaints. *Journal of Personality and Social Psychology, 43,* 1088–1097.

Sabatelli, R. M., Buck, R., & Kenny, D. A. (1986). A social relations analysis of nonverbal communication accuracy in married couples. *Journal of Personality, 54,* 513–527.

Salovey, P., Mayer, J. D., Caruso, D., & Lopes, P. N. (in press). Measuring emotional intelligence as a set of abilities with the MSCEIT. In S. J. Lopez & C. R. Snyder (Eds.), *Handbook of positive psychology assessment.* Washington, DC: American Psychological Association.

Schag, D., Loo, C., & Levin, M. M. (1978). The Group Assessment of Interpersonal Traits (GAIT): Differentiation of measures and their relationship to behavioral response modes. *American Journal of Community Psychology, 6,* 47–62.

Scherer, K. R., & Wallbott, H. G. (1994). Evidence for universality and cultural variation of differential emotion response patterning. *Journal of Personality and Social Psychology, 66,* 310–328.

Snodgrass, S. E. (1985). Women's intuition: The effect of subordinate role on interpersonal sensitivity. *Journal of Personality and Social Psychology, 49,* 146–155.

Snodgrass, S. E. (1992). Further effects of role versus gender on interpersonal sensitivity. *Journal of Personality and Social Psychology, 62,* 154–158.

Snodgrass, S. E., Hecht, M. A., & Ploutz-Snyder, R. (1998). Interpersonal sensitivity: Expressivity or perceptivity? *Journal of Personality and Social Psychology,* 74, 238–249.

Snyder, M. (1974). Self-monitoring of expressive behavior. *Journal of Personality and Social Psychology, 30,* 526–537.

Tickle-Degnen, L. (1998). Working well with others: The prediction of students' clinical performance. *American Journal of Occupational Therapy, 52,* 133–142.

Underwood, M. K., Coie, J. D., & Herbsman, C. R. (1992). Display rules for anger and aggression in school-age children. *Child Development, 63,* 366–380.

Wagner, H. L., MacDonald, C. J., & Manstead, A. S. (1986). Communication of individual emotions by spontaneous facial expressions. *Journal of Personality and Social Psychology, 50,* 737–743.

Walden, T. A., & Field, T. M. (1982). Discrimination of facial expressions by preschool children. *Child Development, 53,* 1312–1319.

Walker-Andrews, A. S. (1997). Infants' perception of expressive behaviors: Differentiation of multimodal information. *Psychological Bulletin, 121,* 437–456.

Wallbott, H. G. (1991). Recognition of emotion from facial expression via imitation?: Some indirect evidence for an old theory. *British Journal of Social Psychology, 30,* 207–219.

Watson, S. G. (1972). Judgment of emotion from facial and contextual cue combinations. *Journal of Personality and Social Psychology, 24,* 334–342.

Zajonc, R. B. (1985). Emotion and facial efference: A theory reclaimed. *Science, 228,* 15–21.

Zebrowitz, L. A. (1997). *Reading faces.* Boulder, CO: Westview Press.

Zuckerman, M., DePaulo, B. M., & Rosenthal, R. (1986). Humans as deceivers and lie detectors. In P. D. Blanck, R. Buck, & R. Rosenthal (Eds.), *Nonverbal communication in the clinical context* (pp. 13–35). University Park, PA: Pennsylvania State University.

Zuckerman, M., Hall, J. A., DeFrank, R. S., & Rosenthal, R. (1976). Encoding and decoding of spontaneous and posed facial expressions. *Journal of Personality and Social Psychology, 34,* 966–977.

Zuckerman, M., Lipets, M. S., Koivumaki, J. H., & Rosenthal, R. (1975). Encoding and decoding nonverbal cues of emotion. *Journal of Personality and Social Psychology, 32,* 1068–1076.

Zuckerman, M., & Przewuzman, S. J. (1979). Decoding and encoding facial expressions in preschool-age children. *Environmental Psychology and Nonverbal Behavior, 3,* 147–163.

CHAPTER 3

Extinction, Inhibition, and Emotional Intelligence

JAMES B. NELSON
MARK E. BOUTON

Feelings seldom, if ever, occur in a vacuum. Rather, the emotions people feel almost always occur in the presence of a myriad of stimuli that arouse and shape them. The powers of emotional stimuli are often acquired through an individual's experience, which gives them their meaning. That is, the emotional power of stimuli is often *learned*. The purpose of this chapter is to present and discuss some current thinking about the basic learning processes applicable to emotions and what they might mean for an understanding of emotional intelligence.

It has never been controversial to think that basic learning processes have important implications for understanding emotion. For example, classical conditioning is still widely seen as the fundamental process through which new cues can come to arouse or trigger emotions (e.g., Bouton, Mineka, & Barlow, 2001; Lang, 1995; LeDoux, 1996; Mineka, 1985; Rescorla & Solomon, 1967). Through classical conditioning, neutral stimuli (conditional stimuli, or CSs) thus acquire a kind of emotional meaning; they come to trigger a variety of responses, including emotional responses, when they are associated with other stimuli that unconditionally elicit emotional states (unconditional stimuli, or USs). The other side of classical conditioning, *extinction*, is equally important in understanding the emotional value we attach to stimuli. In extinction, we learn to stop responding to trigger cues that are no longer associated with the emotion-arousing US. Given the change and flux in the world, there could be little adaptation to changing contingencies without a process like extinction.

We believe that the processes involved in conditioning and extinction may be fundamental to understanding emotional intelligence. For example, emotionally intelligent people are said to have the ability to manage or regulate their emotions effectively (e.g., Feldman-Barrett & Gross, 2001; Mayer, Salovey, & Caruso, 2000). But what skills are involved in that regulation, and how are they acquired? First, although emotional regulation undoubtedly involves a number of different psychological processes (e.g., Feldman-Barrett & Gross, 2001; Matthews & Zeidner, 2000; Mayer & Salovey, 1995; Mayer, Salovey, & Caruso, 2000; Salovey, Hee, & Mayer, 1993), we suspect that an "intelligent" regulation system must minimally involve inhibitory processes that allow it to control or suppress an emotion that might already be in progress. Second, the system must be able to discriminate: Emotions may be functional in some situations but inappropriate in others, and an intelligent system must be sensitive to the difference. Third, the system must be able to adapt to changes that occur over time: Just as emotions might be functional in some situations and not others, so they might be functional at some times but not others. Inhibition, discrimination, and adaptation to change are processes that presumably underlie all emotional intelligence. We will show that all three are also a fundamental part of conditioning and extinction.

Psychological processes are sometimes characterized as either "automatic" or "controlled," and this distinction has found its way into recent discussions of emotional intelligence. For example, Feldman Barrett and Gross (2001) have suggested that automatic emotional responses function well in most situations, but when an emotional response does not match a given situation, controlled processes might come into play as we deliberately intervene to modify the expression of the emotion. The fact that classical conditioning typically involves the elicitation of responses might make it natural to think that it is a mechanism restricted to automatic, as opposed to controlled, processing. However, we believe our discussion of conditioning may apply equally well to both automatic and controlled processes. Classical conditioning involves much more than the simple elicitation of responses (see Bouton, 1994; Rescorla, 1988), and in addition to being an important behavioral phenomenon, it can be viewed as a *method* for studying more general associative learning processes that may be widely represented in psychological functioning. For example, we describe how associative processes intervene to create a match when there is a mismatch between emotion and situation. This is, after all, the state of affairs that starts the process of extinction.

We also discuss how the same associative processes can contribute to human causal judgments, stereotyping, and operant learning (which is the set of mechanisms involved in selecting and acquiring voluntary actions). To the extent that the matching of emotions to the environment, causal judgment, stereotyping, and voluntary action require controlled processes, then what we describe here may be equally germane to controlled as well as automatic processes.

The primary aim of the chapter, then, is to focus on recent work from the laboratory on emotional conditioning and extinction and what it might mean for emotional intelligence and emotional regulation. We mainly, but not exclusively, focus on research on classical conditioning as it has been studied in behavioral studies with animals. We are especially interested in how emotions and their resulting behaviors are influenced by the background "context" in which trigger cues are encountered. The relevant research has uncovered one or two surprises. It suggests, for example, that classically conditioned emotional responses are especially sensitive to the context after extinction has occurred. Theoretically, this means that the context may help regulate emotion by controlling inhibitory processes. Conditioning research continues to provide an important method for testing theories of emotional learning and memory, and it may offer several insights into how emotions are tuned to, and regulated by, their environments.

THE RENEWAL EFFECT: LOSS OF INHIBITION AS A CONSEQUENCE OF CONTEXT CHANGE

A rather interesting feature of emotions aroused in the laboratory is that the background context in which a trigger cue is presented often seems to have little influence. For example, when an emotion-arousing cue is presented in a context in which it has never been presented before, it often arouses the emotion to the same degree as it did in the original context (e.g., Bouton & King, 1983; Bouton & Nelson, 1994; Bouton & Peck, 1989; Bouton & Swartzentruber, 1986; Kaye & Mackintosh, 1990; Kaye, Preston, Szabo, Druiff, & Mackintosh, 1987; Nelson & Bouton, 1997). The power of trigger cues thus seems to transfer very well across contexts. However, as suggested earlier, the picture changes substantially after extinction has occurred. At this point the context becomes a crucial determinant of responding to trigger cues.

These ideas are well illustrated by experiments on a phenomenon called the *renewal effect*. A typical experiment on renewal is conducted with rat subjects. In an initial phase, a potential trigger cue (e.g., a tone or a light) is paired with an emotion-arousing unconditional stimulus (e.g., shock or food). These pairings, and subsequent extinction, usually take place in distinct Skinner boxes housed in different locations in the laboratory. We usually call the context in which conditioning occurs "Context A." As a result of the CS–US pairings, the CS acquires the ability to elicit a variety of emotional, affective reactions associated with the US (Rescorla & Solomon, 1967), such as fear with a shock US or "hope" or excitement with food (Mowrer, 1960; see also Hilgard & Bower, 1975, for an overview). After the cues come to elicit an emotional response reliably, extinction begins—the trigger is now presented without the US. In a typical renewal experiment, extinction is conducted either in the context where the original pairings occurred or in a different (counterbalanced) context ("Context B"). During the course of extinction, the context exerts surprisingly little control over the triggering of emotionally based behaviors. As mentioned earlier, with few exceptions (e.g., Honey, Willis, & Hall 1990; Rauhut, Thomas, & Ayres, 2001) emotional responses elicited by trigger cues are equally evident in the context where they were learned (Context A) and in the other context (Context B).

It is mainly after extinction that the influence of the context becomes evident. When the trigger cues are tested in the context where extinction took place, no responding is observed. However, when the trigger is returned to the context where the original learning took place (Context A), the extinguished responding is "renewed": The trigger cue arouses emotion again (e.g., Bouton & Bolles, 1979a; Bouton & King, 1983; Bouton & Peck, 1989; Brooks & Bouton, 1994; Nakajima, Tanaka, Urshihara, & Imada, 2000; Rauhut et al., 2001; Rosas, Vila, Lugo, & Lopez, 2001). Two examples of the renewal effect are presented in Figure 3.1.

A major implication of the renewal effect is that extinction does not destroy the potential power of an emotional trigger cue. The original meaning connected with the CS remains available in the memory system. Extinction instead involves new learning that adapts the system to the prevailing new contingencies. But the system seems to understand, in a way, that what is true in extinction may not be true in other circumstances. Emotional responses that have changed to match a new situation can still return under the right conditions. Part of the reason is that the context in which extinction takes place appears to acquire the ability to control the inhibition of the original response.

One reason for thinking that learning about the extinction context is specifically important is that it is not necessary to return the trigger stimulus to the original conditioning context to observe renewal af-

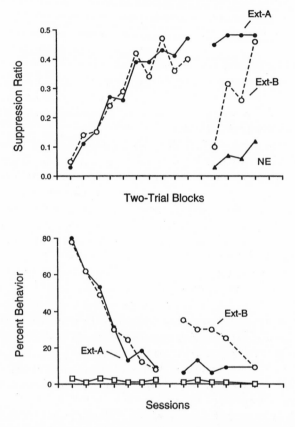

FIGURE 3.1. Renewal of responding in fear conditioning (*top*) and appetitive conditioning (*bottom*). In both experiments conditioning was conducted in Context A and extinction was conducted in either Context A (Ext-A) or a different context (Ext-B). The top panel shows extinction of fear at left. The increasing suppression ratio indicates that behavior initially suppressed by fear increased to a baseline level (0.50). Notice that, as discussed in the text, fear was not affected by a change of context (Ext-B vs. Ext-A). However, when Group Ext-B was returned to the conditioning context, a recovery of fear was observed. (Group NE is a group that received No Extinction.) The bottom panel shows that an appetitive conditioned response, like conditioned fear, was not affected during extinction by a change of context. When Group Ext-B was returned to the conditioning context a renewal of food-related behaviors occurred. Open squares indicate performance of a group that received unpaired CS and US presentations. The top figure is shows data from Bouton and King (1983) and is adapted from Bouton (1997). Copyright 1997 by the American Psychological Association. Adapted by permission. The bottom figure is adapted from Bouton and Peck (1989). Copyright 1989 by the Psychonomic Society. Adapted by permission.

ter extinction. A critical factor appears to be that the cue is tested in a context that is different from the one in which extinction took place. As described earlier, renewal can occur in an A-B-A manner, in which conditioning and extinction take place in different contexts and testing occurs back in the conditioning context (e.g., Bouton & Bolles, 1979a; Bouton & King, 1983; Brooks & Bouton, 1994). But it also occurs in an A-B-C arrangement, in which conditioning and extinction take place in different contexts and testing occurs in a third context (e.g., Bouton & Bolles, 1979a; Bouton & Swartzentruber, 1986; Harris, Jones, Bailey, & Westbrook, 2000). There are some results to suggest that it may even occur when conditioning and extinction take place in the same context and testing occurs in a different one (A-A-B) (e.g., Bouton & Ricker, 1994). The evidence suggests that the strength of the renewal effect is strongest when the trigger is tested in the original context, Context A (Harris et al., 2000). But renewal is partly controlled by an inhibition of responding that is specific to the extinction context. That is, after extinction, emotional responding to the trigger cue is still "on," or ready to happen, unless the context of extinction is present to turn it "off."

The renewal effect is robust and general. It can occur even after extensive extinction involving 84 (Bouton & Swartzentruber, 1989) or 100 (Rauhut et al., 2001) extinction trials (after only 8 and 12 original conditioning trials, respectively). It also occurs in many examples of conditioning, including not only fear conditioning (e.g., Bouton & Bolles, 1979a; Bouton & King, 1983; Harris et al., 2000; Rauhut et al., 2001) and appetitive conditioning (e.g., Bouton & Peck, 1989; Brooks & Bouton, 1994) as shown in Figure 3.1, but also taste-aversion learning, in which a flavor associated with illness triggers disgust responses (e.g., Rosas & Bouton, 1997), and operant conditioning, in which "voluntary" behavior has been reinforced with food (e.g., Nakajima et al., 2000). As we discuss later, it also occurs in human stereotyping and causal learning situations (Kaiser, Miller, & Bouton, 2002; Rosas et al., 2001).

The renewal effect has also been confirmed in a number of other "interference paradigms," besides extinction, in which learning in one phase of an experiment is inhibited by learning in a different phase (Bouton, 1993). For example, the context seems just as important after *counterconditioning*. Peck and Bouton (1990) gave rats either tone–shock or tone–food pairings until the tone reliably elicited either fear or food anticipation (respectively). Then, instead of simple extinction, they gave the animals pairings of the tone with the other US in a second context. That is, animals that had first received tone–shock pairings now received tone–food; animals that had received tone–food now received tone–shock. Either treatment abolished the responding that had developed in the first phase—and replaced it with a new response. However, in either case, following the second (counterconditioning) experience, the original response was renewed when the tone was returned to and tested in the original context. Such an effect suggests that counterconditioning, like extinction, does not involve destruction of the original learning (see Bouton, 1993, 1994; Bouton & Peck, 1992; Brooks, Hale, Nelson, & Bouton, 1995). Following counterconditioning, the first-learned information may also still be available, and the response to the tone is determined by the context. The contexts appeared to select between two available associations (tone–shock and tone–food).

Renewal after counterconditioning may be especially relevant to therapeutic procedures such as systematic desensitization, which were explicitly developed to eliminate unwanted emotion using counterconditioning as the model (Wolpe, 1958). Here, the therapeutic experience is designed to connect a new response to the initially fear-eliciting stimulus. Our point is that this sort of association, like that resulting from simple exposure (extinction) procedures, may still leave a trigger stimulus vulnerable to renewal and thus relapse effects. Changes in context can renew responses after they have been weakened by either extinction or by counterconditioning procedures.

LOSS OF INHIBITION CREATED BY OTHER KINDS OF CONTEXT CHANGE

The foregoing discussion indicates that extinction (and probably other forms of emotional retroactive interference, see Bouton, 1993) is not the same as unlearning. That is, the original learning remains at least partially intact, ready to return to behavior. Its inhibition is enabled by the context. Later we discuss the exact nature of the inhibition controlled by the context; to anticipate, the context seems to control inhibition of the first association by controlling retrieval of the second. But first we focus on a more practical question: What kinds of cues actually constitute the context? Current work suggests that "context" can be many different things. Emotions, and more specifically their retroactive inhibition resulting from procedures like extinction, can be controlled by a number of different kinds of contextual cues.

The Passage of Time

In the research described earlier, the context was the physical context provided by the physical room or apparatuses in which the experiments were conducted. However, Bouton (1988, 1993, 1994) has also suggested that the passage of time can provide a gradually changing context. As many models of forgetting have emphasized, forgetting may occur over time because time creates contextual change (e.g., Estes, 1955; Spear, 1978). Memory retrieval depends on the similarity between the background conditions present during testing and those present during learning. The passage of time causes memory to weaken because contextual change causes retrieval failure.

This idea takes on special meaning when we think of behavior and emotions, the behavioral *output* of memory, rather than memory itself. Bouton (e.g., 1988) noted that the idea can help account for *spontaneous recovery*, another widely known effect that indicates that extinction does not destroy the original learning (e.g., Pavlov, 1927). In spontaneous recovery, extinguished responding can return if time is allowed to pass after extinction (see Brooks, 2000, for a recent example). Spontaneous recovery also occurs when time passes after counterconditioning (Bouton & Peck, 1992); here again, the first-learned meaning of the trigger cue seems to recover and control performance over time. In either extinction or counterconditioning, the suppression (or inhibition) of the original response may be somewhat temporary. The basic idea is that the passage of time between extinction and testing acts as a change in context. Just as extinction performance (and counterconditioned performance) is sensitive to the physical context, so it may be sensitive to the context of time. Spontaneous recovery is the renewal effect that occurs when testing occurs in a new temporal context.

Forgetting created by the passage of time can produce other interesting effects on emotion. Riccio, Richardson, and Ebner (1984; see Bouton, Nelson, & Rosas, 1999, for a recent review) have emphasized the fact that generalization gradients around stimuli tend to flatten as time elapses after conditioning. The term "generalization gradient" describes the tendency for conditioned responding to decrease systematically when an organism is tested with a stimulus that differs increasingly from the one that was used in conditioning. When a generalization gradient "flattens" over time, a response elicited by one stimulus may increasingly come to be elicited by other (similar) stimuli. It is as if we forget the details of the stimulus that was specifically paired with the US and begin responding in a less discriminating manner. One implication is that, at least in principle, emotions may seem to emerge spontaneously to new stimuli that have never triggered them before—even in the absence of a new conditioning experience or new exposure to the US. The passage of time creates a change of context that can cause interesting changes in emotional responding to occur.

Contexts Created by the Expectancy of the US

Some recovery effects, such as *reinstatement* (e.g., Bouton & Bolles, 1979b; Brooks et al., 1995; Rescorla & Heth, 1975), occur in the absence of changes in the physical or temporal context. In reinstatement, responding to an extinguished or counterconditioned cue can return if the animal is merely re-exposed to the original US. It is not necessary to pair the US with the trigger cue: Reinstatement is caused by simply presenting the US again. Our work suggests that the US presentations reinstate the extinguished response because they allow the US to become associated with the current context. The context therefore arouses an expectancy of the US; the presence of this expectancy is what makes the extinguished trigger stimulus excite emotion once more when it is presented again.

For example, in an experiment by Bouton and King (1983, Experiment 2), fear was conditioned and extinguished in rats. Following extinction, the animals received unsignaled shocks in either the context where extinction had taken place or another context. The animals were then tested in the extinction context. Although all animals received unsignaled shocks, only those that received the shocks in the test context (the extinction context) caused reinstated fear to the CS. Thus, learning that the US can happen in the test context was necessary to observe reinstated fear to the CS.

In this case, the context that controls the response to the CS is not physical or temporal, but is essentially an associative feature of the context: It is the expectancy created by the US's association with the context. When the tone is first paired with shock, the animals primarily associate the shock with the tone, but they may also, to a lesser extent, associate it with the background context at the same time. Fear elicited by the background is therefore a feature of the context in which the original tone–shock learning occurs. In the typical scenario, extinction subsequently takes place in a context that is increasingly free of this contextual fear. Thus, one feature of the context of extinction is that it is not fearful. When the shock is delivered again, it makes the context frightening once more. When the tone is then tested there, extinction is lost and fear of the tone returns. Although our example emphasizes fear conditioning, reinstatement is equally evident in learning based on positive stimuli such as food (see Baker, Steinwald, & Bouton, 1991; Bouton & Peck, 1989; Fox & Holland, 1998). Regardless of whether the emotion is negative or positive, an extinguished trigger stimulus can trigger the emotion again in the presence of a context-based expectancy of the US. Other evidence suggests that the associative properties of contexts (what the organism has associated with them) can create discriminative control over how animals respond to trigger cues presented in them (e.g., Bouton, Rosengard, Achenbach, & Peck, 1993; Bouton & Sunsay, 2001).

Interoceptive Contexts Created by Drug States and by Imagination

We also know that internal, "interoceptive," states can serve as contexts. For example, Cunningham (1979) showed that when rats receive fear extinction under the influence of alcohol, they show a recovery of fear when tested in their original sober state. In a more extended series of experiments, Bouton, Kenney, and Rosengard (1990) demonstrated similar effects with the benzodiazepine tranquilizers chlordiazepoxide (Librium) and diazepam (Valium). In those experiments, rats received foot shocks in the presence of a CS while they were in an undrugged state. They then received extinction while under the influence of saline or drug injections. After extinction, the animals exhibited little evidence of fear. However, when exposed to the triggering CS in the absence of the drug, extinguish fear returned. This renewal effect, which can be described as "state-dependent fear extinction," was a function of the drug dosage present in extinction—the stronger the dose, the more profound the eventual renewal effect. It was not eliminated by early exposure to the drug (and the development of some tolerance to it). The results indicate that drugs, like other kinds of background cues, can provide contextual stimuli that control inhibition and extinction. The system seems ready to connect inhibition and extinction to whatever background cues are available, whether they are physical, temporal, or interoceptive.

The implications of these studies seem clear. The use of tranquilizing drugs during therapy can conceivably backfire, in the sense that they make renewal effects possible. There is also a sense in which they suggest a mechanism behind drug abuse. People often try to control or regulate their emotions by taking drugs; an anxious person may be motivated to consume alcohol or Valium for its anxiety-reducing effects. Ironically, though, the effect of the drug may insulate the person from the benefits of extinction that may naturally occur via natural exposure to anxiety trigger cues. In effect, state-dependent extinction protects anxiety from beneficial extinction; the negative emotion returns when the trigger cue is encountered in the absence of the drug, thus creating the motivation to take the drug again. A vicious cycle may ensue.

Recent studies with human participants have demonstrated renewal effects with another "internal" context: a mental one induced through cognitive instruction. Kaiser et al. (2002) have recently demon-

strated renewal effects in people who learned artificial racial stereotypes. Participants played the role of space travelers and learned about
different alien races on different fictitious planets. For example, over a
series of trials on the imaginary planet Alpha-5, participants learned
that certain alien races (e.g., Achmians or Velucians) were associated
with particular behaviors (e.g., were friendly or aggressive). These associations could then be extinguished on a second imaginary planet
(Planet B). For example, participants might then learn that Achmians
were no longer friendly during trials on planet Talos-3. After extinction, the participants were asked to rate the likelihood that different
races would exhibit the various behaviors on Planet A, Planet B, and on
an entirely new Planet C. The tendency to attribute a particular behavioral trait to a particular race can be regarded as a kind of stereotype.
Interestingly, regardless of whether the stereotypes involved positive or
negative traits (e.g., races associated with friendliness vs. aggressive-
ness), the extinguished stereotypes returned when they were tested in
either the original context (Planet A) or the new context (Planet C).
Thus, the extinction of a stereotype did not destroy it. The results suggest that learned stereotypes, another example of associative learning
like classical conditioning, are not necessarily destroyed in extinction,
but may be influenced by similar context-specific inhibition processes.

Rosas et al. (2001) reported related experiments in which human
participants learned about adverse reactions to fictitious drugs. Drugs
and reactions were associated over a series of trials created by exposure
to a series of fictitious medical cases. In the first phase, participants
learned (for example) that the drug "Batim" caused "fever" in the context of "Vanguardia Hospital." In the next phase, subjects might learn
that the drug was associated with "physical energy" in a different context, the "Central Clinic." In a test, the participants were tested for their
beliefs about Batim in the Vanguardia Hospital. When Batim had
caused a different reaction in the other context, there was a robust renewal effect: Batim was still expected to create fever in the Vanguardia
Hospital. Perhaps more surprisingly, participants also showed spontaneous recovery: When the experimenters had the participants return to
the laboratory for testing 48 hours later, a recovery of the originally
learned association also occurred. This recovery occurred when the
learning and testing phases all took place in the same imaginary context. However, the renewal effect added to the spontaneous recovery effect. That is, participants tested (1) in the imaginary context that was
different from the extinction context and (2) after the real 48-hour interval showed stronger recovery than when the context change or retention interval was introduced alone. The results were consistent with
earlier experiments on the additivity of renewal and spontaneous recov-

ery in animals (Rosas & Bouton, 1997). Different types of contexts may thus combine additively.

These experiments with human participants clearly underscore the generality of the renewal effect. It is interesting to reflect on their use of cognitive variables. Stereotypes, which seem to involve a cognitive attribution process, can be seen as another product of the kind of associative learning studied in animal experiments on classical conditioning. And as we emphasized earlier, the experiments demonstrated renewal when the manipulated context—planets for Kaiser et al. (2002) or medical settings for Rosas et al. (2001)—was purely mental, rather than a physical exteroceptive or interoceptive cue. And finally, the form of retroactive inhibition involved in these experiments may also seem rather cognitive. In either case, the original learning was created through purely cognitive input (imaginary pairings of races and behaviors or drugs and reactions), and extinction was created through similarly cognitive input. It is tempting to think that the participants might have used some purely mental operation to suppress the former cognition when the latter was learned. Thus, a further implication of these findings could be that cognitive operations or strategies that we learn to inhibit thoughts or emotions might also depend fundamentally on the context. For all of these reasons, it is not difficult to imagine the possible relevance of these findings to more "cognitive" aspects of emotional regulation.

The results across different associative learning preparations and systems, and with different kinds of contexts, thus seem very general. We believe the common threads suggest important principles for understanding the retrieval and expression of emotions that are elicited by trigger cues. First, in all of these cases, responding to a simple trigger cue was relatively unaffected by a change of context. This is true whether we were studying the evocation of fear reactions, appetitive reactions, stereotypes, or other types of cognitive attributions after original learning. However, when the trigger was then extinguished or associated with another outcome, the new learning seemed especially sensitive to context. The susceptibility of extinction and counterconditioning to contextual change appears to be a basic and ubiquitous process. Physical context (renewal), temporal context (spontaneous recovery), associative context (reinstatement), or interoceptive context changes can all result in a recovery of the original learning.

Contexts Created by Recent Events

There is yet another kind of context that we believe can influence responding to trigger cues. This is the context created by recent events.

Consider another phenomenon that seems important in understanding the regulation of emotion. In *reacquisition,* CS–US pairings can be resumed after extinction. Sometimes these can cause a very rapid return of the extinguished response to the trigger cue (e.g., Napier, Macrae, & Kehoe, 1992). (Rapid reacquisition is another indication that extinction does not destroy the original learning.) However, it is interesting to note that sometimes reacquisition is not rapid at all; it can be slower than the original learning under certain circumstances (e.g., Bouton, 1986; Bouton & Swartzentruber, 1989; Danguir & Nicolaidis, 1977). Our work on this interesting phenomenon has uncovered at least one variable that "selects" between these very different results. Reacquisition is rapid if the original learning has occurred over many trials, so that there has been ample opportunity for a recent trial to predict the outcomes of other trials. That is, responding returns quickly if we have learned to associate a conditioning trial with other conditioning trials: The first few reacquisition trials return the organism to the context prevailing in acquisition. But if acquisition has occurred with very few trials, so that there has been less opportunity to learn this contextual "trial signaling" (Ricker & Bouton, 1996), then reacquisition may not be rapid.

What does this have to do with emotional regulation? Once again, the regulation system seems to discriminate conditions in which it is adaptive to express the emotion (when acquisition conditions prevail) from those when it is not (when extinction conditions prevail). It is another mechanism through which the system tunes itself to the environment. It is also a further mechanism of lapse and relapse (Bouton, 2000). A cigarette smoker or alcoholic may often binge. That is, the person may tend to expose him- or herself periodically to a series of conditioning trials in fairly rapid succession. In this case, smoking or drinking may become associated with the "context" of an earlier smoke or drink—a previous conditioning trial. A smoker who has quit could find him- or herself lapsing one night upon returning to a bar or other situation in which he or she had previously smoked excessively. Because one cigarette provides an additional context for smoking more cigarettes, the mechanism we are talking about causes one cigarette to lead to another—full-blown relapse. Recent events may provide another part of the context that causes recovery of extinguished behavior.

A similar scenario may arise in a more emotional setting. After years of marital trouble marked by repeated fights and emotional outbursts, a couple may seek counseling or make other attempts to improve their marriage. Such a retroactive inhibition experience can be beneficial in the short run. But a single random emotional outburst, like another cigarette, may functionally reintroduce an aspect of the original context and lead to a breakdown of the efforts toward reconciliation.

If one conditioning trial predicts another, as it were, an effective way to prevent relapse (and improve regulation) would be to embed an occasional conditioning trial within a run of extinction trials. Such a procedure would in principle extinguish the relationship between a reinforced trial and more reinforced trials. Recent research suggests that this sort of procedure can indeed slow down rapid reacquisition (Pineño, Frohardt, & Bouton, 2002). Contexts are multifaceted and can have multiple and surprising effects on the effectiveness of trigger cues.

CONTEXT AND THE RETRIEVAL OF
INHIBITION IN EXTINCTION

To explain the various effects of context on extinction, Bouton (1993, 1994) has combined various ideas from learning theory with ideas about the role of context. There is the basic idea, present in most modern theories of conditioning, that during conditioning an excitatory association is formed between the trigger cue (i.e., CS) and the US. Such an association is indicated by the arrow in Figure 3.2. When the trigger cue is presented, it thereby excites or retrieves an explicit or implicit representation of the US. In this way, the trigger arouses the emotion naturally related to the US. During extinction or counterconditioning, the original association is not destroyed. Instead, Bouton adopts the idea that inhibition (e.g., Pavlov, 1927; Pearce & Hall, 1980; Wagner, 1981) is learned during the second learning experience. That association is indicated by the blocked line shown as link 1 in Figure 3.2. When the trigger is now presented, it activates the US through the excitatory association; but that retrieval is also now inhibited by simultaneous activation of the newly learned inhibitory association. The strength of this inhibition regulates the extent to which a representation of the US is activated and an emotion is aroused.

The unique aspect of Bouton's idea is that unlike the originally learned excitatory association, the second-learned inhibition is influenced by the context. That influence is shown in Figure 3.2 by the convergence of input from the trigger cue and the context (link 2). The inhibition is modulated by the context through a mechanism that can be thought to function as an AND gate (cf. Estes, 1976). The context does not directly inhibit the US. Rather, input from the trigger *and* the context in which inhibition was learned are required for the retrieval of inhibition and the regulation of the emotion aroused by the US. When

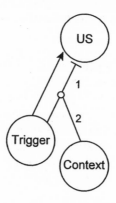

FIGURE 3.2. Model of extinction. The trigger has two types of associations with the US. An excitatory association (*arrow*) is acquired in phase one conditioning, and an inhibitory association (blocked line, Link 1) is acquired during phase two extinction. The inhibitory association is gated and requires input (Link 2) from the context and the trigger for activation.

the trigger is tested outside the context in which the inhibition was acquired, the necessary input from the context is absent and inhibition is not activated. Therefore, the cue once more triggers an emotional response by simple activation of the US. When trigger stimuli are associated with various states of arousal, retrieval of those states is regulated by a context-dependent inhibitory mechanism allowing the clear expression of emotions associated with the new learning.

A possible implication of the Figure 3.2 model is that inhibition may be generally sensitive to contextual change. However, the story is not that simple. Learning theory usually uses the term "inhibition" to mean a purely negative association between a CS and a US. For example, according to many theories (e.g., Rescorla & Wagner, 1972), inhibition is mainly produced when one CS (e.g., a tone) occurs on trials when another CS (e.g., a light) that ordinarily predicts a US is presented without it (e.g., L+/TL–). In effect, the tone, a "conditioned inhibitor," is a pure and unadulterated predictor of "no US." Unfortunately, we have found that such inhibitory learning with the tone is *NOT* context-specific. It is not disrupted at all by a change of context (see Bouton & Nelson, 1994; Nelson & Bouton, 1997). If inhibitory associations are not sensitive to context, then why do they become especially sensitive to context in extinction? One possibility suggested by Bouton (1993) is that context becomes important when the CS acquires a second meaning. According to this analysis, even excitatory associations, which are relatively insensitive to changes in context under ordinary circumstances, can become context dependent if they are the second type of information attached to the trigger.

Nelson (2002) has provided evidence that the order in which associations are learned, rather than their inhibitory or excitatory valence, is indeed the major determinant. In general, either excitatory or inhibitory learning can be context free or context dependent, depending on whether it is the first or second thing learned about a trigger cue. If excitatory conditioning takes place first and inhibitory conditioning takes place second (analogous to the state of affairs in extinction), the second-learned inhibition is dependent on the context for retrieval. However, if inhibitory learning takes place first and excitatory conditioning takes place second, second-learned excitation is now the thing that depends on context for retrieval. In either case, the first-learned association is context free.

Consider an experiment by Nelson (2002) in which rats first received inhibitory conditioning of food with a tone. This inhibitory conditioning was conducted by pairing a visual CS (L) with the delivery of food. However, on some trials a tone (T) was presented along with L, but food did not occur (i.e., L+/TL–). Under these conditions, as described earlier, conditioned inhibition between the tone and the food is acquired (see Bouton & Nelson, 1994; Wagner & Rescorla, 1972). Such inhibition transfers perfectly to a new context. Simple inhibition conditioned to a stimulus seems to be a mechanism by which animals can know, regardless of the context, not to expect food when it ordinarily would occur.

In the second phase of the experiment, the inhibitory tone underwent conventional excitatory conditioning in which it was paired with food. Because inhibition to the tone was acquired in the early parts of the experiment, the excitatory association conditioned later was the second association it acquired—a condition suggested by Bouton (1993) that could lead to context specificity. When the tone was tested in another context, a loss of excitatory conditioning was, in fact, observed. Like second-learned inhibition acquired in extinction, a second-learned excitatory association was also sensitive to changes in context. Control groups that received comparable treatment in the first phase of the experiment without the opportunity to learn inhibition to the tone showed no such loss.

The model proposed by Bouton (1993, 1994) should thus be seen as a more general model accepting the principle that contextual change influences second-learned associations, not merely inhibition. Even excitatory associations, which are usually insensitive to changes in context, can become context dependent if they are the second thing learned about a trigger stimulus. Another way to summarize the idea is to say that contexts control a particular kind of inhibitory process: retroactive inhibition. Retroactive inhibition is created when we learn something at Time 2 that is incompatible with what we learned at Time 1. The second-learned association inhibits the first-learned one. But that inhibition depends in large measure on being in the context where the second thing was learned. This may be the reason that contextual cues are important in controlling memory and behavior in a wide variety of retroactive interference paradigms (Bouton, 1993).

The mechanism described in Figure 3.2 to explain extinction (and other retroactive interference problems) can be seen as a mechanism of emotional intelligence. Through a natural process, learned, emotion-arousing information is regulated by contextually controlled retroactive inhibition that comes into play when a trigger cue acquires a second association or meaning. We emphasize the fact that regulation by context is much less likely prior to the trigger entering a second association. The system seems to treat first-learned experiences as though they are relatively invariant across contexts. When the trigger acquires a second meaning, regulation becomes possible. And this is when the context becomes important. When the trigger stimulus has two possible meanings, context determines the current meaning. It is exactly analogous to how the verbal system determines the meaning of ambiguous words (Bouton, 1994). The context effectively "disambiguates" the meaning of an ambiguous trigger cue by controlling retrieval of the second meaning.

The model proposed by Bouton (1993, 1994) essentially explains recovery effects as retrieval failure. When the stimuli are present outside the context in which extinction takes place, there is a failure to retrieve the regulatory inhibition and a recovery of the original learning is observed. One implication of this is that recovery effects could be reduced by conditions that favor retrieval of the regulating inhibition. Brooks and Bouton (1994) tested this idea using stimuli uniquely correlated with the extinction process. Rats received conditioning and extinction in different contexts. During extinction, some of the rats received additional presentations of another stimulus, a putative retrieval cue, that was simply presented at various times during the session. When the CS was tested back in the conditioning context, renewed responding was observed. But if the cue from extinction was presented just before the test, the renewal was significantly weakened. The idea is that the cue present in extinction served as a retrieval cue, or reminder, of the extinction experience, allowing the retrieval of the regulatory inhibition outside the extinction context. Such a cue has also been shown to attenuate spontaneous recovery (Brooks & Bouton, 1993). The fact that the retrieval cue has similar effects on both phenomena has two interesting implications. First, it supports the idea that renewal and spontaneous recovery are caused by the same mechanism (a failure to retrieve extinction outside the physical or temporal context). Second, it suggests that stimuli that are correlated with the second-learning experience can be used to regulate (inhibit) emotions that may reemerge in new contexts. When we learn a new way of coping with situations and emotions, it may be useful to focus on some token item correlated with the experience that can be taken into new settings.

EMOTIONS AND VOLUNTARY (OPERANT) BEHAVIOR

The preceding discussion has mainly been concerned with the fate of emotions that are aroused by classically conditioned trigger cues. We have noted that such emotions can be regulated by context and inhibitory processes. Of course, even in learning theory, emotions are more than just simple Pavlovian responses: They have another crucial theoretical role as events that motivate or instigate voluntary action (e.g., Rescorla & Solomon, 1967). Classic thinking about avoidance behavior (Mowrer, 1947; see also Ayres, 1998; McAllister & McAllister, 1991) illustrates what we mean. In avoidance learning, the animal learns to avoid exposure to something nasty by performing an action before it is scheduled to happen. According to classic two-factor theory, the avoidance response is learned because it escapes emotion-arousing trigger cues that signal the upcoming nasty event. Fear elicited by the trigger cue thus motivates the behavior. The behavior is also reinforced because it causes fear reduction (it terminates the trigger cue). Classic evidence suggested that organisms learn to work to turn off or dampen aversive emotions (e.g., Miller, 1948). This fact provides a second dimension to the emotion–action interaction: The action that is motivated by emotion further functions to regulate it. Operant learning is the mechanism whereby organisms learn behaviors that regulate emotion.

"Voluntary" action follows principles like those we reviewed earlier for classical conditioning. That is, operant responses are also susceptible to the familiar renewal, reinstatement, and other recovery effects (e.g., see Bouton & Swartzentruber, 1991; Nakajima et al., 2000). Also, operant responses that are motivated by classically conditioned emotions, as discussed in the preceding paragraph, recover when the emotion recovers. To demonstrate how voluntary actions can regulate emotions, and recover along with them, consider an experiment by McAllister, McAllister, Scoles, and Hampton (1986). After fear had been conditioned in rats through many inescapable pairings of a light and shock on one side of a box, a door over a hurdle was opened so that the rat could escape to the other side. When the rat jumped the hurdle, the fear-eliciting light was turned off. Shock was never delivered in this phase. Thus, the jumping behavior of the rat was not an unconditional response to shock or fear. Rather, it was a learned instrumental response that helped terminate (regulate) the fear elicited by the light. In terms of Mowrer's (1947) two-factor theory, the hurdle jump is an action that is reinforced by the termination of the fear-inducing stimulus, which reduces fear. As described earlier, fear motivated the behavior, and fear reduction reinforced it. The behavior was organized to regulate (reduce) fear.

Such a behavior will recover along with the emotion following extinction. After the conditioning of the light and avoidance responding described earlier, the animals underwent extinction training. The extinction trials were actually just like acquisition; the light was turned on, the animals were allowed to escape, and shocks were never delivered. Ultimately, after an average of 208.67 trials in the critical group, extinction occurred. Following extinction, the animals received a single inescapable pairing of the light with shock designed to recondition fear to the light. At this point, the avoidance response could not be made; the only thing being retrained was light–shock association (and thus the emotion aroused by the light). Even though the apparently extinguished behavior could not be performed at the time of the reinstating shock, the avoidance response returned to full strength in later testing when the light was presented and required another 169.33 trials to extinguish. (That number was not significantly different from the initial 208.67.)

The important point, discussed by Falls (1998), is that even though the emotional reaction to the triggering stimulus was extinguished, the capacity to perform an operant response whose learning was motivated by the emotion was retained. Thus, neither the original trigger–US association nor the instrumental action–outcome association was destroyed. This means that an additional effect of the renewal, spontaneous recovery, or reinstatement of extinguished trigger cues may be to cause the recovery of voluntary behaviors whose learning was motivated by the emotion.

But how are we to explain the recovery of the avoidance response itself? One answer is that the strength of avoidance behavior is supposed to be modulated by the strength of the emotion that motivates it. For instance, in so-called "transfer of control" experiments, it can be shown that increasing and decreasing the strength of an emotional state by presenting Pavlovian excitatory and inhibitory trigger cues can increase and decrease the ongoing rate of instrumental responding (e.g., see Rescorla & Solomon, 1967; Trapold & Overmier, 1972; Overmier & Lawry, 1979). This is the sense in which emotions provide a motivational basis for voluntary action.

The motivating effects of emotions are usually seen as energizing them; there is an unconditional invigoration implied. But emotions can also serve as contexts that modulate the behaviors in a more associative sense: They can also provide internal contexts that serve the familiar retrieval function (cf. Overmier & Lawry, 1979). Richardson, Riccio, and Devine (1984) conditioned and then extinguished an avoidance response. In a test phase, some of the rats were then given an injection of adrenocorticotropic hormone (ACTH), a hormone released during stress, while others were given a placebo. ACTH caused a recovery of the extinguished avoidance behavior. Why? One possibility is that natural release of ACTH may have been part of the interoceptive context present during the original (stressful) avoidance learning. After extinction, introduction of ACTH may have returned the animal's original internal context, thus resulting in a renewal of fear and avoidance behavior.

Ahlers and Richardson (1985) tested this idea more directly. During conditioning and extinction some animals received administration of dexamethasone, which blocks the release of the naturally occurring ACTH, and others received saline injections. At the test, the rats received either saline or ACTH injections. For animals that experienced a natural increase in ACTH during conditioning (those that had not received dexamethasone), ACTH at testing resulted in a renewal of the extinguished fear. For animals that did not experience a natural increase in ACTH during conditioning (those that had received dexamethasone injections), ACTH injections at test had no effect. Thus, the effect of the stress hormone produced a renewal effect only when the hormone was a component of the original conditioning episode. It was a part of the context associated with the original avoidance response. Thus, emotions can motivate voluntary action unconditionally, or they can exert control over voluntary action by functioning as a kind of internal context.

These ideas extend the range of things controlled by the factors we discussed earlier. Emotions serve as motivators for voluntary action, and they can serve as contexts as well. The interesting point is that when effects like renewal, spontaneous recovery, and reinstatement occur with trigger cues, we can expect more than just emotion to recover. The behaviors motivated by the emotion, or associated with it through experience, will also reemerge. Thus, if a behavioral strategy has been learned to regulate a negative emotion, then when the emotion recovers through a change in context, the regulating strategy may recover with it. Perhaps good news is thus mixed with the bad. However, it is worth noting that regulatory behaviors are not necessarily "positive." In the abusive marriage example we mentioned earlier, we may imagine that one spouse has learned to suppress or escape negative emotion by using verbal or physical abuse of the other spouse. If anger or frustration is the context (or motivator) of that abuse, any return of anger after therapy may cause a return of the abuse. When emotions return, it is more likely that the originally learned and maladaptive regulatory strategy will return with them. We may expect our recovery effects to have implications for both emotional responding itself and actions that have been learned to deal with it.

CONCLUSION

This chapter has illustrated some implications of recent work in learning theory for our understanding of processes that may underlie emotion and emotional regulation. We started by noting that emotions can be elicited by trigger cues that acquire their power through classical conditioning. We then reviewed research suggesting that the retroactive inhibition of those emotions—regulation of the emotion by subsequently learned conflicting information—is controlled by the context, whether the context is provided by exteroceptive, interoceptive, temporal, or "mental" cues. These findings have a number of implications for understanding recovery and relapse effects (e.g., Bouton, 1988, 2000; Bouton & Nelson, 1998; Bouton & Swartzentruber, 1991). And as we have sketched in the last part of the chapter, they may also have implications for action that has been learned to deal with emotion.

We like to think that the principles that laboratory research has given us provide insight into how the emotional system naturally tunes itself to the environment. Emotions themselves function to get the organism ready for upcoming events (e.g., Bouton et al., 2001; Hollis, 1997). And our point that second-learned information is especially influenced by context makes adaptive sense too. Statistically, events we sample first are more likely to reflect the normal situation. With more samples, we become more likely to sample the exceptions. Our learning system has adapted to these regularities by treating first-learned information as general rules and second-learned information as situation-dependent exceptions. As such, the processes that control emotion are not only lawful, they are organized and sensible (see Bouton, 1994, for further discussion). Research from the learning-theory tradition gives us insight into how emotions are naturally regulated. And it also helps us understand a particular sense in which emotions are "intelligent."

REFERENCES

Ahlers, S. T., & Richardson, R. (1985). Administration of dexamethasone prior to training blocks ACTH-induced recovery of an extinguished avoidance response. *Behavioral Neuroscience, 99,* 760–764.

Ayres, J. J. B. (1998). Fear conditioning and avoidance. In W. O'Donohue (Ed.), *Learning and behavior therapy* (pp. 122–145). Needham Heights, MA: Allyn & Bacon.

Baker, A. G., Steinwald, H., & Bouton, M. E. (1991) Contextual conditioning and reinstatement of extinguished instrumental responding. *Quarterly Journal of Experimental Psychology, 43B,* 199–218.

Bouton, M. E. (1986). Slow reacquisition following the extinction of conditioned suppression. *Learning and Motivation, 17,* 1–15.

Bouton, M. E. (1988). Context and ambiguity in the extinction of emotional learning: Implications for exposure therapy. *Behaviour Research and Therapy, 26,* 137–149.

Bouton, M. E. (1993). Context, time, and memory retrieval in the interference paradigms of Pavlovian learning. *Psychological Bulletin, 114,* 80–99.

Bouton, M. E. (1994). Conditioning, remembering, and forgetting. *Journal of Experimental Psychology: Animal Behavior Processes, 20,* 219–231.

Bouton, M. E. (1997). Signals for whether vs. when an event will occur. In M. E. Bouton & M. S. Fanselow (Eds.), *Learning, motivation, and cognition: The functional behaviorism of Robert C. Bolles* (pp. 385–489). Washington, DC: American Psychological Association.

Bouton, M.E. (2000). A learning theory perspective on lapse, relapse, and the maintenance of behavior change. *Health Psychology, 19,* 57–63.

Bouton, M. E., & Bolles, R. C. (1979a). Contextual control of the extinction of conditioned fear. *Learning and Motivation, 10,* 445–466.

Bouton, M. E., & Bolles, R. C. (1979b). Role of conditioned contextual stimuli in the reinstatement of extinguished fear. *Journal of Experimental Psychology: Animal Behavior Processes, 5,* 368–378.

Bouton, M.E., Kenny, F. A., & Rosengard, C. (1990). State-dependent fear extinction with two benzodiazepine tranquilizers. *Behavioral Neuroscience, 104,* 44–55.

Bouton, M. E., & King, D. A. (1983). Contextual control of the extinction of conditioned fear: Tests for the associative value of the context. *Journal of Experimental Psychology: Animal Behavior Processes, 9*(3), 248–265.

Bouton, M. E., Mineka, S., & Barlow, D. H. (2001). A modern learning theory perspective on the etiology of panic disorder. *Psychological Review, 108,* 4–32.

Bouton, M. E., & Nelson, J. B. (1994). Context specificity of target versus feature inhibition in a feature-negative discrimination. *Journal of Experimental Psychology: Animal Behavior Processes, 20,* 51–65.

Bouton, M. E., & Nelson, J. B. (1998). The role of context in classical conditioning: Some implications for cognitive behavior therapy. In W. O'Donohue (Ed.), *Learning and behavior therapy* (pp. 59–84). Needham Heights, MA: Allyn & Bacon.

Bouton, M. E., Nelson, J. B., & Rosas, J. M. (1999). Stimulus generalization, context change, and forgetting. *Psychological Bulletin, 125,* 171–186.

Bouton, M. E., & Peck, C. A. (1989). Context effects on conditioning, extinction, and reinstatement in and appetitive conditioning preparation. *Animal Learning & Behavior, 17*(2), 188–198.

Bouton, M. E., & Peck, C. A. (1992). Spontaneous recovery in cross-motivational transfer (counterconditioning). *Animal Learning & Behavior, 20,* 313–321.

Bouton, M. E., & Ricker, S. T. (1994). Renewal of extinguished responding in a second context. *Animal Learning & Behavior, 22,* 317–324.

Bouton, M. E., Rosengard, C., Achenbach, G. G., & Peck, C. A. (1993). Effects of contextual conditioning and unconditioned stimulus presentation on performance in appetitive conditioning. *Quarterly Journal of Experimental Psychology, 46B,* 63–95.

Bouton, M. E., & Sunsay, C. (2001). Contextual control of appetitive conditioning: Influence of a contextual stimulus generated by a partial reinforcement procedure. *Quarterly Journal of Experimental Psychology, 54B,* 109–125.

Bouton, M. E., & Swartzentruber, D. (1986). Analysis of the associative and occasion-setting properties of contexts participating in a Pavlovian discrimination. *Journal of Experimental Psychology: Animal Behavior Processes, 12*(4), 333–350.

Bouton, M.E., & Swartzentruber, D. (1989). Slow reacquisition following extinction: Context, encoding, and retrieval mechanisms. *Journal of Experimental Psychology: Animal Behavior Processes, 15,* 43–53.

Bouton, M.E., & Swartzentruber, D. (1991). Sources of relapse after extinction in Pavlovian and instrumental learning. *Clinical Psychology Review, 11,* 123–140.

Brooks, D. C. (2000). Recent and remote extinction cues reduce spontaneous recovery. *Quarterly Journal of Experimental Psychology, 53B,* 24–58.

Brooks, D. C., & Bouton, M. E. (1993). A retrieval cue for extinction attenuates spontaneous recovery. *Journal of Experimental Psychology: Animal Behavior Processes, 19,* 77–89.

Brooks, D. C., & Bouton, M. E. (1994). A retrieval cue for extinction attenuates response recovery (renewal) caused by a return to the conditioning context. *Journal of Experimental Psychology: Animal Behavior Processes, 20,* 366–379.

Brooks, D. C., Hale, B., Nelson, J. B., & Bouton, M.E. (1995). Reinstatement after counterconditioning. *Animal Learning & Behavior, 23,* 383–390.

Cunningham, C. L. (1979). Alcohol as a cue for extinction: State dependency produced by conditioned inhibition. *Animal Learning & Behavior, 7,* 45–52.

Danguir, J., & Nicolaidis, S. (1977). Lack of reacquisition in learned taste aversions. *Animal Learning & Behavior, 5,* 395–397.

Estes, W. K. (1955). Statistical theory of spontaneous recovery and regression. *Psychological Review, 62,* 145–154.

Estes, W. K., (1976). Structural aspects of associative models of memory. In C. N. Cofer (Ed.), *The structure of human memory* (pp. 31–53). New York: Freeman.

Falls, W. A. (1998). Extinction: A review of theory and the evidence suggesting that memories are not erased with nonreinforcement. In W.T. O'Donohue (Ed.), *Learning and behavior therapy* (pp. 205–229). Needham Heights, MA: Allyn & Bacon.

Feldman Barrett, L., & Gross, J. (2001). Emotional intelligence: A process model of emotion representation and regulation. In T. J. Mayne & G. A. Bonanno (Eds.), *Emotions: Current issues and future directions* (pp. 286–310). New York: Guilford Press.

Fox, G. D., & Holland, P. C. (1998). Neurotoxic hippocampal lesions fail to impair reinstatement of an appetitively conditioned response. *Behavioral Neuroscience, 112*, 255–260.

Harris, J. A., Jones, M. L., Bailey, G. K., & Westbrook, R. F. (2000). Contextual control over conditioned responding in an extinction paradigm. *Journal of Experimental Psychology: Animal Behavior Processes, 26*, 174–185.

Hilgard, E. R., & Bower, G. H. (1975). *Theories of learning* (4th ed.). Englewood Cliffs, NJ: Prentice-Hall.

Hollis, K. L. (1997). Contemporary research on Pavlovian conditioning: A "new" functional analysis. *American Psychologist, 52*, 956–965.

Honey, R. C., Willis, A., & Hall, G (1990). Context specificity in pigeon autoshaping. *Learning and Motivation, 21*, 125–136.

Kaiser, C. R., Miller, C. T., & Bouton, M. E. (2002). *Context-specific extinction and inhibition of stereotypes*. Manuscript in preparation.

Kaye, H., & Mackintosh, N. J. (1990). A change of context can enhance performance of an aversive but not of an appetitive conditioned response. *Quarterly Journal of Experimental Psychology, 42B*, 113–134.

Kaye, H., Preston, G., Szabo, L., Druiff, H., & Mackintosh, N. J. (1987). Context specificity of conditioning and latent inhibition: Evidence for a dissociation of latent inhibition and associative interference. *Quarterly Journal of Experimental Psychology, 39B*, 127–145.

Lang, P. J. (1995). The emotion probe: Studies of motivation and attention. *American Psychologist, 50*, 372–385.

Ledoux, J. E. (1996). *The emotional brain: The mysterious underpinnings of emotional life*. New York: Simon & Schuster.

Matthews, G., Zeidner, M. (2000). Emotional intelligence: Adaptation to stressful encounters and health outcomes. In Bar-On, R., & Parker, J. D. A., (Eds). *Handbook of emotional intelligence* (pp. 459–489). San Francisco: Jossey-Bass.

Mayer, J. D., & Salovey, P. (1995). Emotional intelligence and the construction and regulation of feelings. *Applied and Preventive Psychology, 4*, 197–208.

Mayer, J. D., Salovey, P., & Caruso, D. (2000). Models of emotional intelligence. In R. Sternberg (Ed.), *Handbook of intelligence* (pp. 396–420). New York: Cambridge University Press.

McAllister, D. E., & McAllister, R. W. (1991). Fear theory and aversively motivated behavior: Some controversial issues. In M.R. Denny (Ed.), *Fear, avoidance, and phobias: A fundamental analysis* (pp. 135–163). Hillsdale, NJ: Erlbaum.

McAllister, D. E., McAllister, R. W., Scoles, M. T., & Hampton, S. R. (1986). Persistence of fear reducing behavior: Relevance for the conditioning theory of neurosis. *Journal of Abnormal Psychology, 95*, 365–372.

Miller, N. E. (1948). Studies of fear as an acquirable drive: I. Fear as a motivation and fear-reduction as reinforcement in the learning of new responses. *Journal of Experimental Psychology, 38,* 89–101.

Mineka, S. (1985). The frightful complexity of the origin of fears. In F. R. Brush & J. Overmier (Eds.), *Affect, conditioning, and cognition: Essays on the determinants of behavior* (pp. 81–111). Hillsdale NJ: Erlbaum.

Mowrer, O. H. (1947). On the dual nature of learning: A reinterpretation of "conditioning" and "problem solving." *Harvard Educational Review, 17,* 102–150.

Mowrer, O. H. (1960). *Learning theory and behavior.* New York: Wiley.

Nakajima, S., Tanaka, S., Urshihara, K., & Imada, H. (2000). Renewal of extinguished lever-press responses upon return to the training context. *Learning and Motivation, 31,* 416–431.

Napier, R. M., Macrae, M., & Kehoe, E. J. (1992). Rapid reacquisition in conditioning of the rabbit's nictitating membrane response. *Journal of Experimental Psychology: Animal Behavior Processes, 18,* 182–192.

Nelson, J. B. (2002). Context specificity of excitation and inhibition in ambiguous stimuli. *Learning and Motivation, 33,* 284–310.

Nelson, J. B., & Bouton, M. E. (1997). The effects of a context switch following serial and simultaneous feature-negative discriminations. *Learning and Motivation, 28,* 56–84.

Overmier, J. B., & Lawry, J. A. (1979). Pavlovian conditioning and the mediation of behavior. In G. H. Bower (Ed.), *The psychology of learning and motivation* (pp. 1–55). New York: Academic Press.

Pavlov, I. P. (1927). *Conditioned reflexes.* London: Oxford University Press.

Pearce, J. M., & Hall, G. (1980). A model for Pavlovian learning: Variations in the effectiveness of conditioned but not of unconditioned stimuli. *Psychological Review, 87,* 532–552.

Peck, C. A., & Bouton, M. E. (1990). Context and performance in aversive-to-appetitive and appetitive-to-aversive transfer. *Learning and Motivation, 21,* 1–31.

Pineño, O., Frohardt, R. J., & Bouton, M. E. (2002). *Partial reinforcement in extinction retards rapid reacquisition.* Manuscript in preparation.

Rauhut, A. S., Thomas, B. L., & Ayres, J. B. (2001). Treatments that weaken Pavlovian conditioned fear and thwart its renewal in rats: Implications for treating human phobias. *Journal of Experimental Psychology: Animal Behavior Processes, 27,* 99–114.

Rescorla, R. A. (1988). Pavlovian conditioning: It's not what you think it is. *American Psychologist, 43,* 151–160.

Rescorla, R. A., & Heth, C. D. (1975). Reinstatement of fear to an extinguished conditioned stimulus. *Journal of Experimental Psychology: Animal Behavior Processes, 1,* 88–96.

Rescorla, R. A., & Solomon, R. L. (1967). Two-process learning theory: Relationships between Pavlovian conditioning and instrumental learning. *Psychological Review, 74,* 151–182.

Rescorla, R. A., & Wagner, A. R. (1972). A theory of Pavlovian conditioning: Variations in the effectiveness of reinforcement and nonreinforcement. In

A. H. Black & W. F. Prokasy (Eds.), *Classical conditioning II: Current research and theory* (pp. 64–99). New York: Appleton-Century-Crofts.

Riccio, D. C., Richardson, R., & Ebner, D. L. (1984). Memory retrieval deficits based on altered contextual cues: A paradox. *Psychological Bulletin, 96,* 152–165.

Richardson, R., Riccio, D. C., & Devine, L. (1984). ACTH-induced recovery of extinguished avoidance responding. *Physiological Psychology, 12,* 184–192.

Ricker, S. T., & Bouton, M. E. (1996). Reacquisition following extinction in appetitive conditioning. *Animal Learning & Behavior, 24,* 423–436.

Rosas, J. M., & Bouton, M.E. (1997). Renewal of a conditioned taste aversion upon return to the conditioning context after extinction in another one. *Learning and Motivation, 28,* 216–229.

Rosas, J. M., Villa, N. J., Lugo, M., & Lopez, L. (2001). Combined effects of context change and retention interval on interference in causality judgments. *Journal of Experimental Psychology: Animal Behavior Processes, 27,* 153–164.

Salovey, P., Hee, C. K., & Mayer, J. D. (1993). Emotional intelligence and the self-regulation of affect. In D. M., Wegner & J. W. Pennebaker (Eds.), *Handbook of mental control* (pp. 258–277). Upper Saddle River, NJ: Prentice-Hall.

Spear, N. E. (1978). *The processing of memories: Forgetting and retention.* Hillsdale, NJ: Erlbaum.

Trapold, M. A., & Overmier, J. B. (1972). The second learning process in instrumental learning. In A. H. Black & W. F. Prokasy (Eds.), *Classical conditioning II: Current research and theory* (pp. 427–452). New York: Appleton-Century-Crofts.

Wagner, A. R. (1981). SOP: A model of automatic memory processing in animal behavior. In N. E. Spear & R. R. Miller (Eds.), *Information processing in animals: Memory mechanisms* (pp. 5–47). Hillsdale, NJ: Erlbaum.

Wagner, A. R., & Rescorla, R. A. (1972). Inhibition in Pavlovian conditioning: Application of a theory. In R. A. Boakes & M. S. Halliday (Eds.), *Inhibition and learning* (pp. 301–336). London: Academic Press.

Wolpe, J. (1958). *Psychotherapy by reciprocal inhibition.* Stanford, CA: Stanford University Press.

PART II

Using Emotion in Thought and Action

 CHAPTER 4

Affect as Information

An Individual-Differences Approach

CAROL L. GOHM
GERALD L. CLORE

I_s being an "emotional" person desirable or undesirable? Synonyms for the word "emotional" in one thesaurus (Ehrlich, 1994) include "effusive," "fervid," "maudlin," and "mawkish." These words imply that being an emotional person is undesirable. But the synonyms in another thesaurus (Microsoft Word, 2000) include "moving," "touching," "poignant," "exciting," and "arousing." These words imply that being an emotional person may be desirable. Together they suggest that different thesaurus writers have differing implicit theories about emotionality.

A similar difference can be seen across cultures in beliefs about child rearing. Puritan parents in 17th-century America were advised that their children should fear them and that due distance should be maintained, because lavish displays of affection bred contempt and irreverence (Reese, 2000). But the present-day Beng of West Africa "advise parents to teach their children to dish out ribald insults to their grandparents to help the children feel free and familiar with their much older relatives" (DeLoache & Gottlieb, 2000, p. 22). These accounts suggest that different cultures have had differing attitudes toward emotionality.

Related contrasts can also be seen in current psychological research. On the one hand, much research on emotion focuses on the problematic aspects of emotional experience. In the literature on judgment and decision making, emotion has traditionally been seen as a source of unwanted bias. In social psychology, some research focuses on the need to regulate emotion (e.g., Richards & Gross, 2000). However, other research has emphasized the health benefits of expressing emotion (Pennebaker & Bealls, 1986) and the adaptive role of emotional cues in decision making (e.g., Damasio, 1994). Thus, different investigators may also approach emotionality with different attitudes.

So which attitude is the more defensible? Is being emotional and emotionally expressive an adaptive or a maladaptive characteristic? Is the experience of emotion beneficial or harmful, useful or misleading? Investigators of emotion are most likely to answer that neither position is adequate. In particular, the affect-as-information approach to the study of emotion maintains that emotion is neither inherently blessed nor cursed, but is simply information. According to this view, emotional feelings are embodied information reflecting a person's assessment of the personal relevance of his or her current situation. The desirability of being an emotional person depends, therefore, on what one does with the information provided by emotion—one's level of emotional intelligence (Salovey & Mayer, 1990).

THE AFFECT-AS-INFORMATION APPROACH

The affect-as-information hypothesis (Schwarz & Clore, 1983; Clore et al., 2001) is that people routinely use their feelings to make judgments and decisions. People automatically appraise salient aspects of their environment, so that judgments and decisions can be readily made by asking themselves, "How do I feel about it?" (Schwarz & Clore, 1988). The information that feelings convey is about value—that is, about the positive or negative aspect of things. Just as facial expressions of emotion convey such information externally to others, feelings of emotion are seen as conveying it internally to oneself. Unlike affective concepts, which convey positive and negative information cognitively as semantic meaning, affective feelings convey such information as bodily experiences. It seems likely that the physical manifestation of the information is one reason that people find the information from feelings to be especially credible.

Traditionally, theories of judgment (e.g., Anderson, 1981) and attitude (e.g., Ajzen & Fishbein, 1975) assumed that evaluations of objects depended on beliefs about their attributes. Thus, someone might be judged likeable to the extent that others believed he or she had positive attributes (e.g., trustworthiness, loyalty, friendliness, courteousness, kindness). In contrast, the affect-as-information hypothesis assumes that actual liking depends not so much on cognitive beliefs about a person, as on direct, affective experience with the person. It assumes that the critical element in liking is not the conceptualization of the person as positive, but the embodied experience of the person in terms of one's own positive feelings. A problem, however, is that affective beliefs and affective experience go hand in hand, making it difficult to disentangle them to find out whether affective feelings, by themselves, are important or whether their effects are mediated by affective concepts and beliefs.

Research investigating such issues has typically employed induced mood states as a source of feelings that are independent of whatever beliefs are held about a target object. Once affect was varied independently in this way, it became clear that affective feelings were important over and above evaluative beliefs (Gouaux, 1971; Griffit & Veitch, 1971). Subsequently, research has varied as to whether feelings in general were an appropriate basis for judgment (Gasper & Clore, 2000) and whether the particular feelings were attributed to relevant or irrelevant sources (e.g., Schwarz & Clore, 1983). Such studies showed that the critical role of feelings in judgment is that they provide information, information about one's reaction to the object of judgment.

Critics often ask why people would need to be informed by their affective reactions. After all, if emotions result from one's own appraisals, why would information from feelings be needed at all? The answer is that although one is continually engaged in environmental appraisals, the process is largely unconscious. Thus, emotional feelings arise only when something emotionally significant has been detected. According to contemporary dual-process models (e. g., Smith & DeCoster, 1999), emotional appraisals are only one of the many psychological processes of which we remain ignorant until their outcome is recognized consciously. For example, processes in the inner ear generate vestibular signals continuously, but feelings of imbalance intrude on consciousness only as some threshold of instability is exceeded.

According to the affect-as-information approach, affect is an integral part of evaluative judgment. Like other self-generated experiences (e.g., feelings of balance, cold, pain), affective feelings convey, in an embodied form, information about the interface between oneself and one's environment. As such, they are directly useful both as motivation and information. In contrast, most theories of the influence of mood and emotion on cognitive processes (e.g., Bower, 1981; Forgas, 2000; Isen, 1984) have assumed that the role of affect is indirect. In that view, moods are assumed to influence judgment by activating mood-congruent beliefs in memory, and mood-congruent beliefs are assumed to be the real bases of people's evaluative judgments. In contrast, we assume that beliefs reflect feelings. Specifically, feelings serve directly as the information on which judgments are based. The quality of feeling is the implicit evaluation of a situation, and the intensity of feeling is its apparent urgency. Hence, an inability to use such affective information when making judgments should be maladaptive (e.g., Damasio, 1994). If so, then variation among individuals in the extent to which they focus on and use their affective cues should have important consequences, as suggested by the second branch of Mayer and Salovey's (1997) model of emotional intelligence.

In some situations, affective cues are obvious in meaning, and their use obviously appropriate. The fear generated by meeting the proverbial bear in the woods clearly serves as information that a major safety goal has been threatened and as motivation for coping with this fact. However, many situations in life are more complex and subtle. For example, suppose one were interviewing a potential employee whose application listed all of the skills and experience required. However, suppose further that while interviewing her, one experienced negative feelings. What information would those feelings convey? What would they mean? If she happened to have red hair and one's estranged ex-spouse also had red hair, the feelings might be quite irrelevant to the hiring situation. Not hiring her based on this negative affect would be inappropriate and perhaps shortsighted. However, if the same feelings were a reaction to an arrogant attitude on her part, they might be quite relevant to a hiring decision. Thus, the discriminating use of affective cues for judgments and decisions requires an ability to judge when it is relevant and when it is not. That is, the functionality of feelings requires that they generally be attributed to their correct source. In this chapter we review research that we have done on individual differences in this and related processes.

Our study of emotional intelligence from the affect-as-information approach examines individual differences in the use and misuse of affect as information. In the process, we have asked about the differences among people with respect to who trusts their emotions, who attempts to avoid the influence of emotion, and who knows when to attend to and when not to attend to emotional cues. We have also asked whether we could find specific psychological benefits associated with emotional intelligence, and whether the outcomes we discuss have explanations other than emotional intelligence. To date, the research is exploratory and largely correlational, so that the causal direction of the associations that we report, and the psychological processes involved, need to be investigated further.

Much of the research examines people's attitudes toward emotional experiences and their perceptions of their own emotional intelligence. To assess such self-perceptions, we have frequently utilized the

Trait Meta-Mood Scale (TMMS; Salovey, Mayer, Goldman, Turvey, & Palfai, 1995). This scale was proposed early in the development of the current model of emotional intelligence as a self-report measure of beliefs or attitudes about one's moods and emotion, formally termed the "meta-mood experience." The original analyses during scale development supported the existence of three subscales, Clarity, Attention, and Repair. More recently, in a large-scale study, we interrelated 18 self-report measures concerning various aspects of emotion (Gohm & Clore, 2000). We found that the TMMS full scale showed good internal consistency (Cronbach's alpha = .86). Cluster analysis and multidimensional scaling procedures also indicated that the concepts of emotional clarity and emotional attention were empirically separable from each other, as well as from the concepts of emotional intensity and emotional expression. Further, the Clarity and Attention subscales were correlated with self-report measures of similar constructs, the topic to which we turn next.

The Clarity subscale of the TMMS assesses the perceived clarity with which respondents experience their emotions. It asks about the extent to which they believe that they can identify and describe what they are feeling. Items include "I almost always know exactly how I am feeling," "I can't make sense out of my feelings (reverse scored)," and "I am usually very clear about my feelings." Among 141 undergraduates (Gohm & Clore, 2000), scores on the scale were positively correlated with a report of the ability to label emotions ($r = .78$, $p < .01$) and inversely with reported difficulty in identifying emotions ($r = -.68$, $p < .01$) and difficulty in describing emotions ($r = -.59$, $p < .01$). Ability to Label Emotions is a subscale of the Mood Awareness Survey (Swinkels & Guiliano, 1995). Difficulty Identifying and Difficulty Describing Emotions are both subscales of the Toronto Alexithymia Scale (TAS–20; Bagby, Parker, & Taylor, 1994). The Attention subscale of the TMMS assesses the extent to which respondents believe that they attend to and value their emotional experiences. Items include "I pay a lot of attention to how I feel," "People would be better off if they felt less and thought more (reverse scored)," and "Feelings give direction to life." Attention was correlated with a scale of monitoring one's emotions ($r = .57$, $p < .01$) and inversely with a measure of external thinking style ($r = -.49$, $p < .01$). Monitoring Emotions is a subscale of the Mood Awareness Survey (Swinkels & Guiliano, 1995). External Thinking Style is a subscale of the Toronto Alexithymia Scale (Bagby, Parker, & Taylor, 1994). The Repair subscale of the TMMS assesses respondents' beliefs about the degree to which they can moderate their moods. Items include "When I become upset I remind myself of all the pleasures in life," "I try to think good thoughts no matter how badly I feel," and "Although I am sometimes happy, I have a mostly pessimistic outlook (reverse scored)." In another study, Salovey et al. (1995) found that repair was correlated with measures of negative mood regulation ($r = .53$, $p < .01$) and optimism ($r = .57$, $p < .01$). In the research discussed in the following section, we used the total score on these three subscales (Clarity, Attention, and Repair) as a measure of self-perceived emotional intelligence.

COMPARING OBJECTIVE AND SUBJECTIVE MEASURES OF EMOTIONAL INTELLIGENCE

A fundamental supposition of the affect-as-information hypothesis is that in many of life's situations, feelings provide valid and useful information. At least, they *can*, provided that individuals accept and correctly interpret the information. However, not everyone makes good use of this information. Individuals who do not value, attend to, or trust their feelings may reject, or even attempt to correct for their emotions when making evaluations or decisions. If an individual does not understand his or her emotions, or is inaccurate in reading emotional information, such avoidance would be appropriate. However, if a person has accurate emotional information, but does not realize it or distrusts his or her emotional ability, a useful life skill may be wasted. Psychologists have long been concerned about the accuracy of self-evaluation. Most studies have indicated that people tend to overestimate their skills and abilities (Kruger, 1999). In the domain of emotional intelligence, however, our research suggests that the problem lies in underestimating one's ability. Some individuals are emotionally intelligent, but believe themselves not to be.

In a recent study (Gohm, 2000), undergraduates (112 men and 206 women) from the first to the fourth year ($N = 60$, 89, 119, and 43, respectively) completed a self-report measure of emotional intelligence (the TMMS; Salovey et al., 1995) as well as an ability measure of emotional intelligence (the Mayer–Salovey–Caruso Emotional Intelligence Test [MSCEIT]; Mayer, Salovey, & Caruso, 2001). The MSCEIT is based on the model of emotional intelligence developed by Mayer and Salovey (Mayer & Salovey, 1997; Mayer, Salovey, & Caruso, 2000), which is an ability model that views emotional intelligence as the capacity to reason with emotional information. This model divides emotional intelligence into four components: (1) the perception of emotion, (2) the integration of emotion in thought, (3) the understanding of emotion, and (4) the management of emotion. Consistent with the theoretical perspective of the model, the MSCEIT is a performance-based instrument, rather than a measure of self-perceived emotional intelligence.

For example, Perception of Emotion is assessed by asking respondents to judge the emotion expressed in a series of faces, and the emotion elicited by a series of landscapes, and by a series of designs. Emotional Understanding is assessed, for example, by questions about which emotions are blends of other emotions and how emotions progress from one emotion to the next. Emotion Management is partially assessed by asking respondents to choose the best response to various relationship scenarios, such as one's friend getting a promotion that one wanted for oneself. The advantages of this approach include its clear operational definition of emotional intelligence, its imperviousness to faking, and its independence from other assessments of emotional intelligence (see Salovey, Mayer, Caruso, & Lopes, in press).

In this study, self-perceived emotional intelligence (total score on the TMMS) correlated only somewhat with ability (total score on the MSCEIT; $r = .29$, $p < .001$). However, inspection of the scatter plot (confirmed by an equality of variance test) indicated that the variance in the ability measure was much larger among low scorers on the self-report measure. That is, individuals who thought they were emotionally intelligent actually showed the ability, but among individuals who thought they were not emotionally intelligent, there was a wide range of actual ability. Thus, some individuals are emotionally smarter than they think they are. This distrust of their emotional intelligence may moderate processes associated with the experience of emotion, including attributional style, regulation of emotional expression, and accuracy in interpreting others' emotional experience.

Interestingly, neither ability, nor self-perception, nor the accuracy of self-perception, increased over the course of 4 years in college. Ability (MSCEIT scores) was not associated with years in college ($M = 102$, 100, 99, and 94, respectively). Similarly, self-perceived emotional intelligence (TMMS scores) was not different ($M = 3.78$, 3.78, 3.38, and 3.75, respectively). Likewise, the strength of the relation between ability and self-perceived emotional intelligence was not associated with year in college ($r = .40$, .29, .27, and .25, respectively). Although cross-sectional, not longitudinal, these results suggest that emotional intelligence does not automatically improve with life experience, at least not with the experiences typical in college. It is conceivable that more intentional, or effortful, education is required for improvement, although we know very little about how emotional intelligence is acquired and hence how and whether it can be altered. It may be that emotional intelligence is developed primarily in childhood and becomes more stable in early adulthood. Mayer, Caruso, and Salovey (2000) found higher scores in adults as compared with adolescents. Regardless of the source of emotional intelligence, it seems plausible that without trust or belief in the wisdom of their own feelings, individuals may fail to use, or even actively avoid using, the information provided by feelings.

AN INDIVIDUAL-DIFFERENCES TYPOLOGY

In a review of 18 self-report measures concerning various aspects of emotion (Gohm & Clore, 2000), we identified four latent traits: clarity, attention, intensity, and expression. Clarity is the extent to which one can identify and describe feelings. Attention is the extent to which one monitors and values emotional experience. Intensity is the typical magnitude with which one experiences emotions. Expression is the extent to which one outwardly displays emotion. We focused on the first three of these traits and theorized about how these three might moderate the influence of emotion on information processing.

To examine the multivariate influence of these three traits, one could treat them as independent variables in an analysis of variance (ANOVA) or regression model. However, we chose to examine them using cluster analysis. In multiple samples, hierarchical cluster analyses indicated that the traits tend to occur naturally in four specific configurations (Gohm, 1998a, 1998b). That is, based on scores on these three traits, there are four types of persons. We assessed each trait with two instruments in multiple samples. A four-cluster solution was the only set of profiles that consistently replicated, as depicted in Figure 4.1. Therefore, to examine the multivariate influence of these three traits on judgment, we categorized individuals into types according to the profile of their scores on the traits.

One type of person (labeled Hot) scores high on all three traits. That is, individuals with this profile report experiencing their emotions intensely (intensity), valuing and attending to them (attention), and being good at identifying and describing them (clarity). A second type of person (labeled Cool) scores low on all three traits. Individuals with this profile report that their emotions tend to be mild, that they do not value or attend to them, and that they are not good at identifying and describing them. The third type of person (labeled Cerebral) scores low on intensity, average on attention, but high on clarity. Individuals with this profile report experiencing their emotions only mildly, paying an average amount of attention to their emotions, but being good at identifying and describing them. The fourth type of person (labeled Overwhelmed) scores high on intensity, average on attention, but low on clarity. Individuals with this profile report experiencing their emotions intensely, paying an average amount of attention to their feelings, but not being good at identifying and describing them.

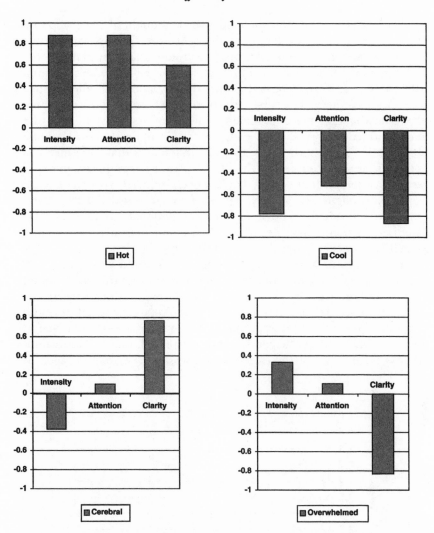

FIGURE 4.1. Mean z scores of three traits for four types of individuals. Intensity is the mean of the z scores on the Affect Intensity Measure (Larsen & Diener, 1987) and the Emotional Intensity Scale (Bachorowski & Braaten, 1994). Attention is the mean of the z scores on attention (Salovey et al., 1995) and monitoring (Swinkels & Guiliano, 1995). Clarity is the mean of the z scores on clarity (Salovey et al., 1995) and labeling (Swinkels & Guiliano, 1995).

This last type, the Overwhelmed, may be thought of as a group who do not believe in the wisdom of feelings. At least, they appear to try to avoid the influence of emotion. We have found that they make mood-relevant judgments that are different from everyone else's (Gohm, 1997, 1998a, 1998b). Repeatedly, when the situation led other participants to make judgments that were consistent with an induced mood, the Overwhelmed made judgments that were inconsistent with the mood induction procedure (see Figure 4.2). In other studies, when the situation led most participants to make judgments that were inconsistent with an induced mood, the Overwhelmed made judgments that were consistent with the mood that had been induced. To explain these contrarian judgments, we have entertained the possibility that Overwhelmed individuals (who have intense emotional reactions but are confused by them) have negative beliefs about the influence of emotion. They appear to view the use of affect in judgment as a bias rather than an ability. As a result, they may attempt to avoid bias by attenuating (getting out of) any mood states in situations that call for reasoned judgment. For instance, in a study (Gohm, 1998a) in which participants were led to believe that they would be doing a large amount of cognitive work (four different experiments by four different researchers), the Overwhelmed participants clearly displayed mood attenuation. That is, by the end of the experimental session, they had engaged in

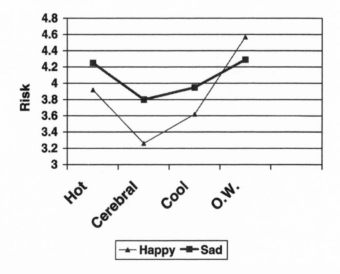

FIGURE 4.2. Mean judgment of risk for each type of individual in each mood condition. From Gohm (1998a). Reprinted by permission of the author.

mood regulation to the extent that participants who had been in the negative mood condition reported being in a better mood than those in the happy condition did. Moreover, their judgments were consistent with their reported moods, so that it was their mood regulation that made them unique, rather than the manner in which they used their feelings in judgment. In another study we found that Overwhelmed types of individuals believed more strongly than others that they were being influenced by their moods (Gohm, 1998c). It seems plausible that this belief motivated them to regulate their mood.

To test the explanation that Overwhelmed individuals regulate their moods because they are motivated to avoid the expected influence of emotion, we manipulated the salience of situational cues concerning the need for mood attenuation (Gohm, 2001). In one condition, individuals were led to believe that they were about to participate in four different experiments by four different researchers (as in the previous study). In another condition, participants were simply told that they would be doing several different tasks. After the mood induction, in the separate experiments condition, we expected the Overwhelmed participants to perceive that they were finished with the initial (mood induction) experiment so that they should get out of their moods in order to perform adequately on the upcoming experiments. In contrast, we expected participants in the single experiment condition to be less likely to punctuate their experience in this way, and hence less likely to regulate mood. The results support the mood regulation explanation. Only individuals classified as Overwhelmed were influenced by this manipulation, showing mood reversal in the multiple experiment but not in the single-experiment condition. Thus, it appears that persons of this type are more concerned than others about the possibility of inappropriate affective influences and so are more likely to regulate or attenuate their feelings. Of course, these findings concerned truly irrelevant feelings that were due to induced mood states. However, we assume that such a distrust of feelings may also prevent such individuals from using the information from their naturally occurring feelings as well. As yet, we have not examined whether Overwhelmed individuals are distrustful of affective information generally or whether their tendency to regulate their feelings reflects an appropriate discrimination of irrelevant from relevant feelings. However, as it happens, their guardedness did not actually insulate them from the influence of mood on their judgments. It led them to change their moods, whereupon their judgments were then governed by affect from their new moods. Such distrust of and confusion about emotion may result in a tendency to avoid emotion-guided thought, which may complicate other areas in the lives of such individuals, an issue to which we turn next.

SUMMING PERCEIVED EMOTIONAL
INTELLIGENCE (TMMS) SCORES

The typology proved very informative in investigating mood regulation and judgment, highlighting effects that were not evident from single-trait analyses. However, it did not prove as informative in the studies reported next. In these, the most interesting effects were related to single traits or to the additive effects of several traits, making the typology analyses redundant. In this section, we report associations with self-reported emotional intelligence as measured by the total score on the TMMS. These effects concern the relationship between emotional intelligence and coping styles, subjective well-being, self-affirming attributions, and relationship quality. Each is discussed briefly.

Perceived Emotional Intelligence and Coping Styles

What if one does trust the wisdom of one's emotions? Does it help one cope with life's stresses? Our initial investigation suggests it may. Specifically, we found that valuing emotional experience and trusting in one's own understanding of and ability to deal with one's emotions (high overall TMMS scores) were associated with the coping styles that are often considered adaptive. In two different samples, self-reported emotional intelligence was related to scores on the COPE scale (Carver, Scheier, & Weintraub, 1989; Gohm & Clore, 2002). Specifically, emotional intelligence was associated with positive reinterpretation and growth ($r = .45$ and .41, p's < .01), active coping ($r = .36$ and .23, p's < .05), planful coping ($r = .27$ and .35, p's < .01), seeking instrumental social support ($r = .28$ and .32, p's < .05), and seeking emotional social support ($r = .39$ and .33, p's < .01). Individuals high in self-reported emotional intelligence reported some tendency to focus on and vent their emotions ($r = .26$ and .22, p's < .05), but this did not lead them to withdraw from the stressful situation behaviorally ($r = -.35$ and $-.26$, p's < .01) or mentally ($r = -.10$ and .04, p's > .23). An emotionally intelligent person would presumably process and express emotions in an appropriate and useful manner. If so, then these associations are consistent with a wise use of the information provided by affect. The results came from an expanded analysis of the data from Gohm and Clore (2002) in which we then looked at the total TMMS score as a measure of self-reported emotional intelligence.

Perceived Emotional Intelligence and Well-Being

Does feeling emotionally intelligent make people happy? Preliminary evidence suggests that it may. To find out, we (Gohm & Clore, 2002) conducted a study in which individuals reported their affective experiences. The results showed that self-perceived emotional intelligence (high TMMS score) was associated with level of happiness ($r = .49$, $p < .01$), percent of time spent being happy ($r = .49$, $p < .01$), more frequent positive affect ($r = .33$, $p < .01$), life satisfaction ($r = .36$, $p < .01$), and self-esteem ($r = .34$, $p < .01$). It was inversely related to general anxiety ($r = -.24$, $p < .01$) and social anxiety ($r = -.30$, $p < .01$). These associations could be due to the beneficial effects of incorporating emotional information into how people manage their lives, including making better judgments and decisions and having more appropriate and successful social interactions than others.

It is also plausible that instead of emotional intelligence causing well-being, the causal direction runs the other way. A person who tends to have mostly positive emotions may find it easier to attend to and value emotion than a person who frequently experiences negative affect. Positive events may increase attention to emotion rather than the reverse (the attention component of the TMMS). Similarly, a person who usually feels positive may find it easier to repair a bad mood (the repair component). Positive emotions may also be easier to label and understand (the clarity component). In addition, self-confidence, self-esteem, or some third variable may conceivably account for both the prevalence of positive emotions and beliefs that one understands one's emotions. Although these reverse influences may also play a role, the extent to which that is the case must await further study. But there are also other ways in which using emotional information may promote positive emotional outcomes. One of these is to make self-affirming attributions.

Perceived Emotional Intelligence and Self-Affirming Attributions

An extended analysis of data from the second sample of Gohm and Clore (2002) shows associations between perceived emotional intelligence and self-affirming attributions for good outcomes. Individuals completed the TMMS as a measure of self-perceived emotional intelligence and the Attributional Style Questionnaire (Peterson et al., 1982) as a measure of explanatory style. The Attributional Style Questionnaire asks respondents to vividly imagine themselves in 12 situations, such as meeting a friend who compliments them on their appearance, looking for a job unsuccessfully for some time, or becoming very rich. For each situation the respondents decide what they feel would be the major cause of the situation if it happened to them and rate the cause on three dimensions, internal versus external ("Is the cause due to something about you or something about other people or circumstances?"), unstable versus stable ("In the future when in this situation, will this cause again be present?"), and local versus global ("Is the cause something that just affects this situation or does it also influence other areas of your life?"). A pessimistic explanatory style in which bad events are attributed to internal, stable, and global causes is associated with poor outcomes, such as depression, poor academic performance (Peterson & Barrett, 1987), and even poor physical health (Peterson & Seligman, 1987). In our sample, individuals who believed in their emotional ability (high TMMS score) tended to make self-affirming (stable, global, and internal) attributions for good outcomes ($r = .34$, $p < .01$). Thus, they presumably benefited from the effects of optimism in general (Peterson, 2000). It is possible that this association reflects general self-confidence and self-esteem. However, such an explanation would not preclude emotional intelligence from being causal. In addition, although they do not suffer from the effects of a pessimistic explanatory style, neither do they avoid taking the blame for negative outcomes ($r = -.08$). Perhaps they are simply accurate in their self-assessments—sometimes accepting responsibility, sometimes not.

Perceived Emotional Intelligence and Relationship Quality

Another domain in which we may expect emotional intelligence to pay dividends is in the quality of interpersonal relationships. One study (Gohm, 1998d) asked whether emotional intelligence improves interpersonal relationships at work. Students were asked to rate how much a number of adjectives described their relationships with their supervisors and the coworker with whom each worked most closely. Some of these adjectives were positive (e.g., friendly, pleasant, and respectful), and some were negative (e.g., awkward, tense, and confusing). Belief in one's own emotional intelligence (TMMS score) was related to the positive aspects of these relationships ($r = .29$, $p < .05$, and $.27$, $p < .07$, for the coworker and supervisor, respectively), but not to the negative aspects ($r = -.05$ and $-.10$, p's $> .49$). The fact that TMMS scores were related to positive but not negative aspects hints that a more general happiness trait may underlie these correlations. However, if that were the case, one would expect the correlations with the negative aspects to be inverse but just as strong. Further, high TMMS scores were associated with general satisfaction with their jobs ($r = .30$, $p < .05$) and with satisfaction with their relationships with the coworkers ($r = .45$, $p < .01$), but not with satisfaction with their pay ($r = -.14$, $p > .33$) or satisfaction with their work schedules ($r = .15$, $p > .32$). Satisfaction with their relationships with their supervisors was not significant ($r = .22$, $p < .15$). This pattern of correlations suggests that high TMMS scores are related to quality interpersonal interactions rather than simply to an underlying tendency to be happy.

A review of the findings from the Gohm and Clore (2002) study shows a rich set of relationships using a summary measure of self-perceived emotional intelligence. The measure is simply a sum of scores on the Emotional Attention, Clarity, and Repair scales of the TMMS. The results suggest that despite the fact that these self-report measures primarily assess beliefs about one's emotional intelligence, they appear to capture relevant aspects of the underlying set of abilities. We turn next to projects focused on the meaning of two of these individual self-perceived characteristics—Attention to Emotion and then Clarity.

ATTENTION TO EMOTION AND MOOD EFFECTS

We have focused on the idea that feelings are functional because they provide information. We have argued that a failure to attend to emotional cues may rob one of important information for judgment, decision, and action. Studies of mood and judgment do show that low scorers on the Attention to Emotion scale of the TMMS do not use their feelings as information in judgments, at least not in laboratory situations, whereas high scorers typically do show mood effects on judgment (Gasper & Clore, 2000). But the story is not quite that simple, as we shall see.

Attention to Emotion and Judgment

Gasper and Clore (2000) included the Attention to Emotion scale of the TMMS in a study of mood and risk estimation. In line with their hypotheses, high and low groups did not differ in the intensity of their moods but did differ in how mood influenced risk estimation. They found higher estimates of risk for negative mood groups only for High Attention, and not for Low Attention, participants. Indeed, there was a trend toward judgmental contrast effects among lows. Whereas the highs used their feelings as information about how worrisome the risks were, lows tended to use the positive or negative event they had described in the induction as an anchor against which to judge the risks. This difference appeared even though highs and lows reported similar moods.

The importance of attention was further seen when an attribution manipulation eliminated mood effects for highs, but created them for lows. Focusing participants on possible sources of their feelings caused highs to stop attending to them but drew the attention of lows, who had focused only on descriptive aspects of the situation.

Attention to Emotion in Problem Solving

In her dissertation, Gasper (1999) did an extensive study of the role of mood in various tasks, including Kahneman and Tversky's heuristic reasoning tasks. She again included the Attention to Emotion scale. Interestingly, she found that lows instead of highs showed mood effects on reasoning. Such effects appeared on more than one processing task. It appeared that paying attention to feelings promoted their use on judgment tasks when such feelings were more or less explicitly relevant. Thus, on judgments tasks that essentially ask, "How do you feel about X?" the more one attends to one's feelings, the more judgments were correlated with feelings. Similarly, such effects were found for some measures in a generative creativity task, where participants used their feelings to judge possible answers.

But the effects were different on reasoning tasks. In those tasks, the individuals who were most likely to use their feelings to guide their solutions were low (rather than high) scorers on the Attention to Emotion scale. Indeed, high scorers tended to show the reverse effects, presumably because attending directly to feelings made them stand out as distinct from the task at hand. Affect-as-information processes depend on people experiencing their feelings as information about the adequacy of their initial approach to the task (Clore et al., 2001). But when they focused on their feelings as feelings, rather than focusing on the task, then the feelings tended not to be experienced as task feedback and reversals of the usual effects appeared.

Thus, whether one uses one's feelings to guide processing depends on whether they are experienced as relevant. In other words, it depends on the implicit attribution that one makes. We expect that when the explicit question concerns one's feelings, as in evaluative judgments, attention to the feelings promotes their use. But in task situations in which problem solving is central, then affective cues most likely seem like task feedback when attending to the task and not to the feelings.

Implications

Should these findings give us pause about training people to pay more attention to their feelings? They suggest that attending to emotion may be of mixed benefit. Presumably, a complete inability to access one's feelings would be disastrous, as implied by Damasio's (1994) observations, but focusing fully on feelings could also be disastrous, as may be the case in addictions and other cravings. In any case, the optimal degree to which one should attend to one's feelings may depend on the task. Knowing what one likes and dislikes, and having ready access to one's feelings, should allow one to be decisive in making judgments and appropriately assertive in social negotiation. But in performance situations, one may often need to focus on the task and allow affective feedback to guide moment-to-moment behavior and processing without direct focus. For example, it seems unlikely that outstanding performances such as breaking the home run record in baseball can be achieved by increasing attention to one's feelings as one stands at the plate.

CLARITY AND PERFORMANCE IN EMERGENCIES

The idea that attending explicitly to emotion may not always promote better performance can perhaps best be seen in emergencies that call for courageous action, or action in the face of fear and distress. Soldiers in combat must act in spite of their fear. Air traffic controllers must not be distracted while directing a tense, complicated sequence of takeoffs and landings. Parents of an injured child must think clearly and not let their distress overcome them. Knowledge about one's emotions, especially about their source and how to avoid overattending to them, may be crucial in such situations. Our research among firefighters suggests that one component of emotional intelligence, clarity about one's emotions, may contribute to the ability to think clearly in a critical situation.

To examine such processes, Gohm and colleagues conducted a research project at a training institute for firefighters. At the Illinois Fire Service Institute, firefighter trainees participate in a series of live-fire exercises. Wearing protective clothing and oxygen breathing equipment, they practice their newly learned skills, including climbing ladders and stairs inside and outside of heat- and smoke-filled buildings, rescuing "victims", and extinguishing fires. Immediately after such drills, trainees who had scored high on clarity (administered earlier during one of their first classroom sessions) reported fewer instances of difficulties in thinking clearly during the exercise, occurrences such as "blanking out," forgetting what they had learned, and being unable to take in all that was happening (Gohm, Baumann, & Sniezek, 2001). This finding was replicated in a sample of career firefighters also participating in a live-fire search-and-rescue exercise (Gohm, Baumann, Sniezek, & Dalal, 2000). It could be the case that firefighters who believe that they understand their emotions also believe that they think clearly under stress, and that both represent wishful thinking rather than accurate belief. However, such a self-enhancement explanation is not likely, because clarity scores were not associated with scores on either prospective or retrospective self-reports of their physical performance (Gohm et al.,

2001). Thus, firefighters who believed that they were good at identifying and labeling their emotions reported an ability to think more clearly, specifically in this intense situation. Presumably, such individuals know that experiencing unpleasant emotions in such a situation is natural and to be expected. Therefore, they are less likely to be distressed by their emotions. As a result, they can use the information provided by their feelings to engage in problem-focused coping, rather than turning away from the task to engage in emotion-focused coping. If one needs to function in a tense, dangerous situation, it may be best *not* to attend unduly to one's fear itself, as opposed to the information it provides about the situation.

The career firefighters who volunteered to engage in the search-and-rescue scenario also wore heart rate monitors under their gear and estimated their heart rates for us (via radio) at several points during the exercise (Gohm et al., 2000). Firefighters who scored high on clarity were also more accurate at estimating their heart rates. Perhaps knowing one internal state (emotional) is associated with knowing another internal state (physical). This association has implications for the relation between emotional intelligence and physical health. To the extent that awareness and accuracy about one's internal physiological state leads to early treatment of illness, which is thought to be the process through which private self-consciousness lessens the adverse effects of stress on health (Mullen & Suls, 1982; Suls & Fletcher, 1985), perhaps teaching emotional intelligence would benefit physical well-being in addition to psychological well-being.

DISCRIMINATING STATE FROM TRAIT EMOTION

As the research with firefighters indicates, there are times when emotions themselves should not be the prime focus of attention and other goals should be allowed to override those activated by emotion. There are also times when momentary affective feelings should be ignored because they are simply irrelevant to the current task. A critical feature of emotional intelligence is the ability to discriminate when one's feelings are relevant. In laboratory research on mood, we often try to diminish people's discriminative ability, because misattributions of affect allow us to study how affective processes work. But in the real world, the ability to make discriminations is surely the essence of emotional intelligence. In this regard, one of the primary goals of psychotherapy is often to help clients determine the meaning and significance of their feelings, or in our language, the "information value." Whether or not affect has clear information value depends in part on the salience of its object, that is, the obviousness of what has triggered the affective response, as can be seen in Table 4.1.

Table 4.1 shows a 2 × 2 matrix of four affective conditions that vary as to whether they are states or dispositions and whether they do or do not have salient objects. Emotions and moods are both states, but emotions have salient objects and moods do not. Attitudes and temperaments are both dispositions, but attitudes have objects and temperaments do not. Thus, sadness can be an emotion because of some specific loss or a mood because of things in general. Similarly, positive affect can come from a positive attitude of liking a specific person or simply from a generally cheerful temperament.

Labeling these conditions as affective simply means that they concern the goodness or badness of things. The information of affective feelings depends in part on the object to which they are attributed. By themselves, they indicate simply that something is (has been appraised as) good or bad. When experienced as a reaction to (attributed to) a specific object, such feelings indicate that the object is good or bad in some way. Moods are useful for studying how current feelings influence evaluative judgment, because their causes are generally not salient. As a result, the information value of the feelings is unconstrained and available for attribution to other plausible causes.

In two experiments, Gasper and Clore (1998) studied the effects of objectless forms of both dispositional (trait anxiety) and state affect (induced mood), examining their effects on risk estimation. Both sources of negative affect tended to increase estimates of risk, but the most interesting results concerned their reactions to the attribution manipulation. They manipulated the object to which participants attributed their feelings by asking some participants questions designed to make the true situational cause salient. In a classroom version of the study, the true cause of state affect was an impending final exam, and in a lab version the true cause was a mood induction procedure in which participants wrote about a happy or sad event they had experienced.

The results were interesting and were identical in both versions. The attribution manipulation, which made salient the true cause of their momentary feelings, reduced risk estimates for the groups that were low in trait anxiety, as expected, but it did not reduce risk esti-

TABLE 4.1. Object Specificity and Duration Distinguish Affective Conditions

	Temporary state	Chronic disposition
Salient object	Emotion	Attitude
Nonsalient object	Mood	Temperament

mates for those high in trait anxiety. If anything, focusing their attention on their feelings by trying to explain them away tended to increase their risk estimates.

These results parallel those of the original Schwarz and Clore (1983) experiments. In those data, situational attributions eliminated mood effects on judgments of life satisfaction, but the influence was apparent only for sadness, not for happiness. According to Diener and Diener (1996), most college students report being happy most of the time. Hence, it appears to be easier to explain away the significance of trait-inconsistent affect than trait-consistent affect. When there are multiple sources of the same affective experiences, an explanation for part of that experience is not sufficient to immunize one's judgment from influence by the rest of it. When the experimenters interviewed participants afterward, highly anxious individuals said that the explanation offered for their feelings was not adequate. They felt that neither the final exam in Study 1 nor the mood induction in Study 2 completely explained their feelings. And, of course, they were right, because they experienced a certain level of chronic anxiety.

These results suggest that chronic or dispositional sources of affect may make it difficult to be discriminating or intelligent about the meaning of one's feelings. After all, the basic information value of anxiety is simply that something is threatening. The feelings themselves are the same whether the perceived threat is physical, psychological, actual, or imagined. Trying to separate different sources of a common pool of affective feelings is like trying to apportion soup with a knife. A chronic background of anxiety or depression should pose serious problems in trying to make appropriate distinctions about the sources of current anxiety and sadness.

SUMMARY

Our research indicates that many individuals who have a reasonable level of emotional intelligence ability (as measured by the MSCEIT) remain unaware (as measured by the TMMS) that they have this ability. Further, individuals who tend to have intense emotional experiences, but find such experiences confusing, behave differently from others around them. They try to exercise control over their feelings, and they make judgments that are different from those of others. In contrast, trusting in one's understanding of emotion was associated with being better able to think clearly in an extreme situation. Similarly, belief in one's own emotional intelligence was associated with psychological well-being, with adaptive coping styles, with a self-affirming attributional style, and with quality relationships. Thus, our research provides support for assumptions underlying emotional intelligence theory. That is, for emotional information to be of value, it may be important for individuals to attend to their emotional experiences, appreciate the value of emotional experience, and trust in their understanding of their own emotions. Individuals in our research who showed evidence of emotional intelligence benefited from this ability. Those who lacked emotional intelligence, or distrusted their own emotional intelligence, suffered from this lack.

AFTERWORD: ON WISDOM, AFFECT, AND THE GOOD

In the foregoing discussion we have taken the position that a pivotal characteristic of affective feelings is that they are informative. They provide information about the goodness and badness of the situations in which they arise. We assume that the positive and negative feelings resulting from ongoing appraisal processes exercise the same kind of influence on judgments and decisions as rewards and punishments are known to exercise on behavior, presumably for the same reason. The reason usually given by psychologists and other social and behavioral scientists for the power of emotion and of reward and punishment is that people are hedonistic. Freud's pleasure principle and Thorndike's reinforcement principle suggest that the ultimate motivation is to approach pleasure and avoid pain. In this view, pleasure and pain constitute the business end of any and all motivation. The same logic has driven the economists' generally unquestioned model of "the rational man," by which they mean the self-interested person.

Probably no one has ever gone broke betting that people would seek pleasure and avoid pain. Nevertheless, the affect-as-information position, taken literally, may offer an alternative view. To the extent that affective experience guides judgments, decisions, and choices because of the information it provides, then one might conclude that people's ultimate motivation is not primarily about approaching pleasure and avoiding pain, but about approaching goodness and avoiding badness. Specifically, the information that affect conveys is, by definition, information about value, about the goodness or badness of things. In this sense, affect generally acts as an adjective rather than as a noun. It modifies and classifies objects into those that are beneficial, enjoyable, or valuable and those that are not. Even when one's goal is pleasure, there is a sense in which the feedback provided by the positive affect that guides behavior does so as information that one is achieving one's goal of pleasure. Positive affect serves then (and always) as information that the outcome of one's endeavors has value. We assume therefore that people are actually motivated by value, and that hedonic pleasures are motivating ultimately because they indicate value. In other words, people are motivated to seek the good and avoid the bad, and the primary function of positive and negative affective feelings is to convey that information in an embodied and hence compelling way.

The error of psychologists, in thinking of pleasure itself as the ultimate motivator, is mirrored in economics by the assumption that people are primarily motivated by money. Money, of course, is motivating not for itself, but because it stands for value. We want it only to the extent that it allows us to purchase value. By itself, devoid of its link to value, it counts for nothing. This is seen when currency becomes inflated so that the value signified by a paper currency decreases. In times of dramatic inflation, when wheelbarrows full of money will not buy a loaf of bread, money looses both its economic and psychological value. Something comparable can be seen in the phenomenon of drug abuse, in which the neurotransmitters, the proximal agents of pleasure, come to lose their value through inflation. What is ruinous about addictive drugs is that the intense rush of pleasure that they initially provide cannot be duplicated except by more drugs, and eventually not even by that. While on the drug, users may feel not only pleasure, but also a sense of euphoria about themselves. What they come to crave, in part, is not simply feelings of pleasure, but what those feelings appear to mean, namely, that they themselves are powerful, lovable, and wonderful beyond their wildest dreams. Such hedonic inflation makes the ordinary affective feedback from everyday activities lose its usual reward value. As a consequence, the activities, places, and people that once gave one's life meaning lose their value as they lose the ability to compete in the drug-inflated dopamine economy. Chasing the currency of value rather than value itself, whether the currency is money or pleasure, leads to misery and meaninglessness. If either money or pleasure were in fact the ultimate human motivation, this could not be so. Thus, we suggest, emotional intelligence at its core requires that one not only attend to one's feelings, but also know what they mean. The secret of the happy life, then, seems to be to find small pleasures in the activities and interpersonal contacts of everyday life, so that these become the objects of affect with the result that they also become objects of value.

ACKNOWLEDGMENTS

Some of the research in this chapter was supported by NSF Grant No. SBR 96-01298 and NIMH Grant No. MH 50074.

REFERENCES

Ajzen, I., & Fishbein, M. (1975). A Bayesian analysis of attribution processes. *Psychological Bulletin, 82,* 261–277.

Anderson, N. H. (1981). *Foundations of information integration theory.* New York: Academic Press.

Bagby, R. M., Parker, J. D., & Taylor, G. J. (1994). The twenty-item Toronto Alexithymia Scale-I. Item selection and cross-validation of the factor structure. *Journal of Psychosomatic Research, 38,* 23–32.

Bachorowski, J., & Braaten, E. B. (1994). Emotional intensity: Measurement and theoretical implications. *Personality and Individual Differences, 17,* 191–199.

Bower, G. (1981). Mood and memory. *American Psychologist, 36,* 129–148.

Carver, C. S., Scheier, M. F., & Weintraub, J. K. (1989). Assessing coping strategies: A theoretically based approach. *Journal of Personality and Social Psychology, 56,* 267–283.

Clore, G. L., Wyer, R. S., Jr., Dienes, B., Gasper, K., Gohm, C. L., & Isbell, L. (2001). Affective feelings as feedback: Some cognitive consequences. In L. L. Martin & G. L. Clore (Eds.), *Theories of mood and cognition: A user's guidebook* (pp. 27–62). Mahwah, NJ: Erlbaum.

Damasio, A. R. (1994). *Descartes' error.* New York: Putnam.

Deloache, J., & Gottlieb, A. (2000). *A world of babies: Imagined child care guides for seven societies.* Cambridge, UK: Cambridge University Press.

Diener, E., & Diener, C. (1996). Most people are happy. *Psychological Science, 7,* 181–185.

Ehrlich, E. (1994). *The highly selective thesaurus for the extraordinarily literate.* New York: HarperCollins.

Forgas, J. P. (2000). Affect and information processing strategies: An interactive relationship. In. J. P. Forgas (Ed.), *Feeling and thinking: The role off affect in social cognition* (pp. 253–280). New York: Cambridge University Press.

Gasper, K. (1999). *How thought and emotional awareness influence the role of affect in processing: When attempts to be reasonable fail.* Doctoral dissertation, University of Illinois at Urbana–Champaign.

Gasper, K., & Clore, G. L. (1998). The persistent use of negative affect by anxious individuals to estimate risk. *Journal of Personality and Social Psychology, 74,* 1350–1363.

Gasper, K., & Clore, G. L. (2000). Do you have to pay attention to your feelings to be influenced by them? *Personality and Social Psychology Bulletin, 26,* 698–711.

Gohm, C. L. (1997). [Mood and judgment using music]. Unpublished raw data.

Gohm, C. L. (1998a). Individual differences in the experience of emotion: Moderators of mood and cognition (doctoral dissertation, University of Illinois at Urbana–Champaign, 1998). *Dissertation Abstracts International, 59*(8-B), 4522.

Gohm, C. L. (1998b). [Mood and judgment emphasizing mood]. Unpublished raw data.

Gohm, C. L. (1998c). [Mood and belief in its influence]. Unpublished raw data.

Gohm, C. L. (1998d). [Personality and work relationships]. Unpublished raw data.

Gohm, C. L. (2000). [Actual and self-reported emotional intelligence]. Unpublished raw data.

Gohm, C. L. (2001, February). Individual differences in mood attenuation: Preparing for the expected influence of affect. In E. C. Pinel (Chair), *Fresh perspectives on affective understanding*. Symposium conducted at the annual meeting of the Society for Personality and Social Psychology, San Antonio, TX.

Gohm, C. L., Baumann, M. R., & Sniezek, J. A. (2001). Personality in extreme situations: Thinking (or not) under acute stress. *Journal of Research in Personality, 35,* 388–399.

Gohm, C. L., Baumann, M. R., Sniezek, J. A., & Dalal, S. (2000, May). *The relation of meta-emotional traits to the availability of cognitive resources among firefighters*. Paper presented at the meeting of the Midwestern Psychological Association, Chicago, IL.

Gohm, C. L., & Clore, G. L. (2000). Individual differences in emotional experience: Mapping available scales to processes. *Personality and Social Psychology Bulletin, 26,* 679–697.

Gohm, C. L., & Clore, G. L. (2002). Four emotion traits and their involvement in attributional style, coping, and well-being. *Cognition and Emotion, 16,* 495–518.

Gouaux, C. (1971). Induced affective states and interpersonal attraction. *Journal of Personality and Social Psychology, 20,* 37–43.

Griffit, W., & Veitch, R. (1971). Hot and crowded: Influence of population density and temperature on interpersonal affective behavior. *Journal of Personality and Social Psychology, 17,* 92–98.

Isen, A. M. (1984). Toward understanding the role of affect in cognition. In R. S. Wyer & T. K. Srull (Eds.), *Handbook of social cognition* (Vol. 3, pp. 179–236). Hillsdale, NJ: Erlbaum.

Kruger, J. (1999). Lake Wobegon be gone! The "below-average effect" and the egocentric nature of comparative ability judgments. *Journal of Personality and Social Psychology, 77,* 221–232.

Larsen, R. J., & Diener, E. (1987). Affect intensity as an individual difference characteristic: A review. *Journal of Research in Personality, 21,* 1–39.

Mayer, J. D., Caruso, D. R., & Salovey, P. (2000). Emotional intelligence meets traditional standards for an intelligence. *Intelligence, 27,* 267–298.

Mayer, J. D., & Salovey, P. (1997). What is emotional intelligence? In P. Salovey & D. Sluyter (Eds.), *Emotional development and emotional intelligence: Educational implications* (pp. 3–34). New York: Basic Books.

Mayer, J. D., Salovey, P., & Caruso, D. R. (2000). Models of emotional intelligence. In R. J. Sternberg (Ed.), *Handbook of intelligence* (2nd ed., pp. 396–420). New York: Cambridge University Press.

Mayer, J. D., Salovey, P., & Caruso, D. R. (2001). *Instruction Manual for the MSCEIT*. North Tonawanda, NY: Multi-Health Systems Inc.

Microsoft Word [computer software]. (2000). Redmond, WA: Microsoft Corporation.

Mullen, B., & Suls, J. (1982). Know thyself: Stressful life changes and the ameliorative effect of private self-consciousness. *Journal of Experimental Social Psychology, 18,* 43–55.

Pennebaker, J. W., & Bealls, S. K. (1986). Confronting a traumatic event: Toward an understanding of inhibition and disease. *Journal of Abnormal Psychology, 95,* 274–281.

Peterson, C. (2000). The future of optimism. *American Psychologist, 55,* 44–55.

Peterson, C., & Barrett, L. C. (1987). Explanatory style and academic performance among university freshmen. *Journal of Personality and Social Psychology, 53,* 603–607.

Peterson, C., & Seligman, M. E. (1987). Explanatory style and illness. *Journal of Personality, 55,* 237–265.

Peterson, C., Semel, A., von Baeyer, C., Abramson, L. Y., Metalsky, G. I., & Seligman, M. E. P. (1982). The attributional style questionnaire. *Cognitive Therapy and Research, 6,* 287–300.

Reese, D. (2000). A parenting manual with words of advice for Puritan mothers. In J. Deloache & A. Gottlieb (Eds.), *A world of babies: Imagined child care guides for seven societies* (pp. 29–54). New York: Cambridge University Press.

Richards, J. M., & Gross, J. J. (2000). Emotion regulation and memory: The cognitive costs of keeping one's cool. *Journal of Personality and Social Psychology, 79,* 410–424.

Salovey, P., & Mayer, J. D. (1990). Emotional intelligence. *Imagination, Cognition and Personality, 9,* 185–211.

Salovey, P., Mayer, J. D., Caruso, D., & Lopes, P. N. (in press). Measuring emotional intelligence as a set of abilities with the MSCEIT. In S. J. Lopez & C. R. Snyder (Eds.), *Handbook of positive psychology assessment.* Washington, DC: American Psychological Association.

Salovey, P., Mayer, J. D., Goldman, S. L., Turvey, C., & Palfai, T. P. (1995). Emotional attention, clarity, and repair: Exploring emotional intelligence using the trait meta-mood scale. In J. Pennebaker (Ed.), *Emotion, disclosure, and health* (pp. 125–154). Washington, DC: American Psychological Association.

Schwarz, N., & Clore, G. L. (1983). Mood, misattribution, and judgments of well-being: Informative and directive functions of affective states. *Journal of Personality and Social Psychology, 45,* 513–523.

Schwarz, N., & Clore, G. L. (1988). How do I feel about it? Informative functions of affective states. In K. Fiedler & J. Forgas (Eds.), *Affect, cognition, and social behavior* (pp. 44–62). Toronto: Hogrefe International.

Smith, E. R., & DeCoster, J. (1999). Associative and rule-based processing: A connectinist interpretation of dual-process models. In S. Chaiken & Y. Trope (Eds.), *Dual-process theories in social psychology* (pp. 323–336). New York: Guilford Press.

Suls, J., & Fletcher, B. (1985). Self-attention, life stress, and illness: A prospective study. *Psychosomatic Medicine, 47,* 469–481.

Swinkels, A., & Giuliano, T. A. (1995). The measurement and conceptualization of mood awareness: Monitoring and labeling one's mood states. *Personality and Social Psychology Bulletin, 21,* 934–949.

CHAPTER 5

The Trouble with Vronsky

Impact Bias in the Forecasting of Future Affective States

DANIEL T. GILBERT
ERIN DRIVER-LINN
TIMOTHY D. WILSON

> Vronsky, meanwhile, although what he had so long
> desired had come to pass, was not altogether happy.
> He soon felt that the fulfillment of his desires gave
> him only one grain of the mountain of happiness he
> had expected. This fulfillment showed him the eternal
> error men make in imagining that their happiness
> depends on the realization of their desires.
> —TOLSTOY (1877/1961, p. 468)

Of all the claims that psychologists have made about human universals, one actually stands a chance of being true: People want to be happy. Different things bring happiness to different people, of course, and cultures vary dramatically in their prescriptions for the good life, but none offers a set of roles and rules that, if followed religiously, guarantees a life of fear and sorrow. Even when people forgo opportunities for happiness—by dieting when they could be eating, or working when they could be sleeping—they are generally doing so in order to enjoy greater happiness in the future. Just about everyone, it seems, prefers pleasure to pain, joy to sadness, satisfaction to frustration, and no psychologist, anthropologist, paleontologist, or historian has ever discovered any culture in any historical epoch whose members generally preferred feeling bad to feeling good. To "prefer" means "to choose or want one thing rather than another because it would be more pleasant" (*Cambridge International Dictionary*, 1995), which is to say that the pursuit of happiness is built into the very definition of preference. In this sense, a preference for pain and sorrow is not so much a diagnosable psychiatric condition as it is an oxymoron.

But if the desire for happiness is universal, the ability to achieve it is not. Most human lives are touched by sorrow, disappointment, resentment, and regret, and many are characterized by them. Why is happiness such a fast moving target? One terribly dull answer is that unhappiness is the consequence of unfulfilled desires and that each of us has plenty of those. We feel certain that we *know* what would make us happy—marriage, divorce, health, money, flattery, power, Belgian chocolate, Cuban cigars—and we naturally think of our unhappiness as the result of a failure to achieve these identifiable ends. We have strong preferences about what the future should bring, we take actions to ensure that it does, and unhappiness sometimes follows because we can't always get what we want. This terribly dull answer would at least be satisfactory were it not for one pesky fact: On those occasions when we take careful aim and get precisely what we were aiming for, we often discover that the rich, robust, and enduring happiness that our achievement was meant to induce is instead thin, fleeting, or absent entirely. Count Vronsky spent several hundred pages of very small type longing for Anna Karenina, but the fulfillment of that passion left him with nothing more than several hundred pages of emptiness.

Could it really be a mistake to expect that happiness will follow the fulfillment of one's desires? It depends, of course, on how accurately one desires. The adverb "accurately" does not normally precede the verb "desire," but if our desires are meant to point us toward those things that, once achieved, will give rise to happiness, then it makes perfectly good sense to think of desires as predictions about the affective consequences of things to come (cf. Berridge & Robinson, 1995). And such predictions, like any, can be wrong. How accurate are human desires? How well do we predict what will make us happy, how happy it will make us, and how long our happiness will last?

IMPACT BIAS

To desire accurately, we must be able to imagine how a particular future circumstance will make us feel—a process called *affective forecasting* (Gilbert & Wilson, 2000). Specifically, we must be able to predict what kind of emotion we will experience ("Will making love with Anna be

boring or exciting?"), how intense that emotion will be ("Mildly exciting or deeply moving?"), and how long the emotion will last ("A moment of passion or a week of euphoria?"). People are relatively accurate in predicting the identities of their future emotions, which is to say
that they can readily distinguish situations that will prove exhilarating
or joyous from those that will evoke anger, annoyance, or ennui
(Robinson & Clore, 2000). On the other hand, people are not so adept
when it comes to predicting the intensity and duration of their emo-
tions (Baron, 1992; Coughlan & Connolly, 2001; Kahneman, 1994;
Kahneman & Snell, 1990, 1992; Loewenstein & Frederick, 1997;
Loewenstein, O'Donoghue, & Rabin, 2000; Loewenstein, Prelec, &
Shatto, 1998; Mellers, 2000; Read & Loewenstein, 1995; Read & van
Leeuwen, 1998; Rottenstreich & Hsee, 2001; Schmitt & Kemper, 1996;
Schwarz, Jacquin, & Telch, 1994; Simonson, 1990; Snell, Gibbs, &
Varey, 1995; Totterdell, Parkinson, Brinner, & Reynolds, 1997; van
Hout & Emmelkamp, 1994; Zeelenberg, van Dijk, Manstead, & van der
Pligt, 1998), and these inaccuracies tend to take a special form. When
people mispredict their affective reactions, they tend to do so by *over-
estimating* the enduring impact that future events will have on their
emotional lives. This *impact bias*[1] has been demonstrated in a variety of
populations (e.g., students, voters, professors, sports fans, medical patients), across a wide range of events (e.g., romantic breakups, personal insults, failed exams, football victories, electoral defeats, relocations,
winning prizes, touching spiders, receiving gifts, being diagnosed with
serious illnesses, failing to secure promotions, failing to lose weight,
reading tragic stories), and by a variety of different investigators
(Buehler & McFarland, 2001; Frederick & Loewenstein, 1999; Gilbert,
Brown, Pinel, & Wilson, 2000; Gilbert, Pinel, Wilson, Blumberg, &
Wheatley, 1998; Loewenstein & Adler, 1995; Loewenstein, Nagin, & Paternoster, 1997; Loewenstein & Schkade, 1999; Mellers & McGraw,
2000; Mellers, Schwartz, & Ritov, 1999; Mitchell, Thompson, Peterson,
& Cronk, 1997; Rachman, 1994; Rachman & Arntz, 1991; Schkade &
Kahneman, 1997; Wilson, Meyers, & Gilbert, 2001; Wilson, Wheatley,
Meyers, Gilbert, & Axsom, 2000b).

Let us be clear from the start: Many events—such as rape, divorce,
or the death of a child—have emotional consequences that may last for
months, years, or even a lifetime, and it would be perverse for anyone
to suggest that such events do not matter. They most certainly do. But

---

[1]We have previously referred to this tendency as the *durability bias*, but this term is clearly
a misnomer inasmuch as people may overestimate the intensity of their emotional reactions at the time an event occurs as well as at later periods. The word "impact" is meant to
suggest that people can overestimate the influence of future events on emotional states,
and yet it is agnostic about the points in time at which such overestimations may occur.

there is considerable evidence to suggest that hedonic reactions to events—even truly tragic events—are shorter-lived than one might expect, and that people typically return to their emotional baselines sooner rather than later. Suh, Diener, and Fujita (1996) measured the correlation between college students' subjective well-being and the number of life events they had experienced in the previous 4 years. Subjective well-being was uncorrelated with the number of negative or positive events a student had experienced 6 months earlier, and the correlations between subjective well-being and events that had occurred within the last 3 months were surprisingly modest. Suh et al. (1996, p. 1091) concluded that "only recent events matter," but even recent events may not matter quite as much as people think they do. A study found that 30% of parents who lost babies as a result of sudden infant death syndrome never experienced significant depression, another study found that 82% of bereaved spouses were doing well just 2 years after the spouse's death (Lund, Caserta, & Diamond, 1989; Wortman, Silver, & Kessler, 1993), and contrary to the expectations of every red-blooded American who has ever lined up at a Seven-Eleven with high hopes and a fistful of dollars, winning large sums of money in the lottery does not seem to make people happy for very long (Brickman, Coates, & Janoff-Bulman, 1978; Kaplan, 1978).

The list goes on, and although we know of dozens of studies that surprise us with the fleeting nature of emotional reactions, we know of none showing that people experience more profound or enduring reactions than one may normally expect. Why do people believe that future events will have greater emotional impact then they actually do?

MISIMAGINED EVENTS

One of the most powerful sources of impact bias is the simplest. *Misconstrual* is the tendency to misimagine important aspects of the event about which one is making predictions. For instance, many of us expect winning a lottery to lead to an enduring increase in happiness because we imagine it providing us with a stress-free existence filled with tropical vacations, fancy cars, gourmet meals, and late nights spent gleefully counting the digits in our bank statement. What we fail to imagine are the tax burdens, the harassment from demanding strangers, the estrangement from our social network, and the deterioration of family relationships, all of which are common among lottery winners (Kaplan, 1978). Many important events, such as marriage, the birth of a child, and terminal illness, are experienced just once or rarely, and we predictably mispredict how such novel events will unfold.

It is not very surprising that we make errors when predicting our reactions to events about which we know little, but it *is* surprising that we fail to appreciate how little we know. Griffin, Dunning, and Ross (1990) asked participants to predict what they would do in a variety of future situations—how much time they would be willing to spend answering questions in a telephone survey, how much money they would be willing to spend to celebrate the end of the term at a restaurant in San Francisco, and so on. Participants also reported how confident they were that each of these predictions was correct. Some participants made the predictions, and others were first asked to describe all the details of the future event they were imagining and then to assume that each of these details was accurate. In other words, some participants were asked to predict their reactions to a generic event whose details were unspecified (dinner at a restaurant), whereas others were asked to predict their reactions to a well-specified event (wine-braised short ribs with roasted root vegetable and parsley coulis at Jardiniere next Tuesday at six). The results showed that the two groups of participants were equally confident in their predictions. Having license to assume the accuracy of all the imagined details of the restaurant experience failed to increase participants' confidence in their predictions, because participants for whom the details were unspecified were *already* as confident as those for whom the details were specified (see also Dunning, Griffin, Milojkovic, & Ross, 1990; Griffin & Ross, 1991). It seems that when we imagine the future, we often do so in the blind spot of the mind's eye, and this tendency can cause us to overestimate our affective responses to the future events we are imagining.

MISREMEMBERED EVENTS

If misconstrual were the sole source of impact bias, then the bias would instantly evaporate when we make forecasts about events that are the same as or similar to those we have experienced before. Alas, learning from experience requires many things, not the least of which is a relatively reliable memory of the experience itself, and research suggests that such memories can be woefully inaccurate. Kahneman, Fredrickson, Schreiber, and Redelmeier (1993) asked participants to submerge their hands in ice water while using an electronic rating scale to rate their moment-to-moment discomfort. Every participant performed both a short trial and a long trial. On the short trial, the participant submerged one hand for 60 seconds in a water bath that was kept at a chilly 14°C. On the long trial, the participant submerged the other hand for 90 seconds in a water bath that was kept at a chilly 14°C for the first 60 seconds, and then surreptitiously warmed to a not-quite-as-chilly 15°C degrees over the course of the remaining 30 seconds. Clearly, the long trial should have been more painful than the short trial if by *more painful* we mean (as people normally do) *more total pain*. And indeed, the particpants' moment-to-moment reports revealed that they experienced equal discomfort for the first 60 seconds on both trials, but much more discomfort in the next 30 seconds if they kept their hands in the water (as they did on the long trial) than if they removed them (as they did on the short trial). Yet, when later asked to remember their experience and say which trial was more uncomfortable, participants tended to say that the short trial was *more* uncomfortable than the long one. In fact, when asked which of the two trials they would rather repeat, 69% of the participants chose the long one (see also Ariely, 1998; Fredrickson, 2000; Fredrickson & Kahneman, 1993). Why would anyone prefer more pain to less? No one does, of course. The long trial had more total pain and thus seems an odd choice to those of us who are standing around with stopwatches. But emotional memory has no stopwatch and thus keeps poor time (Varey & Kahneman, 1992). The long trial was more painful than the short trial, but it had a better finish, and because memories of emotional experiences tend to be based largely on their closing moments, participants remembered the short trial as "the chilly one" and the long trial as "the not-quite-as-chilly one." It is little wonder that women often remember childbirth as a beautiful rather than an agonizing experience (Christensen-Szalanski, 1984) or that unhappy couples remember the early years of their marriages as more unpleasant than they actually were (Holmberg & Holmes, 1994).

After reviewing the literature on emotional memory, Christianson and Safer (1996, p. 235) reached a sobering conclusion: "There are apparently no published studies in which a group of subjects has accurately recalled the intensity and/or frequency of their previously recorded emotions" (see also Feldman-Barrett, 1997). The notoriously labile nature of remembered emotional experience means that we may not always recognize how wrong our forecasts were. Mitchell et al. (1997) asked people who were about to embark on a group bicycling trip through California to predict how they would feel during the trip, to report how they actually felt during the trip, and when the trip was over, to remember how they had felt while it was happening. Although cyclists expected to feel happy during the trip and remembered feeling so, both their predictions and memories were at odds with their experiential reports. Meyers, Wilson, and Gilbert (1999) found a similar result in their study of the 1996 U.S. presidential election. Democrats predicted and remembered experiencing great joy after Bill Clinton's victory, but both their predictions and recollections overestimated the amount of joy they actually reported experiencing at the time. Meyers et al. (1999) found that students did not feel as happy as they expected to feel after performing well on a test, but remembered feeling happier than they actually did. As a result, these students mistakenly predicted that they would feel just as happy if they did well on a similar exam in the future. The bottom line is that memory for emotional experience is imperfect, and in some instances memory and anticipation are more like each other than either is like the experiences they are meant to represent. As such, prior experience with an event does not necessarily provide protection against the impact bias.

UNIMAGINED EVENTS

Errors of imagination and memory are common and powerful, but they are not the only sources of impact bias. Indeed, we tend to overestimate the emotional impact of familiar future events even when we can correctly anticipate every aspect of the time, place, and manner in which the events will unfold. For instance, when Gilbert et al. (1998) asked participants to predict how they would feel a few minutes after receiving negative feedback about their personalities, the participants overestimated the impact of the feedback even though they had thoroughly scrutinized it before making their predictions. When Gilbert et al. (1998) asked participants to predict how they would feel a few minutes after being told that they were not chosen for an attractive job, participants overestimated the impact of receiving that news even though there was nothing particularly mysterious about how the word "No" would sound. When Wilson et al. (2000b) asked die-hard sports fans to predict how they would feel a few days after their favorite football team lost, the fans overestimated the impact of the loss even though they had experienced such losses regularly and often. Why do we overestimate the emotional impact of familiar events whose parameters we can perfectly foresee?

One answer may lie in the way affective forecasts are made. When we attempt to estimate the initial impact of a future event, we often do so by imagining how we would feel if the event were happening now ("It's dreadful to think of the Blue Whales losing the season opener and walking off the field in disgrace") and then correcting our imagined reaction for differences between the temporal locations of the prediction situation and the event (see Elster & Loewenstein, 1992; Loewenstein, Weber, Hsee, & Welch, 2001). This correction allows us to take into account two important parameters. First, it allows us to "add in" the effects of *unique event features*, which are those factors that are likely to influence our feelings at the time of the event but that do not influence our feelings when we imagine the event happening now ("The fact that the opener is being played on my birthday should make me feel a bit better"). Second, it allows us to "subtract out" the effect of *unique prediction features*, which are those factors that are likely to influence our feelings when we imagine the event happening now but that are unlikely to influence our feelings at the time of the event ("I'm in a crummy mood right now because I just paid my taxes, but that will surely pass by September"). In short, correction allows us to consider the differences between now and later and then to adjust our forecasts accordingly.

But there is a problem with adding unique event features and subtracting unique prediction features only after we have first imagined the event happening in the present. When people solve problems by generating an initial solution and then correcting it to take into account additional parameters, their correction is typically insufficient and their final judgment too closely resembles their initial judgment (Gilbert, in press; Gilovich & Savitsky, 1999; Tversky & Kahneman, 1974). This is apparently what happened in a study by Gilbert, Gill, and Wilson (2002), in which participants were asked to predict how much they would enjoy eating a bite of spaghetti and meat sauce the next morning or the next evening. The results suggested that people made these predictions by first imagining how much they would enjoy eating the spaghetti in the present ("Yum!"), using this imagined reaction as an initial prediction of their future reaction, and then adjusting that initial prediction for unique event features ("But spaghetti in the morning would probably be kind of gross") and unique prediction features ("And I'm really hungry now, so just about everything sounds good"). Because participants considered these features only after making a preliminary forecast based on how much they thought they would enjoy eating a bite of spaghetti in the present, their final forecasts were overinfluenced by their current hunger (a unique prediction feature that should have been subtracted out) and underinfluenced by the time of day at which the spaghetti was actually to be eaten (a unique event feature that should have been added in). This was particularly true when participants made their forecasts under cognitive load, which is known to impair correction processes. In a related study, Ebert (2001) asked participants to value prizes ranging from television sets to concert tickets, and they naturally valued the prizes less when they expected to receive them in a month than when they expected to receive them the next day (Laibson, Repetto, & Tobacman, 1998). But when participants made these valuations under cognitive load, they valued the prizes equally highly regardless of when they were to receive them. This result suggests that participants generated values for the prizes by first imagining how they would feel if they received the prizes in the present and then corrected these valuations for the event's actual location in time.

If we predict the intensity of our initial affective reactions to a future event by first introspecting on our affective experience as we think about the event happening now ("Sounds delicious") and then considering factors that distinguish the time of prediction from the time of the event ("But for breakfast? Yuck"), it seems reasonable to suspect that we may predict the duration of our emotional reactions in roughly the same manner. For instance, we may estimate how we will feel a day, or a week, or a month after an event by first imagining our initial reaction to the event, and only then considering *unique event features* (those factors that are likely to influence our feelings when the event happens but that are unlikely to influence our feelings some time later), and *unique postevent features* (those factors that are likely to influence our feelings some time after the event but that are unlikely to influence our feelings when the event happens). So, for example, if we wished to predict how we would feel a week after failing a driver's license test, we might first imagine how we would feel at the time we learned of the failure ("I'd be bummed!") and only then consider those features of the event that are unlikely to be influencing us later ("I won't be hanging around the driver's license bureau like the world's biggest loser, waiting for my mom to come give me a ride home") as well as those aspects of the postevent period that are unlikely to be influencing us at the time of the event ("I'll be surfing on Kaua'i instead"). Figure 5.1 illustrates how affective forecasts of initial intensity and duration may be made by correction.

People use temporal correction to predict the duration of their emotional reactions and hence are particularly unlikely to give unique event and postevent features the weight they are due—a tendency called *focalism* (Schkade & Kahneman, 1997; Wilson et al., 2000b). How we expect to feel 6 hours after our candidate wins the election or our parakeet dies of natural causes should depend on what we think will happen in those 6 hours. If we expect to be watching election returns with like-minded friends or poring over old photos of Tweetie on his favorite perch, our feelings at the postevent period will be quite different than if we expect to be waiting for an airplane or organizing our sock drawer. We may not be able to name each and every one of the things

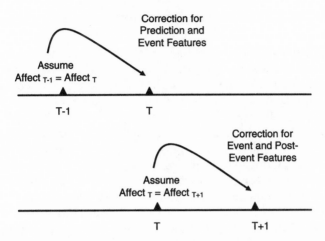

FIGURE 5.1. Forecasts of intensity and duration made by temporal correction.

that will happen between the event and the postevent period for which we are predicting, but the fact that *something* will happen—and that the occurrence of that something will surely influence our emotional state—should at least cause us to moderate our predictions about the enduring impact of the event.

But it doesn't. Wilson et al. (2000b) asked college sports fans to predict how they would feel several days after their school lost a football game and found that fans overestimated the impact of the game. The results showed that they did this in part because they failed to consider the other events that would take place during the days following the game and thus tended to believe that the game would dominate their thoughts and control their emotions far more than it actually did. Interestingly, the impact bias was reduced when fans were made to focus on the postevent factors that they tended naturally to ignore. For example, fans who, just prior to making predictions, were asked to list the activities in which they expected to engage on the days following the game showed a greatly attenuated impact bias. The moral of this story is that emotions are not aroused by football games and then left to decay in a vacuum; rather, they are aroused by football games and then pushed, pulled, dampened, exacerbated, and otherwise altered by postgame pizza, late night parties, and next day hangovers. If we consider the impact of these occurrences only after considering how we will feel at the time of the event, then we are likely to overestimate the duration of our initial reactions.

TRANSFORMED EVENTS

Psychologists from Freud to Festinger, have made much of the fact that people discount, augment, transform, suppress, and rearrange unpleasant information in an attempt to control its emotional consequences. "Rationalization," "dissonance reduction," "motivated reasoning," "positive illusions," "self-deception," "self-enhancement," "self-affirmation," "motivated construal," "ego defense," "self-justification," "self-esteem maintenance," "emotion-based coping," and "terror management" are just a few of the terms that psychologists have used to describe aspects of this tendency (Dunning, 1999; Festinger, 1957; Folkman, 1984; Freud, 1937; Greenwald, 1980; Kunda, 1990; Lyubomirsky, 2001; Pyszczynski, Greenberg, & Solomon, 1997; Steele, 1988; Taylor, 1989; Tesser, 2000; Vaillant, 1993). Although these theoretical constructs differ in important ways, all converge on the notion that people perform psychological work to prevent and abbreviate their experience of negative emotion. This work can take the form of diminishing the importance of negative events ("It's just a football game, after all"), finding meaning in them ("This defeat has taught me the value of loyalty to the home team"), or preventing oneself from thinking about them altogether ("So what's next?"). Most of us, it seems, have what may be thought of as a *psychological immune system*—a system of cognitive mechanisms that transforms our mental representation of negative events so that they give rise to more positive emotions. This system may be curative or prophylactic, truncating our experience of unhappiness or allowing us to avoid it entirely.

One of the most curious things about the psychological immune system is that we seem generally unaware of its influence on our hedonic states (Loewenstein & Adler, 1995; Snell et al., 1995; van Boven, Dunning, & Loewenstein, 2000). When we look forward to events that are sure to bring frustration, sadness, anger, and jealousy, we do not seem to realize that these emotions will not merely subside with the passage of time or be neutralized by subsequent experiences, but that they will be actively antagonized by a host of psychological processes specifically dedicated to their prevention and termination. Our failure to consider these processes can be a problem. For instance, Gilbert et al. (1998) asked participants to predict how they would feel a few minutes after receiving negative personality feedback from a team of seasoned clinicians or from an experimental computer program, and people expected to feel bad—and equally bad—in both cases. Participants who were actually given the negative feedback did not feel as bad as predicted, but more important, those who received the feedback from a clinician felt worse than those who received it from a computer. In another study, Gilbert et al. (1998) asked participants to predict how they would feel a few minutes after reading a tragic story about a toddler who was killed when a playpen collapsed. In one story, the tragedy could easily be blamed on a babysitter who failed to check the safety latch and left the child alone, whereas in another story the babysitter had been appropriately careful and attentive. Participants expected to feel bad—and equally bad—after reading each of the two stories. The results showed that participants did not feel as bad as they predicted, but more importantly, that they felt worse after reading the story that featured a blameless babysitter.

What do these results mean? When people receive negative feedback from an unreliable source or learn about tragedies caused by errant caretakers, they find it relatively easy to explain the negative event in ways that make them feel better (e.g., "Computers can't provide accurate personality assessments, so why should I be upset?" or "The babysitter was careless and I'm not, so an accident like that could never happen to *my* child"). In both of the aforementioned studies, one version of the negative event was more easily defanged than another, and participants made good use of these defanging opportunities when they were available. But the important point is this: Participants who made use of these opportunities did not seem to recognize in prospect that they would do so. In a follow-up study (Gilbert & Ochsner, 2000), participants who received negative personality feedback and participants who were asked to imagine that they had received such feedback were left alone in a room and asked to speak into a tape recorder for 5 minutes. Coding of these tapes revealed that participants who were imagining reacting to negative feedback were more accepting and less defensive than their counterparts, which suggests that they were unable to simulate the operation of their psychological immune systems. In another study (Gilbert & Stalnaker, 2001), participants were asked to predict how accepting they would be (by rating their agreement with items such as "I don't think personality tests are valid"), or how accepting others would be, after receiving positive or negative personality feedback. Participants predicted that they would be about equally accepting in either case, but that others would be much more accepting of positive than negative feedback. Apparently, then, people recognize the existence of the psychological immune system as long as it is not their own (Epley & Dunning, 2000).

The tendency for forecasters to ignore the influence of their psychological immune systems—a tendency called *immune neglect*—may help explain why memory for negative experiences appears to be more accurate than memory for positive experiences. As mentioned earlier, Meyers et al. (1999) found that Democrats misremembered their emotional reactions to Bill Clinton's victory in 1996. But Republicans did not. Similarly, Meyers et al. (1999) found that participants who did well on a test misremembered how they felt upon getting their scores. But participants who did badly did not. Why should this asymmetry have emerged? As it turns out, participants who received negative feedback on the test made themselves feel better by denigrating the validity of the test, and thus, when asked to predict their future reactions to failure on a similar test, they naturally concluded that doing poorly on an invalid test would not make them feel very bad at all. These studies suggest that experience with negative events can cause people to devalue those events, and that a by-product of this fact is that people's subsequent forecasts about the same events are technically more accurate. However, the extent to which people actually learn anything from these affective forecasting errors appears to be limited.

Immune System Dynamics

When a ball rolls off a countertop, it falls. And because there are no forces actively working to hasten or slow its fall, the duration of its descent is a monotonic function of its initial distance from the floor. The higher the countertop from which the ball falls, the longer it takes to hit the floor—and it can *never* take longer for a ball to fall from a low countertop than from a high one. Similarly, if there were no psychological forces actively working to ameliorate negative affect, then its longevity would be a monotonic function of its initial intensity. The more intense the state, the longer it would take to decay, and the decay of a moderate state would never take longer than the decay of an intense one.

The only problem with this rule is that there *are* psychological forces working to ameliorate negative affect and these forces can cause the normally monotonic relation between the intensity and duration of our emotional reactions to become briefly nonmonotonic. The case of physical injury provides a useful analogy. We normally expect the severity of our injuries to determine how long it will take us to recover from them, but because injured people are more likely to take active steps to speed their recoveries when their injuries are particularly severe, there are instances in which they recover more quickly from severe injuries than from mild ones. Anyone who has suffered for years with a trick knee knows that minor dysfunctions often hurt longer than their more severe counterparts, because unlike a trick knee, a shattered patella or a torn ligament exceeds the critical threshold for medical attention and thereby hastens its own mending. The psychological processes that speed recovery from disappointments, insults, failures, and other hedonic afflictions are not unlike the splints and elixirs that speed recovery from physical injury inasmuch as both occur only at critical levels of injury, and the paradoxical result is that we sometimes recover more quickly from truly distressing experiences than from slightly distressing ones (Aronson & Mills, 1958; Gerard & Mathewson, 1966; Zimbardo, 1966). A wife may do the cognitive work necessary to rationalize her husband's infidelity ("Men have to try this sort of thing once to get it out of their systems") but not his annoying habits ("Men often need to experiment with leaving their dirty dishes in the sink"), and the result is that the wife's anger about the husband's disorderliness may actually outlive her anger about his philandering.

Gilbert, Lieberman, and Wilson (2001) demonstrated this effect by arranging for participants to receive personality feedback from another person. Some participants believed they would later meet and interact with the other person, and other participants believed they would not. Forecasters, who were asked to predict how much they would like the other person a few minutes after receiving a negative personality assessment from him or her, predicted that they would dislike the person more if they were expecting to interact than if they were not. These forecasts made good sense. Most of us would probably expect to feel relatively unscathed by the harsh evaluation of an anonymous stranger who knows that he or she will never have to face us, which is approximately equivalent to hearing a few choice words from an angry fellow motorist. On the other hand, when someone who expects to meet us, chat with us, and work with us is willing to tell us beforehand that we are sorely lacking in the attractiveness, intelligence, and friendliness departments, we may reasonably expect to feel wounded. These forecasts are indeed reasonable, but they are also wrong. In fact, experiencers liked the disparaging person more—and not less—when they expected to interact with him or her. Why? Because the distress associated with being insulted by a potential interaction partner is severe enough to trigger the psychological immune system ("I bet he was just kidding with me and is going to make a joke about it when we meet"), whereas the distress associated with being insulted by an insignificant stranger is not. The psychological immune system is a complex system whose dynamics are sometimes difficult to predict. But the failure to predict them may lead forecasters to err.

Choosing Unhappiness

Predictions are usually made with words. But affective forecasts are not just cheap talk, as people are more than willing to put their money where their mouths are. For example, Wilson, Wheatley, and Gilbert

(2000a) asked participants to play a simulated dating game in which they were led to believe that they were competing with another same-sex participant for the affections of an opposite-sex participant. As usual, forecasters predicted that if they lost the dating game, they would be unhappier than experiencers who lost actually were. But in another version of the study forecasters were asked, in addition to making verbal predictions, to decide ahead of time how much of a mood-enhancing drug they would like to take if it turned out that they lost the dating game. Experiencers were told that they had lost the game and, in addition to giving their verbal reports, were asked to select a drug dosage. The results showed that forecasters selected a significantly higher dosage of the drug than did experiencers. Apparently, forecasters really do expect to feel bad when they say they expect to feel bad, and experiencers really do feel fine when they say they feel fine.

Affective forecasts, then, can drive behavior, and when these forecasts are biased by immune neglect, they can lead us to make choices that do not maximize our happiness. For example, Gilbert and Ebert (2002) asked participants to evaluate nine fine art reproductions and then offered to give them one as a gift. Participants were offered a choice between the reproductions they had ranked third and fourth. Some participants (the changeable group) were told that they should, of course, choose the reproduction that they most wanted to keep, but that if they changed their minds any time in the next month, the experimenter would gladly swap the chosen for the unchosen reproduction. Other participants (the unchangeable group) were told that they should choose the reproduction they most wanted to keep and that this choice was final and irreversible. Some of the participants in each group (forecasters) made predictions about how much they would like the chosen reproduction 15 minutes later, whereas other participants (experiencers) waited for 15 minutes and then reported how much they liked the chosen reproduction. Finally, new participants (choosers) were given an introduction to the study and were then asked whether they would prefer to be in the changeable or unchangeable condition.

Consider first the reports of experiencers. Fifteen minutes after making their choices, experiencers in the unchangeable condition reported liking the chosen reproduction more than experiencers in the changeable condition did. Why should this have happened? As we previously saw, the psychological immune system is triggered on some occasions (e.g., when one is insulted by a potential interaction partner) and not on others (e.g., when one is insulted by a stranger). Research suggests that commitment or *unchangeability* is a powerful trigger for the psychological immune system (Frey, 1981; Frey, Kumpf, Irle, & Gniech,

1984; Girard, 1968; Jecker, 1964; cf. Lowe & Steiner, 1968). Our bodies defend against pathogens by attempting first to expel them by coughing, sneezing, tearing, or vomiting, and only when the invasion of the pathogen is irreversible is the physical immune system triggered. Similarly, the mind's first line of defense is to initiate actions that enable us to escape the negative outcomes that threaten our well-being, and it is only when such outcomes are irreversible that the psychological immune system is called on to transform our subjective experience. In short, we attempt to change what we prefer not to accept and then find ways to accept what we cannot change.

This suggests that experiencers should have been more likely to manufacture satisfaction with their gifts when they had no opportunity to swap them than when they did, and that is precisely what happened. Interestingly, however, forecasters did not foresee this effect. Indeed, forecasters—who presumably gave little thought to the sorts of things that might trigger their psychological immune systems—believed they would be just as happy with the chosen reproduction when they could swap it as when they could not. Moreover, choosers, who were introduced to the study and then given the opportunity to be in either the changeable or unchangeable condition, actually had a preference for the changeable condition. In other words, they preferred to be assigned to the condition of the study in which experiencers were the least satisfied. Clearly, the failure to appreciate the dynamics of the psychological immune system may not only impair one's affective forecasts, but may also impair the choices that one bases on them.

Misattributing Happiness

Immune neglect can lead us to predict and choose badly. But it can also influence our deepest beliefs about the causes of the things that happen to us. Because people typically do not realize that they will generate satisfaction with undesirable outcomes, they are occasionally surprised by how well things turn out, and in such instances they may mistakenly credit their self-made fortunes to the intervention of an external agent. In a rather complicated study, Gilbert et al. (2000) asked female participants to perform a visual detection task on a computer and then asked each one to randomly pick one of four other women to be her partner in an upcoming "self-disclosure" game. The participants read four autobiographies, and then some were asked to state how much they would like each of the four partners (the committed group) while others made no such statement (the uncommitted group). The autobiographies were then placed in separate folders, and each participant randomly chose one. The experimenter used sleight of hand to ensure that each participant chose a folder containing the autobiography of an unfavorable partner. The experimenter then falsely confessed that during the visual detection task, the participant had been subliminally primed in an attempt to cause him or her to pick the best partner (cf. Yzerbyt, Schadron, Leyens, & Rocher, 1994). Participants then reported how much they liked the partner they had chosen and how much they thought the subliminal prime had influenced that choice. As expected, uncommitted participants liked their partners more than did committed participants, presumably because it was easier to generate satisfaction with a partner whom they had not publicly denounced. More interestingly, uncommitted participants were also more likely to believe that their choices had been influenced by the subliminal prime. In other words, uncommitted participants were able to generate satisfaction with an unfavorable partner, but because they did not realize they had generated their own satisfaction, they credited the "lucky choice" to an external influence.

People who generate satisfaction with an unfavorable outcome are not only prone to believe that an external agent has influenced their outcomes, but they are also prone to believe that the agent had special insight into their wants and needs. For instance, participants in another study (Gilbert et al., 2000) were introduced to two SmartRadios—computer programs that ostensibly comb the airwaves and use personality information to choose music that their owners will enjoy hearing. Participants listened to a pleasant and an unpleasant musical selection, and some rated the two selections (committed group) whereas others did not (uncommitted groups). Participants then learned that one of the SmartRadios had deliberated long and hard and had concluded that they would like the unpleasant music, which they would therefore be forced to hear several times in a row. Next, participants were told that the entire procedure would be repeated and that this time they could decide which of the two SmartRadios would make their next musical selection for them. As expected, participants in the uncommitted group were more than twice as likely as participants in the committed group to stay with the SmartRadio that had previously subjected them to a cacophony of noise. Why? As described earlier, uncommitted participants found it easier than did committed participants to generate satisfaction with the unpleasant music that the first SmartRadio had chosen. But because they did not know they had generated this satisfaction, they mistakenly concluded that the first SmartRadio had keen insight into their musical tastes and thus "reelected" it to choose for them again. It is perhaps no coincidence that omnipotence (the ability to influence a person's outcomes) and omniscience (the ability to know what a person wants) are two of the attributes traditionally associated with deity. These results demonstrate just one of the potentially important consequences of the failure to appreciate key aspects of our own psychology (Wilson, 1985).

Explaining Happiness

Most organisms achieve pleasure by following a few simple rules (e.g., "If the last behavior increased pleasure, repeat it, and if not, don't"). People are unique among organisms in that they cognize the world and develop deep, rich, theoretical understandings of the causes of their pleasures and pain, presumably because doing so enables them to repeat their pleasurable *experiences* rather than merely repeating the *behaviors* that led to them and hoping for the best. Whether an event is positive ("I just got promoted!") or negative ("I just got demoted!"), pinpointing its antecedent conditions and developing a causal narrative that ties those antecedents to their consequents ("The boss must have seen my annual sales report and taken this action to send me a message") enables the person to predict and control the event's reoccurrence ("I better do more—or less—of the same next quarter").

One of the side effects of all this explanatory activity is that events that initially strike us as extraordinary and unusual are quickly transformed into events that seem more ordinary, explicable, normal, and perhaps even a little dull. An investor may be uncertain whether technology stocks will rise or fall in the coming quarter, and she may be delighted when the NASDAQ closes at a record high. But once this happens, she is likely to generate explanations for the outcome ("The hard winter caused people to stay indoors, thus pushing Internet sales up and traditional retail down"), and the plausibility of these explanations may lead her to believe that, to some extent, the outcome was inevitable (Fischoff, 1975). Similarly, when people are given surprising feedback about their abilities, they spontaneously generate explanations for the feedback, thus rendering it so inevitable that they cannot stop believing it even when they are later told it was false (Ross, Lepper, & Hubbard, 1975). When experimental manipulations prevent people from generating explanations for such feedback, this tendency is eradicated or diminished (Anderson, Lepper, & Ross, 1980; Fleming & Arrowood, 1979). These and other phenomena suggest that when puzzling events occur, we quickly work to unpuzzle them, and that one consequence of this is that the events seem in retrospect more ordinary than they did in prospect.

One of the fundamental laws of emotion is that extraordinary events are more likely than ordinary events to evoke emotional responses (Berns, McClure, Pagnoni, & Montague, 2001; Frijda, 1988; Zajonc,

1998). The paradox is that although we are driven to explain the things that happen to us so that we can repeat our best experiences and avoid repeating our worst, the process of explaining experiences robs them of some of their hedonic power. This attenuation of hedonic power is welcome when the event is unpleasant. Tragedies, failures, and other mishaps becomes less painful when we make sense of them, which is why therapists generally believe that clients must understand the things that have happened to them if they are to overcome their distress (Wortman & Silver, 1989). But if the imperative to make sense of unusual events helps us recover from adversity, it may also cause us to recover from prosperity. What seems like an extraordinary success or an unexpected bit of luck quickly becomes inevitable and mundane as its antecedents are discovered and it is woven into a causal narrative, and that which initially filled us with joy quickly loses its capacity to do so.

Unfortunately, this fact is often lost on forecasters, who seem to know as little about the power of explanation to ameliorate good feelings as bad. Wilson, Centerbar, and Gilbert (2001) invited participants to chat over the internet with three other students of the opposite sex who were ostensibly at other universities (but who were actually bits of computer code). Each participant typed out answers to questions about his or her background and values and watched as the "other students" presumably did the same. Participants were then asked to select one of the other students as the person whom they would most like to have as a best friend and to write a paragraph explaining why they had made that choice. These paragraphs were presumably shared, and each participant was told that all three of the other students had selected him or her as a best friend. They were shown three flattering and distinctive paragraphs explaining these choices. In the revealed condition, participants were told which student wrote each explanation ("Paul was the one who said you were cute, Ringo was the one who said you were witty . . ."), whereas in the anonymous condition, participants received the same information but were not told which student wrote each explanation. Participants reported their emotional states just after reading the explanations and then again 15 minutes later. Finally, a new group of participants (forecasters) was asked to predict how they would feel in each condition, and another group of participants (choosers) was asked to decide whether they would like to be in the revealed or anonymous condition.

The results showed that participants in both the revealed and anonymous conditions were very happy immediately after receiving the feedback, but that participants in the anonymous condition stayed happy longer. Presumably, participants in the revealed condition were able to generate causal stories that explained why they had received each piece of positive feedback ("Ringo was the guy from Liverpool who wanted to be a drummer, so it makes sense that he valued my artistic sensitivity"), and these stories made the other students' choices more explicable and inevitable, and thus less surprising and exciting. Participants in the anonymous condition presumably found it more difficult to generate such stories ("Was it George or Paul who thought I was cute?") and thus the titillating tingle of social success endured. Interestingly, forecasters predicted precisely the opposite pattern of results and expected to be happier in the revealed than the anonymous condition. Choosers naturally fell into line with forecasters: One hundred percent asked to be assigned to the revealed condition! Clearly, the causal explanations we generate for surprising events may have the unusual side effect of neutering those events, and for the most part, we do not realize this will happen. Our ignorance of this fundamental truth can cause us to mispredict our emotional reactions and to choose circumstances that do not maximize our happiness.

Errors of Transformation

The research described thus far suggests that our failure to anticipate the extent to which psychological processes will transform our experience of events can lead us to make a variety of errors that may take many different forms. Figure 5.2 offers a taxonomic scheme that helps explain why such errors manifest as they do. Each panel shows two valenced dimensions on which a pair of outcomes, A and B, may or may not differ. The upper dimension represents a person's forecast of how much he or she will enjoy each of these outcomes at some particular time in the future (A_f and B_f), and the lower dimension represents his or her experienced enjoyment of the two outcomes at that time (A_e and B_e). The first panel illustrates the rational baseline case in which a forecaster's predictions about his or her liking of a relatively positive and relatively negative outcome are perfectly realized.

This rational baseline may be contrasted with the second panel, which illustrates a *minimization error*. This error occurs when forecasters underestimate the difference between the hedonic experiences that the two outcomes will produce. For example, participants in the study by Gilbert and Ebert (2002) decided which of two fine art reproductions they would take home and were or were not given the opportunity to change their minds later. Although participants predicted that they would be equally happy with their chosen reproduction under these two conditions ($A_f = B_f$), they were actually happier when they were not given the opportunity to change their minds ($A_e > B_e$). Similarly, participants in the study by Gilbert et al. (1998) underestimated the differ-

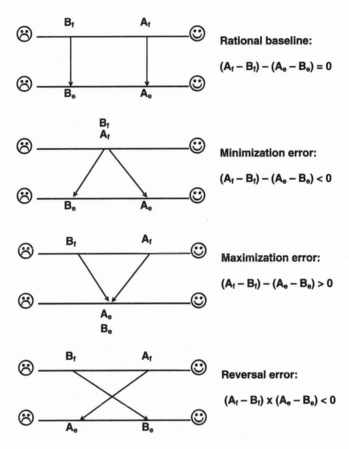

Rational baseline:

$$(A_f - B_f) - (A_e - B_e) = 0$$

Minimization error:

$$(A_f - B_f) - (A_e - B_e) < 0$$

Maximization error:

$$(A_f - B_f) - (A_e - B_e) > 0$$

Reversal error:

$$(A_f - B_f) \times (A_e - B_e) < 0$$

FIGURE 5.2. Forecasting errors produced by the failure to anticipate psychological transformations.

ence between the hedonic experiences of receiving negative feedback from a computer or a clinician, as well as the difference between the experiences of reading a tragic story in which a person could or could not be blamed for the tragedy. Each of these is an instance of minimization.

The third panel illustrates the *maximization error,* which occurs when forecasters overestimate the difference between the hedonic experiences of two outcomes. For example, in the studies of Gilbert et al. (1998), professors overestimated the difference between the hedonic experiences of getting and not getting tenure, students overestimated the difference between the hedonic experiences of maintaining or losing a romantic relationship, and voters overestimated the difference between the hedonic experiences of voting for the winning or losing candidate in an election. In each of these instances, forecasters considered one outcome superior to another ($A_f > B_f$), and experiencers reported that the two outcomes were, in fact, the same ($A_e = B_e$).

Finally, the fourth panel illustrates a *reversal error*. Minimization and maximization errors occur when forecasters mispredict the *magnitude* of the difference between the hedonic experiences of two outcomes, but reversal errors occurs when forecasters mispredict the *direction* of that difference—that is, when the apparently worse outcome ($A_f > B_f$) leads to more satisfaction than the apparently better outcome ($A_e < B_e$). For example, in the studies of Gilbert et al. (2001), participants predicted that they would dislike a person who insulted them more when they expected to have an interaction with that person than when they did not. But because the psychological immune system works harder to optimize one's feelings toward a partner than toward a stranger, participants' experiences of these two outcomes were precisely the opposite.

Why does impact bias take these three forms? Every outcome may be thought of as having two attributes: prepotency and transformability. *Prepotency* refers to the intrinsic hedonic properties of the outcome—in other words, it refers to the hedonic experience that the outcome would normally produce in the absence of any psychological transformation. Sucrose is more pleasurable than quinine to most mammalian palates, and just about everyone prefers orgasms to torture, profits to losses, and praise to castigation. Outcomes have immutable attributes that are experienced by virtually everyone as positive or negative, and those attributes determine the outcome's prepotency. *Transformability*, on the other hand, refers to the likelihood that a person will be motivated and able to transform the subjective experience of the outcome's objective attributes. Some outcomes (such as a receiving negative personality feedback from a computer) are easily transformed, whereas others (such as receiving the same feedback from a team of clinicians) are less so. Some outcomes (such as a being insulted by a partner) are especially likely to activate the processes that transform subjective experience, whereas others (such as being insulted by a stranger) are not. The net hedonic effect of any outcome is a joint function of these two parameters: the feelings an outcome normally produces (prepotency) and the success of the person's efforts to preclude, enhance, or alter those feelings (transformability).

With these parameters in mind, it is possible to predict the form that impact bias will take in a particular instance. Minimization errors are observed in those studies that vary the transformability of outcomes (e.g., the source of personality feedback) while holding constant their prepotency (e.g., the valence of the personality feedback). Because forecasters tend to ignore transformability and emphasize prepotency when predicting their hedonic experience, they tend in such situations to underestimate the difference between the hedonic experiences that the two outcomes will produce. Conversely, maximization errors are observed in those studies that vary the prepotency of the outcomes (e.g., the valence of a tenure decision) while holding constant their transformability (e.g., the source of the tenure decision). Again, because forecasters tend to ignore transformability and base their forecasts instead on prepotency, they tend in these situations to overestimate the difference between the hedonic experiences that the outcomes will produce. Finally, reversal errors are observed in those studies that vary both the transformability and the prepotency of the outcomes. For example, a person's expectations of future interaction with another person can influence both the prepotency of an insult (i.e., a partner's insult may be more hurtful than a stranger's) and the transformability of that insult (i.e., people work harder to excuse the misdeeds of partners than those of strangers). Because expectations of future interaction increase both the prepotency and the transformability of an insult, forecasts and experiences are pulled in opposite directions, and reversal errors result. What this taxonomic scheme suggests, then, is that when people ignore transformability in favor of prepotency, they can make a variety of errors. Research shows that forecasting errors do, in fact, follow the patterns predicted by this simple conceptual scheme.

CONCLUSION

As Mark Twain ostensibly observed, "The art of prophecy is very difficult, especially with regard to the future" (McDonald, 1991). Because the future is inscrutable, most of us blithely accept the fact that tomorrow will bring fortunes and misfortunes that are now beyond our ken. But if we *could* know what was to happen, most of us believe that we would have a damned good idea of how we would feel about it. Windfalls are better than pratfalls, A's are better than C's, December 25 is better than April 15, and everything is better than a Republican administration. Our uncertainty about how the future will be is rivaled only by our certainty about how it should be. Alas, as Count Vronsky learned the hard way, forecasting future feelings is every bit as dubious as predicting the events to which those feelings are responses. The research described in this chapter suggests that our ability to imagine the future, remember the past, and foresee the transformations that events will undergo as we interrogate and explain them, is limited, and hence our ability to predict our own emotional reactions to future events is limited as well.

Understanding when and why we will feel pride, love, jealousy, and rage is a key component of emotional intelligence (Mayer & Salovey, 1997), and it is only natural that research on failures of affective forecasting should cause us to wonder how our forecasting abilities may be improved. Research suggests that a variety of manipulations may serve to ameliorate the impact bias (Buehler & McFarland, 2001; Wilson et al., 2000b). The pressing question is not whether we can improve affective forecasting abilities, but whether we should *want to*. Research demonstrates that predictions of future emotions can be wrong and that these mispredictions can have untoward consequences, but it is entirely possible that when the errors we study in isolation are embedded in the complex web of ordinary events, they may serve some larger purpose of which we are unaware. Inferential errors are like weevils on crops—dangerous pests that any right-minded person should be eager to dispatch. But after the DDT has been generously applied, we may discover that frogs eat weevils, birds eat frogs, snakes eat birds, bears eat snakes, and that as a result of our rush to annihilate that which seemed so desperately in need of it, a once vibrant ecosystem is now devoid of life. In other words, important things that are not measured in experiments—such as our willingness to marry despite the responsibilities and constraints, to go to war despite the threat of injury and death, or to raise children despite the pooping and howling—may well depend on our *inability* to predict how we will feel in the future. Before we design programs to improve emotional intelligence by eradicating errors in affective forecasting, we had best be sure that what appears to be an inferential pest is not actually a vital piece of the psychological food chain.

ACKNOWLEDGMENTS

The research reported herein was supported by research Grant No. RO1-MH56075 from the National Institute of Mental Health to Daniel Gilbert and Timothy Wilson.

REFERENCES

Anderson, C. A., Lepper, M. R., & Ross, L. (1980). Perseverance of social theories: The role of explanation in the persistence of discredited information. *Journal of Personality and Social Psychology, 39,* 1037–1049.

Ariely, D. (1998). Combining experiences over time: The effects of duration, intensity changes and on-line measurements on retrospective pain evaluations. *Journal of Behavioral Decision Making, 11,* 19–45.

Aronson, E., & Mills, J. (1958). The effect of severity of initiation on liking for a group. *Journal of Abnormal and Social Psychology, 59*, 177–181.

Baron, J. (1992). The effects of normative beliefs on anticipated emotions. *Journal of Personality and Social Psychology, 63*, 320–330.

Berns, G. S., McClure, S. M., Pagnoni, G., & Montague, P. R. (2001). Predictability modulates human brain response to reward. *Journal of Neuroscience, 21*, 2793–2798.

Berridge, K. C., & Robinson, T. E. (1995). The mind of an addicted brain: Neural sensitization of wanting versus liking. *Current Directions in Psychological Science, 4*, 71–76.

Brickman, P., Coates, D., & Janoff-Bulman, R. J. (1978). Lottery winners and accident victims: Is happiness relative? *Journal of Personality and Social Psychology, 36*, 917–927.

Buehler, R., & McFarland, C. (2001). Intensity bias in affective forecasting: The role of temporal focus. *Personality and Social Psychology Bulletin, 27*, 1480–1493.

Cambridge international dictionary of English. (1995). Cambridge, UK: Cambridge University Press.

Christensen-Szalanski, J. J. (1984). Discount functions and the measurement of patients' values: Women's decisions during childbirth. *Medical Decision Making, 4*, 47–58.

Christianson, S. A., & Safer, M. A. (1996). Emotional events and emotion in autobiographical memory. In D. Rubin (Ed.), *Remembering our past: Studies in autobiographical memory* (pp. 218–243). Cambridge, UK: Cambridge University Press.

Coughlan, R., & Connolly, T. (2001). Predicting affective reponses to unexpected outcomes. *Organizational Behavior and Human Decision Processes, 85*, 211–225.

Dunning, D. (1999). A newer look: Motivated social cognition and the schematic representation of social concepts. *Psychological Inquiry, 10*, 1–11.

Dunning, D., Griffin, D. W., Milojkovic, J., & Ross, L. (1990). The overconfidence effect in social prediction. *Journal of Personality and Social Psychology, 58*, 568–581.

Ebert, J. E. (2001). The role of cognitive resources in the valuation of near and far future events. *Acta Psychologica, 108*, 155–171.

Elster, J., & Loewenstein, G. F. (1992). Utility from memory and anticipation. In G. F. Loewenstein & J. Elster (Eds.), *Choice over time* (pp. 213–234). New York: Russell Sage Foundation.

Epley, N., & Dunning, D. (2000). Feeling "holier than thou": Are self-serving assessments produced by errors in self- or social prediction? *Journal of Personality and Social Psychology, 79*, 861–875.

Feldman-Barrett, L. (1997). The relationships among momentary emotion experiences, personality descriptions, and retrospective ratings of emotion. *Personality and Social Psychology Bulletin, 23*, 1100–1110.

Festinger, L. (1957). *A theory of cognitive dissonance.* Stanford, CA: Stanford University Press.

Fischoff, B. (1975). Hindsight ≠ foresight: The effects of outcome knowledge on judgment under uncertainty. *Journal of Experimental Psychology: Human Perception and Performance, 1,* 288–299.

Fleming, J., & Arrowood, A. J. (1979). Information processing and the perseverance of discredited self-perceptions. *Personality and Social Psychology Bulletin, 5,* 201–205.

Folkman, S. (1984). Personal control and stress and coping processes: A theoretical analysis. *Journal of Personality and Social Psychology, 46,* 839–852.

Frederick, S., & Loewenstein, G. F. (1999). Hedonic adaptation. In D. Kahneman, E. Diener, & N. Schwartz (Eds.), *Well-being: The foundations of hedonic psychology* (pp. 302–329). New York: Russell Sage Foundation.

Fredrickson, B. L. (2000). Extracting meaning from past affective experiences: The importance of peaks, ends, and specific emotions. *Cognition and Emotion, 14,* 577–606.

Fredrickson, B. L., & Kahneman, D. (1993). Duration neglect in retrospective evaluations of affective episodes. *Journal of Personality and Social Psychology, 65,* 45–55.

Freud, A. (1937). *The ego and the mechanisms of defense.* London: Hogarth Press.

Frey, D. (1981). Reversible and irreversible decisions: Preference for consonant information as a function of attractiveness of decision alternatives. *Personality and Social Psychology Bulletin, 7,* 621–626.

Frey, D., Kumpf, M., Irle, M., & Gniech, G. (1984). Re-evaluation of decision alternatives dependent upon the reversibility of a decision and the passage of time. *European Journal of Social Psychology, 14,* 447–450.

Frijda, N. H. (1988). The laws of emotion. *American Psychologist, 43,* 349–358.

Gerard, H. B., & Mathewson, G. C. (1966). The effects of severity of initiation on liking for a group: A replication. *Journal of Experimental Social Psychology, 2,* 278–287.

Gilbert, D. T. (in press). Inferential correction. In T. Gilovich, D. W. Griffin, & D. Kahneman (Eds.), *The psychology of judgment: Heuristics and biases.* Cambridge, UK: Cambridge University Press.

Gilbert, D. T., Brown, R. P., Pinel, E. C., & Wilson, T. D. (2000). The illusion of external agency. *Journal of Personality and Social Psychology, 79,* 690–700.

Gilbert, D. T., & Ebert, J. E. (2002). Decisions and revisions: The affective forecasting of changeable outcomes. *Journal of Personality and Social Psychology, 82,* 503–514.

Gilbert, D. T., Gill, M. J., & Wilson, T. D. (2002). The future is now: Temporal correction in affective forecasting. *Organizational Behavior and Human Decision Processes, 88,* 430–444.

Gilbert, D. T., Lieberman, M. D., & Wilson, T. D. (2001). *The peculiar longevity of things not so bad.* Unpublished manuscript, Harvard University.

Gilbert, D. T., & Ochsner, K. N. (2000). Unpublished raw data. Harvard University.

Gilbert, D. T., Pinel, E. C., Wilson, T. D., Blumberg, S. J., & Wheatley, T. P. (1998). Immune neglect: A source of durability bias in affective forecasting. *Journal of Personality and Social Psychology, 75,* 617–638.

Gilbert, D. T., & Stalnaker, M. (2001). Unpublished raw data. Harvard University.

Gilbert, D. T., & Wilson, T. D. (2000). Miswanting: Some problems in the forecasting of future affective states. In J. Forgas (Ed.), *Feeling and thinking: The role of affect in social cognition* (pp. 178–197). Cambridge, UK: Cambridge University Press.

Gilovich, T., & Savitsky, K. (1999). The spotlight effect and the illusion of transparency: Egocentric assessments of how we are seen by others. *Current Directions in Psychological Science, 8,* 165–168.

Girard, G. (1968). Décision révocable et fuite du conflit. *Bulletin du CERP, 18,* 245–251.

Greenwald, A. G. (1980). The totalitarian ego: Fabrication and revision of personal history. *American Psychologist, 35,* 603–618.

Griffin, D. W., Dunning, D., & Ross, L. (1990). The role of construal processes in overconfident predictions about the self and others. *Journal of Personality and Social Psychology, 59,* 1128–1139.

Griffin, D. W., & Ross, L. (1991). Subjective construal, social inference, and human misunderstanding. In M. Zanna (Ed.), *Advances in experimental social psychology* (Vol. 24, pp. 319–356). New York: Academic Press.

Holmberg, D., & Holmes, J. G. (1994). Reconstruction of relationship memories: A mental models approach. In N. Schwarz & N. Sudman (Eds.), *Autobiographical memory and the validity of retrospective reports* (pp. 267–288). New York: Springer-Verlag.

Jecker, J. D. (1964). Selective exposure to new information. In L. Festinger (Ed.), *Conflict, decision, and dissonance* (pp. 65–82). Stanford, CA: Stanford University Press.

Kahneman, D. (1994). New challenges to the rationality assumption. *Journal of Institutional and Theoretical Economics, 150,* 18–36.

Kahneman, D., Fredrickson, B. L., Schreiber, C. A., & Redelmeier, D. A. (1993). When more pain is preferred to less: Adding a better ending. *Psychological Science, 4,* 401–405.

Kahneman, D., & Snell, J. (1990). Predicting utility. In R. Hogarth (Ed.), *Insights in decision making* (pp. 295–310). Chicago: University of Chicago Press.

Kahneman, D., & Snell, J. (1992). Predicting a change in taste: Do people know what they will like? *Journal of Behavioral Decision Making, 5,* 187–200.

Kaplan, H. R. (1978). *Lottery winners: How they won and how winning changed their lives.* New York: Harper & Row.

Kunda, Z. (1990). The case for motivated reasoning. *Psychological Bulletin, 108,* 480–498.

Laibson, D., Repetto, A., & Tobacman, J. (1998). Self-control and saving for retirement. *Brookings Papers on Economic Activity, 1,* 91–196.

Loewenstein, G. F., & Adler, D. (1995). A bias in the prediction of tastes. *Economic Journal, 105,* 929–937.

Loewenstein, G. F., & Frederick, S. (1997). Predicting reactions to environmental change. In M. H. Bazerman, D. M. Messick, A. E. Tenbrusel, & K. A. Wade-Benzoni (Eds.), *Environment, ethics, and behavior* (pp. 52–72). San Francisco: New Lexington Press.

Loewenstein, G. F., Nagin, D., & Paternoster, R. (1997). The effect of sexual arousal on sexual forcefulness. *Journal of Research in Crime and Delinquency, 34,* 443–473.

Loewenstein, G. F., O'Donoghue, T., & Rabin, M. (2000). *Projection bias in predicting future utility.* Unpublished manuscript, Carnegie-Mellon University.

Loewenstein, G. F., Prelec, D., & Shatto, C. (1998). *Hot/cold intrapersonal empathy gaps and the under-prediction of curiosity.* Unpublished manuscript, Carnegie-Mellon University.

Loewenstein, G. F., & Schkade, D. (1999). Wouldn't it be nice?: Predicting future feelings. In D. Kahneman, E. Diener, & N. Schwartz (Eds.), *Well-being: The foundations of hedonic psychology* (pp. 85–105). New York: Russell Sage Foundation Press.

Loewenstein, G. F., Weber, E. U., Hsee, C. K., & Welch, N. (2001). Risk as feelings. *Psychological Bulletin, 127,* 267–286.

Lowe, R. E., & Steiner, I. D. (1968). Some effects of the reversibility and consequences of decision on postdecision information preferences. *Journal of Personality and Social Psychology, 8,* 172–179.

Lund, D. A., Caserta, M. S., & Diamond, M. F. (1989). Impact of spousal bereavement on the subjective well-being of older adults. In D. A. Lund (Ed.), *Older bereaved spouses: Research with practical implications* (pp. 3–15). New York: Hemisphere.

Lyubomirsky, S. (2001). Why are some people happier than others? The role of cognitive and motivational processes in well-being. *American Psychologist, 56,* 239–249.

Mayer, J. D., & Salovey, P. (1997). What is emotional intelligence? In P. Salovey & D. Sluyter (Eds.), *Emotional development and emotional intelligence: Implications for educators* (pp. 3–31). New York: Basic Books.

McDonald, K. A. (1991, September 4). Many of Mark Twain's famed humorous sayings are found to have been misattributed to him. *Chronicle of Higher Education,* p. A8.

Mellers, B. A. (2000). Choice and the relative pleasure of consequences. *Psychological Bulletin, 126,* 910–924.

Mellers, B. A., & McGraw, A. P. (2000). *Anticipated emotions as guides to choice.* Unpublished manuscript, Ohio State University.

Mellers, B. A., Schwartz, A., & Ritov, I. (1999). Emotion-based choice. *Journal of Experimental Psychology: General, 128,* 332–345.

Meyers, J., Wilson, T. D., & Gilbert, D. T. (1999). Unpublished raw data. University of Virginia

Mitchell, T. R., Thompson, L., Peterson, E., & Cronk, R. (1997). Temporal adjustments in the evaluation of events: The "rosy view." *Journal of Experimental Social Psychology, 33,* 421–448.

Pyszczynski, T., Greenberg, J., & Solomon, S. (1997). Why do we need what we need? A terror management perspective on the roots of human social motivation. *Psychological Inquiry, 8,* 1–20.

Rachman, S. (1994). The overprediction of fear: A review. *Behaviour Research and Therapy, 32,* 683–690.

Rachman, S., & Arntz, A. (1991). The overprediction and underprediction of pain. *Clinical Psychology Review, 11,* 339–355.

Read, D., & Loewenstein, G. F. (1995). Diversification bias: Explaining the discrepancy in variety seeking between combined and separated choices. *Journal of Experimental Psychology: Applied, 1,* 34–49.

Read, D., & van Leeuwen, B. (1998). Predicting hunger: The effects of appetite and delay on choice. *Organizational Behavior and Human Decision Processes, 76,* 189–205.

Robinson, M. D., & Clore, G. L. (2000). Simulation, scenarios, and emotional appraisal: Testing the convergence of real and imagined reactions to emotional stimuli. *Personality and Social Psychology Bulletin, 27,* 1520–1532.

Ross, L., Lepper, M. R., & Hubbard, M. (1975). Perseverance in self-perception and social perception: Biased attribution processes in the debriefing paradigm. *Journal of Personality and Social Psychology, 32,* 880–892.

Rottenstreich, Y., & Hsee, K. (2001). Money, kisses, and electric shocks: On the affective psychology of risk. *Psychological Science, 12,* 185–190.

Schkade, D. A., & Kahneman, D. (1997). Does living in California make people happy? A focusing illusion in judgments of life satisfaction. *Psychological Science, 9,* 340–346.

Schmitt, D. R., & Kemper, T. D. (1996). Preference for different sequences of increasing or decreasing rewards. *Organizational Behavior and Human Decision Processes, 66,* 89–101.

Schwarz, N. B., Jacquin, K., & Telch, M. J. (1994). The overprediction of fear and panic in panic disorder. *Behavior and Research Therapy, 32,* 701–707.

Simonson, I. (1990). The effect of purchase quantity and timing on variety-seeking behavior. *Journal of Marketing Research, 27,* 150–162.

Snell, J., Gibbs, B. J., & Varey, C. (1995). Intuitive hedonics: Consumer beliefs about the dynamics of liking. *Journal of Consumer Psychology, 4,* 33–60.

Steele, C. M. (1988). The psychology of self-affirmation: Sustaining the integrity of self. In L. Berkowitz (Ed.), *Advances in experimental social psychology* (Vol. 21, pp. 261–302). New York: Academic Press.

Suh, E., Diener, E., & Fujita, F. (1996). Events and subjective well-being: Only recent events matter. *Journal of Personality and Social Psychology, 70,* 1091–1102.

Taylor, S. E. (1989). *Positive illusions.* New York: Basic Books.

Tesser, A. (2000). On the confluence of self-esteem maintenance mechanisms. *Personality and Social Psychology Review, 4,* 290–299.

Tolstoy, L. (1961). *Anna Karenina* (D. Magarshack, Trans.). New York: Signet. (Original work published 1877)

Totterdell, P., Parkinson, B., Brinner, R. B., & Reynolds, S. (1997). Forecasting feelings: The accuracy and effects of self-predictions on mood. *Journal of Social Behavior and Personality, 12,* 631–650.

Tversky, A., & Kahneman, D. (1974). Judgment under uncertainty: Heuristics and biases. *Science, 185,* 1124–1131.

Vaillant, G. (1993). *The wisdom of the ego.* Cambridge, MA: Harvard University Press.

van Boven, L., Dunning, D., & Loewenstein, G. F. (2000). Egocentric empathy gaps between owners and buyers: Misperceptions of the endowment effect. *Journal of Personality and Social Psychology, 79,* 66–76.

van Hout, W. J. P. J., & Emmelkamp, P. M. G. (1994). Overprediction of fear in panic disorder patients with agoraphobia: Does the mismatch model generalize to exposure in vivo therapy? *Behavioral Research and Therapy, 32,* 723–734.

Varey, C., & Kahneman, D. (1992). Experiences extended across time: Evaluation of moments and episodes. *Journal of Behavioral Decision Making, 5,* 169–185.

Wilson, T. D. (1985). Strangers to ourselves: The origins and accuracy of beliefs about one's own mental states. In J. H. Harvey & G. Weary (Eds.), *Attribution: Basic issues and applications* (pp. 9–36). Orlando, FL: Academic Press.

Wilson, T. D., Centerbar, D., & Gilbert, D. T. (2001). Unpublished raw data. University of Virginia.

Wilson, T. D., Meyers, J., & Gilbert, D. T. (2001). Lessons from the past: Do people learn from experience that emotional reactions are short-lived? *Personality and Social Psychology Bulletin, 27,* 1648–1661.

Wilson, T. D., Wheatley, T., & Gilbert, D. T. (2000a). Unpublished raw data. University of Virginia.

Wilson, T. D., Wheatley, T., Meyers, J., Gilbert, D. T., & Axsom, D. (2000b). Focalism: A source of durability bias in affective forecasting. *Journal of Personality and Social Psychology, 78,* 821–836.

Wortman, C. B., & Silver, R. C. (1989). The myths of coping with loss. *Journal of Consulting and Clinical Psychology, 57,* 349–357.

Wortman, C. B., Silver, R. C., & Kessler, R. C. (1993). The meaning of loss and adjustment to bereavement. In M. S. Stroebe & R. O. Hansson (Eds.), *Handbook of bereavment: Theory, research, and intervention* (pp. 349–366). Cambridge, UK: Cambridge University Press.

Yzerbyt, V. Y., Schadron, G., Leyens, J. P., & Rocher, S. (1994). Social judgeability: The impact of meta-informational cues on the use of stereotypes. *Journal of Personality and Social Psychology, 66,* 48–55.

Zajonc, R. B. (1998). Emotions. In D. T. Gilbert, S. T. Fiske, & G. Lindzey (Eds.), *The handbook of social psychology* (Vol. 1, 4th ed., pp. 591–632). New York: McGraw Hill.

Zeelenberg, M., van Dijk, W. W., Manstead, A. S. R., & van der Pligt, J. (1998). The experience of regret and disappointment. *Cognition and Emotion, 12,* 221–230.

Zimbardo, P. G. (1966). Control of pain motivation by cognitive dissonance. *Science, 151,* 217–219.

Situated Cognition and the Wisdom in Feelings

Cognitive Tuning

NORBERT SCHWARZ

This chapter addresses the influence of moods, emotions, bodily sensations, and environmental cues on individuals' spontaneously adopted reasoning styles. Before you read on, I invite you to take the quiz presented in Table 6.1. You will probably find some of the questions rather odd—and the correct answers at the bottom of the table surprising. Yet these answers are supported by solid experimental research, reviewed in this chapter. Moreover, a growing body of literature suggests that emotionally intelligent persons may have a tacit understanding of some of these processes and may deliberately manage their moods to facilitate task performance (see the contributions in Ciarrochi, Forges, & Mayer, 2001). In fact, the questions presented in Table 6.1 bear some similarity with items of the Mayer–Salovey–Caruso Emotional Intelligence Test (MSCEIT; Mayer, Salovey, & Caruso, in press), a test of emotional intelligence.

But *why* would our performance on a wide variety of cognitive tasks be influenced by variables like our moods, the color of the paper on which the task is presented, or whether we press a hand upward or downward against the table? This question is the focus of the present chapter. I propose that these variables share one crucial characteristic: They provide affective cues that inform us about the benign or problematic nature of the situation. Our thought processes, in turn, are tuned to meet these situational requirements, which is highly adaptive.

TABLE 6.1. Quiz

A. Suppose you need to solve *analytical tasks* taken from the Graduate Record Exam. Which of the following would you prefer?
   1. Work on the tasks while being
      (a) in a happy mood; (b) in a sad mood; (c) no preference
   2. Have the tasks presented to you on
      (a) red paper; (b) blue paper; (c) no preference
   3. While working on the tasks, press one hand
      (a) downward against the top of the table; (b) upward against the underside of the table; (c) no preference

B. Suppose you want to solve *creativity tasks* that require playful, divergent thinking? Which of the following would you prefer?
   1. Work on the tasks while being
      (a) in a happy mood; (b) in a sad mood; (c) no preference
   2. While working on the tasks, press one hand
      (a) downward against the top of the table; (b) upward against the underside of the table; (c) no preference

C. Suppose you read a persuasive message. Under which conditions would it be most likely that you are *not* persuaded by *weak* arguments, but *are* persuaded by *strong* arguments?
   1. When you read the arguments while in a
      (a) happy mood; (b) sad mood; (c) makes no difference
   2. When the arguments are printed on
      (a) red paper; (b) blue paper; (c) makes no difference

Correct answers: A. 1b; 2b; 3a; B. 1a; 2b; C. 1b; 2b.

When the situation is characterized as problematic, we are likely to adopt a systematic, bottom-up processing style with close attention to the details at hand. In contrast, when the situation is characterized as benign, we are likely to rely on our usual routines, adopting a top-down processing style with less attention to the details at hand. Although these spontaneously adopted processing styles can be overridden by task demands and important goals, they are likely to influence our cognitive performance under many circumstances. Next, I develop this logic in more detail and provide a selective review of relevant experimental findings.

SITUATED COGNITION: COGNITIVE PROCESSES ARE TUNED TO MEET SITUATIONAL REQUIREMENTS

"My thinking is first and last and always for the sake of my doing," noted William James (1890, p. 333) more than a century ago. From this perspective, human cognition stands in the service of action, and a growing body of research supports this assertion (for a review, see Smith & Semin, 2001). To serve human action in adaptive ways, our cognitive processes are responsive to the environment in which we pursue our goals. This responsiveness ranges from the higher accessibility of knowledge relevant to a given situation (see Yeh & Barsalou, 2000) to the choice of processing strategies that meet situational requirements (e.g., Wegner & Vallacher, 1986). For example, when things go smoothly and we face no hurdles in the pursuit of our goals, we are likely to rely on our preexisting knowledge structures and routines, which have served us well in the past. Once things go wrong, however, we abandon this reliance on our usual routines and focus on the specifics at hand to determine what went wrong and what can be done about it. Hence, our actions, and the context in which we pursue them, are represented at a greater level of detail when things go wrong than when things go well (see Wegner & Vallacher, 1986).

Taken by itself, this observation is not surprising—after all, problems need attention. The very same phenomenon, however, may be at the heart of the more surprising findings presented in Table 6.1, when we assume that feelings, bodily sensations, or environmental cues provide information about the benign or problematic nature of our current situation. This proposal is consistent with many theories of emotion.

FEELINGS ALERT US TO SITUATIONAL REQUIREMENTS

Cognitively oriented emotion researchers generally assume that "emotions exist for the sake of signaling states of the world that have to be responded to, or that no longer need response and action" (Frijda, 1988, p. 354). Similarly, mood researchers typically assume that moods reflect the general state of the organism (Nowlis & Nowlis, 1956), an assumption that prompted Jacobsen (1957) to refer to moods as "barometers of the ego." If so, we may expect that our feelings serve *informative functions*. This expectation has been supported by a large body of research, ranging from the impact of feelings on evaluative judgment to the choice of different processing strategies (for a review see Schwarz & Clore, 1996; see Gohm & Clore, Chapter 4, this volume). This chapter is solely concerned with the latter influence.

Moods

We usually feel bad when we encounter a threat of negative or a lack of positive outcomes, and feel good when we obtain positive outcomes and are not threatened by negative ones. Hence, our moods reflect the state of our environment; being in a bad mood signals a problematic situation, whereas being in a good mood signals a benign situation. These signals have cognitive and motivational consequences, which are highly adaptive under most circumstances.

When facing a problematic situation, we are usually motivated to do something about it. Any attempt to change the situation, however, initially requires a careful assessment of its features, an analysis of their causal links, detailed explorations of possible mechanisms of change, and an anticipation of the potential outcomes of any action that might be initiated. Consistent with these conjectures, being in a negative affective state is associated with a narrowed focus of attention (e.g., Broadbent, 1971; Bruner, Matter, & Papanek, 1955; Easterbrook, 1959) and a higher level of spontaneous causal reasoning (e.g., Bohner, Bless, Schwarz, & Strack, 1988), paralleling the observation that failure to obtain a desired outcome shifts attention to a lower level of abstraction (e.g., Wegner & Vallacher, 1986). These influences foster bottom-up, data-driven processing. Moreover, it may seem unwise to rely on our usual routines and preexisting general knowledge structures without further consideration of the specifics under these conditions, thus discouraging top-down strategies. Finally, we may be unlikely to take risks in a situation that is already marked problematic and may therefore avoid simple heuristics and uncertain solutions.

Conversely, when we face a benign situation that poses no particular problem, we may see little need to engage in detailed analyses and may rely on our usual routines and preexisting knowledge structures, which served us well in the past. This encourages less effortful, top-down processing as a default, *unless* current goals require otherwise. In pursuing such goals, we may be willing to take some risk, given that the general situation is considered safe. As a result, we may prefer simple heuristics over more effortful, detail-oriented judgmental strategies, may explore new procedures and possibilities and pursue unusual, creative associations.

In combination, these conjectures suggest that our cognitive processes are tuned to meet the situational requirements signaled by our feelings (Schwarz, 1990; Schwarz & Clore, 1996; see also Bless, 1997; Fiedler, 1988). Note that this cognitive tuning hypothesis does *not* entail that happy individuals are somehow unable, or generally unwilling, to engage in systematic processing. Rather, it means only that the mood *itself* does not signal a situation that poses particular processing requirements. Hence, the spontaneously adopted heuristic processing style and reliance on preexisting knowledge structures should be easy to override, rendering processing in happy moods more flexible than processing in sad moods. In contrast, the systematic processing style fostered by negative moods should be difficult to override, reflecting that it would be maladaptive to ignore a potential "problem" signal (see Bless & Schwarz, 1999; Schwarz, 2001, for more detailed discussions).

The assumption that our moods inform us about the nature of the situation predicts that their influence will be eliminated when the informational value of the mood is called into question. Empirically, this is the case. When we are aware, for example, that we may feel bad only because of the lousy weather, our bad mood carries little information about the task at hand and its influence on task performance is attenuated or eliminated (e.g., Sinclair, Mark, & Clore, 1994). This finding parallels the observation that mood effects on evaluative judgment are eliminated under similar conditions (e.g., Schwarz & Clore, 1983), consistent with the informative functions logic. Note that this finding is incompatible with competing approaches that trace mood effects on processing style to mood-congruent recall. These approaches (Isen, 1987; Mackie & Worth, 1989) draw on variants of Bower's (1981) network model of affect and memory and assume that being in a good mood facilitates the recall of positive material from memory. Positive material stored in memory is believed to be more tightly organized and interconnected than negative material, resulting in the recall of a large amount of information. This extensive recall, in turn, is assumed by some authors to tax individuals' cognitive capacity, thus interfering with detail-oriented processing in happy moods, forcing individuals to rely on simplifying heuristics (e.g., Mackie & Worth, 1989). In contrast, others (e.g., Isen, 1987) assume that this extensive recall of interconnected material results in a more "complex cognitive context" (Isen, 1987, p. 237) that facilitates novel associations between disparate ideas in working memory, which are actively explored when individuals are in a good mood. The available data do not provide consistent support for either of these assumptions. In general, negative events have been found to elicit more causal analysis and rumination than positive events, presumably resulting in more interconnected representations of negative material (see Clore, Schwarz, & Conway, 1994, for a more detailed discussion). Moreover, other researchers have suggested that being in a sad (rather than happy) mood is more likely to tax individuals' cognitive capacity (e.g., Ellis & Ashbrook, 1988). Neither of these assumptions, however, can account for the observation that mood effects on processing style are eliminated when the informational value of the mood is undermined. In addition, memory-based accounts of processing style effects are incompatible with recent research that documents parallel effects for the information provided by bodily feedback and situational cues. Before I turn to these parallels, however, it is useful to illustrate the differences in processing style elicited by being in a happy and a sad mood with a prototypical example.

An Illustration: Moods and the Use of Scripts

Our knowledge about many everyday situations is represented in memory in the form of *scripts,* that is, general knowledge structures pertaining to what transpires in social settings like a restaurant (Schank & Abelson, 1977). If happy moods increase, and sad moods decrease, our tendency to rely on the "usual routines," we may expect that individuals in a happy mood are more likely to rely on an applicable script than individuals in a sad mood. Empirically, this is the case.

Employing a dual-task paradigm, Bless, Clore, et al. (1996) had happy and sad participants listen to a tape-recorded story about having dinner at a restaurant that contained script-consistent as well as script-inconsistent information. While listening to the story, participants worked on a concentration test that required them to mark certain letters on a work sheet. Good performance on the concentration test required detail-oriented processing; in contrast, the restaurant story could be understood by engaging *either* in script-driven top-down processing or in data-driven bottom-up processing. As predicted, happy participants were likely to recognize previously heard script-inconsistent information and showed high rates of erroneous recognition of previously not presented script-consistent information. This pattern indicates that they relied on their general knowledge about restaurant visits in encoding the information, rendering unusual acts highly salient and memorable. As usual, however, this reliance on general knowledge structures came at the expense of increased intrusion errors. Neither of these effects was obtained for sad participants, indicating that they were less likely to draw on the script. Given that top-down processing is less taxing than bottom-up processing, we may further expect that happy participants do better on a secondary task. Confirming this prediction, happy participants outperformed sad participants on the concentration test.

In combination, these findings indicate that moods influence the spontaneously adopted processing style under conditions where different processing styles are compatible with the individual's goals and task demands, as was the case for comprehending the restaurant story. Under these conditions, sad individuals are likely to spontaneously adopt a systematic, detail-oriented, bottom-up strategy that is usually adaptive in problematic situations, whereas happy individuals rely on a less effortful top-down strategy. Yet when task demands (as in the case of the concentration test, Bless, Clore, et al., 1996) or explicit instructions (e.g., Bless,

Bohner, Schwarz, & Strack, 1990) require detail-oriented processing, happy individuals are able and willing to engage in the effort.

Bodily Feedback

The cognitive tuning logic has recently been extended to *bodily sensations,* which may also signal benign or problematic situations (Friedman & Förster, 2000). In general, people try to approach situations that are characterized by a promise of positive, or a lack of negative, outcomes. Conversely, they try to avoid situations that entail a threat of negative outcomes or a lack of positive ones. If so, bodily responses that are typically associated with approach situations may elicit the heuristic, top-down processing style spontaneously preferred in benign situations. In contrast, bodily responses that are typically associated with avoidance situations may elicit the systematic, bottom-up processing style spontaneously preferred in problematic situations. A bodily response that is closely associated with approach is the contraction of the arm flexor, which is involved in pulling an object closer to the self. Conversely, contraction of the arm extensor is involved in pushing an object away from the self and is closely associated with avoidance. Hence, arm flexion provides bodily feedback that is usually associated with approaching positive stimuli, whereas arm extension provides bodily feedback that is usually associated with avoiding negative stimuli (see Cacioppo, Priester, & Berntson, 1993; Priester, Cacioppo, & Petty, 1996). In fact, affectively neutral stimuli encoded during arm flexion are later preferred over neutral stimuli encoded during arm extension, presumably reflecting the approach–avoidance information provided by the bodily feedback (Cacioppo et al., 1993; see also Chen & Bargh, 1999).

In a series of ingenious experiments, Friedman and Förster (2000) took advantage of this association. They asked seated participants to press the right palm upward against the bottom of a table (arm flexion) or downward against the top of the table (arm extension). Although these movements engage the same muscles, they have no surface similarity to pulling an object closer or pushing it away, thus avoiding the introduction of demand characteristics. As theoretically predicted, arm flexion fostered a heuristic processing style, whereas arm extension fostered a systematic processing style. I return to the results of these studies later.

Affective Environmental Cues

If the impact of moods and bodily sensations on processing style is mediated by the affective information they provide about a situation, we may assume that external, affectively laden situational cues may exert a similar influence. Empirically, this is again the case. For example, Soldat, Sinclair, and Mark (1997; see also Sinclair, Soldat, & Mark, 1998) presented reasoning tasks from the Graduate Record Examination on colored paper and observed that an upbeat red fostered heuristic processing, whereas a depressing blue fostered systematic processing (see Mayer, DiPaolo, & Salovey, 1990, for a discussion of the affective tone of colors). Similarly, Ottati, Terkildsen, and Hubbard (1997) observed that communicators who deliver a message with a happy, smiling face are likely to evoke a heuristic processing style in their audience, whereas communicators who deliver the same message with a somber face are likely to evoke a systematic processing style. I return to these findings later.

Summary

Our strategies of information processing are tuned to meet the requirements of the specific situation. Information that characterizes the situation as problematic fosters the spontaneous adoption of a systematic, detail-oriented, bottom-up processing style. In contrast, information that characterizes the situation as benign fosters the spontaneous adoption of a top-down processing style that relies on preexisting knowledge structures and routines, unless currently active goals require otherwise. The "benign" or "problematic" signal can be external (e.g., situational cues or encountered hurdles) or internal (e.g., moods or bodily feedback), with similar effects observed in either case.

How the processing style elicited by these signals influences task performance depends on the characteristics of the task: Task performance is facilitated when the evoked style matches task requirements, but impeded when it mismatches task requirements. Next, I illustrate the pervasive influence of feelings on task performance, drawing on research into persuasion, stereotyping, and problem solving.

FEELINGS AND TASK PERFORMANCE

Persuasion

How would your happy or sad mood influence your susceptibility to a persuasive message? A common intuition suggests that recipients in a bad mood may be more critical than recipients in a happy mood and hence less influenced by any persuasive message. Empirically, however, this is not the case. Instead, the specific influence of mood on persuasion depends on the strength of the persuasive arguments in ways that are consistent with common dual-process models of persuasion.

As a large body of research in the context of Eagly and Chaiken's (1993) heuristic-systematic model and Petty and Cacioppo's (1986) elaboration likelihood model demonstrated, a message that presents strong arguments is generally more persuasive than a message that presents weak arguments. This observation, however, holds only when recipients are motivated and able to systematically process the content of the message, in which case they generate agreeing thoughts in response to strong arguments and disagreeing thoughts in response to weak arguments. If recipients do not engage in such "elaborative" or "systematic" processing of message content, the advantage of strong over weak arguments is eliminated. Accordingly, one may explore the impact of mood states on processing strategies by testing the relative impact of argument strength under different mood states. Several researchers followed this strategy (see Bless & Schwarz, 1999; Schwarz, Bless, & Bohner, 1991; and Schwarz & Clore, 1996, for more extensive reviews).

These studies consistently showed that individuals in a happy mood are less likely to engage in systematic elaboration of a counterattitudinal message than individuals in a nonmanipulated or a sad mood (e.g., Bless et al., 1990; Bless, Mackie, & Schwarz, 1992; Bohner, Crow, Erb, & Schwarz, 1992; Mackie & Worth, 1989; Worth & Mackie, 1987). Hence, happy recipients are moderately and equally persuaded by strong as well as weak arguments. Moreover, their cognitive responses show no differences as a function of argument strength, and they report similar proportions of agreeing or disagreeing thoughts in response to strong or weak arguments. In contrast, sad recipients are strongly persuaded by strong arguments, but not by weak arguments. In addition, sad recipients report more disagreeing thoughts in response to weak arguments and more agreeing thoughts in response to strong messages. Figure 6.1 shows the pattern usually obtained.

Complementing these investigations into argument strength, Worth and Mackie (1987) observed that happy recipients were more likely than sad individuals to rely on heuristic strategies in assessing the validity of the message, paying attention to cues like the communicator's status or expertise in forming a judgment (e.g., Worth & Mackie, 1987). In combination, the reviewed findings indicate that a strong message fares better with a sad audience than with a happy audience. But if communicators have nothing compelling to say, they are well advised to put recipients in a good mood, providing some cues that indicate high expertise and trustworthiness.

But how confident can we be that the observed effects reflect the

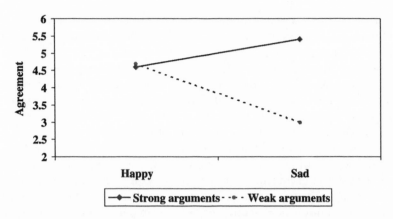

FIGURE 6.1. Persuasion as a function of mood and argument strength. Adapted from Bless, Bohner, Schwarz, and Strack (1990, Experiment 1). Copyright 1990 by the Society for Personality and Social Psychology. Adapted by permission of Sage Publications.

informative functions of moods rather than another process?[1] According to the feelings-as-information logic (Schwarz, 1990; Gohm & Clore, Chapter 4, this volume), the observed effects of mood on processing style will be eliminated when participants become aware that their feelings are due to a source that is irrelevant to their task, thus calling the feelings' informational value into question. A study by Sinclair et al., (1994) supports this prediction. Specifically, students were approached on early spring days when the weather was sunny and pleasant, or cloudy and unpleasant, and were presented with strong or weak persuasive messages. To discredit the informational implications of participants' mood, Sinclair and colleagues did or did not draw their attention to the weather, following a procedure previously used by Schwarz and Clore (1983). When participants' attention was *not* drawn to the weather, the usually obtained interactive effects of mood and message quality were observed. In this case, sad participants were persuaded by strong but not weak messages, whereas happy participants were moderately but equally persuaded by both. However, when the weather was made salient as a potential cause of their momentary feelings, mood no longer played a role and a main effect of message quality emerged.

As already noted in the context of individuals' reliance on scripts (Bless, Clore, et al., 1996), the impact of moods on processing style is not inevitable and can be overridden by other variables. Accordingly,

---

[1]For a comparative discussion of different theoretical approaches, which exceeds the scope of this chapter, see Martin and Clore (2001) and Schwarz and Clore (1996).

explicit instructions to pay attention to the arguments (e.g., Bless et al., 1990), or the promise that carefully thinking about the message would make one feel good (e.g., Wegener, Petty, & Smith, 1995), have been found to elicit systematic message processing in happy recipients. What characterizes the information processing of happy individuals is not a general cognitive or motivational impairment, but a tendency to spontaneously rely on simplifying strategies and general knowledge structures in the absence of goals that require otherwise.

Paralleling the effects of recipients' moods, Ottati et al. (1997) observed that the same message is less likely to be scrutinized when presented by a communicator with a smiling, happy face than when presented by a communicator with a neutral, somber face. They suggested that the communicator's conveyed affect can serve informative functions that parallel recipients' own moods. Further illustrating the power of environmental affective cues, Soldat and Sinclair (2001) had participants read persuasive messages printed on colored paper. The selection of colors was based on affect ratings, and participants perceived the selected hue of blue as conveying negative affect, but the selected hue of red as conveying positive affect. As expected, participants were persuaded by strong arguments, but not by weak arguments, when the message was presented on blue paper. Yet, both types of arguments were similarly persuasive when the message was presented on red paper.

In sum, both internal (moods) and external (facial expressions, color) affective signals have been found to influence the processing of persuasive messages. Throughout, negative affective signals increase systematic processing. In contrast, positive affective signals decrease systematic processing and foster reliance on heuristic cues.

Stereotyping and Impression Formation

Paralleling the distinction between heuristic and systematic processing strategies in the persuasion domain, models of person perception distinguish between two different processing strategies involved in impression formation (Brewer, 1988; Fiske & Neuberg, 1990). At one extreme, judgments may be primarily based on the implications of the target person's category membership, with little attention to the person's specific behaviors. Such judgments are formed in a top-down manner by relying on one's general knowledge about the category, that is, one's stereotype of the group. At the other extreme, judgments may be primarily based on individuating information about the target person, with little impact of information about the person's category membership. Such judgments are formed in a bottom-up manner, with close attention to the specific information pertaining to the person. Hence, we may expect that happy individuals are more likely to engage in stereotyping than sad individuals, in contrast to what common intuition would suggest.

A growing body of research supports this prediction (see Bless, Schwarz, & Kemmelmeier, 1996, for a review). For example, Bodenhausen (1993) presented participants in different moods with descriptions of an alleged student misconduct and asked them to determine the target person's guilt. Participants in a happy mood rated the offender as more guilty when he was identified as a member of a group that is stereotypically associated with the described offense than when he was not. In contrast, the guilt judgments of participants in a neutral or sad mood were not affected by the offender's category membership. Similarly, Edwards and Weary (1993) observed that nondepressed individuals were more likely to rely on category membership information than chronically depressed individuals, who seemed to engage in a more effortful analysis of the individuating information provided to them. In a similar vein, Sinclair (1988) found that participants in a sad mood made more use of detailed performance information. Sad participants were also less likely to show halo effects and more likely to be accurate in a performance appraisal task than those in happy moods, with neutral mood participants falling in between. In addition, sad participants have been found to show less pronounced primacy effects in impression formation tasks than happy participants (Sinclair & Mark, 1992). Finally, Hildebrand-Saints and Weary (1989) observed that chronically depressed individuals sought more, and more diagnostic, information about another person than nondepressed participants. Moreover, depressed participants did so independent of whether they expected to interact with the person in the future, whereas nondepressed participants' information search increased when future interaction was expected.

In combination, these findings again indicate that being in a sad mood fosters the spontaneous adoption of a systematic, bottom-up processing style, whereas being in a happy mood fosters the spontaneous adoption of a heuristic, top-down processing style. Further paralleling the results observed in the persuasion domain, happy individuals' reliance on category membership information can be overridden by manipulations that increase their processing motivation, such as personal accountability for their judgments (Bodenhausen, Kramer, & Süsser, 1994, Experiment 4) or an anticipated interaction with the target person (e.g., Hildebrand-Saints & Weary, 1989).

Quite obviously, the observation that happy moods increase stereotyping runs counter to common intuition as well as the traditional social psychological assumption that we are more likely to stereotype a group the more negative we feel about it (see Allport, 1954). The apparent contradiction, however, may be misleading. The negative feelings elicited by a disliked group may be quite different from the diffuse sad moods induced in the reviewed experiments (for a discussion, see Bodenhausen, 1993). Unfortunately, attempts to test the influence of target-elicited (rather than incidental) feelings by presenting information about liked and disliked groups face serious methodological challenges. Most notably, the groups will necessarily differ in ways other than the feelings they evoke, rendering it difficult to isolate the role of feelings. It is hoped that future research will shed light on this issue.

Categorization

Theoretically, the detail-oriented, bottom-up processing style associated with negative moods should foster the formation of fine-grained, narrow categories, whereas the top-down, heuristic processing style associated with positive moods should foster the formation of more inclusive categories. Numerous studies are consistent with this prediction (for reviews, see Isen, 1987; Schwarz & Clore, 1996). For example, Isen and Daubman (1984) observed that happy participants were more likely to include unusual exemplars in a category than participants in a neutral mood, assigning, for example "feet" and "camel" to the category "vehicles," and "cane" to the category "clothing." Moreover, happy individuals sorted colored chips into a smaller number of piles, again indicating more inclusive categorization. Reversing the categorization task, Hirt, Levine, McDonald, Melton, and Martin (1997) provided participants with a category and asked them to list exemplars. As expected, happy participants listed more unusual exemplars than sad participants, again indicating more inclusive categorization.

Studies drawing on bodily approach–avoidance signals rather than moods again parallel these findings. Using the arm flexion–extension task described earlier, Friedman and Förster (2000, Experiment 6) observed that participants who were induced to flex their arms provided more inclusive categorizations on Isen and Daubman's (1984) task, relative to a control. Conversely, participants who were induced to extend their arms provided less inclusive categorizations relative to a control. These differences were observed in the absence of any differences on mood measures, suggesting that the observed results are indeed due to the information provided by the bodily feedback rather than any changes in participants' mood.

Creative Problem Solving

As may be expected on the basis of the categorization findings, happy individuals typically outperform sad or neutral-mood individuals on creativity tasks, such as Mednick's (1962) remote associates test (e.g., Isen, Daubman, & Nowicki, 1987). Similarly, happy participants list more unusual first associates in response to neutral words than sad or neutral-mood participants (e.g., Isen, Johnson, Metz, & Robinson, 1985).

The results of Friedman and Förster's (2000) ingenious studies on bodily feedback again parallel these findings. As theoretically predicted, the approach feedback provided by arm flexion facilitated creative problem solving across several tasks, whereas the avoidance feedback provided by arm extension impeded it. Specifically, participants who flexed their arms were more likely to break the set than participants who extended their arms, resulting in better performance on Witkin, Oltman, Raskin, and Karp's (1971) Embedded Figure Test (Friedman & Förster, 2000, Experiment 1) as well as Ekstrom, French, Harman, and Dermen's (1976) Snowy Picture Test (Experiment 2). The Embedded Figure Test requires the identification of figures hidden in complex visual patterns, whereas the Snowy Picture Test requires the identification of familiar objects hidden in patterns of visual noise ("snow"). Performance on both tasks is facilitated by the application of familiar concepts to the hidden figures while disregarding irrelevant detail and breaking the set imposed by the distractor. Accordingly, the top-down processing fostered by positive affective cues improves performance on these tasks, whereas the bottom-up processing fostered by negative affective cues impedes it. Finally, arm flexion improved the perceptual restructuring of fragmented visual images on Ekstrom, French, Harman, and Dermen's (1976) Gestalt Completion Test (Friedman & Förster, 2000, Experiments 3 and 4). Both breaking the set and restructuring have traditionally been assumed to play a central role in creative insight. Hence, the emotionally intelligent person may want to press his or her hand upward (rather than downward) against the table when the task requires divergent and creative thinking.

In combination with the categorization findings, these results suggest that being in a happy mood, or receiving approach feedback, should facilitate creative performance on insight tasks (see Isen, 1987). This proposal has received considerable support in the mood domain. For example, Isen and Daubman (1984) observed in a highly influential experiment that being in a happy mood facilitated performance on Duncker's (1945) candle task, relative to being in a neutral or sad mood (see Greene & Noice, 1988, for a replication). Isen (1987) suggested that this finding reflects that happy moods facilitate the recall of diverse material from memory, resulting in a more "complex cognitive context" that facilitates novel connections and insights. Alternatively, the cognitive tuning assumption (Schwarz, 1990) suggests that being in a good mood signals a benign situation that is conducive to playful exploration, which is discouraged by the problem signal provided by negative moods. The most diagnostic test of these competing accounts would be experiments that vary the perceived informational value of participants' mood. Unfortunately, such studies are not available, nor are studies that test the impact of bodily approach–avoidance feedback on traditional insight tasks, like Duncker's candle problem. Overall, however, the accumulating body of evidence across different reasoning tasks suggests that the cognitive tuning assumption may provide a parsimonious account for the diverse set of findings.

Analytic Reasoning Tasks

If being in a sad mood fosters systematic, detail-oriented processing, we may assume that sad moods facilitate performance on analytic reasoning tasks. The bulk of the available evidence is again consistent with this prediction (see Clore et al., 1994; Schwarz & Skurnik, in press, for reviews). For example, Fiedler (1988) reported that sad participants produced fewer inconsistencies in multiattribute decision tasks than happy participants. Specifically, the latter were twice as likely than the former to violate transitivity by producing inconsistent triads of the form $A > B$ and $B > C$, but $A < C$. Similarly, Melton (1995) observed that happy participants performed worse on syllogisms than participants in a neutral mood. Specifically, happy participants were more likely to select an unqualified conclusion and to give answers consistent with the atmosphere heuristic, drawing on their general knowledge about the content domain rather than on the specifics of the task.

Extending the cognitive tuning logic to bodily feedback, Friedman and Förster (2000, Experiment 7) predicted that bodily avoidance feedback would improve performance on analytical reasoning tasks taken from the Graduate Record Exam (GRE), relative to bodily approach feedback. Their data confirmed this prediction, and participants in the arm extension (avoidance) condition solved nearly twice as many problems correctly as participants in the arm flexion (approach) condition. Hence, the emotionally intelligent person may want to press his or her hand downward (rather than upward) against the table while working on analytical tasks.

Finally, Soldat et al. (1997) presented analytic reasoning tasks, also taken from the GRE, on paper that had an upbeat red, or a somewhat depressing blue, color. Across several replications, they observed that participants performed better when the tasks were printed on blue rather than red paper, with white paper falling in between. The performance advantage of blue paper was most pronounced for complex tasks, which posed higher processing demands. Paralleling these laboratory findings, Sinclair et al. (1998) found that students did better on an exam when the exam was printed on blue rather than red paper, in particular for difficult questions.

An important outcome is that neither the bodily feedback in Friedman and Förster's (2000) studies nor the color cues used in Soldat and colleagues' (1997) study resulted in changes in participants' self-reported mood. In combination, these findings indicate that subtle cues, like bodily feedback or the affective connotation of the paper on which the task is presented, can serve as "problem" signals that elicit the more systematic reasoning style usually associated with negative moods.

In contrast to the preceding findings, mostly based on analytic reasoning tasks from the GRE, other studies revealed performance deficits under depressed affect across a variety of mathematics and complex logic tasks (for a review see Clore et al., 1994). Theoretically, mixed findings are to be expected for such tasks because none of the hypothesized processes will *necessarily* result in improved performance. For example, greater attention to detail per se will not improve performance if the application of an algorithm is needed to which the individual does not have access. Moreover, greater attention to detail may increase the risk that the individual gets sidetracked by irrelevant features. Similarly, the top-down processing strategies fostered by positive affective information may facilitate or impede performance, depending on whether the available heuristic is applicable to the current task. Hence, inconsistent results are to be expected in this domain. Nevertheless, performance on analytic reasoning tasks is likely to be facilitated by the detail-oriented processing style fostered by negative affective cues when the person has access to the relevant algorithm, making its systematic application to the details at hand the crucial feature of success. Under such conditions, an emotionally intelligent person may deliberately avoid positive moods, preferring instead the mildly negative moods that facilitate systematic processing.

BEYOND VALENCE: SPECIFIC EMOTIONS

To date, the influence of affective information on individuals' processing style has been primarily investigated by manipulating the global positive versus negative affective cues discussed so far. However, the feelings-as-information logic applies to specific emotions as well, although with some important constraints. These constraints derive from the nature of specific emotions (see DeSteno & Braverman, Chapter 8, this volume).

Theoretically, emotions are thought to reflect the ongoing, implicit appraisal of situations with respect to positive or negative implications for the individual's goals and concerns (e.g., Arnold, 1960). They have a specific referent (what we feel emotional about) and are usually characterized by a short rise time, high intensity, and limited duration. In contrast, the concept of mood refers to the feeling state itself when the object or cause is not the focus of attention. In fact, people are often unaware of the causes of their moods, which may include minor events (like finding a dime; e.g., Isen, 1987) as well as background variables like a lack of daylight or exercise (see Thayer, 1996). Hence, moods lack a specific referent and they usually come about gradually, are of low intensity, and may endure for some time (for a more detailed discussions of these conceptual distinctions, see Clore et al., 1994). We may therefore misread our moods as a response to a wide variety of contexts, which accounts for their pervasive influence. In contrast, we are usually aware of what we feel emotional about and are hence less likely to misread our emotions as a response to some unrelated stimulus (see Keltner, Locke, & Audrain, 1993, for experimental support).

Accordingly, a feelings-as-information analysis suggests that the influence of emotions is more specific than the influence of global moods in two ways: First, the influence of emotions is more likely to be limited to the specific emotion-eliciting event, whereas the influence of moods is likely to generalize to across many unrelated targets (e.g., Keltner et al., 1993). Second, the information provided by emotions is more specific than the information provided by moods. Theoretically, moods provide a global "benign" versus "problematic" signal, as discussed earlier. In contrast, the experience of an emotion signals that the specific appraisal pattern underlying the emotion has been met. For example, feeling angry does not merely tell us that "something" went wrong. Instead, it tells us that another person is responsible for what went wrong, because the appraisal pattern underlying anger entails the attribution of responsibility to an actor. If so, the specific appraisal pattern underlying a given emotion should allow us to understand which processing requirements are conveyed by this emotion, thus paving the way for an analysis of this emotion's likely influence on individuals' processing styles.

Several authors have recently pursued such an extension of the cognitive tuning assumptions (Schwarz, 1990) to specific emotions (Lerner & Keltner, 2000; Ragunathan & Pham, 1999; Tiedens & Linton, 2001), although the few available findings are limited to negative emotions. They converge on the conclusion that different negative emotions have different effects, which can be predicted on the basis of the underlying appraisal pattern. For example, Tiedens and Linton (2001) observed in a persuasion paradigm that sad individuals engaged in systematic message processing, whereas angry individuals did not. They suggested that this difference indicates that the appraisal pattern underlying sadness entails uncertainty, which triggers more extensive reasoning, whereas the appraisal pattern underlying anger does not.

Given these initial results, I am optimistic that detailed analyses of the processing requirements entailed in specific appraisal patterns will go a long way in specifying the impact of emotions on individuals' spontaneously adopted processing strategies. Whether a particular strategy facilitates or impedes performance on a given task will depend on the match or mismatch between the strategy and task characteristics, as seen in the preceding review.

CONCLUDING REMARKS

As this selective review indicates, our feelings can profoundly influence how we approach a reasoning task. Such influences can be conceptualized by considering the informative functions of feelings and environmental cues. When a sad mood, bodily avoidance feedback, or a negative environmental cue alerts us that our current situation may be problematic, we are likely to engage in the detail-oriented, bottom-up processing that is usually adaptive in handling problematic situations. Conversely, when a happy mood, bodily approach feedback, or a positive environmental cue informs us that the situation is benign, we are likely to rely on our usual routines that have served us well in the past. These effects are not observed when the informational value of our feelings for the task at hand is called into question. Moreover, the observed influence of feelings can be overridden by the individual's goals or explicit task demands. From this perspective, the influence of feelings on reasoning is best thought of as an element of situated cognition: Like many other elements of a given situation, our feelings inform us about the processing requirements we face—and our thought processes are tuned to meet these requirements.

ACKNOWLEDGMENT

Preparation of this chapter was supported through a fellowship from the Center for Advanced Study in the Behavioral Sciences, which is gratefully acknowledged.

REFERENCES

Allport, G. W. (1954). *The nature of prejudice.* Boston: MA: Addison-Wesley.

Arnold, M. B. (1960). *Emotion and personality.* New York: Columbia University Press.

Bless, H. (1997). *Stimmung und Denken* [Mood and reasoning]. Bern, Switzerland: Huber.

Bless, H., Bohner, G., Schwarz, N., & Strack, F. (1990). Mood and persuasion: A cognitive response analysis. *Personality and Social Psychology Bulletin, 16,* 331–345.

Bless, H., Clore, G. L., Schwarz, N., Golisano, V., Rabe, C., & Wölk, M. (1996). Mood and the use of scripts: Does being in a happy mood really lead to mindlessness? *Journal of Personality and Social Psychology, 71,* 665–679.

Bless, H., Mackie, D. M., & Schwarz, N. (1992). Mood effects on encoding and judgmental processes in persuasion. *Journal of Personality and Social Psychology, 63,* 585–595.

Bless, H., & Schwarz, N. (1999). Sufficient and necessary conditions in dual-process models: The case of mood and information processing. In S. Chaiken and Y. Trope (Eds.), *Dual process theories in social psychology* (pp. 423–440). New York: Guilford Press.

Bless, H., Schwarz, N., & Kemmelmeier, M. (1996). Mood and stereotyping: The impact of moods on the use of general knowledge structures. *European Review of Social Psychology, 7,* 63–93.

Bodenhausen, G. V. (1993). Emotions, arousal, and stereotypic judgments: A heuristic model of affect and stereotyping. In D. M. Makcie & D. L. Hamilton (Eds.), *Affect, cognition, and stereotyping* (pp. 13–37). San Diego, CA: Academic Press.

Bodenhausen, G. V., Kramer, G. P., & Süsser, K. (1994). Happiness and stereotypic thinking in social judgment. *Journal of Personality and Social Psychology, 66,* 621–632.

Bohner, G., Bless, H., Schwarz, N., & Strack, F. (1988). What triggers causal attributions? The impact of valence and subjective probability. *European Journal of Social Psychology, 18,* 335–345.

Bohner, G., Crow, K., Erb, H.-P., & Schwarz, N. (1992). Affect and persuasion: Mood effects on the processing of message content and context cues and on subsequent behavior. *European Journal of Social Psychology, 22,* 511–530.

Bower, G. H. (1981). Mood and memory. *American Psychologist, 36,* 129–148.

Brewer, M. B. (1988). A dual process model of impression formation. In T. K. Srull & R. S. Wyer (Eds.), *Advances in social cognition* (Vol. 1, pp. 1–36). Hillsdale, NJ: Erlbaum.

Broadbent, D. E. (1971). *Decision and stress.* London: Academic Press.

Bruner, J. S., Matter, J., & Papanek, M. L. (1955). Breadth of learning as a function of drive-level and maintenance. *Psychological Review, 62,* 1–10.

Cacioppo, J. T., Priester, J. R., & Berntson, G. G. (1993). Rudimentary determinants of attitudes: II. Arm flexion and extension have differential effects on attitudes. *Journal of Personality and Social Psychology, 65,* 5–17.

Chen, M., & Bargh, J. A. (1999). Consequences of automatic evaluations: Immediate behavioral predispositions to approach or avoid the stimulus. *Personality and Social Psychology Bulletin, 25,* 215–224.

Clore, G. L., Schwarz, N., & Conway, M. (1994). Affective causes and consequences of social information processing. In R. S. Wyer & T. K. Srull (Eds.), *Handbook of social cognition* (2nd ed., Vol. 1, pp. 323–418). Hillsdale, NJ: Erlbaum.

Duncker, K. (1945). On problem solving. *Psychological Monographs, 58*(5, Whole Issue, No. 270).

Eagly, A. H., & Chaiken, S. (1993). *The psychology of attitudes.* Fort Worth, TX: Harcourt Brace Jovanovich.

Easterbrook, J. A. (1959). The effect of emotion on cue utilization and the organization of behavior. *Psychological Review, 66,* 183–201.

Edwards, J. A., & Weary, G. (1993). Depression and the impression-formation continuum: Piecemeal processing despite the availability of category information. *Journal of Personality and Social Psychology, 64,* 636–645.

Ekstrom, R. B., French, J. W., Harman, H. H., & Dermen, D. (1976). *Manual for kit of factor-referenced cognitive tests.* Princeton, NJ: Educational Testing Service.

Ellis, H. C., & Ashbrook, P. W. (1988). Resource allocation model of the effects of depressed mood states on memory. In K. Fiedler & J. Forgas (Eds.), *Affect, cognition, and social behavior* (pp. 25–42). Toronto: C. J. Hogrefe.

Fiedler, K. (1988). Emotional mood, cognitive style, and behavior regulation. In K. Fiedler & J. Forgas (Eds.), *Affect, cognition, and social behavior* (pp. 100–119). Toronto: Hogrefe International.

Fiske, S. T., & Neuberg, S. L. (1990). A continuum of impression formation, from category-based to individuating processes: Influences of information and motivation on attention and interpretation. In M. P. Zanna (Ed.), *Advances in experimental social psychology* (Vol. 23, pp. 1–74). San Diego, CA: Academic Press.

Friedman, R. S., & Förster, J. (2000). The effects of approach and avoidance motor actions on the elements of creative insight. *Journal of Personality and Social Psychology, 79,* 477–492.

Frijda, N. H. (1988). The laws of emotion. *American Psychologist, 43,* 349–358.

Greene, T. R., & Noice, H. (1988). Influence of positive affect upon creative thinking and problem solving in children. *Psychological Reports, 63,* 895–898.

Hildebrand-Saints, L., & Weary, G. (1989). Depression and social information gathering. *Personality and Social Psychology Bulletin, 15,* 150–160.

Hirt, E. R., Levine, G. M., McDonald, H. E., Melton, R. J., & Martin, L. L. (1997). The role of mood in quantitative and qualitative aspects of performance: Single or multiple mechanisms? *Journal of Experimental Social Psychology, 33,* 602–629.

Isen, A. M. (1987). Positive affect, cognitive processes, and social behavior. In L. Berkowitz (Ed.), *Advances in experimental social psychology.* (Vol. 20, pp. 203–253). New York: Academic Press.

Isen, A. M., & Daubman, K. A. (1984). The influence of affect on categorization. *Journal of Personality and Social Psychology, 47,* 1206–1217.

Isen, A. M., Daubman, K. A., & Nowicki, G. P. (1987). Positive affect facilitates creative problem solving. *Journal of Personality and Social Psychology, 52,* 1122–1131.

Isen, A. M., Johnson, M. M. S., Mertz, E., & Robertson, G. F. (1985). The influence of positive affect on the unusualness of word associations. *Journal of Personality and Social Psychology, 48,* 1413–1426.

Jacobsen, E. (1957). Normal and pathological moods: Their nature and function. In R. S. Eisler, A. F. Freud, H. Hartman, & E. Kris (Eds.), *The psychoanalytic study of the child* (pp. 73–113). New York: International Universities Press.

James, W. (1890). *The principles of psychology* (Vol. 2). New York: Henry Holt.

Keltner, D., Locke, K. D., & Audrain, P. C. (1993). The influence of attributions on the relevance of negative feelings to satisfaction. *Personality and Social Psychology Bulletin, 19,* 21–30.

Lerner, J. S., & Keltner, D. (2000). Beyond valence: Toward a model of emotion-specific influences on judgment and choice. *Cognition and Emotion, 14,* 473–492.

Mackie, D. M., & Worth, L. T. (1989). Cognitive deficits and the mediation of positive affect in persuasion. *Journal of Personality and Social Psychology, 57,* 27–40.

Martin, L. L., & Clore, G. L. (Eds.) (2001). *Theories of mood and cognition: A user's guidebook.* Mahwah, NJ: Erlbaum.

Mayer, J. D., DiPaolo, M., & Salovey, P. (1990). Perceiving affective content in ambiguous visual stimuli—A component of emotional intelligence. *Journal of Personality Assessment, 54,* 772–781.

Mayer, J. D., Salovey, P., & Caruso, D. R. (in press). *Technical manual for the MS-CEIT V. 2. 0.* Toronto: MHS.

Mednick, S. T. (1962). The associative basis of the creative process. *Psychological Review, 69,* 220–232.

Melton, R. J. (1995). The role of positive affect in syllogism performance. *Personality and Social Psychology Bulletin, 21,* 788–794.

Nowlis, V., & Nowlis, H. H. (1956). The description and analysis of mood. *Annals of the New York Academy of Sciences, 65,* 345–355.

Ottati, V., Terkildsen, N., & Hubbard, C. (1997). Happy faces elicit heuristic processing in a televised impression formation task: A cognitive tuning account. *Personality and Social Psychology Bulletin, 23,* 1144–1156.

Petty, R., & Cacioppo, J. (1986). *Communication and persuasion: Central and peripheral routes to attitude change.* New York: Springer Verlag.

Priester, J. R., Cacioppo, J. T., & Petty, R. E. (1996). The influence of motor processes on attitudes toward novel versus familiar semantic stimuli. *Personality and Social Psychology Bulletin, 22,* 442–447.

Raghunathan, R., & Pham, M. T. (1999). All negative moods are not created equal: Motivational influences of anxiety and sadness on decision making. *Organizational Behavior and Human Decision Performance, 79,* 56–77.

Schank, R., & Abelson, R. (1977). *Scripts, plans, goals and understanding: An inquiry into human knowledge structures.* Hillsdale, NJ: Erlbaum.

Schwarz, N. (1990). Feelings as information: Informational and motivational functions of affective states. In E. T. Higgins & R. M. Sorrentino (Eds.), *Handbook of motivation and cognition: Foundations of social behavior* (Vol. 2, pp. 527–561). New York: Guilford Press.

Schwarz, N. (2001). Feelings as information: Implications for affective influences on information processing. In L. L. Martin & G. L. Clore (Eds.), *Theories of mood and cognition: A user's handbook* (pp. 159–176). Mahwah, NJ: Erlbaum.

Schwarz, N., Bless, H., & Bohner, G. (1991). Mood and persuasion: Affective states influence the processing of persuasive communications. In M. Zanna (Ed.), *Advances in Experimental Social Psychology* (Vol. 24, pp. 161–199). San Diego, CA: Academic Press.

Schwarz, N., & Clore, G. L. (1983). Mood, misattribution, and judgments of well-being: Informative and directive functions of affective states. *Journal of Personality and Social Psychology, 45,* 513–523.

Schwarz, N., & Clore, G. L. (1996). Feelings and phenomenal experiences. In E. T. Higgins & A. W. Kruglanski (Eds.), *Social psychology: Handbook of basic principles* (pp. 433–465). New York: Guilford Press.

Schwarz, N., & Skurnik, I. (in press). Feeling and thinking: Implications for problem solving. In J. Davidson & R. Sternberg (Eds.), *The nature of problem solving.* Cambridge, UK: Cambridge University Press.

Sinclair, R. C. (1988). Mood, categorization breadth, and performance appraisal: The effects of order of information acquisition and affective state on halo, accuracy, information retrieval, and evaluations. *Organizational Behavior and Human Decision Processes, 42,* 22–46.

Sinclair, R. C., & Mark, M. M. (1992). The influence of mood state on judgment and action: Effects on persuasion, categorization, social justice, person perception, and judgmental accuracy. In L. L. Martin & A. Tesser (Eds.), *The construction of social judgment* (pp. 165–193). Hillsdale, NJ: Erlbaum.

Sinclair, R. C., Mark, M. M., & Clore, G. L. (1994). Mood-related persuasion depends on misattributions. *Social Cognition, 12,* 309–326.

Sinclair, R. C., & Soldat, A. S. (2001). *Colors, smiles, and frowns: External affective cues can directly affect responses to persuasive communications in a mood-like manner without affecting mood.* Unpublished manuscript, University of Alberta.

Sinclair, R. C., Soldat, A. S., & Mark, M. M. (1998). Affective cues and processing strategy: Color coded forms influence performance. *Teaching of Psychology, 25,* 130–132.

Smith, E. R., & Semin, G. R. (2001). *The foundations of socially situated action: Socially situated cognition.* Unpublished manuscript, Department of Psychology, Purdue University, West Lafayette, IN.

Soldat, A. S., & Sinclair, R. C. (2001). *Colors, smiles, and frowns: External affective cues can directly affect responses to persuasive communications in a mood-like manner without affecting mood.* Unpublished manuscript, University of Alberta.

Soldat, A. S., Sinclair, R. C., & Mark, M. M. (1997). Color as an environmental processing cue: External affective cues can directly affect processing strategy without affecting mood. *Social Cognition, 15,* 55–71.

Thayer, R. E. (1996). *The origin of everyday moods.* New York: Oxford University Press.

Tiedens, L. Z., & Linton, S. (2001). Judgment under emotional certainty and uncertainty: The effects of specific emotions on information processing. *Journal of Personality and Social Psychology, 81,* 973–988.

Wegner, D. M., & Vallacher, R. R. (1986). Action identification. In R. M. Sorrentino & E. T. Higgins (Eds.), *Handbook of motivation and cognition: Foundations of social behavior.* New York: Guilford Press.

Wegener, D. T., Petty, R. E., & Smith, S. M. (1995). Positive mood can increase or decrease message scrutiny. *Journal of Personality and Social Psychology, 69,* 5–15.

Witkin, H. A., Oltman, P. K., Raskin, E., & Karp, S. A. (1971). *A manual for the embedded figures test.* Palo Alto, CA: Consulting Psychologist Press.

Worth, L. T., & Mackie, D. M. (1987). Cognitive mediation of positive mood in persuasion. *Social Cognition, 5,* 76–94.

Yeh, W., & Barsalou, L. W. (2000). *The situated nature of concepts.* Unpublished manuscript, Department of Psychology, Emory University, Atlanta, GA.

CHAPTER 7

Emotional Response Categorization as Emotionally Intelligent Behavior

PAULA M. NIEDENTHAL
NATHALIE DALLE
ANETTE ROHMANN

One sign of intelligence in humans and other species is the ability to group things in the world together and to call them or treat them as instances of the same category. Both the ability to learn categories at all and the use of categories in daily life are intelligent acts. The ability to learn categories demonstrates that individuals can distinguish similarities and differences between objects and events. And individuals separate out the wheat from the chaff; that is, they discriminate between those respects for similarity and difference that are useful from those that are not (e.g., Medin, Goldstone, & Gentner, 1993; Mervis & Rosch, 1981). For example, distinguishing mushrooms from flowers, and poisonous mushrooms from nonpoisonous ones, is useful, whereas distinguishing things that weigh more than 1,000 tons from things that weigh less than 1,000 tons is (for most people, most of the time) not useful, though it depends, certainly, on context. Moreover, in the learning of categories, individuals reveal that they can selectively attend effectively. Thus, even though certain things are orange in color, such as monarch butterflies, tiger lilies, and some cats, and the color orange is certainly attention getting, people do not typically learn and use the category "orange things" (even though they can construct that category if they are asked to do so, for instance, when playing the American television game show "Family Feud").

The reasons that the use of categories, once learned, is intelligent behavior have been outlined many times in relation to both object and social categories (e.g., Cantor & Michel, 1979). Categories provide individuals with a knowledge base from which to treat "new" objects or events as things about which something is already known, and this knowledge base substantially streamlines information processing. If one already possesses the category "brasserie," for example, then the next instance of this category that is encountered can, in a way, be ignored unless it is relevant to ones' present goals. Individuals do not need to stop and assess the importance and meaning of each object or person that they encounter. That is, to continue with the example of a brasserie, individuals do not have to ask themselves, "Can I have something to eat here?" Furthermore, categories provide the basis for induction (e.g., Gelman & Markman, 1987; Rips, 1975). Although individuals are sometimes wrong in their inductive reasoning in any given instance, more often than not they are right (if one considers all natural and artifactual categories). And being able to go beyond the information given helps them to avoid freezing in their tracks and trying to figure out what might happen next. Instead, they can take relatively informed action. Categories thus provide individuals with the basis of a flow of behavior, a sort of confidence that allows life to move seamlessly and even effortlessly along.

In this chapter we consider another way in which the learning and use of categories is intelligent. Specifically, we examine the intelligence of one of the bases on which categories are formed. Do things belong together because they share perceptually similar features? Or because the instances of the category all conform to a common theory? Both bases of categorization seem to exist (e.g., Murphy & Medin, 1985; Rosch, 1975). But the grounds for conceptual structure are more extensive than the two just suggested. Although perceptual similarity and theory are the most well known and most carefully researched types of conceptual coherence, Niedenthal and her colleagues (e.g., Niedenthal, Halberstadt, & Innes-Ker, 1999; Niedenthal & Halberstadt, 2000a, 2000b) have recently argued that individuals also ground categories in emotional response. Thus, sometimes, at least temporarily, objects, people, and events that elicit or have elicited the same emotions in an individual are grouped together and treated as the same kind of thing. The use of emotional response categories, we argue, reflects emotional intelligence.

Related to the construction of emotional response categories per se is the selective use of them. Using emotional response categories in all circumstances would be decidedly unintelligent. But most individuals, except perhaps those who suffer from certain kinds of clinical disorders, do not use such categories indiscriminately (Niedenthal et al., 1999). Emotional response categorization is most likely to occur during states of emotion, and, as we shall see, this is certainly functional. Finally, the organization, or structure, of emotional response categories is also important in the assessment of the intelligence of emotional response categorization. The possible ways in which emotional information is organized in memory are numerous. We argue that one particular structure is the most emotionally intelligent, given the general functions of categorization.

EMOTIONAL RESPONSE CATEGORIZATION: THEORY AND EVIDENCE

Emotional response categorization is the mental grouping together of objects and events that elicit the same emotion, and the treatment of those objects and events as "the same kind of thing." In laying out a theory of this behavior, Niedenthal and colleagues (1999) propose, first, that discrete emotions probably ground emotional response categories. Second, they argue that individuals substantially increase their reliance on emotional response equivalence in using categories when they are in an emotional state. That is, emotional response categorization is observed when individuals are experiencing emotional feelings. Third, they propose a mechanistic account of emotional response categorization. In particular, they suggest that during emotional states individuals selectively attend to emotional response information, clustering into groups those stimuli that are associated with the same emotional response.

The first assertion, that discrete emotions organize emotional categories, is based on already existing empirical evidence. Rather than being the specific subject of our reseach, this assertion largely guided the development of emotion manipulation procedures and the conceptual and perceptual stimuli (see Niedenthal & Setterlund, 1994; Halberstadt & Niedenthal, 1997; and Niedenthal et al., 1999, for details about the development of the materials). We discuss the idea that emotional response categories are grounded in discrete emotions, and why such categorization is intelligent behavior, in a later section. In the following two sections of this chapter we review recent empirical evidence for the second two assertions, that emotional states reorganize the conceptual space, creating links between diverse but emotionally equivalent ideas, and that this is due to selective attention to emotional responses to and aspects of stimuli.

Reorganization of Conceptual Space during Emotional States

In the current view, when individuals are experiencing emotional states, they tend to equate represented concepts and perceived objects on the basis of the emotional response that is associated with them in memory or evoked by them, respectively. In a series of empirical demonstrations of this process, Niedenthal and colleagues (1999) manipulated the emotional states of experimental participants and then gave them a chance to rely on taxonomic relations or emotional equivalence in performing a categorization task.

The categorization task was a triad task based on a technique developed by Gentner (1988). Individuals are presented with a series of trials in which they see first, a target concept. The target concept is associated (in a consensual way, although this is necessary only for efficiency in experimentation) with a discrete emotional response. Then the participants see two comparison concepts and indicate which of the two is most similar to the target. The comparison concepts are carefully chosen so that one shares only a taxonomic or associative relation to the target and is itself emotionally neutral. The other comparison concept is chosen so that it has no other relation to the target concept save the emotional response with which it is associated. For example, the target concept *ambulance,* which is consensually associated with sadness, may have been paired with the concept *unemployment* (emotionally related concept) and the concept *truck* (taxonomically related concept). The triads are developed so that neither comparison concept is ever named as most similar to the target more than 90% of the time by individuals in rather neutral emotional states.

In the first experiment (Niedenthal et al., 1999, Experiment 1), participants were exposed to happiness, sadness, or neutral emotion inductions (a between-participants manipulation in this and all subsequently described experiments) involving a combination of film and music. Participants then performed a triad task in which target concepts were happy or sad, as were the emotionally related comparison concepts. We call these "happy" and "sad" triads, respectively. Filler triads, in which all three concepts were rather neutral and shared other kinds of analogical relations (Gentner, 1988), were also included in the task in order to disguise the interest in emotion. For example, the target *hat* was paired with the concept *socks,* as a taxonomically related concept, and *roof,* which shares an anological-relational similarity to the target. Pretesting had shown that the Gentner (1988) triads were largely composed of neutral concepts. As illustrated in Figure 7.1, participants in the emotions conditions relied on emotional equivalence in their groupings significantly more than did participants in the neutral condi-

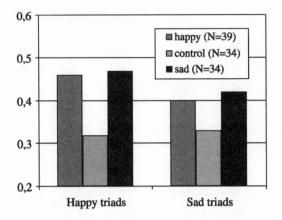

FIGURE 7.1. Percent of happy and sad triad trials on which the emotion concept was judged as most similar to the target concept by participants in happy,
control, and sad emotion induction conditions. Adapted from Niedenthal, Halberstadt, and Innes-Ker (1999, Experiment 1). Copyright 1999 by the American
Psychological Association. Adapted by permission.

tion. Specifically, individuals in the happy and the sad conditions were
more likely than those in the neutral control condition to group together *puppy* and *parade* as most similar to each other than they were to
group together *puppy* and *beetle*. Individuals in the happy and sad conditions were also more likely than those in the neutral control condition
to group *graver digger* with *breakup* rather than with *lumberjack*. A second
experiment (Niedenthal et al., 1999, Experiment 3) generalized the
basic effect to the emotion of fear and to triads that included concepts
related to fear. In that experiment, participants viewed films and listened to music designed to induce fear, sadness, or neutral emotion.
All participants then performed a triad task that included sad and fear
triads, as well as the neutral filler triads. The pattern of findings looked
exactly like that of the first experiment, in that individuals experiencing
emotions grouped together concepts on the basis of emotional equivalence significantly more than did participants experiencing neutral
feelings.

The two experiments described thus far seem to provide good evidence that, consistent with the second assertion of the theory of emotional response categorization, during emotional states conceptual relations are temporarily organized around emotion categories. Concepts
and stimuli appear to go together because they are associated with the
same emotional response, rather than because of other taxonomic or

associative relations. Still, there are several questions that arise from critical consideration of these methods and findings. We examine some of these questions next, in turn.

One Big Emotion Category?

The first question is, does the behavior observed by Niedenthal et al. (1999) have anything to do with discrete categories of emotional response? The triads that composed the triad task in the experiments just described were constructed so that only emotional groupings around specific emotions—happy things with other happy things, or sad things with other sad things—were technically possible. But it could be that all concepts that were emotional (or arousing), regardless of whether they were related to the same discrete emotion, would have been grouped together as similar by individuals experiencing emotional states. Perhaps during emotional states individuals group emotional objects, events, and people into one big (rather unuseful and messy) emotion category.

This question was addressed in a third experiment (Niedenthal et al., 1999, Experiment 2) in which the targets in some triads were associated with one emotion (e.g., happiness) and the emotional comparison concept was associated with an entirely different emotion (e.g., sadness). For example, *kiss* (a concept associated with happiness) may have been paired with *handshake* (a taxonomically related concept) and *ambulance* (a concept associated with sadness). If individuals grouped the emotional comparison concept with the target when considering these "mixed" triads, they would be ignoring the specific type of emotion and just be using a category of "emotional things." Participants in the experiment were again assigned to conditions in which either happiness, sadness, or neutral emotion was induced, and they then completed the modified triad task. This time analyses revealed no effect of emotion condition. That is, individuals in states of happiness and sadness were no more likely than those in a neutral state to group a happy thing with a sad one. And the incidence of such groupings was, in any event, very low. It seems that individuals were intelligent enough to focus on the similarity between the concept of *beach* and *valley* rather than *beach* and *poverty* (Niedenthal et al., 1999). Of course, the results of the study suggest that individuals in emotional states do not use one big emotion category to organize their world when they are experiencing strong emotions. They do not, however, provide unequivocal evidence that participants in the initial experiments were in fact using discrete emotion categories as opposed to other more subordinate or superordinate emotion-based categories. This latter issue should be addressed in future research.

Emotions or Emotion Knowledge?

A second question that arises from the findings of Niedenthal and colleagues (1999) is whether this categorization behavior is caused by the actual experience of emotional feelings. In the experiments just described, the experimental strategy involved inducing emotional states in the first part of a "multipart study" and then, in a second, engaging the participant in the triad task. In interpreting the effects of emotion on categorization, we worry about a nagging alternative: Perhaps the effect is not due to emotions at all, but rather to semantic emotion concepts, that is, declarative knowledge about emotions, activated directly by the content of the induction procedure or self-activated by the attributional processes of the experimental participant (Clore et al., 2001; Wyer & Carlston, 1979).

Research by Innes-Ker and Niedenthal (in press) was recently conducted to test this possibility. The research took the following course: First, a sentence unscrambling task was developed that contained a series of five-word sets. Four words in each set could be organized into a phrase related to happiness (e.g., "the audience was ecstatic," "she shouted with exuberance," "a long pleasure cruise"), sadness (e.g., " the man felt lonely," "she had strong regrets"), or a neutral idea for the control set. There were 30 emotional sentences and 15 filler sentences in each version of the task, and each version was designed to prime only one emotion concept (happiness, sadness, or neutral). Sentence unscrambling tasks have been employed successfully to activate concepts such as kindness and hostility (Srull & Wyer, 1979), gender stereotypes (Banaji, Hardin, & Rothman, 1993), and stereotypes of the elderly (Bargh, Chen, & Burrows, 1996; Dijksterhuis et al., 1998; Stapel, Koomen, & Van der Plight, 1996).

A pilot study was then conducted to investigate the effects of the sentence unscrambling task on emotional state. In the study, participants unscrambled one version of the task and then completed a measure of current emotional state. This pilot study showed that there was no effect of unscrambling sentences about happiness or sadness on emotional state, as would be predicted by many hierarchical theories of emotion processing (e.g., Buck, 1985; Leventhal & Scherer, 1987; see Niedenthal, Rohmann, & Dalle, 2002, for discussion). A second pilot study was also conducted in which semantic priming due to the sentence task was observed. Specifically, participants unscrambled either happy, sad, or neutral sentences and then performed a lexical decision task. In a lexical decision task, letter strings are presented on a computer screen and the individual must indicate as quickly as possible if the string forms a real word or not. Prior processing of a related concept or word will facilitate a "word" judgment. In the present task the words were related to happiness, sadness, or neutral ideas (but were not contained in any sentences in any version of the sentence unscrambling task). As expected, participants who had unscrambled happy sentences made lexical decisions about happy words faster than other participants. And those who had unscrambled sad sentences made lexical decisions about sad words faster than other participants. These results provide evidence that the unscrambling task primed the semantic category of interest.

Consequently, a larger-scale experiment was conducted to examine the influence of exposure to the sentences, and thus the priming of emotion concepts, on emotional response categorization (Innes-Ker & Niedenthal, in press, Experiment 2). In that experiment individuals were exposed either to the sentence unscrambling task (happy, sad, or neutral) or to a typical emotion induction involving the use of films and music (happy, sad, or neutral). They then performed a triad task that contained happy and sad triads. The results of the experiment are illustrated in Figure 7.2. As can be seen, in the emotion induction conditions, Innes-Ker and Niedenthal (in press) replicated the original Niedenthal et al. (1999) Experiment 1. Specifically, individuals in happy and sad

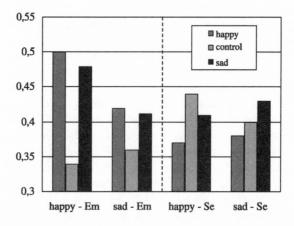

FIGURE 7.2. Percent of happy and sad triad trials, in the films/music emotion induction conditions (Em) and the sentences conditions (Se), on which the target concept was judged as most similar to the emotion concept.

emotional states used emotional response categorization to a significantly greater degree than did individuals in a neutral state. This finding did not, however, extend to the sentence unscrambling conditions. Individuals who had unscrambled sentences that primed semantic concepts of happiness and sadness did not use emotional categorization more often than did individuals who had unscrambled neutral sentences.

The result just described is consistent with that of an experiment reported by Niedenthal et al. (1999), which also tried to address the possibility that the activation of semantic emotion knowledge during an emotion induction is the mechanism responsible for emotional response categorization. In that study, participants were exposed to happy, sad, and neutral films, but half of the participants in each condition were prevented from experiencing emotional reactions to the films. Emotional reactions were short-circuited, as verified by a manipulation check of emotional state, by means of a processing goal (e.g., Blascovich et al., 1993). The processing goal was to count in their heads the number of times the camera changed point of view within each film segment. The idea of the processing goal was that individuals were exposed to the semantic content of the movies, and thus ideas about or associated with emotions, without that exposure being accompanied by emotional feelings.

After seeing happy, sad, or neutral films either with this goal, or with no goal, all participants performed a triad task that contained happy and neutral triads. Participants in the films/music conditions organized the available concepts into emotional response (e.g., happy) categories rather than taxonomic or associative (but nonemotional) categories significantly more often than did participants in the neutral condition. In contrast, in the goal conditions, no differences in the categorizations of participants who had viewed the happy, sad, and neutral films were observed. Thus, simple exposure to the content of films that typically elicit strong feelings of happiness or sadness did not enhance the likelihood that individuals categorize according to emotional response.[1]

---

[1]It is important to note that it could not be claimed that participants who watched the films with a processing goal failed to process the content of the emotional films. A follow-up study demonstrated that participants with and without the processing goal recalled the details of the content of the films with equal accuracy. In addition, there were no differences in participants' ratings of the emotional tone of the films or of the emotions likely to be evoked in viewers of the films. On the other hand, participants who watched the films with the processing goal did not experience the same emotional reactions as did the participants with no processing goal. In fact, in the goal conditions there were no differences in self-reported emotional state of the happy, sad, and neutral films. Thus, goal condition participants showed a clear grasp of the story, and they knew that the films were emotional and would induce certain emotions in a viewer, but they did not themselves feel those emotions after having viewed the films.

Together the two studies just described seem to suggest, therefore, that emotional response categorization is caused by, or at least requires the presence of, emotional feelings. The mere activation of semantic knowledge about a single discrete emotion does not cause the behavior.

Selective Attention to the Emotional Features of Objects

The third assertion of the theory of emotional response categorization is that the phenomenon relies on the mechanism of selective attention. Specifically, along with their perceptual features and conceptual associations, objects and events are represented in terms of the emotional responses they have evoked. Perceivers, however, can attend to this aspect of objects and events to a greater or lesser extent. And they can attend to emotional responses more or less than to other, nonemotional, aspects of a stimulus or stimulus representation. When perceivers selectively attend to emotional responses to objects, persons, and events, they then tend to accord greater weight to the responses in categorization (e.g., Kruschke, 1992; Medin & Schaffer, 1978; Nosofsky, 1986, 1992; Smith, 1989; Smith & Zarate, 1992).

There is already a good deal of evidence that emotional, particularly negative, stimuli attract attention and that this effect is more marked among individuals in chronic emotional states. Negative words categorically interfere with processing in a Stroop task (Pratto & John, 1991), and there are other interactions between emotion traits such as anxiety and phobia and the emotional nature of stimuli in such experiments (see Derryberry & Tucker, 1994; Hope, Rapee, Heimberg, & Dombeck, 1990; Mogg, Mathews, & Weinman, 1989; Watts, McKenna, Sharrock, & Trezise, 1986). For example, MacLeod, Mathews, and Tata (1986) instructed participants to monitor a computer screen for a small dot, which sometimes appeared on the screen following the appearance of a threat or a neutral word. Individuals who suffered from anxiety detected the dot faster when it replaced a threat word than when it replaced a neutral word. This was not observed among nonanxious or depressed individuals. During states of anxiety, attention is allocated to objects that match the perceiver's current affective state in emotional tone. The research is important because the tasks employed require neutral responses to neutral stimuli, which eliminates response bias as an alternative account of the findings (Dalgleish & Watts, 1990).

Thus, it appears that individuals, particularly those in emotional states, attend to emotion-eliciting stimuli and features of such stimuli. However, allocating attention to emotional response information does not necessarily guarantee that this information will be overweighted in, or even used in, judgment. An individual may orient attention to emotional information or the emotional aspect of a stimulus without using the information or aspect in judgment at all. If the changes in categorization demonstrated in the triad studies are due to selective attention, individuals must not only be orienting attention toward emotional information, but also giving greater weight to the information in judgment.

In a series of studies, Halberstadt and Niedenthal (1997) used individual difference multidimensional scaling (INDSCAL; Carroll & Chang, 1970) to evaluate the use of emotional information in similarity judgments. The goal of the general multidimensional scaling (MDS) model is to reveal a latent psychological structure in a set of stimuli by maximizing the correspondence between paired similarity judgments and interstimulus distances in a multidimensional space. The INDSCAL model also allows for the evaluation of individual differences in the extent to which each dimension is weighted in judgment by each participant in the experiment. The differences are represented as perceiver-specific weights that are applied to the overall stimulus space based on the entire sample group. The weights distort the group space, stretching or shrinking it to correspond to each perceiver's idiosyncratic use of the stimulus dimensions (see Arabie, Carroll, & DeSarbo, 1987, for more details).

Evaluation of a selective attention account of emotional response categorization can be accomplished with INSCAL because the dimension weights in the model represent the use of specific stimulus dimensions, and not merely the allocation of attention to those dimensions. If during emotional states perceivers attend to and use emotional responses to the experimental stimuli in judgment, and at the same time they ignore other, nonemotion-related features, this should be revealed in the dimension weights output by an INDSCAL model of their similarity judgments. Specifically, an interaction between the dimensions output by the model and the emotional state of the perceiver is predicted, such that people in emotional states weight emotion-related aspects of the stimuli more heavily, and nonemotional aspects (e.g., gender) less heavily, than control participants. This interaction would reflect the distortion of psychological space into emotional response-based categories.

Halberstadt and Niedenthal (1997) used this MDS approach to test the selective attention account of emotional response categorization. The stimuli were photographs of the faces of male and female actors expressing happiness and sadness. In an initial study, 10 faces were used, and each appeared twice in the stimulus set, once expressing happiness and once expressing sadness. Emotionally expressive faces were used because emotional expressions are strongly associated with specific

emotional responses and have, in fact, been shown to produce these responses in the perceiver through processes of mimicry and contagion
(e.g., Hatfield, Cacioppo, & Rapson, 1993; Haviland & Lelwica, 1987).
The procedure involved an emotion induction with the use of selections of classical music. Participants then judged the similarity between
every pair of the stimulus faces on continuous scales.

    Similarity judgments were analyzed using a three-dimensional
INDSCAL model. Unsurprisingly, the two dimensions that accounted
for the most variance were the explicitly manipulated dimensions of
emotional expression and gender. The third dimension appeared to be
"head orientation," although an exact interpretation of it was not necessary. In an analysis of the weighting of the three dimensions in the
different emotion conditions, dimension use indeed interacted with
emotional state. Consistent with the findings of the triad experiments,
both happy and sad participants weighted emotional expressions more
heavily, and the other two dimensions less heavily, in their judgments of
similarity than did the neutral participants. And the happy and sad
groups did not differ from each other. The results were also replicated
in two additional studies (Halberstadt & Niedenthal, 1997, Experiments 1 and 2). The result is illustrated in Figure 7.3.

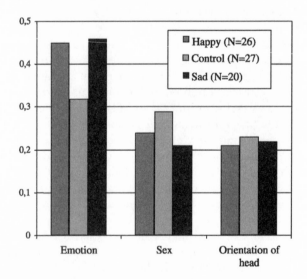

FIGURE 7.3. Attention weights revealed by the scaling of judgments of similar-
ity between pairs of faces by happy, sad, and neutral condition participants.
Adapted from Halberstadt and Niedenthal (1997). Copyright 1997 by the
American Psychological Association. Adapted by permission.

The similarity data from the MDS studies thus support and extend the interpretation of the triad experiments. Just as happy and sad people rated emotionally equivalent concepts as more similar in the triad task, they also rated pairs of faces that expressed the same emotion as more similar in paired similarity rating. More important, the MDS analyses provide direct evidence for the process of selective attention that is proposed to produce these differences. People in emotional states weighted the stimulus information, basing their judgments more on emotional expressions, and less on other, nonemotion-related aspects of the faces, than nonemotional perceivers. The similarity ratings confirmed that the differences in dimension use translated into clustering of same-emotion stimuli, in what we have termed "emotional response categories."

A General Emotions Effect or Emotion Congruence?

A final question raised by the initial demonstrations of emotional response categorization, and explorations into the underlying mechanism, concerns the symmetry of the effect across emotional stimuli for individuals in a specific emotional state. That is, why do experimental participants in sad states use happy categories and weight happy information in judgment to the same degree as people in happy states? And why do people in happy states use sad categories and weight sad information in judgment to the same degree as people in sad states? After all, many studies of emotion–cognition interactions demonstrate an emotion congruence effect whereby an emotional state causes privileged processing (usually facilitated processing) of emotion-congruent information.

In fact, the strongest demonstrations of emotion-congruent processing rely on tasks that were designed to measure automatic spread of activation, such as the lexical decision task in which individuals must decide whether a target set of letters is actually a real word (e.g., Niedenthal & Setterlund, 1994). Priming due to passive spread of activation is a well-documented effect, and certain tasks, such as lexical decision and word naming, are particularly appropriate for assessing it (Meyer & Schvaneveldt, 1971; Neely, 1976, 1977). Some social psychologists also assess priming with tasks in which exposure to priming stimuli occurs in one task and spread of activation is measured in a second. Often the second involves the presentation of an ambiguous stimulus and the measurement of the use of the primed concept in the interpretation of that ambiguous stimulus (e.g., Bargh & Pietromonaco, 1982; Devine, 1989; Stapel et al., 1996).

Neither the triad task nor the similarity task, as used in the research reported here, tests the mechanism of spreading activation. As we have argued, these tasks appear to assess selective attention. Selective attention is at least sometimes under conscious control. In addition, by most accounts, selective attention to a dimension that characterizes stimuli (e.g., color, size)—due, for instance, to prior training or sensitization—is assumed to be spread over the entire dimension, not just a portion of it. So, if attention is directed to color, this means that all colors are attended to more than other possible stimulus features, such as size. The result of attention to a particular dimension is to increase the discriminability of stimuli in terms of that entire dimension and to decrease discriminability on other, relatively unattended dimensions. Thus, stimuli with similar values on the attended-to aspect appear more similar overall, whereas stimuli with discrepant values appear relatively dissimilar.

It is important to note that both automatic spread of activation to emotion-congruent concepts and selective attention to emotional stimuli (from all categories of emotional response) can operate during emotional states and may influence some aspects of performance on categorization tasks. For example, it may be the case that once the stimulus or concept is encoded, selective attention to the emotional aspect of the concept or stimulus, regardless of its correspondence to the currently experienced emotional state, occurs. On the other hand, the "once encoded" part is important. It is reasonable to predict that during sad states, individuals actually encode sad concepts or perceived stimuli for use in a comparative judgment more efficiently than do individuals in happy states. Similarly, during happy states individuals may actually encode happy concepts or perceived stimuli for use in a comparative judgment more efficiently than do individuals in sad states. Thus, for instance, if the triad task were completed under time pressure, an emotion congruence effect of emotional response categorization might well be observed. That is, individuals in happy states may have the time to selectively prefer emotional equivalence when processing happy triads, but not show this same preference when processing sad triads. Similarly, individuals in sad states may have the time to selectively use emotional equivalence when evaluating sad triads, but not happy ones. This hypothesis is the subject of ongoing research by Innes-Ker, Dalle, and Niedenthal.

Generalization to Naturally Induced Emotions and French Concepts

The emotional response categorization initially observed by Niedenthal and colleagues (1999) was recently generalized in two ways. First, both films for emotion induction and triad stimuli were developed for use in

France. Unsurprisingly, the things that make American and French people feel happy and sad are not exactly the same things. When we used subtitled American film comedies to induce happiness in French people, we failed miserably. On the other hand, when French students watched film clips of the celebration on the Champs-Elyseés after the French national soccer team won the World Cup championship in 1998, all individuals—even those with no particular interest in soccer—became extremely happy. (Of course, other Francophones, such as Belgians, became decidedly unhappy when forced to remember this event). Similarly, when we used the triad task developed in the United States with French experimental participants, we discovered that our concepts were not classified correctly for French individuals. Parades in France, for instance, do not traditionally involve floats and candy for children. And, perhaps consequently, parades are not associated with joy. Although one of us (P. N.) can recall Fourth of July parades in small Wisconsin towns in which she rode on 4-H floats and picked up candy that was thrown by passing clowns, her graduate students in France have no such memories. They recall *défilés* on military holidays in which aging men who served in one of the two world wars paraded through the streets wearing their uniforms and holding long-unused guns. And they recall this rather dryly. For French people, therefore, the use of the concept *parade* as one associated with joy would be a grave error. Table 7.1 lists examples of triads developed for use in France. Of course, these may also make sense to Americans. However, it was not the case that the concepts developed by Niedenthal and colleagues (1999) for American participants would be similarly responded to by French participants.

Two studies have been completed with the materials developed in France. First, the general effect of emotional response categorization was replicated in the laboratory (Dalle & Niedenthal, in press). As in Niedenthal and colleagues' (1999) Experiment 1, experimental participants were brought into the laboratory and randomly assigned to re-

TABLE 7.1. Examples of Happy and Sad Triads

Happy triads
   . . . **bébé:** vacances, bourgeon (*baby: vacation, bud*)
   . . . **Noël:** câlin, Pentcôte (*Christmas: cuddle, Pentacost*)
   . . . **champagne:** liberté, fontaine (*champaign: freedom, fountain*)

Sad triads
   . . . **ambulance:** chômage, camion (*ambulance: unemployment, truck*)
   . . . **sanglot:** Alzheimer, rivière (*tear: Alzheimer's, river*)
   . . . **cercueil:** défaite, boîte (*coffin: defeat, box*)

Note. English translations are in *italics.* The target concept is presented in **bold,** followed by the emotionally related and then the semantically related concepts.

ceive happy, sad, or neutral film/music emotion inductions. Following the inductions, they completed a triad task that was composed of happy, sad, and neutral filler triads. A manipulation check of emotional state showed that participants performed the triad task during the desired states. It is important to note that analysis of responses on the triad task replicated the previous findings exactly. Individuals assigned to emotion conditions used emotional equivalence significantly more than did individuals in the neutral condition.

Once the stimuli had been developed and the basic laboratory finding replicated, other generalizations and extensions of the work were possible. For example, an implication of the laboratory research by Niedenthal and colleagues (1999) is that people who are feeling strong emotional states due to naturally occurring events in their lives actually organize their perceptual and conceptual worlds differently from those who are feeling relatively neutral. For example, people feeling naturally induced states of fear should perceive equivalences among objects that evoke the same emotion to a much greater degree than normal. A quasi-experimental field study was designed to test just this implication, and it examined, in particular, the emotion of happiness (Niedenthal & Dalle, 2001). There are a number of social situations in which, a researcher can be pretty sure, the majority of the individuals present will be feeling a strong discrete emotion, with relatively small variability. The social situation that Niedenthal and Dalle chose was weddings. At weddings, at least in France, the invitees are typically very happy. The receptions are most often big celebrative affairs that last, if not all night, at least until the wee hours of the morning. In fact, if invitees leave before 4:00 or 5:00 A.M., the bride and groom may consider their reception to have been a failure. Thus, right after the ceremony itself, the invitees are in a very good mood in anticipation of a great fête. In the field study, experimenters intervened after the ceremony (and before the invitees had begun to drink) and asked individuals to complete a triads questionnaire that included happy and sad triads, as well as neutral filler triads that were direct translations of those used in previous research. Individuals were then asked to fill out a mood scale (which was a translated version of the Brief Mood Introspection Scale; Mayer & Gaschke, 1988).

For a control condition, other individuals were approached as they walked in the street by the university with which Dalle and Niedenthal are affiliated, on a day that was not remarkable in terms of weather, news, or other events. These individuals also completed the triads questionnaire and the mood scale. The wedding invitees were very happy, whereas the individuals in the street were feeling, on average, rather neutral. When responses to the triad task were examined, the emotional response categorization effect was observed. As can be seen in Figure 7.4, individuals at the wedding also showed a significantly greater use of emotional equivalence in categorization than did neutral-feeling passersby around the university (both, it should be noted, represented approximately the same age group and gender distribution; see Niedenthal and Dalle, 2001).

The foregoing sections of this chapter presented experimental findings that together demonstrate that during emotional states individuals selectively attend to emotional response information and in so doing create categories of things that belong together because they elicit the same emotion. The recent research conducted in French, and in the field in France, suggests that emotional response categorization is a robust phenomenon that is observed not only inside the laboratory, but also outside the laboratory and outside the United States. In the next section we make a case for the utility of emotional response categorization for a full account of emotional intelligence.

EMOTIONAL CATEGORIZATION AND INTELLIGENCE

Emotional intelligence has been defined as "the ability to process emotion-laden information competently and to use it to guide cognitive activities like problem-solving and to focus energy on required behaviors" (Salovey, Mayer, and Caruso, 2002). More specifically, Mayer and

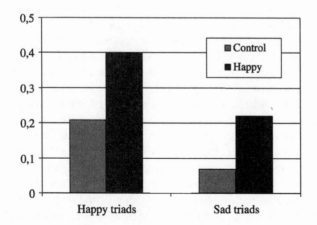

FIGURE 7.4. Percentage of trials on which emotional concepts were selected as most similar to the target concept by happy wedding goers and neutral-mood control participants for happy and sad critical triads.

Salovey (1997) distinguish four different branches of emotional intelligence: perceiving and expressing emotion, assimilating emotion in thought, understanding emotions, and reflectively regulating emotions. How does emotional response categorization fit here? Is emotional response categorization emotionally intelligent behavior? Does it make sense to group things together that evoke the same emotional response, or is it slightly crazy and maladaptive?

Hahn and Chater (1997) recently noted that "a hypothetical concept 'drib' which grouped together a particular lightbulb, Polly the pet parrot, the English channel and the ozone layer would seem to be a useless, and highly bizarre concept precisely because the items it groups together are not at all similar" (p. 43). If Hahn and Chater think that the proposed drib is too bizarre to exist, then what about a category, proposed by Niedenthal and Dalle (2001), that grouped together "one's grandmother's house, Easter dinners, kittens, and summer evening rain showers, because these objects and events all elicit the same feelings of joy"? Is the latter emotional response category too bizarre to exist? Or, to turn the reasoning on its head, would it clearly indicate bizarreness if the category did exist?

We do not think so. We argue that the use of emotional response categories, during emotional states, according to the discrete emotions, and by individuals who do not suffer from affective disorders, is emotionally intelligent behavior. And its use under these conditions is emotionally intelligent for several reasons. First, as demonstrated in the previous section of this chapter, when in a state of emotion, individuals selectively attend to emotional response information (Halberstadt & Niedenthal, 1997). This process supports the identification of emotional reactions in the self and emotional features in the environment, a skill that is related to the first branch, perceiving and expressing emotions, of Mayer and Salovey's (1997) framework. Furthermore, because individuals are often unaware of the source of their own and others' emotions, the onset of an emotion can prompt a search for its cause. It would be useful, particularly in an ambiguous situation, for stimuli to be mentally grouped together according to the emotional responses they elicit, so that the source of an emotional state can be more readily determined. By sorting the environment into categories of things that elicit sadness, happiness, fear, anger, and so on, individuals who are feeling sad, for example, can more easily explain their emotional state by focusing their search on candidate stimuli. In this way, emotional response categorization supports the making of fine distinctions among emotional stimuli and emotional responses. In addition, by sorting stimuli into emotion categories, sad people can also better differentiate their present state from contrasting emotional states, as well as differentiating the stimuli that will be useful for dealing or coping with the emotion from those that will only make it worse (see also Frijda, 1986, 1993).

Some support for this latter idea was reported by Derryberry (1989, 1993). In his research, Derryberry (1993) found emotion-congruence effects in an attention task such that success and failure motivated attention to spatial locations associated with positive and negative values, respectively. In addition, however, he also observed emotion incongruent processing whereby failure feedback increased attention to positive cues and success feedback increased attention to negative cues (Derryberry, 1989). Derryberry and Tucker (1994, p. 175) note: "By promoting both kinds of complementary influences, the motivational state can promote more balanced and flexible processing. The individual is prepared for improving as well as deteriorating conditions." Of course, it is the emotionally intelligent individual who is thus prepared and attending to the emotional significance of different stimuli.

The foregoing analysis suggests that emotional response categorization is also related to the fourth branch, emotion regulation, of Mayer and Salovey's (1997) framework for emotional intelligence. In responding with an empathic emotion to another individual's plight, a perceiver not only identifies the emotion and distinguishes it from others, but can also make use of his or her emotional response categories in taking regulatory action. First, the perceiver will be able to see the person's predicament in terms of emotionally related situations, situations that have perhaps no other basis of similarity other than their associated emotion and would normally not be seen as similar to the person's predicament. Second, such a categorization will highlight the specific action to take to deal with and regulate the emotion (Izard, 1977; Plutchik, 1984; Tomkins, 1962, 1963). Even if the perceiver has never been in this precise situation before, the action that should be taken will be similar to actions successfully taken in past situations in which the same emotional was experienced.

The suggested adaptive behavior function of emotional response categorization is particularly plausible if emotional categories of emotionally intelligent individuals are organized around discrete emotions. To be useful in supporting action, categories must be general enough to permit abstraction to new instances, yet specific enough to provide accurate information about how to respond to those instances (Malt, 1995; Rosch, 1975). The most useful level of categorization can vary, of course, depending on characteristics of the person and the situation. For example, classifying a transport vehicle as a *truck* may be adequate if one is deciding what to buy for a toddler for his birthday, whereas this categorization is insufficient if one is renting a vehicle from a local moving company (Niedenthal & Cantor, 1984). A functional classification must provide information relevant to the context in which the person and stimulus interact. In the case of emotional response categories, the appropriate organizational level is likely to be around the discrete emotions. It would seem less useful for all stimuli that arouse negative emotion, for example, to be classified in terms of their general negativity, even if they arguably require a core behavioral response (e.g., "avoidance"; Davidson, 1992; Davidson & Tomarken, 1989). This categorization is simply not useful enough. The behavioral implications of the stimuli that cause fear, for example, are quite different from those that cause anger, sadness, or disgust (e.g., Frijda, 1986; Izard, 1977; Plutchik, 1984; Tomkins, 1962, 1963). Thus, in terms of the role of emotional response categories in problem solving, and specifically in regulating the emotional state of the self or another person, an organization of concepts by discrete emotions is likely to be the most adaptive.

In sum, the use of emotional response categorization seems to be intimately connected to the concept of emotional intlligence. There may well be variability across individuals in their tendency to rely on emotional categorization during emotional states. Those who can and do should manage taxing social interactions more smoothy. First, the emotional expression of the person(s) present in the interaction will be more easily recognized and isolated. Second, because of the accessibility of memories of situations associated with the same emotional response, an individual will find examples from his or her own life to share, thereby displaying empathy, a skill that has been shown to be correlated with emotional intelligence (Mayer, Caruso, & Salovey, 2000). And finally, access to those emotionally related experiences will provide the basis for adaptive action to take in the service of regulating the emotional experience of the other individual(s).

CONCLUSION

In this chapter we reviewed a program of research indicating that during emotional states, individuals are more likely to form categories around discrete emotions such as sadness, happiness and fear, than when they are feeling more neutral. Conceptual relations seem to change at those times such that other sorts of connections are deemphasized. We also provided some evidence that emotional response categorization is due to changes in selective attention to stimuli and features of stimuli. Emotional states seem to be associated with greater attention to emotional stimuli and features. When example emotional response categories are considered, at first pass one might consider such categories to be rather crazy or at least unintelligent. We have argued that emotional response categorization is intelligent. Things that evoke the same emotion typically require similar types of behavioral responses. They often have similar meaning with regard to the individuals' goals. So, at least during the emotional state, the reorganization of the conceptual space into discrete emotion categories is a smart thing to do. In the spirit of the present volume, we would argue that it is an emotionally intelligent thing to do.

ACKNOWLEDGMENT

Preparation of this chapter was supported by a Programme Cognitique–2000 grant from the Minister of Research and Technology, France.

REFERENCES

Arabie, P., Carroll, J. D., & DeSarbo, W. S. (1987). *Three-way scaling and clustering.* Beverly Hills, CA: Sage.

Banaji, M. R., Hardin, C., & Rothman, A. J. (1993). Implicit stereotyping in person judgment. *Journal of Personality and Social Psychology, 65,* 272–281.

Bargh, J. A., Chen, M., & Burrows, L. (1996). Automaticity of social behavior: Direct effects of trait construct and stereotype activation on action. *Journal of Personality and Social Psychology, 71,* 230–244.

Bargh, J. A., & Pietromonaco, P. (1982). Automatic information processing and social perception: The influence of trait information presented outside of conscious awareness on impression formation. *Journal of Personality and Social Psychology, 43,* 437–449.

Blascovich, J., Ernst, J. M., Tomaka, J., Kelsey, R. M., Salomon, K. L., & Fazio, R. H. (1993). Attitude accessibility as a moderator of autonomic reactivity during decision making. *Journal of Personality and Social Psychology, 64,* 165–176.

Buck, R. (1985). Prime theory: An integrated view of motivation and emotion. *Psychological Review, 92,* 389–413.

Cantor, N., & Michel, W. (1979). Prototypes in person perception. In L. Berkowitz (Ed.), *Advances in experimental social psychology* (Vol. 12). New York: Academic Press.

Carroll, J. D., & Chang, J. J. (1970). Analysis of individual differences in multidimensional scaling via an N-way generalization of Eckart-Young decomposition. *Psychometrika, 35,* 283–319.

Clore, G. L., Wyer, R. S., Dienes, B., Gasper, K., Gohm, C., & Isbell, L. (2001). Affective feelings as feedback: Some cognitive consequences. In L. L. Martin & G. L. Clore (Eds.), *Theories of mood and cognition* (pp. 27–62). Mahwah, NJ: Erlbaum.

Dalgleish, T., & Watts, F. N. (1990). Biases of attention and memory disorders of anxiety and depression. *Clinical Psychology Review, 10,* 589–604.

Dalle, N., & Niedenthal, P. M. (in press). Le reorganisation de l'espace concep-tual au cours des états émotionnel. *L'année Psychologique.*

Davidson, R. J. (1992). Emotion and affective style: Hemispheric substrates. *Psychological Science, 3,* 39–43.

Davidson, R. J., & Tomarken, A. J. (1989). Laterality and emotion: An electro-physiological approach. In F. Boller & J. Grafman (Eds.), *Handbook of neuropsychology* (pp. 419–442). Amsterdam: Elsevier.

Derryberry, D. (1989). Effects of goal-related motivational states on the spatial orienting of attention. *Acta Psychologica, 72,* 199–220.

Derryberry, D. (1993). Attentional consequences of outcome-related motiva-tional states: Congruent, incongruent and focusing effects. *Motivation and Emotion, 17,* 65–89.

Derryberry, D., & Tucker, D. M. (1994). Motivating the focus of attention. In P. M. Niedenthal & S. Kitayama (Eds.), *The heart's eye: Emotional influences in perception and attention* (pp. 167–196). San Diego, CA: Academic Press.

Devine, P. G. (1989). Stereotypes and prejudice: Their automatic and con-trolled components. *Journal of Personality and Social Psychology, 56,* 5–18.

Dijksterhuis, A., Spears, R., Postmes, T., Stapel, D. A., Koomen, W., van Knip-penberg, A., & Scheepers, D. (1998). Seeing one thing and doing another: Contrast effects in automatic behavior. *Journal of Personality and Social Psychology, 75,* 861–871.

Frijda, N. H. (1986). *The emotions.* London: Cambridge University Press.

Frijda, N. H. (1993). The place of appraisal in emotion [Special issue: Appraisal and beyond: The issue of cognitive determinants of emotion]. *Cognition and Emotion, 7,* 357–384.

Gelman, S. A., & Markman, E. M. (1987). Young children's inductions from natural kinds: The role of categories and appearances. *Child Development, 58,* 1532–1541.

Gentner, D. (1988). Metaphor as structure mapping: The relational shift. *Child Development, 59,* 47–59.

Hahn, U., & Chater, N. (1997). Concepts and similarity. In K. Lamberts & D. Shanks (Eds.), *Knowledge, concepts, and categories* (pp. 43–92). Cambridge: MIT Press.

Halberstadt, J. B., & Niedenthal, P. M. (1997). Emotional state and the use of stimulus dimensions in judgment. *Journal of Personality and Social Psychology, 72,* 1017–1033.

Hatfield, E., Cacioppo, J. T., & Rapson, R. L. (1993). Emotional contagion. *Current Directions in Psychological Science, 2,* 96–99.

Haviland, J., & Lelwica, M. (1987). The induced affect response: 10-week-old in-fants' responses to three emotion expressions. *Developmental Psychology, 23,* 97–104.

Hope, D. A., Rapee, R. M., Heimberg, R. G., & Dombeck, M. J. (1990). Repre-sentations of the self in social phobia: Vulnerability to social threat. *Cognitive Therapy Research, 14,* 177–189.

Innes-Ker, Å. H., & Niedenthal, P. M. (in press). Emotion concepts and emo-tional states in social judgment and categorization. *Journal of Personality and Social Psychology.*

Izard, C. E. (1977). *Human emotions*. New York: Plenum Press.

Kruschke, J. K. (1992). ALCOVE: An exemplar based connectionist model of category learning. *Psychological Review, 99*, 22–44.

Leventhal, H., & Scherer, K. (1987). The relationship of emotion to cognition: A functional approach to a semantic controversy. *Cognition and Emotion, 1*, 3–28.

MacLeod, C., Mathews, A. M., & Tata, P. (1986). Attentional bias in emotional disorders. *Journal of Abnormal Psychology, 95*, 15–20.

Malt, B. (1995). Category coherence in cross-cultural perspective. *Cognitive Psychology, 29*, 85–148.

Mayer, J. D., Caruso, D. R., & Salovey, P. (2000). Emotional intelligence meets traditional standards for an intelligence. *Intelligence, 27*(4), 267–298.

Mayer, J. D., & Gaschke, Y. N. (1988). The experience and meta-experience of mood. *Journal of Personality and Social Psychology, 55*, 102–111.

Mayer, J. D., & Salovey, P. (1997). What is emotional intelligence? In P. Salovey & D. Sluyter (Eds.), *Emotional development and emotional intelligence: Implications for educators* (pp. 3–31). New York: Basic Books.

Medin, D. L., Goldstone, R. L., & Gentner, D. (1993). Respects for similarity. *Psychological Review, 100*, 254–278.

Medin, D. L., & Schaffer, M. M. (1978). Contact theory of classification learning. *Psychological Review, 85*, 207–238.

Mervis, C. B., & Rosch, E. (1981). Categorization of natural objects. *Annual Review of Psychology, 32*, 89–115.

Meyer, D. E., & Schvaneveldt, R. W. (1971) Facilitation in recognizing pairs of words: Evidence of a dependence between retrieval operations. *Journal of Experimental Psychology, 90*, 227–234.

Mogg, K., Mathews, A., & Weinman, J. (1989). Selective processing of threat cues in anxiety states: A replication. *Behaviour Research and Therapy, 27*, 317–323.

Murphy, G. L., & Medin, D. L. (1985). The role of theories in conceptual coherence. *Psychological Review, 92*, 289–316.

Neely, J. H. (1976). Semantic priming and retrieval from lexical memory: Evidence for facilitatory and inhibitory process. *Memory and Cognition, 4*, 648–654.

Neely, J. H. (1977). Semantic priming and retrieval from lexical memory: Roles of inhibitionless spreading activation and limited-capacity attention. *Journal of Experimental Psychology: General, 106*, 226–254.

Niedenthal, P. M., & Cantor, N. (1984). Making use of social prototypes: From fuzzy concepts to firm decisions. *Fuzzy Sets and Systems, 14*, 5–27.

Niedenthal, P. M., & Dalle, N. (2001). Le mariage de mon meilleur ami : Emotional response categorization during naturally induced emotional states. *European Journal of Social Psychology, 31*, 737–742.

Niedenthal, P. M., & Halberstadt, J. B. (2000a). Grounding categories in emotional response. In J. Forgas (Ed.), *Feeling and thinking: The role of affect in social cognition* (pp. 357–386). Cambridge, UK: Cambridge University Press.

Niedenthal, P. M., & Halberstadt, J. B. (2000b). Emotional response as conceptual coherence. In E. Eich, J. F. Kihlstrom, G. H. Bower, J. P. Forgas, & P. M. Niedenthal *Cognition/emotion interactions.* New York: Oxford University Press.

Niedenthal, P. M., Halberstadt, J. B., & Innes-Ker, Å. H. (1999). Emotional response categorization. *Psychological Review 106,* 337–361.

Niedenthal, P. M., Rohmann, A., & Dalle, N. (2002). What is primed by emotion words and emotion concepts? In J. Musch & K. C. Klauer (Eds.), *The psychology of evaluation: Affective processing in priming, conditioning, and Stroop tasks.* Mahwah, NJ: Erlbaum.

Niedenthal, P. M., & Setterlund, M. B. (1994). Emotion congruence in perception. *Personality and Social Psychology Bulletin, 20,* 401–410.

Nosofsky, R. M. (1986) Attention, similarity, and the identification/categorization relationship. *Journal of Experimental Psychology: General, 115,* 39–57.

Nosofsky, R. M. (1992). Exemplar-based approach to relating categorization, identification and recognition. In F. G. Ashby (Ed.), *Multidimensional models of perception and cognition* (pp. 363–393). Hillsdale, NJ: Erlbaum.

Plutchik, R. (1984). A psychoevolutionary theory of emotions. *Social Science Information, 21,* 529–553.

Pratto F., & John, O. P. (1991). Automatic vigilance: The attention-grabbing power of negative information. *Journal of Personality and Social Psychology, 61,* 381–391.

Rips, L. J. (1975). Inductive judgments about natural categories. *Journal of Verbal Learning and Verbal Behavior, 14,* 665–681.

Rosch, E. (1975). Cognitive representations of semantic categories. *Journal of Experimental Psychology: Human Perception and Performance, 1,* 303–322.

Salovey, P., Mayer, J. D., & Caruso, D. (2002). The positive psychology of emotional intelligence. In C. R. Snyder & S. J. Lopez (Eds.), *The handbook of positive psychology.* New York: Oxford University Press.

Smith, E. R., & Zarate, M. A. (1992) Exemplar-based model of social judgment. *Psychological Review, 99,* 3–21.

Smith, L. B. (1989). From global similarities to kinds of similarities: The construction of dimension in development. In S. Vosniadou & A. Ortony (Eds.), *Similarity and analogical reasoning* (pp. 146–178). New York: Cambridge University Press.

Srull, T. K., & Wyer, R. S. (1979). The role of category accessibility in the interpretation of information about persons: Some determinants and implications. *Journal of Personality and Social Psychology, 37,* 1660–1672.

Stapel, D. A., Koomen, W., & Van der Plight, J. (1996). The referents of trait inferences: The impact of trait concepts versus actor-trait links on subsequent judgments. *Journal of Personality and Social Psychology, 70,* 437–450.

Tomkins, S. S. (1962). *Affect, imagery, consciousness: Vol. 1. The positive affects.* New York: Springer Verlag.

Tomkins, S. S. (1963). *Affect, imagery, consciousness: Vol. 2. The negative affects.* New York: Springer Verlag.

Watts, F. N., McKenna, F. P., Sharrock, R., & Trezise, L. (1986). Colour naming of phobia-related words. *British Journal of Psychology, 77,* 97–108.

Wyer, R. S., & Carlston, D. E. (1979). *Social cognition, inference, and attribution.* Hillsdale, NJ: Erlbaum.

Emotion and Persuasion

Thoughts on the Role of
Emotional Intelligence

DAVID DeSTENO
JULIA BRAVERMAN

In the middle part of the 20th century, many attitude researchers were intent on discerning the role played by intelligence in
persuasibility (McGuire, 1969). At its heart, the central question of this
endeavor was quite simple: Were highly intelligent individuals less likely
to be influenced by persuasive appeals? The answer, however, was not
to be quite as straightforward. The findings of studies examining this
issue ran the gamut; some revealed higher intelligence to be associated
with decreased persuasibility (e.g., Cooper & Dinerman, 1951), some
with increased persuasibility (e.g., Hovland, Lumsdaine, & Sheffield,
1949), and some with neither outcome (e.g., Hovland, Janis, & Kelley,
1953; Janis & Field, 1959). Such findings, as one can imagine, left the
field in a quandary.

In response to this dilemma, McGuire (1968) theorized that the
apparently fickle influence of intelligence on attitude change might not
reflect the insignificance of this individual difference to the question at
hand, but might mask a more complex system of relations linking intelligence to persuasibility. Indeed, McGuire demonstrated that intelligence does influence responses to persuasive messages, but it does so
through different processes that may, at times, be oppositional. Specifically, he noted that although higher intelligence increases the facility
with which individuals receive and comprehend the information con-

tained in persuasive appeals, it also enhances both their ability to mount counterarguments and their confidence in their initial attitudes. Thus, higher intelligence is associated with processes that both augment and diminish the probability of attitude change, with the result being a curvilinear relation between intelligence and persuasibility.

Given this analysis, questions concerning the role of intelligence and many other individual difference variables thought to be involved in attitude change (e.g., self-esteem) necessarily moved from the realm of a search for their respective simple, direct effects on persuasion to one involving an examination of the multiple routes through which each might affect attitude change (Chaiken, Liberman, & Eagly, 1989; Petty & Cacioppo, 1986; Petty & Wegener, 1998). In the present case, if we are to conceive of emotional intelligence (EI) as an individual difference that reflects a set of abilities and skills with respect to a particular area, much like general intelligence (cf. Mayer, Caruso, & Salovey, 1999; Salovey, Mayer, Caruso, & Lopes, in press), then the parallels between the study of EI-based influences on persuasion and earlier studies involving general (i.e., analytic) intelligence become quite clear. Echoing McGuire's perspective, we believe that it is very unlikely that EI has a single, direct effect on persuasibility, especially given the vast amount of research documenting the multiple roles played by affect in attitude change (Petty, DeSteno, & Rucker, 2001; Petty & Wegener, 1998; Wegener & Petty, 1996). The question of interest in the present case, therefore, should not focus on whether those high in EI are more or less influenced by persuasive appeals, but rather on an examination of the multiple processes by which EI may influence attitude change.

Given the nascent nature of scientific study of the EI construct, very little empirical work has directly examined the influence of EI on psychological phenomena related to persuasion. Consequently, this chapter attempts to provide prospective answers to the preceding question based on present knowledge of the influence of the emotional system on persuasion and to stimulate research aimed at understanding how differences in EI shape responses to persuasive appeals. To that end, we first provide a brief review of current models of attitude change and follow with a discussion of the multiple processes through which EI may exert influence on the cognitive machinations involved in persuasion.

PERSUASION MODELS: A MULTIPLE-PROCESS APPROACH

Although there are individual differences in the tendency to evaluate objects (Jarvis & Petty, 1996), it is well accepted that humans possess a general propensity to appraise positively or negatively most stimuli with which they come in contact (Bargh, Chaiken, Govender, & Pratto, 1992; Bargh, Chaiken, Raymond, & Hymes, 1996). Contemporary definitions of the term "attitude" consequently refer to an overall evaluation (positive or negative) of an object, wherein this global evaluation may vary on a number of dimensions (e.g., extremity, strength) and may represent a composite of the evaluative appraisals attached to some set of the object's basic attributes (Eagly & Chaiken, 1998; Petty & Wegener, 1998). Such evaluations, however, need not be static once formed. Indeed, whole industries and campaigns are built on this fact. The question of import, therefore, surrounds not *whether* but *how* attitudes change.

At present, attitude research has coalesced around the view that persuasion occurs through two primary types of mental processes: those requiring high levels of cognitive effort and those requiring low levels of cognitive effort (see Schwarz, Chapter 6, this volume). This distinction forms the basis of both the elaboration-likelihood model (ELM; Petty & Cacioppo, 1986) and the heuristic–systematic model (HSM; Chaiken et al., 1989) of attitude change. In this chapter, we use the ELM as a framework for discussing the possible effects of EI on persuasion; however, the majority of claims can be accommodated using the HSM framework as well.

Figure 8.1 depicts a generalized model of the processes theorized to be involved in attitude change, modified to highlight the role of EI. At its heart are the classes of mediating mechanisms specified by the ELM.[1] In brief, central (or high) elaboration mechanisms represent processes by which attitude-relevant information is effortfully considered. For example, attitude change resulting from a careful analysis of the policy positions espoused by a political candidate would be indicative of persuasion through the central route. Peripheral (or low) elaboration mechanisms represent processes by which attitudes shift through heuristic (i.e., low effort) mental activity. For example, forming a positive view of a specific brand of soft drink simply because Tiger Woods drinks it in a television commercial indicates persuasion through the peripheral route. In this case, choosing a specific brand is not based on careful consideration of the qualities of the beverage, but on the assumption that Tiger knows best. In many cases, however, attitude change does not result from one type of process working in isolation. Elaboration occurs across a continuum, and therefore both central and

---

[1]Given that a detailed discussion of the specifics of the ELM are beyond the scope of this chapter, readers are referred to Petty and Cacioppo (1986) and Petty and Wegener (1999) for a full exposition of the model.

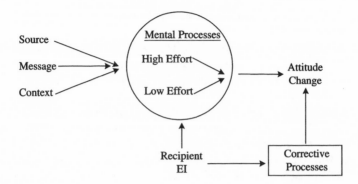

FIGURE 8.1. Generalized model of attitude change as a function of recipient differences in EI.

peripheral processes may exert differential levels of influence simultaneously to produce persuasion (Petty & Cacioppo, 1986; Petty & Wegener, 1999).

Given this framework, investigation of the factors underlying persuasion necessarily turns to (1) the nature of the information that serves as input into these processes and (2) the factors that determine the relative predominance of one class of processes over another. In general, attitude researchers have suggested that four types of independent variables are relevant to these issues (Eagly & Chaiken, 1993; Petty & Wegener, 1998). First and foremost, information of some type (i.e., a message) must enter the system for persuasion to occur. This information, moreover, comes from a specific source (e.g., celebrity, scientist, specific ethnic group member, the object itself) and is received by a specific recipient (e.g., one high or low in self-esteem or need for cognition) in a specific context (e.g., positive mood, cognitive distraction). As depicted in Figure 8.1, these four types of variables, either singly or synergistically, shape attitude change through their use as information and/or their influence on the level of elaboration in the system. For purposes of this chapter, however, we constrain recipient variability to reflect only variability in EI.

Given a specific combination of these variables, attitude change occurs as a function of the differential processing of the relevant information by central and peripheral mediating mechanisms. Central mechanisms, for example, may utilize information contained in the message itself (e.g., factual claims); peripheral mechanisms rely on less issue-relevant information (e.g., the celebrity of the message's source) to induce persuasion. It is not the case, however, that specific types of variables only influence a specific type of mechanism. Rather, the same variable (e.g., mood state) can serve distinct roles, depending on the level of elaboration employed by the system. For example, under high elaboration conditions, positive mood may lead to biased recall of mood-congruent information during mental deliberations concerning a politician's past statements; however, under low elaboration conditions, it may serve simply as a cue that the recipient likes the politician (cf. Petty, Schumann, Richman, & Strathman, 1993; Schwarz & Clore, 1983, 1996).

As Petty and colleagues have noted (Petty & Cacioppo, 1986; Petty & Wegener, 1999), it is important to consider not only that each class of variables is capable of playing multiple roles at different levels of elaboration, but also that each may exert an influence on determining the level of elaboration evoked in the system. For example, messages coming from members of stigmatized groups (i.e., a source variable) tend to evoke higher levels of elaboration than do messages from members of nonstigmatized groups (Petty, Fleming, & White, 1999). Similarly, positive and negative mood states (i.e., a context variable) have been shown to influence the degree of effort devoted to the processing of persuasive appeals (Bless, Bohner, Schwarz, & Strack, 1990; Wegener, Petty, & Smith, 1995).

Persuasion attempts do not always go undetected, however. As noted by McGuire (1968, 1969), one of the factors that produce the curvilinear relation between intelligence and attitude change observed by some investigators is the ability of highly intelligent individuals to recognize the persuasion attempt and to develop counterarguments against its message. Reflecting this notion, contemporary research in social cognition has revealed a propensity for individuals to attempt, under certain conditions, to correct many types of judgments and evaluations for perceived biasing factors (Martin, Seta, & Crelia, 1990; Schwarz & Bless, 1992; Wegener & Petty, 1997; Wilson & Brekke, 1994). Consequently, as shown in Figure 8.1, the final attitude resulting from exposure to a persuasive appeal will be a joint function of output from ELM mechanisms and any corrective processes in which an individual engages (Petty & Wegener, 1998).

THE ROLE OF EMOTIONAL INTELLIGENCE

The experience of emotion has been shown to play a role in each of the aforementioned processes. From serving as input to central and peripheral mechanisms, to influencing the level of elaboration devoted to the processing of a persuasive appeal, to engendering corrective responses from those who suspect their judgments to have been biased by their feelings, emotion stands as one of the principal factors that guide attitude change (Petty et al., 2001; Petty & Wegener, 1998; Schwarz, Bless, & Bohner, 1991). Given this significance, it stands to reason that any individual differences in abilities relevant to the perception, experience, and management of emotion may also impact attitude change. However, as is the case with general intelligence, the effects of such differences in EI are probably quite complex. In the rest of this chapter, we set out some initial conjectures regarding the role played by EI in regard to the relevant mechanisms of persuasion. As indicated in Figure 8.1, we restrict the influence of the recipient factor on persuasive and corrective processes to reflect only variability in EI; this restriction, of course, does not preclude the interaction of EI with other individual differences (e.g., need for cognition, general intelligence, self-esteem) in the production of joint effects on persuasion.

The Role of EI in High-Effort Processes

Under conditions of high cognitive effort, persuasion is mediated by processes involving the careful consideration of information contained in persuasive appeals (Petty & Cacioppo, 1986). Emotion-based influences on such central mechanisms can be categorized into two broad classes: relevant and incidental (Petty et al., 2001). Relevant effects refer to cases wherein one's emotional response to the attitude object represents a valued piece of information that enters into the assessment of the merit of the object (see Gohm and Clore, Chapter 4, this volume). Incidental effects refer to those wherein an extant emotional state, having arisen for reasons entirely separate from consideration of the attitude object, nonetheless biases the cognitive processing of information stemming from the persuasive appeal. We examine each type of emotion-based effect in turn, with an eye to the possible role of EI.

Emotion-relevant effects on persuasion derive from the simple fact that certain stimuli evoke emotional responses upon their perception or consideration and that for a subset of these stimuli, such responses may represent attributes deemed relevant for attitude determination (Martin, Abend, Sedikides, & Green, 1997; Petty & Cacioppo, 1986). For example, in considering the merits of a specific piece of artwork, an individual may take into consideration not only factors such as the materials used and the craftsmanship of the artist, but also the emotional state that this piece produces. That is, he or she may decide that the feeling state the object evokes is a central piece of information in determining its value and, consequently, utilize this information in attitude formation.

For those high in EI, the use of emotion information in this fashion should be accentuated. Given that part of the EI construct entails an increased ability to perceive emotional states both in oneself and in others, utilization of emotional responses as relevant attributes in the evaluation of attitude objects should increase among those high in EI. After all, a central link in the persuasion chain involves reception of the relevant information (McGuire, 1968, 1969). For those low in EI, the utilization of information stemming from their emotional responses to stimuli should be attenuated. Unlike those high in EI, these individuals have difficulty in recognizing and interpreting their emotions, making effortful consideration of this information as an attribute of the attitude object difficult or impossible. Moreover, given that high-EI individuals are expected to have greater facility in the recall of emotion-relevant experiences, attitudes held by these individuals that have been shaped by relevant emotional responses are more likely to evidence increased strength and longevity. That is, the greater accessibility of emotion-relevant information among those high in EI should lead to quicker activation (i.e., strength) of attitudes based on emotional responses (cf. Fazio, 1995).

As noted earlier, emotional states that are present during the consideration of a persuasive message do not always stem from the attitude object itself; rather, they may be entirely incidental to it. For example, one may see an advertisement for a political candidate while watching a comedy special on television, or read an ad for a mutual fund after reading a magazine article detailing the results of a natural disaster. In such cases, emotional states have been shown to shape attitudes in spite of their irrelevance to the attitude object (DeSteno, Petty, Rucker, & Wegener, 2002; Petty et al., 1993; Petty et al., 2001). This influence stems from the ability of these emotional states to bias the processing of information germane to consideration of the attitude object.

Effortful consideration of a persuasive message necessarily entails the generation of thoughts concerning the received information. As noted by Greenwald (1968), such thoughts, or cognitive responses, may themselves exert a strong influence on attitude change. For example, when an individual systematically considers the attributes of a political candidate in working memory, other information associated with this person may also enter into the person's awareness and thereby exert an influence on his or her attitude toward the candidate. Following this logic, it becomes clear that if the nature of the recalled information is biased (e.g., more positive than negative information is retrieved from memory), so too will be the direction of attitude change (Petty & Cacioppo, 1986). Indeed, Petty and his colleagues (Petty et al., 1993) demonstrated that positive mood, because of its ability to increase the accessibility of positively valenced information in memory (cf. Bower &

Forgas, 2001), resulted in greater persuasion as a function of the cognitive responses generated under conditions of high elaboration. That is, positive mood resulted in increased recall of positive information, which led to an increase of positive attributes related to the attitude object in working memory, which led to a more positive attitude toward the object in question.

Because individuals high in EI can be expected both to experience emotional states more fully and to devote more attention to the emotion-relevant aspects of stimuli when encoding them in memory, these individuals should evidence a greater susceptibility to biased processing induced by their incidental emotional states at the time of message reception. That is, emotional states should result in increased accessibility of similarly valenced attributes of the attitude object in the memories of high-EI individuals as compared with those with low EI. Such an increase in positively or negatively toned cognitive responses should, in turn, result in increased attitude change in the respective direction (Petty et al., 1993; Petty et al., 2001; cf. Greenwald, 1968).

High-EI individuals are also expected to identify and differentiate between discrete emotional states more clearly than are low-EI individuals. Such a skill suggests that these individuals may demonstrate greater susceptibility to the effects of specific emotions on biased processing. Work by Niedenthal and colleagues has revealed that the experience of discrete emotional states facilitates the recall of semantic information possessing a matching emotional overtone; anger, for example, increases the accessibility of anger-relevant semantic information (Niedenthal, Halberstadt, & Setterlund, 1997; Niedenthal & Setterlund, 1994; see also Niedenthal, Dalle, and Rohmann, Chapter 7, in this volume). To the extent that a negative emotional state is more clearly experienced as fear or anger (as opposed to a simple negative mood), it may function more efficiently in enhancing recall for cognitive responses possessing a similar emotional overtone. The effectiveness of such specificity in responding will, of course, depend on the nature of the message. However, to the extent that the tone of a message matches the specific emotional state of a high-EI individual, one may expect increased susceptibility to the persuasion attempt (cf. DeSteno et al., 2002)

A final way that we envision EI influencing persuasion revolves around the issue of attitude structure. Fishbein and Ajzen's *theory of reasoned action* stipulates that the two primary determinants of an attitude involve evaluations of its attributes/outcomes and estimates concerning the likelihood that it possesses or will result in these attributes/outcomes (Ajzen & Fishbein, 1980; Fishbein & Ajzen, 1975). For example, an individual's attitude toward a presidential candidate is a function of both that individual's evaluation of the proposals espoused by this candidate and his or her belief that the candidate will bring those proposals to fruition. Such expectancy-value models have shown success in predicting attitude change and behavior (Eagly & Chaiken, 1998), and, consequently, any process that is capable of altering either the value or likelihood attached to specific attributes of an object can also be expected to result in a change of attitude toward that object.

With respect to affect-based influences, it has been repeatedly shown that positive and negative moods bias likelihood expectations concerning the existence or occurrence of valenced attributes and outcomes (Johnson & Tversky, 1983; Mayer, Gaschke, Braverman, & Evans, 1992). Sad individuals, for example, demonstrate an increased belief that negative events are likely to occur. Given this bias, it stands to reason that if an individual's expectations concerning the likelihood that a certain attitude object possesses specific positive attributes or leads to specific positive outcomes increase, that person's attitude toward this object should become more positive as well. Such a determination, of course, would necessarily require a good deal of cognitive effort and thereby occur under conditions of high elaboration.

Following this logic, we expect that individuals high in EI would demonstrate greater susceptibility to affect-induced attitude change as a function of mood-induced biases involving the expectancies attached to specific attributes of the attitude object. For example, because of their tendency to experience emotional states more fully, high-EI individuals in a positive mood should evidence greater expectancies that a political candidate possesses positive qualities and plans successful policy initiatives than would their low-EI counterparts. More vivid emotional experiences should translate into greater use of affect as a source of information in the computation of such expectancies, provided that individuals do not harbor suspicion that these states might bias their judgments (Clore, Gasper, & Garvin, 2001; Schwarz & Clore, 1996).

Recent research on the influence of affective states on likelihood judgments has demonstrated that this biasing effect may function in an emotion-specific fashion and, thereby, has begun to suggest another way in which individual differences in EI might also moderate attitude change. Given that discrete negative emotions (e.g., sadness, anger) have been shown to elevate differentially likelihood estimates for events that match their specific emotional overtones (DeSteno, Petty, Wegener, & Rucker, 2000), it may be the case that high-EI individuals will once again be more susceptible to persuasive appeals relying on the evocation of discrete emotional states. Indeed, recent work has shown that the experience of specific emotions enhances persuasion for messages matching these states in emotional overtone as a function of biased expectancy judgments among individuals who are effortfully considering the messages (DeSteno et al., 2002). Consequently, it may be the case that high-EI individuals demonstrate greater persuasion in response to messages such as fear appeals. These appeals, for example, usually strive to evoke feelings of dread while also presenting information concerning anxiety-provoking consequences. To the extent that a negative emotional state is more clearly experienced as fear (as opposed to a simple negative mood), it may function more effectively in biasing expectancies concerning the occurrence of anxiety-provoking events.

The Role of EI in Low-Effort Processes

People do not always devote a great deal of attention and effort toward the contemplation of persuasive messages. Sometimes, for example, individuals may need to make a quick judgment; other times, they simply may not be interested enough in the message to think about it carefully. Such situations and the corresponding lack of elaboration they induce do not imply that persuasion will be diminished, but rather that it will occur through different mechanisms (Chaiken et al., 1989; Petty & Cacioppo, 1986; Petty & Wegener, 1999). Although many mechanisms associated with the peripheral route to persuasion have been identified, two stand out as relevant to receiver differences in EI, given their relevance to emotion-based influences on persuasion: classical conditioning and the misattribution of affect.

For the past 60 years, researchers have demonstrated that attitude change can occur through the repeated pairings of a specific object with other pleasant or unpleasant stimuli (Razran, 1940; Staats & Staats, 1958; Zanna, Kiesler, & Pilkonis, 1970). Following the principles of classical conditioning, this change is believed to occur through the development of an association between the attitude object and some hedonic consequence. It is important to note, however, that the learning of this association does not require high amounts of cognitive effort. Rather, such conditioning processes have been demonstrated to occur completely outside conscious awareness (Krosnick, Bets, Jussim, & Lynn, 1992) and to influence the evaluation of attitude objects for which effortful consideration was unlikely (Cacioppo, Marshall-Goodell, Tassinary, & Petty, 1992; Priester, Cacioppo, & Petty, 1996).

With regard to EI, we would expect those with high levels to evidence greater attitude change in response to persuasion tactics that manipulate the emotional context associated with the perception of an attitude object. Such heightened susceptibility should result from both their increased tendencies to experience emotional states more vividly and to perceive the covariation between specific stimuli and their emotional consequences. For example, upon repeated presentations of the image of a particular beverage accompanied by enjoyable music, high-EI individuals should tend to evidence greater positive attitudes toward this beverage than should their low-EI counterparts. In this example, the entry of a bottle of soda into awareness will usually not lead to its effortful consideration; thus attitude change will be constrained to peripheral mechanisms. High-EI individuals can be expected to have a greater emotional response toward the music accompanying visual perception of the soda bottle and therefore more readily come to associate their resulting pleasant state with the presence of this object.

The second peripheral mechanism by which recipient differences in EI may moderate persuasibility is the misattribution of affective responses. As documented by Schwarz and Clore (1996), individuals utilize their affective states as cues in determining their evaluation of attitude objects under conditions in which cognitive effort is low. For example, college students were shown to be more receptive to a persuasive message advocating requirements for comprehensive examinations at their institution on days with pleasant weather than on days with inclement weather (Sinclair, Mark, & Clore, 1994). Rather than effortfully evaluating the complicated persuasive appeal, students simply misattributed their positive or negative moods resulting from the weather to their consideration of the appeal. Here again, we would expect those high in EI to be more susceptible to this misattribution bias, given their tendencies to experience their emotional states more fully. Indeed, recent work has indicated a positive relation between attention afforded to affective states and the tendency to succumb to the misattribution bias (Gasper & Clore, 2000; see also Gohm and Clore, Chapter 4, in this volume).

Susceptibility to the misattribution bias can be overcome, however, if one is aware of the true source of his or her emotional state and thus becomes less likely to misattribute that state to some incidental object (Clore et al., 2001; Schwarz & Clore, 1996). It may be argued, therefore, that high-EI individuals may be less influenced by this bias, given their ability to perceive more accurately the causes of their emotional states. We concur with this view; however, such a correction process would occur subsequent to the suspicion of bias, and hence we reserve consideration of this issue for the discussion of emotion-relevant correction processes later in this chapter.

The Role of EI in Determining the Level of Processing Effort

The previous two sections describe the multiple ways in which emotion can influence persuasion at high and low levels of elaboration as a function of recipient differences in EI. Although it is true that given certain contingencies, the level of cognitive effort devoted to the processing of a persuasive message will be constrained to be high (e.g., the message involves a topic of high personal relevance) or low (e.g., the individual is distracted while receiving the message), many times the level of elaboration is more malleable and responsive to subtler contextual factors such as an individual's emotional state (Petty & Cacioppo, 1986; Petty & Wegener, 1999). Incidental emotions, then, serve not only to influence central or peripheral mechanisms directly, but also to determine the types of mechanisms utilized in any given situation (Petty et al., 2001; Schwarz & Clore, 1996).

According to Schwarz and colleagues' cognitive-tuning framework (Clore, Schwarz, & Conway, 1994; Schwarz, 1990; Schwarz & Clore, 1996), the experience of positive affect signals a safe environment in which high levels of cognitive effort need not occur; no problems exist to be solved. Negative states, however, signal the existence of some threat that, in turn, should motivate an individual to engage in more effortful processing aimed at remediation of the problem. In line with this view, most research has revealed that individuals tend to devote more energy to many types of cognitive tasks when experiencing sad, as opposed to happy, affective states (Clore et al., 1994; Schwarz & Clore, 1996). Persuasion, accordingly, may be more likely to occur through effortful mechanisms when recipients are feeling sad (Bless et al. 1990; Bohner, Crow, Erb, & Schwarz, 1992; Mackie & Worth, 1989).

There is, however, some debate on this point. Although not disavowing the ability of emotional states to influence processing level, Wegener and colleagues have challenged the cognitive-tuning framework by demonstrating that positive affective states need not always lead to decreased elaboration in considering a persuasive message (Wegener et al., 1995). Specifically, Wegener and colleagues noted that the majority of persuasive appeals used in previous research focused on negative topics (e.g., dangers of nuclear power, institution of mandatory college examinations). When these researchers presented happy individuals with a positive message, they found evidence of increased processing effort. Wegener and colleagues argued that choice of elaboration level was driven by a desire to maximize hedonic rewards. According to this view, individuals in positive states should exert effort only on tasks that will maintain or increase their present positive states. In short, when people are happy, they do not want to have their moods deflated by thinking hard about negative information.

Although disagreeing on the exact nature of how affective states may influence the processing level in which an individual engages, these frameworks highlight the fact that emotions do exert an influence on the adoption of effortful or heuristic processing mechanisms. The question, from our perspective, then becomes how recipient differences in EI may interact with the contextual factor of emotional state in the determination of elaboration level. In answering this question, it becomes important to consider a characteristic of high-EI individuals that has not yet been invoked: the ability to engage in or detach from specific emotional states as a function of their usefulness for the task at hand.

If the driving motivation in a situation involves emotion regulation with respect to the maintenance or increase of a pleasant affective state, those high in EI are more likely to take the necessary steps to accomplish this goal because of their increased awareness of the hedonic consequences of specific activities. If they are already experiencing a pleasant state, they should be more likely than low-EI individuals (1) to process persuasive messages involving negative information peripherally and (2) to process persuasive messages involving positive information centrally in order to preserve this state (cf. Wegener et al., 1995).

The primary task of a message recipient, however, may not always involve mood maintenance. In certain situations, accuracy in cognitive processing may take precedence; one may wish to ensure that any attitude change is carefully considered. Given that those high in EI are expected to understand more clearly the consequences of their affective states for problem solving, they may deliberately modify their emotional states in an effort to facilitate the processing of a persuasive message. For example, when confronted with an appeal concerning a negative topic, high-EI individuals experiencing a positive affective state may recognize their lack of impetus to contemplate negative information. However, if they believe that it is important to do so, they may attempt to attenuate the positivity of their emotional state (i.e., become a bit more serious) in order to facilitate a more deliberative approach.

The Role of EI in Attitude Correction

To this point, we have argued that high-EI individuals would be more susceptible to emotion-induced biases resulting from both high- and low-effort cognitive processes as a result of several factors associated with heightened experience and understanding of emotional states. However, with the increased knowledge of the causes and consequences of emotional states that is the hallmark of EI likely comes the potential to suspect, monitor, and correct for any perceived biases to which a person believes she or he has succumbed. The utilization of such corrective processes has the potential to modify greatly the preceding statement regarding the heightened susceptibility of those high in EI. As depicted in Figure 8.1, such processes may moderate the influence of emotion-relevant persuasive mechanisms on any resulting attitude.

The notion that individuals, under certain conditions, strive to adjust their judgments for biasing influences has received increasing attention of late. Indeed, in many realms of judgment, there is mounting evidence that given ample suspicion of bias and the cognitive resources to combat it, individuals will attempt to correct their responses in an effort to achieve accuracy (Martin et al., 1990; Strack, Schwarz, Bless, Kübler, & Wänke, 1993; Wegener & Petty, 1995, 1997; Wilson & Brekke, 1994). Findings have shown that individuals believe that their emotional states are capable of biasing their judgments (DeSteno et al., 2000; Johnson & Tverksy, 1983) and, consequently, attempt to adjust their decisions for the presence of such bias when it is suspected (Berkowitz & Troccoli, 1990; DeSteno et al., 2000; Lambert, Khan, Lickel, & Fricke, 1997; Schwarz & Clore, 1983). Given these findings, we expect that high-EI individuals are more likely to anticipate the presence of emotion-induced biases in their judgments and to react against them when motivated to do so. Moreover, as evidence of differential correction for the biasing influence of discrete emotional states has emerged (DeSteno et al., 2000), high-EI individuals can also be expected to engage in emotion-specific, as opposed to simply valence-based, correction processes.

For example, a high-EI individual, because of her awareness of her current angry state and of the consequences that the experience of anger may have held for her past judgments, may anticipate that her hostile feelings are negatively coloring her view of a person with whom she is interacting. If arriving at an accurate evaluation of this other person is important to her, she may adjust her negative attitude toward this person in an attempt to eradicate the suspected bias and thereby moderate her resulting attitude. In making this claim, we are not asserting that high-EI individuals have an understanding of the workings of the cognitive mechanisms involved in attitude change, but simply that they have expectations concerning the ultimate effects that specific emotions may have on the accuracy of their attitudes.

The utilization of corrective processes requires increased cognitive effort and is therefore more likely to occur under conditions of high elaboration (cf. Martin et al., 1990; Wegener & Petty, 1997). However, given that elaboration occurs along a continuum and that both central and peripheral mechanisms can function simultaneously (Petty & Wegener, 1998, 1999), correction for emotion-induced biases may occur along a range of elaborative effort. The result of such processes is the attenuation of the influence of emotion on the persuasibility of high-EI individuals under conditions wherein accuracy is valued.

INTEGRATION AND IMPLICATIONS

We began this chapter by harking back to the debate concerning the role of general intelligence in attitude change. In so doing, we discussed McGuire's (1968, 1969) insightful resolution to the morass of findings documenting positive and negative relations of intelligence to individual differences in persuasibility. In short, McGuire noted that intelligence plays two roles: the facilitator and the inhibitor. The end result therefore becomes one of a curvilinear relation linking intelligence to susceptibility to persuasion. In the present case, we argue that individual differences in EI should function in a similar fashion; EI, much like general intelligence, represents a combination of specific abilities and skills (cf. Mayer, 2001; Mayer et al., 1999; Salovey et al., in press).

In support of this argument, we have reviewed much of what is known about the multiple ways in which emotions can enhance or inhibit persuasion. Under conditions of both high and low elaboration, high-EI individuals can be expected to demonstrate increased susceptibility to the influence of relevant and incidental emotional states because of their heightened experience of emotion and greater use of emotion-relevant information and cues stemming from both themselves and their environment. However, the same individuals, given their knowledge of the causes and consequences of emotional states, can also be expected to demonstrate resistance to emotion-induced biases in the persuasion process. Consequently, the relevant question becomes not "Are those high in EI more or less persuadable," but "Under what conditions are those high in EI more or less persuadable?"

The answer, we believe, is likely to hinge on other contextual factors in the environment. That is, although the general relation between recipient EI and persuasibility can be expected to be curvilinear, the damping of attitude change in any given situation depends primarily on whether corrective processes are activated (see Figure 8.2). Although it is true that high-EI individuals are more likely to invoke such strategies to remove bias, their ability to do so rests on three factors: (1) their suspicion of bias, (2) their ability to engage in the effort to remove bias, and (3) their motivation to remove bias (cf. Martin et al., 1990; Wegener & Petty, 1997). The first factor is clearly more likely to occur among those high in EI; the remaining two, however, bear no association to the EI continuum. For example, a high-EI individual may be unable to devote cognitive resources to the removal of bias because of constraints

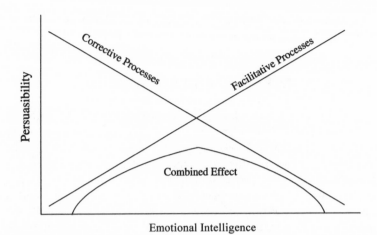

FIGURE 8.2. Persuasibility in response to emotion-relevant attitude information as a function of EI-associated facilitative, corrective, and combinatory processes.

on cognitive capacity, fatigue, or limited time. Moreover, he or she may not be motivated to engage in correction because of a lack of interest in the judgment at hand. Therefore, the exact relation of EI to persuasibility should vary as a function of the specific context; it may be linearly positive, linearly negative, or nonmonotonic in a given situation as a function of the corrective processes invoked to combat the facilitative effects of EI on emotion-induced attitude change.

In conducting this initial foray into consideration of the role of EI in attitude change, we realize that we may have raised many more questions than answers. Indeed, the relation of EI to attitude change can be expected to take many forms, depending on other influences and constraints in the immediate environment. EI's conflicting effects, however, should not be taken to imply the futility of examining its influence on persuasion. To the contrary, they point to the richness of this construct in moderating the function of many emotion-relevant processes already known to induce persuasion. We believe, therefore, that investigation of the effects of recipient differences in EI promises to provide another fruitful strategy for revealing both how and why attitudes change.

REFERENCES

Ajzen, I., & Fishbein, M. (1980). *Understanding attitudes and predicting social behavior.* Englewood Cliffs, NJ: Prentice-Hall.

Bargh, J. A., Chaiken, S., Govender, R., & Pratto, F. (1992). The generality of automatic attitude activation effect. *Journal of Personality and Social Psychology, 82,* 893–912.

Bargh, J. A., Chaiken, S., Raymond, P., & Hymes, C. (1996). The automatic evaluation effect: Unconditionally automatic attitude activation with a pronunciation task. *Journal of Experimental Social Psychology, 32,* 185–210.

Berkowitz, L., & Troccoli, B. T. (1990). Feelings, direction of attention, and expressed evaluations of others. *Cognition and Emotion, 4,* 305–325.

Bless, H., Bohner, G., Schwarz, N., & Strack, F. (1990). Mood and persuasion: A cognitive response analysis. *Personality and Social Psychology Bulletin, 16,* 331–345.

Bohner, G., Crow, K., Erb, H. P., & Schwarz, N. (1992). Affect and persuasion: Mood effects on the processing of message content and context cues and on subsequent behavior. *European Journal of Social Psychology, 22,* 551–530.

Bower, G. H., & Forgas, J. P. (2001). Mood and social memory. In J. P. Forgas (Ed.), *Handbook of affect and social cognition* (pp. 95–120). Mahwah, NJ: Erlbaum.

Cacioppo, J. T., Marshall-Goodell, B. S., Tassinary, L. G., & Petty, R. E. (1992). Rudimentary determinants of attitudes: Classical conditioning is more effective when prior knowledge about the attitude stimulus is low than high. *Journal of Experimental Social Psychology, 28,* 207–233.

Chaiken, S., Liberman, A., & Eagly, A. H. (1989). Heuristic and systematic processing within and beyond the persuasion context. In J. S. Uleman & J. A. Bargh (Eds.), *Unintended thought* (pp. 212–252). New York: Guilford Press.

Clore, G. L., Gasper, K., & Garvin, E. (2001). Affect as information. In J. P. Forgas (Ed.), *Handbook of affect and social cognition* (pp. 121–144). Mahwah, NJ: Erlbaum.

Clore, G. L., Schwarz, N., & Conway, M. (1994). Affective causes and consequences of social information processing. In R. S. Wyer & T. K. Srull (Eds.), *Handbook of social cognition* (Vol. 1, pp. 323–417). Mahwah, NJ: Erlbaum.

Cooper, E., & Dinerman, H. (1951). Analysis of the film *Don't be a sucker.* A study of communication. *Public Opinion Quarterly, 15,* 243–264.

DeSteno, D., Petty, R. E., Rucker, D. D., & Wegener, D. T. (2002). *Emotion specificity in persuasion.* Unpublished manuscript.

DeSteno, D., Petty, R. E., Wegener, D. T., & Rucker, D. D. (2000). Beyond valence in the perception of likelihood: The role of emotion specificity. *Journal of Personality and Social Psychology, 78,* 397–416.

Eagly, A. H., & Chaiken, S. (1993). *The psychology of attitudes.* New York: Harcourt Brace Jovanovich.

Eagly, A. H., & Chaiken, S. (1998). Attitude structure and function. In D. T. Gilbert, S. T. Fiske, & G. Lindzey (Eds.), *Handbook of social psychology* (4th ed., Vol. 1, pp. 269–322). Boston: McGraw-Hill.

Fazio, R. H. (1995). Attitudes as object-evaluaiton associations: Determinants, consequences, and correlates of attitude accessibility. In R. E. Petty & J. A. Krosnick (Eds.), *Attitude strength: Antecedents and consequences* (pp. 247–282). Mahwah, NJ: Erlbaum.

Fishbein, M., & Ajzen, I. (1975). *Belief, attitude, intention, and behavior: An introduction to theory and research.* Reading, MA: Addison-Wesley.

Gasper, K., & Clore, G. L. (2000). Do you have to pay attention to your feelings to be influenced by them? *Personality and Social Psychology Bulletin, 26,* 698–711.

Greenwald, A. G. (1968). Cognitive learning, cognitive response to persuasion, and attitude change. In A. G. Greenwald, T. C. Brock, & T. M. Ostrom (Eds.), *Psychological foundations of attitudes* (pp. 147–170). New York: Academic Press.

Hovland, C. I., Janis, I. L., & Kelley, H. H. (1953). *Communication and persuasion: Psychological studies of opinion change.* New Haven, CT: Yale University Press.

Hovland, C. I., Lumsdaine, A. A., & Sheffield, F. D. (1949). *Experiments on mass communication.* Princeton, NJ: Princeton University Press.

Janis, I. L., & Field, P. B. (1959). Sex differences and personality factors related to persuasibility. In C. I. Hovland & I. L. Janis (Eds.), *Personality and persuasibility* (pp. 55–68). New Haven, CT: Yale University Press.

Jarvis, W. B. G., & Petty, R. E. (1996). The need to evaluate. *Journal of Personality and Social Psychology, 70,* 172–194.

Johnson, E. J., & Tversky, A. (1983). Affect, generalization, and the perception of risk. *Journal of Personality and Social Psychology, 45,* 20–31.

Krosnick, J. A., Betz, A. L., Jussim, L. J., & Lynn, A. R. (1992). Subliminal conditioning of attitudes. *Personality and Social Psychology Bulletin, 18,* 152–162.

Lambert, A. J., Khan, S. R., Lickel, B. A., & Fricke, K. (1997). Mood and the correction of positive versus negative stereotypes. *Journal of Personality and Social Psychology, 72,* 1002–1016.

Mackie, D. M., & Worth, L. (1989). Processing deficits and the mediation of positive affect in persuasion. *Journal of Personality and Social Psychology, 57,* 27–40.

Martin, L. L., Abend, T. A., Sedikides, C., & Green, J. (1997). How would I feel if . . . ? Mood as input to a role fulfillment evaluation process. *Journal of Personality and Social Psychology, 73,* 242–253.

Martin, L. L., Seta, J. J., & Crelia, R. A. (1990). Assimilation and contrast as a function of people's willingness and ability to expend effort in forming an impression. *Journal of Personality and Social Psychology, 59,* 27–37.

Mayer, J. D. (2001). Emotion, intelligence, and emotional intelligence. In J. P. Forgas (Ed.), *Handbook of affect and social cognition* (pp. 410–431). Mahwah, NJ: Erlbaum.

Mayer, J. D., Caruso, D. R., & Salovey, P. (1999). Emotional intelligence meets traditional standards for an intelligence. *Intelligence, 17,* 433–442.

Mayer, J. D., Gaschke, Y. N., Braverman, D. L., & Evans, T. W. (1992). Mood-congruent judgment is a general effect. *Journal of Personality and Social Psychology, 63,* 119–132.

McGuire, W. J. (1968). Personality and susceptibility to social influence. In E. F. Borgatta & W. W. Lambert (Eds.), *Handbook of personality theory and research* (pp. 1130–1187). Chicago: Rand McNally.

McGuire, W. J. (1969). The nature of attitudes and attitude change. In G. Lindzey & E. Aronson (Eds.), *Handbook of social psychology* (2nd ed., Vol. 3, pp. 136–314). Reading, MA: Addison-Wesley.

Niedenthal, P. M., Halberstadt, J. B., & Setterlund, M. B. (1997). Being happy and seeing "happy": Emotional state mediates visual word recognition. *Cognition and Emotion, 11,* 403–432.

Niedenthal, P. M., & Setterlund, M. B. (1994). Emotion congruence in perception. *Personality and Social Psychology Bulletin, 20,* 401–410.

Petty, R. E., & Cacioppo, J. T. (1986). The elaboration likelihood model of persuasion. In L. Berkowitz (Ed.), *Advances in experimental social psychology* (Vol. 19, pp. 123–205). New York: Academic Press.

Petty, R. E., DeSteno, D., & Rucker, D. D. (2001). The role of affect in attitude change. In J. P. Forgas (Ed.), *Handbook of affect and social cognition* (pp. 212–233). Mahwah, NJ: Erlbaum.

Petty, R. E., Fleming, M. A., & White, P. H. (1999). Stigmatized sources and persuasion: Prejudice as a determinant of argument scrutiny. *Journal of Personality and Social Psychology, 76,* 19–34.

Petty, R. E., Schumann, D. W., Richman, S. A., & Strathman, A. J. (1993). Positive mood and persuasion: Different roles for affect under high- and low-elaboration conditions. *Journal of Personality and Social Psychology, 64,* 5–20.

Petty, R. E., & Wegener, D. T. (1998). Attitude change: Multiple roles for persuasion variables. In D. T. Gilbert, S. T. Fiske, & G. Lindzey (Eds.), *Handbook of social psychology* (4th ed., Vol. 1, pp. 323–390). Boston: McGraw-Hill.

Petty, R. E., & Wegener, D. T. (1999). The elaboration likelihood model: Current status and controversies. In S. Chaiken & Y. Trope (Eds.), *Dual-process theories in social psychology* (pp. 41–72). New York: Guilford Press.

Priester, J. R., Cacioppo, J. T., & Petty, R. E. (1996). The influence of motor processes on attitudes toward novel versus familiar semantic stimuli. *Personality and Social Psychology Bulletin, 22,* 442–447.

Razran, G. H. S. (1940). Conditioned response changes in rating and appraising sociopolitical slogans. *Psychological Bulletin, 37,* 481.

Salovey, P., Mayer, J. D., Caruso, D., & Lopes, P. N. (in press). Measuring emotional intelligence as a set of abilities with the MSCEIT. In S. J. Lopez & C. R. Snyder (Eds.), *Handbook of positive psychology assessment.* Washington, DC: American Psychological Association.

Schwarz, N. (1990). Feelings as information: Informational and motivational functions of affective states. In E. T. Higgins & R. M. Sorrentino (Eds.), *Handbook of motivation and cognition: Foundations of social behavior* (Vol. 2, pp. 527–561). New York: Guilford Press.

Schwarz, N., & Bless, H. (1992). Constructing reality and its alternatives: An inclusion/exclusion model of assimilation and contrast effects in social judgment. In L. L. Martin & A. Tesser (Eds.), *The construction of social judgments* (pp. 217–245). Mahwah, NJ: Erlbaum.

Schwarz, N., Bless, H., & Bohner, G. (1991). Mood and persuasion: Affective states influence the processing of persuasive communications. In M. P. Zanna (Ed.), *Advances in experimental social psychology* (Vol. 24, pp. 161–201). San Diego, CA: Academic Press.

Schwarz, N., & Clore, G. (1983). Mood, misattribution, and judgments of well-being: Informative and directive functions of affective states. *Journal of Personality and Social Psychology, 45,* 513–523.

Schwarz, N., & Clore, G. (1996). Feelings and phenomenal experiences. In E. T. Higgins & A. W. Kruglanski (Eds.), *Social psychology: Handbook of basic principles* (pp. 433–465). New York: Guilford Press.

Sinclair, R. C., Mark, M. M., & Clore, G. L. (1994). Mood related persuasion depends on (mis)attributions. *Social Cognition, 12*, 309–326.

Staats, A. W., & Staats, C. K. (1958). Attitudes established by classical conditioning. *Journal of Abnormal and Social Psychology, 57*, 37–40.

Strack, F., Schwarz, N., Bless, H., Kübler, A., & Wänke, M. (1993). Awareness of the influence as a determinant of assimilation versus contrast. *European Journal of Social Psychology, 23*, 53–62.

Wegener, D. T., & Petty, R. E. (1995). Flexible correction processes in social judgment: The role of naïve theories in corrections for perceived bias. *Journal of Personality and Social Psychology, 68*, 36–51.

Wegener, D. T., & Petty, R. E. (1996). Effects of mood on persuasion processes: Enhancing, reducing, and biasing scrutiny of attitude-relevant information. In L. L. Martin & A. Tesser (Eds.), *Striving and feeling: Interactions between goals and affect* (pp. 329–362). Mahwah, NJ: Erlbaum.

Wegener, D. T., & Petty, R. E. (1997). The flexible correction model: The role of naïve theories of bias in bias correction. In M. P. Zanna (Ed.), *Advances in experimental social psychology* (Vol. 29, pp. 141–208). Mahwah, NJ: Erlbaum.

Wegener, D. T., Petty, R. E., & Smith, S. M. (1995). Positive mood can increase or decrease message scrutiny: The hedonic contingency view of mood and message processing. *Journal of Personality and Social Psychology, 69*, 5–15.

Wilson, T. D., & Brekke, N. (1994). Mental contamination and mental correction: Unwanted influences on judgments and evaluations. *Psychological Bulletin, 116*, 117–142.

Zanna, M. P., Kiesler, C. A., & Pilkonis, P. A. (1970). Positive and negative attitudinal affect established by classical conditioning. *Journal of Personality and Social Psychology, 14*, 321–328.

CHAPTER 9

The Role of Emotion in Strategic Behavior
Insights from Psychopathology

CARY R. SAVAGE

Investigations of emotional and cognitive processes have traditionally fallen within separate domains of cognitive neuroscience. Each has tended to emphasize different regions of the brain and different mental operations. Recent advances in both fields, however, have shown that there is actually much more overlap than previously appreciated, in terms of both the mental operations engaged and the neural regions activated in their support. Cognitive and emotional neural systems work together to inform and mediate intelligent strategic behavior. In fact, one of the central purposes of emotion is to assist cognitive processing and strategic behavior (e.g., Damasio, 1994). Psychiatric conditions provide compelling examples of how this process can go wrong. This chapter describes a perspective on psychopathology that emphasizes ways in which individuals place either too much or too little weight on their emotions in guiding strategic behavior. These disruptions in the way emotions are used to inform behavior have profound consequences for cognitive and social functioning. The focus is primarily on obsessive–compulsive disorder (OCD), but comparisons are also made to other forms of psychopathology.

OBSESSIVE–COMPULSIVE DISORDER

"Did I lock the door as I left the house this morning?"; "What about the stove—did I turn it off?"; "That public toilet was so disgusting I still feel dirty even though I washed my hands." Everyone experiences similar thoughts at some point in time. For the most part, they are transitory and cause little real concern. For some individuals, however, these doubts and associated rituals are severe and disabling. For example, consider the individual who feels compelled to get out of the car every time it hits a bump in the road to verify that the "bump" was not an unlucky pedestrian. Or the person who fears that a loved one will die if signatures are not written in "exactly the right way" on bank checks. Or the deeply religious person who repeatedly counts by threes in an attempt to neutralize intrusive blasphemous thoughts and images. Although these individuals usually have some understanding that their intrusive thoughts are bizarre and impossible, they cannot stop worrying about them and engaging in rituals in an effort to reduce anxiety. In these more extreme forms, the person may be diagnosed with OCD. Their fears may be reasonable, and even protective, when experienced in proportion to the real threat—they represent fundamental concerns of protecting self, loved ones, and fellow human beings. However, in OCD, they are taken to the extreme.

Clinical Features

The diagnostic criteria for OCD include the presence of obsessions and/or compulsions that cause significant distress, are time-consuming (more than 1 hour a day), and interfere with normal occupational and social functioning (American Psychiatric Association, 1994). "Obsessions" are the recurrent intrusive thoughts—usually perceived as senseless or threatening—that patients attempt to ignore, suppress, or neutralize with compulsive behaviors. Although the contents of obsessions may seem bizarre to the outside observer, patients themselves recognize that they are inappropriate and products of their own minds. This is an important feature, because it differentiates OCD from delusional conditions. "Compulsions" are the repetitive behaviors (e.g., checking, cleaning) that patients perform, either in response to obsessions or according to rigid stereotypic rules. Compulsive behaviors are usually designed to reduce anxiety associated with obsessions or in some way prevent a dreaded event, but they can also be performed in response to a more vague sense of urgency.

The symptoms of OCD can be expressed in a number of different ways, with various combinations of obsessions and/or compulsions.

Two prototypic symptom subtypes are checking and cleaning. Individuals with predominately *checking* symptoms suffer from obsessive thoughts that they have either done something, or neglected to do something, that will lead to great harm to themselves or others. For example, a patient may worry that he or she will forget to lock the door and that some catastrophic event will ensue, such as someone breaking in and harming loved ones. In response to this obsession, the patient engages in repetitive compulsive behaviors, such as checking to make sure the door is locked. Even after deliberate attempts to "remember" locking the door, the patient feels overwhelmed by doubt and checks the door again. Such checking behavior may become ritualized, such that he or she goes through a rigid sequence of checks, which are still ineffective at reducing the doubt and anxiety. In more severe cases, this can lead to real-life "catastrophe," such as job loss, because so much time is spent in compulsive rituals. This is an example of how OCD patients misinterpret risk (Steketee, Frost, & Cohen, 1998)—job loss resulting from chronic lateness is a more real and probable danger than home invasion, yet the latter is much more compelling to the patient.

Patients with predominately *cleaning* rituals suffer from obsessive thoughts about possible contamination and wash in an attempt to reduce anxiety. For example, a patient may fear contracting human immunodeficiency virus (HIV), even by casual contact such as hand shaking or from doorknobs. Although he or she has an intellectual understanding that such transmission is impossible, the intrusive thoughts and fears persist. In response to these obsessions, the patient engages in repetitive hand washing designed to reduce anxiety. These behaviors can also become ritualized; for example, body parts may be washed a certain number of times or in a designated order. These rituals are ultimately ineffective in reducing anxiety, yet difficult to resist.

The hallmark symptoms of OCD—chronic doubt, repetitive checking, mental rumination, cognitive inflexibility, and ritualistic behavior—suggest that brain dysfunction and neuropsychological impairment underlie this condition. Frontal–striatal networks in the brain are central to current neurobiological theories of OCD. The following section provides a brief overview of the structure and function of these frontal–striatal networks and, in the process, introduces the reader to the terminology of neuroanatomy and neuropsychology. This review provides a foundation for the discussions to follow.

Structure and Function of Frontal–Striatal Networks

The frontal–striatal system consists of cerebral cortical regions, subcortical nuclei collectively known as the basal ganglia and thalamus, and the white matter interconnections between these areas. Cortical–basal ganglia networks are organized into segregated parallel circuits that originate with projections from widespread regions of the cortex to separate components of striatum (caudate nucleus [CN], putamen, and nucleus accumbens; Alexander, Crutcher, & DeLong, 1990; Wise, Murray, & Gerfen, 1996). These cortical–striatal projections are massive, with as many as 10,000 cortical inputs converging on a single striatal neuron (Graybiel, 1998). The striatum can be thought of as a "convergence zone," where widespread, but functionally related, regions of the cortex project to small neuronal compartments (Graybiel, 1998). Figure 9.1 illustrates frontal–striatal networks in pictorial and diagrammatic form.

The top half of the figure emphasizes the organization of cortical projection territories. Although most regions of cortex (frontal, temporal, parietal, occipital) initially project through the striatum, the cortical target of output from the thalamus is almost exclusively to the frontal cortex. Thus, these networks are anatomically connected in such a way that enables them to modulate activity in the frontal and prefrontal cortex (Wise et al., 1996). Although there are at least five distinct circuits (Alexander et al., 1990), it is useful to group them into three functional categories based on the organization of the frontal and prefrontal cortex: (1) *motor networks,* which include reciprocal connections with primary motor and premotor cortical areas; (2) *prefrontal networks,* which include reciprocal connections with the dorsolateral and lateral orbitofrontal cortex (OFC); and (3) *limbic networks,* which include reciprocal connections with the paralimbic frontal cortex, including the anterior cingulate cortex (ACC) and medial OFC (Alexander et al., 1990).

Frontal–striatal networks remain functionally and anatomically segregated as they project from compartments of the striatum through the globus pallidus and substantia nigra, pars reticulata to thalamic nuclei, where they are closed via reciprocal projections back to the cortex. These systems are necessarily simplified for the current discussion. The reader is referred to Alexander et al. (1990) and Wise et al. (1996) for more thorough descriptions of frontal–striatal anatomy. For the purposes of this discussion, it must be kept in mind that patterns of anatomic connectivity place these networks in a position of importance for regulating prefrontal and paralimbic cortical activity, and thereby affecting cognitive and affective information processing. Disruption of prefrontal and paralimbic networks is probably central to the manifestation of OCD as a disorder of both cognitive and emotional dysregulation (Cummings, 1993; Weinberger, 1993; Zald & Kim, 1996a, 1996b). The anatomic structure of these systems highlights the interdependence of affective and cognitive operations in the brain.

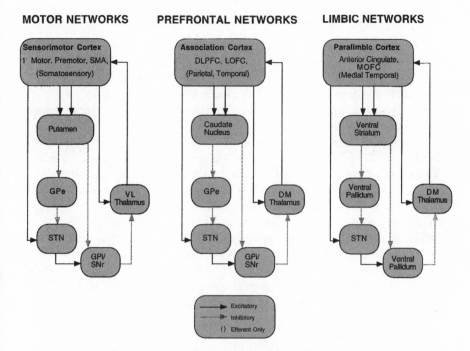

FIGURE 9.1. This figure illustrates the structural and functional organization of frontal–striatal networks. The top section depicts frontal and prefrontal regions of the human cerebral cortex that form the "closed-loop" components of frontal–striatal circuits. The functional organization of the frontal–striatal system is largely defined by the nature of these cortical groups. A diagrammatic representation of motor and prefrontal networks in the frontal–striatal system is also provided, based on the circuit diagrams of Alexander et al. (1990). A distinction is made here between networks that project through putamen and subserve motor processes, networks that project through caudate nucleus and subserve cognitive (prefrontal) processes, and networks that project through ventral striatum and modulate limbic functions. Prefrontal and paralimbic networks are most implicated in OCD. SMA, supplementary motor area; DLPFC, dorsolateral prefrontal cortex; LOFC, lateral orbitofrontal cortex; MOFC, medial orbitofrontal cortex; GPe, external capsule of the globus pallidus; GPi, internal capsule of the globus pallidus; STN, subthalamic nucleus; SNr, substantia nigra, pars reticulata; VL Thalamus, ventrolateral nucleus of the thalamus; DM Thalamus, dorsomedial nucleus of the thalamus.

Neurobiolgy of OCD

The current understanding of OCD as a disorder of brain function in frontal–striatal networks comes from numerous convergent sources, especially from case reports of patients with neurological disorders and from functional neuroimaging studies.

Neurological Case Reports

There are numerous case reports noting associations between OCD or OCD-like behavior and neurological disorders such as Tourette's disorder, postencephalitic and idiopathic Parkinson's disease, Huntington's disease, Sydenham's chorea, and cases of focal prefrontal and striatal lesions (Berthier, Kulisevsky, Gironell, & Heras, 1996; Coffey, Jones, & Shapiro, 1998; Cummings & Cunningham, 1992; Daniele et al., 1997; Donovan & Barry, 1994; Laplane et al., 1989; Savage, 1997; Swoboda & Jenike, 1995; Weilburg et al., 1989; Williams, Owen, & Heath, 1988). The earliest report was probably the original 1885 communication by Gilles de la Tourette that described Tourette's disorder—a neurologic disorder characterized by motor and vocal tics—and noted its frequent association with obsessions and compulsive behaviors (de la Tourette, 1885). Reports have recently appeared in the literature regarding variants of OCD and tic disorders with childhood onset that are secondary to streptococcal infection, known as pediatric autoimmune neuropsychiatric disorders associated with streptococcal infections (PANDAS; Swedo et al., 1998). PANDAS is an autoimmune disorder arising from the production of antineuronal antibodies against human striatum in response to infection.

Eslinger and Damasio (1985) presented a now-famous case report of a patient with bilateral OFC lesions secondary to removal of a large meningioma. Although the patient's behavior was not presented as an example of OCD-like behavior, the similarities are remarkable, including features of repetitive behavior, indecisiveness, and compulsive hoarding:

> He [the patient] needed about 2 hours to get ready for work in the morning, and some days were consumed entirely by shaving and hair washing. Deciding where to dine might take hours, as he discussed each restaurant's seating plan, particulars of menu, atmosphere, and management. He would drive to each restaurant to see how busy it was, but even then he could not finally decide which to choose. Purchasing small items required in-depth consideration of brands, prices, and the best method of purchase. He clung to outdated and useless possessions, refusing to part with dead houseplants, old phone books, six broken fans, five broken television sets, three bags of empty orange juice concentrate cans, 15 cigarette lighters, and countless stacks of old newspapers. (p. 1732)

In a 1994 book, *Descartes' Error: Emotion, Reason, and the Human Brain,* A. R. Damasio describes an even more famous case—the story of Phineas Gage. Gage was a railroad worker who sustained a dramatic injury in 1848 when an iron rod was shot through his skull in an accidental explosion. Although surviving 11 years, Gage underwent many personality changes; among them, according to Damasio's review of the case, was "abnormal collecting behavior." Modern reconstruction of Gage's injury by Hannah Damasio and colleagues (Damasio, Grabowski, Frank, Galaburda, & Damasio, 1994) indicates that ventromedial sectors of the prefrontal cortex, especially the OFC, were probably most directly affected. Thus, Gage may have been the first documented case highlighting a relationship between the OFC and OCD-like behavior.

Functional Imaging Studies

Functional neuroimaging approaches, including positron emission tomography (PET), functional magnetic resonance imaging (fMRI), and event-related potentials (ERPs), have provided evidence of abnormal brain function in patients with OCD during resting states, during symptomatic provocation, and, most recently, during cognitive activation (see Rauch & Savage, 1997; Saxena, Brody, Schwartz, & Baxter, 1998, for reviews). PET studies of OCD acquired during resting states have consistently indicated abnormally increased activity, relative to healthy control subjects, in the OFC (Baxter et al., 1987; Benkelfat et al., 1990; Nordahl et al., 1989), CN (Baxter et al., 1987; Benkelfat et al., 1990), and ACC (Perani et al., 1995; Machlin et al., 1991). Hyperfunction has also been noted with the use of electrophysiological methods, such as ERP, to demonstrate shorter waveform latencies, particularly in components believed to arise from cortical–subcortical interactions (Savage et al., 1994). Metabolic abnormalities in the OFC and CN of patients with OCD normalize following successful treatment with serotonergic reuptake inhibitors (Baxter et al., 1992) or behavior therapy (Schwartz, Stoessel, Baxter, Martin, & Phelps, 1996). Baseline metabolic activity in the OFC has also been shown to predict treatment response to pharmacotherapy and behavior therapy (Brody et al., 1998).

PET studies have examined blood flow changes associated with states of OCD symptom provocation. For example, Rauch and colleagues (1994) measured regional cerebral blood flow with PET while they provoked obsessions in patients with OCD with contamination concerns. Participants in this study were instructed to touch a "contaminated" object during one image acquisition and to touch a "clean" object during another. In this way, blood flow could be compared between two conditions that were identical in perceptual stimulation, but differed in the strength of obsession. During obsessive states, subjects with OCD showed increased blood flow in the right CN, bilateral OFC, and ACC. Activity in the left OFC correlated with the severity of obsessional symptoms. In follow-up PET studies, Rauch et al. (1995, 1996; Rauch, Savage, Alpert, Fischman, & Jenike, 1997) showed that changes in the CN and lateral OFC were unique to OCD as compared with two other anxiety disorders—simple phobia and posttraumatic stress disorder—whereas the ACC activation was common to all three. This suggests that the CN and OFC mediate OCD symptoms specifically, whereas the ACC is more widely implicated in anxious states.

Neuropsychological Features of OCD

Recent neuropsychological studies are beginning to paint a clear and consistent picture of the cognitive deficits associated with OCD. This section provides a summary of the general neuropsychological features of OCD, organized according to the two domains of function most consistently affected: executive function and episodic memory.

Executive Function

The term "executive function" describes a diverse set of high-level cognitive processes that regulate more elementary perceptual, motor, and memory operations. These functions enable individuals to appreciate the overall context of the environment and use this understanding to make plans, implement strategic action, and monitor and flexibly shift behavior when it is no longer appropriate (e.g., see Lezak, 1995). Consider as an example the Wisconsin Card Sorting Test (WCST; Heaton, Chelune, Talley, Kay, & Curtiss, 1993), which is in some ways a prototypical measure of executive functioning. This test consists of four stimulus cards printed with various symbols: one red triangle, two green stars, three yellow crosses, and four blue circles. Subjects are presented with a deck of cards, each card printed with one of four symbols in one of four colors, and instructed to match these cards to the stimulus cards according to an unstated rule (either color, shape, or number). Subjects are not told what the rule is, but they are given feedback after each response as to whether it was correct or incorrect. After 10 consecutive correct responses, the previously correct rule is changed and a new rule must be derived. Therefore, to successfully complete the WCST, subjects must deduce the abstract rules, apply these rules to sort the cards, maintain the response patterns as long as appropriate, and flexibly change behavior when the old response rules are no longer appropriate—all examples of executive functioning.

Investigators have long suspected that OCD is associated with executive function disturbances inasmuch as so many of its central features are reminiscent of classic "frontal lobe" symptoms, such as behavioral inflexibility and stereotypy (Stuss & Benson, 1986). Recent experimental findings have, for the most part, verified these observations. Disturbances in executive functioning have been shown on a variety of different tests, including the Trail Making Test, Part B (Aronowitz et al., 1994), the Category Test (Insel, Donnelly, Lalakea, Alterman, & Murphy, 1983), visual attention tests (Nelson, Early, & Haller, 1993; Dirson, Bouvard, Cottraux, & Martin, 1995), selective attention tests (Clayton, Richards, & Edwards, 1999), self-paced working memory tests (Martin, Wiggs, Altemus, Rubenstein, & Murphy, 1995), Stroop test (Hartston & Swerdlow, 1999), and organizational measures from the Rey–Osterrieth Complex Figure Test (RCFT; Behar et al., 1984; Deckersbach, Otto, Savage, Baer, & Jenike, 2000; Savage et al., 1999; Savage et al., 2000). These measures tap into various aspects of executive functioning, such as the ability to plan, implement strategic action, and monitor and flexibly shift behavior when it is no longer appropriate.

There have been some inconsistencies in findings with the WCST, one of the classic measures of executive functioning described earlier. Some studies have found increased perseveration (difficulty shifting set when the rules change) on the WCST in groups of patients with OCD (Malloy, 1987; Head, Bolton, & Hymas, 1989; Harvey, 1986), and others have not (e.g., Abbruzzese, Ferri, & Scarone, 1995; Boone, Ananth, Philpott, Kaur, & Djenderedjian, 1991; Deckersbach et al., 2000; Gross-Isseroff et al., 1996; Zielinski, Taylor, & Juzwin, 1991). Abbruzzese and colleagues recently compared executive functioning in groups of individuals with OCD with schizophrenic patient groups (Abbruzzese, Bellodi, Ferri, & Scarone, 1995; Abbruzzese, Ferri, & Scarone, 1997). They found that schizophrenic patients were selectively impaired on the WCST, whereas patients with OCD were selectively impaired on an Object Alternation Test (OAT). In the OAT, subjects have to locate an object (e.g., a token) hidden under one of two covers. Following a correct response, the object is moved to the other location and the subject must again locate the object. Subjects are therefore required to continually "shift" away from the most recently reinforced position to the opposite location after each correct response. Findings from the Abbruzzese et al. studies were interpreted to reflect dorsolateral prefrontal cortex (DLPFC) dysfunction in the schizophrenic group and OFC dysfunction in the group with OCD. Gross-Isseroff et al. (1996) also showed that patients with OCD were impaired on the OAT but normal on the WCST. Cavedini, Ferri, Scarone, and Bellodi (1998) compared performance of patients with OCD to a group with major depression and found that the group with OCD had significantly more perseverative responses on the OAT. Thus, the most consistent findings of executive dysfunction in OCD are those using measures believed to be most sensitive to OFC function.

Recent studies of OCD indicate that executive function deficits are pronounced on measures that stress strategic processing and working memory, especially when patients are given minimal direction and feedback. For example, Veale, Sahakian, Owen, and Marks (1996) used the Tower of London Test to show that subjects with OCD had delays in generating alternate strategies following initially incorrect responses. They attributed this slowing to difficulty in shifting mental set. Purcell, Maruff, Kyrios, and Pantelis (1998a, 1998b) found that patients with OCD experienced difficulties on computerized measures of spatial working memory, especially those that required the ability to organize and execute strategies in the presence of minimal external structure. Schmidtke, Schorb, Winkelmann, and Hohagen (1998) reported that subjects with OCD were impaired on measures of controlled attention (a Digit Connection Task) and strategic flexibility (Weight Sorting Task). Overall, results point to impairment in several aspects of executive functioning, especially those requiring the ability to prioritize, to plan and initiate strategic behavior, and to self-monitor and shift mental set in the presence of minimal external feedback.

Episodic Memory

"Episodic memory" refers to the ability to encode, store, and retrieve information that is associated with a distinct place and time. Episodic memory is illustrated when subjects are read a list of words and then, after some delay, instructed to repeat all the words they can remember from the previously learned list. To do this, they must think back to the original learning episode and retrieve information specific to that event.

Groups with OCD are consistently found to be impaired on episodic memory tests, especially on measures using nonverbal stimuli. Problems have been noted on a number of tests of nonverbal memory, including the Visual Reproduction subtest of the Weschsler Memory Scale (WMS; Boone et al., 1991; Christensen, Kim, Dysken, & Hoover, 1992), Delayed Recognition Span Test (Savage et al., 1996), Benton Visual Retention Test (Aronowitz et al., 1994; Cohen et al., 1996), Recurring Figures Test (Zielinski et al., 1991), Korsi's Block Test (Zielinski et al., 1991), Memory Efficiency Battery (Dirson et al., 1995), Stylus Maze Learning (Behar et al., 1984), and recall conditions of the RCFT (Boone et al., 1991; Savage et al., 1999; Savage et al., 2000; Deckersbach et al., 2000).

The Centrality of Executive Dysfunction

Many factors influence the ability to encode, store, and retrieve episodic memories. Memory studies in patients with frontal–striatal neurological dysfunction (e.g., patients with frontal lesions) point to abnormalities in the "strategic" aspects of episodic memory, which are closely tied to executive functioning (Gershberg & Shimamura, 1995; Savage, 1998). For example, these patients have difficulty using semantic organizational attributes of stimuli (e.g., categorical similarities between words in a list) to facilitate the learning and retrieval of episodic memories. Given evidence of frontal–striatal dysfunction in OCD, it is likely that executive dysfunction plays a central role here as well (Savage, 1998).

Savage et al. (1999) used the RCFT (Osterrieth, 1944) to examine the effects of executive disturbance on memory in patients with OCD and healthy controls. Because of the complexity of the RCFT stimulus figure, subjects must carefully plan and organize their drawings; these organizational strategies can be quantified and used to evaluate strategic memory functioning. The RCFT stimulus figure is illustrated in Figure 9.2, along with its core organizational elements.

The most efficient organizational approach on the RCFT is based on the core configural elements illustrated in Figure 9.2—well-organized subjects draw these before they draw more isolated details. Examining this figure reveals how an organized drawing strategy may lead to better memory. First, there are fewer parts to remember in a well-organized drawing; once subjects recall the five configural elements of the figure, they can fill in a few remaining details to achieve high scores. Second, these configural elements are highly "meaningful" to perceptual systems (i.e., rectangle, diagonal "X," horizontal and vertical lines "+," triangle). Information encoded into episodic memory thereby has substantial perceptual structure that makes it easier to retrieve.

Participants in this study were instructed to copy the figure with colored pencils, which were changed every 15 seconds in order to capture the sequence of construction. The authors developed a scoring system whereby subjects received points for constructing each of the configural elements (illustrated in Figure 9.2) as whole units. Using this approach, it was shown that subjects with OCD were impaired in their use of organizational strategies in the copy condition and that they recalled less on immediate and delayed testing. Retention rates from immediate to delayed recall were normal. Figure 9.3 shows drawings of the RCFT figure taken from three representative subjects with OCD. It illustrates the general finding from this study: Patients with poor organizational strategies at copy were the ones who later had difficulty recalling the figure. Multiple regression modeling of these data confirmed that

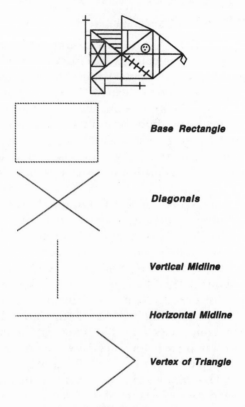

FIGURE 9.2. Illustration of the RCFT figure and the core configural elements—the base rectangle, diagonals, vertical midline, horizontal midline, and vertex of the triangle on the right. These configural elements form the core features of a well-organized approach on the RCFT.

copy organizational strategies statistically mediated group differences in immediate recall. Thus, the cognitive deficit in this study involved planning and organization, a strategic executive function, which had secondary effects on memory.

In a second study, Savage et al. (2000) used the California Verbal Learning Test (CVLT; Delis, Kramer, Kaplan, & Ober, 1987), in addition to the RCFT, to examine memory and organizational processes in patients with OCD. In the CVLT, subjects hear a list of 16 words containing imbedded semantic categories (e.g., fruit, clothing, tools). Subjects are not informed of this structure, and the list is presented so that no two words from the same category appear together. The degree to which subjects spontaneously use semantic organizational strategies can be evalu-

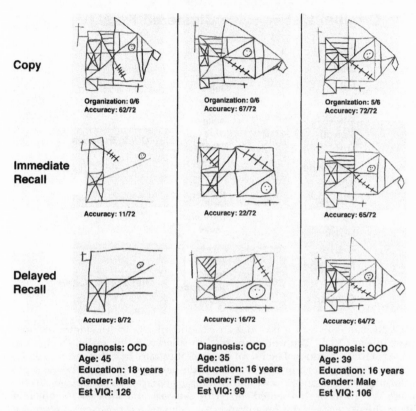

FIGURE 9.3. RCFT drawings of three patients with OCD from a recent study (Savage et al., 1999), illustrating copy, immediate recall, and delayed recall performance conditions. Organization and accuracy scores are provided under the drawings, and demographic information is provided for each patient. Patients 1 and 2 were selected as examples of typical subjects with OCD with poor organization in the copy condition, who later had difficulty recalling the figure on immediate and delayed testing. Patient 3 was provided as an example of a patient with OCD with good organization in the copy condition and good recall at immediate and delayed testing. Multiple regression analyses indicated that group differences in immediate recall were mediated by abnormal copy organizational strategies in the OCD group.

ated by examining how frequently they group words from the same category together during free recall (semantic clustering). Figure 9.4 provides an example of a verbal memory test, patterned after the CVLT. It illustrates the way word lists can be semantically grouped at recall.

Patients with OCD recalled significantly fewer words on the CVLT than control subjects, across all learning trials and on delayed free recall

Original List	Clustered Recall	
Cola	Milk	
Doll	Cola	*Drinks*
Glue	Coffee	
Journal	Juice	
Blocks	Ruler	
Pencil	Glue	*Office Supplies*
Milk	Stapler	
Magazine	Pencil	
Juice	Blocks	
Stapler	Doll	*Toys*
Jacks	Crayons	
Book	Jacks	
Coffee		
Newspaper	Magazine	
Ruler	Book	*Reading Materials*
Crayons	Newspaper	
	Journal	

FIGURE 9.4. This figure provides an example of a word list similar to those used in the CVLT. The words are read to subjects in the order on the left, mixed across categories. The list on the right illustrates how these words can be actively reorganized according to semantically based groups—in this case, types of drinks, office supplies, toys, and reading materials—during free recall. Because the words are presented mixed by category and subjects are not told about the presence of this organization, participants must *spontaneously* impose an organizational structure during free recall.

measures. They also showed less semantic clustering across all five learning trials. In addition, results with the RCFT replicated previous findings of impaired organizational strategies and reduced immediate recall. Investigators examined the mediating effects of strategic processing, using the copy organization score from the RCFT and the semantic clustering score from the CVLT as mediators (independent variables) in multiple regression analyses of free recall. These strategy measures statistically mediated group differences in both verbal and nonverbal free recall, providing additional evidence for the importance of strategic processing deficits in OCD. Cabrera, McNally, and Savage (2001) recently extended this finding by showing that patients with OCD focus less on semantic gist when recalling verbal passages than healthy control subjects.

These findings indicate that one central deficit in OCD—difficulty in mobilizing effective behavioral strategies in novel or ambiguous situations—affects other abilities such as memory. There is another interesting characteristic of patients' performance on the CVLT: Their scores improve disproportionately when they are provided with external structure in the form of category cues and are completely normal when patients are given recognition trials. This suggests that patients with OCD may primarily have problems with the capacity to *spontaneously* impose strategies. The ability of normal subjects to spontaneously apply strategies during verbal learning has recently been tied to functioning in the OFC by a PET study (Savage et al., 2001). Thus, the OFC may play an especially critical role in the failures of patients with OCD to use effective strategies. A brief review of the role of the OFC in cognition will further strengthen this connection.

THE ROLE OF THE ORBITOFRONTAL CORTEX IN COGNITION

The animal literature has implicated the OFC in processes supporting stimulus–reward reversal and monitoring the incentive value of reinforcers (Dias, Robbins, & Roberts, 1997; Gallagher, McMahan, & Schoenbaum, 1999). Furthermore, OFC activity occurs most prominently early in the course of learning, before animals show reliable behavioral discriminations, indicating that the animals are using anticipated future outcome to guide current goal-directed behavior (Shoenbaum, Chiba, & Gallagher, 1998; Lipton, Alvarez, & Eichenbaum, 1999). Humans with OFC lesions also show a number cognitive impairments, especially in novel or poorly structured situations (Damasio, 1996; Eslinger & Damasio, 1985; Rolls, 1996; Rolls, Hornack, & McGrath, 1994). For example, in "gambling" paradigms (Bechara, Tranel, Damasio, & Damasio, 1996; Bechara, Damasio, Tranel, & Damasio, 1997; Bechara, Damasio, Tranel, & Anderson, 1998), patients with OFC lesions consistently play from decks associated with immediate gain but long-term loss. In addition, normal subjects develop anticipatory skin conductance responses (SCRs) prior to card selection, even before they are able to explicitly describe the rules, but patients with OFC lesions do not (Bechara et al., 1996, 1997). An interesting aspect of patients with OFC lesions is that they seem to "understand" that they are making bad choices, yet they persist with ineffective strategies. This is reminiscent of patients with OCD who have insight into their symptoms but are unable to resist them.

Taken together, these studies indicate that the OFC supports the mobilization of effective strategies early during the course of learning in novel or ambiguous situations. This is probably not a deliberate operation, because it occurs very early during learning, before subjects are able to describe what they are doing. Damasio (e.g., 1996) has described the OFC as an "emotional helping" system that allocates processing resources so that executive systems can engage effective strategies. He also hypothesizes that OFC function is critical in guiding behavior based on anticipated future consequences. Interestingly, the OFC has recently been implicated with fMRI in "guessing" operations on a task, based on the Bechara gambling paradigm, in which subjects are instructed to make their best educated "guess" regarding the upcoming card suit or color (Elliott, Rees, & Dolan, 1999). Specifically, OFC activation was associated with increased guessing demands, as subjects had to factor in past instances of success and failure over a number of trials to predict what the next card would be. This finding is consistent with Damasio's hypothesis that the mental signal from the OFC is somewhat akin to a hunch—a subtle feeling that guides an individual toward making a particular decision (Damasio, 1994). In these circumstances the person may not actually be consciously aware of experiencing an emotional state per se, yet the emotion nonetheless influences behavior.

A recent PET study has also identified an important role for the OFC in the ability to use effective strategies during verbal learning (Savage et al., 2001). Subjects in this study encoded two semantically related word lists that were presented so that no two words from the same category occurred together. During one condition, participants could spontaneously impose strategies, whereas in the other they were specifically instructed to use semantic organizational strategies (regroup the words together by category). In a third condition, subjects encoded unrelated word lists. This design thereby manipulated semantic organization in a graded fashion and studied brain systems supporting the spontaneous and directed use of strategies. The graded contrast (directed > spontaneous > unrelated) identified regions of activation in the left inferior prefrontal cortex (IPFC) and left DLPFC, which are directly implicated in the processes supporting semantic organization. Notably, this study also identified strong correlations ($r = .94$ to $.96$; Figure 9.5) between blood flow in the OFC during the first spontaneous encoding condition and behavioral measures of semantic organization assessed during free recall. Thus, blood flow in the OFC predicted which subjects would later use effective semantic strategies.

THE ROLE OF THE ORBITOFRONTAL CORTEX IN OBSESSIVE–COMPULSIVE DISORDER

Taken together, findings indicate that when presented with complex or ambiguous situations, patients with OCD tend to focus on details in iso-

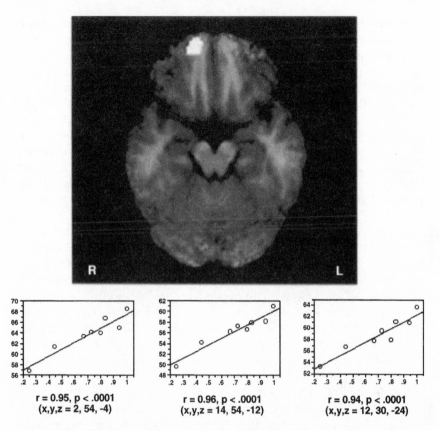

FIGURE 9.5. A PET statistical map from a study (Savage et al., 2001) examining neural systems supporting spontaneous and directed strategy application during verbal learning. In this analysis, correlations were calculated between blood flow during the initial encoding condition and subsequent spontaneous use of semantic clustering strategies during immediate recall. The top of the figure is the area of maximal activation (x, y, z = 14, 54, –12), coregistered with an averaged structural MRI image. The lower half of the figure provides a graphic depiction of the three regions of maximal covariation between blood flow during encoding and spontaneous use of effective strategy. Changes in activity in the ventromedial prefrontal cortex, especially the OFC, predicted which subjects would spontaneously initiate semantic organizational strategies.

lation at the expense of important organizational information. Most normal subjects benefit from latent structure by spontaneously grouping stimuli according to fundamental organizing features. For example, word lists can be subdivided into groups of words with shared categorical membership (see Figure 9.4), and complex designs can be broken down into simpler units that are perceptually meaningful (e.g., squares, triangles, diagonals; see Figure 9.2). Subjects with OCD do not appear to spontaneously detect and/or apply organizational structure as a means of improving encoding and retrieval to the same degree as normal subjects. Instead, they preferentially process details—whether disjointed pieces of a figure or individual words in semantic isolation from the others. This style is epitomized by the expression "He cannot see the forest for the trees." It refers to a tendency to miss the big picture—the unified whole of a situation—because of attention to minutia. As a group, patients with OCD are so focused on details that they miss the larger organizational attributes inherent in the environment. This manifests during formal cognitive testing and in everyday situations, where patients focus on obsessional concerns at the expense of other facets of life.

Based on the literature reviewed here, there is now evidence linking these strategic processing failures to dysfunction in frontal–striatal networks, especially projection networks centered on the OFC. As noted earlier, the OFC is anatomically positioned as a convergence zone for emotional (limbic) and cognitive (prefrontal) information. It is connected in such a way as to use limbic information to determine the motivational significance of stimuli (Rolls, 1996) and then initiate executive processes mediated in other regions of the prefrontal cortex. These abilities are most critical in novel or unstructured situations in which individuals must resolve conflicts between competing choices on the basis of ambiguous or competing information (e.g., Bechara et al., 1998). The OFC is a central neural region where emotions may impact strategic behavior. Interestingly, there is now evidence that performance on the Bechara gambling paradigm predicts response to treatment with selective serotonin reuptake inhibitors in patients with OCD (Cavedini et al., 2001).

Chronic hyperfunction of OFC networks in OCD may interfere with the ability to use emotional information to guide effective strategic behavior. A helpful analogy is provided by the volume controls of a stereo amplifier. If the controls are turned all the way up, it is very difficult to detect small changes in volume. By comparison, if the volume is kept at more modest levels, one can perceive very small changes in loudness. The "signals" from the OFC are probably quite subtle. Effective decision making is influenced by small changes in affective or somatic states, possibly at levels too small to be consciously detected under most circumstances (Damasio, 1996). One must have an appropriate baseline level of activation in order to have adequate "signal to noise" to detect subtle informative changes in affective state. This process may be overwhelmed in OCD, such that emotions have little informative content—that is, the "volume is always on high."

OTHER PSYCHIATRIC DISORDERS

The model proposed here states that, secondary to dysregulation of OFC neural networks, individuals with OCD have difficulty using subtle changes in affective state to guide effective decision making. Other psychiatric conditions have also been linked to OFC dysfunction and may provide useful comparative data. For example, impulse control problems and antisocial personality disorder have been tied to prefrontal dysfunction, particularly in the OFC. Subjects with antisocial personality disorder have reduced prefrontal cortical volumes and decreased somatic responsivity (as measured by SCRs) to disturbing images (Raine, Lencz, Bihrle, LaCasse, & Colletti, 2000). Alcohol and stimulant abusers are found to be impaired on the Bechara gambling paradigm (Bechara et al., 2001) and other measures of OFC function (Dinn & Harris, 2000; Lapierre, Braun, & Hodgins, 1995). Harris and Dinn (1998) proposed that OCD and antisocial personality disorder might represent two extremes of a continuum of OFC function, with OCD groups showing abnormal hyperactivity in the OFC and antisocial groups showing hypoactivity in the same areas. They also found that both groups were impaired on an object alternation test, a measure tied to OFC dysfunction (Freedman, Black, Ebert, & Binns, 1998). Thus, these psychiatric conditions that appear so different may actually represent opposite ends of the same spectrum. In OCD, strategic processing is flooded by affect, whereas in impulse control disorders and antisocial personality, emotion has too little access to cognitive systems. Both extremes are clearly dysfunctional and lead to impaired cognitive and social functioning.

SUMMARY

The clinical and neuropsychological features of OCD highlight the functional interdependence of cognitive and emotional processing. This chapter reviewed clinical and neuropsychological findings in OCD and proposed how they might be related to dysfunction in frontal–striatal networks, especially those converging on the OFC. Evidence is mounting that the OFC is a key neuroanatomical gateway for the connection between the limbic system (emotion) and the prefrontal cortex (cognition). In optimal conditions, affective state informs cognitive processing and strategic behavior is enhanced by taking emotions into consideration. However, in some disorders, such as OCD, cognitive processing is overwhelmed by a limbic system on high alert and the affective state provides little guidance for strategic behavior. Individuals may even be misled by their emotions into making poor decisions. In other conditions, such as antisocial and impulse control disorders, there may be too little access to feelings. Both extremes result in ineffective strategic behavior.

Emotions can be informative, or they can be misleading. What is most adaptive is a balanced access to emotional information—neither too much nor too little. We pay attention to our hunches but are not imprisoned by our fears. In this balance lies the "wisdom in feeling."

REFERENCES

Abbruzzese, M., Bellodi, L., Ferri, S., & Scarone, S. (1995). Frontal lobe dysfunction in schizophrenia and obsessive–compulsive disorder: A neuropsychological study. *Brain and Cognition, 27,* 202–212.

Abbruzzese, M., Ferri, S., & Scarone, S. (1995). Wisconsin Card Sorting Test performance in obsessive–compulsive disorder: No evidence for involvement of dorsolateral prefrontal cortex. *Psychiatry Research, 58,* 37–43.

Abbruzzese, M., Ferri, S., & Scarone, S. (1997). The selective breakdown of frontal functions in patients with obsessive–compulsive disorder and in patients with schizophrenia: A double dissociation experimental finding. *Neuropsychologia, 35,* 907–912.

Alexander, G. E., Crutcher, M. D., & DeLong, M. R. (1990). Basal ganglia-thalamocortical circuits: Parallel substrates for motor, oculomotor, "prefrontal" and "limbic" functions. *Progress in Brain Research, 85,* 119–146.

American Psychiatric Association. (1994). *Diagnostic and statistical manual of mental disorders* (4th ed.). Washington, DC: Author.

Aronowitz, B. R., Hollander, E., DeCaria, C., Cohen, L., Saoud, J. B., & Stein, D. (1994). Neuropsychology of obsessive–compulsive disorder: Preliminary findings. *Neuropsychiatry, Neuropsychology and Behavioral Neurology, 7,* 81–86.

Baxter, L. R., Phelps, M. E., Mazziotta, J. C., Guze, B. H., Schwartz, J. M., & Selin, C. E. (1987). Local cerebral glucose metabolic rates in obsessive–compulsive disorder: A comparison with rates in unipolar depression and in normal controls. *Archives of General Psychiatry, 44,* 211–218.

Baxter, L. R., Schwartz, J. M., Bergman, K. S., Szuba, M. P., Guze, B. H., Mazziotta, J. C., Alazraki, A., Selin, C. E., Ferng, H. K., & Munford, P. (1992). Caudate glucose metabolic rate changes with both drug and behavior therapy for obsessive–compulsive disorder. *Archives of General Psychiatry, 49,* 681–689.

Bechara, A., Damasio, H., Tranel, D., & Anderson, S. W. (1998). Dissociation of working memory from decision making within the human prefrontal cortex. *Journal of Neuroscience, 18,* 428–437.

Bechara, A., Damasio, H., Tranel, D., & Damasio, A. R. (1997). Deciding advantageously before knowing the advantageous strategy. *Science, 275,* 1293–1294.

Bechara, A., Dolan, S., Denburg, N., Hindes, A., Anderson, S. W., & Nathan, P.

E. (2001). Decision-making deficits, linked to a dysfunctional ventromedial prefrontal cortex, revealed in alcohol and stimulant abusers. *Neuropsychologia, 39,* 376–389.

Bechara, A., Tranel, D., Damasio, H., & Damasio, A. R. (1996). Failure to respond autonomically to anticipated future outcomes following damage to prefrontal cortex. *Cerebral Cortex, 6,* 215–225.

Behar, D., Rapoport, J. L., Berg, C. J., Denckla, M. B., Mann, L., Cox, C., Fedio, P., Zahn, T., & Wolfman, M. G. (1984). Computerized tomography and neuropsychological test measures in adolescents with obsessive–compulsive disorder. *American Journal of Psychiatry, 141,* 363–369.

Benkelfat, C., Nordahl, T. E., Semple, W. E., King, C., Murphy, D. L., & Cohen, R. M. (1990). Local cerebral glucose metabolic rates in obsessive–compulsive disorder. *Archives of General Psychiatry, 47,* 840–848.

Berthier, M. L., Kulisevsky, J., Gironell, A., & Heras, J. A. (1996). Obsessive–compulsive disorder associated with brain lesions: Clinical phenomenology, cognitive function, and anatomic correlates. *Neurology, 47,* 353–361.

Boone, K. B., Ananth, J., Philpott, L., Kaur, A., & Djenderedjian, A. (1991). Neuropsychological characteristics of nondepressed adults with obsessive–compulsive disorder. *Neuropsychiatry, Neuropsychology and Behavioral Neurology, 4,* 96–109.

Brody, A. L., Saxena, S., Schwartz, J. M., Stoessel, P. W., Maidment, K., Phelps, M. E., & Baxter, L. R. (1998). FDG-PET predictors of response to behavioral therapy and pharmacotherapy in obsessive–compulsive disorder. *Psychiatry Research, 84,* 1–6.

Cabrera, A. R., McNally, R. J., & Savage, C. R. (2001). Missing the forest for the trees? Deficient memory for linguistic gist in obsessive–compulsive disorder. *Psychological Medicine, 31,* 1089–1094.

Cavedini, P., Ferri, S., Scarone, S., & Bellodi, L. (1998). Frontal lobe dysfunction in obsessive–compulsive disorder and major depression: A clinical-neuropsychological study. *Psychiatry Research, 78,* 21–28.

Cavedini, P., Riboldi, G., D'Annucci, A., Belotti, P., Cisima, M., & Bellodi, L. (2001). Decision-making heterogeneity in obsessive–compulsive disorder: Ventromedial prefrontal cortex function predicts different treatment outcomes. *Neuropsychologia, 40,* 205–211.

Christensen, K. J., Kim, S. W., Dysken, M. W., & Hoover, K. M. (1992). Neuropsychological performance in obsessive–compulsive disorder. *Biological Psychiatry, 31,* 4–18.

Clayton, I. C., Richards, J. C., & Edwards, C. J. (1999). Selective attention in obsessive–compulsive disorder. *Journal of Abnormal Psychology, 108,* 171–175.

Coffey, B. J., Jones, J., & Shapiro, S. (1998). Tourette's disorder and obsessive–compulsive disorder: Clinical similarities and differences. In M. A. Jenike, L. Baer, & W. E. Minichiello (Eds.), *Obsessive–compulsive disorders: Practical management* (3rd ed., pp. 143–161). St. Louis: Mosby.

Cohen, L. J., Hollander, E., DeCaria, C. M., Stein, D. J., Simeon, D., Liebowitz, M. R., & Aronowitz, B. R. (1996). Specificity of neuropsychological impairment in obsessive–compulsive disorder: A comparison with social phobic and normal control subjects. *Journal of Neuropsychiatry and Clinical Neuroscience, 8,* 82–85.

Cummings, J. L. (1993). Frontal subcortical circuits and human behavior. *Archives of Neurology, 50,* 873–880.

Cummings, J. L., & Cunningham, K. (1992). Obsessive–compulsive disorder in Huntington's disease. *Biological Psychiatry, 31,* 263–270.

Damasio, A. R. (1994). *Descartes' error: Emotion, reason, and the human brain.* New York: Avon Books.

Damasio, A. R. (1996). The somatic marker hypothesis and the possible functions of prefrontal cortex. *Philosophical Transactions of the Royal Society of London, 351,* 1413–1420.

Damasio, H., Grabowski, R., Frank, A. M., Galaburda, A. M., & Damasio, A. R. (1994). The return of Phineas Gage: The skull of a famous patient yields clues about the brain, *Science, 264,* 1102–1105.

Daniele, A., Bartolomeo, P., Cassetta, E., Bentivoglio, A. R., Gainotti, G., Albanese, A., & Partolomeo, B. (1997). Obsessive–compulsive behaviour and cognitive impairment in a parkinsonian patient after left putaminal lesion. *Journal of Neurology, Neurosurgery, and Psychiatry, 62,* 288–289.

Deckersbach, T., Otto, M. W., Savage, C. R., Baer, L., & Jenike, M. A. (2000). The relationship between semantic organization and memory in obsessive–compulsive disorder. *Psychotherapy and Psychosomatics, 69,* 101–107.

de la Tourette, G. (1885). Etude sur une affection nerveuse, caracterisée par de l'incoordination motoric accompagnée d'echolalie et de coprolalie. *Archives Neurologique, 9,* 19–42; 158–200.

Delis, D. C., Kramer, J. H., Kaplan, E., & Ober, B. A. (1987). *California Verbal Learning Test: Manual.* San Antonio, TX: Psychological Corporation.

Dias, R., Robbins, T. W., & Roberts, A. C. (1997). Dissociable forms of inhibitory control within prefrontal cortex with an analog of the Wisconsin Card Sort Test: Restriction to novel situations and independence from "on-line" processing. *Journal of Neuroscience, 17,* 9285–9297.

Dinn, W. M., & Harris, C. L. (2000). Neurocognitive function in antisocial personality disorder. *Psychiatry Research, 97,* 173–190.

Dirson, S., Bouvard, M., Cottraux, J., & Martin, R. (1995). Visual memory impairment in patients with obsessive–compulsive disorder: A controlled study. *Psychotherapy and Psychosomatics, 63,* 22–31.

Donovan, N., & Barry, J. J. (1994). Compulsive symptoms associated with frontal lobe injury. *American Journal of Psychiatry, 151,* 618.

Elliott, R., Rees, G., & Dolan, R. J. (1999). Ventromedial prefrontal cortex mediates guessing. *Neuropsychologia, 37,* 403–411.

Eslinger, P. J., & Damasio, A. R. (1985). Severe disturbance of higher cognition after bilateral frontal lobe ablation: Patient EVR. *Neurology, 35,* 1731–1741.

Freedman, M., Black, S., Ebert, P., & Binns, M. (1998). Orbitofrontal function, object alternation, and perseveration. *Cerebral Cortex, 8,* 18–27.

Gallagher, M., McMahan, R. W., & Schoenbaum, G. (1999). Orbitofrontal cortex and representation of incentive value in associative learning. *Journal of Neuroscience, 19,* 6610–6614.

Gershberg, F. B., & Shimamura, A. P. (1995). Impaired use of organizational strategies in free recall following frontal lobe damage. *Neuropsychologia, 13,* 1305–1333.

Graybiel, A. M. (1998). The basal ganglia and chunking of action repertoires. *Neurobiology of Learning and Memory, 70,* 119–136.

Gross-Isseroff, R., Sasson, Y., Voet, H., Hendler, T., Luca-Haimovici, K., Kandel-Sussman, H., & Zohar, J. (1996). Alternation learning in obsessive–compulsive disorder. *Biological Psychiatry, 39,* 733–738.

Harris, C. L., & Dinn, W. (1998, April). *Orbitofrontal dysfunction: A connectionist model of a neurobehavioral continuum.* Paper presented at the annual meeting of the Cognitive Neuroscience Society, San Francisco, CA.

Hartston, H. J., & Swerdlow, N. R. (1999). Visuospatial priming and Stroop performance in patients with obsessive–compulsive disorder. *Neuropsychology, 13,* 447–457.

Harvey, N. S. (1986). Impaired cognitive set-shifting in obsessive–compulsive neurosis. *IRCS Medical Science, 14,* 936–937.

Head, D., Bolton, D., & Hymas, N. (1989). Deficit in cognitive shifting ability in patients with obsessive–compulsive disorders. *Biological Psychiatry, 25,* 929–937.

Heaton, R. K., Chelune, G. J., Talley, J. L., Kay, G. G., & Curtiss, G. (1993). *Wisconsin Card Sorting Test manual: Revised and expanded.* Tampa, FL: Psychological Assessment Resources.

Insel, T. R., Donnely, E. F., Lalakea, M. L., Alterman, I. S., & Murphy, D. L. (1983). Neurological and neuropsychological studies of patients with obsessive–compulsive disorder. *Biological Psychiatry, 18,* 741–751.

Lapierre, D., Braun, C. M. J., & Hodgins, S. (1995). Ventral frontal deficits in psychopathy: Neuropsychological test findings. *Neuropsychologia, 33,* 139–151.

Laplane, D., Levasseur, M., Pillon, B., Dubois, B., Baulac, M., Mazoyer, B., Tran Dinh, S., Gette, G., Danze, F., & Baron, J. C. (1989). Obsessive–compulsive and other behavioural changes with bilateral basal ganglia lesions. *Brain, 112,* 699–725.

Lezak, M. D. (1995). *Neuropsychological assessment* (3rd ed.). New York: Oxford University Press.

Lipton, P. A., Alvarez, P., & Eichenbaum, H. (1999). Crossmodal associative memory representations in rodent orbitofrontal cortex. *Neuron, 22,* 349–359.

Machlin, S. R., Harris, G. J., Pearlson, G. D., Hoehn-Saric, R., Jeffery, P., & Camargo, E. E. (1991). Elevated medial-frontal cerebral blood flow in obsessive–compulsive patients: A SPECT study. *American Journal of Psychiatry, 148,* 1240–1242.

Malloy, P. (1987). Frontal lobe dysfunction in obsessive–compulsive disorder. In E. Perecmam (Ed.), *The frontal lobes revisited* (pp. 207–223). New York: IRBN Press.

Martin, A., Wiggs, C. L., Altemus, M., Rubenstein, C., & Murphy, D. (1995). Working memory as assessed by subject-ordered tasks in patients with obsessive–compulsive disorder. *Journal of Clinical and Experimental Neuropsychology, 17,* 786–792.

Nelson, E., Early, T. S., & Haller, J. W. (1993). Visual attention in obsessive–compulsive disorder. *Psychiatry Research, 49,* 183–196.

Nordahl, T. E., Benkelfat, C., Semple, W., Gross, M., King, A. C., & Cohen, R. M. (1989). Cerebral glucose metabolic rates in obsessive–compulsive disorder. *Neuropsychopharmacology, 2,* 23–28.

Osterrieth, P. A. (1944). Le test de copie d'une figure complex: Contribution à l'étude de la perception et de la memoire [The test of copying a complex figure: A contribution to the study of perception and memory]. *Archives de Psychologie, 30,* 286–350.

Perani, D., Colombo, C., Bressi, S., Bonfanti, A., Grassi, F., Scarone, S., Bellodi, L., Smeraldi, E., & Fazio, F. (1995). FDG PET study in obsessive–compulsive disorder: A clinical metabolic correlation study after treatment. *British Journal of Psychiatry, 166,* 244–250.

Purcell, R., Maruff, P., Kyrios, M., & Pantelis, C. (1998a). Cognitive deficits in obsessive–compulsive disorder on tests of frontal–striatal function. *Biological Psychiatry, 43,* 348–357.

Purcell, R., Maruff, P., Kyrios, M., & Pantelis, C. (1998b). Neuropsychological deficits in obsessive–compulsive disorder: A comparison with unipolar depression, panic disorder, and normal controls. *Archives of General Psychiatry, 55,* 415–423.

Raine, A., Lencz, T., Bihrle, S., LaCasse, L., & Colletti, P. (2000). Reduced prefrontal gray matter volume and reduced autonomic activity in antisocial personality disorder. *Archives of General Psychiatry, 57,* 119–127.

Rauch, S. L., Jenike, M. A., Alpert, N. M., Baer, L., Breiter, H. C., Savage, C. R., & Fischman, A. J. (1994). Regional cerebral blood flow measured during symptom provocation in obsessive–compulsive disorder using ^{15}O-labeled CO_2 and positron emission tomography, *Archives of General Psychiatry, 51,* 62–70.

Rauch, S. L., & Savage, C. R. (1997). Neuroimaging and neuropsychology of the striatum: Bridging basic science and clinical practice. *Psychiatric Clinics of North America, 20,* 741–768.

Rauch, S. L., Savage, C. R., Alpert, N. M., Fischman, A. J., & Jenike, M. A. (1997). The functional neuroanatomy of anxiety: A study of three disorders using positron emission tomography and symptom provocation. *Biological Psychiatry, 42,* 446–452.

Rauch, S. L., Savage, C. R., Alpert, N. M., Miguel, E. C., Baer, L., Breiter, H. C., Fischman, A. J., Manzo, P. A., Moretti, C., & Jenike, M. A. (1995). A positron emission tomographic study of simple phobic symptom provocation. *Archives of General Psychiatry, 52,* 20–28.

Rauch, S. L., van der Kolk, B. A., Fisler, R. E., Alpert, N. M., Orr, S. P., Savage, C. R., Fischman, A. J., Jenike, M. A., & Pitman, R. K. (1996). A symptom provocation study of posttraumatic stress disorder using positron emission tomography and script-driven imagery. *Archives of General Psychiatry, 53,* 380–387.

Rolls, E. T. (1996). The orbitofrontal cortex. *Philosophical Transactions of the Royal Society of London, 351,* 1433–1444.

Rolls, E. T., Hornak, J., & McGrath, W. J. (1994). Emotion-related learning in patients with social and emotional changes associated with frontal lobe damage. *Journal of Neurology, Neurosurgery, and Psychiatry, 57,* 1518–1524.

Savage, C. R. (1997). Neuropsychology of subcortical dementias. *Psychiatric Clinics of North America, 20,* 911–931.

Savage, C. R. (1998). Neuropsychology of obsessive–compulsive disorder: Research findings and treatment implications. In M. A. Jenike, L. Baer, & W. E. Minichiello (Eds.), *Obsessive–compulsive disorders: Practical management* (3rd ed., pp. 254–275). St Louis: Mosby.

Savage, C. R., Baer, L., Keuthen, N. J., Brown, H. D., Rauch, S. L., & Jenike, M. A. (1999). Organizational strategies mediate nonverbal memory impairment in obsessive–compulsive disorder. *Biological Psychiatry, 45,* 905–916.

Savage, C. R., Deckersbach, T., Heckers, S., Wagner, A. D., Schacter, D. L., Alpert, N. M., Fischman, A. J., & Rauch, S. L. (2001). Prefrontal systems underlying spontaneous and directed strategic memory processes. *Brain, 124,* 219–231.

Savage, C. R., Deckersbach, T., Wilhelm, S., Rauch, S. L., Baer, L., Reid, T., & Jenike, M. A. (2000). Strategic processing and episodic memory impairment in obsessive–compulsive disorder. *Neuropsychology, 14,* 141–151.

Savage, C. R., Keuthen, N. J., Jenike, M. A., Brown, H. D., Baer, L., Kendrick, A. D., Miguel, E. C., Rauch, S. L., & Albert, M. S. (1996). Recall and recognition memory in obsessive–compulsive disorder. *Journal of Neuropsychiatry and Clinical Neuroscience, 8,* 99–103.

Savage, C. R., Weilburg, J. B., Duffy, F. H., Baer, L., Shera, D. M., & Jenike, M. A. (1994). Low-level sensory processing in obsessive–compulsive disorder: An evoked potential study. *Biological Psychiatry, 35,* 247–252.

Saxena, S., Brody, A. L., Schwartz, J. M., & Baxter, L. R. (1998). Neuroimaging and frontal–subcortical circuitry in obsessive–compulsive disorder. *British Journal of Psychiatry, 173*(Suppl. 35), 26–37.

Schmidtke, K., Schorb, A., Winkelmann, G., & Hohagen, F. (1998). Cognitive frontal lobe dysfunction in obsessive–compulsive disorder. *Biological Psychiatry, 43,* 666–673.

Schoenbaum, G., Chiba, A. A., & Gallagher, M. (1998). Orbitofrontal cortex and basolateral amygdala encode expected outcomes during learning. *Nature: Neuroscience, 1,* 155–159.

Schwartz, J. M., Stoessel, P. W., Baxter, L. R., Martin, K. M., & Phelps, M. E. (1996). Systematic changes in cerebral glucose metabolic rate after successful behavior modification. *Archives of General Psychiatry, 53,* 109–113.

Steketee, G. S., Frost, R. O., & Cohen, I. (1998). Beliefs in obsessive–compulsive disorder. *Journal of Anxiety Disorders, 12,* 525–537.

Stuss, D. T., & Benson, D. F. (1986). *The frontal lobes.* New York: Raven Press.

Swedo, S. E., Leonard, H. L., Garvey, M., Mittleman, B., Allen, A. J., Perlmutter, S., Lougee, L., Dow, S., Zamkoff, J., & Dubbert, B. K. (1998). Pediatric autoimmune neuropsychiatric disorders associated with streptococcal infections: Clinical description of the first 50 cases. *American Journal of Psychiatry, 155,* 264–271.

Swobota, K. J., & Jenike, M. A. (1995). Frontal abnormalities in patients with obsessive–compulsive disorder: The role of structural lesions in obsessive–compulsive behavior. *Neurology, 45,* 2130–2134.

Veale, D. M., Sahakian, B. J., Owen, A. M., & Marks, I. M. (1996). Specific cognitive deficits in tests sensitive to frontal lobe dysfunction in obsessive–compulsive disorder. *Psychological Medicine, 26,* 1261–1269.

Weilburg, J. B., Mesulam, M. M., Weintraub, S., Buonanno, F., Jenike, M. A., & Stakes, J. W. (1989). Focal striatal abnormalities in a patient with obsessive–compulsive disorder. *Archives of Neurology, 46,* 233–235.

Weinberger, D. R. (1993). A connectionist approach to the prefrontal cortex. *Journal of Neuropsychiatry and Clinical Neurosciences, 5,* 241–253.

Williams, A. C., Owen, C., & Heath, D. A. (1988). A compulsive movement disorder with cavitation of caudae nucleus. *Journal of Neurology, Neurosurgery, and Psychiatry, 51,* 447–448.

Wise, S. P., Murray, E. A., & Gerfen, C. R. (1996). The frontal cortex-basal ganglia system in primates. *Critical Reviews in Neurobiology, 10,* 317–356.

Zald, D. H., & Kim, S. W. (1996a). Anatomy and function of the orbital frontal cortex: I. Anatomy, neurocircuitry, and obsessive–compulsive disorder. *Journal of Neuropsychiatry and Clinical Neuroscience, 8,* 125–138.

Zald, D. H., & Kim, S. W. (1996b). Anatomy and function of the orbital frontal cortex: II. Function and relevance to obsessive–compulsive disorder. *Journal of Neuropsychiatry and Clinical Neuroscience, 8,* 249–261.

Zielinski, C. M., Taylor, M. A., & Juzwin, K. R. (1991). Neuropsychological deficits in obsessive–compulsive disorder. Neuropsychiatry, *Neuropsychology, and Behavioral Neurology, 4,* 110–126.

PART III

Understanding Emotion

"Why Is She Crying?"

*Children's Understanding of Emotion
from Preschool to Preadolescence*

SUSANNE A. DENHAM
ANITA KOCHANOFF

At 7:15 a.m., controlled chaos reigns. Breakfast must be eaten by adults, grade-schoolers, preschoolers, even the dog, and then the humans depart in different directions for their daily activities. Not surprisingly, the understanding of emotions often figures prominently in everyone's interactions. This morning is no exception. Brent, age 8, flings himself into his chair, scowling, as Lauren, age 4, her mouth full of cereal, sneezes. Twelve-year-old Erica leaps up, knocking over her chair. "Look what she did! There's milk all over my new blouse!" she yells to be heard over Lauren's giggles. Mother suddenly sits down and flatly states, "I am counting to 10, and when I'm finished, everyone needs to be eating breakfast. You all need to get to school, and I need to get to work. And Brent, just what *is* your problem?" Dad swings into the room carrying a briefcase and grabs a cookie from the cookie jar as he announces that he will be home late. He smiles and breezes out the door. The children are all momentarily quiet—eating as instructed—except for Lauren's whimpering, "Daddy forgot my kiss." They stare at Mother as tears begin sliding down her face.

Because social interactions and relationships are guided, even defined, by emotional transactions (Denham, 1998; Halberstadt, Denham, & Dunsmore, 2001; Saarni, 1999), understanding of emotions fig-

ures prominently in this set of breakfast encounters. When anyone ex-
hibits emotion within a dyad or group, emotional expressiveness conveys important information, and our example abounds with instances
in which understanding emotions helps to determine the flow and outcome of interaction. Even children as young as Lauren are active participants in the social world and continually make interpretations and attributions of their own and others' behaviors, including emotional ones
(Dodge, Pettit, McClaskey, & Brown, 1986; Miller & Aloise, 1989). Such
understanding of self and others can be a powerful determinant of
behavior. Thus, we contend that emotion knowledge lies at the heart
of emotional intelligence and is central to the contribution of emotional intelligence to children's social competence (Brenner & Salovey,
1997).

As put forward in Halberstadt et al.'s (2001) model of affective social competence, a process view of the application of emotion knowledge guides and illuminates our view of this linkage. At the most basic
level, there must be an initial perception or appraisal that another individual is sending affective information—missing such information defi-
nitely puts one at a disadvantage (e.g., if the children miss their mother's muted anger as she begins to count to 10, they may err seriously by
ignoring her, or even worse, by laughing at the suddenness with which
she sits down). Once perceived, the other's affective message must be
interpreted accurately; at this and all other levels of affective information processing, errors can lead to both intrapersonal and social difficulties—for example, if Lauren is so tickled by sneezing milk every-
where that she considers Erica's verbal and physical cues as shared
delight rather than fury, she risks her sister's heightened wrath. After
one perceives and interprets emotional information, it must be understood within the constraints of display rules and applied within the "ongoing flow" of the context (e.g., Erica may be the only child who really
understands the unstated connection between Dad's behavior and
Mother's tears, and no one but Mother picks up on Brent's scowl as
being important enough for comment). The key to all these information processing steps is to receive, as clearly and nonredundantly as possible, the emotional messages of others. Only after these steps can one
review one's goals and make choices about emotional behavior enactment (Lemerise & Arsenio, 2000).

More detailed aspects of emotional information sometimes need
to be processed as well. For example, realizing that inner and outer
emotional states may differ, and that different individuals have differing emotional "styles," can be very important. Perhaps everyone, even
Lauren, knows that Brent is a grouch every morning, and Mother's
commenting on his scowl really is more indicative of her own internal

state than of his. Or maybe Erica and Mother, unlike Lauren, realize that Brent is trying to hide, with a more "manly" scowl, his distressed ruminating over striking out at last evening's softball game.

Finally, it is tricky to manage true *or* false emotional signals from others. One must be able to ignore false affective messages if ignoring benefits one's goals, or to accept them as real if that is advantageous. One must also (1) pick up real, relevant, helpful messages, (2) ignore real but irrelevant messages, and (3) somehow deal with real and relevant but not helpful messages. Deciding on the truth/falsity and relevance/irrelevance of an emotional message is not easy. For example, where do Mother's tears reside on these continua? Perhaps the best thing for the children to do, at the moment, is just to ignore Mother's tears as a momentary "blip."

In sum, there can be numerous processing components of successful emotion knowledge. During the early years it is likely that the most fundamental of these—perceiving/appraising, interpreting, and taking context into account—are central to children's learning. As children mature, they are able to add the layers of complexity previously enumerated to their emotion knowledge.

Given these considerations, our *first goal* in this chapter is to enumerate the specific elements of emotion knowledge that support the processes just described (Denham, 1998; Halberstadt et al., 2001). Our *second goal* is to couch more detailed descriptions of these elements within the social developmental tasks of each epoch. That is, the defining social issues of each age help clarify the roles played by developing emotion knowledge within each period. For each type of emotion knowledge, we describe and evaluate existing research on the contribution of emotional competence to social competence, using the dual framework of developmentally appropriate aspects of emotion knowledge, as applied within equally developmentally appropriate social relationships. Third, we consider potential causal mechanisms that may contribute to the development of emotion knowledge. Finally, we identify gaps in theory, methodology, and evidence, to suggest future directions.

ELEMENTS OF EMOTION KNOWLEDGE

Researchers are increasingly probing more deeply into children's conceptions about emotions (e.g., Fabes, Eisenberg, McCormick, & Wilson, 1988; Strayer, 1986). Findings reveal that changes in emotion understanding occur from preschool through grade school years. These changes are evident in nine areas of emotion understanding, which we describe in turn.

Noticing an emotional signal is the first area of emotion knowledge (Halberstadt et al., 2001); it may develop at different rates for different people, and there are different developmental trajectories for different signals (e.g., face vs. voice). After noticing that there is an emotional signal to interpret, children first must be able to (1) label emotional expressions both verbally and nonverbally, (2) identify emotion-eliciting situations, and (3) infer the causes of emotion-eliciting situations and the consequences of specific emotions. Then, to even more accurately interpret emotional information, children learn to recognize that others' emotional experiences can differ from their own, that personalized information may be needed to interpret the information accurately. Finally, the ongoing flow of children's increasingly complex social interactions requires knowledge of (1) others' possible dissemblance and the display rules of family and culture, (2) a flexible range of emotion regulation strategies, (3) simultaneous emotions that may conflict, and (4) complex emotions. The emergence of these abilities corresponds to changes in developmentally appropriate tasks of children's social relationships in their emotional lives.

Preschoolers' Emotional Lives

Preschoolers express emotions vividly and frequently. Emotions, whether their own or others', are central experiences in their lives—immediate, salient, and important in their social transactions. Not surprisingly, their most important social tasks include managing emotional arousal so that coordination of play is possible (Gottman & Mettetal, 1986). Succeeding at this social task calls for emotion knowledge. For example, if arguments are to be resolved so that play can continue, children may need to perceive and talk about their playmates' displeasure. To avoid the disorganization of a tantrum, a preschooler may need to think reflectively about a distressing situation. In these ways, emotion knowledge supports preschoolers' attempts to deal with and communicate about the emotions experienced by themselves and others (Dodge, 1989). Emotion knowledge also allows them to selectively attend to other aspects of social experiences. Hence, its unfolding is quite critical for young children. Preschoolers come to comprehend the expressions, situations, causes, and consequences of emotions, which we now describe.

Labeling Emotional Expressions

At the most rudimentary level, preschoolers need to be able to identify the expressions of emotion that they see during social interactions. When Lauren sees a friend struggling to move a chair out of the path of her tricycle, her own actions may depend on knowing whether the friend is exhibiting merely physical effort or accompanying anger as well. Across this age period, preschoolers do become increasingly adept at labeling emotional expressions. Specifically, their abilities to verbally label and nonverbally recognize emotional expressions increase from 2 to 4½ years of age (Denham & Couchoud, 1990). Emotional situations and attendant facial expressions may be learned together, with the first distinction learned being the difference between being happy and not being happy, feeling good versus feeling bad (Bullock & Russell, 1984, 1985). In accord with this possibility, young children's recognition of happy expressions and situations is greater than recognition of negative emotions, with their understanding anger and fear slowly emerging from a "not happy/sad" emotion category (see also Camras & Allison, 1985; Stifter & Fox, 1987). Although children and adults usually share similar sets of central defining characteristics for each discrete emotion, young children's categories are broader, "fuzzier," including more peripheral concepts, especially for negative emotions.

In short, young children become increasingly able to discern important differences between expressions of differing emotions; attaining this ability to differentiate expressions is a vital component of their overall emotion knowledge. However, simply understanding expressions of emotion is not always definitive. In the overall effort to comprehend one's own or others' emotions, situational and other contextual information can be even more important, especially when expressions may be masked or dissembled.

Identifying Emotion-Eliciting Situations

When they can comprehend emotional situations as well as expressions, preschoolers improve their options for understanding the emotions in their social environment. Understanding the events that can elicit emotion, as well as accompanying expressions, increases preschoolers' flexibility in interpreting emotional signals in their environment. If Lauren had been paying attention, she could have noted, "When we don't listen, Mommy feels bad," and adjusted her behavior. Thus, understanding causal factors in emotional situations improves over the preschool period. Little by little, children separate angry situations from sad ones (Denham & Couchoud, 1990; Fabes, Eisenberg, Nyman, & Michealieu, 1991), with fear situations presenting the most difficulty (Brody & Harrison, 1987).

Understanding expressions and eliciting situations for discrete emotions is particularly adaptive for preschoolers (and relatively complete prior to later childhood), because they witness and experience fairly vivid, clear demonstrations of these very feelings. But young children go even further than recognizing the expressions and eliciting situations for discrete emotions—they make more complex attributions about emotions' causes and reason more intricately about their consequences for behavior.

Comprehending Causes of Emotions

Along with perceiving the situational elicitors of emotions, young children begin to use the contextual information found in their everyday experiences to create theories about the causes of happiness, sadness, and anger. Preschoolers, especially those who are 4 years old and older, cite causes for familiar emotions that are similar to those given by adults (Fabes et al., 1988, 1991; Strayer, 1986). If asked, Lauren could probably point out that Brent gets mad because he doesn't want to go to school, but that Daddy is happy to go to work.

Realizing that an emotion's cause can vary depending on the person experiencing it, and that potential elicitors have uniquely individual effects, preschoolers ascribe different causes to different emotions. For example, they cite nonsocial events for their happiness, such as playing with toys, social causes for their sadness and anger, like wanting Mom and being punched, respectively, and fantasy causes for their fear. They build on early understanding of more general emotional situations to create scenarios depicting the causes for specific persons' particular feelings (e.g., self, peer, parent; Dunn & Hughes, 1998).

Thus, children become more able to understand the causal complexities of emotion throughout the preschool period. Through their increased social sensitivity and experience, older preschoolers also develop strategies for appraising others' emotions when available cues are less salient and consensual. Five-year-olds are more likely than 3- and 4-year-olds to focus their explanations of emotions on personal dispositions as opposed to goal states—"She had a bad day" instead of "She didn't want Billy to play with her." Knowing more abstract causes for emotion, less idiosyncratic than those of younger preschoolers, can be useful in actual interaction with friends (Fabes et al., 1991). Knowing the expression, likely context, and causes of emotions is important, but still does not tell the full story. One must also understand the consequences of emotion.

Understanding the Consequences of Emotion

Young children also realize the consequences of many emotions; for example, a securely attached 3-year-old knows that a parent will comfort her when she is upset. Clearly, knowing why an emotion is expressed (its cause) and its likely aftermath (its consequence in terms of the behavior of self or others) aids a child in learning to regulate the behavior and emotions of self and to react to the emotions of others. Discerning consequences of emotion can help a child know what to do when experiencing or witnessing emotion. Lauren could probably accurately assert, "When I'm scared, I could look for Mom"; "When my friend is mad, I get out of the way".

Thus, preschoolers can distinguish the causes of emotions from their consequences when completing stories about why a protagonist felt an emotion and what the protagonist did as a result (Denham, 1998; Russell, 1990); for example, fathers "dance when they're happy," mothers "lie in their beds" when sad, and fathers "give spankings" when angry. What do people do as a consequence of someone else's emotions? Four- and 5-year-olds attribute plausible, nonrandom parental reactions to their own emotions (Denham, 1997), such as their parents' matching their own happiness, performing pragmatic action after sadness, punishing anger, and comforting or acting to alleviate a fear-eliciting stimulus. These investigations suggest that preschoolers have fairly solid conceptions of the behavioral consequences of emotions for both self and others. Given the advantages of consequential knowledge of emotions, it is unfortunate that no research we know of follows these abilities into grade school years.

Sophisticated Understanding of the Emotional Experience of Others

Sometimes knowing about expressions of emotions, emotion-eliciting situations, and even the causes and consequences of emotions, is not enough to interpret accurately the emotional signals of others. Information specific to a particular person in a particular situation may be needed. Although this aspect of emotion knowledge is very important, it can be quite difficult to acquire and use; Lauren may not yet understand that Brent actually gets mad when punished, instead of sad or scared.

In a series of thought-provoking inquiries, Gnepp and colleagues described the information needed in deciding what emotion another person is experiencing or will experience in a given situation (Gnepp, 1989; Gnepp & Chilamkurti, 1988; Gnepp & Gould, 1985; Gnepp, McKee, & Domanic, 1987). Important elements of emotional information are whether (1) the situation is equivocal (i.e., may elicit more than one emotion), (2) there are conflicting cues in the person's expressive patterns and the situation, and (3) person-specific information is needed.

Regarding *equivocality*, the first question is whether the situation has a single strong emotional determinant common across persons. Young children clearly are capable of such determinations. But some situations do not have a strong emotion–event association. Different people feel different emotions during some emotion-eliciting events. One child is happy to encounter a large, friendly looking dog, panting and "smiling" with mouth open. Another child is terrified in the same situation. More personal information is needed in order to know how the person is feeling, and preschoolers are becoming aware of this need. Preschoolers are beginning to recognize the equivocality inherent in some emotion situations, even if they cannot always identify it spontaneously—especially if the necessary personalized inferences fit with their earliest distinctions between emotions, "good" feelings versus "bad" feelings, and, in "bad" feelings, sadness versus anger. The ability to detect and use information about equivocal situations continues to develop through grade school (Gnepp et al., 1987).

Even if a situation is not emotionally equivocal, the person experiencing the event may react *atypically*—there may be a conflict between situational and expressive knowledge. A person may smile when seeing a spider dropping into the room on a strand of web. However, interpreting a reaction as atypical requires a rather sophisticated decision, namely *resolving* conflicting expressive and situational cues to emotions rather than relying on one cue or another. Young children do not perform such problem solving easily or well; they usually still prefer simple, script-based understanding emotion (i.e., they most successfully apply common explanations for emotions, such as, "When we get ice cream, we feel happy.")

However, over time, older preschoolers come to weight expressive and situational sources of emotional information strategically, much as they come to utilize multiple sources of information in nonsocial cognitive tasks (Hoffner & Badzinski, 1989; Wiggers & Van Lieshout, 1985). One of their means of resolving conflicting emotion cues is attributing an idiosyncratic perspective—"She is smiling because she likes shots." Such attribution of idiosyncrasy may be a precursor to understanding the psychological causes of atypical reactions to emotion-eliciting situations (Gnepp, 1989), an ability fully attained only during grade school. The valences of expressions and situations also make a difference. Both preschoolers and early grade school children are less able to resolve an anomalous positive expression paired with a negative situation, such as smiling while getting an injection, than a negative expression paired with a positive situation, such as crying at a birthday party.

If using complex information to attribute emotions to others is so difficult, what kinds of personal information can preschoolers use successfully in interpreting atypical emotions? First, they can use *unique normative information,* such as, "Sarah lives in Green Valley, where all people are friendly with tigers and play games with them all the time" (Gnepp, Klayman, & Trabasso, 1982). When asked how Sarah would feel, preschoolers used unique normative information about liking tigers to modify their responses to a normally unequivocal situation. Preschoolers are also becoming aware that normative cultural categories like age and gender moderate emotions experienced in differing situations. For example, a boy may not be overjoyed to receive a doll as a gift. Second, information about *personality characteristics* that are stable across time and situations can be especially useful. Gnepp and Chilamkurti (1988) told children stories in which the protagonist was honest, clownish, helpful, cruel, shy, or selfish. Only children 6 years old and older used such information to answer questions about feelings in situations that normally could be considered unequivocal: How would a clownish person feel if he wore one black shoe and one white shoe to school and everybody laughed? Third, other *person-specific information* is sometimes needed. Gnepp and colleagues (1982) provided stories in which characters' behavioral dispositions modified normally strong emotion–event associations—"Mark eats grass whenever he can. It's dinnertime and Mother says they're having grass for dinner. How will Mark feel?" Four- and 5-year-olds were able to utilize such information, with responses reflecting the unique perspective of the story character.

In summary, preschoolers are acquiring much emotion knowledge to assist them in social interactions with family and peers. However, it is equally clear that many of the finer nuances of emotion knowledge are either just emerging for them or not yet within their repertoire at all. The pressing concerns of middle childhood, along with input from socializers, cognitive development, and sheer experience with their own and others' emotions (which we discuss later), pave the way for further development of more finely nuanced emotion knowledge.

Grade-Schoolers' Emotional Lives

As grade-schoolers become aware of a social network larger than the dyad, their social developmental task centers more on peer group acceptance and creating lasting dyadic friendships, than on coordinating play. Peer norms for social acceptance are complex and finely tuned, with inclusion by one's peers and avoiding rejection or embarrassment paramount (Gottman & Mettetal, 1986). In this context, emotions are not often expressed as directly and vividly as before; older children learn that their goals are not always met by freely showing their most intense feelings. Brent's sulky demeanor, muted as it is, would not escape the notice of his peers.

Intimate friendships also require older children to use emotion understanding in new ways, specifically to converse about complex aspects of emotion knowledge—display rules, ambivalence, and social emotions. Emotion-colored accounts are compared, contrasted, and validated as friends help each other to sort out their shared and idiosyncratic feelings. Conflict processes also rear their not-necessarily-ugly heads, with conversations replete with emotion talk about regulating anger, jealousy, shame, guilt, and hurt feelings. Many of the telephone calls with which Erica constantly ties up the family telephone focus on feelings, whether she realizes it or not. Thus, older children's increasing emotion knowledge unfolds within the new context of their social group. In the following discussion, we highlight age-specific elements of emotion knowledge as described earlier.

Emotion Knowledge: Beyond Preschool

Virtually all grade-schoolers have a large corpus of data for the *expressions of common emotions*. At the same time, for many of the complicated emotions and modes of expressiveness facing grade-schoolers (e.g., dissembled emotions, expressions of shame; see the following sections), specific facial expressions are somewhat indistinct. These factors render expression knowledge less central than it was during preschool. Nonetheless, some improvement does occur; for example, Gosselin and Simard (1999) found that older children were more successful than preschoolers at distinguishing expressions of fear and surprise.

Regarding *causal emotion knowledge,* older children continue to elaborate on their earlier foundation of causal emotion knowledge. For example, Berti, Garattoni, and Venturini (2000) have found that 7- and 9-year-olds' understanding of the causes of sadness, guilt, and shame exceeds that of 5-year-olds. Similarly, Harris, Olthof, Meerum Terwogt, and Hardman (1987) found that English, Dutch, and Nepali 5- to 14-year-olds extended their causal understanding of emotions to social emotions such as pride, worry, and jealousy, emotions that cannot be linked with a discrete facial expression.

In terms of the *person-specific information* sometimes needed to interpret emotion, grade schoolers utilize information on *individuals' past history and differing emotional styles* much more successfully than young children. Gnepp and Gould (1985) told stories in which person-specific information was embedded in descriptions of the person's past experiences—"Robin's best friend said she didn't like her anymore. Next day, Robin saw her best friend on the playground. How did she feel?" Five-year-olds made more situational inferences, "... happy, because they could play together," than personalized ones, "... sad, because her friend didn't like her anymore." Older children were more able to make accurate personalized inferences.

So far, however, all of the types of emotion knowledge discussed have pertained to the accurate perception and interpretation of emotional information in self or others. The types of emotion knowledge subsequently accrued involve more complexity—realizing that inner and outer emotional states may differ, that cognitive regulation of emotion is possible, that ambivalence may occur; distinguishing the truth or falsity, the relevance or irrelevance, of others' emotional signals.

Knowledge of Emotion Display Rules

Along with growing understanding of others' personalized reasons for emotions, older children increasingly need to follow and understand cultural, familial, and personal rules for expression of emotion. They learn to mask, minimize, or substitute one emotion for another. Even before such rules are understood, however, children understand attempts at hiding emotion completely (i.e., dissemblance).

Knowledge of Dissemblance

Hiding emotions by masking can be advantageous to young children as soon as they realize that they can pose expression voluntarily. Knowing when and when not to show emotions is immeasurably valuable in maintaining social relations. Such dissemblance does not require knowledge of display rules that are normative to a family or culture, but merely the need to send a signal that differs from the emotion felt. Although young children recognize situations that call for dissemblance, this understanding continues to develop through grade school. In one study (Gross & Harris, 1988), both preschoolers and grade-schoolers understood the *real* feelings of a protagonist—whether the protagonist needed to dissemble or not. But the transition to full understanding of dissemblance was not complete until after the preschool period. Six-year-olds easily referred to unobservable phenomena, such as motives and intentions, in explaining dissemblance: "She looked like she felt OK, not sad, so that the other children wouldn't laugh and call her a baby." They understood that where there was any deception at all, the protagonist would *appear to feel* a way that was different from his or her true emotions (i.e., "just OK"). Preschoolers are more likely to think that appearance cannot differ from reality, that "what you feel is what I see" (Harris, Donnelly, Guz, & Pitt Watson, 1986).

Display Rule Knowledge

Dissemblance is not the only way in which children modify their expressiveness. They also may modify their emotional displays, expressing an emotion that differs from the one felt, to conform to socially or personally appropriate display rules. Some reports suggest that during early childhood, the understanding of these specific rules is rudimentary at best (e.g., Gnepp & Hess, 1986). Evidence from this line of research suggests that few children understand, even by first grade, specific prosocial or self-protective rules for minimizing, masking, or substituting emotional expressions; only older grade-school children comprehend display rules serving these functions. Brent may begin to understand that he should not show the full force of his bad temper with his friends if he wishes to keep them.

Despite this assertion, close to half the preschool children in Gnepp and Hess' (1986) study cited at least verbal, if not expressive, rules for regulating emotion (e.g., verbal masking in "I don't care that I lost this silly contest"). Even more important, investigators using developmentally appropriate methodological simplifications have found that even young children may begin to understand display rules as they begin to use them (Banerjee, 1997; Josephs, 1994). Given the sparse nature of research and conflicting claims of that exist, these elements of emotion knowledge clearly remain ripe for further investigation.

Knowledge of Emotion Regulation Strategies

Sometimes one needs to know not how to deal with an emotion's effect on others, as in understanding dissemblance and display rule usage, but how to deal with its very experience and expression oneself (see Gross & John, Chapter 12, this volume). The emotional experiences that signal the attainment or thwarting of a goal act as intrapersonal regulators. Generally, unless a specific social goal violates the premise, we want to feel better and look more positive when we feel and express negative emotions; when we feel and express positive ones, we want to continue feeling good and signaling our good spirits. Preschoolers are learning about the strategies to regulate the emotions of both self and others: They are learning how to change emotions, both negative and positive. In line with adults' notions, they deem anger and sadness most changeworthy, and happiness least. They can generate specific nurturant and aggressive strategies to change sadness and anger, including physical, verbal, social, material, and helping/hindering strategies (Denham, 1998; Fabes et al., 1988).

Preschoolers also come to understand that regulation efforts differ in effectiveness, and begin to at least recognize some cognitive strategies to deal with emotions, such as "remembering a happy time" and "telling yourself how to feel better." However, they do not often generate cognitive strategies on their own (cf. Banerjee, 1997). To help her feel better, Lauren is more likely to offer Mom a grape from the breakfast fruit bowl than she is to advise her to "think about something pretty." This inability to generate strategies spontaneously is parallel to preschoolers' inability to take into account personalized information about emotion spontaneously, suggesting that less sophisticated cognitive development is the root of these limitations. Although cognitive means of changing emotion never predominate across the whole 4- to 15-year age range, older children have the advantage of experience and cognitive ability in this regard (Brown, Covell, & Abramovitch, 1991).

Another means of regulating emotion is the mere passage of time. Although, like adults, they may overestimate the duration of negative emotions (Gilbert, Pinel, Wilson, Blumberg, & Wheatley, 1998), grade school children can describe the unilinear waning of happiness, sadness, or anger at five time points subsequent to an emotion-eliciting event (Brown et al., 1991; Harris, Guz, Lipian, & Man Shu, 1985; Meerum Terwogt & Olthof, 1989). Brent, insulted by the class bully yesterday, may be able to realize that the sting of the snub will lessen by this weekend. Erica is even more likely to see that she will not remain mad at Lauren for long. But for younger children like Lauren, the whole idea of time is rather foreign, and superimposing another difficult set of concepts, emotion regulation, may result in cognitive "overload."

Knowledge of Simultaneity of Emotions and Ambivalence

For older children and adults, it is not uncommon to experience "mixed emotions," as when Erica is somewhat amused at Lauren's antics, but mostly annoyed at the fact that her blouse is soiled (see Lane & Pollermann, Chapter 11, this volume). It is in grade school that children are generally considered to show the first "true" understanding of simultaneous and ambivalent emotions. Harter and colleagues propose a cognitive developmental sequence based on the valence of two felt emotions and the number of targets toward which the two emotions are directed (Harter & Whitesell, 1989). In this model, children progress through four levels of understanding beginning at age 7, when children comprehend that two emotions of the same valence can be directed toward the same target, such as Brent's sadness and anger when the class bully tears up his homework. By age 11 children can acknowledge that

feelings of opposite valences can be expressed toward the same target—
for example, Erica's anger at her mother for taking away a privilege
while loving her all the same.

But because young children's expressiveness is becoming more in-
tricate as they leave the preschool period, they may begin to experience
simultaneous emotions and ambivalence themselves and begin to understand them. Thus, there is some question as to whether Harter and
Whitesell's (1989) work underestimates younger children's actual understanding of multiple or conflicting emotions. The findings in one
key set of studies show that procedural improvements preserve Harter
and Whitesell's (1989) sequence, but accelerate it (Wintre, Polivy, &
Murray, 1990; Wintre & Vallance, 1994). As with other complex aspects
of emotion knowledge, young children can recognize and explain conflicting emotions before they can spontaneously talk about them
(Gordis, Rosen, & Grand, 1989).

Although preschoolers are beginning to comprehend so many sophisticated aspects of emotional life, their reliance on facial expression
to interpret emotions ("Faces can't go up and down at the same time")
and their growing theories of mind ("You can't think two ways") impedes their ability to understand ambivalence (Wellman & Woolley,
1990). They may need to "unlearn" some of their most cherished
propositions about internal states to move forward in this area. Again,
asking questions via more age-appropriate methodology has revealed
that preschoolers have more knowledge than previously supposed
(Donaldson & Westerman, 1986; Peng, Johnson, Pollock, Glasspool, &
Harris, 1992). Given special assistance in visualizing how mixed emotions are experienced/expressed, for example, young children are capable of identifying and talking about them (Kestenbaum & Gelman,
1995).

Despite the controversy over Harter and Whitesell's (1989) chron-
ology, it is clear that older children are more adept at identifying the
complicated aspects of multiple emotions (Harris, 1989; Meerum Terwogt, Koops, Oosterhoff, & Olthof, 1986; Olthof, Meerum Terwogt,
Van Eck, & Koops, 1987). Understanding this complexity in emotions
facilitates a leap in both self-awareness and the ability to get along with
others.

Knowledge of Complex Emotions

Another significant accomplishment in the domain of emotion knowledge is understanding the more complex emotions, particularly sociomoral emotions like guilt and shame, and self-referent and social

emotions like pride, embarrassment, and empathy. Because young children and their peers are beginning to express complex emotions, they have some understanding of them, but it is still quite limited. Even older preschoolers are unable to cite pride, guilt, or shame specifically in relevant success, failure, and transgression experiences—pride at a gymnastic feat or resisting temptation, or guilt for stealing a few coins out of the coin jar in the parents' bedroom (Arsenio & Lover, 1995; Harter & Whitesell, 1989; Nunner-Winkler & Sodian, 1988). Children do not use correct emotional terms, or even descriptions, of their own and others' pride or shame until at least age 6. For example, preschoolers report happiness or excitement, rather than pride, for the gymnastic feat; Lauren would not say she felt guilty about getting milk on Erica's blouse, even if she did—she would say she felt "bad." Even early grade-schoolers report feeling bad, scared, or worried about detection, and the likelihood of punishment, after stealing. They do not use terms referring to guilt. Moreover, although children entering grade school may understand the valence associated with social emotions, they have little knowledge of the kinds of situations that evoke them (Russell & Paris, 1994).

A further complication exists in this area. Four-year-olds through kindergartners usually judge a wrongdoer's feelings on the outcome of his or her actions, using a naïve desire-based causal analysis—a person is happy if he or she does not get caught, but angry if caught. They give what has been dubbed the "happy victimizer" response. However, they do not expect a character, even an ill-motivated one, to feel good if he or she has harmed another person by accident or observed someone being hurt. The very nature of wrongdoing sometimes elicits mixed emotions, even into adulthood (Murgatroyd & Robinson, 1993). But, as noted earlier, preschoolers' understanding of potentially mixed and ambivalent emotional experiences is far from perfect. Adding complex moral themes to the mix just makes reasoning all the more difficult. During grade school years, these concepts remain difficult, but newer research (e.g., Berti et al., 2000) suggests that knowledge of complex emotions continues to improve through grade school.

EMOTION KNOWLEDGE AND SUCCESSFUL SOCIAL INTERACTIONS

Of what use do children put these aspects of emotion knowledge? When they strategically apply emotion knowledge, they more often succeed in peer and other social interactions. This is true both in preschool and grade school. We may expect that the aspects of emotion knowledge that are emerging at each age level will be particularly associated with success in each period's social tasks.

Preschoolers' Emotion Knowledge and Social Competence

Thus, preschoolers' understanding of emotion expressions and situations is related to their positive peer status, to teachers' views of their social competence, and to their prosocial reactions to emotions (Denham & Couchoud, 1991; Denham, McKinley, Couchoud, & Holt, 1990; Roberts & Strayer, 1996; Smith, 2001). In particular, children who can identify the expression on a peer's face or comprehend the emotions elicited by common social situations are more likely to react prosocially to their peers' displays of emotion. If Lauren sees one peer bickering with another and correctly deduces that the peer suddenly experiences sadness or fear, rather than intensified anger, she may comfort her friend rather than retreat or enter the fray. Others may find interactions with such an emotionally knowledgeable agemate very satisfying, rendering Lauren more likable. Similarly, teachers may be attuned to the behavioral evidence of Lauren's emotion knowledge and evaluate it positively—the use of emotion language, the sympathetic reaction. Emotion knowledge allows a preschooler to react appropriately to others, bolstering his or her relationships.

Consonant with our line of reasoning, emotion situation knowledge is related to a number of discrete aspects of social competence related to the management of emotional arousal and coordination of play. For example, this aspect of preschoolers' emotion knowledge is associated with conflict resolution, cooperative shared pretending, and successful communication (Dunn & Cutting, 1999; Dunn & Herrera, 1997). Further, young children's understanding of emotion situations is *negatively* related to nonconstructive anger reactions during peer interaction (Garner & Estep, 2001). Child–friend conversation about emotion also is related to cooperative interaction (Brown, Donelan-McCall, & Dunn, 1996), and preschoolers' spontaneous use of emotion language is related to higher-quality peer interactions and greater peer acceptance (Fabes, Eisenberg, Hanish, & Spinrad, 2001; Garner & Estep, 2001). In Dunn and colleagues' studies (Dunn & Cutting, 1999; Dunn & Herrera, 1997), both the child's and friends' emotion knowledge made independent contributions to positive interaction. Finally, the positive play within friendships, that is itself predicted by knowledge of emotional expressions and situations, predicts understanding of mixed emotions at the end of the preschool period (Dunn, Brown, & Maguire, 1995), suggestive of a bidirectional relation.

Other types of positive social behavior, sometimes within other relationships, are also related to preschoolers' emotion knowledge. Preschoolers' understanding of emotion expressions and situations is related to the use of reasoned argument, and caregiving, with siblings (Dunn, Slomkowski, Donelan, & Herrera, 1995; Garner, Jones, & Miner, 1994). Ability to understand emotion situations and to draw low-level personalized inferences of emotion is also positively related to teachers' ratings of smooth adjustment to Head Start (Shields et al., 2001).

Finally, preschoolers with identified aggression problems have been found to show specific deficits in understanding emotion expressions and situations (Hughes, Dunn, & White, 1998). Arsenio, Cooperman, and Lover (2000) elucidate more details in this relation; in their study, aggression mediated the association between lack of emotion expression and situation understanding and lower levels of peer acceptance. Barth and Bastiani (1997; see also Schultz, Izard, & Ackerman, 1999) uncovered a subtle relation that may underlie aggressive children's social difficulties: Preschoolers' mistaken perceptions of peers' expressions as angry—a recognition bias similar to the hostile attribution bias of later years—are associated with negative social behavior. We have obtained similar results in earlier work, where confusing happiness with any negative emotion, or confusing negative emotions, was negatively related to sociometric likeability (Denham et al., 1990).

Grade-Schoolers' Emotion Knowledge and Social Competence

According to our theoretical expectations, specific aspects of emotion knowledge should be central to social competence in grade school. Grade-schoolers' emotional lives are replete with display rule usage and the experience of complex emotions; thus, it is these aspects of emotion knowledge that we expect to find related to older children's social competence. Consistent with our predictions, older children's understanding of prosocial display rules is related to (1) prosocial behavior, (2) prosocial responses to hypothetical conflicts, and (3) teacher- and peer-rated social competence (Garner, 1996, 1999; Jones, Bowling, & Cumberland, 1998; McDowell & Parke, 2000).

Several studies (e.g., Dodge, Lochman, Harnish, Bates, & Pettit, 1997) suggest a relation between deficits in emotion knowledge and older children's behavior problems. Dodge et al. (1997) found that reactively aggressive children, those who behave aggressively when provoked, had deficits in the ability to interpret the emotion cues inherent in social encounters. Perhaps Brent is still resentful and ready to continue fighting even after the class bully makes a peace overture (because he did not process emotion information accurately). Even more specifically, Greer (1997) found that early-onset conduct-disordered children performed poorly on quickly identifying expressions of emotion. However, findings relating older children's social competence, in whatever form, and emotion knowledge remain few in number.

MECHANISMS UNDERLYING THE DEVELOPMENT OF EMOTION KNOWLEDGE

It is crucial to understand the elements of emotion knowledge that develop from ages 3 to 12. But just as important is unearthing the mechanisms that support the development of such important aspects of children's emotional competence. We suggest that the most important mechanisms are likely to be either interpersonal or intrapersonal. Interpersonal mechanisms contributing to emotion knowledge are likely to include socialization by parents, throughout childhood, and by peers, especially during grade school. Intrapersonal mechanisms that we consider include cognitive development, most specifically the development of Theory of Mind.

Socializers: Parents and Peers

Socialization of emotions is ubiquitous in children's everyday contact with parents and peers. Parenting and peer interaction elicit a variety of emotions that children observe. Further, children's emotions especially often require some kind of parental reaction, and negotiating the world of emotions is considered by some parents to be an important area of teaching (Dix, 1991; Eisenberg & Fabes, 1994; Eisenberg, Fabes, & Murphy, 1996; Eisenberg et al., 1999; Gottman, Katz, & Hooven, 1997). Friends also learn much by watching each other's emotions in the unique situations of peer life—where gossip and avoiding embarrassment are now very important and socially competent responses to important social situations, such as group entry, are to be somewhat wary and emotionally unflappable. Friends also value and validate each other's emotion-colored evaluations of their social experiences and their understandings about local norms for emotion.

Thus, children have much to learn from others about the appropriate expression of emotions, possible reactions to others' positive and negative emotions, the nature of emotional expression, and the types of situations that are likely to elicit emotions. Accordingly, we focus on three possible mechanisms of socialization of emotion knowledge: expression of emotions, reactions to children's emotions, and teaching about emotions (Halberstadt, 1991). We first present findings on parents as emotion socializers, then suggest possibilities for the largely absent research on friends as emotion socializers.

Contributions of Parental Expressiveness

Parental expressiveness teaches the child which emotions are acceptable in the family and in certain contexts. By modeling various emotions, moderately expressive parents give children information about the nature of happiness, sadness, anger, and fear—their expression, likely eliciting situations, and more personalized causes. Mothers and fathers capable of maintaining relatively positive affect during challenging circumstances also may be able to make the world of emotions accessible to their children (Denham, Zoller, & Couchoud, 1994; Parke, Cassidy, Burks, Carson, & Boyum, 1992).

Conversely, parental expressiveness can make it more difficult to address issues of emotion altogether. Although exposure to well-modulated negative emotion can be positively related to understanding of emotion (Garner et al., 1994), parents' frequent and intense negative emotions may disturb children, as well as discourage self-reflection, so that little is learned about emotions (Denham, 1998). It is easy to imagine the confusion and pain of children relentlessly exposed to parents' negative emotions; the mother cited at the beginning of this chapter needs to attend to her own emotional well-being not only for her own benefit, but for the emotional development of her children. Likewise, parents whose expressiveness is quite limited impart little information about emotions; if Dad regularly shows little emotion, his contribution to the children's emotion knowledge may be restricted.

Only a small amount of work has been done on parental emotions' specific contributions to more advanced levels of emotion understanding, such as display rule knowledge. Kindergartners' knowledge of display rules—in situations like losing a game, seeing someone in silly pajamas—was associated with mothers' self-reported emotional expressiveness, even after children's age and receptive language ability were statistically controlled (Jones et al., 1998). Knowledge of self-protective display rules was related to maternal negative emotions like anger and contempt. When children knew that their mothers might react intensely, even explosively, they knew ways to "cover up" emotions to avoid trouble. Less happy mothers may also require their children to be more in control of their expressiveness; Brent received such a message from Mom as he slumped into his chair at the breakfast table. In contrast, prosocial display rules were negatively predicted by maternal negative emotions like sadness. Morose, emotionally self-focused mothers were less able to convey to children how expressiveness can be managed for kindness' sake.

Contributions of Parental Reactions to Children's Emotions

Parents' contingent reactions to their children's emotional displays are also highly salient to the acquisition of emotion knowledge throughout childhood (although, as usual, there is more research on socialization of preschoolers' emotion knowledge). These contingent reactions help the child in differentiating among emotions. Children of parents who encourage emotional expression have more access to their own emotions than those of parents who value maintenance of a more stoic, unemotional mien, and thus come to understand emotions better (Gottman et al., 1997). In contrast, parents' negative responsiveness, such as reacting with anger to a child's sadness or anger, or with happiness to the child's sadness, constitutes punitive socialization of emotion that hampers the process of learning about emotion. One pattern of negative responsiveness initiates escalating cycles of negativity, such as when Mom snaps at Brent; the other constitutes "making fun" of the child. Neither encourages children to learn about the emotional aspects of life (Denham et al., 1994). Other types of punitive socialization, such as directly or indirectly telling the child to stop expressing emotion or ignoring the child's emotions, are also negative predictors of emotion knowledge from preschool to grade school (Denham, Mitchell-Copeland, Strandberg, Auerbach, & Blair, 1997; Garner et al., 1994; McDowell & Parke, 2000).

Contributions of Parental Teaching/Coaching about Emotions

A final aspect of emotion socialization is the most direct—what parents say may impact their children's emotion knowledge. In its simplest form, coaching consists of verbally explaining an emotion and its relation to an observed event or expression. It may also include directing children's attention to salient emotional cues, helping them to understand and manage their own responses, and analyzing the entire social interaction into manageable components. As extensively outlined by Gottman and colleagues (Gottman et al., 1997), parents who are emotion coaches are aware of emotions, particularly negative ones. They talk about them in a differentiated manner and assist their children in experiencing, identifying, and regulating them when necessary. In contrast, dismissing parents may want to be helpful, but ignore children's emotions in an effort to "make it better." Alternatively, dismissing parents may actively punish children for showing or querying about emotions.

Conversations about feelings are important contexts for coaching children about emotions and how to manage them (Bretherton, Fritz, Zahn-Waxler, & Ridgeway, 1986; Brown & Dunn, 1992). Discussing emotions provides children with reflective distance from feeling states themselves, and space in which to interpret and evaluate their feelings and to reflect on causes and consequences. Verbal give-and-take about emotional experience within the scaffolded context of chatting with a parent helps the young child to formulate a coherent body of knowledge about emotional expressions, situations, and causes (Denham et al., 1994; Dunn, Brown, & Beardsall, 1991; Dunn, Brown, Slomkowski, Fesla, & Youngblade, 1991). Such associations between mothers' emotion language and preschoolers' emotion knowledge are often independent of the child's linguistic ability.

More specifically, mothers who not only talk about emotions, but also explain them, have children who are better at understanding emotions (Denham et al., 1994; Dunn, Brown, Slomkowski, et al., 1991). Their highlighting personally relevant information by repeating the child's utterances or explaining their own feelings (e.g., "You make me sad when you don't sit still") also arouses the child and captures his or her attention. If Mom takes time to reflect on the emotional events of the morning, especially her own tears, Lauren may learn a lot about personalized causes of emotions, for example. Unfortunately, extensions of such research to grade school children and their parents have not yet appeared.

Potential Contributions of Friends' Expressiveness

In general, contributions of friends' socialization of emotion are yet to be studied, as unambiguously important as the topic seems. However, we can make some educated guesses as to how friends' emotion socialization probably operates. Our goal here is to point out the possibilities and, we hope, to spur new investigation. Thus, similar to the parental mechanism, friends' emotional expressiveness shows grade-schoolers exactly which emotions are acceptable in the peer context. By modeling various emotional experiences, often those that adhere to the grade school peer culture's "cool rule," friends can give children information about the nature of display rules, successful and unsuccessful regulation strategies, the occurrence of ambivalence, and nuances of guilt, shame, pride, and empathy. When Erica sees her best friend's reaction to another girl's hurt feelings, she sees what is acceptable in their peer group.

Potential Contributions of Friends' Reactions to Children's Emotions

Close friends also react to grade-schoolers' emotions. In this more horizontal friendship relationship, they can help each other sort out which of their feelings are shared and which are purely idiosyncratic reactions to emotions. They can comfort ("Don't worry about that test; you'll do better next time") and exhort ("Stop crying—everybody's looking you!") may both predict emotion knowledge. Friends' reactions may have "more message" and "less fear" than parents'. For example, if a friend had slept over and joined her at breakfast, Erica could learn much from her reaction when Lauren sneezed milk all over her. Messages as subtle as the friend's slight frown or rolled eyes when Erica yelled at Lauren could convey totally different meanings (i.e., disapproval or sympathetic dismay, respectively).

Potential Contributions of Friends' Teaching/Coaching about Emotions

Finally, friends are becoming grade-schoolers' "best bets" for confiding emotional experiences. Grade-schoolers are especially likely to disclose to their friends the emotional understandings and experiences they may hide from others, helping each other acquire emotional competencies (Asher, Parker, & Walker, 1996). Friends may use emotion talk in several ways. First, they partake in negative gossip to solidify their identities in the peer group, broaching the subject of potential insecurities without actually naming them. One can imagine emotion talk occurring during such gossip, functioning within the put-downs ("She's such a little crybaby") or statements of group norms ("I hate it when he blows up like that, don't you?"). Second, they share amity and support—approval of a friend, sympathy, and affection could easily include emotion language. Third, relationship talk also goes on, along with self-disclosure; these aspects of conversation may be replete with emotion talk. In fact, children probably converse with friends about the very aspects of emotion understanding undergoing rapid development at this age—knowledge of display rules, ambivalence, and complex emotions like guilt and shame. It is easy to envision Brent ruminating with a friend over the bully's attack on him: "He made me so mad!" "Yeah, and he's scary when he runs at somebody yelling like that. I would have been really scared if he did that to me."

Cognitive Development and Theory of Mind

Contributions to emotion knowledge that are made by socializers, potent as they may be, do not preclude more internal mechanisms driving development (see, for example, Lane & Pollermann, Chapter 11, this volume). As their cognitive and language abilities mature, preschoolers are more able to construct coherent understandings about their own and others' feelings (Harris, 1989, 1993).

One special cognitive ability that fuels such understanding is *Theory of Mind* (Astington, Harris, & Olson, 1988; see Blair, Chapter 17, this volume). The ability to infer mental states in others and to see them as the basis for overt action has been regarded as evidence that children have a Theory of Mind. Until age 3, children know only one world, the one that accords with their experience. Their Theory of Mind is relatively primitive; young preschoolers have some grasp of their own feelings and desires, they comprehend that *objects* may really not be as they look, and know that emotions are personal internal states (Wellman & Banerjee, 1991). By age 4, however, they begin to understand that different people can experience the same world in different ways, and that each person may therefore have a distinctive belief about reality. They come to understand how end results like actions and emotions are produced by individually unique beliefs and desires. The ability to mentally represent other people's psychological states lies at the heart of this development. It is clear that such ability is central to acquisition of emotion knowledge and that, at the same time, it allows social interaction to become much more sophisticated.

There is some debate as to whether Theory of Mind is inborn or constructed during the child's early years. Whatever the answer to this debate, several abilities form its foundation: self-awareness, capacity for pretense, ability to distinguish reality from pretense (Harris, 1989). Thus, we see that very specific aspects of cognitive development may fuel children's social cognitive abilities to understand emotion. As noted in regard to socialization mechanisms, however, much more information is needed on older children's Theory of Mind and cognitive abilities supporting their new developments in emotion knowledge.

NEW DIRECTIONS: FURTHER THINKING, FURTHER RESEARCH

Because of the ever-present nature of emotion at the core of social interaction and well-being, discerning the nature of linkages from emotional to social competence is a vital task for developmentalists. We have seen a number of areas where there are gaps in research, such as in the more complex aspects of grade-schoolers' emotion knowledge and its socialization. There are also many areas in which developmentally appropriate methodologies are needed to assess emotion knowledge across childhood. In order to flesh out our knowledge so as to make a difference in children's lives both contemporaneously and predictively, we need even more details, especially for delineating elements of both preschoolers' and grade-schoolers' emotion knowledge in a complementary fashion, learning more about the grade school emotion knowledge–social competence link, and expanding our understanding of how the more sophisticated elements of emotion knowledge (e.g., mixed emotions, complex emotions) contribute to social functioning. We also need information of the sort gathered here for other cultural and ethnic groups, to generalize our findings and make them more useful. However, applied suggestions can be made; for example, teaching about feelings may be especially helpful for preschoolers.

Over and above these needs, we argue for viewing children's emotion knowledge as part of the social information processing database, especially for young children just venturing into sustained and independent peer interaction. Such information is equivalent to the "emotional content of children's database of knowledge about social situations" (Lemerise & Arsenio, 2000, p. 115). Children amass age-appropriate aspects of emotion knowledge, then use affect–event linkages to anticipate future emotional consequences for self or others, and plan their behavior accordingly (Arsenio & Lover, 1995). Although emotion is only now being incorporated into the social information processing model, earlier research strongly suggests that children's understanding of emotion is central to the database of social knowledge they use during social interaction (e.g., Denham et al., 1990). Although preschoolers' social information processing is likely to be relatively unsophisticated, this early database of emotional understanding forms the hub of its efficient working.

We can speculate as to how emotion knowledge is accessed at each step of Lemerise and Arsenio's (2000) model. An observant child coordinates his or her own behavior through processing information about others' emotions and their impact. By recognizing her mother's emotions (the encoding step in Lemerise and Arsenio's model), Lauren is in a position to understand how any interaction with Mother is likely to proceed. Such understanding also can trigger empathic responsiveness; seeing the emotional import of tears, she may sympathize with Mother even while not completely understanding her plight. Conversely, misattributing Mother's facial expression or its target can lead to difficulties; mistaking her anger for sadness could lead Brent to explode.

Interpreting this encoded emotional information is the next step in the social information processing model. But inability to understand the other's emotion or its target, or to empathize, can lead to a cascading pursuit of destructive goals. If Erica considers that Mother is crying because "she just doesn't understand me" (not that Mother is just momentarily overwhelmed), for example, a hostile encounter may ensue.

Even response generation, evaluation, and decisions are impacted by the ability to understand emotions of self and others. What are the emotional consequences of a particular chosen behavior? Will Mother stop crying if Erica cleans up the breakfast table? Finally, behavior enactment does not foreclose the need to understand emotions. One needs to be able to read the emotional cues inherent in others' reactions to one's chosen behavior in order to modify it. If everyone ignores Brent as he continues to pout, what should he do? He did not get the emotional response he expected and needs to refine his own emotional message. In sum, children's interpretations and attributions about their own and others' emotions can affect children's emotional arousal and emotion-related behavior, which then feed back to affect subsequent cognitions, emotions, and behaviors (Denham, 1998; Graham, Hudley, & Williams, 1992). Even in this depiction, however, we have not specifically mentioned, for example, knowledge of multiple emotion and complex emotions.

More emotion-relevant on-line tests of social information processing are needed for preschool and older age ranges. For example, in a manner similar to the assessment of the steps in Lemerise and Arsenio's (2000) model, children may be presented with tests of the following: (1) whether they encode the specific emotion cues relevant to the interaction at hand (and even whether they encode those irrelevant to the interaction at hand; (2) whether they interpret the emotion accurately, in terms of causality, intentionality, and relevance, for example; (3) whether their encoding and interpretation of the emotion cues lead to empathic processing; (4) how their interpretations affect their goals for interaction; and finally, (5) how situationally relevant emotion cues change after behavior enactment.

Another aspect of emotion knowledge is also key and needs to be assessed in a parallel manner, even though we have only tangentially discussed it here: knowledge of one's own emotions as experienced. Really understanding one's own goals, intentions, and behaviors within social interaction requires clear knowledge of what one is feeling and why, and what this means for one's behavior (Halberstadt et al., 2001). Relatedly, an area of emotional competence as a whole has not been addressed in this chapter, but is crucial to understanding the impact of emotions in social information processing (Lemerise & Arsenio, 2000): one's own emotionality and ability to regulate it. It should be clear that the emotionally relevant social information processing of Brent, in our ongoing example, would be affected by his own expressivity and means of dealing with it—does witnessing Mother's sadness kindle his own generalized annoyance or anxiety, making it more difficult for him to access his emotion knowledge database and behavioral repertoire? Is he aware of his emotional responses to his mother? Alternately, does he become anxious at seeing his mother frustrated, but regulate this anxiety via self-talk? Both emotional expressivity and regulation are clearly pieces of the puzzle that need to be attended to in future assessment of emotion knowledge within social information processing.

Finally, the notion of emotion knowledge possibly leading to social *in*competence needs to be tackled. In a recent commentary, Arsenio and Lemerise (2001) assert that bullies (who are usually "proactively" rather than "reactively" aggressive) show an asymmetry in their social information processing involving intentions. They care about the intentions and moral legitimacy, and presumably the emotional outcomes, of others' actions, but not their own; they are not bothered about using illegitimate aggression to advance their goals at the expense of others'. Moreover, even when they are successful at some level of emotion knowledge (and they often are not), their empathic responses are impaired. Perhaps, as noted earlier, expression and regulation of one's own emotions may interact with one's emotion knowledge, so that emotion knowledge in the presence of faulty regulation/responsiveness predicts social *in*competence rather than the reverse.

In this chapter we have delineated many developments in children's emotion knowledge; we suggest stepping back and viewing these elements of emotion knowledge from a broader social information processing perspective. Our report suggests that continued research on elements of emotion knowledge may ultimately have important implications for application.

REFERENCES

Arsenio, W. F., Cooperman, S., & Lover, A. (2000). Affective predictors of preschoolers' aggression and peer acceptance: Direct and indirect effects. *Developmental Psychology, 36,* 438–448.

Arsenio, W. F., & Lemerise, E. A. (2001). Varieties of childhood bullying: Values, emotion processes and social competence. *Social Development, 10,* 57–74.

Arsenio, W. F., & Lover, A. (1995). Children's conceptions of sociomoral affect: Happy victimizers, mixed emotions, and other expressions. In M. Killen & D. Hart (Eds.), *Morality in everyday life: Developmental perspectives* (pp. 87–128). New York: Cambridge University Press.

Asher, S. R., Parker, J. G., & Walker, D. L. (1996). Distinguishing friendship from acceptance: Implications for intervention and assessment. In W. M. Bukowski, A. Newcomb, & W. W. Hartup (Eds.), *The company they keep:*

Friendship in childhood and adolescence (pp. 366–406). Cambridge, UK: Cambridge University Press.

Astington, J. W., Harris, P. L., & Olson, D. R. (1988). *Developing theories of mind.* Cambridge, UK: Cambridge University Press.

Banerjee, M. (1997). Hidden emotions: Preschoolers' knowledge of appearance–reality and emotion display rules. *Social Development, 15,* 107–132.

Barth, J. M., & Bastiani, A. (1997). A longitudinal study of emotional recognition and preschool children's social behavior. *Merrill-Palmer Quarterly, 43,* 107–128.

Berti, A. E., Garattoni, C., & Venturini, B. (2000). The understanding of sadness, guilt, and shame in 5-, 7-, and 9-year-old children. *Genetic, Social, and General Psychology Monographs, 126,* 293–318.

Brenner, E.M., & Salovey, P. (1997). Emotion regulation during childhood: Developmental, interpersonal, and individual considerations. In P. Salovey & D. J. Sluyter (Eds.), *Emotional devolopment and emotional intelligence* (pp. 168–192). New York: Basic Books.

Bretherton, I., Fritz, J., Zahn-Waxler, C., & Ridgeway, D. (1986). Learning to talk about emotions: A functionalist perspective. *Child Development, 57,* 529–548.

Brody, L. R., & Harrison, R. H. (1987). Developmental changes in children's abilities to match and label emotionally laden situations. *Motivation and Emotion, 11,* 347–365.

Brown, J. R., Donelan-McCall, N., & Dunn, J. (1996). Why talk about mental states? The significance of children's conversations with friends, siblings, and mothers. *Child Development, 67,* 836–849.

Brown, J. R., & Dunn, J. (1992). Talk with your mother or your sibling? Developmental changes in early family conversations about feelings. *Child Development, 63,* 336–349.

Brown, K., Covell, K., & Abramovitch, R. (1991). Time course and control of emotion: Age differences in understanding and recognition. *Merrill-Palmer Quarterly, 37,* 273–287.

Bullock, M., & Russell, J. (1984). Preschool children's interpretations of facial expressions of emotion. *International Journal of Behavioral Development, 7,* 193–214.

Bullock, M., & Russell, J. (1985). Further evidence on preschoolers' interpretation of facial expressions. *International Journal of Behavioral Development, 8,* 15–38.

Camras, L. A., & Allison, K. (1985). Children's understanding of emotional facial expressions and verbal labels. *Journal of Nonverbal Behavior, 9,* 84–94.

Denham, S. A. (1997). "When I have a bad dream, Mommy holds me": Preschoolers' consequential thinking about emotions and social competence. *International Journal of Behavioral Development, 20,* 301–319.

Denham, S. A. (1998). *Emotional development in young children.* New York: Guilford Press.

Denham, S. A., & Couchoud, E. A. (1990). Young preschoolers' understanding of emotion. *Child Study Journal, 20,* 171–192.

Denham, S. A., & Couchoud, E. A. (1991). Social-emotional contributors to preschoolers' responses to an adult's negative emotions. *Journal of Child Psychology and Psychiatry, 32,* 595–608.

Denham, S. A., McKinley, M., Couchoud, E. A., & Holt, R. (1990). Emotional and behavioral predictors of peer status in young preschoolers. *Child Development, 61,* 1145–1152.

Denham, S. A., Mitchell-Copeland, J., Strandberg, K., Auerbach, S., & Blair, K. (1997). Parental contributions to preschoolers' emotional competence: Direct and indirect effects. *Motivation and Emotion, 21,* 65–86.

Denham, S. A., Zoller, D., & Couchoud, E. A. (1994). Socialization of preschoolers' understanding of emotion. *Developmental Psychology, 30,* 928–936.

Dix, T. (1991). The affective organization of parenting: Adaptive and maladaptative processes. *Psychological Bulletin, 110,* 3–25.

Dodge, K. A. (1989). Coordinating responses to aversive stimuli introduction to a special section on the development of emotion regulation. *Developmental Psychology, 25,* 339–342.

Dodge, K. A., Lochman, J. E., Harnish, J. D., Bates, J. E., & Pettit, G. S. (1997). Reactive and proactive aggression in school children and psychiatrically impaired chronically assaultive youth. *Journal of Abnormal Psychology, 106,* 37–51.

Dodge, K. A., Pettit, G., McClaskey, C. B, & Brown, M. M. (1986). Social competence in children. *Monographs of SRCD, 51*(b), 1–85.

Donaldson, S. K., & Westerman, M. A. (1986). Development of children's understanding of ambivalence and causal theories of emotions. *Developmental Psychology, 22,* 655–662.

Dunn, J., Brown, J. R., & Beardsall, L. (1991). Family talk about feeling states and children's later understanding of others' emotions. *Developmental Psychology, 27,* 448–455.

Dunn, J., Brown, J., & Maguire, M. (1995). The development of children's moral sensibility: Individual differences and emotion understanding. *Developmental Psychology, 31,* 649–659.

Dunn, J., Brown, J., Slomkowski, C., Fesla, C., & Youngblade, L. (1991). Young children's understanding of other peoples' feelings and beliefs: Individual differences and their antecedents. *Child Development, 62,* 1352–1366.

Dunn, J., & Cutting, A. L. (1999). Understanding others and individual differences in friendship interactions in young children. *Social Development, 8,* 201–219.

Dunn, J., & Herrera, C. (1997). Conflict resolution with friends, siblings, and mothers: A developmental perspective. *Aggressive Behavior, 23,* 343–357.

Dunn, J., & Hughes, C. (1998). Young children's understanding of emotions within close relationships. *Cognition and Emotion, 12,* 171–190.

Dunn, J., Slomkowski, C., Donelan, N., & Herrera, C. (1995). Young children's understanding of other people's feelings and beliefs: Individual differences and their antecedents. *Child Development, 62,* 1352–1366.

Eisenberg, N., & Fabes, R. A. (1994). Mothers' reactions to children's negative emotions: Relations to children's temperament and anger behavior. *Merrill-Palmer Quarterly, 40,* 138–156.

Eisenberg, N., Fabes, R. A., & Murphy, B. C. (1996). Parents' reactions to children's negative emotions: Relations to children's social competence and comforting behavior. *Child Development, 67,* 2227–2247.

Eisenberg, N., Fabes, R. A., Shepard, S. A., Guthrie, I. K., Murphy, B. C., & Reiser, M. (1999). Parental reactions to children's negative emotions: Longitudinal relations to quality of children's social functioning. *Child Development, 70,* 513–534.

Fabes, R. A., Eisenberg, N., Hanish, L. D., & Spinrad, T. L. (2001). Preschoolers' spontaneous emotion vocabulary: Relations to likability. *Early Education and Development, 12,* 11–27.

Fabes, R. A., Eisenberg, N., McCormick, S. E., & Wilson, M. S. (1988). Preschoolers' attributions of the situational determinants of others' naturally occurring emotions. *Developmental Psychology, 24,* 376–385.

Fabes, R. A., Eisenberg, N., Nyman, M., & Michealieu, Q. (1991). Young children's appraisal of others spontaneous emotional reactions. *Developmental Psychology, 27,* 858–866.

Garner, P. W. (1996). The relations of emotional role taking, affective/moral attributions, and emotional display rule knowledge to low-income school-age children's social competence. *Journal of Applied Developmental Psychology, 17,* 19–36.

Garner, P. W. (1999). Continuity in emotion knowledge from preschool to middle-childhood and relation to emotion socialization. *Motivation and Emotion, 23,* 247–266.

Garner, P. W., & Estep, K. M. (2001). Emotional competence, emotion socialization, and young children's peer-related social competence. *Early Education and Development, 12,* 29–48.

Garner, P. W., Jones, D. C., & Miner, J. L. (1994). Social competence among low-income preschoolers: Emotion socialization practices and social cognitive correlates. *Child Development, 65,* 622–637.

Gilbert, D. T., Pinel, E. C., Wilson, T. D., Blumberg, S. J., & Wheatley, T. P. (1998). Immune neglect: A source of durability bias in affective forecasting. *Journal of Personality and Social Psychology, 75,* 617–638.

Gnepp, J. (1989). Personalized inferences of emotions and appraisals: Component processes and correlates. *Developmental Psychology, 25,* 277–288.

Gnepp, J., & Chilamkurti, C. (1988). Children's use of personality attributions to predict other people's emotional and behavioral reactions. *Child Development, 59,* 743–754.

Gnepp, J., & Gould, M. E. (1985). The development of personalized inferences: Understanding other people's emotional reactions in light of their prior experiences. *Child Development, 56,* 1455–1464.

Gnepp, J., & Hess, D. L. R. (1986). Children's understanding of verbal and facial display rules. *Developmental Psychology, 22,* 103–108.

Gnepp, J., Klayman, J., & Trabasso, T. (1982). A hierarchy of information sources for inferring emotional reactions. *Journal of Experimental Child Psychology, 33,* 111–123.

Gnepp, J., McKee, E., & Domanic, J. A. (1987). Children's use of situational information to infer emotion: Understanding emotionally equivocal situations. *Developmental Psychology, 23,* 114–123.

Gordis, F., Rosen, A. B., & Grand, S. (1989). *Young children's understanding of si-multaneous conflicting emotions.* Poster presented at the biennial meetings of the Society for Research in Child Development, Kansas City, MO.

Gosselin, P., & Simard, J. (1999). Children's knowledge of facial expression of emotions: Distinguishing fear and surprise. *Journal of Genetic Psychology, 10,* 181–193.

Gottman, J., Katz, L., & Hooven, C. (1997). *Meta-emotion: How families communicate emotionally.* Mahwah, NJ: LEA.

Gottman, J. M., & Mettetal, G. (1986). Speculations about social and affective development of friendship and acquaintanceship through adolescence. In J. M. Gottman & J. Parker (Eds.), *Conversations of friends: Speculations on affective development* (pp. 192–237). New York: Cambridge University Press.

Graham, S., Hudley, C., & Williams, E. (1992). Attributional and emotional determinants of aggression among African-American and Latino young adolescents. *Developmental Psychology, 28,* 731–740.

Greer, A. E. (1997). *Emotional development in children with child-onset and adolescent-onset conduct disorder.* Unpublished doctoral dissertation, University of Iowa, Iowa City, IA.

Gross, D., & Harris, P. (1988). Understanding false beliefs about emotion. *International Journal of Behavioral Development, 11,* 475–488.

Halberstadt, A. G. (1991). Socialization of expressiveness: Family influences in particular and a model in general. In R. S. Feldman & S. Rime (Eds.), *Fundamentals of emotional expressiveness* (pp. 106–162). Cambridge, UK: Cambridge University Press.

Halberstadt, A. G., Denham, S. A., & Dunsmore, J. (2001). Affective social competence. *Social Development, 10,* 79–119.

Harris, P. L. (1989). *Children and emotion: The development of psychological understanding.* Oxford, UK: Basil Blackwell.

Harris, P. L. (1993). Understanding emotion. In M. Lewis & J. Haviland (Eds.), *Handbook of emotions* (pp. 237–246). New York: Guilford Press.

Harris, P. L., Donnelly, K., Guz, G. R., Pitt Watson, R. (1986). Children's understanding of the distinction between real and apparent emotion. *Child Development, 57,* 895–909.

Harris, P. L., Guz, G. R., Lipian, M. S., & Man Shu, Z. (1985). Insight into the time course of emotion among Western and Chinese children. *Child Development, 56,* 972–988.

Harris, P. L., Olthof, T., Meerum Terwogt, M., & Hardman, C. E. (1987). Children's knowledge of the situations that provoke emotion. *International Journal of Behavioral Development, 10,* 319–343.

Harter, S., & Whitesell, N. R. (1989). Developmental changes in children's understanding of single, multiple, and blended emotion concepts. In P. Harris & C. Saarni (Eds.), *Children's understanding of emotion* (pp. 81–116). Cambridge, UK: Cambridge University Press.

Hoffner, C., & Badzinski, D. M. (1989). Children's integration of facial and situational cues to emotion. *Child Development, 60,* 415–422.

Hughes, C., Dunn, J., & White, A. (1998). Trick or treat? Uneven understanding of mind and emotion and executive dysfunction in "hard-to-manage" preschoolers. *Journal of Child Psychology and Psychiatry, 39,* 981–994.

Jones, D. C., Bowling, B., & Cumberland, A. (1998). The development of display rule knowledge: Linkages with family expressiveness and social competence. *Child Development, 69,* 1209–1222.

Josephs, I. (1994). Display rule behavior and understanding in preschool children. *Journal of Nonverbal Behavior, 18,* 301–326.

Kestenbaum, R., & Gelman, S. (1995). Preschool children's identification and understanding of mixed emotions. *Cognitive Development, 10,* 443–458.

Lemerise, E., & Arsenio, W. F. (2000). An integrated model of emotion processes and cognition in social information processing. *Child Development, 71,* 107–118.

McDowell, D. J., & Parke, R. D. (2000). Differential knowledge of display rules for positive and negative emotions: Influences from parents, influences on peers. *Social Development, 9,* 415–432.

Meerum Terwogt, M., Koops, W., Oosterhoff, T., & Olthof, T. (1986). Development in processing of multiple emotional situations. *Journal of Genetic Psychology, 113,* 109–119.

Meerum Terwogt, M., & Olthof, T. (1989). Awareness and self-regulation of emotion in young children. In C. Saarni & P. Harris (Eds.), *Children's understanding of emotion* (pp. 209–237). New York: Cambridge University Press.

Miller, P. H., & Aloise, P. A. (1989). Young children's understanding of the psychological causes of behavior: A review. *Child Development, 60,* 257–285.

Murgatroyd, S. J., & Robinson, E. J. (1993). Children's judgments of emotions following moral transgression. *International Journal of Behavioral Development, 16,* 93–111.

Nunner-Winkler, G., & Sodian, B. (1988). Children's understanding of moral emotions. *Child Development, 59,* 1323–1338.

Olthof, T., Meerum Terwogt, M., Van Eck, O. V., & Koops, W. (1987). Children's knowledge of the integration of successive emotions. *Perceptual and Motor Skills, 65,* 407–414.

Parke, R. D., Cassidy, J., Burks, V. M., Carson, J. L., & Boyum, L. (1992). Familial contribution to peer competence among young children: The role of interactive and affective processes. In R. D. Parke & G. W. Ladd (Eds.), *Family–peer relationships: Modes of linkage* (pp. 107–134). Hillsdale, NJ: Erlbaum.

Peng, M., Johnson, C. N., Pollock, J., Glasspool, R., & Harris, P. L. (1992). Training young children to acknowledge mixed emotions. *Cognition and Emotion, 6,* 387–401.

Roberts, W., & Strayer, J. (1996). Empathy, emotional expressiveness, and prosocial behavior. *Child Development, 67,* 449–470.

Russell, J. A. (1990). The preschooler's understanding of the causes and consequences of emotion. *Child Development, 61,* 1872–1881.

Russell, J. A., & Paris, F. A. (1994). Do children acquire concepts for complex emotions abruptly? *International Journal of Behavioral Development, 17,* 349–365.

Saarni, C. (1999). *The development of emotional competence.* New York: Guilford Press.

Schultz, D., Izard, C. E., & Ackerman, B. P. (1999). Children's anger attribution biases: Relations to family environment and social adjustment. *Social Development, 9,* 284–301.

Shields, A., Dickstein, S., Seifer, R., Guisti, L., Magee, K. D., & Spritz, B. (2001). Emotional competence and early school adjustment: A study of preschoolers at risk. *Early Education and Development, 12,* 73–96.

Smith, M. (2001). Social and emotional competencies: Contributions to young African-American children's peer acceptance. *Early Education and Development, 12,* 49–72.

Stifter, C., & Fox, N. (1987). Preschoolers' ability to identify and label emotions. *Journal of Nonverbal Behavior, 10,* 255–266.

Strayer, J. (1986). Children's attributions regarding the situational determinants of emotion in self and others. *Developmental Psychology, 22,* 649–654.

Wellman, H. M., & Banerjee, M. (1991). Mind and emotion: Children's understanding of the emotional consequences of beliefs and desires. *British Journal of Developmental Psychology, 9,* 191–214.

Wellman, H. M., & Woolley, J. D. (1990). From simple desires to ordinary beliefs: The early development of everyday psychology. *Cognition, 35,* 245–275.

Wiggers, M., & Van Lieshout, C. F. (1985). Development of recognition of emotions: Children's reliance on situational and facial expressive cues. *Developmental Psychology, 21,* 338–349.

Wintre, M., Polivy, J., & Murray, M. A. (1990). Self-predictions of emotional response patterns: Age, sex, and situational determinants. *Child Development, 61,* 1124–1133.

Wintre, M., & Vallance, D. D. (1994). A developmental sequence in the comprehension of emotions: Multiple emotions, intensity and valence. *Developmental Psychology, 30,* 509–514.

CHAPTER 11

Complexity of Emotion Representations

RICHARD D. LANE
BRANKA ZEI POLLERMANN

Wisdom connotes intelligence, the ability to differentiate and understand the relationships between things in the world, tempered by the refinement in one's understanding based on real-life experiences. As such, wisdom can be acquired only through hard-won experience and the recognition that conventional beliefs may be misleading. From this perspective, emotional responses are inherently wise. Emotional responses result from a complex cognitive process consisting of an evaluation of the extent to which goals are being met in interaction with the environment. The usefulness and adaptive value of emotions derives from their phylogenetic origin as rapid and automatic solutions to common problems in adaptation (Tooby & Cosmides, 1990). In this sense, emotions reflect experience across the evolutionary time scale. Furthermore, one's emotional responses may be surprising, as they may be inconsistent with one's own conscious beliefs or expectations. Major life decisions may best be made by relying on one's gut feelings. In this sense, emotions (in contrast to feelings or conscious emotional experiences) are wise because they represent a rapid integration of multiple sources of information and provide an instantaneous assessment about the significance to a person of his or her actual or anticipated interactions with the environment.

The degree to which the inherent wisdom of emotions can be put to purposeful use, however, is a function of the degree to which emotional responses are consciously experienced, attended to, and reflected upon. The autonomic, neuroendocrine, musculoskeletal, perceptual, and mnemonic processes that are automatically set in motion during an emotional response may not be consciously experienced or recognized. Even if an emotional response is associated with a conscious experience or feeling, the person having the emotional response may not attend to it. In that case, the information inherent in the emotional response (e.g., the inherent desire to correct a wrong implicit in an anger response) cannot be explicitly incorporated into conscious thought. In the absence of reflective thought, emotional learning can certainly still occur, but it will necessarily proceed automatically and influence one's future behavior and emotional responses in a manner that is not within one's conscious control.

If the subjective experience or feeling associated with an emotional response *is* attended to, however, there will be considerable variability across individuals in the nature of the information extracted from the experience during off-line reflection. In this chapter we propose that the complexity of the conceptual framework that one has for one's own emotional life will determine both the degree to which that experience can be represented mentally in a complex fashion and the complexity of the on-line emotional experience. As such, the degree to which feelings are informative and can serve as a useful guide in adaptive behavior will be a function of the complexity of the conceptual framework that one has created for one's own emotional life. A primary goal of this chapter is to explain this idea in greater detail.

We begin by reviewing the theoretical background of a cognitive–developmental framework called "levels of emotional awareness." An extension of the theory is presented that places the original model in a somewhat broader context by demonstrating how levels of emotional awareness constitute one manifestation of a larger phenomenon involving the conceptual organization of emotion. Next, empirical data supporting the levels of emotional awareness framework are presented. We then conclude by addressing the implications of this new perspective for emotion research. One major implication is that the conceptual organization of emotions is the primary determinant of the wisdom in feelings.

THE ORIGIN OF COMPLEX REPRESENTATIONS
OF EMOTIONAL STATES

In this section, we expand on previous theoretical formulations of the emotional awareness construct to place it in a broader and more up-to-date context. Inherent in this approach is the concept that the complexity of the representations of emotional states increases developmentally. The goals of this section are to describe what is meant by complexity, explain how it arises, and explain why a conceptual framework of one's own emotional life includes what it does.

One can begin by asking a very simple question. How does a child come to know what he or she is feeling and what other people may be feeling? Emotional responses are highly complex phenomena including autonomic, neuroendocrine, musculoskeletal, perceptual, mnemonic, and experiential processes that are automatically set in motion during an emotional response. Any or all of these phenomena may serve as a substrate for cognitive processing. But early in development, emotional responses are relatively undifferentiated whole-body responses that are sensorimotor in character. Since Piaget discovered that intelligence (Piaget, 1936) derives from a general coordination of sensorimotor patterns, it seemed reasonable to hypothesize that understanding of the internal world of emotions develops according to classic principles of the development of intelligence.

Piaget's fundamental epistemological position is that awareness of the subject's own actions/reactions (like any other knowledge) is constructed; that is, it results from cognitive processes in general and metacognition in particular (Piaget, 1974). By virtue of a developmental process, a person can become aware of the full complexity of his or her own and others' emotional responses.

Lane and Schwartz (1987) proposed that an individual's ability to recognize and describe emotion in oneself and others, called emotional awareness, is a cognitive skill that undergoes a developmental process similar to that which Piaget described for cognition in general. A fundamental tenet of this model is that individual differences in emotional awareness reflect variations in the degree of differentiation and integration of the schemata used to process emotional information, whether that information comes from the external world or the internal world through introspection.

The model posited five "levels of emotional awareness," which share the structural characteristics of Piaget's stages of cognitive development (Piaget, 1937). The five levels of emotional awareness are, in ascending order, (1) awareness of physical sensations, (2) action tendencies, (3) single emotions, (4) blends of emotions, and (5) blends of blends of emotional experience (the capacity to appreciate complexity in the experiences of self and other). The hierarchical relationship between the levels is depicted in Figure 11.1.

Emotional awareness is considered to be a separate line of cognitive development that may proceed somewhat independently from

FIGURE 11.1. The hierarchical relationship between the five levels of emotional awareness.

other cognitive domains. The concept that development can proceed at different rates in different domains of knowledge is known as *horizontal decalage*. In principle, it is entirely possible that a developmental arrest can occur in one domain while development in other domains of intelligence continues unabated.

The relationship between awareness and experience requires comment. Awareness involves directing attention to the contents of experience and retrospectively creating representations off-line. These representations are then automatically used as assimilatory schemes when emotional responses occur on-line. The contents of conscious experience will therefore be determined by these representational schemata.

The five levels therefore describe the cognitive organization of emotional experience. They describe traits, although they may also be used to describe states. The levels are hierarchically related, in that functioning at each level adds to and modifies the functions of previous levels but does not eliminate them. For example, level 4 experiences should be associated with more differentiated representations of somatic sensations (level 1) than level 2 experiences. The feelings associated with a given emotional response can be thought of as a construction consisting of each of the levels of awareness up to and including the highest level attained.

The development of representational schemata is facilitated by the language or other semiotic mode used to describe emotion. This perspective draws on the work on symbol formation by Werner and Kaplan (1963), who maintained that the way the world becomes known to an observer is influenced by the way in which it is represented symbolically. Thus, the nature of conscious emotional experience, and the ability to appreciate complexity in one's own experience and that of others, is influenced by how emotion is represented.

This position is also consistent with that of Piaget's followers such as Karmiloff-Smith (1992), who holds that the development of knowledge proceeds through a process called "representational redescription." In essence, cognitive development from this theoretical perspective consists of the transformation of knowledge from implicit (procedural, sensorimotor) to explicit (conscious thought) representations through the use of language or another semiotic mode. This transformation renders thought more flexible, adaptable, and creative. This viewpoint is consistent with the theory that the way language is used to describe emotion modifies what one knows about emotion and how emotion is experienced consciously.

FROM SENSORIMOTOR TO CONCEPTUAL REPRESENTATIONS

The cognitive "instruments" that allow for the transformation of sensorimotor schemes to conceptual representations are of two kinds (Piaget & Garcia, 1983): empirical abstraction and reflective abstraction (in the sense of reflecting upon). Each abstraction mechanism leads to qualitatively different types of knowledge.

Applied to the knowledge and awareness of emotion, the first type of knowledge is constructed through "empirical abstraction," that is, from direct perception/ proprioception of emotional arousal. In this process a person selects one or several features from the whole global event. The abstracted features depend on which assimilatory schemata have been used as well as on his or her level of coding capacities (establishing relations, correspondences, etc.). At this level a person typically describes successive actions as observational facts. Such a nonreflective level of consciousness includes a person's actions and/or action tendencies, possibly including expressive reactions (voice, face, muscular tensing, etc.).

Assuming functional continuity between sensorimotor intelligence and conceptual thought, Piaget (1972, p. 253) gives four conditions for the transformation of sensorimotor schemes into conceptual schemes: (1) a general acceleration of movements (which is a sign of the beginning of interiorization, that is, of an anticipatory representation of an action scheme); (2) awareness of the structure of the anticipatory scheme, which involves generalization, hierarchical classification, and serial ordering; (3) a system of signs allowing the construction of general concepts necessary for categorizations and serial ordering; and (4) the socialization of representations by virtue of the use of language, which places individual thought into an objective and socially shared reality.

The second type of knowledge is constructed through "reflective abstraction" (Piaget, 1977). The latter involves meta-cognitive treatment of lower-level representations, their relationships, and their coordinations. Such reflecting upon one's own first-level representations includes understanding, deductions (causal explanations, necessities), and drawing inferences (implications, logical connections). At this level a person may typically say, "I am sure I saw and felt . . . , then I told myself . . . , I then had the idea . . . , I concluded that. . . .") "Reflective abstraction" (*abstraction réfléchissante*) is considered to be the main mechanism of conceptualization.

To a large extent the verbalization of emotional experiences can be considered a consciousness-raising process that elevates the procedural dimension of emotion onto a representational level, allowing for more flexible mental handling of emotional contents. The shifting of sensorimotor contents onto a representational level requires conceptualization, which in turn involves reconstruction. The latter follows the same stages as those observed on the practical sensorimotor level: for example, from egocentrism to decentration, from subjectivity to objectivity, from nondifferentiation and noncoordination to differentiation and coordination. Conceptualization is facilitated by the use of language as a semiotic system that "translates" concepts into communicable and conventionalized entities. Linguistic signs facilitate the representational redescription of sensorimotor action schemes through the mechanism of generalization, thus allowing the construction of abstract representational entities free of any concrete content.

Ferdinand de Saussure's (1949/1972) theory of language considers language as a categorizing principle in that the concepts it denotes are by definition categories that the mind has constructed (through extralinguistic and/or linguistic experience) and that the speaking community has conventionalized. Language is also a form of socialized thought in the sense that the precise semantic value of each linguistic sign is conditioned and/or limited by the coexistence of all the other signs available in a given language used by a given speaking community in a given culture.

Verbal description of one's emotions necessarily involves reflecting upon one's own internal experience and expressing it by means of a culturally shared semiotic system. The mere use of language in describing or expressing emotions helps establish a network of differences and similarities between various emotional representations and concepts.

At the highest level, which is the result of reciprocal assimilations of the contents of the second level, a person is able to elaborate operations on operations. The full combinatorial capacity consists of the operations involving four possible transformations, the so-called INCR group, consisting of Identical, Inverse (or Negation), Reciprocal, and Correlative transformations. The INCR group is considered to be a form of equilibrium (or stable level) of a person's operational behaviors. A person is able to have a theory and envisage several different explanatory models for a problem.

Thus, the cognitive "instruments" that make abstract thought possible are essential for the transformation of sensorimotor aspects of emotion into differentiated, conscious experiences. At the highest level, by virtue of the INCR group, emotional information can be manipulated freely independent of the original interoceptive or exteroceptive stimuli.

CONCEPTUAL ORGANIZATION OF EMOTION

Through the process of reflective abstraction involving verbal representations, a framework of emotion knowledge develops. It is a conceptual framework in the sense that each emotion becomes a conceptual entity in its own right, with its own associated features. These include what the experience of having the feeling is like and how it feels in the body, what the outward signs of the emotion are, what causes the feeling, what enhances or diminishes the feeling, how the emotional state is related to overt behavior, and how social context influences what is (or should be) expressed. With development, more and more of these features become part of each individual emotion concept and more distinctions are made between different emotions, leading to an expansion in the conceptual repertoire of emotions. *In essence, a network of interrelated schemata for processing emotional information develops.*

As noted earlier, the process of developing complex mental representations of emotional states proceeds off-line. However, the schemata that develop constitute the "programs" for processing emotional information on-line, which includes the orchestration of each emotional response. As such, the entire panoply of functions involved in emotion gets coordinated into more and more complex schemata. Thus, phenomena that will covary in terms of their degree of differentiation and complexity include the ability to recognize emotion stimuli (either verbally or nonverbally), the range of emotional experience, the extent of one's emotional vocabulary, the capacity for accurate empathy, and the capacity for emotion self-regulation in the service of adaptive social behavior (see also Denham & Kochanoff, Chapter 10, this volume).

THE LEVELS OF EMOTIONAL AWARENESS SCALE: PSYCHOMETRIC FINDINGS

The Levels of Emotional Awareness Scale (LEAS) is a written performance measure that asks a person to describe his or her anticipated feelings and those of another person in each of 20 scenes described in two to four sentences (Lane, Quinlan, Schwartz, Walker, & Zeitlin, 1990). Scoring is based on specific structural criteria aimed at determining the degree of differentiation in the use of emotion words (the degree of specificity in the terms used and the range of emotions described) and the differentiation of self from other. The scoring involves essentially no inference by raters. Because the scoring system evaluates the structure of experience and not its content, individuals cannot modify their responses to enhance their scores, as is the case with some self-report instruments. A glossary of words at each level was created to guide scoring.

Each of the 20 scenes receives a score of 0 to 5, corresponding to the cognitive–developmental theory of emotional awareness that underlies the LEAS (Lane & Schwartz, 1987). A score of 0 is assigned when nonaffective words are used or when the word "feel" is used to describe a thought rather than a feeling. A score of 1 is assigned when words indicating physiological cues are used in the description of feelings (e.g., "I'd feel tired"). A score of 2 is assigned when words are used that convey relatively undifferentiated emotion (e.g., "I'd feel bad") or when the word "feel" is used to convey an action tendency (e.g., "I'd feel like punching the wall"). A score of 3 is assigned when one word conveying a typical differentiated emotion is used (e.g., happy, sad, angry, etc.). A score of 4 is assigned when two or more level 3 words are used in a way that conveys greater emotional differentiation than would either word alone. Respondents receive a separate score for the "self" response and for the "other" response, ranging from 0 to 4. In addition, a total LEAS score is given to each scene equal to the higher of the self and other scores. A score of 5 is assigned to the total when self and other each receive a score of 4 and are differentiated from one another; thus, a maximum total LEAS score of 100 is possible.

To date, eight separate psychometric studies have been conducted with the LEAS. The first study in Yale undergraduates ($N = 94$) enabled us to examine the reliability of the LEAS and its correlation with other psychological tests (Lane et al., 1990). The second study involved students at Chicago Medical School (CMS) ($N = 57$) and focused on the correlation with the Levy Chimeric Faces Test (Lane, Kevley, DuBois, Shamasundara, & Schwartz, 1995). The third study, in Arizona and Minnesota ($N = 385$), established norms for the scale (Lane et al.,

1996). A fourth study with University of Arizona undergraduates ($N =$ 215) involved additional psychometric and psychophysiologic assessments. The fifth and sixth studies were conducted in collaboration with Lisa Feldman Barrett at Boston College. In addition, two international studies were conducted: a study of 331 German students (Wrana et al., 1998) and a Canadian study of 30 subjects with borderline personality disorder and 40 control subjects (Levine, Marziali, & Hood, 1997). The findings from these studies are selectively reviewed here.

The LEAS has consistently been shown to have high interrater reliability and internal consistency (Lane et al., 1998). The test–retest reliability at 2 weeks has been recently shown to be quite good ($N = 135$, Spearman–Brown $r = .67$, $p < .001$). Norms for age, sex, and socioeconomic status have been established based on the study completed in Arizona and Minnesota.

In the Yale study we administered two instruments that, like the LEAS, are cognitive–developmental measures based on Piaget's model: the Sentence Completion Test of Ego Development by Loevinger (Loevinger & Wessler, 1970; Loevinger, Wessler, & Redmore, 1970) and the cognitive complexity of the description of parents by Blatt and colleagues (Blatt, Wein, Chevron, & Quinlan, 1979). The LEAS correlated moderately ($r = .37$ and $r = .36$, respectively) and significantly ($p < .01$) in the predicted direction in both cases. These results support the claim that the LEAS is measuring a cognitive–developmental continuum and that the LEAS is not identical to these other measures.

A key question is whether the LEAS is simply another measure of verbal ability. In the Yale sample the LEAS correlated $r = .38$ ($p < .001$) with the vocabulary subtest of the Wechsler Adult Intelligence Scale (WAIS). In the CMS study the LEAS correlated $r = .17$ (NS) with the Shipley Institute of Living Scale (Shipley, 1940), a multiple-choice measure of verbal ability. These data suggest that verbal ability may contribute to LEAS performance. However, several studies have now been conducted demonstrating that when verbal ability is controlled, significant effects are still observed. For example, LEAS scores in men and women could be compared in all eight studies. In three of these studies measures of verbal ability, including the WAIS vocabulary subtest and the Shipley Institute of Living Scale, were also obtained. In each study women scored higher than men on the LEAS ($p < .01$), even when controlling for verbal ability ($p < .05$) (Barrett, Lane, Sechrest, & Schwartz, 2000). Thus, the finding that women score higher than men on the LEAS is a highly stable and generalizable finding.

Although the LEAS captures important phenomena independent of verbal ability, it would be inappropriate to always covary verbal ability in any study involving the LEAS. As Weiskrantz (2000) discusses, it may be that activation of the commentary system (as opposed to the actual production of the commentary response) generates awareness. As such, removing variance due to language-related ability may encroach upon the core of emotional awareness.

Lisa Feldman Barrett administered the LEAS and the Weinberger Adjustment Inventory to 63 subjects at Pennsylvania State University and 55 subjects at Boston College. In both samples the LEAS correlated significantly ($p < .05$, 2-tailed) with self-restraint, one of three superordinate dimensions of the scale. The LEAS also correlated significantly with impulse control, ($r = .35$, $p < .01$, 2-tailed, and $r = .30$, $p < .05$, 2-tailed), a component of self-restraint that involves the tendency to think before acting. Self-restraint refers directly to suppression of egoistic desires in the interest of long-term goals and relations with others. This replication in independent samples indicates that greater emotional awareness is associated with greater self-reported impulse control, and is consistent with the theory that functioning at higher levels of emotional awareness (levels 3–5) modulates function at lower levels (actions and action tendencies at level 2).

Evidence for the discriminant validity of the LEAS is provided by data from the Norms study and the Arizona undergraduate study. In both studies ($n = 385$ and $n = 215$, respectively) the Affect Intensity Measure (Larsen & Diener, 1987), a trait measure of the tendency to experience emotions intensely, did not correlate significantly with the LEAS despite the large sample sizes. Thus, inadequate statistical power cannot explain the lack of correlation. The LEAS also does not correlate significantly with measures of negative affect, such as the Taylor Manifest Anxiety Scale and the Beck Depression Inventory. These results are consistent with the view that the LEAS measures the structure or complexity and not the intensity or valence of affective experience.

BEHAVIORAL AND NEURAL CORRELATES OF THE LEAS

A key assumption in this work on emotional awareness is that language promotes the development of schemata for the processing of emotional information, whether that information comes from the internal or external world. Once the schemata are established, they should affect the processing of emotional information whether the information is verbal or nonverbal. Thus, the LEAS should correlate with the ability to recognize and categorize external emotional stimuli. Furthermore, this correlation should hold whether the external stimulus and the response are purely verbal or purely nonverbal.

These hypotheses were tested in the Norms study by use of the Perception of Affect Task (PAT), a set of four emotion recognition tasks (35 items each) developed by Jim Rau and Alfred Kaszniak at the University of Arizona (Rau, 1993). The first subtask consists of stimuli describing an emotional situation without the use of emotion words. For example, "The man looked at the photograph of his recently departed wife." The response involves choosing one from an array of seven terms ("happy," "sad," "angry," "afraid," "disgust," "neutral," "surprise") to characterize how the person in question was feeling. The fourth subtask is purely nonverbal. The stimuli consist of photographs of faces developed by Ekman (1982), each of which depicts an individual emotion. The response consists of selecting one from an array of seven photographs depicting emotional scenes without faces (e.g., two people standing arm-in-arm by a grave with their backs to the camera). The other two subtasks involve a verbal stimulus (sentence) and a nonverbal response (from an array of seven faces), and a nonverbal stimulus (face) and a verbal response (from an array of seven words).

Across the entire scale, the correlation between the LEAS and the PAT was high ($r = .43$, $n = 385$, $p < .001$), accounting for about 18% of the variance. Furthermore, significant correlations were observed between the LEAS and each of the PAT subtasks. When dividing the sample into upper (high), middle, and lower thirds on the LEAS, the high-LEAS subjects scored higher on each of the PAT subtasks than the low-LEAS subjects. Thus, high LEAS scores were associated with better emotion recognition no matter whether the task was purely verbal or purely nonverbal (Lane et al., 1996). Furthermore, when combining results for each of the seven emotion categories across the four subtasks (there were five stimuli of each emotion type in each subtask), the same findings for high-, moderate-, and low-LEAS subjects were observed (Lane, Sechrest, Riedel, Shapiro & Kaszniak 2000). These findings support the claim that the LEAS is: (1) a measure of the cognitive–developmental schemata used to process emotional information, whether the information is verbal or nonverbal, (2) a measure of the complexity of experience, and (3) not merely a measure of verbal ability.

To explore the underlying functional neuroanatomy of emotional awareness, we administered the LEAS to participants in a positron emission tomography (PET) study of emotion (Lane et al., 1998). Participants included 12 right-handed female volunteers who were free of medical, neurological, or psychiatric abnormalities. The LEAS and other psychometric instruments were completed prior to PET imaging. Happiness, sadness, disgust, and three neutral control conditions were induced by film and recall of personal experiences (12 conditions). Twelve PET images of blood flow were obtained in each person using the ECAT 951/31 scanner (Siemens, Knoxville, TN), 40 mCi intravenous bolus injections of ^{15}O-water, a 15-second uptake period, 60-second scans, and an interscan interval of 10 minutes.

To examine neural activity attributable to emotion generally, rather than to specific emotions, one can subtract the 3 neutral conditions from the 3 emotion conditions in a given stimulus modality (film or recall). This difference, which can be calculated separately for the 6 film and 6 recall conditions, identifies regions of the brain where blood flow changes specifically attributable to emotion occur. These blood flow changes, which indicate neural activity in particular regions, can then be correlated with the LEAS scores to identify regions of the brain that are associated with emotional awareness during emotional arousal.

Findings from this covariate analysis revealed one cluster for film-induced emotion with a maximum located in the right midcingulate cortex (Brodmann's area [BA] 23; coordinates of maximum = [16, −18, 32]; $z = 3.40$; $p < .001$ uncorrected). For recall-induced emotion, the most statistically significant cluster was located in the right anterior cingulate cortex (BA 24; coordinates of maximum = [16, 6, 30]; $z = 2.82$; $p < .005$ uncorrected). An analysis was then performed to identify areas of significant overlap between the two covariance analyses. With a height threshold of $z = 3.09$, $p < .001$, and an extent threshold of 5 voxels, a single cluster was observed in the right anterior cingulate cortex (BA 24) maximal at [14, 6, 30].

Traditionally, the anterior cingulate cortex was thought to have a primarily affective function (Papez, 1937; Vogt, Finch, & Olson, 1992). However, in addition to a role in emotion regulation, it is now recognized to play important roles in attention, pain, response selection, maternal behavior, vocalization, skeletomotor function, and autonomic control (Vogt & Gabriel, 1993). The multiple functions of the anterior cingulate cortex no doubt contribute to the significant changes in activation that have been observed in a variety of studies. How can these different functions be reconciled with the present findings involving emotional awareness?

One answer may be that these various functions of the anterior cingulate cortex may reflect its superordinate role in executive control of attention and motor responses (Lane et al., 1998). According to this view, emotion, pain, or other salient exteroceptive or interoceptive stimuli provide moment-to-moment guidance regarding the most suitable allocation of attentional resources for the purpose of optimizing motor responses in interaction with the environment. The conscious experience of emotion may occur concomitantly and automatically as attention is redirected by emotion. As such, a role of the anterior cingulate cortex in the conscious experience of emotion fits well with its other functions, but suggests that this role is not exclusive to emotion.

To the extent that people who are more emotionally aware attend more to internal and external emotion cues, the cognitive processing of this information can contribute to ongoing emotional development.

IMPLICATIONS FOR THEORY AND RESEARCH

Emotional Intelligence

Emotional intelligence may be broadly defined as the ability to use emotional information in a constructive and adaptive manner. Emotional information consists of one's own subjective emotional responses as well as the information conveyed by the emotional responses of others. This definition of emotional intelligence is consistent with that of the creators of the construct, who view emotional intelligence as a set of mental abilities (Salovey & Mayer, 1990; Mayer & Salovey, 1997; Mayer, Salovey & Caruso, 1999). These include the ability to perceive emotions, access and generate emotion to assist thought, understand and reason about emotion, and reflectively regulate emotions to promote emotional and intellectual growth.

It should be evident from the earlier discussion of theory that the conceptual organization of one's own emotional life is the core of emotional intelligence. The mental abilities associated with emotional intelligence are all derived from this core. Put in another way, the same principles and processes that govern cognition or intelligence in the usual sense apply to all other domains of intelligence as well, including emotional intelligence. The advantage of the perspective proposed here is that it provides a coherent explanation for the universe of phenomena that are captured by the concept of emotional intelligence. Furthermore, it explains their interrelationship and the principles that define and govern the degree to which someone is emotionally intelligent.

Assessment of the Conceptual Organization of Emotion

If the conceptual organization of one's emotional life is the core of emotional intelligence, this has implications for how emotional intelligence, and related phenomena, are assessed. Currently, emotional intelligence assessment consists of determining accuracy in emotion recognition judgments, making imaginative connections between emotions and concrete objects, assessing the ability to use emotions in decision making, and the like (Mayer, Salovey, & Caruso, 1999).

The first question is how best to assess the conceptual organization of emotion in any given person. Although a Piagetian approach has been used to chart the development of intelligence in a variety of cognitive domains, the fact is that such an approach to emotions has never been undertaken with children or adults. Piaget's (1926/1947) clinical method consists of asking children questions and using their responses to tease out the extent of their conceptual understanding. It is reasonable to predict that the development of a conceptual system for emotions will follow the same principles that govern other areas of cognitive development.

The most efficient way to assess the conceptual organization of emotion remains to be determined. However, for practical reasons it would be ideal to develop specific tasks for this purpose and to develop tasks that would be applicable to adults. An example of such a task is an emotional verbal fluency task, in which the individual is asked to name as many emotion or emotion-related words as possible in a given time period (e.g., 1 or 2 minutes). The emotion terms generated are an indirect index of the conceptual distinctions that the individual has made in the emotion domain. Performance on this task would clearly be influenced by verbal ability. However, individual differences in this domain of intelligence are considerable, and, as demonstrated earlier, verbal ability accounts for only a part of the variance in emotional awareness. Creative nonverbal methods would be needed to explore the conceptual distinctions in emotion made by children in the first 1–2 years of life.

A corollary of this approach is that standard methods of assessing emotional experience may be misguided if one is interested in relating self-reported experience to emotional intelligence. Specifically, typical scales used to assess emotional experience specify the emotion terms in advance and request a rating of intensity or frequency. An important reason that such scales exist is that they are time-efficient and have face validity. What is lost in such an approach, such as the Positive and Negative Affect Scale (PANAS; Watson, Clark, & Tellegan, 1988) is that the conceptual structure of the emotion world is largely prespecified by the selection of the emotion terms, or conceptual distinctions, in advance. An enormous amount of information—information that may be critically important in detecting individual differences in emotional intelligence—is therefore lost. The LEAS was created with exactly this limitation in existing emotion measures in mind.

Alexithymia Revisited

Emotional intelligence is a powerful concept because there is such a wide range of function in this domain in adults. One of us (R. D. L.) has previously postulated that alexithymia, a clinical condition meaning lack of words (or symbols) for emotion, is fundamentally a developmental deficit consisting of a relative absence of emotional experience rather than a lack of words for emotion (Lane, Ahern, Schwartz & Kaszniak, 1997; see also Taylor, Bagby, & Luminet, 2000). One of the obstacles to having alexithymia recognized as a valid clinical entity is the difficulty in explaining exactly in what way a symbolization deficit is the core problem. For example, if on a self-report scale of emotional experience a subject scores in the normal range, does that exclude the possibility of alexithymia? The answer is no, but explaining why that is the case has been challenging. Leaders in this area of research discuss alexithymia as a deficit in the capacity to cognitively elaborate emotions (Taylor, Bagby, & Parker, 1997). The latter position is consistent with the view that the subjective experience of emotion is no different in alexithymic individuals as compared with other individuals, a view to which one of us (R. D. L.) has taken exception (Lane et al., 2000).

If one redefines alexithymia as a deficit in the conceptual organization of emotion, its multiple manifestations become much clearer. As noted earlier, a conceptual deficit is associated with a deficit in the complexity of subjective experience. It is also associated with a deficit in emotion recognition ability, a lack of empathy, a narrowed range of emotional expressions, a limited emotional vocabulary, deficits in the capacity for adaptive social behavior, and limitations in the capacity for emotion self-regulation. Perhaps this new conceptual understanding of alexithymia can lead to more accurate identification of alexithymic individuals and the ability to place the manifestations of alexithymia on a firmer empirical footing.

Another important aspect of the alexithymia construct is its central and peripheral physiological substrates. The concept of alexithymia arose in an attempt to understand the psychological traits that predispose an individual to somatic disease (Taylor, Bagby, & Parker, 1997). The way in which the physiology of emotion may differ in alexithymic compared to nonalexithymic individuals is not well understood, in part because findings have been contradictory. However, any such comparison is dependent upon the ability to classify individuals accurately as having or not having alexithymia. In our view, such methods based on the conceptualization of the condition described earlier have not yet been developed. Once they are, however, the study of alexithymia will permit the investigation of a question that is critical to affect science, namely, the relation between cortical and subcortical structures in the elaboration of emotional responses.

Neuroscience of Emotion and the Complexity of Emotion Representations

One of the challenges in the neuroscience of emotion is to understand how cortical and subcortical structures work together to elaborate emotional responses. As noted previously, we have observed that greater emotional awareness is associated with greater activity in the dorsal anterior cingulate cortex. We have also observed in other studies that the rostral anterior cingulate cortex is preferentially activated while one is attending to one's own emotional states (Lane, Fink, Chua, & Dolan, 1997). We interpret the latter finding in light of Frith and Frith's notion of the paracingulate sulcus as a principal site where the capacity for mentalizing is instantiated (Frith & Frith, 1999). "Mentalizing" refers to the capacity to infer the mental states of others, a cognitive function that may be impaired or absent in patients with autism or autistic spectrum disorders (Baron-Cohen, 1997). One of us (R. D. L.) has previously hypothesized that emotional responses are generated outside of conscious awareness and that the process of experiencing and knowing one's own emotional responses involves higher cortical centers. Specific emphasis has been placed on the dorsal and rostral areas of the anterior cingulate cortex as having differential roles in the phenomenal and reflective awareness of emotions, respectively (Lane, 2000).

To the extent that the paracingulate sulcus participates in establishing mental representations of mental states, intriguing possibilities are raised by the question of how activity in this brain area may vary as a function of the level of one's conceptual framework for understanding one's own emotions. This question has not been addressed previously in empirical research; answers therefore must necessarily be speculative. Frith and Frith (1999) hypothesize that the ability to mentalize evolved from the action system for the purpose of identifying the *intensions* of conspecifics and anticipating their future actions. We know that emotional states may fundamentally consist of action tendencies (Frijda, 1986), which can be construed as equivalent to the intensions of the self. This dovetails beautifully with the Piagetian perspective on cognitive development in that all mental representations at the conceptual level are fundamentally derived from action schemes. It is therefore reasonable to consider, as a first approximation, that the paracingulate sulcus is a substructure within the prefrontal cortex that participates in mediating the representations of mental states (including emotional states) of both self and other. We do not yet know whether different areas of the paracingulate sulcus mediate representations of self or other, or whether the psychological capacity to differentiate between the mental states of self and other is reflected concretely in topographical differentiation of function within this region. Another possibility is that the same subregion within the paracingulate sulcus is responsible for the mental representation of one's own emotional states, but that the psychological differentiation of one's own emotional states may be paralleled by differentiation in the structures with which the paracingulate sulcus receives and sends inputs at different moments in time. One may hypothesize, for example, that the neuroanatomical correlate of a more advanced conceptual framework of one's own emotional life is a greater variety of patterns of neural activity during emotional arousal that have activation of the paracingulate sulcus as a common denominator.

The relation between cortical and subcortical structures in the elaboration of emotional responses raises a fundamental issue, and an important difference, in the epistemology of the external material world and the internal world of emotion. A Piagetian perspective tells us that the outer world becomes known as a function of the assimilatory capacity of one's schemata. The degree to which one has simple or complex schemata for processing exteroceptive stimuli in no way alters the nature of the stimuli to be perceived. However, in the case of the internal world of emotions, the "material reality" that is to be perceived consists of activity in the subcortical generators of emotional responses, the visceral responses that they engender, and the proprioceptive feedback from these responses. According to the model described earlier, this information is processed by cortical structures that have bidirectional connections with the subcortical generators of emotional responses. As such, a dynamic equilibrium between bottom-up and top-down processes may be established between the activity of cortical and subcortical structures so that *the nature of subcortical function is modulated by the cortical structures.* As such, in the case of knowledge about the internal world of emotion, that which is perceived is fundamentally altered by the perceptual apparatus. The difference between exteroceptive and interoceptive cognition, however, is that in the former case the mere act of perception does not constitute an intervention upon the external world, whereas in the latter case of the internal world of emotion it does. In any case, an implication of this line of thought is that the pattern of subcortical activity observed during a given type of emotional arousal varies across individuals as a function of the developmental level of their conceptual organization of their own emotional lives. Furthermore, it may not be that there is one absolute pattern characteristic of each individual level, but rather that the relative patterns of activation across different emotional states vary (become more differentiated) across developmental levels.

Conceptual Organization Is Culture Dependent

Current evidence suggests that there is both commonality and variability across cultures in the emotions that are considered "basic" or fundamental (Schweder, 1993). One way of understanding cross-cultural differences in emotion is that cultures differ in the conceptual framework with which emotional information is processed. The neuroscientific considerations just discussed therefore raise the possibility that fundamental emotions vary across cultures because subcortically generated emotional responses are filtered through higher cortical centers, which are likely highly modifiable through cultural influences. The similarities and differences across cultures may therefore correspond to subcortical and cortical mechanisms, respectively. The nature of the culturally specific stimuli that do or do not evoke emotions may also be learned and may involve plasticity of the neural centers that feed into those areas that generate emotional responses.

An example of the complex questions raised in this area of research is determining whether neurasthenia (a 19th-century diagnosis very similar to the current chronic fatigue syndrome) and depression are the same psychobiological entity. The former has been interpreted by Kleinman as a somatic presentation of depression that is characteristic of non-Western cultures (Kleinman, 1986). An important empirical question is whether the functional neuroanatomy of neurasthenia is equal to depression minus its cortical components (a failure to incorporate cortical mechanisms in the distress network), depression plus different cortical components (e.g., anterior insula, an area that specializes in visceral interoception [Augustine, 1996], rather than ventromedial prefrontal cortex [Damasio, 1994]), or differing cortical *and* subcortical activity based on cortical–subcortical interactions that are bidirectional, reflecting both bottom-up and top-down influences. As noted earlier, we favor the third alternative. Determining whether neurasthenia and depression are different diseases would require addressing issues such as natural history, family history, response to treatment, and the like. Nevertheless, neuroimaging research would be informative in this regard and would be highly relevant to broader questions about the universality of emotional processes.

Another important question is whether the somatizing, neurasthenic pattern would be associated with a lower level of emotional awareness using the LEAS. Although the norm in cultures like Bali is for adults to seek a more uniform rather than a more differentiated experience (R. Schweder, personal communication, November 2000), that may simply illustrate the plasticity and dependence on environmental input of cortical circuitry. To the extent that greater psychological differentiation is acquired through practice, the cultural norm in Bali may be an expression of the general principle that one must "use it or lose it."

Promoting Emotional Growth

In this chapter we have proposed a model of emotional development that places primary emphasis on the development of a conceptual framework of one's own emotional life. To the extent that this is the core of emotional intelligence, with all of its implications for emotion regulation, it is worthy of serious consideration as an approach that can be taught and promoted at the elementary school level. It may also be used to formulate "how to" guides for parents about how best to assist their children with the emotional challenges they face (Elias et al., 1997).

A somewhat more complicated question is how to promote the emotional growth of adults who manifest a delay in this domain of cognitive development. Alexithymia may be the prime example of such a developmental delay. The literature indicates that alexithymic individuals are notoriously difficult to treat in traditional forms of psychotherapy (Taylor, Bagby, & Parker, 1997). In fact, no effective treatments of alexithymia have been reported. This may be because it is first necessary to understand the nature of the deficit before an effective intervention method can be implemented. Specifically, our model suggests that a therapeutic program for alexithymia consists of facilitating the development of complex representations of the subject's emotional life at the conceptual level. This will involve much more than simply finding verbal labels for emotional states; rather, it will consist of transforming representations of emotion that are fragmentary and stuck at the sensorimotor level into a framework of more complex conceptual representations. This will involve developing an appreciation of what different emotional states feel like, how they differ from one another, what kinds of situations bring them on in general, and for alexithymic individuals in particular, the external indicators of such states, the factors that amplify or attenuate them, the behavioral or mental actions that can be taken to modify the intensity of such states, and the proper handling of the expression of such states as a function of the social circumstances of the individual.

CONCLUSION

In this chapter we have extended the theory of levels of emotional awareness by describing how the levels constitute one manifestation of a larger phenomenon involving the conceptual organization of emotion. This extension places the emotional awareness framework squarely within the domain of intelligence more broadly construed, and at the same time helps to clarify how it is related to emotional intelligence. The conceptual organization of emotion helps to explain variability in a wide variety of phenomena related to emotion, including the complexity of subjective emotional experience, the ability to recognize emotions, the range of emotional expressions, the extent of a person's emotional vocabulary, and the capacities for empathy, adaptive social behavior, and emotion self-regulation. This viewpoint also provides a new perspective on a variety of issues, including the neural substrates of emotion, cross-cultural differences in the manifestations of emotion, the process of normative emotional development, and the conceptualization and treatment of clinical phenomena such as alexithymia.

REFERENCES

Augustine, J. R. (1996). Circuitry and functional aspects of the insular lobe in primates including humans. *Brain Research Reviews, 22,* 229–244.

Baron-Cohen, S. (1997). *Mindblindness: An essay on autism and Theory of Mind.* Cambridge, MA: MIT Press.

Barrett, L. F., Lane, R. D., Sechrest, L., & Schwartz, G. E. (2000). Sex differences in emotional awareness. *Personality and Social Psychology Bulletin, 26,* 1027–1035.

Blatt, S. J., Wein, S. J., Chevron, E., & Quinlan, D. M. (1979). Parental representations and depression in normal young adults. *Journal of Abnormal Psychology, 88,* 388–397.

Damasio, A. R. (1994). *Descartes' error: Emotion, reason, and the human brain.* New York: Putnam's.

Ekman, P. (1982). *Emotion in the human face* (2nd ed.). New York: Cambridge University Press.

Elias, M. J., Zins, J. E., Weissberg, R. P., Frey, K. S., Greenberg, M. T., Haynes, N. M., Kessler, R., Schwab-Stone, M. E., & Shriver, T. P. (1997). *Promoting social and emotional learning: Guidelines for educators.* Alexandria, VA: Association for Supervision and Curriculum Development.

Frijda, N. (1986). *The emotions.* Cambridge, UK: Cambridge University Press.

Frith, C. D., & Frith, U. (1999). Interacting minds: A biological basis. *Science, 286*(5445), 1692–1695.

Karmiloff-Smith, A. (1992). *Beyond modularity: A developmental perspective on cognitive science.* Cambridge, MA: MIT Press.

Kleinman, A. (1986). *The social origins of distress and disease.* New Haven, CT: Yale University Press.

Lane, R. D. (2000). Neural correlates of conscious emotional experience. In R. Lane, L. Nadel, G. Ahern, J. Allen, A. Kaszniak, S. Rapscak, & G. E. Schwartz (Eds.), *Cognitive neuroscience of emotion* (pp. 345–370). New York: Oxford University Press.

Lane, R. D., Ahern, G. L., Schwartz, G. E., & Kaszniak, A. W. (1997). Is alexithymia the emotional equivalent of blindsight? *Biological Psychiatry, 42,* 834–844.

Lane, R. D., Fink, G. R., Chua, P. M. L., & Dolan, R. J. (1997). Neural activation during selective attention to subjective emotional responses. *Neuroreport, 8*(18), 3969–3972.

Lane, R. D., Kevley, L. S., DuBois, M. A., Shamasundara, P., & Schwartz, G. E. (1995). Levels of emotional awareness and the degree of right hemispheric dominance in the perception of facial emotion. *Neuropsychologia, 33,* 525–528.

Lane, R. D., Quinlan, D. M., Schwartz, G. E., Walker, P. A., & Zeitlin, S. B. (1990). The Levels of Emotional Awareness Scale: A cognitive–developmental measure of emotion. *Journal of Personality Assessment, 55*(1&2), 124–134.

Lane, R. D., Reiman, E. M., Axelrod, B., Yun, L.-S., Holmes, A., & Schwartz, G. E. (1998). Neural correlates of levels of emotional awareness: Evidence of an interaction between emotion and attention in the anterior cingulate cortex. *Journal of Cognitive Neuroscience, 10*(4), 525–535.

Lane, R. D., & Schwartz, G. E. (1987). Levels of emotional awareness: A cognitive–developmental theory and its application to psychopathology. *American Journal of Psychiatry, 144,* 133–143.

Lane R. D., Sechrest, L., Riedel, R., Shapiro, D., & Kasmap, A. (2000). Pervasive emotion recognition deficit common to alexithymia and the repressive coping style. *Psychosomatic Medicine, 62,* 492–501.

Lane, R. D., Sechrest, L., Reidel, R., Weldon, V., Kasmap, A., & Schwartz, G. E. (1996). Impaired verbal and nonverbal emotion recognition in alexithymia. *Psychosomatic Medicine, 58,* 203–210.

Larsen, R. J., & Diener, E. (1987). Affect intensity as an individual difference characteristic: A review. *Journal of Research in Personality, 21,* 1–39.

Levine, D., Marziali, E., & Hood, J. (1997). Emotion processing in borderline personality disorders. *Journal of Nervous and Mental Disease, 185*(4), 240–246.

Loevinger, J., & Wessler, R. (1970). *Measuring ego development: Vol. I. Construction and use of a sentence completion test.* San Francisco: Jossey-Bass.

Loevinger, J., Wessler, R., & Redmore, C. (1970). *Measuring ego development: Vol. II. Scoring manual for women and girls.* San Francisco: Jossey-Bass.

Mayer, J. D., & Salovey, P. (1997). What is emotional intelligence? In P. Salovey & D. J. Sluyter (Eds.), *Emotional development and emotional intelligence* (pp. 3–31). New York: Basic Books.

Mayer, J. D., Salovey, P., & Caruso, D. (1999). Models of emotional intelligence. In R. J. Sternberg (Ed.), *Handbook of human intelligence* (2nd ed., pp. 396–421). New York: Cambridge University Press.

Papez, J. W. (1937). A proposed mechanism of emotion. *Archives of Neurology and Psychiatry, 38,* 725–734.

Piaget, J. (1936). *La naissance de l'intelligence chez l'enfant.* Neuchâtel: Delachaux et Niestlé.

Piaget, J. (1937). *La construction du réel.* Neuchâtel: Delachaux et Niestlé.

Piaget, J. (1947). *La représentation du monde chez l'infant.* Paris: Presses Universitaires de France. (Original work published 1926)

Piaget, J. (1972). *La formation du symbole chez l'enfant.* Neuchâtel: Delachaux et Niestlé. [English translation: (1951). *Play, dreams and imitation in childhood* (C. Gattegno & F. M. Hodgson, Trans.). New York: Norton, 1962 (Reprint).]

Piaget, J. (1974). *La prise de conscience.* Paris: Presses Universitaires de France. [English translation: (1976). *The grasp of consciousness: Action and concept in the young child* (S. Wedgwood, Trans.). Cambridge, MA: Harvard University Press.]

Piaget, J. (1977). *Recherches sur l'abstraction réfléchissante, Ire partie: l'abstraction des relations logico-arithmétiques.* Paris: Presses Universitaires de France.

Piaget, J., & Garcia, R. (1983). *Psychogenèse et histoire des sciences.* Paris: Flamarion. [English translation: (1983). *Psychogenesis and the history of science* (H. Feider, Trans.). New York: Columbia University Press.]

Rau, J. C. (1993). Perception of verbal and nonverbal affective stimuli in complex partial seizure disorder. *Dissertation Abstracts International (B), 54,* 506-B

Salovey, P., & Mayer, J. D. (1990). Emotional intelligence. *Imagination, Cognition and Personality, 9,* 185–211.

Saussure, de, F. (1972). *Cours de linguistiques générale [A course in general linguistics].* (4th ed.). Paris: Payot. (Original work published 1949)

Schweder, R. A. (1993). The cultural psychology of the emotions. In M. Lewis & J. M. Haviland (Eds.), *Handbook of emotions* (pp. 417–431). New York: Guilford Press.

Shipley, W. (1940). A self-administering scale for measuring intellectual impairment and deterioration. *Journal of Psychology, 9,* 371–377.

Taylor, G. J., Bagby, R. M., & Luminet, O. (2000). Assessment of alexithymia: Self-report and observer-rate measures. In R. Bar-On & J. D. A. Parker (Eds.), *The handbook of emotional intelligence* (pp. 310–319). San Francisco: Jossey-Bass.

Taylor, G. J., Bagby, R. M., & Parker, J. D. A. (1997). *Disorders of affect regulation: Alexithymia in medical and psychiatric illness.* Cambridge, UK: Cambridge University Press.

Tooby, J., & Cosmides, L. (1990). The past explains the present: Emotional adaptations and the structure of ancestral environment. *Ethology and Sociobiology, 11,* 375–424.

Vogt, B. A., Finch, D. M., & Olson, C. R. (1992). Functional heterogeneity in cingulate cortex: The anterior executive and posterior evaluative regions. *Cerebral Cortex, 2*(6), 435–443.

Vogt, B. A., & Gabriel, M. (1993). *Neurobiology of cingulate cortex and limbic thalamus.* Boston: Birkhauser.

Watson, D., Clark, L. A., & Tellegan, A. (1988). Development and validation of brief measures of positive and negative affect: The PANAS Scales. *Journal of Personality and Social Psychology, 54,* 1063–1070.

Weiskrantz, L. (2000). Blindsight: Implications for the conscious experience emotion. In R. Lane, L. Nadel, G. Ahern, J. Allen, A. Kasczniak, S. Rapscak,

& G. E. Schwartz (Eds.), *Cognitive neuroscience of emotion* (pp. 277–295). New York: Oxford University Press.

Werner, H., & Kaplan, B. (1963). *Symbol formation: An organismic-developmental approach to language and the expression of thought.* New York: Wiley.

Wrana, C., Thomas, W., Heindichs, G., Huber, M., Obliers, R., Koerfer, A., & Köhle, K. (1998, March). *Levels of Emotional Awareness Scale (LEAS): Ein beitrag zur empirischen überprüfung von validität und reliabilität einer deutschen fassung.* Postervortrag bei der 47 Arbeitstagung des Deutschen Kollegiums für Psychosomatische Medizin, Leipzig.

Managing Emotion

 CHAPTER 12

Wise Emotion Regulation

JAMES J. GROSS
OLIVER P. JOHN

Evolutionary perspectives hold that emotions serve a number of important functions, such as preparing for vigorous action, fine-tuning cognition, and communicating with others. This view of emotions as functional has provided a much-needed corrective to the long-standing view of emotions as dysfunctional and disruptive (Gross & Keltner, 1999). However, functional analyses may lull the unwary into believing that emotions are *always* helpful. This conclusion would seriously miss the mark. After all, who hasn't become so anxious that he has mucked up an important talk? Or laughed when she should have kept a stiff upper lip? Or become so angry that he couldn't think straight? Indeed, many forms of psychopathology described in the *Diagnostic and Statistical Manual of Mental Disorders* (American Psychiatric Association, 1994) may be conceptualized as disorders of emotion regulation (Gross & Levenson, 1997).

Emotions both help *and* hinder functioning. Thus, it is becoming increasingly clear that the critical question is not whether emotions are good or bad, but what makes a given emotion helpful or unhelpful in a particular context (Parrott, 2001). This more nuanced conception of the value of emotions also recognizes that people are by no means passive as emotions come and go. Individuals actively regulate their emotions, shaping them in an attempt to capitalize on their good features while minimizing their bad features (Gross, 1998b). This is important because emotions such as fear, amusement, and anger are evolutionary "best guesses" as to what an individual in a certain situation should do (Tooby & Cosmides, 1990), and not surefire winning solutions to every challenging problem we face. Part of the "wisdom of the body" is that we are able to modify our emotions (Cannon, 1932). Indeed, optimal emotional responding requires that individuals shape their emotions by regulating how these emotions are experienced or expressed.

In this chapter we consider the role of emotion regulation in adaptation. More specifically, we contrast two specific, theoretically defined forms of emotion regulation and show their divergent consequences for cognitive, affective, and social functioning. Our general thesis is that different emotion regulation strategies may have profoundly different implications for well-being. We should emphasize at the outset that we do not believe that any one form of emotion regulation is always better than any other. However, our research suggests that different strategies may have such different consequences that they have quite different implications for well-being. To set the stage for our discussion of emotion regulation, we first describe our conception of emotions as response tendencies and present a process model of emotion regulation that we use to organize the rich variety of ways people regulate their emotions. In the second section, we narrow our focus to two particular forms of emotion regulation—reappraisal and suppression—and draw upon both laboratory and individual-difference studies to examine more closely the cognitive, affective, and social consequences of these two forms of emotion regulation. Finally, in the third section, we discuss implications of these findings for a broader conception of the role emotion regulation plays in emotionally intelligent behavior (Salovey & Mayer, 1990).

EMOTION AND EMOTION REGULATION

Based on a distillation of points of convergence among emotion researchers (see Gross, 1999a), we view emotion as originating with the evaluation of external or internal emotion cues. Sometimes emotions are triggered automatically, such as when we recoil fearfully from a snake (LeDoux, 1994). At other times, emotions arise only after considerable meaning analysis, such as when we grow angry after hearing a demeaning remark or an off-color joke (Lazarus, 1991). In either case, the evaluations, when associated with a coordinated set of behavioral, experiential, and physiological emotional response tendencies, bias how we respond to perceived challenges and opportunities. However, these response tendencies are not all there is to the story: We can modulate these incipient response tendencies, thereby modifying our manifest responses.

In this view, emotions are modes of responding that have more or less well-defined trajectories (involving an automatic set of responses) that may be modified by an executive mode of functioning that is, at least initially, deliberate and flexible (Feldman Barrett & Gross, 2001). Because our automatic emotional responses often dovetail nicely with the demands of our varying life circumstances, these automatically executed responses serve us well much of the time.

However, there are times when our emotional responses are likely to do more harm than good, either because we have misunderstood the situation or because the general-purpose solution provided by our emotional responses is insensitive to the important particulars of the situation. When we find that our emotional responses are not well matched to a given circumstance, we may try to intervene to modify our experience or expression of emotion. And it is this malleability of our emotional modes of responding that permits us to regulate or adjust our responses in such a way that our responses better match our goals in a particular situation.

Emotion Regulation in Everyday Life

To explore how emotion regulation takes place in everyday life, we asked undergraduate research participants to describe, either in writing or in a semistructured interview, a recent occasion on which they tried to alter their emotions. Respondents had no difficulty whatsoever describing such an episode. A particularly common form of emotion regulation was decreasing negative emotions by altering one's thoughts. One such example follows:

> "I was feeling bad and I decided that I didn't want to feel bad anymore. So I was just talking to myself and telling myself that it was OK and why what I was thinking was wrong and why it didn't make sense and stuff. [I was trying to change] the negative thinking. I tried to tell myself contrary thoughts. I tried to think of things that are opposite of what [was] making me feel down."

However, respondents also described situations in which they attempted to change their thinking so as to increase emotion, either negative or positive. One particularly poignant episode involving an attempt to increase negative emotion follows:

> "My father [is very ill] and can't talk or move his left side. My mother left to run an errand and I had to care for him and my . . . nephew for about an hour. My father has always been very demanding, so when he began hitting the side of the bed, for the nth

time that day, I ignored him. After a while I went in to check on him. I saw a tear running down his cheek and I felt an overwhelming sense of guilt. He tried to communicate by writing, but I couldn't understand. A couple minutes later, my mother returned and checked on him. She said that he didn't really need anything. That nothing was wrong and he was just being his usual self. So I tried to get rid of the guilt by hardening myself with bad memories of him. It worked. . . ."

Other emotion regulation episodes focused on changing the outward signs of emotions. Sometimes respondents described trying to decrease emotion-expressive behavior. An example of such an episode follows:

"I was feeling really stressed because I had a paper due the next day but then, I had a friend who was coming over . . . and so even though she was here and I was really, really stressed I tried my hardest to act like I was OK and just tried to show her a good time. I tried to talk to her even though inside, I was paranoid that I was wasting my time because I needed to do my paper. [I was trying to change] my facial expression . . . my tone of voice."

Respondents also mentioned occasions on which they tried to decrease positive signs of emotion. For example:

"I was set up on a date with this girl and I was telling myself the whole time before the date like, 'OK, don't get excited, because you don't want to like her because you'll take a chance of her not liking you back, right?' . . . I was really excited and really . . . like I was back in high school or something. [I was] very excited though I didn't want to portray that excitement then. I was trying to change how I would project the emotions. . . . I couldn't change the emotions themselves, so I was trying to just mask them, and make sure that they didn't just come flowing out of me."

Taken together, these emotion-regulatory vignettes make it clear that emotion regulation involves more than down-regulating negative emotions (Gross, 1999b). Indeed, people say that they try to initiate, increase, maintain, and decrease both negative and positive emotions (Parrott, 1993). When thinking about emotion regulation, it also is important to recognize that emotion regulation involves more than altering emotion experience (e.g., trying to improve a bad mood). Emotions are multicomponential processes that involve changes in subjective experience, expressive behavior, and physiological responding. Emotion regulation involves attempts to influence one or more of these three components. Furthermore, although an interview method such as the one mentioned earlier ensured that the examples of emotion regulation given here were conscious, it is easy to imagine emotion regulation that occurs outside of consciousness. For example, one may mask disappointment at an unattractive present (Cole, 1986) or turn attention away from upsetting material (Boden & Baumeister, 1997) without even thinking about it.

A Process Model of Emotion Regulation

As the preceding examples suggest, there are many ways to go about regulating emotions. How can we make sense of the potentially limitless number of emotion regulation strategies? According to Gross's (1998b) process model of emotion regulation, specific strategies can be differentiated along the time line of the unfolding emotional response. That is, strategies differ in *when* they have their primary impact on the emotion-generative process, as shown in Figure 12.1.

At the broadest level, we can distinguish between *antecedent-focused* and *response-focused* emotion regulation strategies. *Antecedent-focused* strategies are things we do before the emotion response tendencies have become fully activated and have changed our behavior and peripheral physiological responding. An example of antecedent-focused regulation is viewing an admissions interview as an opportunity to see how much you like the school, rather than a test of your worth. *Response-focused* strategies are things we do once an emotion is already under way, after the response tendencies have been generated. An example of response-focused regulation is keeping a poker face while holding a great hand during an exciting card game.

As shown in Figure 12.1, five more specific emotion regulation strategies can be located within this broad scheme (Gross, 1998b, 2001). The first of these strategies is *situation selection*, denoted in Figure 12.1 by the solid line toward situation 1 (S1) rather than situation 2 (S2). Situation selection refers to approaching or avoiding certain people, places, or things so as to regulate emotion. For example, you may decide to have dinner with a friend who always makes you laugh the night before a big exam (S1), rather than going to the last-minute study session with other nervous students (S2). Of course, many factors go into the selection of one situation versus another, but to the extent that a situation's expected emotional impact plays a role in its selection, we regard this as a form of emotion regulation.

Once selected, a situation may be tailored so as to modify its emo-

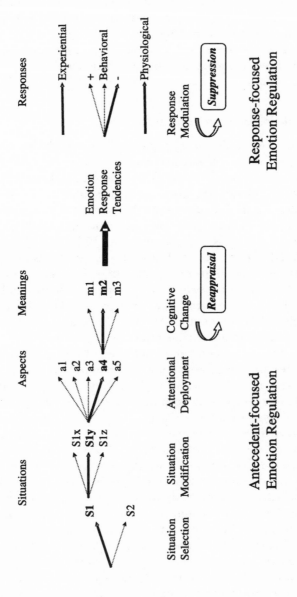

FIGURE 12.1. A process model of emotion regulation. Two specific emotion regulation strategies—reappraisal and suppression—are the primary focus here. From Gross (2001). Copyright 2001 by the American Psychological Society. Reprinted by permission of Blackwell Publishing.

tional impact, creating either S1x, S1y, or S1z. This constitutes *situation modification,* which has also been referred to as problem-focused coping (Lazarus & Folkman, 1984) or as primary control (Rothbaum, Weisz, & Snyder, 1982). For example, continuing with the example of the exam, if you are talking with your friend the night before a big exam, and he asks whether you are ready for the exam, you can make it clear that you would rather talk about something (anything!) else.

Third, situations have different aspects (e.g., a1, a2, a3, a4, a5), and *attentional deployment* is used to select which of the many aspects of the situation you focus on. An example is distracting yourself from a conversation that has taken an upsetting turn, by counting ceiling tiles. Other types of attentional deployment include concentrating attention on a particular topic or task (see Csikszentmihalyi, 1975), or ruminating (Nolen-Hoeksema, 1993).

Once you have focused on a particular aspect of the situation, *cognitive change* may be used, which refers to selecting which of the many possible meanings (e.g., m1, m2, m3) you will attach to that aspect. For example, you may remind yourself that "it's only a test" (m2), rather than seeing the exam as a measure of your value as a human being (m1). Cognitive change also may be used to magnify rather than minimize the emotional response; it may also be used to change the type of emotion as well as its intensity. The personal meaning you assign to the situation is crucial, because it powerfully influences which experiential, behavioral, and physiological response tendencies will be generated in the particular situation.

Finally, *response modulation* refers to attempts to influence emotion response tendencies once they already have been elicited. Response modulation is illustrated in Figure 12.1 by decreasing expressive behavior (–). In our example of the exam, response modulation may take the form of hiding your embarrassment after doing poorly on the exam. It may also take the form of altering experiential or physiological components of emotion as well.

THE CONSEQUENCES OF EMOTION REGULATION

Our description of five points in the emotion generative process at which emotion can be regulated makes it clear that there are a great many different ways a person can go about regulating emotion. A pressing question is whether some emotion regulation strategies have more to recommend them than others. Are there better and worse ways to regulate emotion?

To answer this question, we have used the process conception of emotion regulation described earlier to distinguish between antecedent-focused emotion regulation (situation selection, situation modification, attentional deployment, and cognitive change) and response-focused emotion regulation (response modulation). Using this broad temporal distinction, we have conducted a series of experimental and individual-difference studies to examine two theoretically derived forms of emotion regulation. So far, we have focused on two forms of down-regulation, as decreasing emotion is a most common and highly valued emotion regulation goal. The first is a form of antecedent-focused emotion regulation, namely, cognitive reappraisal, which refers to construing a potentially emotion-eliciting situation in nonemotional terms. The second is a form of response-focused emotion regulation, namely, expressive suppression, which refers to inhibiting ongoing emotion-expressive behavior.

As shown in Table 12.1, our aim has been to coordinate experimental and individual-difference studies in order to understand better the consequences of reappraisal and suppression. In our experimental studies, we have manipulated reappraisal by instructing participants to view emotion-eliciting material with the detached interest of a medical professional. We have manipulated suppression by instructing participants to view emotion-eliciting material while trying not to let their feelings show. In our individual-difference studies, we have used a new measure called the Emotion Regulation Questionnaire (for details, see Gross & John, 2002). This 10-item questionnaire has two scales: One assesses the extent to which an individual uses reappraisal, and the other assesses the extent to which an individual uses suppression. As shown in Table 12.1, an example of a reappraisal item is "I control my emotions by changing

TABLE 12.1. Experimental and Individual-Difference Studies of Reappraisal and Suppression

Study design	Reappraisal	Suppression
	Instructions	
Experimental manipulation	"We would like you to view the [upcoming stimulus] with the detached interest of a medical professional."	"If you have any feelings as you watch the [upcoming stimulus] please try your best not to let those feelings show."
	Questionnaire items	
Individual differences	"I control my emotions by *changing the way I think* about the situation I'm in."	"I control my emotions by *not expressing them.*"

the way I think about the situation I'm in." An example item from the suppression scale is "I control my emotions by not expressing them." These brief scales have satisfactory reliabilities, whether the participants are college students or adults in late middle age. Moreover, the reappraisal and suppression scales are essentially unrelated (mean $r = -.01$). Reappraisal and suppression are thus two independent strategies for down-regulating emotions, such that individuals may habitually use one, both, or neither of them. Finally, these individual-difference measures are relatively independent of socially desirable responding.

By comparing two common strategies for down-regulating negative emotions, we can ask whether different emotion regulation strategies indeed produce different profiles of consequences. The logic of our comparative design hinges on the premise that whereas antecedent-focused forms of emotion regulation (such as reappraisal) principally concern whether or not emotion response tendencies *are triggered*, response-focused strategies (such as suppression) concern how emotion response tendencies *are modulated once they have been triggered*. How do the strategies of reappraisal and suppression differ cognitively, affectively, and socially?

Cognitively, we expect reappraisal to interrupt emotion generation so early on that a relatively large impact on the resultant emotion can be made at relatively little cognitive cost. By contrast, suppression likely requires ongoing efforts as the individual seeks to modify emotional responses as they arise, a requirement that translates into greater cognitive costs for suppression than for reappraisal.

Affectively, when used to decrease negative emotion, we expect reappraisal successfully to turn down the experiential, behavioral, and even the physiological consequences of negative emotion. Similarly, when used to enhance positive emotion, we expect reappraisal to increase experiential, behavioral, and physiological responding. Suppression, by contrast, should decrease both negative and positive emotion-expressive behavior, but have little impact on emotion experience. In view of the effort associated with ongoing attempts to manage emotion response tendencies as they arise, we also expect suppression to lead to increased physiological responding.

Socially, if reappraisal is in fact able to decrease the experience and expression of negative emotions successfully while also enhancing the experience and expression of positive emotions, we expect reappraisal to be socially beneficial. Suppression, by contrast, should have social costs, both because it leads to decreases in negative and positive emotion-expressive behavior and because it produces a state in which individuals are feeling something different from what they are communicating to their interaction partners.

In the following sections we review a series of coordinated experimental and individual difference studies designed to test these general predictions. Although no one study is conclusive, we believe that the cumulative findings across diverse studies support our claim that these two strategies for down-regulating negative emotion have importantly different consequences.

Cognitive Consequences of Emotion Regulation

Emotions usually arise when something important to an individual is at stake. At such times, a high level of cognitive performance is often desirable (Richards & Gross, 2000). Given that emotions may need to be regulated in such circumstances, how should suppression and reappraisal affect an individual's ability to perform well cognitively?

Suppression is a form of emotion regulation that requires self-monitoring and self-corrective action throughout an emotional event. Such monitoring requires a continuous outlay of cognitive resources, reducing the resources available for processing events so that they can later be remembered. Reappraisal, by contrast, is evoked early in the emotion-generative process. Therefore, this strategy typically does not require continuous self-regulatory effort during an emotional event. This would make costly self-regulation unnecessary, leaving memory intact.

We tested these predictions regarding the cognitive consequences of emotion regulation on memory in three interlocking laboratory and individual-difference studies (Richards & Gross, 2000). In the first study we focused on suppression. Participants were shown a short film clip known to elicit negative emotion. This film depicts a husband who confesses to his wife that he has had an extramarital affair. A fight ensues, which is witnessed by their young child, who begins to cry. Half of the participants were randomly assigned to inhibit emotion-expressive behavior during the film clip (suppress), whereas the other participants simply watched the film (control). To assess the cognitive impact of suppression, after participants had viewed the film, we administered a surprise cued-recognition test for auditory and visual details contained in the film. We also asked participants how confident they were about each of their responses to the memory test. As predicted, suppression led to reliable decrements (as compared with the control condition) in both objective memory and memory confidence ratings.

In a second study we examined the cognitive consequences of both suppression and reappraisal. Our goals in this study were to assess the impact of regulating differing levels of emotion and to begin to test the mechanisms by which emotion regulation might be affecting cognitive performance on our memory tests. Participants watched a series of slides that elicited either high or low levels of negative emotion. As in Study 1, some of the participants were randomly assigned to view the slides while inhibiting their ongoing emotion-expressive behavior (suppress). Others were simply asked to watch the slides (control). Still others were randomly assigned to view the slides with the detached interest of a medical professional (reappraise). As slides were presented, participants were provided with information about each slide. Then, after viewing the slides, participants were given two types of memory tests. The first—a nonverbal memory test—involved a series of photo spreads, and the participants' task was to identify which of four photos corresponded to a slide seen in the viewing phase. The second—a verbal memory test—required that participants write down the information associated with each slide as it was presented for a second time. As predicted, suppression participants performed less well on the verbal memory test than control participants. By contrast, reappraisal had no impact on verbal memory. Importantly, the effect of suppression on verbal memory was just as pronounced for the low-emotion as for the high-emotion slides, suggesting that it is the process of engaging in suppression that is cognitively costly, rather than the amount of emotion that is actually suppressed. Interestingly, suppression had no reliable impact on nonverbal memory, suggesting that the cognitive costs of suppression are due to the verbal demands of self-instructions issued during the course of suppression (e.g., "I need to keep my face still"; "Oops—I let that one slip").

To examine whether individual differences in emotion regulation would have the same consequences for memory as our laboratory manipulations, we examined the impact of individual differences in reappraisal and suppression on memory. We measured individual differences in habitual reappraisal and suppression using the Emotion Regulation Questionnaire (Gross & John, 2002). We assessed memory using two measures that were selected to assess memory for contexts in which we thought it likely that individual differences in emotion regulation might be evident. The first was a self-report measure of memory for conversations (Hermann & Neisser, 1978). The second was an objectively scored free-recall test for spontaneous emotion regulation episodes that occurred over a 2-week period and had been reported daily. As expected, we found that individuals who scored higher on the suppression scale reported having worse memory. They also performed worse on an objective memory test in which they were asked to recall events they had listed in a daily diary 1 week earlier. By contrast, reappraisal had no effects on either self-reported or objective memory. It is important that these memory findings withstood the use of control measures including neuroticism and social desirability. These individual-difference findings converge nicely with the results of our experimental studies and suggest that whereas suppression is cognitively costly, reappraisal is not.

Affective Consequences of Emotion Regulation

One of the major aims of emotion regulation is to influence the way emotions are felt or expressed. Do different forms of emotion regulation have demonstrably different effects on the experiential, behavioral, and physiological components of the emotional response?

Because reappraisal involves cognitively transforming a potentially emotion-eliciting situation, we expect that reappraisal that takes the form of leading an individual to reconstrue the event in less emotional terms will lead to decreases in emotion experience, expressive behavior, and physiological responding. By contrast, expressive suppression requires that an individual actively work against the ongoing emotion-expressive behavior that is generated as the emotion unfolds. This line of reasoning suggests that the decreases in expressive behavior that are associated with suppression may give rise to an increase in autonomic nervous system activation consequent to the effort expended to regulate emotion-expressive behavior.

To test whether reappraisal and suppression would have different consequences for behavioral, experiential, and physiological responses, we used a short film that showed an arm amputation to elicit disgust (Gross, 1998a). We administered specific instructions to participants who had been randomly assigned to one of three experimental conditions. In the first, subjects were asked to *think* about what they were seeing in such a way that they did not feel anything at all (reappraise). In the second, subjects were asked to *hide* their emotional reactions (suppress). In the third, subjects simply watched the film (control).

Suppression and reappraisal could indeed be distinguished. Suppression decreased disgust-expressive behavior and increased sympathetic activation of the cardiovascular and electrodermal systems. Like suppression, reappraisal decreased expressive behavior. Unlike suppression, however, reappraisal had no observable consequences in terms of sympathetic activation of the cardiovascular or electrodermal system. Whereas suppress participants showed greater increases in sympathetic activation than watch or reappraise subjects, the latter two groups did not differ from one another. Also unlike suppression, reappraisal decreased disgust experience, whereas suppression had no effect on disgust experience. These findings show that how one goes about achieving a certain emotion regulatory goal may be as important a determinant of the affective consequences of one's efforts as the goal one is trying to achieve—not showing emotion may exact a higher physiological cost than other regulatory strategies.

Related studies have examined the boundary conditions of the effects of suppression. These studies (Gross & Levenson, 1993, 1997) have examined a second negative emotion—sadness—as well as a positive emotion, namely, amusement. Consistent with expectations, suppressing sadness and amusement led to increased sympathetic activation of the cardiovascular system, including increased systolic and diastolic blood pressure, and decreased finger pulse amplitude, finger temperature, and pulse transit times. Increased sympathetic activation of the cardiovascular system thus appears to be the common core to emotion suppression across both positive and negative emotion contexts.

An interesting and unexpected finding was that whereas suppressing negative emotion-expressive behavior had no impact on negative emotion experience (disgust in one study, sadness in the other), suppressing positive emotion did have an impact on positive emotion experience. More specifically, inhibiting amusement-expressive behavior decreased reports of amusement experience. This was true both in a context that predominantly elicited amusement (an amusement film) and in a context in which there were lower levels of amusement (a sadness film that evoked a bit of secondary amusement). This finding jibes with prior scattered reports from the facial feedback tradition that inhibiting amusement (e.g., McCanne & Anderson, 1987; Strack, Martin, & Stepper, 1988) and pride (e.g., Stepper & Strack, 1993) expressive behavior leads to decreases in the self-reports of these positive emotions. It is not clear why suppressing positive emotions such as amusement and pride has a different impact on emotion experience than suppressing negative emotions such as sadness and disgust.

Replicated laboratory findings concerning the differential impact of suppression and reappraisal suggest the possibility that individual differences in these two emotion regulation strategies should have discernible affective consequences. More specifically, based on our model of emotion regulation and on the experimental literature, we hypothesized that individuals who habitually suppress should have lesser negative and positive emotion-expressive behavior. Given the apparently asymmetric relations between emotion experience and emotion expression for negative versus positive emotions, we further hypothesized that individuals who habitually suppress should have comparable levels of negative emotion experience, but lesser positive emotion experience. By contrast, we expected that individuals who habitually reappraise should have lesser negative emotion experience and expression, and greater positive emotion experience and expression.

To test these predictions, Gross and John (2002) used the Emotion Regulation Questionnaire (described earlier) to assess individual differences in suppression and reappraisal and obtained self- ratings of emotion experience and expression, as well as peer-ratings of emotion expression. As predicted, suppression was associated with lower levels of positive emotion experience and expression. Relations between suppression and negative emotion expression also followed expectations, with suppression being associated with lesser negative emotion-expressive behavior. Findings regarding suppression and negative emotion experience were mixed, showing either no effects or positive effects; that is, the more individuals said they suppressed, the more negative emotion they said they felt. Reappraisal, by contrast, was associated with greater positive emotion experience and expression, and lesser negative emotion experience and expression. As with suppression, self-reports and peer reports converged nicely with the results of previous experimental studies.

An important question is whether these affective consequences are ephemeral—resulting in slight and transient changes in temporary emotion experience—or whether their effects accumulate and impact long-term well-being. To assess the impact of habitual suppression and reappraisal on adaptation, Gross and John (2002) related their individual difference measures of these two emotion regulation strategies to indicators of personal functioning: life satisfaction, well-being, and depression. In each case, suppression was associated with negative outcomes, whereas reappraisal was associated with positive outcomes. Together with the experimental findings described earlier, these findings provide strong evidence that suppression and reappraisal have strikingly divergent consequences for affective responding.

Social Consequences of Emotion Regulation

To date, research on emotion regulation has focused on the effects regulation has on the regulator. However, emotion regulation often occurs in social contexts. In light of the differing cognitive and affective consequences of reappraisal and suppression, how might these two emotion regulation strategies influence social interaction?

Suppression, in particular, seems to be a blunt instrument—one that decreases both negative and positive emotion-expressive behavior. Suppression further compromises social responsiveness by producing a memory impairment for social information presented while the individual is regulating emotions (Richards & Gross, 2000). These considerations led us to predict that suppression would have negative social consequences. By contrast, reappraisal seems to increase positive emotion experience and expression and decrease negative emotion experience and expression, with no discernible cognitive consequences. These considerations led us to predict that reappraisal would not have adverse social consequences.

To study the social impact of these two forms of emotion regulation, we focused on one important social context, namely, an interaction in which two people discuss an upsetting topic. In this context, reappraisal should selectively alter the meaning of the potentially upsetting situation in such a way that it decreased the reappraiser's negative—but not positive—emotion-expressive behavior. By contrast, we expected that suppression would decrease both negative and positive emotion-expressive behavior. Given the differential impact of reappraisal and suppression, we expected that suppression—but not reappraisal—would lead to negative reactions from others.

To test this prediction, we asked unacquainted pairs of women to watch an upsetting film and then discuss their reactions (Butler et al., 2002). Unbeknownst to the other, one member of each dyad had been asked to either suppress, reappraise, or interact naturally with her conversation partner. We expected suppression to decrease the emotional responsiveness of the regulator. Because emotional responsiveness is a key element of social support, and social support decreases physiological responses to stressors (Uchino, Cacioppo, & Kiecolt-Glaser, 1996), the diminished emotional responsiveness shown by suppression participants should produce large physiological responses in their interaction partners. By contrast, we did not expect reappraisal participants to show decreased emotional responsiveness. We therefore expected that the interaction partners of reappraisal participants would have physiological responses comparable to those of control participants.

As predicted, partners of suppression participants showed greater increases in blood pressure than partners of participants who were either reappraising or acting naturally. Thus, interacting with a partner who shows little emotional responsiveness is more physiologically activating than interacting with a partner who shows greater emotion. An important question is whether these findings, which were based on a laboratory interaction between two unacquainted women, would generalize beyond this context. Would these social consequences of emotion regulation be discernable with the use of an individual-differences approach?

To find out, Gross and John (2002) related individual differences in suppression and reappraisal to measures of social functioning, including social support, coping, and being liked by one's peers. Individuals who habitually suppress were less likely to share either their negative or their positive emotions with others than were individuals who reappraised. Suppression was also associated with poorer social support and lesser use of instrumental and emotional social support coping. Finally, suppression and reappraisal were differentially related to both self-reports and others' reports of how well liked a person was, so that individuals who tended to use reappraisal were more likely to be liked than individuals who used suppression. Together with the experimental findings, these individual difference findings indicate that in the social domain, too, reappraisal may have more to recommend it than suppression.

IMPLICATIONS AND FUTURE DIRECTIONS

From violence in the schoolyards to deadly "road rage" on the highways, we regularly see the awful consequences of failures of emotion regulation. In the past two decades a literature has emerged that has begun to examine emotion regulation empirically (Gross, 1998a). This literature promises a much-needed theoretical and empirical framework to examine the costs and benefits of different forms of emotion regulation and dysregulation. In this chapter we have described five points in the emotion-generative process at which emotions can be regulated: (1) selection of the situation, (2) modification of the situation, (3) deployment of attention, (4) change of cognitions, and (5) modulation of responses.

To illustrate the divergent consequences of attempts to intervene at varying points in the emotion-generative process, we have focused on two forms of emotion regulation—reappraisal and suppression. Using both experimental and correlational studies, we have shown that suppression consumes cognitive resources, impairing memory for information presented during the emotion regulation period. Reappraisal, by contrast, appears to have no such cognitive consequences. In the affective domain, we have shown that suppression decreases not only negative but also positive emotion-expressive behavior. Worse, suppression appears to have little impact on negative emotion experience, while decreasing positive emotion experience. Suppression is also associated with increased sympathetic activation of the cardiovascular system that appears to be out of keeping with metabolic demand. By contrast, reappraisal decreases negative emotion experience and expression, while increasing positive emotion experience and expression. Unlike suppression, reappraisal is not associated with increased sympathetic activation. Even in the social domain, suppression appears to have less desirable consequences than reappraisal. As compared with reappraisal, suppression leads individuals to share less of their positive and negative emotions, resulting in weakened social support and even their being less liked. Also unlike reappraisal, suppression leads to increased blood pressure in social partners.

Implications for Emotionally Intelligent Behavior

Classical conceptions of intelligence have emphasized cold, cognitive operations (Feldman Barrett & Gross, 2001). Contemporary research and theorizing in the area of emotional intelligence has highlighted the importance of motivational and emotional factors and, in particular, has explicitly drawn emotion regulation into the realm of emotional intelligence. We regard our research on emotion regulation as an important—albeit preliminary—step toward a clearer understanding of how different emotion regulation strategies may be more or less helpful in a particular adaptive context.

We must emphasize that we regard suppression and reappraisal as but two of a large family of emotion regulatory processes. Many other widely used and important forms of emotion regulation have yet to be thoroughly analyzed, but it is our hope that our experimental and individual-differences analyses of suppression and reappraisal may provide a reference point for future research on other, related forms of emotion regulation.

It is important to note that although we have found that the profile of consequences associated with reappraisal seems to be consistently more attractive than the profile of consequences associated with suppression, we think it likely that there are many times when suppression is either the only or the best option. Occasionally, there simply may not be time to cognitively reevaluate a rapidly developing situation, making reappraisal an unworkable choice. Although we do not yet have the data to demonstrate this, we believe that it is the flexible application of a range of emotion regulatory strategies that is associated with adaptive success. Better to be able to suppress, reappraise, or use yet other forms of emotion regulation, than not be able to use these strategies. As long as the short- and longer-term costs and benefits of each form of emotion regulation are kept in mind, we suspect that each will have its place in the arsenal of emotion regulatory strategies for the emotionally intelligent individual.

Directions for Future Research

Empirical research on the adaptive consequences of differing forms of emotion regulation has only just begun, and a number of important directions for future research remain. In our view, five of these research directions stand out as particularly important: (1) looking at how the consequences of different forms of emotion regulation vary according to a particular individual's habitual patterns of emotion regulation, (2) exploring emotion regulation in psychopathology, (3) analyzing emotion regulation over the life span, (4) assessing the longer-term health consequences of emotion regulation, and (5) examining other forms of self-regulation.

In this review we have integrated experimental and individual-differences approaches to the study of emotion regulation (Underwood, 1975). However, important questions remain concerning the interaction of individual differences and basic emotion regulatory processes. For example: Does expressive suppression have the same profile of consequences when individuals high and low in habitual use of expressive suppression are compared? Is expressive suppression harder (or easier) for individuals who typically engage in suppression as compared with those who typically do not? Analyses of individual differences in how often different emotion regulatory strategies are used should be complemented by an analysis of not just frequency of emotion regulation, but capability. What may prove important is not just whether one typically suppresses or reappraises, but how capable one is at regulating in each manner when one so desires.

As noted in our introduction, there is now a growing consensus that many forms of psychopathology involve emotion dysregulation. However, even in disorders that are manifested affective disorders, such as major depressive disorder, it is not yet known precisely how emotion is dysregulated. A second important direction for future research, therefore, is a more thoroughgoing application of the tools of affective science to the domain of psychopathology. Such research promises to help translate our growing understanding of basic emotion regulatory processes into clearer statements and models concerning the nature of emotion dysregulation in the wide array of psychopathological conditions that involve difficulties with emotional responding.

A third important direction for future research is to increase the contact between adult and child emotion regulation research. Emotion regulation is by no means only for adults. There is a large body of literature on emotion regulation in infancy and childhood, and life span developmental scholars are beginning to chart the waxing and waning of emotion regulatory processes in the adult years as well. It will be important, therefore, to ask what individuals of differing ages can do—and want to do—to regulate their emotions. For example, temperament researchers have made a compelling case for early-appearing individual differences in emotional responding and regulation (e.g., Derryberry &

Rothbart, 1984). How do these initial differences give rise to different emotion trajectories as infants begin to be able to approach, withdraw from, or alter their local environment? As infants grow into childhood, how do they learn social rules governing which emotions they may experience and express? Even in adulthood, emotion regulation continues to develop as adults learn to fine-tune their emotion-expressive displays to match the demands of home and work. For example, physicians learn to regulate strong emotion aroused by injuries and corpses, and flight attendants learn to overcome feelings of anger when dealing with rude passengers. In later years, emotion regulation takes the form of preferring to spend time with familiar others rather than strangers, which may represent a shift in preferred means of emotion regulation (Gross et al., 1997).

A fourth important direction for future research is to explore the longer-term consequences of various emotion regulation strategies, particularly for physical health. The findings reviewed here have largely focused on immediate and shorter-term effects. However, if there are consistent individual differences in emotion and emotion regulation, we expect that such differences will have cumulative effects. For example, each time emotion is suppressed, physiological responses are magnified. Any one physiological response of increased intensity is unlikely to have deleterious consequences, but if such responses recur day after day after day, there may be adverse health consequences. A recent study illustrates how such a hypothesis may be tested. Heart attack survivors were divided into four groups, depending on their scores on measures of distress and the tendency to inhibit emotion (Denollet et al., 1996). The subgroup scoring high on both distress and inhibition had a significantly higher death rate (27%) than other patients (7%). This finding suggests that suppression may well prove to have important cumulative consequences for health as well.

Finally, a fifth direction for future research concerns how emotion regulation relates to other important forms of self-regulation. It is not yet clear whether processes that regulate emotional impulses should be distinguished from those that regulate impulses associated with hunger, thirst, aggression, and sexual arousal. Advances in theory, computational models, and autonomic and central nervous system measurement all promise to help sharpen the points of convergence and divergence across differing modes of self-regulation. These issues seem certain to attract continued interest, as researchers with a variety of interests (e.g., weight loss, substance abuse, aggression, emotion regulation; see Baumeister & Heatherton, 1996) work to better understand which forms of self-regulation are most likely to promote healthy adaptation.

ACKNOWLEDGMENTS

This chapter draws on Gross (2001) and Feldman Barrett and Gross (2001). Preparation of this chapter was supported by Grant Nos. MH53859 and MH43948 from the National Institute of Mental Health.

REFERENCES

American Psychiatric Association. (1994). *Diagnostic and statistical manual of mental disorders* (4th ed.). Washington DC: Author.

Baumeister, R. F., & Heatherton, T. F. (1996). Self-regulation failure: An overview. *Psychological Inquiry, 7,* 1–15.

Boden, J. M., & Baumeister, R. F. (1997). Repressive coping: Distraction using pleasant thoughts and memories. *Journal of Personality and Social Psychology, 73,* 45–62.

Butler, E. A., Egloff, B., Wilhelm, F. H., Smith, N. C., Erickson, E. A., & Gross, J. J. (2002). *The social consequences of expressive suppression.* Manuscript submitted for publication.

Cannon, W. (1932). *The wisdom of the body.* New York: Norton.

Cole, P. M. (1986). Children's spontaneous control of facial expression. *Child Development, 57,* 1309–1321.

Csikszentmihalyi, M. (1975). *Beyond boredom and anxiety: The experience of play in work and games.* San Francisco: Jossey-Bass.

Denollet, J., Sys, S. U., Stroobant, N., Rombouts, H., Gillebert, T. C., & Brutsaert, D. L. (1996). Personality as independent predictor of long-term mortality in patients with coronary heart disease. *Lancet, 347,* 417–421.

Derryberry, D., & Rothbart, M. K. (1984). Emotion, attention, and temperament. In C. E. Izard, J. Kagan, & R. B. Zajonc (Eds.), *Emotions, cognitions, and behavior* (pp. 132–166). Cambridge, UK: Cambridge University Press.

Feldman Barrett, L., & Gross, J. J. (2001). Emotional intelligence: A process model of emotion representation and regulation. In T. J. Mayne & G. A. Bonanno (Eds.), *Emotions: Current issues and future directions* (pp. 286–310). New York: Guilford Press.

Gross, J. J. (1998a). Antecedent- and response-focused emotion regulation: Divergent consequences for experience, expression, and physiology. *Journal of Personality and Social Psychology, 74,* 224–237.

Gross, J. J. (1998b). The emerging field of emotion regulation: An integrative review. *Review of General Psychology, 2,* 271–299.

Gross, J. J. (1999a). Emotion and emotion regulation. In L. A. Pervin & O. P. John (Eds.), *Handbook of personality: Theory and research* (2nd ed., pp. 525–552). New York: Guilford Press.

Gross, J. J. (1999b). Emotion regulation: Past, present, future. *Cognition and Emotion, 13,* 551–573.

Gross, J. J. (2001). Emotion regulation in adulthood: Timing is everything. *Current Directions in Psychological Science, 10,* 214–219.

Gross, J. J., Carstensen, L. L., Pasupathi, M., Tsai, J., Gottestam, K., & Hsu,

A. Y. C. (1997). Emotion and aging: Experience, expression, and control. *Psychology and Aging, 12,* 590–599.

Gross, J. J., & John, O. P. (2002). *Individual differences in two emotion regulation processes: Implications for affect, relationships, and well-being.* Manuscript submitted for publication.

Gross, J. J., & Keltner, D. (Eds.). (1999, September). Functional accounts of emotion [Special issue]. *Cognition and Emotion, 13.*

Gross, J. J., & Levenson, R. W. (1993). Emotional suppression: Physiology, self-report, and expressive behavior. *Journal of Personality and Social Psychology, 64,* 970–986.

Gross, J. J., & Levenson, R. W. (1997). Hiding feelings: The acute effects of inhibiting negative and positive emotion. *Journal of Abnormal Psychology, 106,* 95–103.

Herrmann, D., & Neisser, U. (1978). An inventory of everyday memory experiences. In M. M. Gruneberg, P. E. Morris, & R. N. Sykes (Eds.), *Practical aspects of memory* (pp. 35–51). London: Academic Press.

Lazarus, R. S. (1991). *Emotion and adaptation.* Oxford: Oxford University Press.

Lazarus, R. S., & Folkman, S. (1984). *Stress, appraisal and coping.* New York: Springer.

LeDoux, J. E. (1994, June). Emotion, memory and the brain. *Scientific American, 270,* 50–57.

McCanne, T. R., & Anderson, J. A. (1987). Emotional responding following experimental manipulation of facial electromyographic activity. *Journal of Personality and Social Psychology, 52,* 759–768.

Nolen-Hoeksema, S. (1993). Sex differences in control of depression. In D. M. Wegner & J. W. Pennebaker (Eds.), *Handbook of mental control* (pp. 306–324). Englewood Cliffs, NJ: Prentice-Hall.

Parrott, W. G. (1993). Beyond hedonism: Motives for inhibiting good moods and for maintaining bad moods. In D. M. Wegner & J. W. Pennebaker (Eds.), *Handbook of mental control* (pp. 278–308). Englewood Cliffs, NJ: Prentice-Hall.

Parrott, W. G. (2001). Implications of dysfunctional emotions for understanding how emotions function. *Review of General Psychology, 5,* 180–186.

Richards, J. M., & Gross, J. J. (2000). Emotion regulation and memory: The cognitive costs of keeping one's cool. *Journal of Personality and Social Psychology, 79,* 410–424.

Rothbaum, F., Weisz, J. R., & Snyder, S. S. (1982). Changing the world and changing the self: A two-process model of perceived control. *Journal of Personality and Social Psychology, 42,* 5–37.

Salovey, P., & Mayer, J. D. (1990). Emotional intelligence. *Imagination, Cognition and Personality, 9,* 185–211.

Stepper, S., & Strack, F. (1993). Proprioceptive determinants of emotional and nonemotional feelings. *Journal of Personality and Social Psychology, 64,* 211–220.

Strack, F., Martin, L. L., & Stepper, S. (1988). Inhibiting and facilitating conditions of the human smile: A nonobtrusive test of the facial feedback hypothesis. *Journal of Personality and Social Psychology, 54,* 768–777.

Tooby, J., & Cosmides, L. (1990). The past explains the present: Emotional adaptations and the structure of ancestral environments. *Ethology and Sociobiology, 11,* 375–424.

Uchino, B. N., Cacioppo, J. T., & Kiecolt-Glaser, J. K. (1996). The relationship between social support and physiological processes: A review with emphasis on underlying mechanisms and implications for health. *Psychological Bulletin, 119,* 488–531.

Underwood, B. J. (1975). Individual differences as a crucible in theory construction. *Amercian Psychologist, 30,* 128–134.

Positive Emotions and Emotional Intelligence

MICHELE M. TUGADE
BARBARA L. FREDRICKSON

Positive emotions are a part of everyday life. Sometimes certain positive emotions are experienced more intensely than others; at other times, it may not be appropriate or even adaptively useful to feel positive emotions at all. What accounts for knowing when positive emotions are appropriate, when they are not, and how best to utilize them in one's life? Are there such things as "wise" knowledge and use of positive emotions? We think so. The answer may lie in the construct of *emotional intelligence*. According to the framework of emotional intelligence, one must be competent at understanding one's emotions; be able to process emotional information accurately and efficiently; and have the insight to skillfully use one's emotions to solve problems, make plans, and achieve in one's life (Salovey & Mayer, 1989–1990). Positive emotions are related to each of these aspects in important ways.

What role do positive emotions play in emotional intelligence? In this chapter, we first discuss the adaptive significance of positive emotions and then explore the possibility that there are individual differences in the ability to "intelligently" use positive emotions as a means of guiding and understanding one's behavior and experience. Next we examine whether such individual differences may be rooted in underlying skills that can be learned and thereby contribute to people's efforts to improve their own mental and physical health. Then we review studies that indicate that the use of positive emotions can lead to enhanced well-being over time. Finally, we consider whether current theories of emotional intelligence should be modified to incorporate the role of positive emotions in the theory more explicitly.

THE ADAPTIVE SIGNIFICANCE
OF POSITIVE EMOTIONS

Traditional approaches to the study of emotions have tended to overlook and even ignore positive emotions. With greater attention given to the study of negative emotions, many emotion theorists often simply squeezed positive emotions under the umbrella of general emotion models (Fredrickson, 1998). Sensing that traditional approaches to emotion did not do justice to positive emotions, Fredrickson developed an alternative model for positive emotions that better captures their unique effects. Fredrickson calls this the *broaden-and-build theory* of positive emotions, because positive emotions appear to *broaden* people's momentary thought–action repertoires and *build* their enduring personal resources (Fredrickson, 1998, 2001).

Fredrickson contrasts this new model with traditional models of emotion based on specific action tendencies. Specific action tendencies, according to Fredrickson, work well to describe the form and function of negative emotions and should be retained for models of this subset of emotions. Specific action tendencies narrow a person's momentary thought–action repertoire by calling to mind an urge to act in a particular way (e.g., escape in fear, attack in anger, expel in disgust). In a life-threatening situation, a narrowed thought–action repertoire promotes quick and decisive action that carries direct and immediate benefit. Specific action tendencies called forth by negative emotions represent the sort of actions that worked best to save our ancestors' lives and limbs in similar situations.

Yet positive emotions seldom occur in life-threatening situations. As such, a psychological process that narrows a person's momentary thought–action repertoire to promote quick and decisive action may not be needed. Instead, Fredrickson has argued that positive emotions have a complementary effect: They *broaden* people's momentary thought–action repertoires, widening the array of the thoughts and actions that come to mind: to play and create when experiencing joy, to explore when experiencing interest, to savor and integrate when experiencing contentment, and to combine play, exploration, and savoring when experiencing love (Fredrickson, 1998).

Support for the hypothesis that experiences of positive emotions broaden a person's momentary thought–action repertoire can be drawn from studies that have examined the cognitive and behavioral effects of positive states. Work by Isen and colleagues is particularly valuable in demonstrating that positive emotions produce patterns of thought that are notably unusual (Isen, Johnson, Mertz, & Robinson, 1985), flexible and inclusive (Isen & Daubman, 1984), creative (Isen, Daubman, & Nowicki, 1987), and receptive (Estrada, Isen, & Young, 1997). Testing the effects of positive states on behavior, Isen and colleagues have shown that positive emotions produce more creative (Isen et al., 1987) and variable (Kahn & Isen, 1993) actions.

In further support of the broadening hypothesis, Fredrickson and Branigan (2001) found that positive emotions do indeed broaden an individual's thought–action repertoire. In their study, participants were experimentally induced to experience joy, contentment, fear, anger, or neutrality, after which they listed all the things they would like to do right then (a measure of breadth in participants' thought–action repertoires). Those experiencing joy and contentment listed significantly more things, relative to those experiencing fear and anger and relative to those experiencing neutrality. Moreover, those in the two negative emotion conditions also named significantly fewer things than those in the neutral control condition (Fredrickson & Branigan, 2001). So, distinct positive emotions expand the array of thoughts and actions that come to mind, whereas distinct negative emotions taper this same array.

Taken together, these studies indicate that positive emotions appear to "enlarge" the cognitive context (Isen, 1987), an effect linked to increases in brain dopamine levels (Ashby, Isen, & Turken, 1999). Fredrickson (1998, 2001) has argued that the broadened mind-sets that accompany positive emotions, in turn, carry indirect and long-term adaptive benefits, because broadening *builds* enduring personal resources. These resources include physical resources (e.g., improved health, longevity), social resources (e.g., friendships, social support networks), intellectual resources (e.g., expert knowledge, intellectual complexity), and psychological resources (e.g., resilience, optimism, creativity). Importantly, the personal resources accrued during states of positive emotions are durable. They outlast the transient emotional states that led to their acquisition. In consequence, then, the often incidental effect of experiencing a positive emotion is an increase in one's personal resources. These resources can be drawn on in subsequent moments and in different emotional states. So, through experiences of positive emotions, people *transform* themselves, becoming more creative, knowledgeable, resilient, socially integrated, and healthy individuals.

This "building" effect of positive emotions is particularly useful in contexts of chronic stress, where such resources can often become depleted. Research on positive emotions in the context of coping and negative emotion regulation is beginning to gain attention. Like work on emotions theory, traditional research on coping theory has largely been focused on the management of negative emotions without taking into account the coping processes associated with positive emotions. The broaden-and-build theory provides a conceptual framework for understanding the coping process by illuminating how positive emotions can help restore and build on depleted personal resources.

Folkman, Moskowitz, and their colleagues have been among the first to provide empirical support for the prediction that positive emotions are important facilitators of adaptive coping and adjustment to acute and chronic stress (Billings, Folkman, Acree, & Moskowitz, 2000; Folkman, 1997; Moskowitz, Folkman, Colette, & Vittinghoff, 1996; for a review see Folkman & Moskowitz, 2000). Their longitudinal research focuses on the psychological responses associated with caregiving and bereavement among partners of men with AIDS. Participants in their study were found to have significantly elevated levels of depressed mood throughout caregiving, which persisted through bereavement—findings expected in this research. Surprisingly, however, with the exception of the time immediately before and after their partners' deaths, caregivers also reported experiences of positive mood at the same frequency of their negative mood (Folkman, 1997). This finding at first seems counterintuitive: Why would someone facing the enormous stresses of caregiving and bereavement experience any positive emotions at all? The seemingly counterintuitive logic behind these findings, in fact, provides a lens through which to understand the adaptive role of positive emotions in the coping process. The occurrence of positive emotions amid adversity may provide the necessary psychological rest to help buffer against stress, replenish, and restore further coping abilities (Lazarus, Kanner, & Folkman, 1980).

Folkman and Moskowitz (2000) highlight three kinds of coping related to the occurrence and maintenance of positive affect: (1) positive reappraisal (finding a "silver lining"), (2) problem-focused coping (efforts directed at solving or managing the distressing problem), and (3) infusing ordinary events with positive meaning (e.g., appreciating a compliment). An important finding in the study on AIDS-related caregiving was that these coping mechanisms were consistently associated with increases in positive emotion (distinct from decreases in distress; Moskowitz, Folkman, Collette, Vittinghoff, 1996). Moreover, coping that resulted in increased positive emotions was associated with lower levels of physical symptoms during times of stress, whereas coping that resulted in increased negative emotions was linked to higher levels of physical symptoms among the caregivers (Billings, Folkman, Acree, &

Moskowitz, 2000). In related work by others, similar coping strategies have been shown to predict increases in psychological well-being and health (e.g., Affleck & Tennen, 1996; Davis, Nolen-Hoeksema, & Larson, 1998; for a review, see also Park & Folkman, 1997).

Research conducted by Folkman, Moskowitz, and colleagues, then, provides a useful complement to Fredrickson's (1998, 2001) broaden-and-build theory. Recall that the broaden-and-build theory posits that under stressful conditions, negative emotions *narrow* one's momentary thought–action repertoire, which results in cardiovascular reactivity that prepares the body for specific action. In contrast, positive emotions *broaden* one's thought–action repertoire, "undoing" this bodily preparation for specific action. By consequence of broadening one's thoughts and actions, the theory posits, positive emotions *build* that individual's personal resources (Fredrickson, 1998, 2001). This perspective on positive emotions helps explain why those who experience positive emotions in the midst of stress are able to benefit from their broadened mind-sets and successfully regulate their negative emotional experiences, which in turn produces beneficial consequences for their psychological and physiological well-being.

This *undoing effect* of positive emotions reflects one type of emotion regulation, one of the four components of emotional intelligence theory. Fredrickson and colleagues have tested the undoing effect by experimentally inducing a high-arousal negative emotion in all participants (Fredrickson & Levenson, 1998; Fredrickson, Mancuso, Branigan, & Tugade, 2000). In one study (Fredrickson et al., 2000), participants prepared a speech under time pressure, each believing that the speech would be videotaped and evaluated by peers. This task induced the subjective experience of anxiety, along with increases in heart rate, peripheral vasoconstriction, and systolic and diastolic blood pressure. Into this context of anxiety-related sympathetic arousal, we randomly assigned participants to view one of four films (joy, contentment, neutrality, sadness).

The undoing hypothesis predicts that those who experience positive emotions on the heels of a high-activation negative emotion will show the fastest cardiovascular recovery. We tested this by measuring the time elapsed from the start of the randomly assigned film until the cardiovascular reactions induced by the negative emotion returned to baseline levels. In three independent samples, participants in the two positive emotion conditions (joy and contentment) exhibited faster cardiovascular recovery than those in the neutral control condition, and faster than those in the sadness condition, who exhibited the most protracted recovery (Fredrickson & Levenson, 1998; Fredrickson et al., 2000). These findings indicate that positive emotions have the unique ability to physiologically down-regulate lingering negative emotional arousal. Although the precise cognitive and physiological mechanisms of the undoing effect remain unknown, the broaden-and-build theory suggests that broadening at the cognitive level may mediate undoing at the cardiovascular level. Phenomenologically, positive emotions may help people place the events in their lives in a broader context, lessening the resonance of any particular negative event.

Evidence for the undoing effect of positive emotions suggests that people may enhance their psychological well-being, and perhaps also their physical health, by cultivating experiences of positive emotions at opportune moments to cope with negative emotions (Fredrickson, 2000a). This idea can be supported by experiments showing that positive affect facilitates attention to negative self-relevant information (Trope & Neter, 1994; Trope & Pomerantz, 1998; Reed & Aspinwall, 1998; for a review, see Aspinwall, 1998). Extrapolating from these findings, Aspinwall (2001) describes how positive affect and positive beliefs serve as resources for people coping with adversity (see also Taylor, Kemeny, Reed, Bower, & Gruenewald, 2000). For instance, Aspinwall argues that in the face of stress, optimists and people experiencing positive affect expect positive outcomes and therefore aim to achieve them. As such, they are more likely to use active coping (e.g., problem solving) and are less likely to use avoidance coping (e.g., disregarding the problem). Active coping efforts in turn provide people with the necessary feedback to discover which strategies are effective, helping them to conserve current resources and build new ones toward efficient coping (Aspinwall, 2001). Taken together, these studies suggest that positive emotions may indeed have adaptive benefits in the coping process. Further research in this area is needed to explore the characteristics of individuals who contribute to their ability to generate and sustain positive emotions in stressful contexts.

INTELLIGENT USE OF POSITIVE EMOTIONS

The emotional intelligence framework suggests that there may be individual differences in people's abilities to cognitively represent their emotions and exert effective control over their emotional lives, allowing some to more effectively manage their emotions during stressful situations (Feldman Barrett & Gross, 2001; Salovey, Hsee, & Mayer, 1993). At one end of the spectrum there are individuals who are consistently hampered by their inability to cope with stress, never quite able to recover from negative life events. At the other end are individuals who quickly and efficiently rebound from stressful experiences, being able to move on despite adverse circumstances. Thus, individuals may differ in how they perceive, express, understand, and manage emotional phenomena. In other words, *emotional intelligence* may be a key factor differentiating those individuals who are able to successfully cope with stressful encounters from those who face setbacks from similar experiences (Salovey, Bedell, Detweiler, & Mayer, 1999).

Given the evidence showing that positive emotions indeed produce beneficial outcomes in the coping process (e.g., Folkman & Moskowitz, 2000; Fredrickson, 2000a), it is possible that certain individuals have a greater tendency to draw on positive emotions in times of stress, intuitively understanding and using positive emotions to their advantage. Psychologically resilient people—who are described as "emotionally intelligent" (Salovey et al., 1999)—appear to be likely candidates for this type of intuition.

RESILIENT INDIVIDUALS REFLECT EMOTIONAL INTELLIGENCE

Psychological resilience is characterized by the ability to bounce back from negative emotional experiences and by flexible adaptation to changing situational demands (Block & Kremen, 1996; Lazarus, 1993). Those with low resilience are said to have a difficult time coping with negative experiences and are unable to recover from them (e.g., Klohnen, 1996; Rutter, 1987). In contrast, those with high resilience are said to be able to "ride out the storm," handle anxiety, and tolerate frustration even when faced with episodes of distressing emotional experience (Carver, 1998; Saarni, 1999).

Individual differences in psychological resilience predict differential outcomes in emotion regulation. For instance, relative to those less resilient, highly resilient individuals restore self-esteem after failure (Wolin & Wolin, 1993), show more creative problem solving when handling stressful situations (Demos, 1989; Cohler, 1987; Murphy & Moriarty, 1976), and elicit more positive responses from social support networks to help buffer against negative emotional experiences (Demos, 1989; Werner & Smith, 1992). Moreover, highly resilient individuals demonstrate greater personal insight by having the ability to judge their own strengths and limitations during difficult times (Wolin & Wolin, 1993). Thus, it appears that resilient individuals may effectively recognize their own feelings and those of others and utilize their emotion knowledge to effectively manage their emotional experiences (Kumpfer, 1999; Masten, Best, & Garmezy, 1990). That is, resilient individuals appear to have emotional intelligence.

Researchers have utilized both observer evaluations and self-reports to investigate individual differences in psychological resilience. There has been convergence in the data, indicating that resilient individuals have optimistic, zestful, and energetic approaches to life, are curious and open to new experiences, and are characterized by high positive emotionality (Block & Kremen, 1996; Klohnen, 1996). Thus, based on these findings, it seems clear that positive emotionality is an important element of psychological resilience.

Thus, for resilient people, understanding the benefits of positive emotions may be key to effective emotion regulation. Support for this prediction can be demonstrated in their knowledge and use of positive emotions to cope. Recent research indicates that individual differences in resilience predict the ability to harness the beneficial effects of positive emotions to one's advantage when coping with negative emotional experiences. For instance, researchers describe resilient individuals as happy and energetic people who frequently use humor as a coping strategy (e.g., Werner & Smith, 1992; Wolin & Wolin, 1993), which has been shown to help people cope effectively with stressful circumstances (e.g., Martin & Lefcourt, 1983; Nezu, Nezu, & Blisset, 1988). Likewise, Masten et al. (1990) have found that resilient children under high stress exhibit higher scores on humor generation than those less resilient facing equally high levels of stress. These findings demonstrate that coping by means of humor, a strategy associated with positive emotions, allows resilient people to reduce stress and restore perspective, as well as remain engaging to others, thereby maintaining positive social support networks (Kumpfer, 1999). Beyond humor, resilient individuals have been shown to use other coping strategies that elicit positive emotions to regulate negative emotional situations. For instance, during heightened levels of stress they use strategies such as relaxation (allowing time to interpret and assess problems), exploration (to consider behavioral alternatives), and hopeful, optimistic thinking (having faith in their ability to overcome adversity) as means of regulating negative emotional experiences (Werner & Smith, 1992). Taken together, these findings indicate that positive emotions may have advantages in the coping process by creating broadened mind-sets useful for coping and, consequently, building personal resources that may be valuable in future coping efforts.

Our own work has demonstrated that psychologically resilient individuals are physiologically resilient as well, and that positive emotions are useful in achieving this outcome. Theoretical descriptions of psychological resilience indicate that resilient individuals are able to "bounce back" from stressful experiences quickly and efficiently (Carver, 1998; Lazarus, 1993). This theoretical definition suggests that, as compared with their less resilient counterparts, resilient individuals would exhibit faster cardiovascular recovery from negative emotional arousal. In addition, together with our work on the undoing hypothesis (Fredrickson & Levenson, 1998; Fredrickson et al., 2000), the broaden-and-build theory suggests that this ability to "bounce back" to cardiovascular baseline may be fueled by experiences of positive emotion.

To test these hypotheses, we used the same time-pressured speech preparation task (described earlier) to induce a high-activation negative emotion in volunteer participants. We measured psychological resilience using Block and Kremen's (1996) self-report scale. Interestingly, resilience did *not* predict the levels of anxiety participants reported experiencing during the speech task, or the magnitude of their cardiovascular reactions to the stressful task, both of which were considerable. Resilience did, however, predict participants' reports of positive emotions. Before the speech task was even introduced, the more resilient individuals reported higher levels of preexisting positive affect on an initial mood measure. And when later asked how they felt during the time-pressured speech preparation phase, the more resilient individuals reported that, along with their high anxiety, they also experienced higher levels of happiness and interest.

As predicted by the theoretical definition of psychological resilience, the more resilient participants exhibited significantly faster returns to baseline levels of cardiovascular activation following the speech task. Moreover, as predicted by the broaden-and-build theory, this difference in time to achieve cardiovascular recovery was mediated by differences in self-reported positive emotions (Tugade & Fredrickson, 2002). Thus, our resilient participants appeared to have recruited positive emotions (intentionally or unintentionally) to physiologically regulate their negative emotional arousal.

These findings were used to extend current theories of psychological resilience through exploration of the construct's physiological qualities. In our study, a parallel between psychological and physiological resilience emerged: Those who rated themselves as having high abilities to effectively rebound from stressful encounters also demonstrated this quality physiologically, by quickly returning to baseline levels of physiological responding after negative emotional arousal. Furthermore, it appears that the experience of positive emotions aids resilient individuals in achieving accelerated cardiovascular recovery from negative emotional arousal. Thus, resilient individuals may have an intuitive understanding of the benefits that positive emotions confer. That is, they—wittingly or unwittingly—may use positive emotions "intelligently" to regulate negative emotional experiences.

It is important to note that despite these individual differences in the *frequency* of intelligently using positive emotions to cope with stress, the capacity for momentary experiences of positive emotions is something that all humans share (Fredrickson, 2000b). This capacity, according to the broaden-and-build theory (Fredrickson, 1998, 2001), is an evolved psychological adaptation. Thus, all people (not just resilient people) share the capacity to experience the beneficial repercussions associated with positive emotions. Resilient people simply use this capacity more often. Even so, many questions remain: Do resilient individuals intentionally recruit positive emotions to cope? If so, how do they do it? Can these strategies be taught to less resilient individuals? These questions lay the groundwork for subsequent studies.

Research has shown that in order to understand how an individual will cope in response to a situation, it is important to know how that individual interprets the situation (e.g., Lazarus & Folkman, 1984). Thus, examining cognitive appraisals can enrich our understanding of how positive emotions and positive appraisals influence the coping process. Cognitive appraisals may also help explain individual differences in resilience. For instance, differences may arise in appraisals of the controllability of an event, the extent to which an event violates one's goals, and the extent to which an event is appraised as threatening versus challenging. Moreover, research has shown that positive appraisal styles (i.e., the tendency to interpret events in a positive light) have strong implications for emotion regulation, showing that they aid in efficient emotion regulation in both the short term (e.g., taking a college examination,) and the long term (e.g., dealing with breast cancer or a death of a friend; Folkman, Lazarus, Dunkel-Schetter, DeLongis, & Gruen, 1986; Lazarus & Folkman, 1984; Park & Folkman, 1997).

Two types of appraisals that have received attention in the stress and coping literature as having different psychological and physiological consequences are those involving *threat* versus *challenge* (Lazarus & Folkman, 1984; Tomaka, Blascovich, Kibler, & Ernst, 1997). With threat appraisals, people's perception of danger exceeds the perception of their abilities or resources to cope with the stressor. In contrast, with challenge appraisals, people's perception of danger does not exceed the perception of resources or abilities to cope. Presumably, threatened individuals perceive the potential for loss—with little, if anything, to be gained—in the situation. Challenged individuals, in contrast, perceive the possibility of gain (i.e., positive incentives or avoidance of harm) as well as loss in the situation (Lazarus & Folkman, 1984).

In our initial study that tested the physiological consequences of positive emotions and psychological resilience (described earlier), self-reports revealed that the more resilient individuals appraised a stressful speech task as less threatening, as compared with those less resilient. Perhaps in consequence, resilient participants experienced higher levels of positive emotion during the stressful task. Experiences of positive emotions in turn produced faster cardiovascular recovery after the task.

Can individuals with low psychological resilience learn how to use positive emotions during stress to cope effectively in stressful situations? To explore this question, we conducted a follow-up study in which cognitive appraisals were manipulated by randomly assigning participants to hear different instruction sets that emphasized ideals related to challenge or threat. We predicted that, as compared with those with greater resilience, those with less resilience would benefit most from the use of challenge appraisals in the face of stressful situations.

We used the same speech preparation task to induce negative emotional experience. Across all participants, the greatest emotion experienced during the speech task was anxiety. As in the previous study, the groups did *not* differ in self-reported levels of anxiety, nor in magnitude of cardiovascular reactivity in response to the task, indicating that regardless of their level of resilience or the appraisal condition to which they were assigned, all participants experienced the speech task as equally stressful, both subjectively and physiologically. Group differences did emerge, however, in subjective reports of positive emotionality. Specifically, amid the high anxiety they experienced, those with low resilience who were assigned to appraise the speech task as a challenge reported feeling more amused, happy, and "psyched-up," as compared with those with low resilience who were assigned to appraise the task as threat. Among participants with high resilience, "challenge" and "threat" groups did not differ in self-reported positive emotionality.

We then examined group differences in rates of cardiovascular recovery from the speech task. Among participants with low resilience, those who interpreted the task as a challenge experienced faster cardiovascular recovery from the arousal caused by the task, as compared with those who interpreted the task as a threat. However, among highly resilient participants, recovery was equally fast, regardless of whether the task was interpreted as a challenge or a threat. Moreover, as predicted by the broaden-and-build theory, for those with low resilience, positive emotions mediated the effect of appraisals on recovery (Tugade & Fredrickson, 2002).

These findings highlight the importance of positive emotions and positive appraisals in the emotion regulation processes of resilient individuals. Expanding on the undoing hypothesis of positive emotions (Fredrickson & Levenson, 1998; Fredrickson et al., 2000) and cognitive appraisal theories of stress and coping (e.g., Lazarus & Folkman, 1984; Tomaka et al., 1997), findings from this study provide support for the prediction that positive emotions and appraisals of challenge (versus threat) are important factors that contribute to psychological resilience. Indeed, these findings are especially promising, because they suggest that those with low levels of psychological resilience are not necessarily destined to poor emotion regulation and its consequences: With the use of positive appraisals that generate positive emotions, they also have the capacity to effectively regulate negative emotional experiences. These results imply that interventions that promote positive appraisal styles may be especially useful for those with lower levels of psychological resilience.

POSITIVE EMOTIONS IN EVERYDAY LIFE

Up to this point, readers may wonder how the wise use of positive emotions can be reflected in the circumstances of everyday life. People are faced with positive and negative events over the course of their lives, all of which can influence their emotional and physical well-being. Even seemingly uneventful or ordinary occurrences can have significant effects, depending on how individuals construe these situations and the contexts in which they occur. In their research on caregivers of people with AIDS, for example, Folkman and Moskowitz (Folkman, 1997; Moskowitz et al., 1996) found that even amid their distress, a majority of participants were able to find positive meaning in ordinary events, whether they were planned events (e.g., being thankful for friendship during a social gathering) or more random (e.g., appreciating a flower along one's path).

In their longitudinal study, Folkman and Moskowitz interviewed the caregivers and found that more than 99% of participants had no problem recalling a positive event that helped them get through their days (Folkman, 1997). Folkman and Moskowitz (2000) suggest that infusing ordinary events with positive meaning may be an adaptive form of coping. When a negative event occurs, the individual psychologically creates a positive event or reinterprets a commonplace event more positively, as a way of buffering the negative consequences of the negative event. Notably, according to these authors, it is likely that the ability of the caregivers in their study to find positive meaning in run-of-the-mill events did not occur by accident. Rather, these caregivers may have purposefully looked to positive aspects of their lives as a way of coping with their distress. According to Folkman and Moskowitz (2000), this positive reappraisal generated experiences of positive emotion even amid stress. These experiences of positive emotion gave them the needed psychological lift to help them continue and move forward in their lives. Similar results can be seen in research pointing to the benefits of seeking visual art, music, and nature to momentarily liberate oneself from stress and uplift one's psychological well-being in preparation for further coping efforts ahead. For instance, visual and musical art have been shown to be related to the release of unexpressed emotions in women coping with breast cancer (Predeger, 1996), and they are said to help urban minority youth develop resiliency against sources of daily stress (Canino, 1995). Similarly, leisure activities and environments, particularly in nature (e.g., hiking outdoors), have been shown to facilitate coping with daily sources of stress (Ulrich, Dimberg, & Driver, 1991).

In line with the broaden-and-build theory of positive emotions, finding positive meaning in negative circumstances broadens one's scope of attention and cognition, which should aid in effective coping. Contemporary theorists have begun to include positive-meaning finding and stress-related growth in their models of stress and coping (e.g., Folkman, 1997; Park & Folkman, 1997). For example, Taylor's (1983) model of cognitive adaptation emphasizes the adaptive value of positively reinterpreting stressful experiences. Positive reappraisal involves strategies for reframing an event to see it in a more positive light. Applying this coping mechanism, cognitive behavioral therapists have encouraged individuals to use positive reappraisal strategies to assist them in confronting and dealing with difficult situations (e.g., Eifert & Wilson, 1991; Kuyken & Brewin, 1994).

Tennen and Affleck (1999) have made major contributions to this area of research with studies showing that benefit-finding enhances emotional and physical adaptation in the face of adversity. For example, they have found that benefit-finding is related to less negative affect in cancer patients, less depression and greater meaningfulness in life in stroke victims, and greater psychological adjustment in women with breast cancer (see Tennen & Affleck, 1999, for a review). This reconstruction of meaning leads to a renewal of faith and a redefinition of the self in relation to others (Calhoun & Tedeschi, 2001; Tedeschi, Park, & Calhoun, 1998; Wolin & Wolin, 1993). Taken together, these studies provide further demonstrations of how coping strategies that use positive emotions wisely can be rewarding to an individual in otherwise stressful situations.

The broaden-and-build theory (Fredrickson, 1998, 2001) may help explain how particular strategies that cultivate positive meaning and positive emotions can enhance coping outcomes. Strategies that elicit positive emotions, the theory suggests, broaden the scope of attention and cognition, which in turn should facilitate coping (Fredrickson, 2000a). Coping benefits are likely to accrue because the broadening effects of positive emotion increase the likelihood that individuals find positive meaning in stressful circumstances. It is important to note that the relation between positive meaning and positive emotions is considered reciprocal: Not only does finding positive meaning trigger positive emotion, but positive emotions—because they broaden thinking—should increase the likelihood of finding positive meaning in subsequent events (Fredrickson, 2000a). Thus, the broadening effects of positive emotions may provide the cognitive context for finding positive meaning, which in turn, can help individuals cope with adversity.

To test these hypothesized effects, we asked undergraduate research participants to provide us with narratives about "the most important personal problem" they were currently facing (adapted from Moos, 1988). Then, participants responded to the following questions: Why do you think you are facing these circumstances?; What is the significance of these current circumstances?; What kind of sense can you make of these circumstances?; and Will there be any long-term consequences of these circumstances? Participants then rated the degree of benefit finding, positive reappraisal, and positive meaning they experienced in response to the problem they described. Finally, we assessed individual differences in psychological resilience using Block and Kremen's (1996) resiliency scale. This scale assesses the extent to which an individual can modify his or her responses to changing situational demands.

We discovered that individual differences in psychological resilience predicted the ability to find positive meaning in the problems of daily life. An important finding in our study was that highly resilient and less resilient individuals reported equal levels of frustration in response to the problem they described. Differences emerged, however, in participants' reports of positive emotions: Even before they were asked to describe their most important current problem, highly resilient participants reported higher levels of positive affect on an initial mood measure. Then, when they were asked about how they felt in response to the problem they described, highly resilient individuals reported feeling more happiness amid their high level of frustration as compared with those less resilient. As predicted by the broaden-and-build theory of positive emotions, positive-meaning finding was mediated by differences in positive emotions (Tugade & Fredrickson, 2002).

In sum, as we expected, highly resilient individuals were better able to find positive meaning in the problems of their daily life, more so than their less resilient peers. For resilient people, positive-meaning finding may reflect insight about the benefits of positive emotions in helping to adapt to, and overcome, stressful circumstances. Moreover, the experience of positive emotions may contribute to people's ability to learn from negative life events, to be optimistic about their resolve, to find benefits, and to grow from negative experiences. Although past literature and data from this study suggest the possibility that resilient individuals intentionally recruit positive emotions in times of stress (e.g., using humor to cope, finding positive meaning in negative circumstances), empirical studies remain to be conducted to test whether the "intelligent" use of positive emotions is an automatic or controlled process.

Findings from this study illuminate how positive emotions can produce increasing benefits over time. As the broaden-and-build theory posits (Fredrickson, 1998, 2001), finding positive meaning amid stress can build personal resources, such as strengthened relationships and enhanced values (by inspiring more courage, tolerance, and wisdom; cf. Tennen & Affleck, 1999; Janoff-Bulman, 1992). In time, such resources can foster further experiences of positive emotions, which in turn can build even further personal resources that will contribute to future positive emotional experiences.

POSITIVE EMOTIONS TRIGGER UPWARD SPIRALS TOWARD IMPROVED EMOTIONAL WELL-BEING

Preliminary evidence, then, suggests that positive emotions may fuel individual differences in resilience. Noting that psychological resilience is an enduring personal resource, the broaden-and-build theory makes the bolder prediction that experiences of positive emotions may also, over time, build psychological resilience, not just reflect it. That is, to the extent that positive emotions broaden the scopes of attention and cognition, enabling flexible and creative thinking, they should also augment people's enduring coping resources (Aspinwall, 1998, 2001; Isen, 1990). In turn, by building this psychological resource, positive emotions should enhance people's subsequent emotional well-being. Consistent with this view, studies have shown that people who experience positive emotions during bereavement are more likely to develop long-term plans and goals. Together with positive emotions, plans and goals predict greater psychological well-being 12 months postbereavement (Stein, Folkman, Trabasso, & Richards, 1997; for related work, see Bonanno & Keltner, 1997).

The suspected reciprocal relations between positive emotions, broadened thinking, and positive meaning suggest that, over time, the effects of positive emotions should accumulate and compound: The broadened attention and cognition triggered by earlier experiences of positive emotion should facilitate coping with adversity, and this improved coping should predict future experiences of positive emotion. As this cycle continues, people build their psychological resilience and enhance their emotional well-being.

The cognitive literature on depression has already documented a *downward spiral* in which depressed mood and the narrowed, pessimistic thinking it engenders influence one another reciprocally, over time leading to ever worsening moods, and even clinical levels of depression (Peterson & Seligman, 1984). The broaden-and-build theory predicts a comparable *upward spiral* in which positive emotions and the broadened thinking they engender also influence one another reciprocally, leading to appreciable increases in emotional well-being over time. Positive emotions may trigger these upward spirals, in part, by building resilience and influencing the ways people cope with adversity. (For a complementary discussion of upward spirals, see Aspinwall, 1998, 2001.)

Fredrickson and Joiner (2002) conducted an initial prospective test of the hypothesis that, through cognitive broadening, positive emotions produce an upward spiral toward enhanced emotional well-being. Positive and negative emotions were assessed, as well as a concept called broad-minded coping, at two time points, 5 weeks apart. Broad-minded coping was tapped by items such as "Think of different ways to deal with the problem" and "Try to step back from the situation and be more objective."

Data revealed clear evidence for an upward spiral. Individuals who experienced more positive emotions than others became, over time, more resilient to adversity, as indexed by increases in broad-minded coping. These enhanced coping skills, in turn, predicted increased positive emotions over time (Fredrickson & Joiner, 2002).

These findings suggest that positive emotions and broad-minded coping mutually build on one another: Positive emotions not only make people feel good in the present, but also—through their effects on broadened thinking—increase the likelihood that people will feel good in the future. Because broad-minded coping is a form of psychological resilience, these data are consistent with the prediction, drawn from the broaden-and-build theory, that momentary experiences of positive emotion can build enduring psychological resources and trigger upward spirals toward enhanced emotional well-being.

SUMMARY AND CONCLUSIONS

The broaden-and-build theory (Fredrickson, 1998, 2001) posits that positive emotions are useful in several ways. They guide present behavior, by broadening one's attention and cognition, setting the stage for creative, explorative, and innovative pursuits. Moreover, positive emotions build personal and social resources to help individuals achieve better lives in the future. Like the broaden-and-build theory, emotional intelligence theory marks the intersection between two fundamental components of psychology: the cognitive and the emotional systems. By linking the two theories, it becomes apparent that the knowledge and use of positive emotions constitute an important skill set for effective personal and social functioning.

Given the beneficial effects of positive emotions and emotional intelligence on physical and psychological well-being, it may be useful to modify current theories of emotional intelligence to include a discussion of positive emotions. To date, most research and theory about emotional intelligence focuses on recognizing, understanding, and managing *negative* emotions in the service of effective interpersonal and intrapersonal functioning, with little mention of how *positive* emotions may be important to the construct of emotional intelligence. However, as we have shown in this chapter, the ability to recognize and use positive emotions to manage negative circumstances can have beneficial effects on one's well-being. Thus, understanding these benefits and using positive emotions to one's advantage during times of stress may exemplify emotional intelligence.

It is likely that an emotionally intelligent person can fully appreciate the advantages of positive emotions. One of the main determinants of the intelligent management of emotions is having access to one's own emotional life (Mayer & Salovey, 1993). This involves the ability to draw on one's feelings as means of understanding and guiding one's behavior. However, our data also suggest that emotionally intelligent skills may be taught and interventions developed to promote them. In other words, a person may learn to develop internal models of emotion that include standards of effective emotional functioning. More specifically, interventions may be used to teach individuals how to utilize effectively their knowledge of positive emotions at opportune moments to optimize their well-being as well as their personal and social growth.

In sum, investigating the broaden-and-build theory of positive emotions in conjunction with emotional intelligence theory provides greater insight into the reasons that certain emotionally intelligent individuals are able to effectively function within society while others may not fare as well. These individuals may possess complex understandings of their positive emotions and use this knowledge to adapt resourcefully in response to negative stimuli. It is also conceivable that emotionally intelligent individuals proactively cultivate positive emotions as paths toward development and growth, a direct implication of the broaden-

and-build theory. Thus, positive emotions are key resources that should be recognized for their worth—although positive emotions are a part of everyday life, they are not merely experiences that produce momentary pleasures. Indeed, they also appear essential for effective and optimal personal and social functioning.

REFERENCES

Affleck, G., & Tennen, H. (1996). Construing benefits from adversity: Adaptaional significance and dispositional underpinnings. *Journal of Personality, 64,* 899–922.

Ashby, F. G., Isen, A. M., & Turken, A. U. (1999). A neurophysological theory of positive affect and its influence on cognition. *Psychological Review, 106,* 529–550.

Aspinwall, L. G. (1998). Rethinking the role of positive affect in self-regulation. *Motivation and Emotion: Special Issue: Positive Affect and Self-Regulation: I, 22,* 1–32.

Aspinwall, L. G. (2001). Dealing with adversity: Self-regulation, coping, adaptation, and health. In A. Tesser & N. Schwarz (Eds.), *The Blackwell handbook of social psychology: Vol. 1. Intrapersonal processes* (pp. 591–614). Malden, MA: Blackwell.

Billings, D. W., Folkman, S., Acree, M., & Moskowitz, J. T. (2000). Coping and physical health during caregiving: The roles of positive and negative affect. *Journal of Personality and Social Psychology, 79,* 131–142.

Block, J., & Kremen, A. M. (1996). IQ and ego-resiliency: Conceptual and empirical connections and separateness. *Journal of Personality and Social Psychology, 70,* 349–361.

Bonanno, G. A., & Keltner, D. (1997). Facial expressions of emotion and the course of conjugal bereavement. *Journal of Abnormal Psychology, 106,* 126–137.

Calhoun, L. G., & Tedeschi, R. G. (2001). Posttraumatic growth: The positive lessons of loss. In R. A. Neimeyer (Ed.), *Meaning reconstruction and the experience of loss.* (pp. 157–172). Washington, DC: American Psychological Association.

Canino, I. A. (1995). Coping with stress through art: A program for urban minority children. In H. W. Harris, H. C. Blue, & E. H. Griffith (Eds.), *Racial and ethnic identity: Psychological development and creative expression.* New York: Routledge.

Carver, C. S. (1998). Resilience and thriving: Issues, models and linkages. *Journal of Social Issues, 54,* 245–266.

Cohler, B. J. (1987). Adversity, resilience, and the study of lives. In E. J. Anthony & B. J. Cohler (Eds.), *The invulnerable child.* (pp. 363–424). New York: Guilford Press.

Davis, C. G., Nolen-Hoeksema, S., & Larson, J. (1998) Making sense of loss and benefiting from experience: Two construals of meaning. *Journal of Personality and Social Psychology, 75,* 561–574.

Demos. E. V. (1989). Resiliency in infancy. In T. F. Dugan & R. Cole (Eds.), *The child in our times: Studies in the development of resiliency* (pp. 3–22). Philadelphia: Brunner/Mazel.

Eifert, G. H., & Wilson, P. H. (1991). The triple response approach to assessment: A conceptual and methodological reappraisal. *Behaviour Research and Therapy, 29,* 283–292.

Estrada, C. A., Isen, A. M., & Young, M. J. (1997). Positive affect facilitates integration of information and decreases anchoring in reasoning among physicians. *Organizational Behavior and Human Decision Processes, 72,* 117–135.

Feldman Barrett, L., & Gross, J. (2001). Emotional intelligence: A process model of emotion representation and regulation. In T. Mayne & G. Bonanno (Eds.), *Emotions: Current issues and future directions* (pp. 286–310). New York: Guilford Press.

Folkman, S. (1997). Positive psychological states and coping with severe stress. *Social Science and Medicine, 45,* 1207–1221.

Folkman, S., Lazarus, R. S., Dunkel-Schetter, C., DeLongis, A., & Gruen, R. (1986). Dynamics of a stressful encounter: Cognitive appraisal, coping, and encounter outcomes. *Journal of Personality and Social Psychology, 50,* 992–1003.

Folkman, S., & Moskowitz, J. T. (2000). Positive affect and the other side of coping. *American Psychologist, 55,* 647–654.

Fredrickson, B. L. (1998). What good are positive emotions? *Review of General Psychology: Special Issue: New Directions in Research on Emotion, 2,* 300–319.

Fredrickson, B. L. (2000a). Cultivating positive emotions to optimize health and well-being. *Prevention and Treatment, 3.* Available on the World Wide Web: *http://journals. apa. org/prevention.*

Fredrickson, B. L. (2000b). Cultivating research on positive emotions. *Prevention and Treatment, 3.* Available on the World Wide Web: *http://journals. apa. org/prevention.*

Fredrickson, B. L. (2001). The role of positive emotions in positive psychology: The broaden-and-build theory of positive emotions. *American Psychologist, 56,* 218–226.

Fredrickson, B. L., & Branigan, C. (2001). *Positive emotions broaden the scope of attention and thought–action repertoires: Evidence for the broaden-and-build model.* Manuscript under review.

Fredrickson, B. L., & Joiner, T. (2002). Positive emotions trigger upward spirals toward emotional well-being. *Psychological Science, 13,* 172–175.

Fredrickson, B. L., & Levenson, R. W. (1998). Positive emotions speed recovery from the cardiovascular sequelae of negative emotions. *Cognition and Emotion, 12,* 191–220.

Fredrickson, B. L., Mancuso, R. A., Branigan, C., & Tugade, M. M. (2000). The undoing effect of positive emotions. *Motivation and Emotion, 24,* 237–258.

Isen, A. M. (1987). Positive affect, cognitive processes, and social behavior. *Advances in Experimental Social Psychology, 20,* 203–253.

Isen, A. M. (1990). The influence of positive and negative affect on cognitive organization: Some implications for development. In N. L. Stein, B. Leventhal, & T. Trabasso. (Eds.), *Psychological and biological approaches to emotion* (pp. 75–94). Hillsdale, NJ: Erlbaum.

Isen, A. M., & Daubman, K. A. (1984). The influence of affect on categorization. *Journal of Personality and Social Psychology, 47,* 1206–1217.

Isen, A. M., Daubman, K. A., & Nowicki, G. P. (1987). Positive affect facilitates creative problem solving. *Journal of Personality and Social Psychology, 52,* 1122–1131.

Isen, A. M., Johnson, M. M. S., Mertz, E., & Robinson, G. F. (1985). The influence of positive affect on the unusualness of word associations. *Journal of Personality and Social Psychology, 48,* 1413–1426.

Janoff-Bulman, R. (1992). *Shattered assumptions: Towards a new psychology of trauma.* New York: Free Press.

Kahn, B. E., & Isen, A. M. (1993). The influence of positive affect on variety seeking among safe, enjoyable products. *Journal of Consumer Research, 20,* 275–270.

Klohnen, E. C. (1996). Conceptual analysis and measurement of the construct of ego-resiliency. *Journal of Personality and Social Psychology, 70,* 1067–1079.

Kumpfer, K. L. (1999). Factors and processes contributing to resilience: The resilience framework. In M. D. Glantz & J. L. Johnson (Eds.), *Resilience and development: Positive life adaptations* (pp. 179–224). New York: Kluwer Academic/Plenum Publishers.

Kuyken, W., & Brewin, C. R. (1994). Stress and coping in depressed women. *Cognitive Therapy and Research, 18,* 403–412.

Lazarus, R. S. (1993). From psychological stress to the emotions: A history of changing outlooks. *Annual Review of Psychology, 44,* 1–21.

Lazarus, R. S., & Folkman, S. (1984). *Stress, appraisal and coping.* New York: Springer.

Lazarus, R. S., Kanner, A. D., & Folkman, S. (1980). Emotions: A cognitive-phenomenological analysis. In R. Plutchik & H. Kellerman (Eds.), *Theories of emotion* (pp. 189–217). New York: Academic Press.

Martin, R. A., & Lefcourt, H. M. (1983). Sense of humor as a moderator of the relation between stressors and moods. *Journal of Personality and Social Psychology, 45,* 1313–1324.

Masten, A. S., Best, K. M., & Garmezy, N. (1990). Resilience and development: Contributions from the study of children who overcome adversity. *Development and Psychopathology, 2,* 425–444.

Mayer, J. D., & Salovey, P. (1993). The intelligence of emotional intelligence. *Intelligence, 17,* 433–442.

Moos, R. H. (1988). *Coping responses inventory manual.* Palo Alto, CA: Stanford University and Department of Veterans Affairs Medical Centers.

Moskowitz, J. T., Folkman, S., Collette, L, & Vittinghoff, E. (1996). Coping and mood during AIDS-related caregiving and bereavement. *Annals of Behavioral Medicine, 18,* 49–57.

Murphy, L. B., & Moriarty, A. E. (1976). *Vulnerability, coping and growth from infancy to adolescence.* New Haven: Yale University Press.

Nezu, A. M., Nezu, C. M., & Blissett, S. E. (1988). Sense of humor as a moderator of the relation between stressful events and psychological distress: A prospective analysis. *Journal of Personality and Social Psychology, 54,* 520–525.

Park, C. L, & Folkman, S. (1997). Meaning in the context of stress and coping. *Review of General Psychology, 1,* 115–144.

Peterson, C., & Seligman, M. E. P. (1984). Causal explanations as a risk factor for depression: Theory and evidence. *Psychological Review, 91,* 347–374.

Predeger, E. (1996). Womanspirit: A journey into healing through art in breast cancer. *Advances in Nursing Science, 18,* 48–58.

Reed, M. B., & Aspinwall, L. G. (1998). Self-affirmation reduces biased processing of health-risk information. *Motivation and Emotion: Special Issue: Positive Affect and Self-Regulation, 22,* 99–132.

Rutter, M. (1987). Psychosocial resilience and protective mechanisms. *American Journal of Orthopsychiatry, 57,* 316–331.

Saarni, C. (1999). *The development of emotional competence.* New York: Guilford Press.

Salovey, P., Bedell, B. T., Detweiler, J. B., & Mayer, J. D. (1999). Coping intelligently: Emotional intelligence and the coping process. In C. R. Snyder (Ed.), *Coping: The psychology of what works* (pp. 141–164). New York: Oxford University Press.

Salovey, P., Hsee, C. K., & Mayer, J. D. (1993). Emotional intelligence and the self-regulation of affect. In D. M. Wegner & J. W. Pennebaker (Eds.), *Handbook of mental control* (pp. 258–277). Upper Saddle River, NJ: Prentice-Hall.

Salovey, P., & Mayer, J. D. (1989–1990). Emotional intelligence. *Imagination, Cognition and Personality, 9,* 185–211.

Stein, N. L., Folkman, S., Trabasso, T., & Richards, T. A. (1997). Appraisal and goal processes as predictors of psychological well-being in bereaved caregivers. *Journal of Personality and Social Psychology, 72,* 872–884.

Taylor, S. E. (1983). Adjustment to threatening events: A theory of cognitive adaptation. *American Psychologist, 38,* 1161–1173.

Taylor, S. E., Kemeny, M. E., Reed, G. M., Bower, J. E., & Gruenewald, T. L. (2000). Psychological resources, positive illusions, and health. *American Psychologist, 55,* 99–109.

Tedeschi, R. G., Park, C. L., & Calhoun, L. G. (1998). *Posttraumatic growth: Positive changes in the aftermath of crisis.* Mahwah, NJ: Erlbaum.

Tennen, H., & Affleck, G. (1999). Finding benefits in adversity. In C. R. Snyder (Ed.), *Coping: The psychology of what works* (pp. 279–304). New York: Oxford University Press.

Tomaka, J., Blascovich, J., Kibler, J., & Ernst, J. M. (1997). Cognitive and physiological antecedents of threat and challenge appraisal. *Journal of Personality and Social Psychology, 73,* 63–72.

Trope, Y., & Neter, E. (1994). Reconciling competing motives in self-evaluation: The role of self-control in feedback seeking. *Journal of Personality and Social Psychology, 66,* 646–657.

Trope, Y., & Pomerantz, E. M. (1998). Resolving conflicts among self-evaluative motives: Positive experiences as a resource for overcoming defensiveness. *Motivation and Emotion, 22,* 53–72.

Tugade, M. M., & Fredrickson, B. L. (2002). *Resilient individuals use positive emo-*

tions to bounce back from negative emotional experiences. Manuscript under review.

Ulrich, R. S., Dimberg, U., & Driver, B. L. (1991). Psychophysiological indicators of leisure benefits. In B. L. Driver, P. J. Brown, & G. L. Peterson (Eds.), *Benefits of leisure.* State College, PA: Venture Publishing.

Werner, E., & Smith, R. S. (1992). *Overcoming the odds: High risk children from birth to adulthood.* Ithaca: Cornell University Press.

Wolin, S. J., & Wolin, S. (1993). *Bound and determined: Growing up resilient in a troubled family.* New York: Villard Press.

The Functional Utility of Negative Emotions

W. GERROD PARROTT

The idea that negative emotions can be functional may seem odd or even self-contradictory. Yet it is the thesis of this chapter that negative emotions can indeed be useful and even desirable, and that emotional intelligence includes recognizing and exploiting this utility. If this thesis seems strange, it is probably because of two assumptions that are often made about emotions: first, that emotions are principally feelings, and second, that people are principally hedonistic. These assumptions are fairly common; they are often made both by academics studying emotion and by laypersons in many Western societies. The assumption that emotions are feelings construes negative emotions as unpleasant feelings and positive emotions as pleasant feelings. The assumption of hedonism construes people as seeking pleasure and avoiding pain. The combination of these two assumptions yields the conclusion that people will be motivated to avoid or eliminate negative emotions and to seek or maintain positive emotions.

These two assumptions, however, are at best incomplete and are in some ways outright misleading. There is more to emotions than pleasant or unpleasant feelings, and there is more to human decision making than hedonism (Parrott, 1993). Enlarging one's conception of emotions and decision making alters one's understanding of the functions of negative emotions, and thus of emotional intelligence. Negative emotions have considerable potential to be useful. For this potential to be realized, however, these emotions must appear under the right circumstances, be expressed in ways that are productive in the current situation, be regulated so that their intensity and manifestations are appropriate, and be restrained under circumstances in which they are not helpful. Emotional intelligence, as it is now conceived, entails all of these determinants of functional utility.

This chapter addresses each of these points in turn. The first section describes the nature of emotions, with particular attention to negative emotions. It demonstrates that emotions entail much more than feelings: One's appraisal of one's situation, one's readiness to think and act, and one's effect on others are all modified during emotional states. The next section argues that these properties of negative emotions give them the potential to have functional utility. The rest of the chapter considers how this potential utility can best be realized. I describe a variety of factors that help determine the functional utility of emotions, and show that emotional intelligence is directly related to some of them but only indirectly related to others.

THE NATURE OF NEGATIVE EMOTIONS

Emotions can be understood as involving a constellation of features. These features include an appraisal, readiness to think and act in certain ways, physiological changes, and social signals and dispositions, as well as feelings. The functional utility of emotions is grounded in these changes, so understanding this utility requires appreciation of each of these aspects of emotion.

An appraisal is an assessment of how present circumstances influence one's goals and well-being. An appraisal is cognitive in the sense that it involves meaning and interpretation, but not in the sense that it need be deliberate, verbal, or symbolic. Thus, appraisal is cognitive in a way that is more like perception than like reasoning or knowledge. Appraisal also differs from other types of cognition in that it concerns the personal significance of an event, action, or object, rather than general information about it. It is the implications for one's own cares, concerns, goals, values, or well-being that are appraised (see Frijda, 1986; Lazarus, 1991; Ortony, Clore, & Collins, 1988). Theories of emotional appraisal contend that it is our interpretation of events that determines whether and in what way we become emotional. In other words, appraisals are typically the cause of emotions. Appraisal theories also typically contend that appraisals are an intrinsic part of emotions; they do not merely precede emotions. Part of what it means to have an emotion is to perceive one's circumstances along the lines of the appraisal integral to that emotion (Frijda, 1986; Lazarus, 1991).

Appraisals provide an alternative to feelings for understanding why some emotions are considered "negative" whereas others are considered "positive." Negative emotions—such as fear, sadness, shame, anger, contempt, guilt, disgust, anxiety, disappointment, embarrassment, loneliness, envy, and hatred—share the property of involving an appraisal that something is wrong. One's well-being is threatened, one's goals have to be abandoned, one lacks what one desires, one views oneself as doing wrong or as not projecting the desired appearance to others, and so on. In contrast, positive emotions—happiness, gratitude, pride, love, relief, hope, and so on—involve appraisals that one is meeting one's goals, that a bad event has not come to pass, that one is meeting or exceeding one's own standards, that one's relationship with another is secure, and so on. From this perspective, positive and negative emotions are not so much pleasant and unpleasant hedonic states as they are favorable or unfavorable assessments of one's present circumstances. For this reason even the feeling of emotion involves more than merely pleasure or pain. Emotional feelings may serve as information about one's present state of affairs and may color decision making about how to allocate one's mental and physical resources (Clore & Parrott, 1991; Oatley, 1992; Schwarz, 1990).

In addition to appraisals and feelings, emotions are associated with increased readiness to engage in various kinds of actions and thinking. For example, many negative emotions, such as anxiety and disgust, create a readiness to move away from an object or a threat. Other negative emotions, such as anger and contempt, involve a readiness to oppose or attack. Self-conscious negative emotions such as shame and embarrassment involve a tendency for social withdrawal, whereas emotions such as sadness and sorrow tend to involve giving up opposition to a disliked circumstance or abandoning a goal (Frijda, Kuipers, & ter Schure, 1989). These action tendencies are manifested in a variety of ways. There may be a lower threshold for initiating certain types of action: The fearful person is "jumpy," the irritated person is "snappish," the sad person is subdued and withdrawn. Action tendencies must be defined fairly abstractly; although there are sometimes particular actions that are primed, the tendency is often more general, such as "opposition" or "escape."

Many of the physiological aspects of emotions can be understood as aspects of action readiness. Some emotions involve activation of the sympathetic nervous system—increased heart rate and blood pressure, changes in blood flow, breathing, perspiration, and so on—and these can be understood as preparing the body for physical exertion (Cannon, 1929). Hormonal changes, such as increases in epinephrine, adrenocorticotropic hormone, or corticosteroids, mobilize energy resources and thus also prepare for action (Selye, 1956). Although there is not a clear patterning of physiology that corresponds to particular emotions, physiological changes do seem to correspond to require-ments arising in coping with environmental demands and thus with preparation for action (Frijda, 1986; Ginsburg & Harrington, 1996).

Emotional action tendencies are not limited to physical actions, but include various types of mental readiness as well. The allocation of attention is one mental action that is strongly influenced by emotional states. Anxiety, for example, involves a tendency to be vigilant for threats. Attention is more quickly directed toward threatening stimuli when a person is anxious than when not (Mogg & Bradley, 1999). More generally, negative emotions allocate attention and other cognitive re-sources to plans and goals that need them most urgently (Oatley, 1992). The content of thought can also be biased by emotion. Memory for past events may be skewed toward memories that are congruent with the emotional state, as when a sad person recalls unhappy times or when an angry person recalls previous transgressions (Blaney, 1986). The way a situation is interpreted may also be biased in a way that is congruent with a person's present emotional state, as when a statement or behavior is interpreted differently by sad and happy people (Bower, 1991; Forgas, 1995). Emotions influence not only attention and the content of thought, but the style of thinking as well. Negative emotions have been found to predispose people to adopt a conservative ap-proach to problem solving: careful, methodical, and analytical. Positive emotions have been associated with a more holistic style that is less pre-cise and detail oriented but also more creative, risky, and flexible (Isen, 2000; Schwarz & Bless, 1991).

In addition to their effects on the individuals experiencing the emotions, their effects on others can be seen as well. Emotions may be expressed by facial expression, posture, or voice, and these expressions influence other people in a variety of ways. One person's emotion can influence other people to have the same emotion, so that the emotion spreads from one person to another (Hatfield, Cacioppo, & Rapson, 1994). One person's emotion can also induce a complementary emo-tion in another, as when one person's anger induces another person's fear, or one person's gratitude induces another person's pride (e.g., Dimberg & Ohman, 1996).

The display of emotions is intimately intertwined with cultural norms and meanings, so many effects of emotions can be appreciated only within the context of a particular culture and social setting. Cul-tures tend to treat emotions objectively, in the sense that there are pub-lic standards regarding when certain emotions are allowed, reasonable, or appropriate (Sabini & Silver, 1982). To perform many jobs and so-cial roles correctly, it is necessary to display the correct emotion in the correct manner on the correct occasion (Hochschild, 1979). For these reasons there are social costs and benefits to emotions that are specific to particular cultures and social settings, and these must be considered along with an emotion's other effects.

Although the emphasis of this argument has been to show that emotions consist of more than feelings, it is worth noting that feelings themselves may have functional utility. According to some theorists, emotional feelings function by providing feedback about one's appraisals. Although the details of the appraisals themselves may not be directly accessible to consciousness, emotional feelings may provide a conscious representation of the personal significance of events (Clore & Parrott, 1991; Schwarz, 1990). Moods and emotions may also signal whether the individual presently has the resources to cope with the demands being placed on him or her (Fredrickson, 1998; Morris, 1992).

In summary, emotions modify appraisals of circumstances, preparations for various modes of action and thought, feelings, and expressions and behaviors that influence the emotions and behavior of others. Emotions thus consist of far more than feelings; in fact, many feelings of emotion may be at least partly the result of these other emotional changes (Parrott, 1995). It is because emotions affect people in so many ways that it is possible for them to have functional consequences. The next section presents an outline of these consequences and how they can be either adaptive or maladaptive.

THE FUNCTIONAL (AND DYSFUNCTIONAL) UTILITY OF NEGATIVE EMOTIONS

Negative emotions have the potential for functional utility because there are times when the effects of negative emotions are useful. Recognizing this potential for benefit is the key to understanding why it is neither odd nor self-contradictory to claim that negative emotions can be useful or even desirable. In the simplest case, emotions will have utility if their effects tend to be beneficial under the conditions associated with each emotion's appraisal. For example, anger involves a readiness to be confrontational and antagonistic, and to the extent that confrontation and antagonism are adaptive under conditions that induce anger, this readiness will facilitate adaptive behavior. Similarly, fear involves a readiness to protect oneself and to move away from danger, and disgust involves expulsion and maintaining distance; to the extent that these actions tend to be adaptive under conditions that induce fear and disgust, these emotions too will tend to have functional utility.

The preceding examples illustrate how emotional readiness for physical action can have utility. The other effects of negative emotions also have the potential to function beneficially. For example, reallocating attention can be very functional: In anxiety it enables one to be vigilant for threats; in jealousy it leads one to monitor relationships that may have been taken for granted; in shame it can lead one to monitor others' opinions and to reestablish one's reputation. Negative emotions lead to reallocation of limited mental resources to the goals and projects that most need one's attention (Oatley, 1992).

Emotion's effects on style of thinking have the potential to be useful as well. Negative emotions occur when something has gone wrong or threatens to go wrong. They occur when there is a problem, when goals are at risk, or when resources seem inadequate. Such times may not be the best for exploring new approaches, nor are they times when one can easily afford a mistake. A careful, analytical approach that avoids risk taking may often be most appropriate in times of threat or stress (Schwarz & Bless, 1991; see also Schwarz, Chapter 6, this volume).

The social effects of negative emotions can have a variety of potential benefits. When informing other people of an emergency, a person is more likely to obtain energetic assistance if that person expresses alarm than if he or she appears calm and matter-of-fact. It makes the urgent nature of the situation more real to others and may induce a similar emotion in them, which may in turn facilitate their actions (Hatfield et al., 1994). Such contagion of negative emotions has the potential to produce benefits for the person initiating the social sequence.

The social effects of negative emotions can also be useful when they induce complementary emotions in others. For example, the anger expressed by a bill collector may be effective if it intimidates and scares a customer into paying a bill out of fear of legal and social consequences. Bill collectors who use anger to obtain these social effects are more effective than those who do not (Hochschild, 1983).

Finally, emotional feelings can themselves have functional utility. Their function is often conceived as one of providing information. Emotional feelings can be a source of information about something as specific as a person's attitude toward an object or individual or as general as a person's overall state of well-being (Schwarz, 1990). Although the complexity of evaluating information about a person or event may be too great to be held in conscious awareness, the outcome of one's unconscious appraisal may be learned by paying attention to resulting emotional feelings (Clore & Parrott, 1991). Just as the visual perception of size can be the result of a complex calculation yet be immediately experienced, so too may emotional feelings directly provide information about one's construal of a complex situation as it pertains to one's concerns and resources to cope (Morris, 1992).

In summary, the mental, physical, social, and experiential effects of negative emotions have the *potential* to be adaptive and useful. Whether this potential for usefulness in actualized in everyday life is determined by a variety of factors. Just because negative emotions *can* be adaptive does not mean that they are. The thesis of this chapter is that emotional intelligence is associated with some of the determinants of emotions' functional utility. Exploring this thesis requires that we have some understanding of how emotions produce their effects and why these effects are sometimes functional and other times are not. These two topics turn out to be related, so they will be discussed together next, along with their relation to the concept of emotional intelligence.

EMOTIONAL INTELLIGENCE AND THE DETERMINANTS OF EMOTIONAL FUNCTION AND DYSFUNCTION

To understand how negative emotions can function adaptively, it is useful to consider how they can function maladaptively. It is often easier to notice something when it is causing a problem than when it is working smoothly. When I recently analyzed a sample of dysfunctional emotions (both positive and negative), I identified several factors that commonly determine whether an emotion would be functional or dysfunctional (Parrott, 2001). Appreciating how these factors play a role in causing emotions to be counterproductive is a helpful way to appreciate how they can contribute to producing productive emotions.

Regulation of Intensity

One determinant of an emotion's functionality is the intensity of the emotion. For example, fear can be useful both for fleeing from a predator and for studying for an exam, but not at the same intensity. In the case of fleeing from a predator, a high intensity of fear is useful because frantic action can assist in rapid and energetic escape. In the case of studying, although one can benefit from the mental focus and aversion to distraction that fear provides, such benefits can be overridden by excessive agitation, by motivation to escape the tension in ways other than by studying, and by a progression from excessive fear to hopelessness. In both cases, the fear will be most beneficial if it is regulated to an intensity that is useful for the situation at hand. In some fearful situations, say fear of major surgery that one is about to undergo, there may be nothing at all that the fear can accomplish, and indeed there may only be harm. In such cases, the best emotion management may be to reduce the fear as much as possible and to cultivate positive emotions instead (Cohen & Lazarus, 1973).

Regulation of intensity is perhaps the simplest aspect of self-management of emotion, but its simplicity makes it a good starting point for asking how the concept of emotional intelligence may apply as a determinant of emotional functioning. As formulated by Mayer and Salovey (1997), emotional intelligence is composed of four "branches." The lowest branch involves the ability to perceive emotions accurately in oneself and in others, as well as to express emotions. The second branch pertains to the ways in which emotion guides thinking, such as by prioritizing thinking, directing attention, serving as information about one's attitudes and concerns, and altering one's approach to problem solving. The third aspect of emotional intelligence has to do with one's knowledge of emotions. The fourth and highest branch has to do with self-regulation: the ability to adjust one's emotional state depending on the requirements of the present situation. This fourth branch is clearly relevant to the management of emotional intensity. For negative emotions to function adaptively, their intensity must be regulated so as to be sufficient to produce benefits but not so excessive that they interfere with the task at hand.

The reason that Mayer and Salovey (1997) conceptualized this branch as the "highest" branch of emotional intelligence is that it is the most complex and, in their view, the most reflective and conscious. Although they do not seem to consider higher branches as being based on lower branches, effective self-regulation seems to require abilities from the other branches of emotional intelligence. It seems likely that a woman who is good at appropriately regulating the intensity of her emotions would also be good at perceiving her emotions (Branch 1), at understanding how emotions influence her thinking (Branch 2), and at knowing how emotions progress from one state to another (Branch 3). Such abilities and knowledge appear to be very useful in knowing how best to manage one's emotions. Interestingly, there is now evidence that these subtypes of emotional intelligence correlate. Research on the Multifactor Emotional Intelligence Scale (MEIS) has found that measures of Branch 4 correlate about $r = .5$ with measures of Branch 1, and about $r = .3$ with measures of Branches 2 and 3 (Mayer, Caruso, & Salovey, 1999).

Management of Type of Emotion

More sophisticated emotional management occurs when the type of emotion itself, not merely the intensity of an emotion, is regulated. Such self-management requires a person to be aware of emotional possibilities that are not present and to take steps to achieve the desired emotional state. In the case of negative emotions, such self-management may be hindered by the common contemporary assumptions that people are hedonistic and that emotions are feelings. People nevertheless learn to strive for negative emotions. Some of the reasons for cultivating negative emotions have been foreshadowed by the previous analysis of functional utility, and I have documented elsewhere an extensive list of motives for this striving (Parrott, 1993). A few of these motives are described here to provide a sense of how they relate to emotional intelligence.

Some of the motives, as mentioned earlier, are social. Expressions of negative emotions can inform others that one is unhappy and can elicit offers of sympathy and help. Recall that calls for help are responded to more quickly if one's own negative emotional state is conveyed in the appeal. Negative emotions can also influence others in ways that advance one's goals. Thus, a motive for inducing a negative emotion in oneself is to benefit from these social effects on others.

In addition, experiencing negative emotions oneself can make one more empathetic with unhappy others and appreciate their points of view. When consoling a sad friend, one can take advantage of the cognitive effects of sadness to appreciate better how that friend is experiencing the world and communicate better one's own understanding. This cognitive benefit can supplement the social benefit of appearing concerned and sensitive to the friend's feelings.

This example leads to a further social motive, which concerns cultural rules for emotional expression in public. There are occasions on which it is proper to appear somber (such as at a funeral, in some cultures) or outraged (such as at a protest rally) or afraid (such as when requesting special protection). These expressions are sometimes required by the social setting, sometimes by the particular role one plays within a setting, and sometimes by the rhetorical need to seem sincere. In all these cases, it is not mandatory that one actually experience the emotion, only that one *appear* to experience it. Nevertheless, people often find that actually experiencing the negative emotion is better. It requires less concentration and effort to produce the required effect that way; one benefits from thinking in a style consonant with one's expressions; and one is less likely to make a mistake in expressing the required emotion (Hochschild, 1979; Parrott, 1993).

Other motives for cultivating negative emotions are nonsocial. For example, if one needs to be analytic and cautious, cultivating a moderate level of anxiety may be a sound strategy because it aligns one's motivations and cognitive style with the task at hand. If one finds that one is not working hard enough when in a cheerful, relaxed state, one may steer oneself toward a more angry or anxious mood in order to create a drive and intensity conducive to sustained, focused effort. If one needs to recall facts relevant to a complaint or argument, becoming angry may facilitate memory because of emotion-congruent recall.

Thus, there are cognitive as well as social reasons for seeking out negative emotional states. One may therefore expect emotional intelligence to be related to this ability. Most of the components of emotional intelligence postulated by Mayer and Salovey (1997) appear to be involved in seeking out negative emotional states. Reflective regulation (Branch 4) is central, of course, but most of the other branches appear to be involved as well. Branch 2 includes the ability to generate emotions in oneself in order to benefit from their effects on oneself and on others. Branch 3 taps the appreciation of emotions' meanings and their development over time. One may therefore expect emotional intelligence to be related to individual differences in this type of emotion management.

Managing the Emotional Response

In addition to regulating intensity and seeking negative emotions when they are beneficial, my analysis of dysfunctional emotions suggests another way in which emotional intelligence may be related to emotional management. This third type of management involves modifying emotional responses so that they function beneficially in the particular situation at hand. To understand this type of management and why it is essential, it is important to recognize that the action readiness that accompanies emotions is usually of a broad sort. That is, the readiness for escape that is typically a part of fear can involve quite different actions under different circumstances. Escaping a falling boulder is rather different from escaping a large group of predators—panicked sprinting may work for the former, whereas freezing to avoid detection may be better for the latter. Escaping a falling stock market will not be accomplished by either course, although placing a quick call to one's broker may be a good idea. Fear may facilitate all three escapes, but pointing to a general readiness for escape underexplains how the particular form of escape is brought about. It is not just the choice of running, freezing, or telephoning that is at stake, but the particular manner of each. Whether one turns left or right may matter with the boulder; the fact that a right turn would send one over a 500-meter precipice would be a good thing to remember, for example.

In fact, most emotional action tendencies can be enacted in a variety of ways, and the manner of enactment can strongly influence the emotion's utility (Parrott, 2001). An example such as the falling boulder understates the complexity of human social emotions. For a richer example one may reflect on the variety of ways a person can act out of anger or shame, in which a vast range of actions and subtle nuances of enactment can matter a great deal. For an even richer appreciation of what is at work, one may reflect on acting angry or ashamed when visiting another country where one has only a simple understanding of the local culture, or reflect on the difference between an artful and clumsy expression of anger or shame. The point is that the rules are complex and the social landscape is subtle, and although one can imagine enactments that would have functional utility, one can also easily imagine enactments that would be counterproductive or self-destructive, all motivated by the same emotion.

It is important not only to appreciate that negative emotions can have functional utility, but also to recognize that this utility is not automatic once the appropriate negative emotion has been aroused. Considerable management and intelligence must be brought to bear on the problem at hand (Parrott & Schulkin, 1993). The concept of emotional intelligence may be useful in addressing this issue. The highest branch of emotional intelligence involves reflective management of emotions (Mayer & Salovey, 1997), and it may be productive to conceive of this management as involving the choice and control of emotional responses as well as the choice of emotion and management of its intensity. Other branches contribute to this type of regulation. The ability to read others' expressions accurately (Branch 1) and knowledge of how one emotion transitions to another (Branch 3) are two examples of the components of emotional intelligence that underlie the management of emotional responses.

AUTOMATION AND REGULATION

The importance of emotional management is not always appreciated in contemporary psychology. In the psychological literature one finds two models for understanding how emotions achieve functional utility. The first model construes the effects of emotion as automatic, and their utility as probabilistic. The second model construes the effects of emotions as the outcome of strategy and regulation, and their utility as depending on a series of decisions that occur as emotions unfold. In examining these models, I suggest that each captures part of the truth, but only one makes a place for the types of emotional intelligence discussed in the previous section. The concept of emotional intelligence is more closely related to the model of regulated emotion.

When emotions' functional utility is depicted as a matter of probability, the line of reasoning is as follows: If fear is elicited by an appraisal of danger or threat, and if fear entails physiological and cognitive changes that promote readiness to flee, and if readiness to flee is on average beneficial under circumstances of danger or threat, then fear will on average be adaptive. This probabilistic argument does not require that emotions be regulated. It is entirely compatible with a simple, mechanical view of how emotions work. As long as appraisals are fairly accurate, and as long as emotional reactions are generally beneficial under the conditions that elicit them, then an emotion that simply activates a state of action readiness can have functional utility by improving a person's chances of coping appropriately in the circumstances that confront him or her.

This mechanical view of how emotions work is consistent with some theories of emotion. For example, Johnson-Laird and Oatley describe emotion as "a small and distinctive suite of action plans" (1992, p. 206) "which can invoke the actions of some processors and switch others off. . . . The emotion signal simply propagates globally through the system to set it into one of a small number of emotion modes" (Oatley & Johnson-Laird, 1987, p. 33). On their account, emotions are relatively prepackaged, and when an emotion is activated it switches on its suite of action tendencies.

This probabilistic construal is typical of evolutionary approaches to emotions, too (Tooby & Cosmides, 1990). Negative emotions are viewed as functional if they improve one's odds, if they shift one into a mode of operation that is more likely to be adaptive under the circumstances than are other modes of operation. It is not only the readiness for action that is described by these probabilistic models. All of the effects of emotion can be conceived as part of a "package" that is activated when an emotion occurs. The functional utility of that package is understood in probabilistic terms: It is adaptive in a given environment if on average its benefits exceed its costs.

When introducing the functional utility of negative emotions earlier in this chapter, I mostly used the language of automation; it is simple and direct. Yet despite the convenience, the mechanical view represents an oversimplification. This simplification is apt for some aspects of emotion and can be close enough for some others, but in important ways it is inaccurate to describe human emotions in terms of automatic packages whose function or dysfunction is only a matter of probability. An alternative approach to emotions characterizes them more abstractly as categories of responses that are malleable by context and open to strategy and choice. A variety of theoretical approaches characterize emotions as regulated. For example, some theories depict the symptoms of emotion not as a prepackaged suite, but rather as reactions that can be motivated by an emotional appraisal. According to such accounts, emotional appraisals typically motivate people in certain ways because of the meaning that is projected onto the situation. For example, an anxious man perceives his goals as being threatened; he therefore becomes motivated to be on guard for threats; he perceives himself as unsafe and is unwilling to take risks; he is careful and analytical when solving problems. The reactions occur because of the meaning of the situation, not because a prepackaged reaction has been activated. In principle, a person who is anxious about the consequences of avoiding risk may manifest his or her anxiety by taking more risks, not fewer (Parrott, 1993; Schwarz, 1990).

Schwarz and Clore (1983) also dispute the claim that the cognitive effects of emotion are invariably elicited when an emotion is aroused. In a series of experiments they demonstrated that a mood-congruent bias of judgment does not occur when people believe that the cause of their mood is irrelevant to the judgment they are making. Schwarz and Clore (1983) argue that moods may bias cognition only because of the mediation of an attribution, but not directly. The cognitive symptoms of emotion are viewed as an outcome of attribution and motivation, not as a part of a preassembled package (Parrott, 1993). The automatic model has not been abandoned, because it is consistent with other evidence (e.g., Forgas, 1995), so at present there seems to be a need for both types of models.

Another shortcoming of the automatic model stems from the fact that emotional action readiness is often of a general sort. It has often been suggested that emotions are intermediate between fixed action patterns and completely rational decision making (e.g., de Sousa, 1987; Johnson-Laird & Oatley, 1992). Emotions involve general dispositions such as fleeing, expelling, being vigilant, opposing, or giving up, but, as argued in the previous section, these dispositions underexplain emotional behavior. To where should one flee, and when should one start? How should one go about opposing? Toward what should one be vigilant? Even if these emotional dispositions are "prepackaged," the disposition underspecifies the action to be taken. Further specification and direction must occur before any readiness can result in adaptive action. In Frijda's (1986) theory this point is made explicitly. Frijda argues that emotions are subject to regulation in every stage of their existence. Choices are made about what situations will be entered, about what appraisals will be made, about what motives will exist, and about what responses will occur. Frijda (1986) describes emotions as being "handled," but I prefer to say that emotions are "managed" or "regulated." With any of these terms, it is necessary to clarify that this self-management of emotion need not be either voluntary or conscious. Often it is neither (Parrott, 1993).

According to these theories, more than just probability is involved in determining the functional utility of an emotion. When emotions are viewed as flexible and regulated, their functional utility depends as much on this regulation as it does on the probability that a typical instance of the emotion is useful in the current circumstances.

Each of the two models of emotional utility discussed in this section—probability and regulation—has its place. The probability model fits emotions to the extent that certain features seem constant. The regulation model better captures the ways in which emotions are shaped to fit their circumstances. It is worth noting that under some circumstances the two models become quite similar. For example, under conditions of uncertainty, even the most rational self-regulation must use heuristics and take a guess at the response that has the highest probability of success under the circumstances.

SOME LIMITATIONS OF THE PRESENT CONCEPTION OF EMOTIONAL INTELLIGENCE

In the previous sections I have discussed several determinants of an emotion's functional utility. The three determinants that have been discussed—regulating intensity, deliberately achieving and maintaining a negative emotion where it is appropriate, and managing the emotional response—appear to be related to the concept of emotional intelligence as it has been developed by Mayer and Salovey (1997). In this section I wish to describe several additional determinants of functional utility that do not seem to be as directly associated with emotional intelligence.

The method for identifying these determinants is the same as previously discussed: dysfunctional emotions are compared with functional emotions to determine the factors that influence whether an emotion will function adaptively (Parrott, 2001). However, alongside the three determinants already discussed, there are three others that are less clearly related to emotional intelligence.

The first is the accuracy of the emotional appraisal. Anger may function adaptively when a person has been slighted (Averill, 1979), but if the slight was only imagined and not real, the anger is much more likely to be dysfunctional. Similarly, if one appraises a rejected invitation as a personal rejection by someone with whom one had hoped to establish a serious relationship, the emotion of sadness is likely to follow. This sadness can function adaptively if it leads to abandonment of the goal, analysis of the reasons for failure, and the adoption of more realistic goals. But what if the refusal was not a rejection? What if the person actually *did* have other plans that regrettably could not be cancelled? The sadness is not only unwarranted but likely to be counterproductive. Obviously, no one can completely avoid inaccurate appraisals, but it does seem that there may be individual differences in the overall accuracy of appraisals. For example, consistently inaccurate appraisals for a particular type of emotion is, from a cognitive perspective, the primary symptom of an affective disorder (Beck, 1976).

We should wonder whether an individual difference that is associated with the functional utility of negative emotions is also associated with the concept of emotional intelligence. Unlike the previous determinants of functional utility, this one is not so clearly linked to emotional intelligence. Although it is true that Mayer and Salovey's (1997) Branch 1 is called "perception, appraisal, and expressions of emotion," these authors appear to use "appraisal" to refer to identifying emotions correctly based on their eliciting conditions, not to appraising correctly the eliciting conditions themselves. A person who becomes aware of a bias in his or her appraisals should learn to be wary of certain emotions and to consciously "double-check" when they occur, and that ability would appear to fall under Branch 4, "reflective regulation." Nevertheless, the original bias in appraisal does not seem to be encompassed in Mayer and Salovey's (1997) definition.

Other determinants of emotional function and dysfunction involve the proper allocation of priority to goals. Based on my survey of dysfunctional emotions, it is important for a person to have a good sense of when a goal is important and when it is not, as well as to be able to allocate priority among multiple goals so that his or her emotion is directed toward the goal that is most important and most likely to benefit from attention. That is, emotions do not function adaptively when people become unduly upset about unimportant matters. Furthermore, emotions do not function adaptively when an emotional reaction to a minor goal overrides an emotional reaction to a more important goal. Neither do emotions function adaptively when an emotional reaction to a goal that one cannot influence overrides an emotional reaction to a goal for which one's efforts could make a difference. Having the ability to allocate priorities surely contributes to individual differences in emotional function, yet this ability is not among those in Mayer and Salovey's (1997) definition of emotional intelligence.

Thus, we have components of emotional function that are not contained in the definition of emotional intelligence. What are we to make of this? I think the best conclusion is that we should not expect all of the determinants of function to be part of emotional intelligence. Mayer and Salovey have chosen to try to keep their definition of emotional intelligence from becoming too loose, and I think their strategy is wise. They have done this by insisting that emotional intelligence actually be a kind of intelligence (Mayer et al., 1999). They have restricted this concept from applying to anything and everything that seems linked to the potential benefits of emotions. The price of this precision is that there will be determinants of emotional function that are outside the concept of emotional intelligence. Such determinants may fit the automatic model more than the regulation model.

On the other hand, the appraisals of situations and of goal importance are not exclusively automatic. They have been the topics of philosophical and religious reflection since ancient times and continue to occupy us today (Sorabji, 2000). Such reflections surely constitute what we may call "wisdom," our wisdom about our feelings, and they often include suggestions on how to socialize children and train adults to optimize the utility of their emotions. These reflections and suggestions surely inform what Mayer and Salovey (1997) call "reflective regulation of emotions to promote emotional and intellectual growth" (p. 11)—their description of Branch 4 of emotional intelligence. In this way, wisdom can shape emotion via emotional intelligence.

CONCLUSION

Negative emotions have considerable potential for functional utility. This potential derives from their effects on readiness for physical and mental action, from the information they communicate to self and to others, and from their effects on other people. These effects can be quite beneficial under the conditions that tend to produce negative emotions, for two reasons. One reason is probability: When a situation entails the loss of, or a threat or challenge to, an important goal, the effects of the elicited negative emotion tend to be functional. That is, under circumstances that produce a negative appraisal, the average benefit of the emotion exceeds the average loss based on nothing more than favorable odds. A probabilistic approach to function oversimplifies matters, however, because emotions are not simply present or absent. Rather, they can lead to a variety of actions and expressions, they can occur at various intensities, and they can be sought or resisted. The second reason that emotions can be beneficial has to do with this management and regulation. By managing the type, intensity, and enactment of one's emotional state, a much greater degree of functional utility can be achieved than would be possible by probability alone. These conclusions hold for positive emotions as well.

Emotional intelligence appears to be associated more with the managerial influences than with the probabilistic ones. This is understandable, given that emotional intelligence has been conceived as a type of intelligence. Nevertheless, some of the determinants of functional utility are based on processes that contribute to the probabilistic basis of utility. These include accurate appraisals, a sense of a goal's importance, and the ability to allocate priority among multiple goals. Inasmuch as these abilities fall outside our conception of emotional intelligence, we must conclude that emotional intelligence is but one of many sources of the wisdom in feelings. Yet inasmuch as we see emotional intelligence as applying the most sophisticated human thinking to emotional management, we must conclude that emotional intelligence involves not only the wisdom in feelings, but also the channeling of human wisdom to better shape our feelings.

REFERENCES

Averill, J. R. (1979). Anger. In H. E. Howe Jr. & R. A. Dienstbier (Eds.), *Nebraska symposium on motivation* (Vol. 26, pp. 1–80). Lincoln: University of Nebraska Press.

Beck, A. T. (1976). *Cognitive therapy and the emotional disorders.* New York: International Universities Press.

Blaney, P. H. (1986). Affect and memory: A review. *Psychological Bulletin, 99,* 229–246.

Bower, G. H. (1991). Mood congruity of social judgments. In J. P. Forgas (Ed.), *Emotion and social judgments* (pp. 31–53). Oxford: Pergamon Press.

Cannon, W. B. (1929). *Bodily changes in pain, hunger, fear and rage* (2nd ed.). New York: Appleton.

Clore, G. L., & Parrott, W. G. (1991). Moods and their vicissitudes: Thoughts and feelings as information. In J. P. Forgas (Ed.), *Emotion and social judgments* (pp. 107–123). Oxford: Pergamon Press.

Cohen, F., & Lazarus, R. S. (1973). Active coping processes, coping dispositions, and recovery from surgery. *Psychosomatic Medicine, 35,* 375–389.

de Sousa, R. (1987). *The rationality of emotion.* Cambridge, MA: MIT Press.

Dimberg, U., & Ohman, A. (1996). Behold the wrath: Psychophysiological responses to facial stimuli. *Motivation and Emotion, 20,* 149–182.

Forgas, J. P. (1995). Mood and judgment: The affect infusion model (AIM). *Psychological Bulletin, 117,* 39–66.

Fredrickson, B. L. (1998). What good are positive emotions? *Review of General Psychology, 2,* 300–319.

Frijda, N. H. (1986). *The emotions.* Cambridge, UK: Cambridge University Press.

Frijda, N. H., Kuipers, P., & ter Schure, E. (1989). Relations among emotion, appraisal, and emotional action readiness. *Journal of Personality and Social Psychology, 57,* 212–228.

Ginsburg, G. P., & Harrington, M. E. (1996). Bodily states and context in situated lines of action. In R. Harré & W. G. Parrott (Eds.), *The emotions: Social, cultural and biological dimensions* (pp. 229–258). London: Sage.

Hatfield, E., Cacioppo, J. T., & Rapson, R. L. (1994). *Emotional contagion*. Cambridge, UK: Cambridge University Press.

Hochschild, A. R. (1979). Emotion work, feeling rules, and social structure. *American Journal of Sociology, 85,* 551–575.

Hochschild, A. R. (1983). *The managed heart: The commercialization of human feeling.* Berkeley: University of California Press.

Isen, A. M. (2000). Positive affect and decision making. In M. Lewis & J. M. Haviland-Jones (Eds.), *Handbook of emotions* (2nd ed., pp. 417–435). New York: Guilford Press.

Johnson-Laird, P. N., & Oatley, K. (1992). Basic emotions, rationality, and folk theory. *Cognition and Emotion, 6,* 201–223.

Lazarus, R. S. (1991). *Emotion and adaptation.* New York: Oxford University Press.

Mayer, J. D., Caruso, D. R., & Salovey, P. (1999). Emotional intelligence meets traditional standards for an intelligence. *Intelligence, 27,* 267–298.

Mayer, J. D., & Salovey, P. (1997). What is emotional intelligence? In P. Salovey & D. J. Sluyter (Eds.), *Emotional development and emotional intelligence: Educational implications* (pp. 3–31). New York: Basic Books.

Mogg, K., & Bradley, B. P. (1999). Selective attention and anxiety: A cognitive–motivational perspective. In T. Dalgleish & M. J. Power (Eds.), *Handbook of cognition and emotion* (pp. 145–170). Chichester, UK: Wiley.

Morris, W. N. (1992). A functional analysis of the role of mood in affective systems. In M. S. Clark (Ed.), *Review of personality and social psychology: Vol. 13. Emotion* (pp. 256–293). Newbury Park, CA: Sage.

Oatley, K. (1992). *Best laid schemes: The psychology of emotions.* Cambridge, UK: Cambridge University Press.

Oatley, K., & Johnson-Laird, P. (1987). Towards a cognitive theory of emotions. *Cognition and Emotion, 1,* 29–50.

Ortony, A., Clore, G. L., & Collins, A. (1988). *The cognitive structure of emotions.* Cambridge, UK: Cambridge University Press.

Parrott, W. G. (1993). Beyond hedonism: Motives for inhibiting good moods and for maintaining bad moods. In D. M. Wegner & J. W. Pennebaker (Eds.), *Handbook of mental control* (pp. 278–305). Englewood Cliffs, NJ: Prentice-Hall.

Parrott, W. G. (1995). Emotional experience. In A. S. R. Manstead & M. Hewstone (Eds.), *The Blackwell encyclopedia of social psychology* (pp. 198–203). Oxford: Basil Blackwell.

Parrott, W. G. (2001). The implications of dysfunctional emotions for understanding how emotions function. *Review of General Psychology, 5,* 180–186.

Parrott, W. G., & Schulkin, J. (1993). Psychophysiology and the cognitive nature of the emotions. *Cognition and Emotion, 7,* 43–59.

Sabini, J., & Silver, M. (1982). *Moralities of everyday life.* New York: Oxford University Press.

Schwarz, N. (1990). Feelings as information: Informational and motivational functions of affective states. In R. Sorrentino & E. T. Higgins (Eds.), *Handbook of motivation and cognition* (Vol. 2, pp. 527–561). New York: Guilford Press.

Schwarz, N., & Bless, H. (1991). Happy and mindless, but sad and smart? The impact of affective states on analytic reasoning. In J. P. Forgas (Ed.), *Emotion and social judgments* (pp. 55–71). Oxford: Pergamon Press.

Schwarz, N., & Clore, G. L. (1983). Mood, misattribution, and judgments of well-being: Informative and directive functions of affective states. *Journal of Personality and Social Psychology, 45*, 513–523.

Selye, H. (1956). *The stress of life* (rev. ed.). New York: McGraw-Hill.

Sorabji, R. (2000). *Emotion and peace of mind: From Stoic agitation to Christian temptation.* Oxford: Oxford University Press.

Tooby, J., & Cosmides, L. (1990). The past explains the present: Emotional adaptations and the structure of ancestral environments. *Ethology and Sociobiology, 11*, 375–424.

PART V

Extensions

CHAPTER 15

Toward a Shared Language for Emotion and Emotional Intelligence

JAMES A. RUSSELL
KIMBERLY A. BARCHARD

What is the emotionally intelligent person intelligent about? And what ability does the emotionally intelligent person have? Everyday words like "emotion" and "intelligence" start to answer these questions, but we believe that further progress in the study of emotional intelligence requires a careful analysis of the domain of emotion and of the processes involved in intelligence. "Emotion" and "intelligence" are not scientifically honed concepts but everyday words that evolved for a variety of everyday uses.

In this chapter, our theme is that an understanding of emotional intelligence requires an understanding of emotion. We offer one possible analysis of emotion and discuss how to apply that analysis to understanding the emotional intelligence of an individual. Specifically, we propose here a descriptive framework—concepts for five emotional elements—that can be shared by researchers with different theoretical perspectives on emotion and on emotional intelligence.

We then develop the idea that individuals are more or less intelligent in each of these five elements. Specifically, we discuss individual differences in having, in conceptualizing, in being meta-aware of, and in regulating each of the five elements. These four domains of individual differences can be crossed with the five emotional elements to form a 4 × 5 grid that is a preliminary and (highly) tentative structure of emotional intelligence.

We believe that the time is right for more precise concepts, a more explicit structure, and more testable models in the domain of emotion and emotional intelligence. Toward this end, we offer our definitions and grid as heuristic suggestions. Needless to say, all is subject to improvement, counterproposal, and replacement. Our definitions and structures are not the final word, obviously, but perhaps a step in an interesting direction.

FIVE PSYCHOLOGICAL CONCEPTS TO REPLACE THE TERM "EMOTION"

Unfortunately, there is no agreed-upon account or even definition of the term "emotion" that emotional intelligence researchers can rely on. Indeed, as psychology has developed over the decades, accounts and definitions of emotion have multiplied and diverged. Although everyone knows a clear case of emotion when they see it, no one seems able to locate a clear border between emotions and nonemotions. The concept of emotion has blurry edges, may be culture specific, and is in great need of clarification and perhaps reform. When made operational, it includes reactions ranging from rate of eye-blinking to lifelong love of an offspring. What seem like theoretical or empirical disputes sometimes turn out to be matters of definition.

The word "emotion" brings to mind such examples as fleeing a bear in terror, punching someone's nose in fury, or Romeo eloping with Juliet in love. We eventually consider such events, but we start at a more primitive level of analysis, slowly building our way back to these more prototypical examples. Fleeing the bear and other such prototypical emotions, which we call *emotional episodes,* are the large molecules of interest, but we must first define more elementary particles. By "elementary particles," we mean the most basic units at a psychological level (which we take to complement rather than compete with a neurophysiological level). Table 15.1 lists our five basic concepts.

The five technical concepts for these elements replace the concept of *emotion,* and hereafter we use the term "emotion" as simply a shorthand tag for this list of five technical concepts. The five are prescriptively defined and thus may not capture the way in which either researchers or the person in the street uses the terms we use. Our proposed framework is meant to be as independent as possible of individual theoretical approaches to emotion (including our own). We believe that this framework can assist researchers, even with vastly different theoretical

TABLE 15.1. Five Emotion-Related Terms and Their Prescriptive Definitions

Term	Definition
Objectless Affect	Primitive affective feelings and their associated neurophysiological substrate, not necessarily associated with a particular object
Attributed Affect	Objectless Affect that has been linked to a Specific Object
Perception of Affective Quality	Perception of the capacity of a stimulus to alter Objectless Affect
Emotional Behavior	Any overt activity (instrumental, expressive, physiological) associated with Objectless Affect or Attributed Affect
Emotional Episode	Co-occurrence of the above-listed Events: Objectless Affect attributed to an Object (constituting Attributed Affect), with the Object perceived in terms of Affective Quality and with Emotional Behavior directed at the Object

assumptions, in more clearly stating their areas of agreement and disagreement. Every theory of emotion should find its place somewhere within this framework. Similarly, although our framework derives from past empirical research, we have tried to create a language in which empirically testable propositions can be stated, rather than one with empirical presuppositions.

Objectless Affect

More and more, scholars have come to emphasize that most emotions are *directed at* or are *about* something (here that something is called an Object). To love is to love someone; to be angry is to be angry with someone; to be jealous is to be jealous of someone—at least on most occasions. Nevertheless, some emotion-related states exist without an Object; we refer to these states as "Objectless Affect." An example of Objectless Affect is free-floating anxiety, in which the source of the anxiety is unknown but the feeling exists nonetheless. Everyday examples include feeling tense, calm, alert, depressed, or ebullient—not about anything in particular and for no clear reason.

Objectless Affect consists of raw primitive affective feelings and their neurophysiological substrate. We believe that states of Objectless Affect are an important class and deserve to be isolated and named. Indeed, those theorists who recognize Objectless Affect usually see it as lying at the heart of emotion. Of course, no one uses our term "Objectless Affect." Instead, various terms are used: Objectless Affect is what Thayer (1989) called "activation," what Watson and Tellegen (1985) called "affect," what Morris (1989) called "mood," what Oatley and Johnson-Laird (1987) called "emotion modes," what Izard (1991) called "emotion," what Russell and Feldman Barrett (1999) called "core affect," and what the person on the street calls "a feeling."

Objectless Affect has been approached from two broad perspectives (as has emotion in general): the dimensional and the categorical. The dimensional perspective relies on broad bipolar continua (see Russell & Feldman Barrett, 1999). Various dimensions have been proposed. A very common one is pleasure versus displeasure (closely related to positive–negative, evaluation, approach–avoidance, hedonic tone, and valence). Thus, Objectless Affect includes simply feeling good or bad. Another common dimension is activation versus deactivation (also called activity or arousal). Thus, Objectless Affect includes all those feelings (likely related to proprioceptive feedback) of bodily activation including sweating, muscle tension, fidgeting, butterflies in the stomach, blushing, and the like. It also includes feelings of deactivation such as drowsiness, lethargy, and serenity. Another dimension is stress versus relaxation (contrasting upset and tension with relief and relaxation); Watson and Tellegen (1985) had named this dimension Negative Affect, but recently renamed it Negative Activation (Watson, Wiese, Vaidya, & Tellegen, 1999). Yet another dimension is sadness/depression versus elation and ebullience; Watson and Tellegen (1985) had named this dimension Positive Affect, but recently renamed it Positive Activation.

The number of needed dimensions, their nature, and their relation to each other are topics of current concern. It is fair to say that there is a consensus that the number of dimensions is small. Figure 15.1 shows a recent attempt to reconcile several different models by empirically placing different theorists' dimensions within the same geometric space. In this model, a person always has some Objectless Affect (even if neutral), which can therefore be represented as a point on the map in Figure 15.1. That point ebbs and flows, rarely remaining still.

The categorical perspective describes emotion in terms of discrete (qualitatively distinct) categories. Most theorists assume some fixed number of categories, with the actual number to be discovered through empirical research. Most category theorists focus on Object–directed emotions, but two consider what we call Objectless Affect. Oatley and Johnson-Laird (1987) proposed five discrete categories: happiness, fear, anger, sadness, and disgust. In their account, these five categories

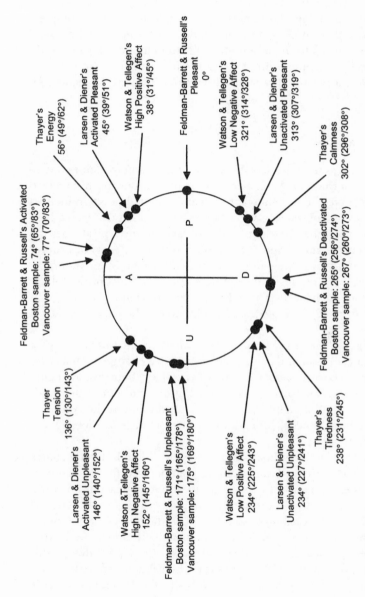

FIGURE 15.1. A circumplex representation of 16 affect construct via CIRCUM. In this representation, two separate analyses are shown superimposed on one another. In both analyses, Pleasant was designated the reference variable and its angle was fixed at 0°; community estimates were constrained to be equivalent for all variables. Figures given are estimates of polar angles (with the 95% confidence interval). *N*s = 198,217. From Yik, Russell, and Feldman Barrett (1999). Copyright 1999 by the American Psychological Association. Reprinted by permission.

Thayer's Energy 56° (49°/62°)

Larsen & Diener's Activated Pleasant 45° (39°/51°)

Watson & Tellegen's High Positive Affect 38° (31°/45°)

Feldman-Barrett & Russell's Pleasant 0°

Watson & Tellegen's Low Negative Affect 321° (314°/328°)

Larsen & Diener's Unactivated Pleasant 313° (307°/319°)

Thayer's Calmness 302° (296°/308°)

Feldman-Barrett & Russell's Deactivated Boston sample: 265° (256°/274°) Vancouver sample: 267° (260°/273°)

Feldman-Barrett & Russell's Activated Boston sample: 74° (65°/83°) Vancouver sample: 77° (70°/83°)

Thayer Tension 136° (130°/143°)

Larsen & Diener's Activated Unpleasant 146° (140°/152°)

Watson &Tellegen's High Negative Affect 152° (145°/160°)

Feldman-Barrett & Russell's Unpleasant Boston sample: 171° (165°/178°) Vancouver sample: 175° (169°/180°)

Watson & Tellegen's Low Positive Affect 234° (225°/243°)

Larsen & Diener's Unactivated Unpleasant 234° (227°/241°)

Thayer's Tiredness 238° (231°/245°)

are basic primitive modes of the brain, occur without an Object, and are the basis of all emotions. Interestingly, Izard (1991) also defined "emotion" in a way that fits our definition of Objectless Affect. For example, Izard considered the state of being sad at the death of someone (in our terms, an Attributed Affect) as an emotion–cognition complex: The sadness is the emotion, and "at the death of someone" is a cognitive structure joined to the emotion. Thus, the emotion per se is without an Object, but acquires one by joining with a cognitive structure. In Izard's theory, a person always has at least one of these Objectless Affects.

Attributed Affect

Although changes in Objectless Affect are caused, a person does not always know what the causes are. There are many reasons for this: Objectless Affect is subject to too many internal and external causal influences to track, and some of the causes are beyond one's ability to detect. Nevertheless, one searches for causal links. Indeed, in the typical case, the search is accurate and simple. One looks up to see a gorgeous sunset and feels genuine pleasure—the pleasure is immediately and automatically attributed to the sunset. We define Attributed Affect by the following properties, each necessary and together sufficient: (1) change in Objectless Affect, (2) an Object, and (3) linking of the Objectless Affect to the Object.

By "link" we mean the process (conscious or unconscious, quick and automatic, or slow and controlled) by which a change in Objectless Affect comes to be associated with an Object. Many theorists have come to think of this linking process as an attribution (and hence the possibility of misattribution) and thus to place attribution at the center of emotion (Keltner, Locke, & Audrain, 1993; Schwarz & Clore, 1983; Weiner, 1985).

Although we define it in a complex way, Attributed Affect includes all commonly experienced and seemingly simple affective reactions to something: feeling happy at a success, sad at a loss, upset at a frustration, enthusiastic at an opportunity, lethargic because of influenza, or bored by a dull film. Attributed Affect is also at the heart of other, more complex emotion-related events. For example, many motives fit the definition of Attributed Affect: One feels displeasure and attributes the displeasure to a deprivation. Most important, Attributed Affect is at the heart of Emotional Episodes; more on this shortly. Attributed Affect is not defined by overt instrumental behavior, although, obviously, the two are linked empirically.

Perception of Affective Quality

When a person opens his or her eyes on the world, a myriad of events and objects appear, and each one has not only sensory, perceptual, and cognitive properties but affective properties as well. For example, a person may find a sunset beautiful, an odor offensive, a melody soothing, a taste delicious, a person boring, an idea exciting, and the temperature of a room uncomfortable. Most objects or events in the world are pleasant or unpleasant, upsetting or relaxing, exciting or depressing. Such words point to the capacity of the object or event to cause pleasure or displeasure, upset or relaxation, excitement or depression—in other words, to cause changes in Objectless Affect. We refer to an object's capacity to create Objectless Affect as that object's Affective Quality. We refer to the process whereby a person perceives an object's Affective Quality as the Perception of Affective Quality.

Perception of Affective Quality contrasts with Objectless Affect in two ways. First, Objectless Affect seems to exist within oneself (I feel glum, or chipper, or tense today), whereas an Affective Quality seems to exist within the Object (it is the sunset that is beautiful, the odor that is offensive, and so on). Second, a person seems to have but one Objectless Affect at a time (or, at most, a small number, in the case of mixed feelings), whereas one perceives simultaneously many objects and events in the world, each with its own Affective Quality.

Of course, there is likely to be an empirical relation between one's Objectless Affect and one's Perception of Affective Quality; the distinction here is a conceptual one. Objectless Affect and Perception of Affective Quality are linked but not in any simple way. One can judge a meal as smelling delicious and simultaneously feel genuine pleasure when receiving that meal. But one can judge the meal as smelling delicious and feel genuine *displeasure* when deprived of that meal. Thus, intensity of pleasure (Objectless Affect) and deliciousness (Affective Quality) can be positively or negatively correlated, depending on circumstances.

Perception of Affective Quality is similarly linked to other classes of emotion in a complex way. For example, Perception of Affective Quality typically accompanies Attributed Affect—one of the conditions of Attributed Affect is that the change in Objectless Affect is attributed to the Object, which is typically the focus of attention. However, Perception of Affective Quality can also occur independently of Objectless Affect. For example, one may recognize that the sunset is beautiful or that a story is funny without feeling pleasure (such observations are common in depression).

Thus far, we have provided simple examples of Perception of Affective Quality. These perceptions can be described with terms analogous to those used to describe Objectless Affect: for example, "pleasant," "unpleasant," "arousing," "soporific," "disgusting," "frightening," "infuriating," and "enjoyable." There are also more complex types of Perception of Affective Quality. We sometimes judge events to be capable of producing shame, embarrassment, envy, pride, jealousy, grief, or other complex emotional episode. These Perceptions of Affective Quality (and perhaps some of the simpler perceptions) are predictions of full Emotional Episodes.

Emotional Behavior

The classes we have defined so far are covert states. We define Emotional Behavior as all overt activity associated with either Objectless Affect or Attributed Affect. Emotional Behavior is a broad and heterogeneous class that includes instrumental actions (fleeing the bear, fighting the enemy, eloping with Juliet), nonverbal expressive signs (gestures, postures, facial movements), verbal and vocal expressions (stating how upset one is, screaming), and visible signs of physiological changes (trembling, tears, sweating). The previous examples are not to be taken as an exhaustive list of mutually exclusive categories, but rather as overlapping illustrations. Clearly, distinctions must be made within the broad class of emotional behavior, and yet how best to carve up this domain is not yet clear.

Emotional Episode

We are now in a position to consider those prototypical examples of emotion that come so readily to mind: fleeing a bear in terror and so on. In these examples, the ingredients we have carefully distinguished all co-occur. The bear appears, the person's Objectless Affect changes from feeling tranquil to agitated, the agitation is quickly linked to the bear, the bear seems capable of inflicting harm, and one flees. Such events are so different from ordinary mundane life—they seem irrational, beyond voluntary control, and animalistic—that emotion has been thought of, in the days of faculty psychology, as stemming from a separate faculty, or, nowadays, as stemming from a separate and more primitive part of the brain.

Emotional Episodes have also been characterized in so many different ways (ranging from fixed action patterns similar to reflexes to socially constructed roles) that it may be impossible to define them in a way that is satisfactory to all theorists. We believe that we can at least take a step in that direction. Most theorists of emotion agree that an Emotional Episode consists of components. Although theories of emotion often add additional components, most theories include the following list as a minimum: An event occurs (which becomes the Object). This event changes Objectless Affect (greatly and obviously in prototypical cases). The Objectless Affect becomes Attributed Affect when the person attributes the change to the Object. One's Emotional Behavior is altered, typically directed at the Object.

Although there are dimensional and categorical approaches to emotion in general, Emotional Episodes are almost always described categorically, and we follow that practice. (We return to the topic of these categories shortly.) For Emotional Episodes, the most fundamental theoretical dispute has to do with the origin of those categories. "Basic emotion" theorists (e.g., Izard, 1991) assume that categories such as fear and anger are natural kinds, by which we mean that the categories are nature's own biologically fixed divisions and are universal to humankind. In this theory, the components all co-occur because they are preprogrammed by a module in a subcortical region of the brain. The components can be disassociated only by additional processes. For example, when the Emotional Episode of anger occurs, certain facial movements naturally occur, unless prevented from doing so by a deliberate attempt to deceive. In contrast, "social construction" theorists (e.g., Averill, 1982) assume that these categories are cultural artifacts, by which we mean that the categories derive from cultural practices that differ from one society to another. The components co-occur because they are specified by cultural rules that are passed from one generation to the next. Again, the components can be disassociated only by additional processes. In either the basic emotion or the social construction theory, the categories exist to be discovered, either in nature or in culture. Stated so starkly, these two theories seem worlds apart. In practice, the two are more difficult to distinguish, perhaps because culturally defined categories are designed to represent nature; for example, the culturally defined categories of *man* and *woman* are defined to capture a biologically based division. Our definition of Emotional Episode is meant to be agnostic in these and related theoretical debates.

Summary

The emotionally intelligent person can be intelligent about various things, and it is helpful to have a list of those things. We propose that the term "emotion" be replaced with five theoretically distinct (although empirically related) concepts. These five are offered in the spirit of developing a language in which theorists of different persuasions can state their claims in ways understandable to one other. For this reason, the definitions we have developed are prescriptive. That is, we have stipulated what the terms mean and do not claim that anyone else uses these terms in the way we do. Our five elements are defined at a psychological level, and the reader may wonder why we have omitted a physiological element. All five elements have a physiological substrate, which must be described and analyzed. Thus, we think of the physiological as a different level of analysis and not as another (sixth) element to be added to our list.

At the heart of our analysis is what we call Objectless Affect. This ingredient is what Perception of Affective Quality predicts, is what becomes Attributed Affect, is linked to Emotional Behavior, and is the core ingredient in an Emotional Episode. In this chapter, we do not propose an account of the processes involved. Instead, we focus on a more preliminary problem of description and definition. The division of emotion into these five concepts provides a finer-grained analysis of emotion. It is a division, we hope, on which an analysis of Emotional Intelligence can be developed.

FOUR BROAD DOMAINS OF INDIVIDUAL DIFFERENCES

Like *emotion*, emotional intelligence (EI) admits of various definitions and accounts. For example, the relation of EI to intelligence more generally remains to be resolved. EI may be a new ability or a new aspect of personality (or both), or it may be redundant with already defined abilities or personality traits. In the same spirit with which we approached emotion, we hope to be as theory neutral as possible in approaching EI. We think of EI as being a broad field of inquiry. That is, much like personality or ability, EI need not be a single entity or unitary process. Rather, the number of dimensions required to describe EI, its relation to the domain of personality, its relation to the domain of cognitive abilities, and so forth, are all left as empirical questions. To remain as theory neutral as possible, we therefore begin simply with a focus on possible domains in which there may exist individual differences in relation to emotion. We suggest that there are individual differences in (1) having emotions, in (2) conceptualizing emotion, in (3) becoming meta-aware of emotion, and in (4) regulating emotion. We first describe these four domains and then turn to individual differences in them.

Having Emotion

Individuals differ in average levels of Objectless Affect, its volatility, and responsiveness to classes of stimuli; in how often they form Attributed

Affect and to what they attribute Objectless Affect; in what stimuli they perceive to have what affective qualities; in what emotional behaviors they enact in which circumstances; and in which Emotional Episodes they engage.

Conceptualizing Emotion

Emotions can exist without being conceptualized, as presumably happens in some species. Human beings nonetheless do conceptualize events in the world, including emotions, largely by grouping into categories and ordering along continua (see Denham & Kochanoff, Chapter 10, this volume). The nature of categories and concepts has been and continues to be the subject of philosophical and scientific debate. For example, some believe that concepts are more or less faithful representations of categories and that categories exist in the external world whether recognized or not. Others, however, believe that categories have no existence independent of someone's concept of them. To keep things simple, we use the term "concept" to represent the mental processes involved in recognizing and understanding categories of events, in our case emotional events.

Words such as "fear," "anger," "love," and "happiness" are tags or labels for emotion concepts. Some, such as "cheerful," "tense," "depressed," "relaxed," and "chipper," apply primarily (although not exclusively) to Objectless Affect. Other words, such as "pleasant," "unpleasant," "exciting," "relaxing," "depressing," "disgusting," "infuriating," "frightening," "inspiring," and "endearing," describe the Perception of Affective Quality. Some, such as "anger," "fear," "jealousy," and "envy," apply to Attributed Affect and Emotional Episodes.

A concept for a type of Emotional Episode can be thought of as a *script* (Fehr & Russell 1984). That is, in a specific Emotional Episode, the components (change in Objectless Affect, attribution, etc.) are known to unfold in a temporal order and possess causal connections. (The script may be called a schema, folk theory, cognitive model, or prototype; for present purposes, we need not distinguish among these various accounts of mental representation.) A script for an Emotional Episode is a knowledge structure that specifies the components and temporal/causal links among those components in a prototypical case of that episode. For example, the script for fear would specify the causes, characteristics, and consequences of the clearest cases of fear. These characteristics would include the Objectless Affect, Attributed Affect, and Emotional Behavior associated with fear. A script for fear is given in Table 15.2.

Prototypical Emotional Episodes of fear are those actual cases that

TABLE 15.2. A Possible Script for the Category of Fear

Component	Example
Antecedent Event (becomes the Object)	The bear appears.
Perception of Affective Quality	Bear appears threatening.
Change in Objectless Affect	Change from tranquility to agitation.
Attribution	Agitation is linked to bear.
Emotional Behavior	Freeze, flee, cry for help.

fit the script extremely well. Emotional Episodes of fear are those actual cases that fit the script well enough to count as a case. The borders between prototypical cases, nonprototypical cases, and noncases are extremely blurry.

Theorists differ on some of the attributes of emotion concepts/scripts. For example, Clore and Ortony (1991) believe that each script possesses both a prototype, which is used to help identify real-world exemplars, and an essence (a list of necessary and sufficient conditions), which is used in reasoning about that emotion. In contrast, Russell (1991) suggests that the prototype alone suffices for both real-world identification and reasoning.

Becoming Meta-Aware

Emotion can simply occur with little or no awareness. For example, a person can be tense and uncomfortable (Objectless Affect), but have his or her attention focused on immediate concerns. The tension and discomfort are on the periphery of consciousness. Similarly, a person's environment may seem gloomy (Perception of Affective Quality) without the person focusing on that gloominess. One can smile or move awkwardly or hastily (Emotional Behavior) without being aware of doing so. It is another matter to *notice* that one is tense and uncomfortable, to notice that one is smiling or moving awkwardly or hastily, or to notice that the environment is gloomy. Although awareness may well be a matter of degree, we draw a simple distinction here between the occurrence of emotion, on the one hand, and a meta-awareness of that emotion on the other.

This distinction is sometimes phrased in terms of levels of consciousness. At the first level of consciousness is the raw feeling of Objectless Affect or the almost reflexive response to a situation that may occur in Emotional Behavior. At the level of what some have called secondary consciousness or meta-consciousness, one notices (attends to and attempts to analyze) the events at the first level of consciousness. Meta-awareness, we propose, draws on emotion concepts and is necessary for labeling an emotion, for putting the emotion in a broader context, and for understanding an emotion (see Lane & Pollermann, Chapter 11, this volume). Put differently, to be jealous of Chris, one can simply feel unpleasant and agitated, attribute that feeling to Chris's actions, and have thoughts of harming Chris. To *know that one is* jealous, one must be meta-aware of these ingredients, with the ingredients interpreted as fitting into the script of jealousy. Thus, one may be jealous of Chris, but sincerely deny feeling jealous because the meta-awareness is lacking: "I'm *not* jealous! I'm just tired of his annoying behavior." Only later may one realize that jealousy is the better interpretation.

Regulating

Regulation is any process aimed at altering thoughts, behaviors, or, in the cases of interest here, emotions (see Gross & John, Chapter 12, this volume). Self-Regulation is a set of self-initiated processes aimed at altering one's own emotion. Other-Regulation is aimed at others. A variety of such processes occur, with varying degrees of success.

THE STRUCTURE OF EMOTIONAL INTELLIGENCE

How are the four domains just described related to the five emotional elements described initially? To pursue this question, we formed a 4 × 5 grid, as seen in Table 15.3. The cells of this grid suggest component processes that together make up EI. The grid may thus expose areas underexplored and lead to more explicit decisions about what is and what is not EI. Each cell may also suggest an area in which measuring instruments could be created. In this section, we therefore use the grid to suggest a taxonomy of measuring instruments. As we progress through this grid, some suggested components seem more like personality traits (or even temperament) and others more like cognitive abilities. We also need to distinguish all these processes as they apply to the self and to others. We begin with the first column.

Emotion Events Themselves

Although it may seem curious to include individual differences in our five emotion elements themselves within the structure of EI, there is some precedent for doing so. One may also consider the appropriateness of the occurrence of one of the five elements, given the context.

TABLE 15.3. The Structure of Emotional Intelligence

	Event	Concept	Meta-Awareness	Regulation
Objectless Affect				
Attributed Affect				
Emotional Behavior				
Perception of Affective Quality				
Emotional Episode				

Objectless Affect

Bar-On (1997) included one's level of happiness as one dimension of EI (to be precise, Emotional Quotient (EQ), which Bar-On defined to include EI). More generally, people differ in the kinds, intensities, and other attributes of Objectless Affect. Such differences are usually termed temperament, mood, and mood disorders. Those with a mood disorder (such as Objectless Affect that fluctuates unpredictably between depression and mania) have a challenging task to which they can apply their abilities. Variations in Objectless Affect can also vary in their appropriateness for the circumstances of their occurrence, both in under- and overreactions.

Attributed Affect

Individuals differ in how frequently they attribute Objectless Affect to specific causes and in the causes they choose. For example, those with an internal locus of control tend to attribute events to themselves; those with an external locus tend to attribute the same events to external causes. Weiner (1985) provided a finer-grained analysis of attribution and applied it specifically to emotion. In Weiner's analysis, for example, gratitude occurs when one attributes a good outcome to the actions of another. Bar-On (1997) and Goleman (1995) included optimism (vs. pessimism) as a dimension of EI. Translating into present terms, we suggest that optimists tend to attribute their failures (or bad feelings in general) to causes that are changeable, whereas pessimists tend to attribute the same events to causes that are stable. The opposite occurs for success.

Perception of Affective Quality

The Perception of an Object's Affective Quality is a prediction of the change in Objectless Affect one will undergo because of that Object. To find someone exciting, boring, scary, or relaxing is to anticipate feeling excited, bored, scared, or relaxed, respectively, in that person's presence. Individuals differ in the frequency of making, and perhaps more important, in the accuracy of, these predictions. Sometimes one is surprised by how one actually feels about something: Although Sally may have looked forward eagerly to her evening with her friend, she may be disappointed with the evening. In their Multifactor Emotional Intelligence Scale, Mayer, Caruso, and Salovey (1999) include scales for differences in perceiving the affective qualities of music, designs, and stories.

Emotional Behavior

Under the title Emotional Behavior, we include a heterogeneous mix, and so there are undoubtedly a number of individual differences involved, from autonomic nervous system lability, to facial or vocal expressiveness, to the specific instrumental actions taken in various emotion-related circumstances, such as confrontational versus conciliatory actions during conflict. EI researchers have pointed to a number of these differences and begun to develop measures of them.

Emotional Episode

Because we defined an Emotional Episode as composed of the first four types of "elementary particles," there may be no additional individual differences to add here. On the other hand, individuals may differ in the patterns of those events. For example, some individuals may frequently show the full prototypical pattern of anger, or fear, or some other category. Another individual may instead show less patterning or idiosyncratic combinations.

Concepts

Individual differences in conceptual knowledge of emotion may be anchored at one end by alexithymia, which literally means lacking in words for emotion. Although considered a psychiatric diagnostic category, alexithymia is assessed along a continuum. Those categorized as alexithymic have difficulty recognizing, describing, and understanding emotions. Conversely, most theorists of EI describe the opposite end of this continuum as those who are better than others at recognizing, understanding, and describing emotions.

There are several self-report questionnaires and maximum-performance tests of knowledge of concepts related to Objectless Affect, Attributed Affect, and Emotional Episodes. These include the Toronto Alexithymia Scale–20 (Bagby, Parker, & Taylor, 1994), especially the Difficulty Describing Feelings and Difficulty Identifying Feelings subscales; the Recognition of Emotion in Self and Recognition of Emotion in Others subscales of Tett, Wang, Gribler, and Martinez (1997); the Levels of Emotional Awareness Scale (Lane, Quinlan, Schwartz, Walker, & Zeitlin, 1990); the Multifactor Emotional Intelligence Scale (MEIS; Mayer, Caruso, et al., 1999), especially the Blends, Progressions, Transitions, and Relativity subscales; and the Mayer–Salovey–Caruso Emotional Intelligence Test (MSCEIT; Mayer, Salovey, & Caruso, 1999) Blends, Progressions, Transitions, and Analogies subscales. Fewer scales related to Perception of Affective Quality exist. These include Tett's Emotional Appropriateness subscale, as well as the MEIS Synesthesia and Feeling Biases subscales, and the MSCEIT Synesthesia, Facilitation, and Sensation Translation subscales. Finally, Tett et al.'s (1997) Recognition of Emotion in Others subscale measures understanding of the Emotional Behavior of other people.

Meta-Awareness

In Meta-Awareness, one focuses on, notices, labels, and takes into account the emotion happening at the primary level. The Trait Meta-Mood Scale (TMMS; Salovey, Mayer, Goldman, Turvey, & Palfai, 1995) Attention subscale, Bernet's (1966) Perception of Affect Based on Body scale, and the Toronto Alexithymia Scale–20 (Bagby et al., 1994) External Orientation subscale likely tap this component. Meta-Awareness of Objectless Affect allows one to take one's mood into account in planning one's activities. Tett et al.'s (1997) Flexible Planning subscale assesses the extent to which the individual makes important life decisions based on emotions.

Meta-Awareness of Attributed Affect may allow one to seek slowly and deliberately the cause of one's Unattributed Affect when the cause is not immediately obvious. Alternatively, one may question the causal attribution made at the primary level (I thought that Joe made me angry; but maybe it was just the stresses of the day). Thus, one may assess how accurately attributions have been made. Meta-Awareness of one's own behavior may mean noticing the impression created on others, one's own style of behaving, and so on. Meta-Awareness of Perceived Affective Quality allows a more deliberate and skeptical approach to judging Affective Quality (I notice that although food from this restaurant tastes good, I feel bad within a few hours, and so perhaps that restaurant is not really very good). Tests of these latter types of Meta-Awareness have yet to be developed.

Regulation

The ability to regulate emotion is widely recognized as central to EI, as seen in Tett et al.'s (1997) Regulation of Emotion in the Self subscale, the MEIS (Mayer, Caruso, et al., 1999) Managing Feeling of Self subscale, and the MSCEIT (Mayer, Salovey, et al., 1999) Emotion Management subscale. Our framework suggests a number of distinctions that point to separable components. For example, we know of no theory of EI that distinguishes Objectless Affect from Attributed Affect, and our framework suggests that this may be a helpful distinction. The strategies and skills involved may be quite different. Sally may focus directly on Objectless Affect, seeking to improve her mood through food, drink, entertainment, and so on. She focuses on Affect Regulation. Jane, in contrast, may focus first on finding the cause of her Objectless Affect (i.e., in moving from Objectless Affect to Attributed Affect). Once the cause is determined, she may focus her efforts specifically on that cause (e.g., her difficulties with her coworkers). She may be said to be focusing on Emotion Regulation.

Self-Regulation of Objectless Affect is a pervasive feature of life. One typically (although not always) seeks to maintain a pleasant mood or alter an unpleasant one (Thayer, Newman, & McCain, 1994). (For a discussion of occasions on which one may seek out an unpleasant mood, see Parrott, 1993.) One typically seeks a level of activation commensurate with anticipated activities, from the stimulus of the morning coffee to the relaxant of the evening brandy. Individuals differ qualitatively in the strategies used and quantitatively in the effectiveness of those strategies. In deciding what to do, where to go, and with whom to be, one anticipates Attributed Affect. Processes involved in anticipating pleasures and displeasures constitute an area of very active concern (Gilbert, 1989).

Other-Regulation of Objectless Affect and Attributed Affect is assessed using self-report measures such as Tett et al.'s (1997) Regulation of Emotion in Others subscale and using maximum-performance tests such as the MEIS (Mayer, Caruso, et al., 1999) Managing Feelings of Others subscale and MSCEIT (Mayer, Salovey, et al., 1999) Emotions in Relationships subscale. Regulation of others' affect will usually but not always be altruistic. For example, imagine that Sally is in a conflict with her colleague. Sally can try to calm the colleague, or she can provoke anger, so that the colleague acts foolishly and rashly.

Regulation of Emotional Behavior, sometimes referred to as Emotion Control, is an area of current study (e.g., Baumeister, Heatherton, & Tice, 1994; Rosenbaum, 1993).

CONCLUDING COMMENT

The grid in Table 15.3 is the simplest organizing tool that we could think of. Forming a grid suggests that EI consists of four levels corresponding to four qualitatively different types of process. Some of these processes logically presuppose others. Presumably, Level 1 (events themselves) occurs first, developmentally and phylogenetically. To refer to individual differences at this level as *intelligence* might be suspect, for it is the intelligence of emotion itself. The second level (concepts) is squarely cognitive, albeit applied to the emotional realm. The next two levels are qualitatively different again. Describing these processes as *levels* raises such questions as whether they develop in parallel, or in ways that depend on one another. Conceptual and empirical analyses of such questions are an exciting frontier in the rapidly unfolding science of emotional intelligence.

REFERENCES

Averill, J. R. (1982). *Anger and aggression: An essay on emotion.* New York: Springer.

Bagby, R. M., Parker, J. D. A., & Taylor, G. J. (1994). The twenty-item Toronto Alexithymia Scale: I. Item selection and cross-validation of the factor structure. *Journal of Psychosomatic Research, 38,* 23–32.

Bar-On, R. (1997). *EQ-i: Bar-On Emotional Quotient Inventory, technical manual.* Toronto, ON: Multi-Health Systems.

Baumeister, R. F., Heatherton, T. F., & Tice, D. M. (1994). *Losing control: How and why people fail at self-regulation.* San Diego, CA: Academic Press.

Bernet, M. (1996, August 12). *Emotional intelligence: Components and correlates.* Paper presented at the 104th convention of the American Psychological Association, Toronto, Canada.

Clore, G. L., & Ortony, A. (1991). What more is there to emotion concepts than prototypes? *Journal of Personality and Social Psychology, 60,* 48–50.

Fehr, B., & Russell, J. A. (1984). Concept of emotion viewed from a prototype perspective. *Journal of Experimental Psychology: General, 113,* 464–486.

Gilbert, D. T. (1989). Thinking lightly about others: Automatic components of the social inference process. In J. S. Uleman & J. A. Bargh (Eds.), *Unintended thought* (pp. 189–211). New York: Guilford Press.

Goleman, D. (1995). *Emotional intelligence.* New York: Bantam Books.

Izard, C. E. (1991). *The psychology of emotion.* New York: Plenum Press.

Keltner, D., Locke, K. D., & Audrain, P. C. (1993). The influence of attributions on the relevance of negative feelings to personal satisfaction. *Personality and Social Psychology Bulletin, 19,* 21–29.

Lane, R. D., Quinlan, D. M., Schwartz, G. E., Walker, P. A., & Zeitlin, S. B. (1990). The Levels of Emotional Awareness Scale: A cognitive–developmental measure of emotion. *Journal of Personality Assessment, 55,* 124–134.

Mayer, J. D., Caruso, D. R., & Salovey, P. (1999). Emotional intelligence meets traditional standards for an intelligence. *Intelligence, 27,* 267–298.

Mayer, J. D., Salovey, P., & Caruso, D. R. (1999). *Instruction manual for the MSCEIT Mayer–Salovey–Caruso Emotional Intelligence Test, research version 1.1.* Toronto, ON: Multi-Health Systems.

Morris, W. N. (1989). *Mood: The frame of mind.* New York: Springer.

Oatley, K., & Johnson-Laird, P. N. (1987). Towards a cognitive theory of emotions. *Cognition and Emotion, 1,* 29–50.

Parrott, W. G. (1993). Beyond hedonism: Motives for inhibiting good moods and for maintaining bad moods. In D. M. Wegner & J. W. Pennebaker (Eds.), *Handbook of mental control* (pp. 278–305). Englewood Cliffs, NJ: Prentice-Hall.

Rosenbaum, M. (1993). The three functions of self-control behaviour: Redressive, reformative, and experiential. *Work and Stress, 7,* 33–46.

Russell, J. A. (1991). In defense of a prototype approach to emotion concepts. *Journal of Personality and Social Psychology, 60,* 37–47.

Russell, J. A., & Feldman Barrett, L. (1999). Core affect, prototypical emotional episodes, and other things called emotion: Dissecting the elephant. *Journal of Personality and Social Psychology, 76,* 805–819.

Salovey, P., Mayer, J. D., Goldman, S. L., Turvey, C., & Palfai, T. P. (1995). Emotional attention, clarity, and repair: Exploring emotional intelligence using the Trait Meta-Mood Scale. In Daniel M. Wegner & James W. Pennebaker (Eds.), *Emotion, disclosure, and health* (pp. 125–154). Washington, DC: American Psychological Association.

Schwarz, N., & Clore, G. L. (1983). Mood, misattribution, and judgments of well-being: Informative and directive functions of affective states. *Journal of Personality and Social Psychology, 45,* 513–523.

Tett, R., Wang, A., Gribler, J., & Martinez, A. (1997, April 4). *Development of self-report measures of emotional intelligence.* Paper presented at the annual convention of the Southeastern Psychological Association, Atlanta, GA.

Thayer, R. E. (1989). *The biopsychology of mood and activation.* New York: Oxford University Press.

Thayer, R. E., Newman, R., & McClain, T. (1994). Self-regulation of mood: Strategies for changing a bad mood, raising energy, and reducing tension. *Journal of Personality and Social Psychology, 67,* 910–925.

Watson, D., & Tellegen, A. (1985). Toward a consensual structure of mood. *Psychological Bulletin, 98,* 219–235.

Watson, D., Wiese, D., Vaidya, J., & Tellegen, A. (1999). The two general activation systems of affect: Structural findings, evolutionary considerations, and psychobiological evidence. *Journal of Personality and Social Psychology, 76,* 820–838.

Weiner, B. (1985). An attributional theory of achievement motivation and emotion. *Psychological Review, 92,* 548–573.

Yik, M. S. M., Russell, J. A., & Feldman Barrett, L. (1999). Structure of self-reported current affect: Integration and beyond. *Journal of Personality and Social Psychology, 77,* 600–619

CHAPTER 16

Sensitivity and Flexibility

Exploring the Knowledge Function
of Automatic Attitudes

MELISSA J. FERGUSON
JOHN A. BARGH

The concept of attitudes is historically one of the most widely studied topics in social psychology (e.g., see Allport, 1935; Eagly & Chaiken, 1993; McGuire, 1986). An attitude has generally been consistently defined throughout the past 7 decades as "a psychological tendency that is expressed by evaluating a particular entity with some degree of favor or disfavor" (Eagly & Chaiken, 1993, p. 1; see also Allport, 1935; Smith, Bruner, & White, 1956; Thompson, Zanna, & Griffin, 1995; Thurstone, 1928). The research activity surrounding this construct has addressed a wide spectrum of topics, such as underlying structure (e.g., Eagly & Chaiken, 1993; Katz & Stotland, 1959; Rosenberg & Hovland, 1960), functionality (e.g., Katz, 1960; Katz & Stotland, 1959; Pratkanis, Breckler, & Greenwald, 1989), the ability of attitudes to predict attitude-relevant behavior (e.g., Elms, 1975; Fishbein & Ajzen, 1974, 1975; Kelman, 1974; Schuman & Johnson, 1976; Wicker, 1969), and methods of attitude measurement (e.g., see Himmelfarb, 1993, for a review).

Though many of these issues are currently being examined, much of the zeitgeist concerns the degree to which the particular measurement of attitudes has consequences for the operationalization and utility of attitudes. More specifically, recent research and theory focus on whether and how attitudes that are activated *outside of awareness* differ from attitudes that are *strategically recalled* (e.g., Ajzen & Sexton, 1999; Banaji, 2001; Cunningham, Preacher, & Banaji, 2001; Devine, 1989; Dovidio, Kawakami, Johnson, Johnson, & Howard, 1997; Fazio, Jackson, Dunton, & Williams, 1995; Klauer, 1998; McConnell & Leibold, 2001; Nesdale & Durkin, 1998; Rudman, Greenwald, Mellott, & Schwartz, 1999; Wilson, Lindsey, & Schooler, 2000; Wittenbrink, Judd, & Park, 1997). For example, to what degree can researchers apply theoretical perspectives on the nature of strategically recalled attitudes to automatically activated attitudes?

In this chapter we extend a traditional analysis of strategic attitudes to automatic attitudes. Researchers and theorists have delineated the ways in which strategic attitudes are functional because of their delivery of affective information concerning the corresponding objects (e.g., Katz, 1960; Pratkanis et al., 1989; Smith, Bruner, & White, 1956). We argue that automatic attitudes can be similarly conceptualized as functional in terms of both their sensitivity to contextual differences in the meaningfulness of objects, and their flexibility in responding to novel objects. We first describe strategic and implicit measurement in general and next consider the particular ways in which both strategic and automatic attitudes can be considered functional. We then turn to recent research concerning the sensitivity and flexibility of automatic attitudes.

STRATEGIC RECALL: EXPLICIT ATTITUDE MEASUREMENT

Attitudes have traditionally been measured by simply asking respondents to report their preferences, feelings, thoughts, and behaviors regarding an issue or object. Although such measurement captures the intentional stance of people (i.e., it measures what people consciously and intentionally report), it generates data that are otherwise fraught with interpretational difficulties. Because people can strategically modify their answers, their "attitudes" can represent factors other than the underlying construct of interest (e.g., Devine, 1989, 1995; Fazio et al., 1995; Greenwald, McGhee, & Schwartz, 1998, Jones & Sigall, 1971; Schuman & Kalton, 1985; Warner, 1965). For example, people may, on some occasions, present themselves as holding socially desirable, egalitarian values even though they demonstrate (socially undesirable) racial prejudices on other, less public occasions (e.g., Sigall & Page, 1971). People may report an attitude according to what they believe the experimenter expects (e.g., Orne, 1962; Rosenthal & Jacobson, 1966) or what the social norms prescribe (e.g., Gaes, Kalle, & Tedeschi, 1978; Ostrom, 1973).

The possibility that respondents can modify their attitudes on explicit measures led researchers to develop more covert explicit attitude measures, wherein the attitude object of interest is not obvious. For example, researchers interested in assessing the extent to which people are racially prejudiced constructed subtle measures of racism that ostensibly tap political conservatism (e.g., McConahay, 1986). This masking of the true construct of interest is intended to minimize the degree to which participants react to social norms and demand effects. If participants believe that the questions pertain to policy preferences, they may not hide or modify their true racially prejudiced attitudes.

AUTOMATIC ATTITUDES: IMPLICIT ATTITUDE MEASUREMENT

Even explicit measures that are subtle, however, do not preclude the possibility that respondents strategically misrepresent their feelings or beliefs in the interest of some attitude-irrelevant factor. The possibility that people alter their explicitly reported attitudes means that such measures are perhaps not capturing "real," or unadulterated, attitudes. This skepticism has encouraged researchers to adopt implicit measures of attitudes (e.g., Bargh, Chaiken, Govender, & Pratto, 1992; Bargh, Chaiken, Raymond, & Hymes, 1996; Fazio, Sanbonmatsu, Powell, & Kardes, 1986; Greenwald et al., 1989; Greenwald et al., 1998; Wittenbrink, Judd, & Park, 1997). Implicit measures can assess the phenomenon of interest without participants being aware that their reactions to objects are being recorded. Because they are unaware of the intent of the measure, they are theoretically unable to react in a socially desirable or demand-laden fashion (though see Glaser & Banaji, 1999).

Implicit measures of attitudes are currently generating numerous research questions (e.g., Banaji, 2001; Fazio et al., 1986; Greenwald et al., 1998). One of the most frequently used implicit attitude measures (e.g., Bargh et al., 1992; Bargh et al., 1996; Fazio et al., 1986; Fazio et al., 1995) entails a sequential priming paradigm (Neely, 1976, 1977) in which prime words that represent attitude objects (e.g., "puppy," "crime") are paired with positively or negatively valenced adjectives (e.g., "generous," "awful"). Within a typical trial, a prime word is presented for a fraction of a second and is then followed by an adjective, to which participants must respond in some way (e.g., evaluation task, lexical decision task). The response times to the positive and negative adjectives are compared as a function of the valence of the preceding primes. This paradigm demonstrates the phenomenon of evaluative or affective priming: Participants' reaction times to adjectives are faster when those adjectives are preceded by similarly (versus dissimilarly) valenced primes.

According to this body of research, an *automatic attitude* consists of evaluative information that is associated with the attitude object in memory (Fazio, 2000; see also Ferguson & Bargh, in press). This interpretation presupposes so-called symbolic, localist models of memory wherein representations of semantically related objects are interconnected within an associative network (e.g., Anderson, 1983; Anderson & Bower, 1973; Collins & Loftus, 1975; Smith, 1996). Upon perception of an attitude object, activation automatically spreads from the object representation to the evaluation of the object, and then possibly to evaluatively similar objects (see Fazio, 2000; Ferguson & Bargh, in press).

Researchers have asserted that the activation of the evaluative information in memory is automatic for two main reasons. The first is that the stimulus-onset asynchrony (SOA) between the prime word and target word in evaluative priming paradigms is too brief a delay to allow strategic (i.e., nonautomatic) responding to occur (e.g., Fazio et al., 1986; cf. Klauer, Rossnagel, & Musch, 1997; Neely, 1976, 1977). The second reason is that according to evaluative priming research, attitudes toward objects can be activated even when the attitude objects are subliminally presented, thereby demonstrating automatic activation (Greenwald, Draine, & Abrams, 1996; Greenwald et al., 1989; Wittenbrink et al., 1997).

Although participants are typically aware of the presentation of the prime words in the sequential priming paradigm, they are unaware that their automatic reactions to the prime words are being measured. This is in clear contrast to explicit attitude measurement, wherein participants are pointedly asked to report their attitudes, which requires them first to estimate their attitude, and then decide whether and how to report that attitude. Because of the contrast in the way in which implicit and explicit attitudes are measured, and the consequent difference in participant's awareness of what is being measured, researchers are systematically exploring what exactly is captured by implicit measurement as compared with explicit measurement. In other words, in what ways, if any, do automatic attitudes (i.e., those measured implicitly) differ from strategic attitudes (i.e., those measured explicitly)?

For example, researchers have studied the extent to which automatic attitudes predict subsequent attitude-relevant behavior (e.g., Fazio et al., 1995; Swanson, Rudman, & Greenwald, 2001), whether automatic attitudes correspond to strategic attitudes (e.g., Cunningham et al., 2001; McConnell & Leibold, 2001), and how automatic attitudes differ from strategic attitudes in terms of stability across time and susceptibility to persuasion and change (e.g., Wilson et al., 2000). The extent to which the traditional conceptualization of attitudes can be applied to implicit attitudes has also been discussed (see Banaji, 2001).

Although there are dimensions along which strategically recalled attitudes differ from implicitly measured attitudes, such as perhaps the immediacy with which the attitudes are invoked, we focus on the possibility that the two types of measurement capture attitudes that are similarly functional for the perceiver. Specifically, given that both strategic and automatic attitudes provide perceivers with affective information regarding the respective objects, we apply the functional perspective on strategic attitudes to those attitudes that are automatically activated.

THE KNOWLEDGE FUNCTION OF AUTOMATIC ATTITUDES: OVERVIEW

Many researchers and theorists have argued that an important function of both strategic and automatic attitudes is the delivery of affective information about the attitude object (Fazio, 1989). Katz (1960) and Smith et al. (1956) referred to such appraisal as the knowledge function and identified it as one of the four primary functions of attitudes. Fazio (1989) claimed that this function is the most important because it refers to all attitudes, regardless of the intensity or direction of the attitude. He states that "regardless of why the individual's attitude took on a particular valence, the mere possession of any attitude is useful to the individual in terms of orienting him or her to the object in question" (p. 172).

This behavioral orientation toward the object is an integral reason that an attitude is conceptualized as functional (e.g., Fazio, 1989; Lewin, 1935; Pratkanis et al., 1989). Attitudes provide evaluative information about the respective objects that then helps orient the person toward the objects in an appropriate manner, whereby the person can avoid threatening or unpleasant objects and approach safe or pleasing objects. Automatic attitudes are thus functional because they can quickly and effortlessly provide vital information to the perceiver, saving him or her the trouble of having to repeatedly and consciously figure out whether an object is safe or dangerous, pleasing or displeasing (Smith et al., 1956, p. 41).

Yet although researchers have discussed the functional nature of automatic attitudes (Fazio, 1989), previous literature suggests that the functional nature of automatic attitudes may be constrained relative to that of strategic attitudes. We discuss two proposed limitations to the function of automatic attitudes. The first limitation concerns the degree to which automatic attitudes are sensitive to the context within which attitude objects are perceived. Specifically, strategic attitudes are widely acknowledged to be context sensitive: A strategic attitude depends on the context in which the object is perceived, and consequently, the goals of the perceiver concerning that object (e.g., see Anderson, 1974; Bem, 1972; Fazio, 1987; Millar & Tesser, 1986; Olson, 1990; Schwarz & Clore, 1983; Strack, 1992; Tesser, 1978; Wilson, Dunn, Kraft, & Lisle, 1989; Wilson & Hodges, 1992). Such sensitivity of explicit attitudes is clearly important because it allows the person to behave in a situation-relevant fashion toward the object, according to his or her goals within the situation.

In contrast, automatic attitudes have sometimes been conceptualized as context independent (e.g., Fazio et al., 1995; Wilson & Hodges, 1992; Wilson et al., 2000), with some recent exceptions (e.g., Dasgupta & Greenwald, 2001; Wittenbrink, Judd, & Park, 2001). Such insensitivity would undermine the functional nature of automatic attitudes because automatic attitudes would be unable to account for situation-specific constraints regarding the object. We address this issue by exploring the sensitivity of automatic attitudes—if the functional nature of automatic attitudes rests on the delivery of information about how to relate to the object (e.g., approach or retreat), the information should be sensitive to the meaning of the object according to different goals of the perceiver. That is, an automatic attitude toward a given object should vary according to the utility of the object for the person, which may change across contexts and time. We review recent research that addresses this issue and suggests that automatic attitudes are contextually sensitive (Ferguson & Bargh, 2002).

The second limitation concerns the extent to which automatic attitudes are flexible to novel attitude objects, or whether they depend solely on preexisting, stored representations of evaluation. Research shows that people can strategically evaluate novel objects and can integrate evaluative information from a variety of different sources (e.g., Anderson & Rosenfeld, 1988; Bechtel & Abrahamsen, 1991; Carlston and Smith, 1996; Fiedler, 1996; Smith, 1996; Smith & DeCoster, 1999). Although work outside the area of attitudes suggests that people can automatically integrate evaluative information (e.g., Fiedler, 1996), the literature on automatic attitudes instead suggests that automatic activation of an attitude depends solely on a stored, preexisting representation of an evaluation, which is associated with the object in memory (Fazio, 2000; Ferguson & Bargh, in press; Wilson et al., 2000). This view suggests that automatic attitudes can be invoked only in response to previously appraised objects.

Furthermore, it is presumed that the construction of an attitude for a novel object requires some degree of conscious effort and thus cannot occur automatically (Fiske & Pavelchak, 1986; Wilson & Hodges, 1992; Wilson et al., 2000). This research suggests that people would be unable to automatically evaluate a novel object because of their inability to integrate multiple sources of evaluative information. To address this issue, we describe recent research that demonstrates that automatic attitudes are constructed in response to novel stimuli, thereby suggesting that automatic attitudes are flexible and constructive (Duckworth, Bargh, Garcia, & Chaiken, in press; Ferguson & Bargh, in press).

SENSITIVITY OF AUTOMATIC ATTITUDES

The primary function of an automatic attitude is that it quickly and effortlessly delivers information about how to relate to the attitude object (Fazio, 1989). For example, an object that evokes negativity can be immediately avoided or at least closely monitored, and an object that provokes positivity can be approached (e.g., Lewin, 1935; Rosenberg, 1956). This evaluative information is essential for how the perceiver understands the environment and structures his or her actions toward a given object (Fazio, 1989). Thus, the automatic evaluation of an object is functional because it guides behavior toward that object.

It is important to note that much theory asserts that behavior toward a given object will depend on the meaningfulness of that object within the situation in which it is encountered. That is, the meaning of an object is determined by the relation of the object to the person's goals within that situation. This perspective suggests that knowledge about objects is context bound (e.g., Fiske, 1992; Glenberg, 1997; Lewin, 1935). For example, Glenberg (1997, p. 5) argues that "to a particular person, the *meaning* of an object, event, or sentence is what that person can do with the object, event, or sentence" (italics added). For example, "depending on the context, a [C]oke bottle can be used to quench thirst, as a weapon, a doorstop, or a vase. That is, *meaning* depends on the context" (Glenberg, 1997, p. 6, italics added).

From this perspective, therefore, the evaluative knowledge about how to relate to an object must be sensitive to one's actual goals concerning that object, which can vary across contexts. If one is thirsty, a Coke bottle can be used to quench thirst and should therefore be evaluated positively. If, on the other hand, one is confronted by a mugger who is holding a Coke bottle as a weapon, the bottle should be evaluated negatively. Lewin (1935, p. 78) presaged this argument by asserting that "the valence of an object usually derives from the fact that the object is a means to the satisfaction of a need, or has indirectly something to do with the satisfaction of a need." The evaluative information of an object should therefore depend on the object's usefulness for the perceiver's goal(s). When an object should be approached, the attitude should be positive, and when the object should be avoided, the attitude should be negative. As Lewin (1935, p. 81) states, "the kind (sign) and strength of the valence of an object or event thus depends directly on the momentary condition of the needs of the individual concerned."

This perspective has been readily applied to explicit attitudes but not, as yet, to automatic attitudes (see Ferguson & Bargh, 2002). In fact, though some recent research has shown that automatic attitudes can vary if different information about the object is made salient (e.g., Dasgupta & Greenwald, 2001; Wittenbrink et al., 2001), other research suggests that automatic attitudes are contextually independent and rigid— largely impervious to change or fluctuation (Wilson & Hodges, 1992; Wilson et al., 2000; cf. Nelson & Bouton, Chapter 3, this volume). To examine the degree to which automatic attitudes are functional in the sense that they provide contextually sensitive information about how to relate to an object, we review some recent research that addresses this issue. We first explore the reasons that automatically activated evaluative knowledge should be context sensitive and then review a series of three studies that demonstrate such sensitivity.

Why Should Automatic Attitudes Be Sensitive to Context?

Much research has demonstrated that explicit attitudes vary according to contextual factors such as mood, previously activated attitude-relevant information, and experimental expectations, for instance (e.g., see Anderson, 1974; Bem, 1972; Fazio, 1987; Millar & Tesser, 1986; Olson, 1990; Schwarz & Clore, 1983; Strack, 1992; Tesser, 1978; Wilson et al., 1989; Wilson & Hodges, 1992). As discussed in the introduction of this chapter, when participants want to please the experimenter and are able to guess how the experimenter wants them to respond, they often respond accordingly (e.g., Orne, 1962; Rosenthal & Jacobson, 1966). Moreover, participants will report more egalitarian attitudes toward marginalized group members if they believe that they will be held accountable or if they want to display a fair and just way of thinking (e.g., Gaes et al., 1978; Ostrom, 1973).

From this body of research, it is evident that when people explicitly and purposefully report their attitudes, the direction and intensity of their attitudes depend on a variety of factors, perhaps including their underlying, unadulterated actual attitudes. The regular fluctuation of explicitly measured attitudes have led some researchers to argue that stored attitudes do not exist, but instead are always constructed on the spot, according to temporarily activated subsets of attitude-relevant information in memory (e.g., Anderson, 1974; Tesser, 1978).

There is no a priori reason to assume that automatically activated evaluative information would not also be sensitive to the context in which the attitude object is measured. Many theorists claim that attitude objects are associated with a complex array of memories, including exemplars (e.g., Abelson, 1976, 1981; Bower, 1981; Eagly & Chaiken, 1993; Fishbein & Ajzen, 1975; Fiske & Pavelchak, 1986; Schank & Abelson, 1977). Given such an array of memories associated with a given attitude object, it seems likely that some object-relevant memories may be positively valenced and others may be negatively valenced (see Dasgupta & Greenwald, 2001). For example, someone may have many positive memories of drinking a sugary soda but may also have negative memories of the harmful effects of ingesting large quantities of caffeine. The context in which the soda product is perceived may determine the nature of the automatic attitude toward the drink, just as the context may influence the explicitly reported attitude.

Recent Research

Three experiments were conducted to test the sensitivity of automatic attitudes. The first two experiments explored the degree to which the framing of attitude objects influences the automatic attitudes toward those objects. Attitude objects that have been used in previous research and are considered to be fairly stable across time were included as the attitude objects of interest (e.g., see Bargh et al., 1992). We included normatively positive and negative attitude objects (e.g., dentist, chocolate). The methodology was largely the same for the two experiments. On each given trial, a prime word that represented an attitude object (i.e., "dentist") was presented for 250 milliseconds and was then followed by the presentation of an adjective (e.g., "generous," "awful"). Participants were asked to rate the adjectives as "good" or "bad" as quickly and accurately as possible.

In both experiments, we were interested in a specific set of attitude objects and wanted to demonstrate that each attitude object of interest could be framed as something safe and pleasing versus dangerous and displeasing, and that the automatic attitude toward that object would reflect the framing. Accordingly, each trial that contained an attitude object of interest (as the prime) was yoked with a preceding trial in which the prime word was semantically related to the subsequent attitude object of interest. Thus, across all trials, we were concerned with only those trials that contained attitude objects of interest. The rest of the trials simply served to *frame* the way in which the attitude objects of interest were perceived.

The critical between-subject manipulation was whether the attitude objects of interest were preceded by attitude objects (as the primes in the preceding trials) that *matched* versus *mismatched* in valence with the traditional valence of the attitude objects of interest. For example, those participants who were in the condition in which the attitude objects were always framed according to their traditional valence would first see a trial with the attitude object *drill* (followed by an adjective), and then in the following trial see the attitude object *dentist* (followed by an adjective). This set of two trials for the attitude object *dentist* would be repeated with multiple positive and negative adjectives. We expected participant's reaction times to the negative adjectives (those that followed "dentist") to be shorter than their reaction times to the positive adjectives (those that followed "dentist") because we expected the word "drill" to frame *dentist* as something painful and negative.

In contrast, those participants who were in the condition in which the attitude objects were framed in an opposite manner to their traditional valence would first see "doctor" (followed by an adjective) and then, in the next trial, see "dentist" (followed by an adjective). In this case, we expected participants' reaction times to the positive adjectives (those that followed "dentist") to be shorter than their reaction times to the negative adjectives (those that followed "dentist") because we expected the word "doctor" to frame the attitude object *dentist* as something safe, helpful, and positive. The critical analysis across all attitude objects of interest was whether the valence of an attitude changed depending on the previously presented, semantically related information in the preceding trial.

In addition, the first experiment also explored the stability of automatic attitudes across two measurement points. Although previous research has demonstrated that automatic attitudes might be unreliable across time (e.g., Cameron, Alvarez, & Bargh, 2000), we hypothesized that such automatic appraisals should be stable, as long as the context within which the attitude object is perceived remains stable. Thus, participants completed the sequential priming paradigm twice in the same experiment. After they completed the paradigm the first time, they completed a number of control measures for approximately half an hour. They then completed the same exact priming paradigm again. We predicted that if the context determines the automatic attitude toward a given attitude object, there should be high and significant correlations between the automatic attitudes in the first measurement and those in the second measurement.

The hypothesis was supported by the pattern of data from each experiment. In the condition in which attitude objects in the preceding trials were evaluatively consistent with the traditional valence of the attitude objects of interest, automatic attitudes toward those attitude objects of interest were consistent with traditional conceptions. The word "dentist" automatically evoked a negative attitude, for instance. Comparatively, in the condition in which the previously presented attitude objects were evaluatively inconsistent with the traditional valence of the attitude objects of interest, automatic attitudes toward those attitude objects were reliably and strongly reversed as compared with the other condition. For these participants, the word "dentist" automatically evoked a positive attitude.

Finally, the first experiment also demonstrated the reliability of the automatic attitude measurement. We examined the reliability by comparing the correlations between reaction times to positive and negative adjectives as a function of the preceding attitude object, across the two time measurements. The correlations were highly positive and significant, thereby suggesting that if the context within which an attitude object is perceived remains constant, the nature of the automatic attitude is reliable. In addition, the automatic attitudes toward the objects of interest in the first measurement significantly predicted the automatic attitudes in the second measurement.

These first two experiments demonstrated that automatically activated attitudes can be completely reversed by manipulating the nature of recently activated, semantically related (to the attitude object) information. When the attitude object was framed as a dangerous or displeasing object (e.g., *drill* highlights the danger of *dentist*), the automatic attitude toward that object was negative. In contrast, when the object was framed as a safe or pleasing object (e.g., *doctor* emphasizes the safety, competence, and prestige of *dentist*), the automatic attitude toward that object was positive. These two experiments demonstrate that the evaluative knowledge that is delivered about an object is sensitive to the meaningfulness of the object to the perceiver. When negative aspects of the object are salient, the evaluative information is negative. When positive aspects of the object are highlighted, the evaluative information is positive. In addition, when the context is held constant, automatic attitudes are highly reliable.

A third experiment was conducted to further examine the degree to which the knowledge that an automatic attitude delivers is sensitive to the goals of the perceiver. Although the previous two experiments suggested that the evaluative information that is automatically activated about an object depends on which aspect of the object is made salient, we wanted to test more directly whether a current activated goal would render some attitude objects more useful than when the goal is not activated. In addition, we were interested in the extent to which automatic attitudes would be responsive to a currently held goal, versus a goal that had already been completed.

In the third experiment, we focused on the goal of achievement. Participants sat in individual cubicles and were told that they were going to play a game in which they would be asked to make words from 15 Scrabble letter tiles. They were all told that they would have 5 minutes to make different words from the letter tiles. There were two between-subject variables. The first concerned whether an achievement goal was induced. Some participants were told that the game measured their verbal skills and their potential to succeed in various academic environments. These participants were also told that their performance would be compared to the performance of other students and so they should do as well as possible.

The same participants were told that they would receive points for their performance. Specifically, they were told that they would receive 1 point for every word, 5 points for every noun, and 7 points for every noun that started with the letter "c." They were instructed to achieve as many points as possible and to write down each word on a separate sheet of paper. The participants were timed, and the experimenter wore a stopwatch that she used in front of them to emphasize the need to work quickly.

The other participants were simply told to make words out of the letters for 5 minutes and that they would be asked questions about the experience of making words after the game was over. They were told that they did not need to write anything down, remember anything, or show the experimenter any of the words, because they would be asked questions later. Nothing about points was mentioned.

After all participants played the game for 5 minutes, they then completed a computer task that consisted of a sequential priming paradigm in which their automatic attitudes toward several attitude objects were measured. These words represented attitude objects that were useful for those who were trying to achieve (e.g., "words," "nouns," "c," "points," "compete").

The second independent variable concerned whether participants were told that they would play a second round of the game after this computer task, or that they were finished with the Scrabble game. Some participants were told that there would be two rounds of the game and that they would play the first 5-minute round and then complete a task that would clear their minds before going onto the second round of the game. The other participants were told that they would play the Scrabble game for 5 minutes, and would then start a computer task. Thus, during the priming paradigm, half of the participants believed that they would play the Scrabble game again in a couple of minutes and the other half believed that they were finished with the game.

The attitude objects presented in the priming paradigm were useful for those participants who were given an achievement goal. We therefore expected that their automatic attitudes toward these attitude objects would be more positive than those of participants for whom these attitude objects were not useful. However, we also predicted that those in the achievement goal condition who expected to play again would demonstrate the most positive attitudes, for these participants still held the goal of performing well in the game. In contrast, those in the achievement condition who thought that they were finished with the game would not evaluate the objects as positively because the objects would no longer be useful for them at that point.

The results supported this hypothesis. According to an analysis of the reaction times to the positive and negative adjectives, automatic attitudes for the objects were reliably more positive for those in the achievement condition who thought that they would be playing again in several minutes, as compared with those of participants in the other three groups. That is, for participants in the achievement condition who thought they would play again, reaction times to the positive adjectives were significantly shorter than reaction times to the negative adjectives. For those in the other three conditions, automatic attitudes toward the objects were marginally negative, as indicated by shorter reaction times to negative versus positive adjectives.

It should be noted that the performance of those in the achievement condition and the two-rounds condition did not differ from the performance of those in the achievement and the one-round condition. An important point, then, is that the interaction described earlier suggests that the positive attitudes toward the objects did not result from a learning mechanism wherein those who performed better with regard to the objects generated more positivity toward the objects. Rather, the findings demonstrate that only those for whom the objects were still useful automatically evaluated the objects as positive. Those for whom the objects were no longer useful evaluated the objects in a neutral to negative manner.

In sum, this recent research illustrates two aspects of the knowledge function of automatic attitudes. The first is that, in general, an automatic attitude toward an object is sensitive to the current utility of that object, according to the context in which it is perceived. For example, if an object is framed as painful or displeasing (e.g., when the word "drill" precedes the attitude object "dentist"), the automatic attitude is negative. The third experiment futher suggests that automatic attitudes are also sensitive to whether a goal is currently in place or has just been completed. These findings indicate that the knowledge provided by automatic attitudes is sensitive to the context in which the respective objects are perceived.

Finally, an important result is that this third experiment also suggests that automatic appraisal does not depend on highly habitual, familiar responses to the attitude object and can instead reflect very recently learned information about that object, which is contrary to previous research (e.g., Bargh, 1989, 1997; Smith & Lerner, 1986). Participants were able to automatically evaluate attitude objects as positive, even when the utility of those objects was learned only 5 minutes prior to the measurement of the attitudes toward those objects.

FLEXIBILITY OF AUTOMATIC ATTITUDES

We now turn to the second dimension concerning the knowledge function of automatic attitudes—namely, the degree to which automatic attitudes are flexible in response to novel information or objects. If the function of automatic attitudes is to deliver evaluative information quickly and effortlessly in order to aid the perceiver in his or her behavior toward the objects as well as his or her understanding of the situation, then it would be an advantage to be able to appraise novel objects. In other words, the ability to automatically integrate evaluative information from individual features of a novel object in order to provide a summary evaluative response to the object, instead of relying solely on preexisting stored representations, seems like an advantage. This would mean that an integration of evaluative information concerning novel objects could occur immediately and without the necessity of conscious attention.

Previous research suggests that automatic attitudes depend on previously stored evaluative associations (e.g., Bargh et al., 1992; Bargh et al., 1996; Fazio et al., 1986; Fiske & Pavelchak, 1986). For example, Fazio et al. (1986) refer to the association between the representation of the attitude object and the representation of the evaluation of that object in their discussion of attitude activation. On this subject, they state, "Just as a knowledge structure concerning some object may consist of bits of information organized in a network of associations to the object, so too may affect be linked to the object. Furthermore, just as activation can spread from one node in the network to another, the present data indicate a spontaneous spreading of activation from the object to the affective association" (p. 236).

In addition, theorists have argued that an automatic activation of more than one evaluative representation requires conscious effort and cannot be accomplished automatically (Fiske & Pavelchak, 1986; Wilson & Hodges, 1992; Wilson et al., 2000). For example, Wilson et al. (2000) argue that some attitudes are stored in memory and can therefore be automatically activated, whereas other attitudes are not stored in memory and require an on-line integration of evaluative information from numerous sources. This integration requires some degree of strategic effort (i.e., is not automatic). According to this perspective, people are able to evaluate novel objects only if they can effortfully integrate information about the features of the object.

No previous research has directly examined the extent to which people are able to automatically evaluate novel objects. For example, although it may seem as though this topic has been addressed by the work of Zajonc and colleagues on mere exposure (e.g., Monahan, Murphy, & Zajonc, 2000; Murphy & Zajonc, 1993), this research has actually shown only that the explicit liking of stimuli increases as the exposure of the stimuli increases. Although this research demonstrates how the frequency of exposure influences a person's explicit positivity toward the stimuli, it does not address whether and how people are automatically evaluating each novel stimulus.

Recent Research

Across four experiments, Duckworth et al. (in press) found evidence that participants were able to nonconsciously and automatically evaluate novel auditory and visual stimuli. In the first two experiments, participants were asked to pronounce a series of adjectives that appeared one at a time in the center of a computer screen. Each adjective was preceded by an auditorily presented attitude object that was either a positive or negative word or nonsense (novel) word. The words were nouns that had been used in previous automatic evaluation experiments (e.g., "cancer," "music"; see Bargh et al., 1992). The nonsense (novel) words were composed of two-syllable utterances and were unfamiliar to the participants. The valence of the novel words was determined by a separate pilot study in which participants explicitly evaluated the novel stimuli (as was the case across all four experiments).

The pattern of data from each experiment demonstrates the signature evaluative priming effect, both when the attitude objects were familiar and when they were novel. Specifically, participants were faster at pronouncing the target adjectives when the preceding attitude objects were of the same (versus opposite) valence, regardless of whether the attitude objects were novel. The results from these two experiments show that people can automatically evaluate novel sounds as good or bad without any corresponding representation of the meaning of those novel sounds in memory.

In the third experiment, Duckworth et al. (in press) used pictorial stimuli as the attitude objects, including pictures of both familiar and novel attitude objects; the novel pictures were abstract art images with which participants were unfamiliar. As predicted, participants pronounced the target adjectives more quickly when the adjectives were preceded by attitude objects of the same (vs. opposite) valence, again, irrespective of the novelty of the pictures. The findings replicated the results from the first two experiments, and suggest that participants are able to automatically appraise novel images as positive or negative.

The fourth experiment addressed the degree to which the findings would generalize to a different response task, rather than pronunciation. Participants were asked to make either approach motions by pulling a lever toward them or avoidance motions by pushing a lever away from them (see Chen & Bargh, 1999; Wentura, Rothermund, & Bak, 2000). Novel abstract art images were used as prime stimuli, as in the third experiment, and appeared one at a time on a computer screen. Participants were told to either push or pull the lever in response to each image. It was expected that if participants were able to automatically evaluate the novel objects, positive evaluations should facilitate approach arm motions, as compared with negative evaluations, and negative evaluations should facilitate avoidance arm motions relative to positive evaluations. The results support this pattern, thereby showing that people are able to automatically evaluate novel stimuli and that this automatic appraisal influences the speed with which participants can behave toward the prime stimuli.

Together, these four experiments suggest that automatic attitudes are flexible in that they can be constructed in response to objects with which participants are unfamiliar. This finding suggests that the automatic appraisal of objects does not require preexisting, stored attitude representations associated with those objects. In addition, the findings suggest that constructive processes in appraisal do not require effortful processing, contrary to some recent theorizing (Wilson & Hodges, 1992; Wilson et al., 2000).

Most important, these experiments suggest a parallel between strategic attitudes and automatic attitudes. Both types of attitudes can refer to novel stimuli, presumably by integrating evaluative information from multiple sources in order to deliver an evaluation about the object as a whole.

CONCLUSION

This chapter has considered the implicit measurement of people's attitudes and the extent to which such automatic attitudes are functional. Researchers have asserted that the delivery of evaluative knowledge about an object is the primary function of attitudes, and that automatic attitudes accomplish this as well and are therefore functional. However, previous research suggests a limit to the extent to which automatic attitudes are functional, relative to strategic attitudes.

In particular, although strategic attitudes are thought to be sensitive to the context in which the attitude object is perceived and measured, automatic attitudes have been conceptualized as stable and impervious to temporary influences of attitude-irrelevant factors (Fazio et al., 1995; Wilson & Hodges, 1992; Wilson et al., 2000). Indeed, the purported stability of implicit attitude measurement is one of the reasons researchers began to prefer it over explicit measurement (e.g., see Banaji, 2001). However, in line with recent research suggesting that automatic attitudes may depend on the attitude-relevant exemplars to which the perceiver is exposed (e.g., Dasgupta & Greenwald, 2001), we reviewed evidence from three experiments that suggest that automatic attitudes are sensitive to the context in which the object is perceived, and consequently, to the current goals of the perceiver. For example, participant's automatic attitudes toward objects depended on whether the attitude objects were framed as safe and pleasing or as dangerous and displeasing. Further, participants' automatic attitudes toward a group of objects were positive when those objects were useful to the participants' goals.

Although strategic attitudes have been conceptualized as flexible and sometimes constructive, automatic attitudes have been presumed to be stable across time and rather inflexible (e.g., Wilson et al., 2000). Moreover, research and theory have suggested that whereas people can strategically evaluate novel objects, they are unable to do so automatically (e.g., Fiske & Pavelchak, 1986; Wilson & Hodges, 1992). In contrast, we reviewed a series of four experiments that demonstrate that people do immediately and automatically appraise objects with which they are unfamiliar. This finding was replicated with two different types of novel stimuli (audibly presented "words," and images) and across two different response tasks (pronunciation and arm movements).

These two sets of studies suggest that automatic attitudes are functional in a sensitive and flexible way. They provide the perceiver with evaluative information about an object in a way that is sensitive to the meaningfulness of the object within the current situation and relative to the person's goals. Further, people seem able to automatically appraise novel objects (i.e., those with no corresponding representation in memory). Together, these findings suggest that automatic attitudes can be considered functional to a similar extent as attitudes that are strategically recalled.

REFERENCES

Abelson, R. P. (1976). Script processing in attitude formation and decision making. In J. S. Carroll & J. W. Payne (Eds.), *Cognition and social behavior* (pp. 33–45). Hillsdale, NJ: Erlbaum.

Abelson, R. P. (1981). Psychological status of the script concept. *American Psychologist, 36,* 715–729.

Ajzen, I., & Sexton, J. (1999). Depth of processing, belief congruence, and attitude–behavior correspondence. In S. Chaiken & Y. Trope (Eds.), *Dual-process theories in social psychology* (pp. 117–138). New York: Guilford Press.

Allport, G. W. (1935). Attitudes. In C. Murchison (Ed.), *Handbook of social psychology* (pp. 798–844). Worcester, MA: Clark University Press.

Anderson, J. R. (1983). *The architecture of cognition.* Cambridge, MA: Harvard University Press.

Anderson, J. R., & Bower, G. H. (1973). *Human associative memory.* Washington, DC: Winston.

Anderson, J. A., & Rosenfeld, E. (1988). *Neurocomputing: Foundations of research.* Cambridge, MA: MIT Press.

Anderson, N. H. (1974). Cognitive algebra: Integration theory applied to social attribution. In L. Berkowitz (Ed.), *Advances in experimental social psychology* (Vol. 7, pp. 1–101). New York: Academic Press.

Banaji, M. R. (2001). Implicit attitudes can be measured. In H. L. Roediger, J. S. Nairne, I. Neither, & A. Surprenant (Eds.), *The nature of remembering: Essays in honor of Robert G. Crowder* (pp. 117–150). Washington, DC: American Psychological Association.

Bargh, J. A. (1989). Conditional automaticity: Varieties of automatic influence in social perception and cognition. In J. S. Uleman & J. A. Bargh (Eds.), *Unintended thought* (pp. 3–51). New York: Guilford Press.

Bargh, J. A. (1990). Auto-motives: Preconscious determinants of social interaction. In E. T. Higgins & R. M. Sorrentino (Eds.), *Handbook of motivation and cognition: Foundations of social behavior* (Vol. 2., pp. 93–130). New York: Guilford Press.

Bargh, J. A. (1997). The automaticity of everyday life. In R. S. Wyer (Ed.), *Advances in social cognition* (Vol. 10, pp. 1–61). Mahwah, NJ: Erlbaum.

Bargh, J. A., Chaiken, S., Govender, R., & Pratto, F. (1992). The generality of the automatic attitude activation effect. *Journal of Personality and Social Psychology, 62,* 893–912.

Bargh, J. A., Chaiken, S., Raymond, P., & Hymes, C. (1996). The automatic evaluation effect: Unconditional automatic attitude activation with a pronunciation task. *Journal of Experimental Social Psychology, 32,* 104–128.

Bechtel, W., & Abrahamsen, A. (1991). *Connectionism and the mind: An introduction to parallel processing in networks.* Oxford, UK: Basil Blackwell.

Bem, D. J. (1972). Self-perception theory. In L. Berkowitz (Ed.), *Advances in experimental social psychology* (Vol. 6, pp. 1–62). New York: Academic Press.

Bower, G. H. (1981). Mood and memory. *American Psychologist, 36,* 129–148.

Cameron, J. A., Alvarez, J. M., & Bargh, J. A. (2000). *Examining the validity of implicit and explicit measures of prejudice: Is there really a bona fide pipeline?* Paper presented at the 1st annual meeting of the Society for Personality and Social Psychology, Nashville, TN.

Carlston, D. E., & Smith, E. R. (1996). Principles of mental representation. In E. T. Higgins & A. W. Kruglanski (Eds.), *Social psychology: Handbook of basic principles* (pp. 184–210). New York: Guilford Press.

Chen, M., & Bargh, J. A. (1999). Consequences of automatic evaluation: Immediate behavioral predispositions to approach and avoid the stimulus. *Personality and Social Psychology Bulletin, 25,* 215–224.

Collins, A. M., & Loftus, E. F. (1975). A spreading-activation theory of semantic processing. *Psychological Review, 82,* 407–428.

Cunningham, W. A., Preacher, K. J., & Banaji, M. R. (2001). Implicit attitude measures: Consistency, stability, and convergent validity. *Psychological Science, 12,* 163–170.

Dasgupta, N., & Greenwald, A. G. (2001). On the malleability of automatic attitudes: Combating automatic prejudice with images of liked and disliked individuals. *Journal of Personality and Social Psychology, 81,* 800–814.

Devine, P. G. (1989). Stereotypes and prejudice: Their automatic and controlled components. *Journal of Personality and Social Psychology, 56,* 5–18.

Devine, P. G. (1995). Prejudice and out-group perception. In A. Tesser (Ed.), *Advanced social psychology* (pp. 467–524). New York: McGraw-Hill.

Dovidio, J. F., Kawakami, K., Johnson, C., Johnson, B., & Howard, A. (1997). On the nature of prejudice: Automatic and controlled processes. *Journal of Experimental Social Psychology, 33,* 510–540.

Duckworth, K., Bargh, J. A., Garcia, M., & Chaiken, S. (in press). The automatic evaluation of novel stimuli. *Psychological Science.*

Eagly, A. H., & Chaiken, S. (1993). *The psychology of attitudes.* Fort Worth, TX: Harcourt Brace Jovanovich.

Elms, A. C. (1975). The crisis of confidence in social psychology. *American Psychologist, 30,* 967–976.

Fazio, R. H. (1987). Self-perception theory: A current perspective. In M. P. Zanna, J. M. Olson, & C. P. Herman (Eds.), *Social influence: The Ontario Symposium* (Vol. 5, pp. 129–150). Hillsdale, NJ: Erlbaum.

Fazio, R. H. (1989). On the power and functionality of attitudes: The role of attitude accessibility. In A. R. Pratkanis, S. J. Breckler, & A. G. Greenwald (Eds.), *Attitude structure and function* (pp. 153–180). Hillsdale, NJ: Erlbaum.

Fazio, R. H. (2000). On the automatic activation of associated evaluations: An overview. *Cognition and Emotion, 14,* 1–27.

Fazio, R. H., Jackson, J. R., Dunton, B. C., & Williams, C. J. (1995). Variability in automatic activation as an unobtrusive measure of racial attitudes. A bona fide pipeline? *Journal of Personality and Social Psychology, 69,* 1013–1027.

Fazio, R. H., Sanbonmatsu, D. M., Powell, M. C., & Kardes, F. R. (1986). On the automatic activation of attitudes. *Journal of Personality and Social Psychology, 50,* 229–238.

Ferguson, M. J., & Bargh, J. A. (in press). The constructive nature of automatic evaluation. In J. Musch & K. C. Klauer (Eds.), *The psychology of evaluation: Affective processes in cognition and emotion.* Hillsdale, NJ: Erlbaum.

Ferguson, M. J., & Bargh, J. A. (2002). *Markers of meaningfulness: A motivational perspective of automatic attitudes.* Unpublished manuscript, New York University.

Fiedler, K. (1996). Explaining and simulating judgment biases as an aggregation phenomenon in probabilistic, multiple-cue environments. *Psychological Review, 103,* 193–214.

Fishbein, M., & Ajzen, I. (1974). Attitudes toward objects as predictors of single and multiple behavioral criteria. *Psychological Review, 81,* 59–74.

Fishbein, M., & Ajzen, I. (1975). *Belief, attitude, intention, and behavior: An introduction to theory and research.* Reading, MA: Addison-Wesley.

Fiske, S. T. (1992). Thinking is for doing: Portraits of social cognition from daguerreotype to laserphoto. *Journal of Personality and Social Psychology, 63,* 877–889.

Fiske, S. T., & Pavelchak, M. A. (1986). Category-based versus piecemeal-based affective responses: Development in schema-triggered affect. In R. M. Sorrentino & E. T. Higgins (Eds.), *Handbook of motivation and cognition: Foundations of social behavior* (pp. 167–203). New York: Guilford Press.

Gaes, G. G., Kalle, R. J., & Tedeschi, J. T. (1978). Impression management in the forced compliance situation. *Journal of Experimental Social Psychology, 14,* 493–510.

Glaser, J., & Banaji, M. R. (1999). When fair is foul and foul is fair: Reverse priming in automatic evaluation. *Journal of Personality and Social Psychology, 77,* 669–687.

Glenberg, A. M. (1997). What memory is for. *Behavioral and Brain Sciences, 20,* 1–55.

Greenwald, A. G., Draine, S. C., & Abrams, R. L. (1996). Three cognitive markers of unconscious semantic activation. *Science, 273,* 1699–1702.

Greenwald, A. G., Klinger, M. R., & Liu, T. J. (1989). Unconscious processing of dichoptically masked words. *Memory and Cognition, 17,* 35–47.

Greenwald, A. G., McGhee, D. E., & Schwarz, J. L. K. (1998). Measuring individual differences in implicit cognition: The Implicit Association Test. *Journal of Personality and Social Psychology, 74,* 1464–1480.

Himmelfarb, S. (1993). The measurement of attitudes. In A. H. Eagly & S. Chaiken (Eds.), *The psychology of attitudes* (pp. 23–84). Fort Worth, TX: Harcourt Brace Jovanovich.

Jones, E. E., & Sigall, H. (1971). The bogus pipeline: A new paradigm for measuring affect and attitude. *Psychological Bulletin, 76,* 349–364.

Katz, D. (1960). The functional approach to the study of attitudes. *Public Opinion Quarterly, 24,* 163–204.

Katz, D., & Stotland, E. (1959). A preliminary statement to a theory of attitude structure and change. In S. Koch (Ed.), *Psychology: A study of a science* (Vol. 3, pp. 423–475). New York: McGraw-Hill.

Kelman, H. C. (1974). Attitudes are alive and well and gainfully employed in the sphere of action. *American Psychologist, 29,* 310–324.

Klauer, K. C. (1998). Affective priming. *European Review of Social Psychology, 8,* 63–107.

Klauer, K. C., Rossnagel, C., & Musch, J. (1997). List context effects in evaluative priming. *Journal of Experimental Psychology: Learning, Memory, and Cognition, 23,* 246–255.

Lewin, K. (1935.). *A dynamic theory of personality.* New York: McGraw-Hill.

McConahay, J. B. (1986). Modern racism, ambivalence, and the Modern Racism Scale. In J. F. Dovidio & S. L. Gaertner (Eds.), *Prejudice, discrimination, and racism* (pp. 91–125). San Diego, CA: Academic Press.

McConnell, A. R., & Leibold, J. M. (2001). Relations among the Implicit Association Test, discriminatory behavior, and explicit measures of racial attitudes. *Journal of Experimental Social Psychology, 37,* 435–442.

McGuire, W. J. (1986). The vicissitudes of attitudes and similar representational constructs in twentieth century psychology. *European Journal of Social Psychology, 16,* 89–130.

Millar, M. G., & Tesser, A. (1986). Thought-induced attitude change: The effects of schema structure and commitment. *Journal of Personality and Social Psychology, 51,* 259–275.

Monahan, J. L., Murphy, S. T., & Zajonc, R. B. (2000). Subliminal mere exposure: Specific, general, and diffuse effects. *Psychological Science, 11,* 462–466.

Murphy, S. T., & Zajonc, R. B. (1993). Affect, cognition, and awareness: Affective priming with optimal and suboptimal stimulus exposures. *Journal of Personality and Social Psychology, 64,* 723–739.

Neely, J. H. (1976). Semantic priming and retrieval from lexical memory: Evidence for faciliatory and inhibitory processes. *Memory and Cognition, 4,* 648–654.

Neely, J. H. (1977). Semantic priming and retrieval from lexical memory: Roles of inhibitionless spreading activation and limited-capacity attention. *Journal of Experimental Psychology: General, 106,* 225–254.

Nesdale, D., & Durkin, K. (1998). Stereotypes and attitudes: Implicit and explicit processes. In K. Kirsner & C. Speelman (Eds.), *Implicit and explicit mental processes* (pp. 219–232). Mahwah, NJ: Erlbaum.

Olson, J. M. (1990). Self-inference processes in emotion. In J. M. Olson & M. P. Zanna (Eds.), *Self-inference processes: The Ontario Symposium* (Vol. 6, pp. 17–42). Hillsdale, NJ: Erlbaum.

Orne, M. T. (1962). On the social psychology of the psychological experiment: With particular reference to demand characteristics and their implications. *American Psychologist, 17,* 776–783.

Ostrom, T. M. (1973). The bogus pipeline: A new *ignis fatuus? Psychological Bulletin, 79,* 252–259.

Pratkanis, A. R., Breckler, S. J., & Greenwald, A. G. (1989). *Attitude structure and function.* Hillsdale, NJ: Erlbaum.

Rosenberg, M. J. (1956). Cognitive structure and attitudinal affect. *Journal of Abnormal and Social Psychology, 53,* 367–372.

Rosenberg, M. J., & Hovland, C. I. (1960). Cognitive, affective, and behavioral components of attitudes. In C. I. Hovland & M. J. Rosenberg (Eds.), *Attitude organization and change: An analysis of consistency among attitude components* (pp. 1–14). New Haven, CT: Yale University Press.

Rosenthal, R., & Jacobson, L. (1966). Teachers' expectancies: Determinants of pupils' IQ gains. *Psychological Reports, 19,* 115–118.

Rudman, L. A., Greenwald, A. G., Mellott, D. S., & Schwartz, J. L. K. (1999). Measuring the automatic components of prejudice: Flexibility and generality of the Implicit Association Test. *Social Cognition, 17,* 437–465.

Schank, R. C., & Abelson, R. P. (1977). *Scripts, plans, goals, and understanding: An inquiry into human knowledge structures.* Hillsdale, NJ: Erlbaum.

Schuman, H., & Johnson, M. P. (1976). Attitudes and behavior. *Annual Review of Sociology, 2,* 161–207.

Schuman, H., & Kalton, G. (1985). Survey methods. In G. Lindzey & E. Aronson (Eds.), *Handbook of social psychology* (3rd ed., Vol. 1, pp. 635–697). New York: Random House.

Schwarz, N., & Clore, G. L. (1983). Mood, misattribution, and judgment of wellbeing: Informative and directive functions of affective states. *Journal of Personality and Social Psychology, 45,* 513–523.

Sigall, H., & Page, R. (1971). Current stereotypes: A little fading, a little faking. *Journal of Personality and Social Psychology, 18,* 247–255.

Smith, E. R. (1996). What do connectionism and social psychology offer each other? *Journal of Personality and Social Psychology, 70,* 893–912.

Smith, E. R., & DeCoster, J. (1999). Associative and rule-based processing: A connectionist interpretation of dual-process models. In S. Chaiken & Y. Trope (Eds.), *Dual-process theories in social psychology* (pp. 323–336). New York: Guilford Press.

Smith, E. R., & Lerner, M. (1986). Development of automatism of social judgments. *Journal of Personality and Social Psychology, 50,* 246–259.

Smith, M. B., Bruner, J. S., & White, R. W. (1956). *Opinions and personality.* New York: Wiley.

Strack, F. (1992). The different routes to social judgments: Experiential versus informational strategies. In L. L. Martin & A. Tesser (Eds.), *The construction of social judgments* (pp. 249–276). Hillsdale, NJ: Erlbaum.

Swanson, J. F., Rudman, L. A., & Greenwald, A. G. (2001). Using the Implicit Association Test to investigate attitude-behaviour consistency for stigmatised behaviour. *Social Cognition, 15,* 207–230.

Tesser, A. (1978). Self-generated attitude change. In L. Berkowitz (Ed.), *Advances in experimental social psychology* (Vol. 11, pp. 289–338). New York: Academic Press.

Thompson, M. M., Zanna, M. P., & Griffin, D. W. (1995). Let's not be indifferent about (attitudinal) ambivalence. In R. E. Petty & J. A. Krosnick (Eds.), *Attitude strength: Antecedents and consequences. Ohio State University series on attitudes and persuasion* (Vol. 4, pp. 361–386). Hillsdale, NJ: Erlbaum.

Thurstone, L. L. (1928). Attitudes can be measured. *American Journal of Sociology, 33,* 529–554.

Warner, S. L. (1965). Randomized response: A survey technique for eliminating evasive answer bias. *Journal of the American Statistical Association, 60,* 63–69.

Wentura, D., Rothermund, K., & Bak, P. (2000). Automatic vigilance: The attention grabbing power of approach- and avoidance-related social information. *Journal of Personality and Social Psychology, 78,* 1024–1037.

Wicker, A. W. (1969). Attitude versus actions: The relationship of verbal and overt behavioral responses to attitude objects. *Journal of Social Issues, 25*(4), 41–78.

Wilson, T. D., Dunn, D. S., Kraft, D., & Lisle, D. J. (1989). Introspection, attitude change, and attitude–behavior consistency: The disruptive effects of explaining why we feel the way we do. In L. Berkowitz (Ed.), *Advances in experimental social psychology* (Vol. 22, pp. 287–343). Orlando, FL: Academic Press.

Wilson, T. D., & Hodges, S. D. (1992). Attitudes as temporary constructions. In A. Tesser & L. Martin (Eds.), *The construction of social judgment* (pp. 37–65). Hillsdale, NJ: Erlbaum.

Wilson, T. D., Lindsey, S., & Schooler, T. Y. (2000). A model of dual attitudes. *Psychological Review, 107,* 101–126.

Wittenbrink, B., Judd, C. M., & Park, B. (1997). Evidence for racial prejudice at the implicit level and its relationship with questionnaire measures. *Journal of Personality and Social Psychology, 72,* 262–274.

Wittenbrink, B., Judd, C. M., & Park, B. (2001). Spontaneous prejudice in context: Variability in automatically activated attitudes. *Journal of Personality and Social Psychology, 81,* 815–827.

CHAPTER 17

Theory of Mind, Autism, and Emotional Intelligence

ROBERT JAMES RICHARD BLAIR

The goal of this chapter is to consider the relationship between Theory of Mind and emotional intelligence. Toward this goal, I provide a brief description of Theory of Mind and then consider the relationship between Theory of Mind and the components of emotional intelligence. This is done mostly through a neuropsychological approach. I consider the implications of data from populations who present with deficits in Theory of Mind (individuals with autism) and emotional intelligence (psychopathic individuals). I ask whether individuals with Theory of Mind impairment necessarily show impairment in emotional intelligence by reviewing work with children with autism. I then consider whether individuals with emotional intelligence impairment necessarily show impairment in Theory of Mind by reviewing work with psychopathic individuals. The chapter closes with an investigation of whether emotional processes play any role in the development of Theory of Mind.

WHAT IS THEORY OF MIND?

Theory of Mind refers to the ability to represent the mental states of others, that is, their thoughts, desires, beliefs, intentions, and knowledge (Frith, 1989; Leslie, 1987; Premack & Woodruff, 1978). Theory of Mind allows the attribution of mental states to self and others in order to explain and predict behavior. As a hypothesis, Theory of Mind has considerable similarity to earlier ideas of role and perspective taking (Chandler, Greenspan, & Barenboim, 1974; Selman, 1980). Role taking was defined as the ability to recognize another person's expectations and desires, predicting how that person may react, and understanding what the person means to communicate. The main difference between the current conceptualization of Theory of Mind and earlier ideas about role and perspective taking is that Theory of Mind is a more tightly specified construct. Activities that were grouped together as forms of role or perspective taking—for example, cognitive and visual perspective taking—have been shown to be computationally distinct and mediated by different neurocognitive systems (Baron-Cohen, 1989; Reed & Peterson, 1990).

The classic measure of Theory of Mind is the Sally–Anne task (Wimmer & Perner, 1983). In this task, the participant is shown two dolls, Sally and Anne, and a basket and a box. The child watches as Sally places her marble in the basket and then leaves the room. While Sally is out, naughty Anne moves Sally's marble from the basket to the box. Then she, too, leaves the room. Now Sally comes back into the room. The child is asked the test question: "Where will Sally look for her marble?" In order to accomplish this task, the child must represent Sally's mental state, her belief that the marble is in the basket. Without this representation, the child will answer on the basis of the marble's real location, that is, in the box. Most healthy developing children from the age of 4 years pass this test (Wimmer & Perner, 1983).

There are two main positions on Theory of Mind: the theory-theory view (e.g., Gopnik & Meltzoff, 1997; Perner, 1991) and the modular view (Leslie, 1987). According to the theory-theory view, children construct mental state concepts (e.g., *belief, misrepresentation*) through the use of domain-general mechanisms for the formation of theories. Effectively, these mechanisms are making theories about other individuals. In contrast, according to the modular view, the Theory of Mind Mechanism (ToMM) is a mechanism that allows the representation of mental states.

The theory-theory view faces several major difficulties. These are not detailed here, but it is worth noting that manipulations of the false belief paradigm that are designed to either decrease the strength of representations of the current state of the object or increase the strength of representations of the false belief, massively influence performance on false belief tasks (see, for a review, Leslie, 2000). Such data can be elegantly explained by the ToMM model but are incompatible with theory-theory views. Moreover, it is difficult to understand from the perspective of modern cognitive neuroscience how a system allowing the representation of the mental states of others is likely to develop as a consequence of the child's forming a theory that this is the case.

However, it is worth considering that some of the debate between the theory-theory and modular camps' positions probably occurs because, in some respects, the positions are models of different phenomena. The theory-theory authors are attempting to describe the child's and adult's semantic knowledge about other individuals' internal states. In contrast, Leslie (2000), in particular, is attempting to detail a model of the computational architecture that is necessary for the representation of the mental states of others.

From a cognitive neuroscience perspective, it is interesting to note that recent animal work has identified medial frontal cortex involvement in the representation of the animal's goals during instrumental learning paradigms (see, for a review, Balleine & Dickinson, 1998). This is intriguing because a series of neuroimaging studies in humans have consistently implicated comparable regions of the medial prefrontal cortex, as well as the temporoparietal junction and the temporal poles, in the representation of the mental states of others (Baron-Cohen, Ring, et al., 1999; Brunet, Sarfati, Hardy-Bayle, & Decety, 2000; Castelli, Happe, Frith, & Frith, 2000; Fletcher et al., 1995; Gallagher et al., 2000; Goel, Grafman, Sadato, & Hallett, 1995; Vogeley et al., 2001; see, for a review, Frith & Frith, 1999). Although there is very little work suggesting that animals can represent the mental states of others, the work of Balleine and Dickinson (1998) raises the interesting possibility that the capacity to represent the mental states of others in humans may incorporate older neurocognitive systems that allow the representation of the mental states (in particular, the goals) of the self. This has led to the suggestion of a neurocognitive architecture whereby a mechanism sensitive to biological motion (potentially involving neurons within the temporoparietal junction) serves to activate systems required for the representation of mental states (Blair, Frith, Smith, Abell, & Cipolotti, 2002; Cipolotti, Robinson, Blair, & Frith, 1999). These systems include the temporal poles and medial frontal cortex. The suggestion follows recent computational accounts of executive functioning where "Task Demand" units represent the task to be achieved and modulate the functioning of posterior systems (Cohen, Braver, & O'Reilly, 1996; Cohen & Servan-Schreiber, 1992). The idea is that Theory of Mind involves a system of neurons that allow the representation of another individual's intention and that this neural activity modulates more posterior representations, perhaps requiring the temporal poles, allowing potential predictions of the other individual's behavior (Blair, in press). This is not to suggest that Theory of Mind can be equated with executive functioning; there are now data that indicate that Theory of Mind is dissociable from executive functioning (Fine, Lumsden, & Blair, 2001; Lough, Gregory, & Hodges, 2001). However, the suggestion is that Theory of Mind may share computational similarities with other executive systems.

According to the perspective briefly described thus far, the theory-theory positions are positions concerning the nature of the posterior representations, the concepts of other individuals, whereas the modular position relates to the way in which neurons in medial frontal cortex interact with posterior systems. I stress this difference here because any discussion of the relationship between emotional intelligence and Theory of Mind could be between emotional intelligence and the ability to represent the mental states of others or emotional intelligence and people's theories about other individuals' internal states. In this chapter, I focus on the relationship between emotional intelligence and the ability to represent the mental states of others.

THEORY OF MIND AND EMOTIONAL INTELLIGENCE

There are two main ways in which the relationship between Theory of Mind and emotional intelligence can be explored. The first is by finding the degree of association between performance on Theory of Mind measures and performance on emotion tasks in normally developing individuals. This approach typically involves correlational analyses of performances on tests designed to assess different cognitive functions. The major problem with this approach is that observed correlations may not indicate functional equivalence of core systems, but only similar developmental trajectories or the functioning of systems that are commonly required for successful performance on both types of task but that are not part of the core systems themselves. This problem is particularly severe in exploring the relationship of other variables with Theory of Mind, as it is highly plausible that much of the variance in Theory of Mind scores, at least if they are obtained through false belief tests, is due to variance in executive, "inhibitory" systems rather than variance in the ability to represent the mental states of others (Leslie, 2000).

The second approach is neuropsychological, which does not face the major problem outlined for the first approach. Within the neuropsychological approach, populations are identified who present with impairment in a specific neurocognitive system and the implications of this impairment are investigated. Individuals with autism are a population who have severe Theory of Mind impairment. So, by studying these individuals, we should be able to ascertain the relationship between Theory of Mind and emotional intelligence.

AUTISM

Autism is a severe developmental disorder described by the American Psychiatric Association's *Diagnostic and Statistical Manual of Mental Disorders* (DSM-IV; American Psychiatric Association, 1994) as "the presence of markedly abnormal or impaired development in social interaction and communication and a markedly restricted repertoire of activities and interests" (p. 66). The main criteria for the diagnosis in DSM-IV can be summarized as qualitative impairment in social communication and restricted and repetitive patterns of behavior and interests. These criteria must be evident before 3 years of age. The incidence rate has been estimated as approximately 4 in 10,000 (Lotter, 1966).

Children with autism have been consistently reported to show Theory of Mind impairment. This was originally observed by Baron-Cohen, Leslie, and Frith (1985). Children with autism and two comparison groups, a mildly retarded population to match for mental age and a chronologically matched (to mental age) population of normally developing children were presented the Sally–Anne task described earlier. Although most of the members of both comparison groups passed this test, 80% of the children with autism failed it. This finding has now been replicated in a number of studies, using real people instead of toys, using a "think" question rather than a "look" question, and using a control group of specifically language-impaired children to rule out a language deficit explanation (Leslie & Frith, 1988; Perner, Frith, Leslie, & Leekam, 1989; see, for a review, Baron-Cohen, 1995).

It is worth noting that the disorder of autism has also been linked with other impairments such as executive dysfunction (e.g., Hughes, Russell, & Robbins, 1994; Liss et al., 2001; see, for a review, Pennington & Ozonoff, 1996) and face processing deficits (e.g., Blair et al., 2002; Klin et al., 1999). However, the regions of the dorsolateral prefrontal cortex that have been linked to the executive dysfunction that children with autism typically show (Pennington & Ozonoff, 1996) are not regions of the brain that are typically linked to emotional processing (see LeDoux, 1998). In addition, face processing and emotional processing have also been demonstrated to be dissociable systems (e.g., Calder, Young, Rowland, & Perrett, 1996). Thus, it would be inappropriate to attribute any impairment, or lack of impairment, in emotional processing to either executive dysfunction or impairment in face recognition.

If Theory of Mind is necessary for the emergence of emotional intelligence, then we can predict that a population who lacks Theory of Mind, individuals with autism, should not show these characteristics. The relationship of Theory of Mind to the elements of emotional intelligence is considered in the following section.

THEORY OF MIND AND EMOTION PERCEPTION

As stated earlier, emotion perception includes the individual's ability to identify the his or her own emotional experiences, the ability to identify another individuals emotional experience from that person's facial expressions or vocal tone, and the ability to identify the emotional signal value attributed to objects such as works of art. As far as I am aware, no work has investigated the emotional signal value attributed to objects such as works of art in individuals with Theory of Mind impairment, and this subelement is not considered in this chapter. However, the relationship of Theory of Mind to the other two subelements of emotion perception are considered in turn.

Theory of Mind and the Identification of the Emotional Experiences of the Self

It is difficult to draw direct conclusions about the ability of an individual to identify his or her own emotional experiences. However, one way in which we can indirectly explore this issue is by looking at an individual's ability to attribute emotions to others. The suggestion is that individuals who show anomalous emotional attributions for particular emotions probably experience these emotions atypically. There has been some work on emotion attribution in children with autism (Baron-Cohen, 1991; Capps, Yirmiya, & Sigman, 1992; Yirmiya, Sigman, Kasari, & Mundy, 1992). This work generally indicates that children with autism do appear capable of appraising emotional experiences if they are relatively simple (Capps et al., 1992) and do not require the representation of the mental states of others (Baron-Cohen, 1991; however, see Yirmiya et al., 1992). This suggests that children with autism can appraise, and potentially experience, at least the emotions of happiness and sadness. However, it may be unlikely that children with autism can experience complex emotions such as pride and embarrassment (Capps et al., 1992). Moreover, unsurprisingly, given their impairment in Theory of Mind, children with autism have difficulty appraising emotional situations in which knowledge of the mental states of the protagonists is important (Baron-Cohen, 1991). Thus, it may be expected that children with autism have difficulty experiencing surprise.

However, it is possible that Theory of Mind is rather more related to emotional experience than the evidence presented thus far suggests. The neural architecture identified through functional imaging studies as being crucial for the representation of the mental states of others' includes the medial frontal cortex. This region has also been shown to be involved in an individual's representation of his or her own mental states (Frith & Frith, 1999). For example, the prefrontal region was activated in a study in which subjects reported self-generated thoughts independent from stimuli in the immediate environment (McGuire, Paulesu, Frackowiak, & Frith, 1996). In addition, Blakemore, Wolpert, and Frith (1998) observed medial frontal cortex activity associated with self-reports of a tickling sensation produced by self-produced tactile stimulation. This finding has led to the suggestion that on-line monitoring of inner states—the subjects' own or others'—may engage specific medial frontal regions, regardless of the specific source of information (Castelli et al., 2000). The consequent prediction is that an individual with impairment in the representation of the mental states of others may also have impairment in the representation of his or her own mental states. In line with this prediction, it has been found that children with autism have impairment in representing their own mental states as well as those of others (Frith & Happé, 1999).

Findings indicating that this region of medial frontal cortex is involved in the representation of the mental states of others and the self (i.e., Theory of Mind is involved in the representation of the mental states of the self) are crucial to note, given that this same region also appears to be involved in the representation of the emotional states of the self. Thus, medial frontal cortical activity is associated with perceived pain (Raineville, Duncan, Price, Carrier, & Bushnell, 1997) and self-reports of emotional responses to pleasant, unpleasant, and neutral pictures (Lane, Fink, Chau, & Dolan, 1997). Moreover, there is one suggestive finding that individuals who self-report reduced emotional experience demonstrate reduced medial frontal cortical activity when viewing emotional visual stimuli (Lane et al., 1998). These results suggest that Theory of Mind, by being involved in the representation of the mental states of the self, may also be crucially involved in emotional experience. Currently, a firm conclusion is not possible.

Theory of Mind and the Identification of Others' Emotional Expression

There have been a considerable number of investigations into the ability of individuals with autism to recognize the emotional expressions of others. Many have reported that children with autism have difficulty recognizing the emotional expressions of others (e.g., Bormann-Kischkel, Vilsmeier, & Baude, 1995; Hobson, 1986; Howard et al., 2000). A recent claim has been that this is specific for fearful expressions (Howard et al., 2000). In addition, children with autism have been found to show difficulties in detecting intermodal correspondence of facial and vocal/ linguistic affect (Hobson, Ouston, & Lee, 1989; Loveland et al., 1995).

However, children with autism have usually been found to be unimpaired in facial affect recognition for any emotion when the control group was matched on verbal mental age (e.g., Adolphs, Sears, & Piven, 2001; Baron-Cohen, Wheelwright, & Joliffe, 1997; Ozonoff, Pennington, & Rogers, 1990; Prior, Dahlstrom, & Squires, 1990). In addition, several studies have found emotion processing impairment to be pronounced only when the emotion is a complex "cognitive" emotion such as surprise or embarrassment (Baron-Cohen, Spitz, & Cross, 1993; Bormann-Kischkel et al., 1995; Capps et al., 1992; Baron-Cohen et al., 1993). Finally, Davies and colleagues (Davies, Bishop, Manstead, & Tantam, 1994) found that high-ability children with autism did show difficulties in facial affect matching tasks relative to controls, and they also found them to show difficulties on nonfacial stimuli matching tasks. Davies et al. (1994) suggested that these findings indicate that there may be a general perceptual deficit in children with autism that is not specific to faces or emotions.

Thus, the bulk of the evidence strongly suggests that Theory of Mind is not related to the identification of the emotional expressions of others. But even if Theory of Mind is not related to the naming of the emotional expressions of others, perhaps it is crucial for appropriate autonomic and behavioral responses to other individuals' emotional expressions.

At least five studies have explored the autonomic and behavioral reactions of individuals with autism to the emotional responses of others (Bacon, Fein, Morris, Waterhouse, & Allen, 1998; Blair, 1999a; Corona, Dissanayake, Arbelle, Wellington, & Sigman, 1998; Dissanayake, Sigman, & Kasari, 1996; Sigman, Kasari, Kwon, & Yirmiya, 1992). In four of these studies, the child with autism was playing with the experimenter and the experimenter feigned an emotional reaction, usually distress (Bacon et al., 1998; Corona et al., 1998; Dissanayake et al., 1996; Sigman et al., 1992). Three of these studies have reported reduced empathic responding in the children with autism (Corona et al., 1998; Dissanayake et al., 1996; Sigman et al., 1992). All three reported that when adults displayed emotional reactions, children with autism looked far less at the adults than was true for mentally retarded and normally developing children of equivalent mental age. Moreover, Corona et al. (1998) found that the children with autism did not show the reduced heart rate observed among the mentally retarded comparison population in reaction to the adult feigning distress.

However, these studies have relied on the participant switching his or her attention to the individual feigning distress. This is potentially a problem, as in many of these studies, the child, particularly if the child is of more limited intellectual ability, has shown limited attention to the face of the experimenter (Bacon et al., 1998; Corona et al., 1998; Dissanayake et al., 1996; Sigman et al., 1992). Indeed, Dissanayake et al. (1996) found that the emotional responsiveness of the children with autism was related to their intellectual ability. Moreover, Bacon et al. (1998) found group differences in empathic responsiveness only for low-functioning children with autism. High-functioning children with autism were as likely as the comparison groups to show empathic concern when the adult simulated distress. The results of Bacon et al. (1998) were of particular interest, as the same participants, both high and low functioning, did show reduced social referencing relative to the comparison groups following the sound of a loud unfamiliar and ambiguous noise; that is, the children with autism were less likely to look toward an adult to elicit clarification in the presence of an ambiguous noise. Attempting to gain additional information from another in an ambiguous situation implies calculation of mental states; it is necessary to calculate that the other may have a different knowledge base from your own. These results indicated that although children with autism did not look toward adults as a source of information in an ambiguous context (i.e., the loud unfamiliar noise), they automatically oriented to adults when presented with a basic emotional stimulus, the sound and display of distress.

Interestingly, the Blair (1999a) study also indicated that children with autism did show autonomic responses to the distress of others if the others' distress was unambiguous and in conditions of low distractibility. Blair (1999a) investigated the psychophysiological responsiveness of children with autism and comparison groups to distress cues (sad faces), threatening stimuli (angry faces and threatening animals), and neutral stimuli (neutral faces and objects). Twenty children with autism and two mental-age-matched comparison groups, consisting of 20 children with moderate learning difficulty and 20 normally developing children, were shown slides of these three types of stimuli, and their electrodermal responses were recorded (Blair, 1999a). The children with autism, like the two comparison groups, showed significantly greater autonomic responses to the distress cues, but not the threatening stimuli, than to the neutral stimuli. These results suggest that Theory of Mind is not a prerequisite for generating autonomic responses to the distress of others.

Theory of Mind and the Use of the Sad/Fearful Emotional Signals of Others

Empathic responses to the distress of others has long been linked to moral socialization (Hoffman, 1988; Eisenberg et al., 1990). Recently, this has been formalized within a neurocognitive model of empathy (Blair, 1995). According to the model, moral socialization occurs through the pairing of the activation of the mechanism by distress cues with representations of the acts that caused the distress cues (i.e., moral transgressions, e.g., one person hitting another). A process of classical conditioning results in these representations of moral transgressions becoming triggers for the mechanism. The appropriately developing child thus initially finds the pain of others aversive and then, through socialization, thoughts of acts that cause pain to others aversive also.

Earlier, I presented evidence that individuals with autism were able to recognize the sad and fearful expressions of others (Adolphs et al., 2001; Baron-Cohen et al., 1997; Ozonoff et al., 1990; Prior et al., 1990). But can children with autism use these signals of the distress of others in order to demonstrate moral socialization? One of the markers demonstrating moral socialization in the normally developing child is the emergence of the moral–conventional distinction (Blair, 1995; Smetana, 1993; Turiel & Wainryb, 1998; Smetana, 1993). The moral–conventional distinction is the distinction that children and adults make in their judgments between moral and conventional transgressions (Smetana, 1993; Turiel & Wainryb, 1998). This distinction is made from the age of 39 months (Smetana & Braeges, 1990) and is found across cultures (Nucci, Turiel, & Encarnacion-Gawrych, 1983; Song, Smetana, & Kim, 1987). Within the literature, moral transgressions (e.g., hitting another, damaging another's property) are defined by their consequences for the rights and welfare of others. Conventional transgressions (e.g., talking in class, dressing in opposite sex clothes) are defined by their consequences for social order. Children and adults generally judge moral transgressions to be more *serious* than conventional transgressions (Smetana & Braeges, 1990). In addition, and more important, modifying the rule conditions (by an authority figure removing the prohibition against the act, for example) affects the permissibility only of conventional transgressions. Even if there is no rule prohibiting the action, individuals generally judge moral transgressions as nonpermissible. In contrast, if there is no rule prohibiting a conventional transgression, they generally judge the act as permissible. Although individuals do not always make the moral–conventional distinction in their judgments of seriousness, they do always make the moral–conventional distinction in their judgments of modifiability. Thus, children have been found to judge some conventional transgressions to be as serious as some moral transgressions at some ages (Stoddart & Turiel, 1985; Turiel, 1983). However, even those children who judged conventional transgressions to be as serious as moral transgressions judged moral transgressions as less rule contingent and less under the jurisdiction of authority than the conventional transgressions.

It is crucial to note that it is the presence of victims that distinguishes moral and conventional transgressions. If a person considers that a transgression will result in a victim, he or she will process that transgression as moral. If the person considers that a transgression will not result in a victim, he or she will process that transgression as conventional. Thus, Smetana (1982) has shown that whether an individual treats abortion as a moral transgression or a conventional transgression is determined by whether he or she judges the act to involve a victim. Similarly, Smetana (1985) has found that unknown transgressions (specified by a nonsense word, i.e., "X has done dool") were processed as moral or conventional according to the specified consequences of the act. Thus, "X has done dool and made Y cry" would be processed as moral, whereas "X has done dool and the teacher told him off" would be processed as conventional. If an individual is responsive to the presence of victims, he or she should make the moral–conventional distinction. On the other hand, if an individual is not sensitive to the distress of victims, he or she will not make the moral–conventional distinction.

So do children with autism make the moral–conventional distinction? I investigated the ability to make this distinction in two groups of 10 children with autism (one group that failed all false belief tasks and one group that passed first order tasks) and two comparison groups (10 children with moderate learning difficulty and 10 typically developing children). All four groups of children, even the least able group of children with autism, made the moral–conventional distinction. That is, they were less likely to permit the moral transgressions than the conventional transgressions under normal—and crucially, under modified—rule conditions. The children with autism, even those who, according to their false belief test results, showed no ability to represent the mental states of others, still prohibited the moral, but not the conventional, transgressions in the absence of prohibitory rules (Blair, 1996). Thus, Theory of Mind does not appear to be crucial for this form of emotional assimilation.

Theory of Mind and the Use of the Angry Emotional Signals of Others

A neurocognitive system that relies on the orbitofrontal cortex (OFC) mediates response reversal as a consequence of changes in reinforcement contingencies (Rolls, 2000; Dias, Robbins, & Roberts, 1996). In addition, it is also suggested that another neurocognitive system that relies on OFC mediates response reversal as a consequence of the emotional signals of others (Blair & Cipolotti, 2000; Blair, 2001). Thus, angry expressions are known to curtail the behavior of others in situations in which social rules or expectations have been violated (Averill, 1982). It is suggested that there is a system that is activated by another individual's angry expressions or, possibly, other negative affect expressions (e.g., the staring expressions of others that can precede a sense of embarrassment and perhaps others' disgusted expressions) or the expectations of another's anger. The suggestion is that activation of this system results in the modulation of current behavioral responding, preventing the individual from engaging in inappropriate behavior.

This position has drawn support from findings that the ventrolateral orbitofrontal cortex (BA47) is activated by negative emotional expressions, in particular anger but also fear and disgust (Blair, Morris, Frith, Perrett, & Dolan, 1999; Kesler/West et al., 2001; Sprengelmeyer, Rausch, Eysel, & Przuntek, 1998). Moreover, patients with social behavioral difficulties following lesions of the frontal, particularly the orbitofrontal, cortex have impairment in expression recognition, particularly for the expression of anger (Blair & Cipolotti, 2000; Hornak, Rolls, & Wade, 1996).

It can be assumed that those components of the system that respond to angry faces are independent of Theory of Mind because children with autism generally show no impairment in their recognition of other individuals' angry expressions (Adolphs et al., 2001; Baron-Cohen et al., 1997; Ozonoff et al., 1990; Prior et al., 1990). However, this system is also supposed to respond to violations of social conventions that are likely to lead to social disapproval (Blair, 2001; Blair & Cipolotti, 2000). This function of the system is likely to occur in synchrony with the neurocognitive architecture that allows Theory of Mind. Thus, to determine whether another individual has violated social norms, it is necessary to calculate whether the action could be construed as a violation and, crucially, whether the action was conducted intentionally. Actions that can be construed as violations but that are initiated unintentionally are generally considered embarrassing rather than social violations (Garland & Brown, 1972; Semin & Manstead, 1982). Thus, for instance, sitting in the seat on a bus that another is about to take is a social norm violation if you do it intentionally, but embarrassing if you trip and fall into the person's place by accident. Following this analysis, we may consider that both the capacity to represent the intentions of others (Theory of Mind) and the capacity to respond to expectancies of another's negative affect are related to the ability to identify norm violations. This is indeed the case. Patients with Theory of Mind impairment have been found to show impairment in the ability to identify norm violations (Baron-Cohen,

O'Riordan, Stone, Jones, & Plaisted, 1999; Dewey, 1991) as have patients with impairment in the capacity to process the angry expressions of others (Blair & Cipolotti, 2000; Stone, Baron-Cohen, & Knight, 1998). Moreover, a recent neuroimaging study of the neural systems involved in processing social norm violations revealed activation of those regions associated with Theory of Mind (described earlier), as well as regions of the orbitofrontal cortex previously found to respond to the angry facial expressions of others (Berthoz, Armony, Blair, & Dolan, in press). Thus, Theory of Mind does appear to be involved in this form of emotional assimilation.

Summary of the Relationship between Theory of Mind and Emotion Perception

In conclusion, the relationship between Theory of Mind and the emotion perception element of emotional intelligence remains unclear, at least in regard to the subelement concerning the ability to identify the emotional experiences of the self. Theoretically, the conclusion rests on whether the representation of the mental states of the self utilizes the same neurocognitive architecture as the representation of the mental states of others; that is, whether Theory of Mind allows the representation of the mind of the self as well as that of others. If Theory of Mind is inextricably linked to conscious experience, then Theory of Mind will, of course, play a role in emotional experience. However, if we can assume that performance on emotion attribution tasks indexes ability to identify the emotional experiences of the self, then we can conclude that Theory of Mind is not a prerequisite for the development/functioning of this ability.

In regard to the ability to identify the emotional expressions of others, it now appears clear that Theory of Mind is not a prerequisite for this ability. Individuals with autism who show pronounced impairment in Theory of Mind do not have impairment in the recognition of the expressions of others. In addition, Theory of Mind does not appear to be crucial for the child to use information about the distress of others in the process of moral socialization. Children with autism, even with pronounced Theory of Mind impairment, show no difficulty with tasks that index the degree of moral socialization such as the moral–conventional distinction paradigm. However, Theory of Mind does appear to be involved in the use of information concerning the negative reactions of others, particularly their anger, in considering social conventional transgressions. Even if children with autism are able to process the angry expressions of other individuals, without information about other individuals' intentions they have great difficulty in processing actions as appropriate or inappropriate (Baron-Cohen et al., 1999; Dewey, 1991).

THEORY OF MIND AND EMOTIONAL REGULATION

Emotional regulation includes the individual's ability to manage his or her own emotional response. This section considers the relationship between Theory of Mind and the systems involved in planning and controlling emotional displays.

Emotional displays include expressions and other forms of emotional behavior such as weeping or "jumping for joy." The initial emotional displays of the very young child have been thought to be almost instinctive displays activated by environmental events (cf. Camras, Malatesta, & Izard, 1991); the emotional displays of very young children are released stimuli to salient emotional stimuli. Then, as the child becomes older, social stimuli, in the proximity of others, become more important in determining whether an expression is displayed (e.g., Jones & Raag, 1989; Tronick, Als, & Adamson, 1979). Indeed, by adulthood, the presence of others massively influences whether an emotional stimulus will generate emotional behavior or not (e.g., Fridlund, 1991; see Figure 17.1).

In addition to the relatively automatic communication of emotion that is a function of the intensity of the emotional stimuli and the presence/absence of other individuals, emotional expressive displays can come under executive control. Indeed, a major task faced by the child in middle childhood is to learn the culture's display rules governing the conditions that are appropriate for the display of specific emotions, that is, situations in which the automatic urge to communicate the emotion currently experienced must be inhibited and either an alternative expression displayed or nothing revealed. In a classic study of the development of display rules/control over emotional expressions, Saarni (1984) demonstrated age-related changes in the ability of children to cover their disappointment at the discovery that their gift for helping out an adult was much less interesting than the gift they had been given for the same type of task the day before.

There is very little systematic data on the relationship of Theory of Mind to the display of emotional expressions. It can probably be safely assumed that Theory of Mind is not associated with the emergence of the display of the emotional expressions of disgust, anger, happiness, sadness, and fear in the first 12 months of life (e.g., Camras et al., 1991; Izard, 1992). Although there is evidence that children can represent at least some mental states during this period (see, for a review,

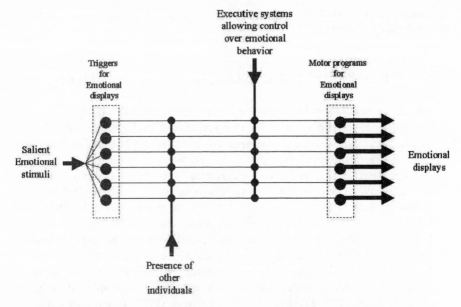

FIGURE 17.1. A model of the control of emotional displays. In this figure, motor programs for emotional displays are triggered by salient emotional stimuli. These will change during development (see Camras et al., 1991). Thus, blowing on a baby's skin may be sufficient to elicit smiling behavior in the infant, whereas the receipt of a pleasing gift may be a more salient stimulus in adulthood. In addition, the production of the motor programs for emotional displays is modulated by the presence of other individuals. Thus, an individual is far more likely to smile at a pleasing video when other individuals are present than if he or she is alone (Fridlund, 1991). This modulation is thought to be relatively automatic. For example, if others are present, the threshold for activation of the emotion display motor programs may be reduced. In addition, to these relatively automatic effects on the display of emotion, Figure 17.1 represents the role of executive systems. These executive systems can be thought of as allowing the suppression of a socially undesirable emotional display (disappointment at a detestable gift) in favor of a socially desirable emotional display (happiness).

Johnson, 2000), this capacity is unlikely to be related to the relatively automatic displays of emotion activated by salient emotional stimuli. Indeed, if, as has been suggested (Camras et al., 1991), the young child's emotional displays are almost instinctive displays activated by environmental events, the only way that Theory of Mind could determine emotional displays would be by assuming that representations of other's mental states have been evolutionarily specified to automatically activate emotional displays. This is very unlikely. Moreover, the evidence suggests that children with autism do show appropriate emotional responsiveness. Thus, although there have been clinical reports that children with autism do not use their emotional expressions in a communicative fashion (e.g., Bartak, Rutter, & Cox, 1975; Wing, 1983), the empirical literature is more equivocal. Indeed, there have even been suggestions that the emotional responsiveness of children with autism is heightened. Thus, for example, Capps and colleagues (Capps, Kasari, Yirmiya, & Sigman, 1993) recorded parental reports of emotional expressiveness as well as reactions to emotionally laden videotapes in children with autism and matched comparison populations. Interestingly, both the data obtained through parental report and the data obtained directly in response to the videotapes indicated that the children with autism displayed more, rather than less, emotional responsiveness. This suggests that Theory of Mind is not related to the production of emotional expressions, although it may be related to the individual's ability to follow social rules regarding when to display these expressions.

What about display rules? It is plausible that the capacity to represent the mental states of others may be important for the individual's learning how he or she should respond in particular social contexts. In addition, representations of the mental states of others may, in healthy individuals, be triggers for the executive systems that allow the implementation of display rules (see Figure 17.1). Perhaps the clinical reports that children with autism do not use their emotional expressions in a communicative fashion relate to the inability of these children to learn and use display rules (e.g., Bartak et al., 1975; Wing, 1983). Indeed, the fact that the children with autism in the study by Capps et al. (1993) actually showed heightened emotional responsiveness to the comparison populations may also indicate that the children were less likely to use display rules to govern their responsiveness. This hypothesis makes a clear prediction that children with autism should have poor control of emotional behavior relative to comparison children in a replication of the classic Saarni (1984) study. However, as far as I am aware, this prediction remains currently untested.

Summary of the Relationship between Theory of Mind and Emotional Regulation

In conclusion, Theory of Mind does not appear to be related to the capacity to actually produce emotional expressions. However, it is likely to be involved in regulating when they are produced. Indeed, in the section assessing the relationship between Theory of Mind and emotional assimilation, I presented data indicating that Theory of Mind was crucial for regulating appropriate social conventional behavior. Displays of emotion are highly governed by a society's conventional rules.

AN ALTERNATIVE APPROACH

In this chapter I have considered the relationship between Theory of Mind and emotional intelligence by examining a population who have a pronounced Theory of Mind impairment and considering which elements of emotional intelligence may be affected by this impairment. However, an alternative way to consider the relationship between Theory of Mind and emotional intelligence is to explore a population with severe difficulties in emotional intelligence and determine whether this population also has Theory of Mind dysfunction. Individuals with psychopathy are a population with severe impairment in emotional intelligence. In the following sections I describe the disorder of psychopathy, findings relevant to emotional intelligence in a population with this disorder, and then consider whether this population presents with any Theory of Mind dysfunction.

PSYCHOPATHY

Psychopathy is a disorder characterized in part by callousness, a diminished capacity for remorse, impulsivity, and poor behavioral controls (Hare, 1991). It is identified in children with the Psychopathy Screening Device (Frick & Hare, in press) and in adults with the Revised Psychopathy Checklist (Hare, 1991). It is important to note that this disorder is not equivalent to the psychiatric diagnosis of conduct disorder or antisocial personality disorder (American Psychiatric Association, 1994). These psychiatric diagnoses are relatively poorly specified and concentrate almost entirely on the antisocial behavior shown by the individual rather than any form of functional impairment. Because of this lack of specification, rates of diagnosis of conduct disorder reach up to 16% of boys in mainstream education (American Psychiatric Association, 1994) and rates of diagnosis of antisocial personality disorder are more than 80% in patients in forensic institutions (Hart & Hare, 1996). Because of these high rates of diagnosis, populations identified with these diagnostic tools are highly heterogeneous and include many individuals with other disorders. Psychopathy, in contrast, is shown by less than 1% of individuals in mainstream education (Blair & Coles, 2000) and less than 30% of individuals incarcerated in forensic institutions

(Hart & Hare, 1996). Thus, individuals with psychopathy are a far more homogeneous population.

Psychopathy, Emotional Intelligence, and Theory of Mind

Individuals with psychopathy can be considered to be a prototypical example of a population with impairment in emotional intelligence. In relation to the elements considered earlier, psychopathic individuals have been shown to have selective difficulties in the recognition of fearful vocal and facial expressions (Blair, Colledge, Murray, & Mitchell, 2001; Stevens, Charman, & Blair, 2001; Blair & Coles, 2000). In addition, psychopathic individuals show reduced autonomic responding to the distress of other individuals (Aniskiewicz, 1979; Blair, 1999b; Blair, Jones, Clark, & Smith, 1997; House & Milligan, 1976). Psychopathic individuals show impairment in emotional learning paradigms (Newman & Schmitt, 1998), in emotional memory (Christianson et al., 1996), in changing their responses as a function of changes in reinforcement contingencies (Blair, Colledge, & Mitchell, 2001; Fisher & Blair, 1998; LaPierre, Braun, & Hodgins, 1995; Newman, Patterson, & Kosson, 1987), and in moral socialization (Blair, 1995; Blair, Monson, & Frederickson, 2001; Wootton, Frick, Shelton, & Silverthorn, 1997).

Psychopathic individuals do not typically have Theory of Mind impairment. Four out of five studies on psychopathic individuals found no indications of Theory of Mind impairment (Blair et al., 1996; Blair & Colledge, in press; Richell et al., in press; Widom, 1978—did not; Widom, 1976—did). Moreover, even in the broader spectrum of antisocial individuals, there is little data suggesting any link between Theory of Mind impairment and antisocial behavior. Hughes, Dunn, and White (1998) did find some indication of Theory of Mind impairment in their "hard-to-manage" preschoolers relative to a comparison group. However, Happé and Frith (1996) found no impairment in children with emotional and behavioral difficulties. Similarly, a study of school bullies found no indications of Theory of Mind impairment (Sutton, Smith, & Swettenham, 1999). Sutton and colleagues also found no relationship between Theory of Mind performance on the advanced eyes task (Baron-Cohen et al., 1997) and disruptive behavior disorder symptoms in children aged 11–13 years (Sutton, Reeves, & Keogh, 2000).

Thus, we see signs of a classic neuropsychological double dissociation (Shallice, 1988). Individuals with autism represent a population with pronounced Theory of Mind impairment but relatively minor indications of difficulties in emotional intelligence. In contrast, psychopathic individuals represent a population with pronounced difficulties in many aspects of emotional intelligence but no indications of Theory of Mind impairment. Such a double dissociation is very powerful evidence that Theory of Mind is independent of most aspects of emotional intelligence.

A FINAL QUESTION: IS EMOTIONAL INTELLIGENCE NECESSARY FOR THE DEVELOPMENT OF THEORY OF MIND?

For as long as autism has been recognized, the idea has existed that the main difficulty for people with autism is an inability to enter into emotional relationships. Thus, Kanner, the psychiatrist who originally described the disorder in 1943, wrote, "These children have come into the world with an innate inability to form the usual, biologically provided affective contact with other people, just as other children come into the world with innate physical or intellectual handicaps" (Kanner, 1943, p. 250). More recently, it has been suggested that the Theory of Mind impairment shown by individuals with autism is a consequence of a deeper impairment that prevents the child from establishing normal interpersonal relatedness with those around him or her (Hobson, 1993), that is, that emotional responding is necessary for the appropriate development of Theory of Mind. Hobson (1993) views autism as primarily an affective and interpersonal impairment that cannot be defined without regard to the child's relationship to caregivers. Disruption to the early processes of joint attention, and particularly of the "triangulation" of attention and emotion involving baby, adult, and object, are postulated to occur in autism because of innate brain abnormalities. Hobson postulates an innate impairment in the ability to perceive and respond to the affective expressions of others, and suggests that as a result of this deficit children with autism do not receive the necessary social experiences in childhood to develop Theory of Mind (Hobson, 1993).

In addition to Hobson's argument that the ability to enter into emotional relationships is necessary for the development of the neurocognitive architecture that allows the representation of the mental states of others, other researchers have focused on the idea that the understanding of another's mental states (i.e., individual's semantic knowledge/theories of Theory of Mind) may relate to "emotional understanding." Although no computational details have been provided, the suggestion has been that there may be conceptual links between understanding beliefs and understanding emotions (e.g., Dunn, 1995). Over the last decade, Dunn and colleagues have conducted a series of studies investigating this issue (Dunn, 1995; Dunn, Brown, & Beardsall, 1991; Cutting & Dunn, 1999; Hughes & Dunn, 1998). Although the results of these studies are mixed, the consensus is that understanding of belief and understanding of emotion are dissociable. Thus, Hughes and Dunn (1998), in their longitudinal study of 50 children aged 47–60 months, did find that individual differences in understanding of both false-belief and emotion were stable over this time period and were significantly related to each other. However, Dunn et al. (1991), in their longitudinal study of 33-month-olds did not find such a relationship. Moreover, Dunn (1995) found that individual differences in each domain at 40 months had distinct sequelae at the end of the children's kindergarten year of school. In addition, Cutting and Dunn (1999) found in their study of 4-year-olds that individual differences in false-belief and emotion understanding were correlated but that these domains did not contribute to each other independently of age, language ability, and family background.

An even more fundamental indication that emotional responding is not necessary for the development of Theory of Mind is provided by work with individuals who do have profound impairment in emotional intelligence, namely, psychopathic individuals. The emotional impairment shown by psychopathic individuals is certainly sufficient to disrupt their emotional bonds with others. In fact, reduced emotional bonding with significant others is one of the defining features of psychopathy (Hare, 1991, 1993). If emotional intelligence, either directly or indirectly, through the mediation of the development of attachments to significant others (cf. Hobson, 1993), is involved in the development of Theory of Mind, then psychopathic individuals should have profound Theory of Mind impairment. Yet psychopathic individuals have been consistently found to show no Theory of Mind impairment (Blair et al., 1996; Blair & Colledge, in press; Richell et al., in press; Widom, 1978; for an exception, see Widom, 1976). Moreover, other populations who show milder impairments in emotional intelligence, such as individuals with emotional and behavioral difficulties, school bullies, or individuals with disruptive behavior disorder symptoms, also show no Theory of Mind impairment (Happé & Frith, 1996; Sutton et al., 2000; Sutton et al., 1999). Thus, the data strongly suggest that emotional intelligence is not necessary for the development of Theory of Mind.

CONCLUSION

This chapter has considered the relationship between Theory of Mind and emotional intelligence from a neuropsychological perspective. I have discussed the implications obtained from two populations: individuals with autism who have profound impairment in Theory of Mind and individuals with psychopathy who have profound impairment in emotional intelligence. The first section of this chapter considered whether children with autism have difficulties in emotional intelligence. I presented data suggesting that this population may have difficulties in (1) the perception of the emotional experience of the self, (2) the emotional assimilation of information about actions likely to anger others and other individuals' intentions to evaluate whether actions are socially appropriate or not, (3) and, connected to (2), the appropriate regulation of emotional displays according to social conventions. However, I also presented data indicating that this population had no difficulties in (1) the perception of the emotional displays of others, (2) the emotional assimilation of information concerning changes in reinforcement contingencies, (3) the assimilation of information concerning the distress of others, and (4) the regulation of emotional displays when these are not governed by social conventions.

These data suggest that Theory of Mind may be related to two elements of emotional intelligence. The first is conscious access to emotional experience. It is possible that the neurocognitive architecture of Theory of Mind is crucial not only for representing the internal states of others but also for representing the internal states of the self (Castelli et al., 2000). The second is assimilation of emotional information and mental state information to determine whether actions are socially appropriate or not. The role of Theory of Mind in this assimilation process may be the reason for much of the socially unusual behavior of individuals with autism.

In contrast, individuals with psychopathy show profound impairment in emotional intelligence. Indeed, all those components of emotional intelligence that are intact in individuals with autism are dysfunctional in individuals with psychopathy. In fact, and interestingly, all those components of emotional intelligence that are dysfunctional in individuals with autism are intact in individuals with psychopathy (see Blair & Cipolotti, 2000). There are currently no reports of generally defective emotional experience in individuals with psychopathy, and they are sensitive to others' anger and accurately identify social conventions.

Thus, there is a double dissociation between Theory of Mind and many aspects of emotional intelligence. Such a double dissociation is very powerful evidence that Theory of Mind is independent of most aspects of emotional intelligence.

ACKNOWLEDGMENTS

This work was supported by a Medical Research Council grant (ref. G9716841) and the Department of Health (VISPED initiative).

REFERENCES

Adolphs, R., Sears, L., & Piven, J. (2001). Abnormal processing of social information from faces in autism. *Journal of Cognitive Neuroscience, 13*(2), 232–40.

American Psychiatric Association. (1994). *Diagnostic and statistical manual of mental disorders* (4th ed.). Washington, DC: Author.

Aniskiewicz, A. S. (1979). Autonomic components of vicarious conditioning and psychopathy. *Journal of Clinical Psychology, 35,* 60–67.

Averill, J. R. (1982). *Anger and aggression: An essay on emotion.* New York: Springer-Verlag.

Bacon, A. L., Fein, D., Morris, R., Waterhouse, L., & Allen, D. (1998). The responses of autistic children to the distress of others. *Journal of Autism and Developmental Disorders, 28*(2), 129–42.

Balleine, B. W., & Dickinson, A. (1998). Goal-directed instrumental action: Contingency and incentive learning and their cortical substrates. *Neuropharmacology, 37*(4–5), 407–419.

Baron-Cohen, S. (1989). Perceptual role taking and protodeclarative pointing in autism. *British Journal of Developmental Psychology, 7*(2), 113–127.

Baron-Cohen, S. (1991). Do people with autism understand what causes emotion? *Child Development, 62,* 385–395.

Baron-Cohen, S. (1995). *Mindblindedness: An essay on autism and theory of mind.* Cambridge, MA: MIT Press.

Baron-Cohen, S., Leslie, A. M., & Frith, U. (1985). Does the autistic child have a "theory of mind"? *Cognition, 21,* 37–46.

Baron-Cohen, S., O'Riordan, M., Stone, V., Jones, R., & Plaisted, K. (1999). Recognition of faux pas by normally developing children and children with Asperger syndrome or high-functioning autism. *Journal of Autism and Developmental Disorders, 29*(5), 407–418.

Baron-Cohen, S., Ring, H. A., Wheelwright, S., Bullmore, E. T., Brammer, M. J., Simmons, A., & Williams, S. C. (1999). Social intelligence in the normal and autistic brain: An fMRI study. *European Journal of Neuroscience, 11*(6), 1891–1898.

Baron-Cohen, S., Spitz, A., & Cross, P. (1993). Do children with autism recognize surprise? A research note. Cognition and Emotion, 7, 507–516.

Baron-Cohen, S., Wheelwright, S., & Joliffe, T. (1997). Is there a "language of the eyes"? Evidence from normal adults, and adults with autism or Asperger syndrome. *Visual Cognition, 4*(3), 311.

Bartak, L., Rutter, M., & Cox, A. (1975). A comparative study of infantile autism and specific developmental language disorder: The children. *British Journal of Psychiatry, 126,* 127–145.

Berthoz, S., Armony, J., Blair, R. J. R., & Dolan, R. (in press). Neural correlates of violation of social norms and embarrassment. *Brain.*

Blair, R. J. R. (1995). A cognitive developmental approach to morality: Investigating the psychopath. *Cognition, 57,* 1–29.

Blair, R. J. R. (1996). Brief report: Morality in the autistic child. *Journal of Autism and Developmental Disorders, 26,* 571–579.

Blair, R. J. R. (1999a). Psycho-physiological responsiveness to the distress of others in children with autism. *Personality and Individual Differences, 26,* 477–485.

Blair, R. J. R. (1999b). Responsiveness to distress cues in the child with psychopathic tendencies. *Personality and Individual Differences, 27,* 135–145.

Blair, R. J. R. (2001). Neuro-cognitive models of aggression, the antisocial personality disorders and psychopathy. *Journal of Neurology, Neurosurgery and Psychiatry, 71,* 1–4.

Blair, R. J. R. (in press). The relationship between Theory of Mind and antisocial behavior. In V. Slaughter & B. Rappacholi (Eds.), *Individual differences in theory of mind: Implications for typical and atypical development.*

Blair, R. J. R., & Cipolotti, L. (2000). Impaired social response reversal: A case of "acquired sociopathy." *Brain, 123,* 1122–1141.

Blair, R. J. R., & Coles, M. (2000). Expression recognition and behavioral problems in early adolescence. *Cognitive Development, 15,* 421–434.

Blair, R. J. R., & Colledge, E. (in press). Selective impairments in social cognition in boys with attention deficit hyperactivity disorder and psychopathic tendencies. *British Journal of Developmental Psychology.*

Blair, R. J. R., Colledge, E., & Mitchell, D. (2001). Somatic markers and response reversal: Is there orbitofrontal cortex dysfunction in boys with psychopathic tendencies? *Journal of Abnormal Child Psychology, 29,* 499–511.

Blair, R. J. R., Colledge, E., Murray, L., & Mitchell, D. (2001). A selective impairment in the processing of sad and fearful expressions in boys with psychopathic tendencies . *Journal of Abnormal Child Psychology, 29,* 491–498.

Blair, R. J. R., Frith, U., Smith, N., Abell, F., & Cipolotti, L. (2002). Fractionation of visual memory: Agency detection and its impairment in Autism. *Neuropsychologia, 90,* 108–118.

Blair, R. J. R., Jones, L., Clark, F., & Smith, M. (1997). The psychopathic individual: A lack of responsiveness to distress cues? *Psychophysiology, 34,* 192–198.

Blair, R. J. R., Monson, J., & Frederickson, N. (2001). Moral reasoning and conduct problems in children with emotional and behavioral difficulties. *Personality and Individual Differences, 31,* 799–811.

Blair, R. J. R., Morris, J. S., Frith, C. D., Perrett, D. I., & Dolan, R. (1999). Dissociable neural responses to facial expressions of sadness and anger. *Brain, 122,* 883–893.

Blair, R. J. R., Sellars, C., Strickland, I., Clark, F., Williams, A., Smith, M., & Jones, L. (1996). Theory of Mind in the psychopath. *Journal of Forensic Psychiatry, 7,* 15–25.

Blakemore, S. J., Wolpert, D. M., & Frith, C. D. (1998). Central cancellation of self-produced tickle sensation. *Nature Neuroscience, 1*(7), 635–40.

Bormann-Kischkel, C., Vilsmeier, M., & Baude, B. (1995). The development of emotional concepts in autism. *Journal of Child Psychology and Psychiatry, 36*(7), 1243–1259.

Brunet, E., Sarfati, Y., Hardy-Bayle, M. C., & Decety, J. (2000). A PET investigation of the attribution of intentions with a nonverbal task. *Neuroimage, 11*(2), 157–66.

Calder, A. J., Young, A. W., Rowland, D., & Perrett, D. I. (1996). Facial emotion recognition after bilateral amygdala damage: Differentially severe impairment of fear. *Cognitive Neuropsychology, 13,* 699–745.

Camras, L. A., Malatesta, C., & Izard, C. E. (1991). *The development of facial expressions in infancy. Fundamentals of nonverbal communication.* Cambridge, UK: Cambridge University Press.

Capps, L., Kasari, C., Yirmiya, N., & Sigman, M. (1993). Parental perception of emotional expressiveness in children with autism. *Journal of Consulting and Clinical Psychology, 61*(3), 475–484.

Capps, L., Yirmiya, N., & Sigman, M. (1992). Understanding of simple and complex emotions in non-retarded children with autism. *Journal of Child Psychology and Psychiatry, 33*(7), 1169–1182.

Castelli, F., Happé, F., Frith, U., & Frith, C. (2000). Movement and mind: A functional imaging study of perception and interpretation of complex intentional movement patterns. *Neuroimage, 12,* 314–325.

Chandler, M. J., Greenspan, S., & Barenboim, C. (1974). Assessment and training of role-taking and referential communication skills in institutionalized, emotionally disturbed children. *Developmental Psychology, 10,* 546–553.

Christianson, S. A., Forth, A. E., Hare, R. D., Strachan, C., Lidberg, L., & Thorell, L. H. (1996). Remembering details of emotional events: A comparison between psychopathic and nonpsychopathic offenders. *Personality and Individual Differences, 20,* 437–443.

Cipolotti, L., Robinson, G., Blair, R. J. R., & Frith, U. (1999). Fractionation of visual memory: Evidence from a case with multiple neuro-developmental impairments. *Neuropsychologia, 37,* 455–465.

Cohen, J. D., Braver, T. S., & O'Reilly, R. C. (1996). A computational approach to prefrontal cortex, cognitive control and schizophrenia: Recent developments and current challenges. *Philosophical Transactions of the Royal Society B, 351,* 1515–1527.

Cohen, J. D., & Servan-Schreiber, D. (1992). Cotext, cortex, and dopamine: A connectionist approach to behavior and biology in schizophrenia. *Psychological Review, 99,* 45–77.

Corona, C., Dissanayake, C., Arbelle, A., Wellington, P., & Sigman, M. (1998). Is affect aversive to young children with autism?: Behavioral and cardiac responses to experimenter distress. *Child Development, 69*(6), 1494–1502.

Cutting, A. L., & Dunn, J. (1999). Theory of Mind, emotion understanding, language, and family background: Individual differences and interrelations. *Child Development, 70*(4), 853–865.

Davies, S., Bishop, D., Manstead, A. S. R., & Tantam, D. (1994). Face perception in children with autism and Asperger's syndrome. *Journal of Child Psychology and Psychiatry and Allied Disciplines, 35*(6), 1033–1057.

Dewey, M. (1991). Living with Asperger's syndrome. In U. Frith (Ed.), *Autism and Asperger's syndrome.* Cambridge, UK: Cambridge University Press.

Dias, R., Robbins, T. W., & Roberts, A. C. (1996). Dissociation in prefrontal cortex of affective and attentional shifts. *Nature, 380,* 69–72.

Dissanayake, C., Sigman, M., & Kasari, C. (1996). Long-term stability of individual differences in the emotional responsiveness of children with autism. *Journal of Child Psychology and Psychiatry and Allied Disciplines, 37*(4), 461–467.

Dunn, J. (1995). Children as psychologists: The later correlates of individual differences in understanding of emotions and other minds. *Cognition and Emotion, 9,* 187–201.

Dunn, J., Brown, J. R., & Beardsall, L. (1991). Family talk about feeling states and children's later understanding of others' emotions. *Developmental Psychology, 27,* 448–455.

Eisenberg, N., Fabes, R., Miller, P. A., Shell, R., Shea, C., & May-Plumlee, T. (1990). Preschoolers' vicarious emotional responding and their situational and dispositional prosocial behavior. *Merrill Palmer Quarterly, 36,* 507–529.

Fine, C., Lumsden, J., & Blair, R. J. (2001). Dissociation between "theory of mind" and executive functions in a patient with early left amygdala damage. *Brain, 124*(Pt 2), 287–298.

Fisher, L., & Blair, R. J. R. (1998). Cognitive impairment and its relationship to psychopathic tendencies in children with emotional and behavioral difficulties. *Journal of Abnormal Child Psychology, 26,* 511–519.

Fletcher, P. C., Happé, F., Frith, U., Baker, S. C., Dolan, R. J., Frackowiak, R. S., & Frith, C. D. (1995). Other minds in the brain: A functional imaging study of "theory of mind" in story comprehension. *Cognition, 57,* 109–128.

Frick, P. J., & Hare, R. D. (in press). *The psychopathy screening device.* Toronto: Multi-Health Systems.

Fridlund, A. J. (1991). Sociality of solitary smiling: Potentiation by an implicit audience. *Journal of Personality and Social Psychology, 60,* 229–246.

Frith, C. D., & Frith, U. (1999). Interacting minds: A biological basis. *Science, 286,* 1692–1695.

Frith, U. (1989). *Autism: Explaining the enigma.* Oxford: Blackwell.

Frith, U., & Happé, F. G. E. (1999). Theory of Mind and self-consciousness: What is it like to be autistic? *Mind and Language, 14*(1), 1–22.

Gallagher, H. L., Happé, F., Brunswick, N., Fletcher, P. C., Frith, U., & Frith, C. D. (2000). Reading the mind in cartoons and stories: An fMRI study of "theory of mind" in verbal and nonverbal tasks. *Neuropsychologia, 38*(1), 11–21.

Garland, H., & Brown, B. R. (1972). Face-saving as affected by subjects' sex, audiences' sex and audience expertise. *Sociometry, 35*(2), 280–289.

Goel, V., Grafman, J., Sadato, N., & Hallett, M. (1995). Modeling other minds. *Neuroreport, 11,* 1741–1746.

Gopnik, A., & Meltzoff, A. N. (1997). *Words, thoughts, and theories.* Cambridge, MA: MIT Press.

Happé, F. G. E., & Frith, U. (1996). Theory of mind and social impairment in children with conduct disorder. *British Journal of Developmental Psychology, 14*(4), 385–398.

Hare, R. D. (1991). *The Hare Psychopathy Checklist—Revised.* Toronto, ON: Multi-Health Systems.

Hare, R. D. (1993). *Without conscience: The disturbing world of the psychopaths among us.* New York: Simon & Schuster.

Hart, S. D., & Hare, R. D. (1996). Psychopathy and antisocial personality disorder. *Current Opinion in Psychiatry, 9,* 129–132.

Hobson, P. (1986). The autistic child's appraisal of expressions of emotion. *Journal of Child Psychology and Psychiatry, 27,* 321–342.

Hobson, R. P. (1993). *Autism and the development of mind.* Hove, East Sussex: Erlbaum.

Hobson, R. P., Ouston, J., & Lee, A. (1989). Naming emotion in faces and voices: Abilities and disabilities in autism and mental retardation. *British Journal of Developmental Psychology, 7*(3), 237–250.

Hoffman, M. L. (1988). Moral development. In M. Bornstein & M. Lamb (Eds.), *Developmental psychology: An advanced textbook* (pp. 497–548). Hillsdale, NJ: Erlbaum.

Hornak, J., Rolls, E. T., & Wade, D. (1996). Face and voice expression identification in patients with emotional and behavioral changes following ventral frontal damage. *Neuropsychologia, 34,* 247–261.

House, T. H., & Milligan, W. L. (1976). Autonomic responses to modeled distress in prison psychopaths. *Journal of Personality and Social Psychology, 34,* 556–560.

Howard, M. A., Cowell, P. E., Boucher, J., Broks, P., Mayes, A., Farrant, A., & Roberts, N. (2000). Convergent neuro-anatomical and behavioral evidence of an amygdala hypothesis of autism. *Neuroreport, 11*(13), 1931–1935.

Hughes, C., & Dunn, J. (1998). Understanding mind and emotion: Longitudinal associations with mental-state talk between young friends. *Developmental Psychology, 34*(5), 1026–1037.

Hughes, C., Dunn, J., & White, A. (1998). Trick or treat?: Uneven understanding of mind and emotion and executive dysfunction in "hard-to-manage" preschoolers. *Journal of Child Psychology and Psychiatry, 39*(7), 981–994.

Hughes, C., Russell, J., & Robbins, T. W. (1994). Evidence for executive dysfunction in autism. *Neuropsychologia, 32,* 477–492.

Izard, C. E. (1992). Basic emotions, relations among emotions, and emotion–cognition relations. *Psychological Review, 99,* 561–565.

Johnson, S. C. (2000). The recognition of mentalistic agents in infancy. *Trends in Cognitive Science, 4*(1), 22–28.

Jones, S. S., & Raag, T. (1989). Smile production in older infants: The importance of a social recipient for the facial signal. *Child Development, 60,* 811–818.

Kanner, L. (1943). Autistic disturbances of affective contact. *Nervous Child, 2,* 217–250.

Kesler/West, M. L., Andersen, A. H., Smith, C. D., Avison, M. J., Davis, C. E., Kryscio, R. J., & Blonder, L. X. (2001). Neural substrates of facial emotion processing using fMRI. *Cognitive Brain Research, 11*(2), 213–226.

Klin, A., Sparrow, S. S., de Bildt, A., Cicchetti, D. V., Cohen, D. J., & Volkmar, F. R. (1999). A normed study of face recognition in autism and related disorders. *Journal of Autism and Developmental Disorders, 29*(6), 499–508.

Lane, R. D., Fink, G. R., Chau, P. M. L., & Dolan, R. J. (1997). Neural activity during selective attention to subjective emotional responses. *Neuroreport, 8,* 3969–3972.

Lane, R. D., Reiman, E. M., Axelrod, B., Yun, L. S., Holmes, A., & Schwartz, G. E. (1998). Neural correlates of levels of emotional awareness: Evidence of an interaction between emotion and attention in the anterior cingulate cortex. *Journal of Cognitive Neuroscience, 10*(4), 525–535.

LaPierre, D., Braun, C. M. J., & Hodgins, S. (1995). Ventral frontal deficits in psychopathy: Neuropsychological test findings. *Neuropsychologia, 33*, 139–151.

LeDoux, J. (1998). *The emotional brain.* New York: Weidenfeld & Nicolson.

Leslie, A. M. (2000). *"Theory of Mind" as a mechanism of selective attention.* Cambridge, MA: MIT Press.

Leslie, A. M. (1987). Pretense and representation: The origins of "Theory of Mind." *Psychological Review, 94,* 412–426.

Leslie, A. M., & Frith, U. (1988). Autistic children's understanding of seeing, knowing and believing. *British Journal of Developmental Psychology, 6,* 315–324.

Liss, M., Fein, D., Allen, D., Dunn, M., Feinstein, C., Morris, R., Waterhouse, L., & Rapin, I. (2001). Executive functioning in high-functioning children with autism. *Journal of Child Psychology and Psychiatry, 42*(2), 261–270.

Lotter, V. (1966). Epidemiology of autistic conditions in young children: I. Prevalence. *Social Psychiatry, 1,* 124–137.

Lough, S., Gregory, C., & Hodges, J. R. (2001). Dissociation of social cognition and executive function in frontal variant frontotemporal dementia. *Neurocase, 7*(2), 123–130.

Loveland, K. A., Tunali, K. B., Chen, R., Brelsford, K. A., Ortegon, P., & Pearson, A. (1995). Intermodal perception of affect in persons with autism or Down syndrome. *Development and Psychopathology, 7*(3), 409–418.

McGuire, P. K., Paulesu, E., Frackowiak, R. S., & Frith, C. D. (1996). Brain activity during stimulus independent thought. *Neuroreport, 7*(13), 2095–2099.

Newman, J. P., Patterson, C. M., & Kosson, D. S. (1987). Response perseveration in psychopaths. *Journal of Abnormal Psychology, 96,* 145–148.

Newman, J. P., & Schmitt, W. A. (1998). Passive avoidance in psychopathic offenders: A replication and extension. *Journal of Abnormal Psychology, 107,* 527–532.

Nucci, L., Turiel, E., & Encarnacion-Gawrych, G. E. (1983). Social interactions and social concepts: Analysis of morality and convention in the Virgin Islands. *Journal of Cross Cultural Psychology, 14,* 469–487.

Ozonoff, S., Pennington, B., & Rogers, S. (1990). Are there emotion perception deficits in young autistic children? *Journal of Child Psychology and Psychiatry, 31,* 343–363.

Pennington, B. F., & Ozonoff, S. (1996). Executive functions and developmental psychopathology. *Journal of Child Psychology and Psychiatry, 37,* 51–87.

Perner, J. (1991). *Understanding the representational mind.* Cambridge, MA: MIT Press.

Perner, J., Frith, U., Leslie, A. M., & Leekam, S. R. (1989). Exploration of the autistic child's theory of mind: Knowledge, belief and communication. *Child Development, 60,* 689–700.

Premack, D., & Woodruff, G. (1978). Does the chimpanzee have a theory of mind? *Behavioural and Brain Sciences, 1*(4), 515–526.

Prior, M., Dahlstrom, B., & Squires, T. (1990). Autistic children's knowledge of thinking and feeling states in other people. *Journal of Autism and Developmental Disorders, 31,* 587–602.

Raineville, P., Duncan, G. H., Price, D. D., Carrier, B., & Bushnell, M. C. (1997). Pain affect encoded in human anterior cingulate but not somatosensory cortex. *Science, 277,* 968–971.

Reed, T., & Peterson, C. (1990). A comparative study of autistic subjects' performance at two levels of visual and cognitive perspective taking. *Journal of Autism and Developmental Disorders, 20,* 555–568.

Richell, R. A., Mitchell, D. G. V., Neuman, C., Leonard, A., Baron-Cohen, S., & Blair, R. J. R. (in press). Theory of Mind and psychopathy: Can psychopathic individuals read the "language of the eyes"? *Neuropsychologia.*

Rolls, E. T. (2000). The orbitofrontal cortex and reward. *Cerebral Cortex, 10,* 284–294.

Saarni, C. (1984). An observational study of children's attempts to monitor their expressive behavior. *Child Development, 55*(4), 1504–1513.

Selman, R. L. (1980). *The Growth of Interpersonal Understanding.* New York: Academic Press.

Semin, G. R., & Manstead, A. S. (1982). The social implications of embarrassment displays and restitution behavior. *European Journal of Social Psychology, 12*(4), 367–377.

Shallice, T. (1988). *From neuropsychology to mental structure.* Cambridge, UK: Cambridge University Press.

Sigman, M. D., Kasari, C., Kwon, J., & Yirmiya, N. (1992). Responses to the negative emotions of others by autistic, mentally retarded, and normal children. *Child Development, 63,* 796–807.

Smetana, J. G. (1982). *Concepts of self and morality: Women's reasoning about abortion.* New York: Praeger.

Smetana, J. G. (1985). Preschool children's conceptions of transgressions: The effects of varying moral and conventional domain-related attributes. *Developmental Psychology, 21,* 18–29.

Smetana, J. G. (1993). Understanding of social rules. In M. Bennett Ied.), *The child as psychologist: An introduction to the development of social cognition* (pp. 111–141). New York: Harvester Wheatsheaf.

Smetana, J. G., & Braeges, J. L. (1990). The development of toddlers' moral and conventional judgments. *MPQ, 36,* 329–346.

Song, M., Smetana, J. G., & Kim, S. Y. (1987). Korean children's conceptions of moral and conventional transgressions. *Developmental Psychology, 23,* 577–582.

Sprengelmeyer, R., Rausch, M., Eysel, U. T., & Przuntek, H. (1998). Neural structures associated with the recognition of facial basic emotions. *Proceedings of the Royal Society of London. B, 265,* 1927–1931.

Stevens, D., Charman, T., & Blair, R. J. R. (2001). Recognition of emotion in facial expressions and vocal tones in children with psychopathic tendencies. *Journal of Genetic Psychology, 162*(2), 201–211.

Stoddart, T., & Turiel, E. (1985). Children's concepts of cross-gender activities. *Child Development, 56,* 1241–1252.

Stone, V. E., Baron-Cohen, S., & Knight, R. T. (1998). Frontal lobe contributions to theory of mind. *Journal of Cognitive Neuroscience, 10*(5), 640–656.

Sutton, J., Reeves, M., & Keogh, E. (2000). Disruptive behavior, avoidance of responsibility and theory of mind. *British Journal of Developmental Psychology,* *18*(1), 1–11.

Sutton, J., Smith, P. K., & Swettenham, J. (1999). Social cognition and bullying: Social inadequacy or skilled manipulation? *British Journal of Developmental Psychology, 17*(3), 435–450.

Tronick, E. Z., Als, H., & Adamson, L. (1979). Structure of early face-to-face communicative intent. In M. Bullowa (Ed.), *Before speech: The beginnings of human communication.* Cambridge, UK: Cambridge University Press.

Turiel, E. (1983). *The development of social knowledge: Morality and Convention.* Cambridge, UK: Cambridge University Press.

Turiel, E., & Wainryb, C. (1998). Concept of freedoms and rights in a traditional, hierachical organized society. *British Journal of Developmental Psychology, 16,* 375–395.

Vogeley, K., Bussfeld, S. P., Newen, A., Herrmann, S., Happé, F., Falkai, P., Maier, W., Shah, N. J., Fink, G. R., & Zilles, K. (2001). Mind reading: Neural mechanisms of theory of mind and self-perspective. *NeuroImage, 14,* 170–181.

Widom, C. S. (1976). Interpersonal and personal construct systems in psychopaths. *Journal of Consulting and Clinical Psychology, 44,* 614–623.

Widom, C. S. (1978). An empirical classification of female offenders. *Criminal Justice and Behavior, 5,* 35–52.

Wimmer, H., & Perner, J. (1983). Beliefs about beliefs: Representation and the constraining function of wrong beliefs in young children's understanding of deception. *Cognition, 13,* 103–128.

Wing, L. (1983). Diagnosis, clinical description and prognosis. Oxford: Peragemon Press.

Wootton, J. M., Frick, P. J., Shelton, K. K., & Silverthorn, P. (1997). Ineffective parenting and childhood conduct problems: The moderating role of callous-unemotional traits. *Journal of Consulting and Clinical Psychology, 65,* 292–300.

Yirmiya, N., Sigman, M. D., Kasari, C., & Mundy, P. (1992). Empathy and cognition in high-functioning children with autism. *Child Development, 63,* 150–160.

Index